ECONOMIC THEORY AND
EXHAUSTIBLE RESOURCES

THE CAMBRIDGE ECONOMIC HANDBOOKS

General Editors

ECONOMIC THEORY AND EXHAUSTIBLE RESOURCES

By

P. S. DASGUPTA

PROFESSOR OF ECONOMICS IN THE UNIVERSITY OF LONDON
AT THE LONDON SCHOOL OF ECONOMICS

G. M. HEAL

PROFESSOR OF ECONOMICS IN THE UNIVERSITY OF SUSSEX

JAMES NISBET & CO. LTD
Digswell Place, Welwyn
CAMBRIDGE UNIVERSITY PRESS

First published 1979
by James Nisbet and Company Limited
Digswell Place, Welwyn, Herts.
and the Cambridge University Press

SBN 0 7202 0313 9 Board
SBN 0 7202 0312 0 Paperback

HC EDITION
AT PB PRICE

Printed in Great Britain at the University Press Oxford

For our children

Bridget, Zubeida and Shamik

PREFACE

A book on the economics of exhaustible resources requires no justification. A long book does. We had originally planned to write a monograph on the subject, more in keeping with the design of the Handbook Series, of which this volume is a member. Had we pursued this approach we would have been forced to assume a knowledge of resource allocation theory, and the book would have applied this directly to the subject matter at hand.[1] But the subject has recently attracted the attention of mathematicians, physicists, engineers, biologists and systems analysts as well, and we wanted to write for them too.

There was in fact another reason. Even the best graduate texts on resource allocation theory are often dry, and it is not uncommon for economics students to fail to see what questions such economic theorizing is designed to answer and why they might be worth asking. It occurred to us that exhaustible natural resources provide one with particularly good examples for illustrating resource allocation theory. There is therefore a good deal of interchange between resource allocation theory and its application to exhaustible resources in the chapters that follow. We have often raised a question that appears naturally to arise when one thinks of such resources, developed the relevant analysis in a more general context, and then gone back to address ourselves to the question we had originally asked. This second reason explains why we have attempted to write a text on resource allocation theory at the same time. It is entirely possible that we have not succeeded, even partially, in carrying out this enterprise. But it was clearly worth a try. At any event, we hope that this book will prove useful to the graduate student were he to use it in conjunction with the more established texts on the subject.

We have not attempted to avoid rigour in the analyses that follow, but we have avoided generality wherever we felt that it would distract the reader from the point we wished to make. The purist will find disquieting our two-asset, constant population model with which we analyse growth possibilities in an economy with exhaustible resources. He will look askance at our reliance on

---

[1] For such an exposition, see Herfindahl and Kneese (1974).

symmetric externalities in Chapters 3, 5, and 12. But we have tried throughout to make clear why we are appealing to what we think are strong special cases and to what extent the results are robust. The Notes at the end of the chapters are addressed directly to this and provide detailed references for more general analyses.

Our reliance on special cases has also enabled us to keep the mathematical analysis well within the reach of first-year graduate students studying economic theory. Nothing more than elementary analysis is assumed. We have avoided appealing directly to the calculus of variations since, for the problem at hand, as in Chapter 10, the arguments can be conducted without an appeal to it.

We have found great difficulty in arriving at a satisfactory title for the book. Our final choice probably goes to the heart of the contents. On occasion we have reported on applied work on the subject. Here our coverage is really rather narrow. Thus, for example, we have not reported on the important recent work of Professor Dale Jorgenson and his associates on energy use in different sectors of the American economy. This is partly because our understanding of these matters is not as expert as we would wish it to be; partly also because it would have taken us far afield and altered the structure of the book.

This book has gone through several drafts. Part of the first draft was written while the authors were visiting Stanford University during 1974–1976. We are most grateful to the US National Science Foundation and the Department of Economics at Stanford for making our visits possible. The first draft was used by us as a basis for lectures to graduate students at the London School of Economics, Stanford University, the University of Sussex and Yale University. We have gained much from the comments of the participants, too numerous to mention individually. For typing and duplication facilities of the several drafts we are most grateful to the London School of Economics, Stanford University and the University of Sussex. Much of the typing was done with great efficiency by Jean Krechnyak at Stanford University, and Jean Middleton and Katie Davis at the London School of Economics.

The authors have worked together on the subject matter of this book for several years now and we are jointly responsible for the book as a whole. However, we have not worked equally on all chapters. Dasgupta is primarily responsible for Chapters 3, 5, 6, 8, 9, 13 and 14; and Heal for Chapters 1, 4, 12, 15 and 16. Chapters 2, 7, 10 and 11 were written jointly.

We owe intellectual debts to many. Our greatest debt is to Frank Hahn who instructed us to write the book and gave us detailed comments on each draft. Our debt to him, we are inclined to believe, exceeds that which is normally accorded by authors to editors of series to which they are contributing. Pradeep Mitra and Robert Solow made extensive comments on the first draft. The final version reflects the impact of their comments. Our debt to Joseph Stiglitz is no less. We have gained much from discussions with him over several years. We have had useful discussions with A. K. Das Gupta, Carol Dasgupta, Paul David, Robert Dorfman, Robert Eastwood, Lucien Foldes, Richard Gilbert, Claude Henry, David Hendry, Farouzeh Khalatbari, Tjalling Koopmans, Eric Maskin, James Meade, David Newbery, William Nordhaus, Nathan Rosenberg, Amartya Sen, Michael Spence, Alister Ulph and John Wise. We are grateful to them all.

Partha Dasgupta

London School of Economics and Political Science.

Geoffrey Heal
July 1978

University of Sussex.

CONTENTS

xiv CONTENTS

CHAPTER 1

A PREVIEW

1. The role of natural resources in the functioning of an economic system has received intermittent attention from economists. The classical economists of the nineteenth century were very much concerned with this issue: both Malthus and Ricardo saw in a country's land the key to many characteristics of its economy. However, in the considerable developments of economic theory that have occurred in the twentieth century, there has been little explicit mention of natural resources. These differences are perhaps not surprising. In the eighteenth and nineteenth centuries, the ownership and productivity of land were evidently of great importance in determining the distribution of income, and the timing and location of the industrial revolution in the United Kingdom were clearly influenced by the exhaustion of certain traditional resource supplies and the availability of alternatives. To nineteenth-century man, it would therefore have seemed unthinkable that one could explain the dynamics of an economy, or analyse the processes of production and exchange, without giving special attention to the role of natural resources.

The economic theorists of the twentieth century have, however, proceeded on the basis of just such an omission, at least until recently: in the works that have exercised a dominant influence on the evolution of economic theory in the last half century— Hicks's *Value and Capital*, Samuelson's *Foundations of Economic Analysis* and the developments of the Arrow–Debreu model— there are few explicit references to natural resources. And indeed one could read the whole of the very extensive literature of the 1950s and 1960s on economic growth in the long run without ever realizing that the availability of natural resources (other than labour) might be a determinant of growth potential. The lack of direct reference to resources in this literature presumably reflects the fact that for the first two-thirds of the twentieth century, resource constraints were not important for most industrialized nations: these either possessed their own resource supplies, which they regarded as adequate, or

1

felt that they could be confident of importing resources in unlimited amounts from developing countries, initially because in many cases they controlled these countries as part of the colonial system, and subsequently because, although independent, the supplying countries remained politically quiescent, with foreign exchange needs so great that they could be counted on to supply unlimited quantities of their principal (and often only) exports.

The wheel has now turned full circle: in the last quarter of the twentieth century, no general text on economics will be complete without a reference to resource depletion. There are many reasons for this abrupt change: some authors would argue that it reflects a shift in the balance of political power between developed and developing countries, and others that it reflects a change in the economic balance in resource markets—a change which will no doubt bring in its wake changes in many traditional political balances. We examine one of the most notable exemplars of this phenomenon—the oil market—in some detail in Chapter 15. The revival of interest in the economic aspects of resource-depletion has been accompanied by some rather widely publicized claims that the tools of economic analysis as forged over the last half century fail to provide an adequate intellectual basis for tackling the problems that arise: we need, or so it is said, newer, more glamorous, more capital-intensive tools such as systems analysis. We hope that our book will disprove this point. It is true that the tools of economic analysis cannot solve all the problems in this area, but this could of course be said of any field of enquiry. However, the important point is that, although economic theory as elaborated in recent years contains very few explicit references to the role of natural resources, it does, occasionally with modification and extensions, provide a very productive framework within which one can analyse many of the questions of current concern—questions such as 'Will the free play of market forces lead to a use of resources that is in any sense rational? Is there a case for government intervention, or even extensive national planning, in relation to activities impinging on resource-use? What are the particular problems in planning such activities?'

Interest in these issues was also stimulated by the appearance of Forrester's book *World Dynamics* and by the subsequent publications of the Club of Rome. These provoked two vocal reactions, neither of which seems entirely appropriate, given the state of our knowledge. There are those who, being persuaded by the numbers in the world models, are convinced that doom lies in wait at the end of the century—unless we act. But when this action is detailed as cutting industrial production and asking developing countries to forgo industrialization, initial sympathy with this concern for the human plight is greatly diminished. We do not profess to know if doom lurks around the corner (for many people round the globe, it is perhaps this side of the corner), but it is clear that the economics of the world models is, to say the least, questionable. There are many central issues concerning the nature of production with exhaustible resources and the role of the price mechanism, which are totally overlooked. Subsequent chapters examine these in some detail.

Partly in response to this apocalyptic vision is the other reaction to the exhaustible resource problem. This is that there is really no problem. As resources become scarce, their prices will rise, and this encourages entrepreneurs to search for cheaper substitutes. Of course there is uncertainty about the success of this search, but the point is that the market generates signals and incentives which ensure that discovery and substitution are carried out at an appropriate intensity. This too is an overly simplistic view, neglecting many major complications connected with the behaviour of markets under conditions of uncertainty and endogenous information. These are also issues that we shall subject to careful scrutiny. Indeed, we now turn to a preview of these and other relevant issues.

2. There are many economically important commodities that could be described as natural resources—land, oil, coal, ores, precious stones, fish populations, areas of scenic beauty, and so on. Our attention in this book is directed not at all of these, but only at those that might be described as exhaustible resources. A resource is exhaustible if it is possible to find a pattern of use which makes its supply dwindle to zero. Obviously oil, coal and ores are exhaustible resources, in that the world's total endowments of these, though large, are certainly finite. Typically the amount available at any given cost increases with the cost, and in some cases may become very large indeed at sufficiently high costs—as in the case of the extraction of minerals from sea water. A fish population is also an exhaustible resource. Although it can potentially reproduce itself or even expand, very intensive fishing can certainly reduce it to zero. Perhaps fertile land is also an exhaustible resource in this sense: if it is over-cropped and badly maintained, soil erosion may reduce it to a wasteland—as happened several millennia ago in parts of what is now the Sahara desert. At certain stages of our analysis, it will prove convenient to distinguish between these two classes of exhaustible resources: we shall do this by referring to the former (oil, minerals, etc.) as strictly exhaustible resources and to the latter (fish populations, possibly land) as renewable resources.

The analytical problems that arise when one starts to ask questions about the depletion of exhaustible resources are extremely wide ranging, and involve many facets of economic theory. Thus, in many cases important issues hinge upon the nature of property rights in the resource. It is often difficult to establish such rights, yet their absence may lead to excessively rapid depletion. This point is exemplified by the case of fish populations: it has long been recognized that unrestricted access by competing fishermen leads to considerable externalities between them (the more one catches, the less is available to others), and hence to a private marginal product in excess of the social, and an over-allocation of resources to fishing. There is also the point that if each boat, or fleet, believes that its competitors will not operate a policy designed to conserve fish stocks for future years, then there is no incentive for it to pursue such a policy itself: for conservation would mean reducing its present catch below the maximum attainable, which in the conditions posited would simply lead to an increase in competitors' catches. Hence whether market forces produce a 'sensible' use pattern for fish populations will depend substantially on the institutional structure within which those forces are constrained. We analyse this kind of issue at some length in Chapters 3 and 5. Oil fields can provide another example of the same problem: if competing companies sink wells into the same oil-bearing rock formation, then there are again externalities between them, which may again reduce the incentives to conserve the stock. Certain states in the USA have passed legislation which is essentially designed to restrict the kinds of property rights that can exist in oil fields, with a view to ensuring that all such externalities are internalized.

Analysing the dynamics of an economy with exhaustible resources requires that one give considerable attention to the nature of the set of consumption paths open to such a system. This in turn requires very careful consideration of the technology of resource use. An intuitively appealing conclusion, and one which is clearly implicit in the various world models of Forrester, Meadows and others, is that if a resource is in some sense 'essential' and is available only in a finite amount, then on all feasible paths consumption must necessarily decline to zero. We shall show that, plausible though this view seems, it may be false. Capital-resource substitution (or 'stock-flow substitution' in the terminology of some of the conservationist literature) may be sufficient to overcome the 'drag' imposed by an essential and exhaustible resource.

Another puzzle whose resolution also hinges upon a careful analysis of the technology of resource use is that of the relationship between economic and thermodynamic concepts of efficiency in the use of resources, particularly energy resources. This has been the source of some confusion in the last few years—probably unnecessarily so, as there are several relatively simple points that can be made about this relationship. All of these essentially technological issues are considered in Chapter 7.

The efficiency with which a market system allocates exhaustible resources between competing uses at different dates is probably the most important single aspect one might wish to analyse. We may be more concerned to achieve a sensible allocation of our oil stocks between present uses and those a generation hence than we are to achieve such a balance for our present stocks of consumer durables; perhaps the reason is that we expect to be able to make more of the latter at future dates if the need arises. Obtaining the correct intertemporal balance does seem to be the crux of the 'problem of exhaustible resources' as usually viewed by the public and by policy makers. Asking whether the market system will strike such a balance takes us into the domain of intertemporal welfare economics. Again, the answer depends very much on the institutional structure of the market system. Certainly one can devise market structures which will get the balance right, but they are very complicated and rather different from the ones we actually have. Specifically, one element of the sufficient conditions for a market system to produce an optimal allocation of exhaustible resources over time is that it should contain a complete set of forward markets, i.e. that there should exist markets on which it is possible to buy and sell the right to have the resource delivered at any future date. Although actual market systems do contain some forward markets, and those that exist are typically for homogeneous non-produced goods such as resources, this complete condition is certainly not met, and theoretical arguments would tend to suggest that as a consequence resource markets may be unstable, and will almost certainly display 'market bias', in the sense of depleting the resource at a rate different from an optimal rate. It is obviously important to try to establish the nature of this discrepancy, and to consider the impact on it of various policies open to governments. These include stabilization measures analogous to the schemes already used for certain agricultural commodities, and a range of fiscal instruments such as profits taxes, depletion allowances, and many others.

The non-existence of a sufficiently comprehensive set of markets is one reason for the existence of market bias; another is of course the more traditional problem of imperfect competition. This requires very careful analysis in an intertemporal setting. It has, for example, been argued that 'monopoly is the conservationist's best friend' because by raising the price of a resource and reducing its supply, it will ensure that the resource is depleted less rapidly than otherwise. We shall see in Chapter 11 that matters are a little more complex, though this simple argument is not entirely misleading. Of course, to be thorough, one has to consider forms of imperfect competition other than pure monopoly, and this as always introduces great complexity and a multitude of possible outcomes. All of these issues are taken up in the central part of the book, and especially in Chapters 4, 6, 8 and 11.

The importance of the time dimension in the present problem suggests very naturally questions about the *efficiency* of allocation over time; but one is at least equally interested in the question of intertemporal equity. If the present generation uses up the whole of the remaining stock of a resource, their successors may be impoverished because of this, Such a situation could be efficient, but many would regard it as grossly unfair. Anyone familiar with basic welfare economics will realize that efficient outcomes need not be equitable, and vice versa. Problems of equity arise in a particularly acute form in the present intertemporal context because those most likely to suffer from an inequitable outcome are those not at present available to press their case. Basic to the problem is a complete inequality in the extent to which the generations affected by a policy are capable of putting their case to those making the decisions. Hence, in analysing these issues, and in attempting to decide how, ideally, depletion should be arranged, we need to clarify our ideas about fairness between generations, and to spell out in detail the implications of these ideas. This forms the subject matter of Chapters 9 and 10.

Uncertainty provides a further complication that is an essential ingredient in any convincing formulation of our problem. It is not unique in this respect; most economic problems, if stated accurately, involve an element of uncertainty. However, as uncertainty is typically compounded by increasing distance into the future, and we have already seen that our analysis must take into account considerations related to the relatively distant future, it is clear that uncertainty will loom particularly large. The balance that our economic system has to strike is between relatively clear-cut present needs, and some rather unclear future needs. The uncertainty about the future has many causes. Partly it stems from an inevitable inability to predict people's tastes and needs. But more specific to the particular problem in hand is uncertainty about future resource stocks and about future technology. The former arises because resource stocks are rarely known with certainty; there have been few periods in the last half century when there have not been important discoveries of many resources. Hence when deciding how fast to use up a resource, we have to realize that our estimates of its availability may increase or decrease over time, in an unpredictable manner. Evidence for the importance of this is provided by the fact that between 1953 and 1972, the world's proven oil reserves rose by a factor of 5·7, while oil consumption rose by a factor of 4. Of course, the evolution of known reserves is certainly not exogenous, but is a response to the allocation of effort to prospecting and development—itself a function of many factors, including expectations about future prices, the tax treatment of exploration expenses and the system used to allocate exploration rights amongst competing firms. Typically this is some form of competitive bidding, but there are many variations possible within this general framework. We discuss some of these issues in Chapters 12 and 14.

The importance of uncertainty about future technology should be self-evident: as a resource becomes scarce and its price rises, efforts to develop substitutes or to find processes which can function without it, or with only minimal amounts, are intensified. Oil again provides an example. One has only to consider the upsurge of research on alternative energy sources following the 1973 Arab oil embargo and the sharp price rises. Naturally, the choice of a depletion policy should depend upon the likelihood of success in these ventures, so that important elements of uncertainty have once again to be confronted directly. These issues are considered at length in the context of a market economy in Chapter 13, and within the framework of a planned economy in Chapters 14 and 16.

3. The foregoing paragraphs have described, admittedly in rather summary form, a sample of the issues we hope to raise in the following chapters. We would not claim to be examining all of the questions that arise in connection with exhaustible resources. We are deliberately concentrating on a range of theoretical issues concerning the performance of the mechanisms by which these resources may be allocated. While many of the empirical questions relating to the likely availability of extra resource supplies or to the chances of technological changes of a major type have been adequately, though perhaps not definitively, studied, there is need for a theoretical framework within which this data can be evaluated. We hope that the arguments of this book go some way towards constructing that framework.

There is another important class of questions that we shall also consider: these are questions relating to what one might describe as the political economy of resource depletion. This is in itself a complex set of issues with many dimensions. Amongst these are strategic issues relating to security; many governments place great importance on being able to control their supplies of resources, a tendency that has been greatly reinforced by turbulent events in the oil market in 1973. This aspect of the political economy of the problem is amenable to our analytical approach; the emphasis on security of supply as an objective of policy could be regarded as a rational response to uncertainty by risk averse governments. One could see it as an attempt to minimize the greatest economic damage that a hostile trading partner could inflict, or to minimize the bargaining power of such a partner. It is analogous to what game theorists know as the 'maximin' strategy in a game of conflict.

Several strands of this complex of problems are concerned with the international distribution of income. Ownership of a large fraction of the world's stock of a resource gives a country, or group of countries if they collaborate, very substantial monopoly power which they may exploit to effect a considerable transfer of income to themselves. This in turn influences relative rates of development, diplomatic relations between buyers and sellers, and the political and military standing of the sellers. One need look no further than the Organization of Petroleum Exporting Countries for illustrations of all these points; and there seems to be little doubt that similar organizations for other resources will follow in the future. The rate at which stocks of a resource are depleted does, of course, influence the chances of such a cartel being formed.

The point is that as stocks are depleted, those remaining tend to become concentrated in a decreasing number of countries, and in general the smaller the number of countries involved, the easier it will be to organize a really effective cartel. The reduction in numbers makes communication and organization easier, and increases the chances of finding that degree of political homogeneity without which successful collaboration is highly unlikely. These chances are further heightened by the fact that the first stocks to be depleted are usu illy those nearest to the consumers, i.e. those in the developed consumer countries. And these are just the countries likely to use their power to break a cartel. The history of OPEC again provides an interesting example of these points: although formed in the early 1960s, its bargaining power remained minimal until consuming countries became seriously worried about long-term supply problems, and was given a considerable boost by the rapid passage of the USA from self-sufficiency in oil to substantial dependence on imports in the early 1970s. (This process is examined in some detail in Chapter 15.)

These and related issues could clearly be pursued at much greater length, and in due course they will be. However, we hope that we have at present said enough to whet the reader's appetite for the more formal and precise analysis of these issues that begins in the next chapter.

4. We wish to end this introductory review by making quite explicit a methodological point which is at least strongly implicit in what follows, but which nevertheless merits distinct and emphatic statement. In much of the succeeding analysis, we make a substantial number of simplifying assumptions, and consequently work with relatively simple models, typically involving no more than four or five variables. The methodological point is that this is not a choice that is forced on us by a desire to maintain comprehensibility by a broad audience. It is a deliberate choice based on the belief— confirmed by the common experience of many members of our profession—that for the purposes of developing a deep and intuitive understanding of the complexities of an economic system, it is best to abstract dramatically and consider only a skeletal representation of the key factors and their interactions. Obviously, which are key factors and which are subsidiary, is in the first instance a matter of judgement, to be verified or rejected by empirical studies. What one aims at in constructing an economic model, whose purpose is the development of understanding at a basic conceptual level (as opposed for example to the prediction of the values to be assumed by a particular set of variables at a future date), is to strip away detail and in the process sacrifice precision, in order to grasp at general principles which would be obscured but by no means invalidated by the inclusion of detail. What one aims at in other words is the construction of a framework which is simple enough to reveal the principles at work but whose basic structure is robust to the kinds of additions and extensions generally needed to implement the analysis in any particular situation. Such an approach is very much in the spirit of a tradition of economic analysis, running from Adam Smith through Keynes to the present, but is sometimes found a little surprising by those inexperienced in the field. It is primarily for this reason that it has seemed to us to merit explicit notice.

CHAPTER 2

RESOURCE ALLOCATION IN A TIMELESS WORLD

Introduction

This chapter is by way of being introductory. It is also the most formal of the chapters in the book. We shall introduce several concepts that will prove essential in discussing the economics of exhaustible natural resources. Since these notions form the basis of resource allocation theory it will prove useful to avoid mentioning exhaustible resources at this stage. This is so for two reasons. One of our aims in this book is to explore the extent to which economics can usefully be applied to analyse the allocation of exhaustible natural resources under various circumstances. As a minimum we must then sketch the theory to which we shall be appealing. This forms our first reason. Our second reason is that while exhaustible resources are much like any other resource, they possess some strong special features. The remainder of this book will analyse these special features. This being so, it is important to make precise what they are special features of.

In this chapter we shall discuss resource allocation in the simplest of environments—one that is timeless and where the agents face no uncertainty. In fact the construction can be reinterpreted to accommodate both time and uncertainty. This will be done in Chapters 4, 8 and 14. It is possible that all readers are familiar with the material of this chapter. If a glance persuades the reader of this he can go directly to Chapter 3.

1. Equilibrium Concepts

We begin by considering a very general environment consisting of n agents (individuals) each of whom has a set A_i $(i = 1, \ldots, n)$ of *acts* from which he may *in principle* choose. For the moment we leave the nature of these acts undefined, though they may typically involve the selection of net consumption bundles or of production plans. a_i stands for the act chosen by individual i, and $a = (a_1, \ldots, a_i, \ldots, a_n)$ denotes the vector of all such choices, one for each individual. In many cases the set of acts actually feasible for individual i will depend on the choices made by others. Thus a downstream firm cannot avail itself of clean water from a river if an upstream firm is emitting water pollutant, and an oil drilling company cannot extract all the oil from a concession if a neighbouring firm slant-drills and taps the same pool. To formalize this point, let us denote by $N=(1, \ldots, n)$ the set of all agents in the environment. Now denote by $a_{N-i}=(a_1, a_2, \ldots, a_{i-1}, a_{i+1}, \ldots, a_n)$ the vector of acts chosen by agents other than i, and by $\phi_i(a_{N-i})$ the set of acts *feasible* for i when others choose a_{N-i}. Obviously $\phi_i(a_{N-i})$ cA_i for all i, and for a vector a of acts to be feasible it must be the case that $a_i \in \phi_i(a_{N-i})$ for $i=1, \ldots, n$.[1] It is worth noting that this framework allows for 'externalities', in the sense that the options open to an individual may depend on the actions of others.

It is quite natural at this stage to leave unspecified the nature of the acts a_i, and consequently the sets A_i and $\phi_i(a_{N-i})$. But it is worth emphasizing that A_i and $\phi_i(a_{N-i})$ are constrained as much by 'natural laws' and the state of knowledge (e.g. that one cannot survive with zero consumption, or that currently energy cannot be supplied by controlled nuclear fusion) as by *legal* sanctions (e.g. that a firm cannot pollute a river if this is prohibited by law and if enforcement of the law is costless). We shall discuss these matters later in this chapter and as well in Chapters 3 and 5.

The next stage in presenting the construction is to turn to the preferences of individuals. Each individual i is assumed to have preferences over both his own acts and the acts of all others.[2] We further assume that these preferences can be represented by a function. Let this be u_i for individual i. Call this i's *utility function*. Then $u_i(a)$ associates with any vector a of acts, a single number, and $u_i(\cdot)$ represents individual i's ranking of alternative vectors of

[1] We write $\phi_i(a_{N-i}) \subseteq A_i$ to denote that $\phi_i(a_{N-i})$ is a subset of A_i. That is, an element of $\phi_i(a_{N-i})$ is an element of A_i. Furthermore, 'ϵ' denotes 'membership'. Thus $a_i \epsilon \phi_i(a_{N-i})$ denotes that a_i is a member of $\phi_i(a_{N-i})$.

[2] To be precise, we define a *preference ordering* of i as a *binary relation*, $\geqslant_i$ (interpreted as being 'at least as good as') defined over all vectors of acts $a \equiv (a_1, \ldots, a_j, \ldots, a_n)$ (with $a_j \epsilon A_j$: $j=1, \ldots, n$) such that (1) $a \geqslant_i a$ for all a (reflexivity); (2) $a \geqslant_i a'$ and $a' \geqslant_i a''$ implies $a \geqslant_i a''$ (transitivity) and (3) for all a and a' (with $a_j a' \epsilon A_j$: $j=1, \ldots, n$) either $a \geqslant_i a'$ or $a' \geqslant_i a$ (completeness). Thus, in our usage of the term a preference ordering is *complete* (i.e. any two vectors of acts are comparable by i). If the binary relation $\geqslant_i$ satisfies (1) and (2) but not (3) we say that i has a *partial* ordering defined over vectors of acts, (see Chapters 9 and 10). If $a \geqslant_i a'$ but *not* $a' \geqslant_i a$ then we write $a >_i a'$ (that is, i *strictly prefers* a to a'). To be accurate, individual preferences ought to be defined over the *consequences* of actions. But we suppose that each set of acts, one for each agent, leads to a unique consequence. Hence we may as well define preferences directly on sets of acts. See also Chapter 13.

acts.[3] Of course, it is quite explicit in this framework that individual i's utility depends not only on his own actions, but also on those of all others. 'Externalities' in consumption are therefore representable within this framework.

We are now concerned here with singling out those states of affairs that can, in some sense, be regarded as *viable*. Several possibilities suggest themselves, and here we consider a few that have been much discussed in recent years. In doing this it will prove helpful to introduce some additional notation. Let M be a subset consisting of M ($0 \leqslant M \leqslant n$) members. Such a subset will be called a *coalition*. The behaviour of coalitions will play an important part in the analysis of viability that follows, for it would seem reasonable that a state of affairs would be viable if no coalition (or at least no coalition of a particular type) can reject it.

To formalize this point, consider a vector a of feasible acts. We say that a can be *upset* by a coalition M if there exists a feasible vector a' with the property that $a'_j = a_j$ for $j \in N - M$ (i.e. for those not in the coalition) and

$$
\begin{aligned}
u_i(a') &\geqslant u_i(a) &&\text{for all } i \in M \\
u_i(a') &> u_i(a) &&\text{for at least one } i \in M.
\end{aligned}
$$

In words, a coalition can upset a feasible vector of acts if it can locate an alternative feasible vector which involves no change in behaviour for those not in the coalition, which improves the lot of at least one member of the coalition, and which makes no member worse off. Although the alternative which can be used to upset a particular vector involves no changes in the acts of those not in the coalition, it may of course change their utilities for better or worse—because these depend, *inter alia*, on a_i for $i \in M$.

Three different notions of viability are based on this concept of upsetting:

(a) If a feasible vector of acts a cannot be upset by the grand coalition of all individuals, then a is said to be *Pareto efficient*;

(b) If a feasible vector of acts cannot be upset by any single-membered coalition, then it is said to be a *Nash equilibrium*;

[3] By this we mean that $a \geqslant_i a'$ if and only if $u_i(a) \geqslant u_i(a')$. In particular, if $a_i > a'$ then $u_i(a) > u_i(a')$. Such a numerical representation need not exist. But it can be shown to exist under certain circumstances. On this, see Debreu (1954, 1959) and Arrow and Hahn (1971). It is clear that if a numerical representation does exist it is not unique. Any monotone increasing function of $u_i(\cdot)$ is a numerical representation of $\geqslant_i$. This is what one means when one says that the individual is assumed to possess 'ordinal utility'.

14   ECONOMIC THEORY AND EXHAUSTIBLE RESOURCES

(c) If a feasible vector of acts cannot be upset by *any* coalition then it is said to be a *strong equilibrium*.

It is useful to see the precise sense in which the three foregoing notions capture different aspects of the idea of viability. Consider a feasible vector of acts $a = (a_1, \ldots, a_i, \ldots, a_n)$. If an individual is allowed to act on his own (and this is allowed under (b) and (c)), he will wish to search and see whether he can choose an alternative act for himself that he prefers. But since both his feasible set of acts and his utility depend on the actions of others he will need to hypothesize the response of the others to his possible moves. The definition of upsetting embodies one such assumption, namely that the remaining agents will not respond at all. Given this assumption, the supposition that individuals act independently leads directly to the concept of Nash equilibrium. If coalitions are prohibitively costly to form (by our definition of a coalition, those of size greater than one, that is!) a Nash equilibrium is the only viable outcome resulting from the notion of upsetting. Not surprisingly, this concept has been widely used in the economics literature, though it often masquerades under alternative titles—Cournot and Edgeworth equilibria for instance.

If all coalitions can costlessly be formed, the strong equilibrium would seem a reasonable candidate for viability. The problem, as we shall see below, is that even in seemingly reasonable constructions a strong equilibrium often does not exist, i.e. every feasible vector of acts is upset by some coalition. One can also see why Pareto efficiency, which is usually not regarded as an equilibrium concept, can be viewed as one. If a vector of acts is not Pareto efficient, then all individuals, collaborating together, can upset it in order to improve on it.

It is of course immediate from the foregoing definitions that, if a vector of acts is a strong equilibrium, it is both a Nash equilibrium and Pareto efficient. It should also be immediate that there is no such necessary relationship between Nash equilibria and the set of vectors of acts that are Pareto efficient. In other words, an outcome that is a Nash equilibrium may well be one that is not Pareto efficient. Likewise, a Pareto efficient outcome may not be viable in the sense of being a Nash equilibrium.

The equilibrium concepts mentioned so far are based on the idea that resistance to upsetting should be a characteristic of an equilibrium: they differ only in the coalitions that are allowed to upset.

There is a possible weakness in this approach, which is that the assumption that a coalition makes about the behaviour of non-members before rejecting a particular vector of acts is perhaps too optimistic. This assumption is that those outside the coalition do not react. In practice, they may wish to retaliate against the coalition. This consideration has led to the following, dramatically conservative, definition.

A feasible vector $\bar{a}$ of acts is *blocked* by a coalition M if there exists a set of acts $a_i{}'$, $i \in M$, one for each member, such that for all feasible vectors a with $a_i = a_i{}'$ for $i \in M$,

$$u_i(a) \geqslant u_i(\bar{a}) \qquad \text{for } i \in M$$
$$u_i(a) > u_i(\bar{a}) \qquad \text{for at least one } i \in M.$$

Obviously this is a much more stringent concept than that of upsetting. For a vector to be blocked by a coalition it has to find a set of acts, one per member of the coalition, which will make no member worse off and at least one member better off *irrespective of what those outside the coalition may feasibly do*. A coalition contemplating blocking therefore has to take into account possible retaliatory acts by outsiders, even though such retaliation may greatly damage those carrying them out. Blocking obviously represents one end of the spectrum of which upsetting constitutes the other.

Three distinct equilibrium notions now follow from the definition of blocking.

(a') A feasible vector of acts is *Pareto efficient* if it cannot be blocked by the grand coalition of all individuals.

(b') A feasible vector of acts is said to be *individually rational* if it cannot be blocked by any single-membered coalition.

(c') A feasible vector of acts is said to be in the *core* if it cannot be blocked by *any* coalition.[4]

In definitions (a) and (a') the impossibility of 'upsetting' and 'blocking' amount to the same thing, since both are concerned only with the set of *all* individuals. As there *are* no individuals outside the coalition it makes no difference what is assumed about 'them'. That is why both notions lead to the same concept, viz. Pareto efficiency. Notice as well that a vector of acts that is in the core is both individually rational and Pareto efficient.

[4] What we have called a core is normally called an α-core. On this, see Aumann (1967).

In general, nothing further can be said about the relationships between these various equilibrium concepts. A good deal more can be asserted, however, if we are to restrict the environment to those where the feasible set of acts for each agent is independent of the acts of others. Thus suppose $\phi_i(a_{N-i}) = A_i$ for all i. Now consider a feasible vector of acts, a. It is then immediate from the definitions that if a cannot be upset by a given coalition, then it cannot be blocked by it either. It follows that if a is a strong equilibrium, it is in the core. By the same token, if a feasible vector of acts is a Nash equilibrium it is also individually rational. In Diagram 2.1 we

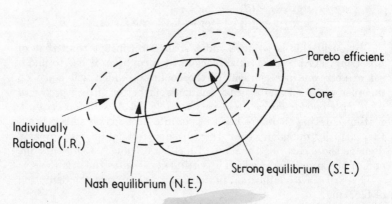

Diagram 2.1

(Enclosed areas denote sets of vectors representing different equilibrium concepts. Relationships between the core and S.E.; and N.E. and I.R. are restricted to the case of $\phi_i(a_{N-i}) = A_i$ for all i)

demonstrate these relationships between the five equilibrium notions that have just been defined.

It would seem then that we are presented with an *embarras de richesses*: there are too many equilibrium notions—not too few.[5] But it would be unreasonable to suppose that a single notion of equilibrium would prove reasonable for all economic environments. In some markets cartels have been known to form; in others, not so. Coalition formation is not costless, and there is obviously a bias in such costs, for some coalitions are easier to form than others. Coalitions among members with religious or cultural ties or within peer groups are presumably easier to form than otherwise. If the

[5] For a sample of other notions of equilibrium, see Luce and Raiffa (1957).

number of individuals is large the costs of communication may be too high for multi-membered-coalitions to form, and such *non-co-operative* equilibrium notions as Nash equilibrium and individually rational outcomes may be the appropriate concepts of viability. But if n is large and only single-membered coalitions are expected to be formed it would seem that the Nash concept possesses an intuitive appeal that the set of individually rational outcomes does not. As we remarked earlier, the notion of blocking is extremely conservative—or risk averse. It is hard to see why an individual, in deciding on whether to make a move, must take into account every feasible act on the part of all others and then make sure that the move makes him better off irrespective of what the others do. It is for such reasons that the notion of a Nash equilibrium has been exploited a good deal in the literature, and we shall appeal to it several times in the chapters that follow.

We have defined several distinct equilibrium notions (or notions of viability). There is no pretence though that an outcome that is viable is necessarily desirable. The fact that a vector of acts is Pareto efficient does not offer sufficient ground for it to be regarded as optimal—or even desirable. Typically, one would be concerned as well with the *distribution* of utilities, and it is possible that a vector of acts sustains an equilibrium in one of the several senses that we have defined, and at the same time yields a distribution of utilities that one may deplore. This is, of course, familiar matter, and we shall not need to dwell on it, except to emphasize a key point that is often overlooked. Each of the five notions of viability that we have enumerated has, quite naturally, been defined relative to the set of *feasible* vectors of acts. As such we have postulated the existence of the sets ϕ_i and A_i without much comment. In general, a change in the definition of feasibility will result in a change in the set of vectors of acts that are equilibria—in any sense of the term. This at once provides a clue to the manner in which public policy can affect equilibrium outcomes—for better or worse. In general, taxes and subsidies, regulations, public production and the establishment of property rights are all designed to alter the feasible sets of acts that individuals face. A major concern of economists has been to analyse how this might best be done under various circumstances. We shall be much concerned with this range of questions in the chapters that follow.

2. The Prisoner's Dilemma: An Example

We have presented various notions of equilibrium in a fairly
abstract setting because it is easiest to see their structure when
presented in a general framework. We now consider a simple and
well-known example of such an environment with a view to exemplifying these notions. The example that we shall consider is widely
known as the prisoner's dilemma game. Its importance lies in the
fact that it sheds a little light on many resource allocation problems.
Here we shall consider this problem in the currently topical context
of fisheries regulation, without going into the precise nature of the
environment that leads to the formulation we present.

Suppose that there are two countries, A and B, that exploit a
fishing ground on the high seas. International law gives neither any
right to control access to this. Marine biologists discover that this
ground has been grossly over-fished in the past, so that a continuation of present fishing levels will lead to its extinction within the
near future. However, the fish species involved reproduce very
rapidly, and the biologists indicate that a two-year ban on all
fishing, together with suitable limits on the catch rate thereafter,
would ensure the long-run survival of the fishery. Each country
therefore has two options: to pass a domestic law banning the use
of this fishery for two years and limiting it thereafter, or to allow
the present domestic catch policy to continue. This range of choices
is unaffected by the other country's choice, so that in terms of our
earlier notation $\phi_i = A_i$, $i = 1, 2$. However, the return that either
country receives as a result of pursuing each of these policies
naturally does depend on what choice the other makes, so that
'utilities' are interdependent although feasible sets are not. There
are four possible combinations of policy choices, and hence four
possible payoffs for each country. These are presented in Table 2.1.
The numbers in this table are purely hypothetical, and represent

Table 2.1

| | Country A | |
Country B	Allow present catch policy of A to continue	Limit fishing
Allow present catch policy of B to continue	(15, 15)	(5, 25)
Limit fishing	(25, 5)	(20, 20)

the relative magnitudes that might be involved. One can think of them as indicating the value of profits derived from the fishery, measured, say in $ million. Of each pair of numbers, the first represents the payoff to A, and the second to B. Thus if both agree to a policy of limitation, then each will attain profits of $20 million. On the other hand, if neither adopts such a policy, then each will attain only $15 million. The off-diagonal elements of the table indicate the outcome if one country unilaterally adopts a policy of restraint. In such a case there is a substantial asymmetry in the outcome. The benefits of the restraint exercised by one country accrue primarily to the other, whose fishermen are left free to take both their usual catch and most of the catch that the other country's fleet would normally take. Thus if B exercises restraint and A does not, the payoffs are $25 million to A and $5 million to B and vice versa. The question we now turn to is this: in the context of this example, which of the equilibrium notions discussed above exist, and what are their characteristics?

The first point to note is that of the four possible outcomes, all are Pareto efficient except that in which both countries allow the present state to continue. It is also easy to verify that this non-Pareto efficient outcome is the unique Nash equilibrium. Clearly, a situation where both limit their fishing is not a Nash equilibrium, since on the assumption that A will limit its fishing, B's optimal choice is to impose no restrictions, raising its own payoff from 20 to 25. Thus the mutual limitation outcome can be upset by either country acting in this way. Likewise, the situation where A exercises restraint and B does not, producing payoffs of $5 million and $25 million respectively, is not a Nash equilibrium, as A can upset it by choosing instead not to exercise restraint and thus raising its payoff by $10 million. A parallel argument establishes that the reciprocal situation where B exercises restraint and A does not, cannot be a Nash equilibrium. Thus the only possible candidate for the role of Nash equilibrium is the outcome where neither country exercises restraint, and indeed it is clear that this is a Nash equilibrium because on the assumption that the other will continue without restriction, neither has any incentive to impose such restrictions itself. Restraint would merely reduce its payoff from $15 million to $5 million, boosting that of the other by $10 million.

Recall now from Diagram 2.1 that if a vector of acts is a strong equilibrium, then it must also be a Nash equilibrium and Pareto efficient. In the prisoner's dilemma problem the only Nash equilibrium outcome is Pareto *in*efficient. It follows that a strong equilibrium does not exist.

We turn now to the equilibrium concepts arrived at from the notion of 'blocking'. Take first the vector of acts consisting of A limiting its fishing and B continuing its present policy. While it cannot be blocked by B (why?) it can be blocked by A, because A can guarantee for itself a return of at least $15 million by continuing its catch policy irrespective of what B proposes to do. It follows that this proposed vector of acts is not individually rational. By a parallel argument it is easily confirmed that the vector of acts consisting of A continuing its present catch policy and B limiting its fishing is not individually rational either. Now consider the case where both countries exercise restraint. It is individually rational. For consider A. It cannot guarantee for itself $20 million if it continues its present policy. Should B also continue as before A will receive only $15 million. Similarly for B. There remains the vector of acts consisting in both countries pursuing their present policy. It is simple to see that this too is individually rational.

In this simple example there are three non-trivial coalitions that can form; namely two single-membered coalitions and the grand coalition of the two. We have seen that the two vectors of acts resulting in the 'utility' pairs (15, 15) and (20, 20) are both individually rational. Of these two, the pair (20, 20) is Pareto efficient. It follows immediately that the vector of acts consisting in both countries exercising restraint is the unique core element. These findings are tabulated below in Table 2.2.

The prisoner's dilemma example has been discussed widely in the literature, and it has been argued very forcefully that there is a definite sense in which the outcome where neither country exercises restraint is the likely outcome. The point about this particular example is that each country finds it in its interests not to restrict its fishing activity, irrespective of what the other does. Thus if the

Table 2.2

Pareto efficient outcomes	(A limits, B limits); (A limits, B does not) and (B limits, A does not)
Nash equilibrium outcomes	(A does not limit, B does not limit)
Strong equilibrium outcomes	Does not exist
Individually rational outcomes	(A limits, B limits); (A does not limit, B does not limit)
Core outcomes	(A limits, B limits)

other country also fails to restrict its fishing, the country under consideration has a payoff of $15 million instead of $5 million, whereas if the other does limit, not limiting pays off to the extent of giving $25 million instead of $20 million. Thus the policy of not restricting fishing is a dominant strategy for each country, though of course the outcome where *neither* exercise restraint is not Pareto efficient.

It has been observed that the two countries could enter into a treaty to restrict fishing, and that in consequence both would be better off than in the Nash equilibrium. It is, however, true that each will have an incentive to break the treaty, so that whether or not the mutual limitation outcome is viable will depend very much on the possibility of guaranteeing that this treaty is observed. The example does illustrate that different equilibrium concepts consist in different sets of outcomes and that whether a given equilibrium notion is in fact viable depends crucially on the social and institutional framework within which the problem is set. If this is such as to facilitate co-operation and the observance of mutually advantageous treaties, then the appropriate equilibrium concept may well be that of the core. But in other less propitious circumstances the non-Pareto efficient Nash equilibrium may result.

It has seemed worth presenting the prisoner's dilemma game at some length partly because it illustrates well the different equilibrium notions presented earlier, and also because there are a number of other important problems in the field of resource management which for pedagogic purposes can be given a similar structure. One could for example consider two drilling companies both drilling into the same oil pool whose geological structure is such that the total amount recoverable declines with the speed of extraction. Then if both deplete the reservoir slowly, both will do well: but if either believes that the other will continue a slow extraction policy, then it has an incentive to deplete fast and obtain a larger fraction of the oil. Similar problems can arise if two countries pollute a body of water which is adjacent to both of them. Issues of this nature will form the basis of the problem of 'the common' which will be discussed in Chapters 3, 5 and 12. What we shall see however is that contrary to what is often claimed, the problem of 'the common', when properly formulated, is *not* a prisoner's dilemma game.

We have completed our general overview of some alternative notions of equilibrium. In the next section we review an important environment, the *private ownership economy*, and discuss a much studied equilibrium notion; that of a *competitive equilibrium*.

3. Competitive Equilibrium of a Private Ownership Economy

The *private ownership economy* has been much discussed in the economics literature.[6] Here we shall sketch its essential features.

Suppose there to be l perfectly divisible commodities (labelled $k = 1, \ldots, l$). They consist of final consumption goods, intermediate goods and services. *Consumers* are n in number (labelled $i = 1, \ldots, n$) and we denote by $x_i = (x_{i1}, \ldots, x_{il})$ the vector of consumption by consumer i—i.e. his *consumption bundle*. For consumers it is usual to represent *demands* by positive numbers and *supplies* by negative

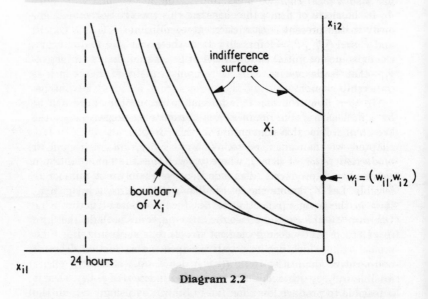

Diagram 2.2

numbers. Thus, for example, the labour service provided by an individual is usually denoted by a negative number. In this chapter we shall follow this convention. In subsequent chapters, where the discussion will proceed by way of examples, we shall not need to follow this convention.

Denote by X_i the set of all physically allowable consumption bundles for consumer i. Thus for example, consumption bundles with more than 24 hours of labour service in a day are ruled out of court, as are bundles that stipulate consumption levels falling short

[6] See the references in the Notes at the end of this chapter.

of subsistence needs. X_i is called the *consumption possibility set* of consumer i. Thus $x_i \in X_i$. In Diagram 2.2, a two-commodity world is represented, with the first good ($k=1$) supplied by the consumer, and the second ($k=2$) being demanded by him. There are several technical assumptions about X_i that are normally made. We shall not tabulate all of them. We shall merely mention one that we shall make use of, namely that, as in Diagram 2.2, X_i is a closed convex set.[7]

In the private ownership economy consumer i possesses an *initial endowment* vector $w_i = (w_{i1}, \ldots, w_{il})$. He has a legal right to w_i. We take it that w_i belongs to X_i. Assume next that consumer i has also a legal right to a fraction θ_{ij} of the net profit of firm j. θ_{ij} is the share of firm j that consumer i owns. It is given exogenously in the present construction. By definition $0 \leqslant \theta_{ij} \leqslant 1$ for all i and j, and $\sum_{i=1}^{n} \theta_{ij} = 1$ for all j. It is these last two features—viz. the existence of initial endowments of goods and shares, i.e. w_i and θ_{ij}—that leads one to call the present construction the private ownership economy.

We turn now to firms. It is normal to denote the *supplies* made by a firm as positive numbers and *demands* by negative numbers. We shall follow this convention in this chapter although in later chapters we shall not need to. We write by $y_j \equiv (y_{j1}, \ldots, y_{jl})$ the *production vector* of firm j, where y_{jk} denotes the net quantity of commodity k produced (demanded) by j. Plainly not all y_j's are feasible. Let Y_j denote the set of all y_j's that are feasible for firm j. It is in the main a reflection of the state of knowledge of j.[8] In Diagram 2.3 the case is presented where a firm uses a single input ($k=1$) to produce a single output ($k=2$). Given an amount of the input $-y_{j1}$ (which is non-negative, since inputs are measured as non-positive quantities) let $f_j(-y_{j1})$ denote the *maximum* output feasible by j. $f_j(\cdot)$ is called the *production function* of j. Of course, it is feasible to produce less than $f_j(-y_{j1})$ even by using $-y_{j1}$ units of

---

[7] X_i is said to be a *convex* set if x_i, $x_i' \in X_i$ and $0 < \alpha < 1$, implies that $\alpha x_i + (1-\alpha)x_i' \in X_i$. That is, a weighted average (with positive weights) of two points in X_i is also a point in X_i. It is *strictly convex* if the weighted average (with positive weights) of any two members of X_i is in the interior of X_i, i.e. one can construct a circle (sufficiently small in radius) with the weighted average as centre, which lies entirely in X_i. X_i is said to be *closed* if the limit of every convergent sequence of points in X_i belongs to X_i. Thus in Diagram 2.2 the boundary of X_i is assumed to belong to X_i. Notice that in the diagram x_{i1} denotes the quantity of *labour* which is supplied by i. Thus his initial endowment of labour is nil (or, to put the matter differently, his initial endowment of *leisure* is 24 hours).

[8] We say, 'in the main' since legal sanctions, e.g. patent barriers, and social sanctions play their part as well in constraining Y_j.

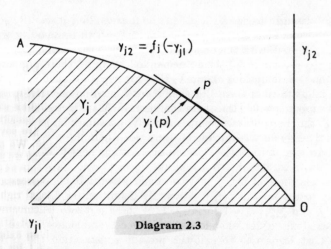

Diagram 2.3

the input. If the firm in fact produces less than this, one says that the firm is producing inefficiently. One does not wish to rule out inefficient production in advance and, in particular, if commodities can be freely disposed of, it is feasible for the firm to produce a *negative* amount of the second commodity, using inputs of the first (i.e. use both as inputs and produce nothing!). In short, for this two commodity example

2.1 $$Y_j = \{y_j | y_{j2} \leqslant f_j(-y_{j1})\}$$ [9]

Y_j is called the *production possibility set* of firm j. As regards the structure of production possibility sets we begin by supposing that $0 \in Y_j$. That is, *inactivity* is feasible. We shall also rule out increasing returns to scale in production and suppose that Y_j is convex (as in Diagrams 2.3 and 2.4). We can now formalize the assumption that commodities are freely disposable: If y_j is feasible (i.e. $y_j \in Y_j$) then if $y_j' \leqslant y_j$ then y_j' is also feasible. In particular, this means that in Diagrams 2.3 and 2.4 the entire south-west quadrant is feasible, (i.e. it is a subset of Y_j). The assumption that Y_j is invariant to the production vectors of other firms (an assumption that we have implicitly made) bears emphasis. The implications of dropping this last and the free-disposal assumption will be studied in Chapter 3.

Two final assumptions about production possibilities that are implicit in Diagrams 2.3 and 2.4 are worth stating explicitly. The

---

[9] The notation in 2.1 says 'the set of all y_j's such that $y_{j2} \leqslant f_j(-y_{j1})$'.

first is that Y_j is closed. Thus, the boundaries, OA in the diagrams belong to Y_j (see 2.1). To bring out the second, let $y_j \in Y_j$. Then $\sum_{j=1}^{m} y_j$ is the total production vector of the economy. Write $y = \sum_{j=1}^{m} y_j$ where $y_j \in Y_j$. The set of all such total production vectors we denote as Y (i.e. $Y = \sum_{j=1}^{m} Y_j$). Clearly $0 \in Y$ (since $0 \in Y_j$ by assumption). Consider a total production vector $y \in Y$ and suppose $y \neq 0$. Then the assumption is that $-y$ does not belong to Y. In the context of our example the assumption says that if, say, the economy is capable of using three units of labour input to produce five units of the consumption good as output, then it is not

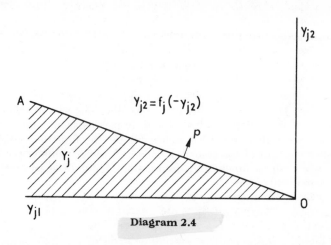

Diagram 2.4

possible to reverse the process and to produce three units of labour output with five units of the consumption good as input. Diagrams 2.3 and 2.4 of course rule out such production reversal. It is a mild assumption.

A distinguishing feature of a competitive equilibrium of a private ownership economy is the role that *prices* play in delineating the feasible sets and payoffs of agents. It is supposed that a market is organized for each and every commodity in the economy, and that a price is quoted for each good. Here we suppose that the cost of establishing a market is negligible.[10] One supposes as well that

[10] This assumption will be dropped in Chapter 3. The implications of dropping this assumption for an intertemporal economy are far reaching. On this, see Hahn (1971, 1973b), Radner (1972), Starrett (1973), Kurz (1974) and Hart (1975).

agents are sufficiently large in number that each consumer and each producer can treat prices parametrically.[11] Let $p = (p_1, \ldots, p_l)$ be a vector of prices in our construction. This is not necessarily an 'equilibrium' price vector.[12] We take it that $p_k \geqslant 0$ for $k = 1, \ldots, l$, with at least one price strictly positive; an assumption that will be justified presently. If $\mathbf{y}_j$ is the production vector of firm j, its *net profit* is expressed as $p \cdot \mathbf{y}_j \equiv \sum_{k=1}^l p_k y_{jk}$.[13] Given p, firm j chooses $\mathbf{y}_j$ from Y_j with a view to maximizing $p \cdot \mathbf{y}_j$. Suppose that a best choice exists. Call this a *supply vector* of j, and write it as $\mathbf{y}_j(p)$. It is unique (given p) if there are *decreasing returns to scale and proportions* in production, as in Diagram 2.3. It is not necessarily unique if there are *constant returns to scale* in production, as in Diagram 2.4. For if p is perpendicular to the straight line OA in Diagram 2.4, the firm makes zero profit (and this is the maximum profit it can make) no matter where it produces on OA. Therefore, so far as the *firm* is concerned, it may as well produce at any point on OA. This last is an argument that we shall use repeatedly in the following chapters.

In the private ownership economy the expenditure that an individual is allowed to undertake is constrained to be no greater than his wealth. This is his *budget constraint*. It is convenient to think of all transfers (e.g. gifts, etc.) as being embodied in his initial endowment vector, w_i. This being so, individual i's wealth is computed as follows.

Given p, the value of his initial endowment vector is $p \cdot w_i = \sum_{k=1}^l p_k w_{ik}$. Moreover, if firms are profit maximizing he receives as his share from the firms an amount equalling $\sum_{j=1} \theta_{ij} \cdot p \cdot \mathbf{y}_j(p) = \sum_{j=1}^m \theta_{ij} \sum_{k=1}^l p_k y_{jk}(p)$. Therefore, his wealth, I_i, is

$$2.2 \qquad I_i = \sum_{k=1}^l p_k w_{ik} + \sum_{j=1}^m \theta_{ij} \sum_{k=1}^l p_k y_{jk}(p).$$

Let x_i be a consumption bundle. Then i is constrained to choose x_i so that

$$2.3 \qquad x_i \in X_i \quad \text{and} \quad p \cdot x_i \leqslant I_i.$$

---

[11] The implications of dropping this last assumption will be studied in Chapter 11.

[12] The assumption that prices are treated parametrically out of 'equilibrium' can only be justified if agents are assumed, in a certain sense, to be unsophisticated calculators. On this, see Arrow (1959). We shall not go into this question here.

[13] Since output is measured as a positive number, and input as a negative number, $p \cdot \mathbf{y}_j$ is indeed net profit. The cost element of the production plan has in fact been netted out in the scalar product.

We take it that i has a preference ordering defined over his consumption possibility set, X_i, and in particular, that the preference ordering can be represented by a *continuous* function, $u_i(x_i)$. This function is, of course, not unique. Any continuous monotone increasing function of $u_i(\cdot)$ is a representation of the ordering as well. In what follows we shall suppose that if $x_i, x_i' \in X_i$ and $x_i \geqslant x_i'$, and that the amount of at least one good is strictly greater, then $u_i(x_i) > u_i(x_i')$. The set of all x_i that yield the same value of $u_i(\cdot)$ defines an *indifference surface* for i (see Diagram 2.2). He is *indifferent* between the x_i's that lie on such a surface. We shall also suppose that the indifference surfaces are strictly convex to the origin (as in Diagram 2.2). Formally this last means that $u_i(x_i)$ is by assumption a strictly quasi-concave function.[14] It should be noted that i's preferences have been defined over X_i. By assumption, then, his preferences are defined solely over *his* consumption vectors. (This will be relaxed in Chapter 3.) We shall suppose, as in Diagram 2.2, that consumers are never satiated. That is, given any $x_i \tau X_i$ there is another consumption vector $x_i \tau X_i$ which i strictly prefers to x_i (i.e. $u_i(x_i) > u_i(x_i)$).

Consumer i aims at selecting his most preferred consumption vector from the set defined by 2.2 and 2.3. We call this most preferred vector his *demand vector*, and express it as $x_i(p)$. Here we take it that it exists. It is unique (i.e. $x_i(p)$ is a single-valued function of p) since indifference surfaces are strictly convex to the origin (see Diagram 2.5). Now if $x_i(p)$ maximizes $u_i(x_i)$ subject to x_i being chosen from within the budget constraint 2.3, Diagram 2.5 suggests at once that the cheapest way consumer i can attain the utility level $u_i \equiv u_i\{x_i(p)\}$ is to 'purchase' $x_i(p)$; or in other words, that any other consumption bundle lying on the same indifference surface as $x_i(p)$ involves greater expenditure. This is in fact generally true (exceptions can arise if w_i lies on the lower boundary of X_i; a case we shall rule out here), and it is a result that we shall appeal to subsequently.

[14] $u_i(x_i)$ is (*strictly*) *quasi-concave* when the following holds: let $u_i(x_i) = u_i(x_i')$, i.e. x_i and x_i' are on an indifference surface. Define $x_i'' = \alpha x_i + (1-\alpha)x_i'$ ($0 < \alpha < 1$), as a weighted average of x_i and x_i' with positive weights. Then $u_i(x_i'') (>) \geqslant u_i(x_i)$. That is, x_i'' is (strictly) preferred to x_i (and x_i'). In words, indifference surfaces are strictly convex to the origins. An equivalent definition is that for any $x_i, x_i' \in X_i$ and $0 < \alpha < 1$ $u_i(\alpha x_i + (1-\alpha)x_i') (>) \geqslant \min \{u_i(x_i), u_i(x_i')\}$; the weighted average of two consumption vectors is (strictly) preferred to the less preferred of the two. In later chapters we shall often suppose that $u_i(x_i)$ is *strictly concave*. This means that if $x_i, x_i' \in X_i$ then for all $\alpha (0 < \alpha < 1)$, $u_i(\alpha x_i + (1-\alpha)x_i') > \alpha u_i(x_i) + (1-\alpha)u_i(x_i')$. It is immediate that if a function is strictly concave, it is strictly quasi-concave.

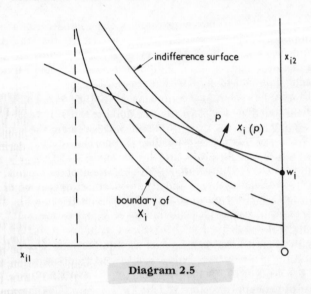

Diagram 2.5

Before defining a competitive equilibrium of a private ownership economy there are three points that need to be discussed. The first is that in order to ensure that each firm has a profit maximizing vector of inputs and outputs (i.e. that a *supply vector* exists) it is necessary to suppose that the price of every commodity is non-negative. This is because we have supposed that free disposal of goods and services is possible. Thus, if the price of some commodity is negative, a firm can in effect raise its profits by demanding more and more of it from the market. Clearly there is no finite limit to the competitive firm's demand for this good. A supply vector will not exist.[15]

The second point is that since by assumption there is no uncertainty and all commodities have a market, there is no trading in shares in firms. Goods are exchanged in the markets, but not shares. The point is that there will be no incentive for share markets to develop since, given a price vector and a policy (viz. production vector) on the part of the firm, the net profit can be calculated by all consumers with unerring accuracy. There will be no difference of

[15] It is possible to dispose of the free-disposal assumption (see, for example, Bergstrom (1975) and Kuhn and Hart (1975)). One can see that negative prices must then be allowed for (think of garbage as a commodity). We ignore these issues here. They will appear in Chapter 3.

opinion among consumers about the value of a production activity and therefore no incentive for trading in shares.

The third point is that the absolute levels of the prices are not of any importance: only relative prices matter in any given agent's decision. Thus, for example, with a price vector p, firm j's profit is $p \cdot y_j$. Then if y_j is profit maximizing at p then it remains so if instead the price vector is αp $(\alpha > 0)$. Moreover, if p is replaced by αp $(\alpha > 0)$ in 2.2 and 2.3 the feasible set of x_i's remain the same.

Since only relative prices matter we can normalize. One approach is to suppose that the prices add up to one (i.e. $\sum_{k=1}^{l} p_k = 1$ with $p_k \geqslant 0$ for $k = 1, \ldots, l$). Another is to choose a *numeraire* good (i.e. its price is set equal to unity) and all prices are expressed relative to this unit of account. This latter approach is a bit trickier, since one needs to be sure that the price of the commodity chosen as the numeraire is not zero.

We now come to the definition of an equilibrium. A *competitive equilibrium of a private ownership economy* is a non-negative price vector, p^*; a set of net demand vectors x_i^* $(=x_i(p^*)$, $i = 1, \ldots, n)$; and a set of net supply vectors y_j^* $(=y_j(p^*)$, $j = 1, \ldots, m)$, such that demand equals supply in the following generalized sense:

2.4
$$\sum_{i=1}^{n} x_i^* \leqslant \sum_{j=1}^{m} y_j^* + \sum_{i=1}^{n} w_i$$

and

2.5
$$p^* \cdot \left(\sum_{j=1}^{m} y_j^* + \sum_{i=1}^{n} w_i - \sum_{i=1}^{n} x_i^* \right) = 0.$$

A careful reading of 2.4 and 2.5 leads to the following interpretation: at a competitive equilibrium (i) total demand for each commodity must be no greater than total supply; (ii) if demand for a commodity is less than its supply in equilibrium, then the commodity is free (its price is nil); and (iii) demand equals supply for a commodity with a positive price. Conditions 2.4 and 2.5 denote the classical 'law of supply and demand'.

The above notion is widely known. It is distinct from the equilibrium notions discussed earlier; for the strong special feature of the competitive environment is the role that prices play in defining legal constraints (viz. the budget constraints of consumers) and objectives (viz. net profits of firms.).

It will be worthwhile emphasizing that if there are constant returns to scale in production for firm j, then at a competitive equilibrium j's net profit is nil. It cannot, of course, be negative, since the firm always has the option of shutting down and choosing $\mathbf{y}_j = \mathbf{0}$. It cannot be positive, since if $\mathbf{p}^* . \mathbf{y}_j^* > 0$ then $\alpha \mathbf{p}^* . \mathbf{y}_j^* > \mathbf{p}_j^* . \mathbf{y}_j^*$ for $\alpha > 1$, and, because of constant returns to scale, $\alpha \mathbf{y}_j^*$ is feasible for j if $\mathbf{y}_j^*$ is feasible. Therefore $\mathbf{y}_j^*$ could not have been profit maximizing. In the following chapters we shall often make use of this feature of constant returns to scale firms.

If the notion of a competitive equilibrium is to be a useful organizing idea, it is necessary to demonstrate that such an equilibrium exists in a fairly wide class of private ownership economies.[16] A significant part of modern mathematical economics consists of a description of less and less restricted environments that possess competitive equilibria.[17] We shall not report on this investigation here. Our purpose is merely to present the background for the special environments to be discussed in subsequent chapters. The environments that we shall discuss later on will be sufficiently simple to allow us often to *compute* competitive equilibria with little effort. But in computing an equilibrium one is, among other things, demonstrating that an equilibrium exists. Since we shall be able to do this for the models that follow, we shall not concern ourselves with a general 'existence theorem'. Instead we *illustrate* the matter here by considering an economy consisting of two goods, a single consumer and a single firm. In Diagram 2.6 this single firm is assumed to possess a constant-returns-to-scale technology. The straight line OA denotes the boundary of Y. Its normal (facing the north-easterly direction) is denoted by the vector $\mathbf{p}^*$. The initial endowment vector of the single consumer is the point B, $(\mathbf{w})$. BC is the straight line through B drawn parallel to OA. We know at once that $\mathbf{p}^*$ must be the equilibrium price vector. Let us check this. With $\mathbf{p}^*$ prices the firm may as well produce at any point on OA (it makes zero net profit at any such point and negative profit if it produces at any point below OA). So it may as well produce at the point marked $\mathbf{y}(\mathbf{p}^*)$. The consumer, facing the price vector $\mathbf{p}^*$, cannot consume at any point in X above the line BC. His budget constraint 2.2 and 2.3 prohibits him from choosing such a point. The shape of his indifference surfaces are such that, in Diagram 2.6, the point represented by $\mathbf{x}(\mathbf{p}^*)$ denotes his most preferred consumption bundle subject to this constraint. But by construction

[16] For details, see Arrow and Debreu (1954).
[17] See, for example, Debreu (1959), Chapter 5.

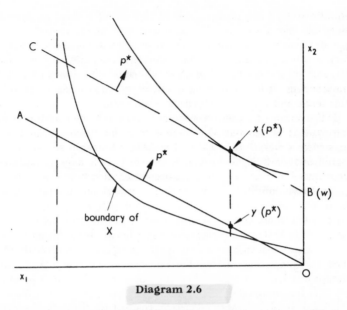

Diagram 2.6

$x(p^*) = y(p^*) + w$. The identification of the competitive equilibrium is complete. It is unique in this simple economy.

4. Competitive Equilibrium and Pareto Efficiency

There are at least three reasons why economists have made such an intensive study of competitive equilibria of a private ownership economy. The first, and probably the most common argument offered, is that it provides a *description* of a property-owning democracy. It is argued that as a first approximation, it may well suffice as a description of some economies one knows. The second reason is quite different, and is not concerned with description at all. The motivation comes from the following observation: the definition of a competitive equilibrium is designed to describe a *coherent* allocation of resources in a decentralized environment where each agent needs know only his mind and endowments, the vector of prices, and therefore his wealth. The question then arises whether it is possible to describe environments where this coherence is logically possible.[18] The third reason stems from the recognition

---

[18] This and the following reason can be found explicitly in Arrow and Hahn (1971), pp. vi–vii.

that the allocation of resources realized at a competitive equilibrium has some virtues, in that it can be regarded as superior to a large class of other feasible allocations. An investigation into the precise sense in which this last is true is patently of interest. It will tell us the sense in which a competitive equilibrium allocation can be used as a benchmark for evaluating other allocations. In this section we investigate this.

Earlier in this chapter we defined Pareto efficiency as an equilibrium notion—a feasible vector of acts being Pareto efficient if it cannot be blocked (upset) by the grand coalition of all agents. Stated equivalently, a feasible vector of acts is Pareto efficient if there does not exist another feasible vector of acts that is preferred by at least one agent and which is judged not inferior by any agent.

Let us translate this for the economy introduced in the last section. The total endowment vector of the economy is $\sum_{i=1}^{n} w_i$. A *feasible allocation* $(x_1, \ldots, x_n, .y_1, , \ldots, y_m)$ is a set of consumption vectors x_i $(i=1, \ldots, n)$, and production vectors y_j $(j=1, \ldots, m)$ such that

2.6a $\qquad x_i \in X_i$ $(i=1, \ldots, n)$ and $y_j \in Y_j$ $(j=1, \ldots, m)$

2.6b $$\sum_{i=1}^{n} x_i \leqslant \sum_{i=1}^{n} w_i + \sum_{j=1}^{m} y_j.$$

The above requires no further discussion. We say that a feasible allocation $(x_1', \ldots, x_n', y_1', \ldots, y_m')$ is *Pareto superior* to the feasible allocation $(x_1, \ldots, x_n, y_1, \ldots, y_m)$ if $u_i(x_i') \geqslant u_i(x_i)$ for all $i=1, \ldots, n$ and $u_i(x_i') > u_i(x_i)$ for at least one i.[19] We say that a feasible allocation is Pareto efficient if there is no feasible allocation Pareto superior to it.

It is now simple to show that under the assumptions made in the last section a competitive equilibrium of a private ownership economy is Pareto efficient. Suppose $(p^*, x_1^*, \ldots, x_n^*, y_1^*, \ldots, y_m^*)$ denotes a competitive equilibrium. We wish to show that no feasible allocation is Pareto superior to it. Thus consider a feasible allocation $(x_1', \ldots, x_n', y_1', \ldots, y_m')$ and suppose that it is Pareto superior. Then since it is feasible it satisfies 2.6, and therefore,

2.7 $$\sum_{i=1}^{n} x_i' \leqslant \sum_{i=1}^{n} w_i + \sum_{j=1}^{m} y_i'.$$

[19] In short, the former allocation can be blocked (upset) by the grand coalition of all consumers.

Since $p^* \geqslant 0$ (equilibrium prices are non-negative) we can multiply both sides of 2.7 by p^* to obtain

$$2.8 \qquad \sum_{i=1}^{n} p^* . x_i' \leqslant \sum_{i=1}^{n} p^* . w_i + \sum_{j=1}^{m} p^* . y_j' .$$

But y^*_j is profit maximizing for firm j at the price vector p^*. Thus

$$2.9 \qquad \sum_{i=1}^{n} p^* . w_i + \sum_{j=1}^{m} p^* . y_j' \leqslant \sum_{i=1}^{n} p^* . w_i + \sum_{j=1}^{m} p^* . y_j^* .$$

Combining 2.8 and 2.9 yields

$$2.10 \quad \sum_{i=1}^{n} p . x_i' \leqslant \sum_{i=1}^{n} p^* . w_i + \sum_{j=1}^{m} p^* . y_j' \leqslant \sum_{i=1}^{n} p^* . w_i + \sum_{j=1}^{m} p^* . y_j^* .$$

As we have supposed that consumers are unsatiated at a competitive equilibrium they will each have exhausted their entire budget. Thus

$$2.11 \quad p^* . x_i^* = p^* . w_i + \sum_{j=1}^{m} \theta_{ij} p^* . y_j^* \qquad \text{for all } i = 1, \ldots, n.$$

Summing equation 2.11 over all consumers yields 2.5, i.e.

$$2.12 \qquad \sum_{i=1}^{n} p^* . x_i^* = \sum_{i=1}^{n} p^* . w_i + \sum_{j=1}^{m} p^* . y_j^*$$

(since $\sum_{i=1}^{n} \theta_{ij} = 1$ for all $j = 1, \ldots, m$).

A scrutiny of 2.10 to 2.12 indicates that there are two possibilities. The first is that for all $i = 1, \ldots, n$

$$2.13 \qquad\qquad p^* . x_i' \leqslant p^* . w_i + \sum_{j=1}^{m} \theta_{ij} p^* . y_j^*$$

in which case, summing 2.13 over all consumers will yield 2.10. But in this case x_i' is within consumer i's budget at equilibrium prices and equilibrium production. Since by hypothesis there is at least one consumer who strictly prefers x_i' to x_i^*, the latter could not have been his utility maximizing purchase (i.e. his demand vector). We have arrived at a contradiction. Hence 2.13 cannot hold for all i.

But if there is at least one consumer for whom $p^*.x_i' > p^*.w_i + \sum_{j=1}^{m} \theta_{ij} p^*.y_j^*$ there must be at least one consumer (say r) for whom the reverse inequality holds, i.e.

2.14
$$p^*.x_r' < p^*.w_r + \sum_{j=1}^{m} \theta_{rj} p^*.y_j^*.$$

and this also leads to a contradiction. To see this notice that by hypothesis $u_r(x_r') \geqslant u_r(x_r^*)$. But this cannot be. For this consumer can purchase a tiny bit more of each commodity than in x_r', and still satisfy his budget constraint. He will strictly prefer this to x_r' and hence to x_r^*. But in this case x_r^* could not have been his utility maximizing purchase at equilibrium prices (p^*) and production (y_j^*). Thus the allocation at a competitive equilibrium is not Pareto inferior to any feasible allocation. It follows that a competitive equilibrium allocation is Pareto efficient.[20]

Although admittedly not negligible, this virtue of competitive equilibria is nevertheless limited. The allocation sustained at a competitive equilibrium depends, among other matters, on the distribution of initial endowments, w_i. There is nothing in the construction describing a private ownership economy to rule out an inequitable initial endowment distribution, giving rise to an inequitable equilibrium allocation.

The following, much deeper, relationship between Pareto efficient allocations and competitive equilibria tells us what public policy is required to alter the feasible sets of consumers so as to ensure that any given Pareto efficient allocation can be sustained as a competitive equilibrium. The proposition is that under certain circumstances (viz. the assumptions made about the private ownership economy of section 3), any Pareto efficient allocation can be sustained as a competitive equilibrium provided the initial endowments have been suitably redistributed among consumers.[21]

To simplify the exposition we shall employ diagrammatic analysis. We shall therefore return to the two-commodity world of section 3. Since neither good can be an intermediate commodity and since we

[20] It is important to realize that at no point in the proof have we needed to assume that consumer indifference surfaces are convex to the origin nor that production possibility sets are convex. We shall need to assume this though for the 'inverse optimum' theorem that follows.

[21] It is this proposition that is appealed to when the claim is made that with appropriate *lump-sum* taxes and subsidies a competitive private ownership economy can sustain an optimum allocation of resources. We shall demonstrate this as well for an intertemporal economy in Chapter 10.

have assumed that consumers are non-satiable the analysis will not be as general as it could be made.[22] Recall that the initial economy-wide endowment vector is $\sum_{i=1}^{n} w_i$. An allocation $(x_1, \ldots, x_n, y_1, \ldots, y_m)$ is feasible if it satisfies 2.6. Let $(\bar{x}_i, \ldots, \bar{x}_n, \bar{y}_1, \ldots, \bar{y}_m)$ be any given Pareto efficient allocation. It is by assumption feasible. Write $(z_1, z_2) \equiv \mathbf{z} \equiv \sum_{i=1}^{n} x_i - \sum_{i=1}^{n} w_i - \sum_{j=1}^{m} y_j$ as the *excess demand vector*. The terminology is obvious. If an allocation is feasible, then (by 2.6), the corresponding excess demand vector must be non-positive (i.e. $\mathbf{z} \leqslant \mathbf{0}$). That is, feasible excess demand vectors must all lie in the south-west quadrant (written as R_-^2) in Diagram 2.7. Now

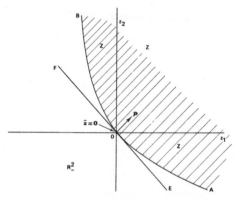

Diagram 2.7

return to the chosen Pareto-efficient allocation. We write the excess demand vector associated with it as $(\bar{z}_1, \bar{z}_2) \equiv \bar{z} \equiv \sum_{i=1}^{n} \bar{x}_i - \sum_{i=1}^{n} w_i - \sum_{j=1}^{m} \bar{y}_j$. Since by assumption consumers are never satiated, it must be the case that $\bar{z} = \mathbf{0}$ (why?). Next consider all *logically possible* allocations (satisfying 2.6a) that are strictly preferred by all consumers $(\bar{x}_1, \ldots, \bar{x}_n, \bar{y}_1, \ldots, \bar{y}_m)$. Let us denote the set of excess demand vectors associated with all such allocations by Z. No such allocation is, of course, feasible, or else the chosen allocation would not have been Pareto efficient. Therefore, all such allocations violate 2.6b. In Diagram 2.7 the curve AB represents the boundary of the

[22] Anticipating matters, the point is that the price vector supporting the chosen Pareto-efficient allocation will be found to be strictly positive. This need not be the case for more general economies. For the general treatment of the problem with finite number of commodities, see Debreu (1959), Chapter 6.

set of all such (unfeasible) allocations. That is, points to the north-east of AB (i.e. points in Z) represent excess demand vectors associated with allocations that are preferred by all consumers to the chosen Pareto efficient allocation.[23] We have drawn this region Z as convex. In fact it is easy to see that Z is convex if consumer utility functions are quasi-concave and if production sets (Y_j) are all convex.[24] In Diagram 2.8 the straight line FE is the tangent to AB at the origin. Let the normal to FE (facing the north-east) be denoted by the vector p. Then it is immediate from the diagram that

2.15
$$p.z \geqslant 0 \quad \text{if} \quad z \in Z$$

and
$$p.z \leqslant 0 \quad \text{if} \quad z \leqslant 0 \text{ (i.e. } z \in R_-^2).$$

From the diagram it is clear that $p \geqslant 0$, (i.e. p_1, $p_2 > 0$). Now, we have argued that

2.16
$$\bar{z} = 0 = \sum_{i=1}^{n} \bar{x}_i - \sum_{i=1}^{n} w_i - \sum_{j=1}^{m} \bar{y}_j.$$

Consider then an excess demand vector $z \in Z$ and let the allocation generating it be $(x_1, \ldots, x_n, y_1, \ldots, y_m)$. Thus

2.17
$$z = \sum_{i=1}^{n} x_i - \sum_{i=1}^{n} w_i - \sum_{j=1}^{m} y_j \in Z.$$

Then by 2.15 we have $p.(z - \bar{z}) \geqslant 0$, (since $p.\bar{z} = p.0 = 0$), which one can write as

2.18
$$\sum_{i=1}^{n} (p.x_i - p.\bar{x}_i) + \sum_{j=1}^{m} (p.\bar{y}_j - p.y_j) \geqslant 0$$

[23] It should be noted that for our simple two commodity economy, the excess demand vector associated with *all* Pareto-efficient allocations is the origin, 0. But the shape of AB—in particular, its slope at the origin—depends on the Pareto-efficient allocation we have singled out for study.

[24] Let $(x_1', \ldots, x_n', y_1', \ldots, y_n')$ and $(x_1'', \ldots, x_n'', y_1'', \ldots, y_m'')$ be two (infeasible) allocations, each being strictly preferred by all consumers to $(x_1, \ldots, x_n, y_1, \ldots, y_m)$. Let $z' = \sum_{i=1}^{n} x_i' - \sum_{i=1}^{n} w_i - \sum_{j=1}^{n} y_j'$ and likewise z'', be the excess demand vectors associated with the two allocations. By definition, they belong to Z. Let $0 < \alpha < 1$. The two (infeasible) allocations, by assumption, satisfy 2.6a. Since X_i and Y_j are both convex (for all i and all j) the allocation $(\alpha x_1' + (1-\alpha)x_1'', \ldots, \alpha x_n' + (1-\alpha)x_n'', \alpha y_1' + (1-\alpha)y_1'', \ldots, \alpha y_m' + (1-\alpha)y_m'')$ also satisfies 2.6a. Since indifferences surfaces are strictly convex to the origin (i.e. $u_i(x_i)$ is strictly quasi-concave) this last allocation is strictly preferred by all consumers to the less preferred of the two out of which it has been constructed. Therefore the excess demand vector associated with this last allocation also belongs to the region in question.

But z was arbitrarily chosen from Z. It follows that each of the $m+n$ terms in 2.18 must be non-negative in order that 2.18 holds. Thus

2.19 $$p \cdot \bar{y}_j \geqslant p \cdot y_j \qquad \text{for all } y_j \in Y_j$$
and
2.20 $\quad p \cdot x_i \geqslant p \cdot \bar{x}_i \qquad$ for all $x_i \in X_i$, and $u_i(x_i) > u_i(\bar{x}_i)$.

But 2.19 says that $\bar{y}_j$ is a profit maximizing production vector for firm j at the price vector p, and 2.20 says that at the price vector p the consumption vector $\bar{x}_i$ prescribed to consumer i by the chosen Pareto-efficient allocation is the cheapest way he can obtain the utility level $u_i(\bar{x}_i)$.[25] For our purposes here, this is another way of saying that if $p \cdot \bar{x}_i$ is the income that i is given then $\bar{x}_i$ is his utility maximizing purchase—when p is the price vector. Therefore, any Pareto-efficient allocation can be sustained as a competitive equilibrium provided the economy's total endowment vector $\sum_{i=1}^{n} w_i$ is allocated among the consumers in a suitable way. The price vector, p, which we have shown 'supports' the chosen Pareto-efficient allocation, is often called an *efficiency price vector*. In the chapters that follow we shall often use this terminology. But the implication of this result is this. We have noted that a (Pareto) efficient allocation is not necessarily an *optimal* allocation. But suppose it is argued (see Chapter 9) that an optimal allocation is Pareto efficient. Then the result says that by a suitable reallocation of initial endowments (often called lump-sum transfers) among consumers the optimum allocation can in principle be attained as a competitive equilibrium. We shall illustrate this possibility in Chapter 10 when we come to the question of the optimal depletion of exhaustible resources.

Notes on Chapter 2

Our aim in this chapter has been to provide a summary of various notions of equilibrium that have been discussed by economists. Several of these we shall appeal to in the chapters that follow. Of particular interest to us will be the notions of Nash equilibrium, of a competitive equilibrium of a private ownership economy, the concept of Pareto efficiency, and their relationships under various circumstances. For splendid expository pieces on the notion of economic equilibria, see Chipman (1965), Arrow (1969), Radner (1970) and Hahn (1973a). Perhaps the most lucid introductions to the properties of a competitive equilibrium of a private ownership economy are to be found in Koopmans (1957), Radner (1972), Malinvaud (1972), Arrow (1974), Hildenbrand and Kirman (1975) and Bliss (1975). Debreu (1959) and Arrow and Hahn (1971) provide a rigorous account of this theory. The role that prices can play in

[25] To justify the latter claim we need to rule out the possibility that there exists $x_i \in X_i$ such that $p \cdot x_i = p \cdot \bar{x}_i$ and $u_i(x_i) > u_i(\bar{x}_i)$. Suppose there exists such an x_i. Then there exists a number $\lambda < 1$ (but sufficiently near unity!) such that $u_i(\lambda x_i) > u_i(x_i)$, and also $p \cdot (\lambda x_i) < p \cdot \bar{x}_i$. But this violates 2.20.

sustaining a Pareto efficient allocation of resources is discussed in Koopmans (1957) and Bliss (1975). For a discussion of the question of how one may locate such prices, see Heal (1973).

The question of the existence of a Nash equilibrium in an abstract social system (as in section 1) was dealt with in the classic articles of Nash (1950) and Debreu (1952). The model has been generalized in different directions by Schaffer and Sonnenschein (1974) and Dasgupta and Maskin (1977). The relationship between a competitive equilibrium of a private ownership economy and a Nash equilibrium of a suitably defined abstract social system was demonstrated in a remarkable paper by Arrow and Debreu (1954). In this paper the authors proceeded first to demonstrate that the set of competitive equilibria of a private ownership economy is identical to the set of Nash equilibria of a social system suitably defined. They then appealed to the theorem regarding the existence of a Nash equilibrium in Debreu (1952) to establish the existence of a competitive equilibrium of a private ownership economy under certain conditions (viz. that production possibility sets of firms and consumption possibility sets of consumers are convex, that preferences are continuous and convex to the origin, etc.) This approach is particularly illuminating, since it reveals the precise sense in which a general competitive equilibrium may be viewed as a Nash equilibrium.

The relationship between competitive equilibria and the set of core allocations of a private ownership economy—an issue we have bypassed—has been explored vigorously in recent years. For a pure exchange economy (i.e. one where there is no production at all) the notion of 'blocking' takes on an intuitively appealing form. The very worst that a complementary coalition can do to a coalition is not to bestow any gifts on the coalition. Given initial endowments, the notion of blocking is then straightforward, and an argument similar to the one we have employed in showing that a competitive equilibrium is Pareto efficient establishes that if consumers have convex preferences a competitive equilibrium is in the core. For economies with production, matters are a little more complicated unless one postulates a constant returns to scale technology that is available to every potential coalition of consumers. On all this see for examples Debreu and Scarf (1963), Aumann (1964), Arrow and Hahn (1971), Böhm (1970) and Hildenbrand and Kirman (1976).

A particularly interesting non-co-operative equilibrium notion that we have not discussed is the one associated with the name of von Stackelberg. It is a variant of the Nash notion and focuses attention on possible asymmetry in the importance of agents. Thus suppose that there are precisely two firms that supply a market. Suppose each plays a Nash game while choosing quantities to sell in the market. Each firm calculates the amount that is most profitable for it to produce contingent on the output of the other. Call this a firm's *reaction curve*. A Nash equilibrium is a pair of output levels such that the output level of each firm maximizes its profit given the other's output level (i.e. the intersection of the two reaction curves); see, for example, Malinvaud (1972). The von Stackelberg approach is to suppose that one of the firms (viz. the 'leader') calculates the reaction curve of the other and *then* chooses its profit maximizing output, while the other calculates its profit maximizing output level contingent on the output of the leader (i.e. the other works on its reaction curve). The von Stackelberg equilibrium would appear a reasonable one to explore in the analysis of markets where cartels have been known to form but where not all firms join the cartel. We shall discuss this at length in Chapter 11.

The prisoner's dilemma game has been much discussed in recent years. It is attributed to A. W. Tucker. To learn why the game has been christened by this title the reader cannot do better than to read the account in Luce and Raiffa (1957). For an application of the game to an analysis of moral conduct, see Sen (1974).

CHAPTER 3

EXTERNALITIES

Introduction

In the previous chapter we discussed several notions that could, under different circumstances, be regarded as equilibria of a social system. Such notions are designed to represent viable outcomes. One that came up for particular scrutiny was the notion of a competitive equilibrium of a private ownership economy. A central feature underlying this concept is the existence of a competitive market for each and every commodity in the economy. Interest in such an equilibrium stems largely from the fact that under certain circumstances it sustains an efficient allocation of resources, in a sense that was made precise in the previous chapter. This provides one with a reason for regarding such an equilibrium as a benchmark with which to compare viable outcomes in other circumstances. The precise sense in which this can be done will occupy a great deal of this book. Now, there are many circumstances in which market solutions do not sustain an efficient allocation of resources. Many such situations can be described by saying that certain essential markets do not exist. Sometimes they just happen not to exist for accidental or historical reasons; sometimes there are logical reasons why they cannot exist; sometimes the nature of the physical situation keeps them from existing, or makes them function wrongly if they do exist. It happens that industries producing (or using) renewable and non-renewable resources are especially vulnerable to these difficulties. We then need to see how one might best analyse such situations. This chapter is concerned with illustrating how these difficulties are likely to arise, how they distort market equilibria away from efficiency, and what sorts of corrective measures are possible. In doing this we shall proceed by way of examples. For a more general treatment of the problem see the references in the Notes at the end of the chapter.

1. Market Equilibrium and Pareto Efficiency

Consider an economy composed of N individuals $(i = 1, 2, 3, \ldots, N)$. There are two commodities in this world, the first of which is of the

39

kind that appeared in the description of the private ownership economy, in the sense that, while an individual's utility depends on the quantity of this commodity he purchases, it does not depend on the amounts purchased by others. We shall tentatively refer to this as a *private* good. The second commodity, it will be supposed, is of a somewhat different nature. We shall suppose that an individual's utility depends not only on the quantity of this commodity that he purchases but that it depends on the amounts that others purchase of it as well. Denoting by x_i the quantity of the private good purchased by individual i and by g_i his purchase of the second commodity we suppose that his preferences over different allocations of these two commodities can be represented by an increasing, strictly concave and differentiable utility function, u_i, where

3.1 $$u_i = u_i(x_i, g_1, g_2, \ldots, g_i, \ldots, g_N).$$

Even a casual inspection of 3.1 suggests that we have already made an important limiting assumption regarding the transaction possibilities in this economy. We have in effect assumed that when individual h purchases g_h units of the second commodity individual i cannot be prevented from consuming g_h and consequently that he does indeed do so. In other words we are supposing that *exclusion* is impossible. This would appear to be a very reasonable assumption for commodities like national defence or law enforcement, for it would be impossible to provide security to one individual in a given region without at the same time providing this service to all the others (although the *benefit* enjoyed by person i when person h purchases a unit of this service could well depend on who person h is). For commodities like television transmission, however, non-excludability is not an appropriate assumption today. Broadcasting companies can now transmit what are often called 'scrambled' waves. In this situation when individual h purchases a programme he purchases a device that 'unscrambles' these waves, enabling him to view the programme. This particular purchase provides no benefit to person i.

In this book we shall not analyse the theory of externalities in any great detail. Rather, we are concerned with those aspects of the theory that have a direct bearing on the economics of natural resources. While 'non-excludability' is a special case, our subsequent examples will suggest that it is *the* special case for our purposes.

Consider then, our simple example with two kinds of commodities. To keep the argument simple, and to contrast the second commodity sharply with the private good, we shall for much of the time consider an important special case of 3.1, where individual i's utility depends on the *total quantity* of this second commodity purchased by everyone. In other words, we shall often restrict ourselves to the case where

$$3.2 \qquad u_i = u_i\left(x_i, \sum_{j=1}^{N} g_j\right).$$

Following traditional terminology we shall refer to the second commodity as a *public* good when i's utility function is of the form 3.2. Each individual is assumed to possess initially one unit of the private good and nothing of the public good. However, individuals can transform the private good into the public good at a fixed rate p. This may be thought of being achieved through trade with the rest of the world at a fixed international price of p units of the private good for each unit of the public good purchased. Alternatively, one may like to think of there being constant returns to scale in domestic production possibilities of converting the private good (say, leisure) into the public good (say, national defence). To present the points that we wish to focus attention on here in as sharp a manner as possible, assume all individuals to be identical, and that in particular,

$$3.3 \qquad u_i(x_i, \sum_{j=1}^{N} g_j) = \log x_i + \log \left(\sum_{j=1}^{N} g_j\right).$$

Individual i is therefore concerned with maximizing 3.3 subject to his budget constraint

$$3.4 \qquad pg_i + x_i \leqslant 1.$$

The question is: what notions of equilibrium seem appropriate for this decentralized economy, and what are their properties? Notice that the notion of a competitive equilibrium in a private ownership economy cannot cope with the problem here in its entirety because while it is plain from the budget constraint 3.4 that individual i chooses x_i and g_i, his utility depends as well on the choice of $g_j(j \neq i)$. This is a type of interaction that simply did not occur in our description of the private ownership economy, although of course, such interactions lay very much at the heart of the general social system studied in the last chapter.

If N is reasonably large it may seem plausible to consider a mixture of the notions of a competitive equilibrium and a Nash equilibrium. Not surprisingly, it is this notion that has been widely discussed in the literature. The central idea in this mixed conception is for each individual to suppose that each of the other individuals will purchase so much (not necessarily the same amounts) of the public good. He would then proceed to make his optimum purchases subject to his budget constraint. An equilibrium would then be a situation where each individual's supposition turned out to be correct. We shall call this mixed conception a *market equilibrium*. In one sense our terminology is somewhat misleading in that a special case of a market equilibrium is one where each and every commodity that enters in the utility functions of individuals and production sets of firms has a market. A yet more special case of this is a competitive equilibrium of a private ownership economy where it is further assumed that every agent is a price taker. Thus what we have called a market equilibrium is characterized as much by a *lack* of markets as by the existence of markets. Nevertheless, in so far as the notion of an equilibrium is a useful organizing idea, a mixed concept stands out probably as a more appropriate description of the world as we know it. Our terminology ought not therefore to be very confusing.

We would wish to study the nature of a market equilibrium for our example. Our very special parametrization of the economy was done solely with a view to being able to compute an equilibrium rather readily. We do this now.

Given that individuals are identical it is plain that one of the market equilibria must be characterized by a symmetrical allocation amongst all the N members of society. Indeed, one can readily verify that this will be the only market equilibrium. Thus let individual i suppose that *each* of the others has purchased $\hat{g}$ of the public good. His problem then reduces to maximizing.

$$\log x_i + \log\{g_i + (N-1)\hat{g}\}$$

by selecting x_i and g_i subject to 3.4. Denoting by λ_i the Lagrange multiplier associated with 3.4 one readily establishes that the necessary (and sufficient, since the utility function is strictly concave and the feasible set is convex) conditions for optimality are

3.5
$$\frac{1}{x_i} = \lambda_i$$

and

3.6
$$\frac{1}{(N-1)\hat{g} + g_i} = \lambda_i p.$$

Now at the market equilibrium one must have $g_i = \hat{g}$. It follows from equations 3.5 and 3.6 that

$$N\hat{g} = \frac{\hat{x}}{p},$$

which on using the budget constraint 3.4 yields

3.7
$$\hat{x} = \frac{N}{1+N} \quad \text{and} \quad \hat{g} = \frac{1}{(1+N)p}.$$

It follows that at the market equilibrium each individual purchases $\hat{x}$ and $\hat{g}$ units of the two commodities as given in 3.7. Notice that if N is large each individual at the equilibrium retains almost all of his initial endowment (the unit quantity of the private good) and transforms only a tiny bit of it in purchasing the public good. Indeed, the total purchase of the public good by the whole economy is $N\hat{g}$ and is thus bounded above by $1/p$.

An obvious question that one can ask is whether this market equilibrium is Pareto efficient. As one might suspect the answer is 'no'. Given that individuals are identical, calculating a Pareto-efficient allocation is simple. We are interested in an efficient allocation that is symmetrical among the individuals. Thus one naturally considers an optimization exercise in which a representative individual chooses for everyone. It follows that the problem is to maximize $\log x + \log Ng$ by choosing x and g subject to the budget constraint

$$pg + x \leqslant 1.$$

It is readily confirmed that the solution $(\tilde{x}, \tilde{g})$ of this problem can be expressed explicitly as

3.8
$$\tilde{x} = \frac{1}{2} \quad \text{and} \quad \tilde{g} = \frac{1}{2p} \quad \text{and therefore} \quad \tilde{g} = \frac{\tilde{x}}{p}.$$

That $(\tilde{x}, \tilde{g})$ is a Pareto-efficient allocation follows directly from the nature of the exercise that we have performed. That it is the case that the market equilibrium allocation 3.7 is not, follows readily from the fact that the utility of a representative individual at the allocation 3.8 is

$$\log \frac{1}{2} + \log \left(\frac{N}{2p} \right) = \log \left(\frac{N}{4p} \right),$$

while his utility at the market equilibrium is

$$\log \left(\frac{N}{1 + N} \right) + \log \left(\frac{N}{p(1 + N)} \right) = \log \left(\frac{N^2}{(1 + N)^2 p} \right)$$

It is of course immediate that

$$\frac{N}{4p} > \frac{N^2}{(1 + N)^2 p} \quad \text{when } N > 1.$$

2. Markets for Externalities

The foregoing example, which we shall explore yet further is, while simple in structure, very instructive. It has, for example, brought out sharply the fact that a market equilibrium can readily be Pareto *in*efficient. This feature would seem to run counter to the account in the last chapter where it was established that a competitive equilibrium of a private ownership economy is Pareto efficient. But there is really no mystery in this. The clue to a resolution of this apparent paradox lies, of course, in recognizing that every commodity that entered the description of a private ownership economy had a market and consequently a price associated with it. Putting it loosely, every commodity in the private ownership economy was assumed 'private'. In our present example, one of the commodities is not of such a variety. At the market equilibrium while individual i pays for only that quantity of the public good that he purchases (namely $\hat{g}$), he in effect consumes $N\hat{g}$. This is another way of saying that we have underspecified the number of 'commodities' in this economy and that some of these commodities have gone unpriced.

Yet another way is to say that at the market equilibrium of our example an individual is not compensated by the others for the benefit he bestows on the others in purchasing a unit of this public good. Given that it *is* a benefit that he is bestowing on others it is not entirely surprising that $\hat{g} < \tilde{g}$ and, therefore, that at the market equilibrium there is an undersupply of the public good compared to the Pareto-efficient allocation. This suggests that if a competitive market is established for each and every commodity that is potentially available in an economy, the allocation attained would be Pareto efficient. It would seem, then, that the notion of *externalities* is linked with the non-existence of markets, and indeed, one could define an externality to occur whenever a decentralized economy has insufficient incentives to create a potential market in some commodity and where, as a result, the market equilibrium is Pareto inefficient. This idea, the case for establishing markets for externalities—and hence, by our definition, obliterating the externalities—is one that has long been advocated. We look into this in the context of our example.

Imagine then that what we ordinarily call individual h's purchase of the 'externality generating' good (g_h) is regarded as the production of N joint outputs, one for each individual in the economy. Thus denote by g_{ih} $(h, i = 1, \ldots, N)$ the quantity of this good consumed by individual i when individual h purchases g_h. In our example we shall have

3.9 $\qquad\qquad g_{ih} = g_h \quad \text{for all } i \text{ and all } h.$

With this notion, individual i's utility can be expressed as

3.10 $\qquad\qquad u_i = u_i(x_i, g_{i1}, g_{i2}, \ldots, g_{ii}, \ldots, g_{iN})$

or as in our special case 3.3 by

3.11 $$u_i = \log x_i + \log \left(\sum_{h=1}^{N} g_{ih} \right).$$

Because of the notation just introduced, the variables appearing in the utility function relating to individual i are proper to him alone and appear in no one else's utility function. What we have, in effect, done is to have increased the number of commodities in the economy from 2 to $2 + N(N-1)$. One can now regard g_{ih} as being a commodity that is private to individual i. In other words, it is a *named* good. With this rather natural extension of the notion of a commodity, externalities have been reduced to ordinary commodities (they are named commodities) and, as one might expect, all the formal theory of the competitive equilibrium of a private ownership economy can be brought to bear on it. We look into this now. Given that we are regarding g_{ih} as a commodity that is produced by h and consumed by i, a competitive market for g_{ih} would entail the establishment of a price that i would have to pay h for i consuming g_{ih}. Of course, condition 3.9 would need to be satisfied for all i and h. But this will emerge as a market clearing condition for these joint products where at an equilibrium demands and supplies of these joint products are matched.

Denote by p_{ih} the price that i pays to h when i consumes the named good g_{ih}. (The sign of p_{ih} is of course an unknown of the problem. If, as in our example, the marginal utility to i of consuming g_{ih} is positive at an equilibrium, then one would suppose that $p_{ih} > 0$; not so if the 'externality' is a 'bad'.) Individual i's budget constraint will now read

$$3.12 \qquad pg_{ii} + x_i + \sum_{\substack{h=1 \\ h \neq i}}^{N} p_{ih}g_{ih} \leqslant 1 + \sum_{\substack{h=1 \\ h \neq i}}^{N} p_{hi}g_{hi}.$$

The only terms that may require explanation are the ones under the summation sign. Now $\sum_{h \neq i} p_{ih}g_{ih}$ is the amount that i is required to pay others for his consuming $g_{ih}(h \neq i)$. But he in turn receives payments from others for his consuming g_{ii}, since g_{ii} is, after all, a joint product, providing h with g_{hi}. It follows that $\sum_{h \neq i} p_{hi}g_{hi}$ is the total amount he receives from others. The upshot is that by this device of creating competitive markets for externalities (and therefore, by our definition, removing the externalities) we have a construction that is exactly akin to the private ownership economy of the last chapter. It will nevertheless be instructive to look a little more closely at a competitive equilibrium with markets for externalities.

Assume for the moment that individual utilities are of the general form 3.10. Individual i is concerned with maximizing 3.10 by choosing x_i and g_{ih} $(h=1, \ldots, N)$ subject to the budget constraint 3.12. At an equilibrium condition 3.9 must hold. Thus the budget constraint can be re-expressed as

$$3.13 \qquad pg_{ii} + x_i + \sum_{h \neq i} p_{ih}g_{ih} \leqslant 1 + \sum_{h \neq i} p_{hi}g_{ii}.$$

Denoting by μ_i the Lagrange multiplier associated with 3.13 it is readily checked that i will select x_i and g_{ih} $(h=1, \ldots, N)$ so as to ensure that

3.14a $$\frac{\partial u_i}{\partial g_{ih}} = \mu_i p_{ih} \qquad (h \neq i)$$

3.14b $$\frac{\partial u_i}{\partial g_{ii}} = \mu_i \left(p - \sum_{\substack{h=1 \\ h \neq i}}^{N} p_{hi} \right) \qquad i = 1, \ldots, N$$

and

3.14c $$\frac{\partial u_i}{\partial x_i} = \mu_i.$$

Notice that equation 3.14b implies that with the introduction of competitive markets for externalities the *net* price that i pays for purchasing g_i $(=g_{ii})$, is not p but rather $(p - \sum_{h \neq i} p_{hi})$, for p is the anonymous market price and $\sum_{h \neq i} p_{hi}$ is what he receives from others for his purchasing g_{ii}.

Using 3.14a in 3.14b one obtains

3.15 $$\frac{1}{\mu_i} \frac{\partial u_i}{\partial g_{ii}} = \left(p - \sum_{h \neq i} \frac{1}{\mu_h} \frac{\partial u_h}{\partial g_{hi}} \right)$$

and hence, from 3.14c that

3.16 $$\sum_{h=1}^{N} \frac{\dfrac{\partial u_h}{\partial g_{hi}}}{\dfrac{\partial u_h}{\partial x_h}} = p, \quad \text{for all } i.$$

Equation 3.16 is the fundamental principle pertaining to the production and allocation of externalities.[1] It expresses the fact that at a competitive equilibrium with a complete set of markets for externalities the ratio of the *sum* of the marginal rates of substitution between the externalities (regarded as a joint product) and the private good is equal to the marginal rate of transformation (p) between them. A competitive equilibrium with a complete set of markets for externalities is often referred to in the literature as a *Lindahl equilibrium*. It is, of course, rather plain that a Lindahl allocation will be Pareto efficient given that with competitive markets for externalities the economy is a private ownership one. We confirm this for our special case.

[1] See Samuelson (1954) and Arrow (1969).

Assume then that individual utilities are of the type 3.11. Given that individuals are identical, common sense dictates that we attempt to locate the general equilibrium prices by considering the possibility that

3.17 $$p_{ih} = \frac{p}{N} \quad \text{for all } i \text{ and } h.$$

One confirms that the price structure as expressed in 3.17 will in fact support an equilibrium. Denote by g_{ii}^* and x_i^* the net quantities of the public good and the private good that i purchases from the anonymous market. The complete symmetry of the model implies that g_{ii}^* and x_i^* are independent of i. Denote them by g^* and x^*. It follows that equation 3.16 reduces to

$$g^* = \frac{x^*}{p}.$$

Using this in the budget constraint 3.13 yields immediately that $x^* = 1/2$ and therefore that $g^* = 1/2p$. But this is simply the Pareto-efficient allocation $(\tilde{x}, \tilde{g})$ calculated earlier.

The efficiency implications of a Lindahl equilibrium have been recognized for a long time. It is for this reason that people have often advocated the desirability of allowing institutions to develop which will permit individuals to transact amongst one another the rights to generate externalities. The question, however, arises whether such competitive markets for externalities can readily be established. Even assuming, as we have done, that actual transactions and calculations can costlessly be carried out, there are at least three immediate reasons why there may be problems in establishing such markets.

1. A precondition for the establishment of a market is the existence and enforcement of property rights. We emphasized this aspect of the problem when discussing the private ownership economy. Now in many cases of externalities it may be impossible (or at any rate difficult) to *define* property rights, let alone establishing them legally and then enforcing them. A consideration of the private ownership economy suggests that the ability to set prices for commodities demands the possibility of excluding non-buyers from the use of the product. Now with externalities this exclusion may be technically impossible or at any rate it may require the use of

considerable resources. Property rights will be difficult to define precisely in such cases. The stringent market clearing condition 3.9 reflects the fact that it is technically impossible to prevent individual $i(i \neq h)$ from consuming g_h when individual h purchases g_h. Public goods like national defence and *open* grangeland and *open* sea will have this property. Externalities like pollution are other important examples. Clean air or clean water or noise pollution going to each individual will have to be treated as a separate commodity and it would have to be possible in *principle* to supply to one and not the other (though, of course, the final equilibrium would involve an equal supply, condition 3.9, to all). But this may be impossible or, anyhow, it may be very costly to make possible. Consider, for example, a locality where the inhabitants have, by law, the right to clean air. Now individual i by himself cannot sell his right to a neighbourhood factory desiring to emit pollution because the factory will be incapable of restricting its pollution to i's property. This is so because the atmosphere is in a constant state of diffusion. It is usually very expensive (via individual air conditioners) to parcel the atmosphere into units occupied by different individuals. But in effect it is this possibility that is required in principle for the price system to be viable for this example. It is at this point that one notices the connection between the problems of defining and enforcing property rights and the possibilities of excluding non-buyers from consuming commodities not purchased by them.

Another common example of the problems of establishing and enforcing property rights is the case of the owners of two adjoining oil fields. While it is easy to envisage the owners as having titles to the *land* they occupy, owning titles to the *oil* underground is an entirely different matter. One usually does not know precisely how much oil lies below a given surface area of land. Add to this the fact that nothing apparently is easier for oil men than syphoning oil from under their neighbour's land without anyone being the wiser, and it is easy to recognize that the quantities of oil that can be extracted over time (and consequently the flow of profits over time) by an oil man will depend on the quantities of oil extracted over time by his neighbour even though the oil market may be perfectly competitive. The problem here lies not so much in enforcing property rights as in defining them. One can no doubt define them by legislating that all the oil that lies under a given parcel of land belongs to the owner (or lessee) of the parcel. But this is not a comforting definition since, given the fluid nature of petroleum, there is a tendency for the oil to migrate within the underground reservoir, particularly so when pressure gradients are caused during the process of extracting it. Thus the source of the problem here lies in the uncertainty as to the original location of a given quantity of oil extracted at a given well. In the face of this problem the United States, for example, has developed a doctrine of property in petroleum known as the 'rule of capture'. According to this doctrine a quantity of petroleum belongs to the landowner (or lessee) who captures it through wells located on his land, regardless of its original location as a natural deposit.

An equivalent way of looking at this example is to recognize that while it is possible to parcel out land amongst various people and thus establish ownership claims, the oil under these adjoining parcels is a common pool to which all owners (or lessees) of these parcels have access. It is not possible for owner i to exclude neighbour j from the oil under i's parcel of land. If neighbour j drills y_j barrels of oil, the extraction possibilities—and consequently the profits—of owner i will depend on y_j. Here j's drilling imposes an externality on i; an external *dis*economy to be sure, since the larger y_j is, the more curtailed are the extraction possibilities for i. We shall analyse the effect of such an externality on the rate of depletion of a common pool in Chapter 12.

2. The second point pertains to the fact that markets for externalities usually involve a small number of buyers and sellers. In our earlier example, the named good g_{hi} has precisely one buyer (h) and one seller (i). Even if one can *define* a competitive equilibrium with markets for externalities (i.e. markets for these named goods), there is no necessary force driving the system to it. It is not enough, as some economists have suggested, to ensure that man h and man i can bargain and transact in the named good g_{hi}. Given that only two individuals are involved there is no presumption that the bargain would result in competitive prices being the outcome, for we are really in the realm of bilateral monopoly. Stating it in another way, each of these externality markets is too 'thin' for a competitive allocation to be the natural outcome.

3. The third point generally rears its head when external diseconomies like pollution are involved. We shall elaborate on it later by means of an example in section 6. But a brief mention at this point would not be out of place. Suppose that property rights can be established and enforced (so that point 1 is irrelevant). Suppose also that we can ignore point 2. It is plainly the case that if we are

to exploit the theory of competitive equilibrium of a private owner-ship economy by introducing named goods, we need to verify that in the space of all named goods production possibilities for the economy as a whole define a convex set. Furthermore, we need to verify that in the space of named goods the utility functions of the individuals are quasi-concave. If either of these convexity assump-tions is violated a competitive equilibrium with markets for extern-alities, while *definable*, may simply not exist. This 'non-convexity' problem did not, of course, arise in the case of our simple example involving a public good. But it often arises in the context of pro-duction possibilities when external diseconomies are involved.[2] As a consequence of such non-convexities one is really in the realm of imperfect competition. It is likely that what one will observe in such situations are prices for externalities that are not independent of quantities demanded and supplied. But this means that we are in the realm of thin markets.

For certain important classes of problems, such as the well-known problem of the common, it is the absence of property rights for certain goods that leads to the underlying non-convexity in production possibilities. For such problems points 1 and 3 are related in that if the appropriate property rights can be established costlessly the underlying non-convexity disappears. We shall note this when analysing the problem of the common in sections 4 and 5. There remains, however, a wide class of circumstances where the non-convexity is fundamental in that it is not due to any inadequate specification of property rights. We shall consider such cases by means of an example in section 6.

These foregoing observations would seem to suggest that to search for Nirvana via competitive markets for externalities is rather like searching for the Holy Grail. An entire class of potential markets for externality may fail to develop simply because of the difficulties in establishing property rights.[3] If externality markets are absent, a question that arises is whether the government can ensure that a market equilibrium is Pareto efficient by a judicious

[2] For a general argument see Starrett (1972).
[3] Where property rights can be readily defined and enforced, both a Lindahl equilibrium and the core can be defined. Of course, neither need exist. Our simple example suggested that a Lindahl equilibrium is in the core of an economy if the externalities are in the form of public goods. That this is indeed so is demonstrated in Foley (1970). For generalizations see Starrett (1973).

selection of taxes and subsidies which alter the prices and incomes that individuals face. We look into this now.

3. Pigouvian Taxes for Correcting Externalities

Return once again to our twice familiar economy with a single private good and a single public good. Denote by t_i the specific subsidy that the government introduces on the purchase of a unit of the public good by individual i, and by τ_i a lump sum tax in terms of the private good that the government imposes on i. (If $t_i < 0$, the subsidy is in fact a tax. Likewise, if $\tau_i < 0$ the lump sum tax is in fact a subsidy.) Given that there are no markets for externalities individual i is concerned with maximizing

$$\log x_i + \log \left(\sum_{j \neq i} g_j + g_i \right)$$

subject to his budget constraint

3.19 $$(p - t_i)g_i + x_i \leqslant 1 - \tau_i$$

where i selects only x_i and g_i. As earlier, his optimal x_i and g_i will depend, among other things, on $g_h(h \neq i)$. In effect, then, we are concerned with describing a market equilibrium where government intervention has altered the prices and endowments of individuals. For the moment we do not inquire into the basis on which the government chooses t_i and τ_i. But given that individuals are identical we know in advance that the government will wish to set the rate of subsidy, t_i, and the lump sum tax τ_i the same for all individuals. Denote them then by t and τ respectively. The computation of the tax equilibrium is simple. We know that at an equilibrium individuals will behave identically. Denote by $\bar{g}$ and $\bar{x}$ the quantities of the public good and the private good that individual $h(h \neq i)$ purchases. Denote by λ_i the Lagrange multiplier associated with 3.19, and one verifies that i will choose g_i and x_i so as to satisfy

3.20 $$\frac{1}{x_i} = \lambda_i$$

and

3.21 $$\frac{1}{(N-1)\bar{g} + g_i} = \frac{p - t}{x_i}.$$

Write $\bar{p} = p - t$. At the equilibrium one has from equation 3.21 the fact that

3.22
$$N\bar{g} = \frac{\bar{x}}{\bar{p}}.$$

But we are trying to arrive at the Pareto-efficient allocation 3.8. It follows from 3.22 that in order for this to be achieved the net price $\bar{p}$ that individuals face must equal p/N. Thus the government must set $t = (N-1)p/N$, which is the subsidy per unit of the public good purchased by an individual. With this net price p/N that an individual faces, his budget constraint 3.19 at the equilibrium will read as

3.23
$$\frac{p}{N}\,\bar{g} + \bar{x} = 1 - \tau.$$

Using 3.22 in 3.23 one obtains

3.24
$$\frac{(1+N)}{N}\,x = 1 - \tau.$$

But the government needs to select τ so as to ensure that each individual ends up consuming exactly as in 3.8. Thus, in fact it needs to ensure that $\bar{x} = 1/2$. It follows from 3.24 that the government must set $\tau = (N-1)/2N$.

We have confirmed that if the government were to impose a lump sum tax of $(N-1)/2N$ on each person and were to establish subsidy of $(N-1)/N \cdot p$ per unit of the public good purchased the resulting market equilibrium would be Pareto efficient. We have finally to check if the government can successfully carry out such a tax subsidy scheme; that is, whether the government's budget is balanced. Given that $\bar{g} = 1/2p$, the government's total expenditure as subsidy payments is

$$\frac{N}{2p}\,\frac{(N-1)}{N}\,p = \frac{(N-1)}{2}.$$

Its gross receipt from the lump sum taxes is, of course,

$$N\tau = \frac{N(N-1)}{2N} = \frac{(N-1)}{2}.$$

The budget is, in fact, balanced.

Strictly from a *formal* point of view our example suggests that, so long as all costs in running an institution are nil, a tax equilibrium and a competitive equilibrium with markets for externalities are equivalent.[4] And yet one should not accept this suggestion without investigating whether the result is robust. Again, from a formal point of view we noted that, since individuals transact in named goods in markets for externalities, the number of commodities purchased and sold by an individual is considerably larger at a Lindahl equilibrium than the number of commodities purchased and sold at a tax equilibrium. To be precise, in our example individual i participated in $2(N-1)$ externality markets $\{g_{ih}(h \neq i)$ and $g_{hi}(h \neq i)\}$ each of which was assumed inoperative at the tax equilibrium. At the tax equilibrium each individual assumed the quantities of the public good purchased by the others as given. They were not quantities over which he had any control. Our general discussion of the existence of a competitive equilibrium in Chapter 2 should now draw our attention to the following point: namely that, if the existence of an equilibrium is to be assured, each individual's utility function will have to be quasi-concave in the space of those commodities whose quantities the individual can control. In our example, of course, the utility function of the representative individual was strictly quasi-concave (in fact strictly concave) whether or not named goods were introduced. But intuition suggests that it may be simple to construct examples where the convexity assumptions fail to be satisfied if named goods are introduced but where they are satisfied if named goods are not introduced. In such cases it is possible that, while a tax equilibrium exists, a Lindahl equilibrium does not.[5]

In fact it emerges that such possibilities can arise rather generally when externalities are of a detrimental kind, like noise or pollution. They arise in an interesting form in the case of free access to a common property known widely as the problem of the common. We touched on this when discussing the problem in establishing property rights for neighbouring oil men. The implication on the rate of depletion of a common oil pool we defer to a later chapter when we have introduced time into our analysis. In the following section we analyse the problem of the common in some detail in

---

[4] For general propositions along these lines see Foley (1970) and Starrett (1972). We emphasize the fact that such an equivalence depends crucially on institutional costs being at least comparable (in our example, strictly zero).

[5] For a general discussion of this point see Starrett and Zeckhauser (1971).

those situations where the intertemporal aspects of the problem can be ignored, without our losing sight of the essential structure of the problem.

4. Common Property Resource, or the Problem of the 'Common'

(i) *The problem:* Imagine a body of water, such as a lake or the open seas. It will be supposed that the body of water derives its value from the marine life it sustains. While the open seas may appear at first sight to be too large in surface area for the common's problem to be relevant, the recent Icelandic fishing dispute should remind us that there are various kinds of aquatic life, like cod and haddock, that are relatively non-migratory in character and are thus localized in different parts of the seas. We are concerned here with a specific species of aquatic life, localized in a specific part of the open sea. In other words, we are concentrating our attention on a specific fishing ground. It will be supposed, as is actually the case, that nobody owns the fishing ground in the open sea. Consequently everyone has an equal right to fish. There is thus free access to the fishing ground. Our interest in focusing attention on aquatic life in discussing the problem of the common lies in the fact that while such species are self-renewable if the size of their population is large enough, the chance of a given species surviving is severely reduced if the population size gets below a certain threshold level. This threshold level varies greatly from species to species and depends as well on the environment in which the species exists. What is known as the 'biotic potential' of many kinds of fish is so large that the threshold level associated with it may be 'very small'. On the other hand, for land animals the threshold level is often 'large'. The analysis that follows pertains not only to fishing from a common fishing ground but as well to hunting or trapping for animals from a common ground. The main point is that given a positive threshold level, the rate of total catch is crucially important in judging whether a particular species is endangered.

Suppose there to be N fishing firms $(i = 1, \ldots, N)$ assumed identical. We shall regard fishing as a production activity in which the catch is the output and labour and fishing equipment are the variable inputs. To simplify, we shall aggregate these variable inputs into one and regard this single input as 'vessels', assumed perfectly divisible. If S is the size of the fishing ground and if there are X vessels on the fishing ground, the total catch, Y, is assumed to satisfy the constraint $Y \leqslant H(X, S)$ where H is a production function with constant returns to scale in the two factors (X and S) with positive but diminishing returns to each factor. Suppose also that $H(0, S) = 0$. Now, the fishing ground is fixed in size. Denote the size by $\bar{S}$. Because of constant returns to scale we note that $H(X, \bar{S}) = \bar{S}H(X/\bar{S}; 1)$. Since $\bar{S}$ is constant for our problem we may as well normalize and set $\bar{S} = 1$. Now write $H(X, 1) = F(X)$. By assumption $F(0) = 0$, $F'(X) > 0$, $F''(X) < 0$, and furthermore, $F(X)$ is bounded above (presumably by the size of the total stock of fish). Notice that these assumptions imply that

$$\frac{F(X)}{X} > F'(X) \quad \text{and that} \quad \lim_{x \to \infty} \frac{F(X)}{X} = 0.$$

(see Diagram 3.1 below).

The assumption of diminishing returns (i.e. $F''(X) < 0$) is crucial to the exercise and it reflects the fact this is a fixed area of the sea which the particular species under consideration inhabits. There is in effect a crowding of vessels. Given that X is the number of vessels on the sea, $F(X)/X$ is the average catch per vessel when the vessels are efficiently manned. If the ith firm owns x_i of these vessels it will be supposed, for simplicity, that its catch is $x_i F(X)/X$. But $X = \sum_{i=1}^{N} x_i$. It follows that, since the average product $F(X)/X$ is a diminishing function of X, the catch accruing to i is dependent

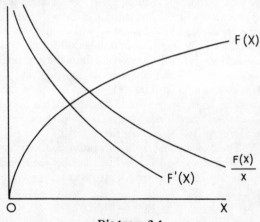

Diagram 3.1

not only on i's input x_i, but as well on the number of vessels introduced by the other firms. Given the diminishing returns it is also the case that the externality that others impose on one is of a detrimental nature; that is, unlike the earlier example, we are in the realm of external diseconomies. Write

$$X_{N-i} \equiv \sum_{\substack{j=1 \\ j \neq i}}^{N} x_j$$

and denote by y_i the ith firm's catch of fish. We have therefore supposed that

3.25
$$y_i \leqslant \frac{x_i F(X_{N-i} + x_i)}{X_{N-i} + x_i}.$$

Assume that the markets for both boats and the catch are perfectly competitive. Choosing the catch as our numeraire good, let p be the rental value of a vessel. Firms are profit maximizing and our first task is to compute the market equilibria. Given that firms are identical the computation is simple enough. As in our earlier example let firm i suppose that each of the other firms will introduce $\hat{x}$ vessels. It follows that i wants to choose x_i with a view to maximizing

3.26
$$\frac{x_i F\{(N-1)\hat{x} + x_i\}}{(N-1)\hat{x} + x_i} - px_i.$$

It follows immediately that it will choose x_i (provided $x_i > 0$) at the solution of this equation

3.27
$$\frac{(N-1)\hat{x}F\{(N-1)\hat{x} + x_i\}}{\{(N-1)\hat{x} + x_i\}^2} + \frac{x_i F'\{(N-1)\hat{x} + x_i\}}{(N-1)\hat{x} + x_i} = p.$$

At this market equilibrium with free access to the fishing ground, condition 3.27 will hold for all i, and by symmetry $x_i = \hat{x}$ for all i. Thus the equilibrium number of boats, $\hat{x}$, per firm is the solution of the equation

3.28
$$\frac{F(Nx)}{Nx} - \frac{1}{N}\left\{\frac{F(Nx)}{Nx} - F'(Nx)\right\} = p.$$

In other words at this market equilibrium the total number of vessels, X, on the sea is the solution to the equation

$$3.29 \qquad \frac{F(X)}{X} - \frac{1}{N}\left\{\frac{F(X)}{X} - F'(X)\right\} = p.$$

Equation 3.28 (or, equivalently, equation 3.29) is the fundamental result of the problem of the common, and the question arises whether a positive value of X satisfies 3.29. It is simple to see that the answer is 'yes' if we were to assume in addition the innocuous condition $F'(0) > p$ (for if not, then it would not be worth anyone's while undertaking to catch the species). The question arises whether the allocation at the market equilibrium as implied by 3.28 is Pareto efficient for these N firms. Again, the answer, as in the previous example, is 'no'. To obtain the symmetric Pareto-efficient allocation for these N firms, one needs to choose x so as to maximize the total net profit

$$3.30 \qquad F(Nx) - pNx,$$

and then dividing this profit equally between them. In other words, the N firms by their joint collusive action 'internalize' the externalities that have resulted as a consequence of the fact that the fishing ground is an unpaid factor in production. Maximizing 3.30 readily yields the condition that x ought to be the solution of the equation

$$3.31 \qquad F'(Nx) = p,$$

or equivalently,

$$3.32 \qquad F'(X) = p.$$

Equation 3.32 is, of course, widely familiar and reflects the efficiency condition that the marginal product of vessels ought to equal their rental price. Denote by $\tilde{x}$ the solution to 3.31, and by $\tilde{X}$ the solution to 3.32. That is, $\tilde{X} = N\tilde{x}$. One can confirm as well that the allocation implied by $\tilde{x}$ is in the core for these N firms, for no coalition of firms can guarantee a profit level as high as that implied at the Pareto efficient outcome with symmetric division of the total profit. If it attempts to block the allocation, the complementary coalition of firms can introduce a 'large' number of vessels (since there is no *legal* limit on the number of vessels a firm can introduce) and thereby push the average product of vessels to a level equal to p.

Denote by $\hat{X}$ the solution of equation 3.29, and let $\hat{X}=N\hat{x}$. Using equation 3.29 one has that

3.33 $\qquad p - F'(\hat{X}) = \frac{(N-1)}{N}\left\{\frac{F(\hat{X})}{\hat{X}} - F'(\hat{X})\right\} > 0.$

Using 3.32 and 3.33 it follows that

$$\tilde{X} < \hat{X} \quad (\text{or } \tilde{x} < \hat{x}).$$

It follows that at the free access market equilibrium there are too many vessels and, therefore, too large a catch; in the sense that each firm's profit could be raised if the firms were to undertake a joint decision to *reduce* their fishing activity and procure a *smaller* catch. Notice as well that at the market equilibrium each firm makes a positive profit. To see this one notes from equation 3.29 that

3.34 $\qquad \frac{F(\hat{X})}{\hat{X}} - p > 0$

and indeed that at the equilibrium each firm's net profit, $\hat{\pi}$, is

3.35 $\qquad \hat{\pi} = \frac{1}{N^2}\{F(\hat{X}) - \hat{X}F'(\hat{X})\} > 0.$

and thus that the average product strictly exceeds the rental price of a vessel (see Diagram 3.2).

It will be noticed that, contrary to what is often claimed, the problem of 'the common' and the resulting sub-optimality of the market equilibrium are *not* formally identical to an N–person version of the prisoner's dilemma game. The key feature of the prisoner's dilemma game, or so we noted, is not only that its unique Nash equilibrium is Pareto inefficient, but also that the Nash equilibrium is characterized by *dominant* strategies on the part of each agent. It is a simple matter to confirm in the foregoing formulation that firms do not possess dominant strategies in the common's problem. Indeed, $\hat{x}$ is the profit maximizing number of vessels for the representative firm only when the remaining firms introduce $(N-1)\hat{x}$ vessels. It is only for pedagogic reasons that in section 2 of the previous chapter we illustrated the prisoner's dilemma game by means of an artificially restricted problem of the common. Nevertheless, the above formulation implies that it is in the interest of each firm

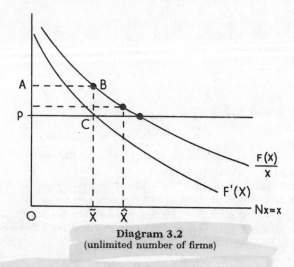

Diagram 3.2
(unlimited number of firms)

to come to an agreement to restrict its input to level $\tilde{x}$; indeed this allocation is in the core while the market equilibrium allocation is not. But it is not in the firms' interests to do so in the absence of a collective agreement. While for this simple symmetric model it may seem that an agreement to introduce only $\tilde{x}$ vessels can easily be reached, whether or not it will be complied with will depend on whether or not the agreement can be *enforced* easily. Enforcement may be costly to administer. Plainly its costliness will vary from context to context.

The fact that the market equilibrium allocation is not in the core and in particular that there is excessive fishing at the equilibrium may appear a bit paradoxical since we have not introduced any monopolistic elements in the market for boats and catch. But it is not difficult to see why the result comes out the way it does. The introduction of an extra boat by a firm alters its catch, of course, but it also inflicts a diseconomy on the other firms in the sense that their catch is reduced. Granted that if N is large this external diseconomy on each of these other firms will be negligible. But the *sum* of these negligible quantities need by no means be negligible. We demonstrate this by deriving the special result that follows when N is arbitrarily large.

Given that p is a constant we may regard the total number of vessels $\hat{X}$ given by the market equilibrium condition 3.29 as simply a function of N. The question arises about the functional form of $\hat{X}$.

Notice first that if $N=1$ then from equations 3.29 and 3.32 we have $\hat{x}=\tilde{x}$ and consequently there is no problem of the common. The problem that we have been discussing arises, as our arguments have shown, only when $N>1$. Thus write the LHS of equation 3.29 as $G(X, N)$. That is

Defines

$$G(\hat{X}, N) \equiv \frac{F(\hat{X})}{\hat{X}} - \frac{1}{N}\left\{\frac{F(\hat{X})}{\hat{X}} - F'(\hat{X})\right\} = p.$$

To keep the argument simple regard N ($\geqslant 1$) as a continuous variable. From equation 3.29 it is immediate that

$$\frac{\partial \hat{X}}{\partial N} = - \frac{\dfrac{\partial G}{\partial N}}{\dfrac{\partial G}{\partial \hat{X}}}.$$

Routine calculation now yields that

$$\frac{\partial \hat{X}}{\partial N} > 0.$$

In other words, $\hat{X}$ is monotonically increasing in $N(N \geqslant 1)$. But it must be bounded above, since, if not, then given that by our assumptions regarding F one has

$$\lim_{\substack{X \to \infty \\ N \to \infty}} G(\hat{X}, N) = 0,$$

equation 3.29 would be violated. It follows that $\hat{X}$ tends to a finite limit as $N \to \infty$, and thus that at the market equilibrium each firm introduces an 'infinitesimal' number of vessels. But at this limit, equation 3.29 reduces to

3.36
$$\frac{F(X)}{X} = p,$$

or, in other words, that in the large numbers case the *average product* of vessels is equated to their rental price at the free access equilibrium (see Diagram 3.3). It follows that in the case of large numbers the profits are diluted to zero at the free access equilibrium.

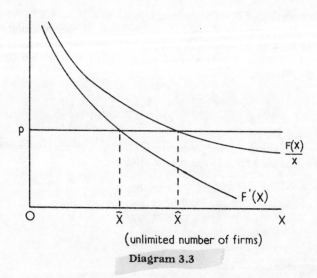

(unlimited number of firms)

Diagram 3.3

The consequences of such over-exploitation of aquatic life at the free access equilibrium can be serious, and possibly disastrous. For suppose that the total population size of such a species is Z, and suppose $\underline{Z}(0 < \underline{Z} < Z)$ is the threshold population size such that below this size the entire species is seriously threatened with extinction. It is entirely possible that

3.37 $$F(N\tilde{x}) < Z - \underline{Z} < F(N\hat{x})$$

$\tilde{x}$ = cooperative eq[…]
$\hat{x}$ = mht equil.

Granted that the arguments leading to 3.37 have relied on firms being singularly myopic in concerning themselves solely with one period's profit. One might wish to argue that firms will not over-exploit if the species is threatened with extinction, since this would cut into future profits. Quite apart from the question of whether firms are as far-sighted as some would like to believe, the introduction of time will not necessarily alter the essentials of the argument. Restricting its catch in order to husband the resource will not really help a firm's future profits much if the competing firms decide to make a killing at one go and virtually wipe out the species. Thus if each firm were to fear that the total catch of all the competing firms will bring the population size below the threshold $\underline{Z}$ it may find it most profitable to join in the rampage and get as much in the first period as possible, and this despite the firm having taken future possibilities into account.[6] In other words such fear could be self-fulfilling, leading to a market equilibrium in which the species is over-exploited in the first period.

In our example we have not imputed any value to the species other than the value that the catch fetches in the market. To put it loosely we have imputed only an economic value to the species. An environmentalist's reaction to our example could be that this merely proves the profit motive of firms to be incompatible with the environmentalist's goals. But inequality 3.37 indicates that it is not quite as simple as that. It is in the interest of each firm to agree to restrict output if that is the only way to get the other firms to do likewise. Profits would be higher by this means. If 3.37 holds, maximization of total profits leads to a catch that is not inconsistent with the environmentalist's goals. In our example if condition 3.37 holds, the guilty party is not the profit motive *per se*. Rather, it is the economic and legal environment in which the profit motive is allowed free play.

So far we have interpreted the inefficiency of the market equilibrium *with free access* as being due to the externalities that each firm inflicts on the others in their production activities. An equivalent way of interpreting this inefficiency is to recognize that the open sea is an asset that is not owned by anyone in particular. Consequently no rental is charged to the different firms for the right to fish. Under common property the sea is a free good for the individual firm. Indeed it is for this reason that we have been referring to the resulting market equilibrium as a free access equilibrium.

(ii) *Competitive markets for named vessels:* Now our earlier discussion of the problems of establishing competitive markets for externalities would suggest that so long as the fishing ground is to remain common property it is doubtful that competitive markets for 'named' *vessels* would develop. Specifically, points 1 and 2 (see pp. 48–50) would seem very relevant for such doubts. But there is in fact an additional reason why one would not wish to rely on the appearance of competitive markets for named vessels. For so long as the fishing ground remains a common property recall that the *i*th firm's production possibilities are represented in 3.25. Recall also that an obvious route in such a situation would be to have competitive markets for 'named' vessels. Thus write

[6] In fact total exhaustion of a potentially renewable resource can rather easily arise even if firms are assumed not to fear that their competitors will be involved in wholesale rampage. In Chapter 5 we shall explore such possibilities.

define: $\qquad\qquad x_{ij} = x_j \quad \text{for } i, j = 1, \ldots, N.$

Consequently 3.25 can be expressed as

$$y_i \leqslant \frac{x_{ii} F\left(\sum\limits_{j=1}^{N} x_{ij}\right)}{\sum\limits_{j=1}^{N} x_{ij}}.$$

The idea then is that firm i can enter into a transaction with firm j supplying i with x_{ij} which is an input in i's production y_i. There are in effect N inputs $(x_{ij}, j=1, \ldots, N)$ in the ith firm's production function. The critical question now is whether the production

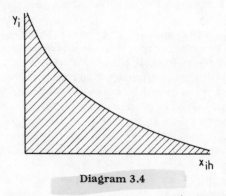

Diagram 3.4

possibilities open to i satisfy the convexity conditions that we assumed in the description of the private ownership economy. It is easy to verify that the answer is 'no'. For consider some $h(\neq i)$ and hold all x_{ij} fixed with $j \neq h$. Then one confirms readily enough that y_i as a function solely of x_{ih} is a declining one (see Diagram 3.4 below). With our assumptions regarding F the curve does not cut the horizontal axis but approaches it gradually. In any event the underlying region is non-convex and one suspects that a Lindahl equilibrium may not exist. That this may indeed happen can easily be argued. Recall that, at a Lindahl equilibrium that we are envisaging here, there will be a price p_{ih} that i must 'pay' h for h supplying each unit of the named commodity x_{ih}. Can p_{ih} be negative (the case where h actually pays i for the right to introduce a unit of x_h)? Not so. For if it were, then i could set $x_{ii}=0$, close down production and demand an unlimited quantity of x_{ih}. This would yield an unlimited profit to i even though i is not actually undertaking any fishing activity. But at a positive price that h is required to pay i, firm h will hardly be willing to supply an unlimited quantity of x_{ih}. Demand and supply of x_{ih} will not match when $p_{ih}<0$ and so p_{ih} cannot be negative at equilibrium. Can p_{ih} equal zero at equilibrium? Again the answer will generally be 'no', for if $p_{ih}=0$ then i will not demand any positive amount of x_{ih} (since x_{ih} is detrimental to i's production). But with no payments required, firm h will generally wish to introduce a positive quantity of x_h ($=x_{ih}$) at its profit maximizing production plan. Again, the supply and demand for the named good x_{ih} will generally not match. The argument is strengthened further if we were to assume that $p_{ih}>0$. The source of the problem lies in that so long as a resource is common property the production possibility set of the representative firm is non-convex in the space of named commodities.

(iii) *Optimum regulations:* Now even though a competitive equilibrium with markets for 'named' vessels is a most unlikely outcome, there are a number of other avenues that we might wish to explore towards achieving an efficient allocation. Analytically, the most direct avenue would be to parcel the fishing ground into N 'plots' of equal size and allow each firm to have proprietary rights over one and only one such plot. By this means the fishing ground ceases to be common property and, as we shall see, so does the non-convexity vanish. We have already noted that for certain resources, such as oil underground, this is technically simply not possible. Our present case of fishing from a body of water raises similar problems, because while by this scheme firm i will not be allowed to fish on firm j's plot (that is, not without paying a competitive rent to j) it will presumably be able to utilize techniques to entice the fish under j's plot to drift into its own. Even so, for the sake of argument let us suppose that private property rights to the plots can costlessly be established and enforced in the catchment area. Recall that we began this section by supposing that efficient catch, Y, is a function of the total number of vessels, X, and the size of the catchment area, S, and that there are constant returns to scale. Thus $Y=H(X, S)$. But the total catchment area is fixed in size at $\bar{S}$. Now if the fishing ground is parcelled out and *if it is costless to protect one's property rights*, firm i faces production possibilities given by $y_i \leqslant H(x_i, \bar{S}/N)$.

But given that H is a function with constant returns to scale one has

$$H\left(x_i, \frac{\bar{S}}{N}\right) = \frac{\bar{S}}{N} H\left(\frac{Nx_i}{\bar{S}}, 1\right) \equiv \frac{\bar{S}}{N} F\left(\frac{Nx_i}{\bar{S}}\right).$$

As before, we may as well normalize and set $\bar{S}=1$. It follows that i is concerned with choosing x_i with a view to maximizing its own net profit, $1/N[F(Nx_i)]-px_i$. Consequently x_i will be chosen at that level for which

3.38 $$F'(Nx_i) = p, \qquad i = 1, \ldots, N.$$

But conditions 3.38 and 3.31 are identical. In other words, the allocation implied by 3.38 is Pareto efficient. Thus if symmetric property rights are established to what was originally a common property fishing ground each firm will introduce precisely $\tilde{x}$ vessels, and each firm will capture a profit equal to $F(N\tilde{x})/N-p\tilde{x}$ which, in turn, will emerge as the competitive rent per plot on the fishing ground. In other words, by assigning property rights on what was originally a common property resource (i.e. the fishing ground) the problem takes on a conventional form.

But given that for many cases it is simply too costly (if not impossible) to devise and enforce private property rights on certain resources, the foregoing avenue is not really a universal way out of the problem. (Imagine the difficulties in enforcing each citizen's right to a clean air-space directly over his private property.) Consequently one is encouraged to look elsewhere.

In the case of the open seas, where the body of water (and consequently, the aquatic life under it), is not owned by anyone, the firms (countries) may agree jointly to impose on themselves a quantity control (that is, a quota system), limit themselves to $\tilde{x}$ vessels per firm (and hence $F(N\tilde{x})/N$ units of catch per firm), and introduce a policing system to ensure that no individual firm cheats. This is often termed the *pure quota scheme*. If, on the other hand, the body of water is a lake located within a well-defined national boundary, there are at least two other schemes that the government might wish to consider in ensuring an efficient outcome. The idea, in each case, is for the government to take charge of the common property resource and to introduce regulations aimed at the attainment of allocative efficiency.

The first, which is often called the *pure licensing scheme*, consists in the government issuing a fixed number, $\overline{X}$, of licences for the total number of vessels that are allowed to be introduced into the catchment area. A market for these licences is then allowed to be developed among the firms. If, as we have been supposing, N is large, it is plausible that the market for these licences is more or less competitive. Let us suppose that this is so. Denote by $\overline{p}$ the competitive price of a licence when $\overline{X}$ is the total number of licences issued. It follows that each firm now faces a rental price $p + \overline{p}$ per vessel. What is done with the government revenue generated by the issue of these licences is a distributional question that we do not go into at this stage. For our actual example, we might, to fix our ideas, wish to consider the firms jointly issuing the total number of licences, $\overline{X}$, allowing a competitive market to develop for them; and then dividing the resulting revenue equally among themselves. We now construct the market equilibrium. If the ith firm were to assume that each of the other firms will introduce $\overline{x}$ vessels, its profit will be defined by

$$\frac{x_i F\{(N-1)\overline{x} + x_i\}}{(N-1)\overline{x} + x_i} - (p + \overline{p})x_i.$$

Consequently x_i would be chosen so as to satisfy the condition

3.39 $\qquad \dfrac{(N-1)\overline{x}F\{(N-1)\overline{x} + x_i\}}{\{(N-1)\overline{x} + x_i\}^2} + \dfrac{x_i F'\{(N-1)\overline{x} + x_i\}}{(N-1)\overline{x} + x_i} = p + \overline{p}.$

If condition 3.39 is to lead to an equilibrium one must have $x_i = \overline{x}$, given that firms are identical. It follows that 3.39 reduces to

3.40 $\qquad \dfrac{(N-1)\overline{x}F(N\overline{x})}{(N\overline{x})^2} + \dfrac{F'(N\overline{x})}{N} = p + \overline{p},$

where $N\overline{x} = \overline{X}$, the number of licences issued. But presumably the government issues precisely $\tilde{X}$ ($= N\tilde{x}$) licences, since it is concerned with sustaining the Pareto-efficient allocation. Recall equation 3.31. It follows that 3.40 reduces to

$$\frac{(N-1)\tilde{x}F(N\tilde{x})}{(N\tilde{x})^2} + \frac{F'(N\tilde{x})}{N} = F'(N\tilde{x}) + p$$

and consequently

$$3.41 \qquad \tilde{p} = \frac{(N-1)}{N} \left\{ \frac{F(N\tilde{x})}{N\tilde{x}} - F'(N\tilde{x}) \right\} > 0$$

where $\tilde{p}$ denotes the equilibrium price of a licence when $\tilde{X}$ licences are issued in all. It follows that if $\tilde{X}$ is the total number of licences issued by the government (regulatory agency) the equilibrium price, $\tilde{p}$, of a licence will be given by 3.41 and faced with this price each firm will find it most profitable to introduce precisely $\tilde{x}$ vessels if it is supposed that the other firms will purchase $(N-1)\tilde{x}$ licences in all. In other words, the government's problem consists solely in the choice of the total number of licences it issues.

An alternative regulatory device, often called the *pure tax scheme*, is in some sense a mirror image of the pure licensing scheme. It is in fact the Pigouvian tax notion discussed in section 3 in the context of external economies. The idea here is that the government (regulatory agency) imposes a tax per vessel (that is, a licensing fee per vessel) introduced by each firm. As in the case of the pure licensing scheme we do not concern ourselves at this stage with what is done with the tax revenue. As before, we might like to suppose that the firms impose a specific tax on themselves and divide the resulting revenue equally among themselves. If this is so and if we can show that there exists a tax equilibrium that is efficient in the sense that each firm finds it most profitable to limit itself to $\tilde{x}$ boats, when it assumes that each of the other firms will limit itself to $\tilde{x}$ boats, then the pure tax scheme and the pure licensing scheme envisaged earlier would be identical.

Denote by t the specific tax imposed on each vessel. If the ith firm were to assume that each of the other firms will introduce $\bar{x}$ vessels, its profit will be defined by

$$\frac{x_i F\{(N-1)\bar{x} + x_i\}}{(N-1)\bar{x} + x_i} - (p+t)x_i.$$

Note that this problem has exactly the same formal structure as the pure licensing scheme

Consequently x_i would be chosen so as to satisfy the condition

$$\frac{(N-1)\bar{x}F\{(N-1)\bar{x} + x_i\}}{\{(N-1)\bar{x} + x_i\}^2} + \frac{x_i\{F'(N-1)\bar{x} + x_i\}}{(N-1)\bar{x} + x_i} = p + t.$$

If this is to lead to an equilibrium one must have $x_i = \bar{x}$ given that firms are identical. It follows that

3.42
$$\frac{(N-1)\bar{x}F(N\bar{x})}{(N\bar{x})^2} + \frac{F'(N\bar{x})}{N} = p + t.$$

But we want to choose t so as to ensure that $x_i = \tilde{x}$ is a possible equilibrium value. In other words, if each firm supposes that each of the others will introduce $\tilde{x}$ boats then $\tilde{x}$ would be its profit maximizing input level. Towards this set t at $\tilde{t}$, where

3.43
$$\tilde{t} = \frac{(N-1)}{N} \left\{ \frac{F(N\tilde{x})}{N\tilde{x}} - F'(N\tilde{x}) \right\}.$$

Using 3.43 in the RHS of 3.42 and setting $\bar{x} = \tilde{x}$ one obtains the condition

$$F'(N\tilde{x}) = p$$

which is precisely what is desired. Comparing equations 3.41 and 3.43 one notes that $\tilde{p} = \tilde{t}$ and, therefore that at the optimum for our problem the competitive price of the licences is equal to the Pigouvian tax per vessel that the government selects. This might suggest that the pure licensing scheme and the pure tax scheme are identical. For our present problem the results obtained by the two schemes are the same. Nevertheless, the schemes are different in spirit. We have noted that in the pure licensing scheme the government dictates the number of licences permitted (that is, the total number of vessels allowed) and the price system developed for this fixed number of licences allocates these licences among the N firms. In the pure tax scheme the government does not dictate directly the total number of vessels allowed on the fishing ground. Profit maximizing firms decide on how many vessels to introduce as a response to the licence fee introduced by the government on each vessel. While for our present problem the pure quota scheme, the pure licensing scheme and the pure tax scheme emerged as being identical in impact at the optimum, we shall note in Chapter 13 that this is not always so.

Notice that at the tax equilibrium the total tax revenue, R, is

3.44
$$R = N\tilde{x}\tilde{t} \equiv \frac{(N-1)}{N} \{F(N\tilde{x}) - N\tilde{x}F'(N\tilde{x})\}$$

$$\equiv \frac{N-1}{N} \{F(\tilde{X}) - \tilde{X}F'(\tilde{X})\}.$$

For large N one has from equation 3.44 that

3.45 $\qquad R \simeq \tilde{R} \equiv F(N\tilde{x}) - N\tilde{x}F'(N\tilde{x}) \equiv F(\tilde{X}) - \tilde{X}F'(\tilde{X}),$

where $\tilde{R}$ is defined in equation 3.45 as the rent that ought to be imputed to the fishing ground. That is, $\tilde{R}$ is the area of the rectangle ABCp in Diagram 3.2. Indeed $\tilde{R}$ would have emerged as the competitive rent of the fishing ground had it not been a common property. Since $R < \tilde{R}$ when N is finite, it is the case that firms would make a positive profit at the tax equilibrium even if the entire tax revenue were expropriated by the government and not returned to the firms on a lump sum basis. The question arises whether firms are better or worse off at the free access equilibrium than they are at the tax equilibrium if the entire tax revenue is expropriated from them by the government. Rather surprisingly, perhaps, it is easy to show that they are unambiguously better off at the free access equilibrium. To see this, note that at the tax equilibrium if the entire tax revenue is expropriated, the total net profit (expressed as $N\tilde{\pi}$) made by the N firms as a whole is

$$N\tilde{\pi} = F(\tilde{X}) - R - p\tilde{X}.$$

Using equations 3.43 and 3.44 in this expression for $N\tilde{\pi}$ one has

$$N\tilde{\pi} = \frac{1}{N} \{F(\tilde{X}) - \tilde{X}F'(\tilde{X})\}$$

and thus that profit per firm is

3.46 $\qquad \tilde{\pi} = \frac{1}{N^2} \{F(\tilde{X}) - \tilde{X}F'(\tilde{X})\}.$

Comparing equations 3.35 and 3.46 and noting that $\tilde{x} < \hat{x}$ one sees readily enough that $\hat{\pi} > \tilde{\pi}$. ✒

One can see the nature of the corrective specific tax 3.43 more heuristically as follows. Recall that the catch obtained by the ith firm is represented by 3.25. Now the marginal loss in catch imposed

Note that $\frac{d}{dx}\left[F(x) - xF'(x) \right] = F'(x) - F'(x) - xF''(x)$

$= -xF''(x) > 0$

on i by the addition of an extra boat by some other firm is $\partial y_i / \partial X_{N-i}$, which routine calculation shows to be

$$3.47 \qquad \frac{\partial y_i}{\partial X_{N-i}} = \frac{x_i}{X} \left\{ F'(X) - \frac{F(X)}{X} \right\}.$$

The corrective tax that needs to be imposed on a given firm is plainly the *sum* of all the marginal losses in catch that are sustained by all the other firms when this firm adds an extra boat to its active fleet.[7] Thus if the ith firm adds an extra boat the total marginal loss, M_L, to all firms is obtained from 3.47 as

$$3.48 \qquad M_L = \frac{X_{N-i}}{X} \left\{ F'(X) - \frac{F(X)}{X} \right\}.$$

Since $M_L < 0$ it is indeed a loss that is being inflicted. When $X = N\tilde{x}$ a glance at 3.43 and 3.48 shows that $t = |M_L|$, where $|M_L|$ is the absolute value of the loss.

Now the marginal benefit, M_B, to the ith firm when it introduces an extra boat is plainly $(\partial y_i / \partial x_i - p)$, which from 3.25 yields

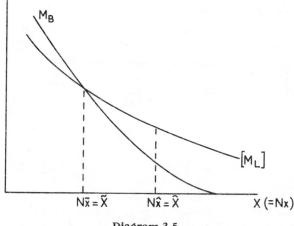

Diagram 3.5

<hr />

[7] Compare this with our example of external *economies*. There we noted that the corrective *subsidy* that was needed to be imposed on the purchase of a unit of the public good by an individual was the sum of the marginal benefits enjoyed by all the other individuals as a consequence.

$$3.49 \qquad M_B = \frac{F(X) + x_i F'(X)}{X} - \frac{x_i F(X)}{X^2} - p.$$

Examining the difference between M_B and $|M_L|$ from 3.48 and 3.49 yields

From 3.48 + 3.49:

$$3.50 \qquad M_B - |M_L| = F'(X) - p.$$

Given the assumptions that have been made about F there is a unique value $(N\tilde{x})$ of X at which expression 3.50 is zero (see Diagrams

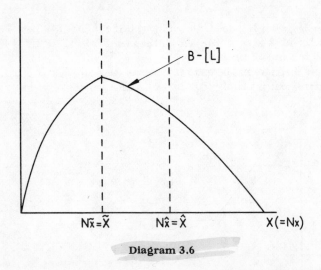

Diagram 3.6

3.5 and 3.6). The tax system is designed to locate this value of X.

The link between designing a tax system that will force profit maximizing firms to operate at what is collectively the desired level of operation (i.e. $N\tilde{x}$), and conducting a social cost–benefit analysis to locate this desired level and thereby to impose a pure licensing system, can also be brought out by this example. Social cost–benefit analysis will signal the need for expanding the level of fishing activity, X, whenever $M_B > |M_L|$ or equivalently, whenever the *total* net benefit curve $B - L$ is increasing.[8] To be precise, if $M_B > |M_L|$ at a given level of activity then a marginal project ΔX (when $\Delta X > 0$) will show positive net social benefits, since $(M_B - |M_L|)\Delta X > 0$. It will be worth undertaking. One would wish to go on accepting such marginal projects until $M_B = |M_L|$. Likewise, if at a level of activity one finds $M_B < |M_L|$ then a marginal project ΔX will be judged desirable only when $\Delta X < 0$, since only for such a 'project' will net social benefit $(M_B - |M_L|)\Delta X$ be positive. In this case as well one would wish to continue to choose such 'projects' until $M_B = |M_L|$.

5. Some Examples of Common Property Resources

We have analysed the problem of the common in the context of individuals hunting for aquatic life from a body of water that is not owned by anyone in society or, to put it equivalently, when the fishing ground is a common property resource. Several other examples would seem to fit the general texture of the arguments that we have developed from this specific context. We have already mentioned that a similar problem occurs when oil men drill for oil from a common underground reservoir and when the rule of capture prevails. The case of hunting or trapping for animals in a common ground is another example. On most occasions the pollution of the atmosphere is also such an instance. The atmosphere's capacity to absorb pollution is, while large, clearly finite. But if individuals are not charged for disposing of pollutants into the atmosphere they enjoy the benefit of a free service, namely the service that the atmosphere performs in absorbing pollutants. Our formal analysis has suggested that this benefit can in fact be largely a mixed blessing in that there is a tendency for the market equilibrium to sustain too much pollution in a sense that can be made precise. In those situations where the individuals can be regarded as roughly identically placed (such as a community of motorists emitting noxious

---

[8] We are calling this social cost–benefit analysis even though benefits and costs are being measured in terms of the profits of the different firms. There is no consumer surplus to be taken into account in the exercise since the market for the catch has been assumed perfectly competitive. The term social cost–benefit analysis could, however, be misleading for this exercise if one wants to impute a value to the aquatic life itself on environmental grounds. We are here restricting attention to the economic value of such animals or rather to the value of the catch. In effect then we are discussing the optimum social management of a common property resource when the resource is socially valued solely in terms of the value of the catch.

fumes from their cars and at the same time preferring clean air to polluted air), our formal analysis of the common's problem will carry over directly. The problem of the common arises as well in the case of individuals drawing water from a common underground reservoir. Under what is known as the 'riparian' doctrine (which is similar to the rule of capture in the case of oil extraction), each owner of a parcel of land is allowed to extract as much water as he desires without regard to its effect on the owners of neighbouring parcels. Thus the doctrine provides no protection to a well-owner from the lowering of the water table caused by his neighbour's action. If in addition, an excessive drawing of water causes salt water intrusion, the ground water basin may well be destroyed. In this event we are confronted with a problem exactly akin to the problem of common property fishing. The grazing of cattle or sheep in a common land has similar features as well, and the free access equilibrium would imply an over-grazing of such property. To the extent that such over-grazing deteriorates the quality of the land (as has happened, for example, in some of the arid grasslands in the Middle East) the curtailment of the total size of the herds grazed is not merely in the economic interests of the grazer but also in the interest of the environmentalist. The problem is analogous to those that our example has already brought out. But our formal analysis, while suggestive, has nevertheless been limited in scope. We have analysed the problem in an entirely static context. This limitation prevents one from describing sharply the fact that common property resources are often eroded gradually over time. In certain cases the total erosion can happen in a matter of a few decades, as in the case of the American bison in its natural habitat, but others take a longer time. The Negev Desert was not created overnight. It is only when we introduce time explicitly into the analysis that we shall be able to analyse the general question of husbanding a potentially renewable resource. We shall go into this in Chapter 5.

The fact that common property resources tend to be exploited at an excessive rate has been recognized for a long time. It would appear that historically property rights for the common property resource were often difficult to establish for a variety of reasons. Here we have emphasized the purely technical difficulties that can often arise, as in the case of oil or water in an underground reservoir, or in the case of a hunting resource that migrates over large areas of land, or indeed as in the case of the atmosphere which is in a constant state of diffusion and movement. But technical difficulty is of course only one possible reason. Custom can play its part. Often the notion of private property rights may be alien to the society in question, particularly so when the resource is vital to its members. Thus, for example, in the medieval manorial economy in England the domestic animals were privately owned but the land the animals grazed was a common property resource. On occasion the problem can be a direct political one as, to take an example, when different nations are involved in exploiting a resource from international waters.

Generally speaking, when the problem of over-exploitation of a common property resource has been recognized and when the resource has continued to remain a common property, attempts have been made to regulate its exploitation via *quantity* controls. Thus, for example, in the United States after years of excessive drilling in the states of Oklahoma, Texas, California and New Mexico, the Conally 'Hot Oil' Act of 1935 was a culmination of two decades of attempts at regulating production of oil via controls on the number of wells drilled, their spatial distances, and even on the quantities extracted.[9] Often, when agricultural land is communally exploited, elaborate quantity controls are devised to prevent over-utilization. Thus, for example, in medieval England the manor would regulate the grazing of domestic animals in the common land by limiting the number of animals grazing, as well as the duration of grazing.[10] More recently, in the United States the Taylor 'Grazing' Act of 1934 was designed precisely to 'stop injury to the public grazing lands by preventing over-grazing' of the open grangelands of the Cascade Range and the Sierra Nevada Mountains.[11] But on occasion the problem is sighted a bit too late. The American whooping crane is now extinct. It is also possible that the bowhead and the right whales have suffered a similar fate.

The problems of devising and enforcing such regulations are plainly acute when nations vie with one another for a common property resource. The 'Cod War' between Iceland and Great Britain is still unresolved. And it can hardly be said that the International Whaling Commission has been spectacularly successful. Established in 1946 with seventeen member countries, the Commission's task is to protect whale species by setting maximum animal catch limits,

[9] For a thorough discussion of petroleum regulations in the United States, see McDonald (1971).
[10] On this, see Lipson (1949), p. 72.
[11] See Foss (1960), p. 61.

designating areas closed for hunting, and setting minimum population size limits below which the species are considered endangered. But the Commission has neither inspection nor enforcement authority. Consequently ignoring the Commission's recommendations appears to have been the single systematic policy followed by some of the member countries.[12] So much so that despite the concern expressed by many over the years, the blue whale species was pretty close to extinction by the early 1960s. A main problem of arriving at an agreed upon regulation (as opposed to enforcing it) is that unlike the formal model that we have studied, 'firms' exploiting a common property resource are generally not identical. For Iceland cod fishing is a major industry; for Great Britain, it is not. Devising a fair regulation in such instances is understandably difficult. Then again, problems arise whenever there are disagreements about technological possibilities. Iceland argues that excessive catches in the past have brought the cod population off its territorial waters down to a dangerously low level. Great Britain does not believe the gloomy statistics.[13] Regulations are difficult to arrive at when the factual basis on which the regulations are to be built is not agreed upon.

These are, of course, among the more spectacular examples. Regulations are, understandably, easier to introduce if the 'firms' exploiting the common property resource do not form a powerful block. Big-game hunters may find a government's assessment of the threshold population size a of given species too high. But if they do not form a powerful political lobby, strong regulations can in fact be enacted. And they often are.

Our simple model describing N identical firms exploiting a common property resource suggests that there are several ways of meeting the problem of over-utilization at a free access equilibrium. We noted that quantity restriction (i.e. specifying the input level $\tilde{x}$ per firm) is identical in impact to introducing an optimal tax on each unit of the input introduced (which in turn is identical in impact to the pure licensing scheme), so long as the tax revenue is distributed evenly among the N firms.[14] A third scheme that we have explored would be to legislate private property rights to the

---

[12] On this, see McVay (1966).

[13] On this, see Shapley (1972).

[14] We shall note later that this equivalence between a quantity mode of regulation and a price mode of regulation does not hold if the central authority's knowledge of technological and economic possibilities is imperfect and when the regulation is plausibly circumscribed. See Chapter 13.

resource. This last, as we have noted, is simply not feasible if the resource is oil or water underground.

But it is certainly feasible with arable or grazing land. When this scheme is introduced the resource ceases to be common property and the problem is solved at one stroke.[15] It would appear that even in early societies land was as often as not privately owned; and even in those where there was free access to land there were often elaborate regulations co-ordinating their utilization by the various members of society.[16] But while it is true that a free access equilibrium is allocationally inefficient, it should by no means be thought that the introduction of property rights on what was originally a common property resource is necessarily a move towards raising welfare. We have seen that when N is finite each firm makes a positive net profit at the free access equilibrium. Introducing the tax that we analysed would certainly be in the interests of efficiency. But we have noted that if not a penny of the tax revenue is paid back to the firms, they are all worse off even though they still make positive profits. Then again, if what was originally a communal property is suddenly expropriated by an 'outsider' who proceeds to exact the full rent from the property accruing to it at the profit maximizing level of activity $N\tilde{x}$, each of the firms is yet worse off since in the other two cases, they were making a positive profit at least and now they are not. This expropriation of a common property resource, while blessed at the altar of efficiency, can have disastrous distributional consequences. The point that is being raised is analytically, of course, a trivial one, but it has been argued by some that it is nevertheless historically rather important. Thus, for example, during the fifteenth and sixteenth centuries the enclosure movement swept the English countryside, thereby putting an end to communal arable land. In its wake it seems were left literally thousands of impoverished peasants whose simple means of livelihood were

[15] These differing schemes, for our model, are identical so long, of course, as the costs involved in sustaining these schemes are equal. In our example we have supposed that such costs are nil. But one should bear in mind that there are administrative costs in establishing and enforcing taxes. At the same time there are costs of policing private property rights (e.g. fences that separate one's grazing ground from one's neighbour's). When contemplating alternative *institutional* systems such cost considerations will presumably matter. For an excellent discussion of such matters, see Dales (1968).

[16] For example in Greco-Roman times land was usually privately owned by a few landlords (see Finley (1973)). We are by no means suggesting that private ownership of land is prompted by recognition of the problem of the common; simply that where land is communally owned regulations toward its utilization often seem to appear.

wrecked and who had consequently to search for industrial employment.

'Communal property . . . was an old Teutonic institution which lived on under cover of feudalism. We have seen how the forcible usurpation of this, generally accompanied by the turning of arable into pasture land, begins at the end of the fifteenth and extends into the sixteenth century. But, at that time, the process was carried on by means of individual acts of violence against which legislation, for a hundred and fifty years, fought in vain . . . The parliamentary form of the robbery is that of Acts for enclosures of commons, in other words, decrees by which the landlords grant themselves the people's land as private property, decrees of expropriation of the people.'[17]

A remarkable feature of the problem of common property resource is the variety of examples that one can rather readily construct in exemplifying it.[18] While the general nature of the problem appears in each such example, one's reaction to the various means of coping with it no doubt depends on the example in question. If the tax proceeds from big-game hunting are expropriated entirely by the government, the resulting distributional impact will not usually stick in one's throat. Not so, presumably, if the 'firms' happen to be individuals eking out an existence from a common property resource. While we have focused attention only on the inefficiency involved in the exploitation of a common property resource, the distributional consequences of alternative mechanisms of removing this inefficiency should certainly be borne in mind when examining any particular case.

6. Asymmetrical Externalities and the Multiplicity of Tax Equilibria

We have analysed the problem of the common at some length because of the importance of the problem and also because of the simplicity of its underlying structure. A distinguishing feature of our

[17] Marx (1961), p. 724. The Marxian thesis regarding the distributional impact of the enclosure movement of the fifteenth and sixteenth centuries has been systematically challenged over the years (see, for example, Kerridge (1969)). For a recent revival of the thesis see the interesting paper by Cohen and Weitzman (1975).

[18] For illuminating early discussion of the problem of the common, see Gordon (1954) and Milliman (1956). Gordon emphasized the common fishery's problem and Milliman those of common water resources. For a popular and dramatic statement of the problem see Hardin (1968).

EXTERNALITIES 79

model of common property resource is the symmetric nature of the externalities. An implication of this assumption of symmetry is that the tax equilibrium is unique. To state this another way, the symmetry assumption implies that the marginal benefit curve (M_B) cuts the marginal loss curve $(|M_L|)$ at a single point (see Diagram 3.5) or, equivalently, that the net benefit curve $(B - |L|)$ as a function of the total number of vessels (X) is single peaked (see Diagram 3.6). This is an amiable property for the problem to have. We noted that marginal social cost–benefit analysis allows one to locate the number of vessels $\tilde{X}$ that ought ideally to be utilized.

Unhappily a great many examples of external diseconomies do not have this simple structure. Consequently it is entirely possible in such cases for there to be a multiplicity of tax equilibria. In other words it is possible in such cases that the net benefit curve has multiple peaks, some of which are merely locally the greatest in value and not globally so.[19] Marginal social cost–benefit analysis in such cases can be treacherous since, depending on the level of activity from which social cost–benefit analysis is begun, the analysis may quite easily lead to a mere local optimum and miss out the global one without anybody being the wiser. We shall illustrate such a possibility by means of an example. The example will also enable us to discuss a number of further issues that are relevant in discussing the theory of externalities.

Suppose that industry α consists of N identical firms, $(i = 1, \ldots, N)$, all located upstream of a river. Firm i utilizes two variable inputs, l_i and x_i, to produce a homogeneous product, y_i. For simplicity we take it that production possibilities open to i are represented by

3.51 $\qquad y_i \leqslant l_i^a x_i^b, \qquad a, b > 0 \quad \text{and} \quad a + b < 1; \qquad i = 1, \ldots, N.$

The production process, however, consists as well in the creation of effluent, e_i, which to be specific, is a transformed product of the input, x_i. This effluent, it is supposed, can only be deposited in the river. A detailed account of production possibilities would have us take into the fact that the quantity of effluent can often be controlled (say, by breaking it down into relatively harmless molecules)

[19] Stating the point in yet another way; the motivation for devising a tax system is to allow the economy to find the optimum of the net benefit curve (assuming, of course, that the government has a clear assessment of how to aggregate individual benefits and costs into social benefits and costs). Formally speaking the taxes are computed from the first order conditions pertaining to the maximum of the net benefit curve. It follows that every local maximum and every local minimum can be established as a tax equilibrium.

with the help of further resources. Here we shall wish to keep the analysis simple. Consequently, we ignore such possibilities of treating the waste and suppose simply that e_i is proportional to x_i, and, in particular that

3.52 $e_i = \mu x_i, \qquad \mu > 0,$[20] $i = 1, \ldots, N.$

Industry β consists of M identical firms ($j = 1, \ldots, M$), all located downstream of this river. For simplicity we suppose that firm j utilizes a variable input, v_j, and a fixed quantity of water to produce a homogeneous product, z_j. But while the quantity of water required is fixed (because, say, the plant size is fixed), its usefulness depends on the quality of the water and, in particular, it is supposed that the less contaminated the water, the more productive it is. Again, a detailed treatment of production possibilities would have us take into account the fact that the contaminated water can often be purified (at least up to a point) by j with the help of further resources. Once again, we shall wish to keep j's production possibilities in a simple form. Thus we ignore such possibilities. Write $E = \sum_{i=1}^{N} e_i$, for the total quantity of effluent in the river. Then we take it that production possibilities open to j can be represented by the form

3.53

$$
\left.
\begin{aligned}
& z_j \leqslant \frac{k(v_j)}{1 + h(E)}, \qquad j = 1, \ldots, M \\[6pt]
& \text{where} \\
& k(0) = 0, \qquad k'(v_j) > 0, \qquad k''(v_j) < 0, \\
& h(0) = 0, \quad \text{and} \quad h'(E) > 0.
\end{aligned}
\right\} \quad \text{[12]}
$$

As in the earlier sections of this chapter we shall be interested in the notion of an equilibrium outcome for these two industries.

[20] To give only an example of how one may wish to capture the fact that treatment of the waste is possible by i one could suppose that i can utilize a further resource z_i to control the waste via the production constraint

$$e_i \geqslant \frac{\mu x_i}{1 + g(z_i)},$$

where $g(0) = 0$ and $g'(z_i) > 0$. In 3.52 it is supposed that $g(z_i) = 0$ for all z_i.

[21] A simple example of how one may wish to capture the fact that j is capable of purifying the river water for its own use would be as follows. Denote by m_j the level of pollution of the water actually used by j in its production of the final good. Let s_j denote a variable input in its water purification plant. Then we could suppose that

$$m_j \geqslant \frac{h(E)}{1 + r(s_j)} \quad \text{and} \quad z_j \leqslant \frac{k(v_j)}{1 + m_j}$$

where $r(0) = 0$ and $r'(s_j) > 0$. In 3.53 we are supposing that such purification possibilities do not exist and, therefore, that $r(s_j) = 0$ for all s_j.

Again, as in our earlier examples let us cushion these two industries from the outside world by supposing that they trade with the rest of the world at fixed prices. Thus denote by p_y, p_l and p_x the prices of the single output and the two variable inputs involved in industry α, and by p_z and p_v the prices of the single output and the single variable input involved in industry β.

An important feature in which our present example differs from the example of the 'common' is the asymmetrical nature of the interaction between the two industries. There is a temptation to say that so long as $\sum_{i=1}^{N} e_i > 0$ industry α imposes an externality on industry β and not the other way around, and common parlance would describe the interaction in precisely such a manner. We shall note presently that the matter is somewhat more ambiguous than common parlance would suggest and that it depends critically on the precise specification of property rights. Even so, it is plain that a distinguishing feature of the present example is the asymmetry in the interaction.

If both N and M are reasonably large it may seem plausible to contemplate once again the notion of a market equilibrium which we introduced in section 1. We shall compute such equilibria in what follows. Given that firms are profit maximizing each firm will produce efficiently. Consider firm i in industry α. Let A (a constant) denote the cost that i has to bear on its fixed capital. Net profit for i can then be denoted as $(p_y y_i - p_l l_i - p_x x_i - A)$, which, on using 3.51 can be expressed as

3.54 $$p_y l_i^a x_i^b - p_l l_i - p_x x_i - A.$$

Firm i is concerned with maximizing 3.54 by choosing l_i and x_i. The critical question pertains to the *admissible* set of values of these two variables. Now so far as l_i is concerned, presumably it can take any non-negative value that i chooses. But what of x_i? For note 3.52. The admissible range of values for x_i will plainly depend on the law pertaining to the amount of pollution that i is allowed to deposit into the river. For example, if industry β has a right to *pure* river water then *in the absence of any negotiations* between firm i and industry β, x_i will have to be set at zero. Now as we are considering the market equilibrium in the sense that we have defined it we take it by definition that there are no negotiations. The equilibrium that we are studying is a non-co-operative one. It is, therefore, informative to suppose that i chooses l_i only, and to express i's maximized profit, π_α^i as a function of the quantity of pollution, e_i ($=\mu x_i$) that it deposits into the river. This procedure will enable us to describe the set of market equilibria as a function of the precise pollution rights specified by law. Thus write

$$3.55 \qquad \pi_\alpha^i(e_i) = \max_{l_i} \left(\frac{p_y l_i^a e_i^b}{\mu^b} - p_l l_i - p_x \frac{e_i}{\mu} - A \right).$$

Given that by assumption $a+b<1$ (see 3.51) it is simple to check that $\pi_\alpha^i(e_i)$ is a concave function. In Diagram 3.7 a typical functional form of π_α^i is presented. The diagram also contains the resulting form of the marginal profit function $d\pi_\alpha^i(e_i)/de_i$.

Consider now firm j in industry β. If we were to take it that the total level of pollution in the river is E, its net profit ($p_z z_j - p_v v_j$), can, on using 3.53 be denoted as

$$3.56 \qquad p_z \frac{k(v_j)}{1 + h(E)} - p_v v_j.$$

(We assume, for simplicity, that j incurs no fixed cost.) Firm j is concerned with maximizing 3.56 by a judicious choice of v_j. Denoting by π_β^i the maximized value of profit we have, by definition

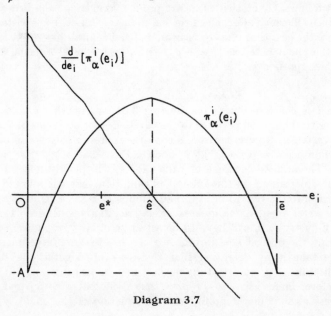

Diagram 3.7

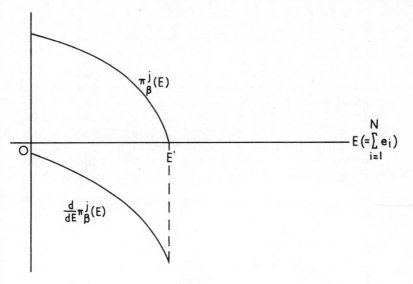

Diagram 3.8

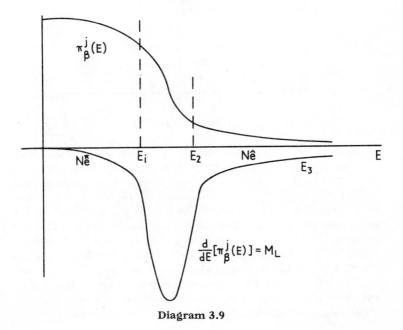

Diagram 3.9

3.57
$$\pi_\beta^j(E) \equiv \max_{v_j} \left\{ \frac{p_z k(v_j)}{1 + h(E)} - p_v v_j \right\}.$$

It is immediate from the RHS of 3.57 that $\pi_\beta^j(E)$ is a declining function of E. But it can never be negative, since j always has the option of setting $v_j = 0$ and thereby closing down its operation. In Diagrams 3.8 and 3.9 two plausible forms of π_β^j are presented. The diagrams also depict the corresponding shapes of $d\pi_\beta^i(E)/dE$, the marginal impact of E on j's maximized profit level.

In Diagram 3.8 it is supposed that up to the pollution level E', π_β^j is concave and that for all $E > E'$ one has $\pi_\beta^j = 0$. Diagram 3.9

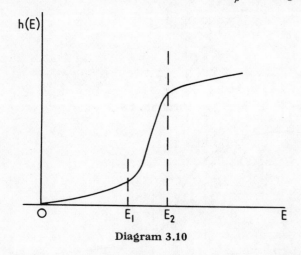

Diagram 3.10

portrays a more interesting situation. Recall 3.53. Apart from asserting that $h(0) = 0$ and $h'(E) > 0$ we have left the functional form of h unspecified. In many situations it is plausible to suppose that $h(E)$ has the shape depicted in Diagram 3.10. The situation captured by Diagram 3.10 is one where up to a total pollution level E_1 the water impurity does not affect production possibilities in industry β by much. In other words, up to E_1, $h'(E)$ is rather 'low' (though positive). Over the range E_1 to E_2^- the water impurity begins to affect production possibilities in industry β quite seriously. That is to say $h'(E)$ is 'large'. Beyond E_2 it is supposed that h more or less flattens out. Most of the damage has already been done. Now if $h(E)$ has the form depicted in Diagram 3.10, then it is immediate from 3.57

that $\pi_\beta^j(E)$ will have the form drawn in Diagram 3.9. Up to a level of pollution E_1 maximum profit, π_β, declines very slowly. It declines dramatically over the range E_1 to E_2 during which the marginal impact of E is great. Beyond E_2 maximum profit declines slowly, possibly to zero for large enough values of E (say for $E \geqslant E_3$). In either case (i.e. Diagrams 3.8 or 3.9) π_β^j is a non-concave function if the entire non-negative range of E is contemplated. In what follows we shall, to be specific, take it that $\pi_\beta^j(E)$ has the functional form depicted in Diagram 3.9.

We have described the profit functions of the representative firms in the two industries and it remains to characterize the market equilibria. As one might be inclined to guess, the structure of the market equilibria depends critically on the specification of pollution rights. Suppose, to take an extreme example, that in this economy the law recognizes pollutor's rights but not the rights of the pollutees. That is to say, suppose that industry β has no legal *right* to pure water. Recall that we are attempting to describe an equilibrium that is characterized by an absence of negotiations between firms. Since by law firm i can pollute as much as it likes without penalty it will come to pollute up to the level $\hat{e}$ (see Diagram 3.7) at which $\pi_\alpha^i(e_i)$ is maximized. Total pollution in the river will therefore be $N\hat{e}$. Turning to industry β, so long as $N\hat{e} < E_3$ (see Diagram 3.9) firm j will find it profitable to undertake production. The interesting situation is one where this is indeed so. Thus in the case where the pollutor has the right to pollute indefinitely the market equilibrium is characterized by a total pollution level $N\hat{e}$. Total profit for the two industries taken together at the equilibrium can be read off from Diagrams 3.7 and 3.9 and can be expressed as

$$3.58 \qquad\qquad \pi(\hat{e}) \equiv N\pi_\alpha^i(\hat{e}) + M\pi_\beta^j(N\hat{e}).$$

We shall presently compare $\pi(\hat{e})$ with maximum total profit for the two industries taken together; that is, with a Pareto-efficient allocation. But for the moment consider an altered legal structure, one where there are some rights for the pollutees as well. It is supposed that the law recognizes that it must not empower the pollutee with the right to pure river water (i.e. $E = 0$) since in the absence of negotiations (that is, at a market equilibrium), industry α will be forced to close down and absorb a total loss NA. Consequently the law empowers the pollutee with only partial rights, in that it allows firm i in the industry to pollute only up to a level e^*

(>0) with impunity. In other words, e^* is the *benchmark* level of pollution per firm in industry α.[22] Now if $0 < e^* < \hat{e}$ (see Diagram 3.7) and if, as we are supposing, there are no negotiations between firms, then i will deposit precisely e^* units of pollution, since π_α^i is increasing at e^*.[23] It follows that at a market equilibrium total pollution will be at the level Ne^*. Consequently total profit for the industries taken together is

$$3.59 \qquad \pi(e^*) = N\pi_\alpha^i(e^*) + M\pi_\beta^j(Ne^*)$$

(see Diagrams 3.7 and 3.9). Notice that $\pi_\alpha^i(e^*) \neq \pi_\alpha^i(\hat{e})$, $\pi_\beta(e^*) \neq \pi_\beta^j(\hat{e})$, and in general that $\pi(e^*) \neq \pi(\hat{e})$. Notice also that the lower the benchmark level of pollution, e^*, the more the equilibrium distribution favours industry β. We conclude that at a market equilibrium *both* the total profit for the two industries taken together, as well as the distribution of this profit between the two industries, depend on the specification of pollution rights.[24]

In what follows we shall be concerned, for simplicity, with the size of total profits (sum of producers' surpluses). In other words, we shall be concerned with Pareto-efficient allocations. It is rather plain that a market equilibrium will be Pareto *inefficient* unless, by fluke or design, e^* has been chosen so as to support a Pareto-efficient outcome. So the first question to ask is whether a Lindahl equilibrium can exist for this problem. In fact it is rather easy to check that it does not. For recall that a Lindahl equilibrium will consist of competitive markets for named commodities, e_{ji}, where in equilibrium

$$3.60 \qquad e_i = e_{ji}, \qquad i = 1, \ldots, N \quad \text{and} \quad j = 1, \ldots M.$$

To say that firm i in industry has been empowered by law with a benchmark level of pollution, e^*, is a way of saying that i has an initial endowment, e^*, of pollution rights. Denote by p_{ji} the price that firm i in industry α has to pay firm j in industry β for a unit of pollution that i deposits into the river. Thus, in fact, if i deposits

[22] We are supposing that it is costless to monitor the quantity of effluent generated by *each* firm in industry α.

[23] If $e^* > \hat{e}$ then i will deposit precisely $\hat{e}$, since π_α^i is a declining function beyond $\hat{e}$.

[24] This feature is, of course, true as well in the case of the problem of the common. We did not emphasize it in the discussion of the common's problem, however, because the problem there is characterized by a simple and unambiguous set of property rights; namely that each firm has the right to exploit the common property to any extent it chooses. That is, the law ascribes full rights to the polluter.

e_i ($=e_{ji}$) units, its net payment to j is $p_{ji}(e_i-e^*)$. Now it is plain that at an equilibrium p_{ji} cannot be positive. For with $p_{ji}>0$ firm j will be encouraged to undertake little or no production activity but to earn all its profits by selling pollution rights to i; the more it sells, the higher its profits. But i will hardly wish to purchase an unlimited quantity of pollution rights, most certainly not beyond the level $\bar{e}$ at which $\pi_\alpha^i=-A$ (see Diagram 3.7), and actually at a level less than $\bar{e}$. Demand and supply of e_{ji} will not match, and consequently an equilibrium cannot be sustained with $p_{ji}>0$. Notice next that p_{ji} cannot be zero in equilibrium since in this case there is in fact no cash transfer between i and j. Consequently j will demand that $e_{ji}=0$ while i would wish to supply e_{ji} at a level $\hat{e}$. The argument is reinforced if $p_{ji}<0$. One concludes that a Lindahl equilibrium for our problem does not exist. The source of the problem, as one would be inclined to guess, is that in the space of named commodities firm j's production possibility set is non-convex. This can be readily confirmed by considering 3.53. Holding constant v_j and all except one named commodity e_{ji} one can describe production possibilities as circumscribed by the curve in Diagram 3.11. The set is, of course, non-convex.

The question that arises next pertains, as in our earlier examples, to the kinds of regulatory measure that will ensure that a market equilibrium sustains an efficient allocation. Now it can be checked that given our characterization of production possibilities for the

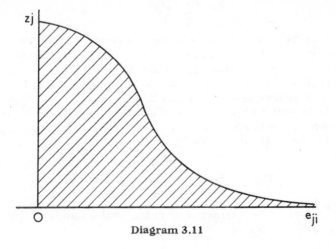

Diagram 3.11

two industries the pure quota rule, the pure licensing scheme and the pure pollution tax scheme will all in principle work for this problem. To illustrate this, consider for example the pure tax scheme. The regulatory agency, would wish to impose a specific tax, t, per unit of effluent, e_i ($\geqslant 0$) that i deposits in the river. *Given t, i's profit will read as*

$$\frac{p_y l_j^a e_i^b}{\mu^b} - p_l l_i - \left(\frac{p_x + \mu t}{\mu}\right) e_i - A,$$

and consequently i will be concerned with selecting l_i and e_i optimally, *with no constraint on either variable.* The regulator's problem consists in choosing the correct value of t, where, by a correct value, we mean one that sustains a Pareto-efficient outcome. This is precisely what was aimed at in the previous examples. However, a source of worry for this example is that unlike the problem of the common there may be computational difficulties in *locating* an efficient regulatory measure. This is a point we raised at the very beginning of this section and it is time to elaborate on it. In order to do this it will be useful to simplify the example and suppose that $N = M$. Given that firms in a given industry are identical, one is concerned with those allocations in which firms in a given industry behave identically. Recall Diagram 3.9. Denote by

$$M_L \equiv \frac{d}{dE}\{\pi_\beta^j(E)\} < 0,$$

the marginal loss to firm j due to an increase in river pollution and, therefore, by $NM_L(E)$ the *sum* of the marginal losses to the firms in industry β (see Diagram 3.9). Denote by $N|M_L(E)|$ the absolute value of this loss. Using Diagram 3.9 the general shape of this can easily be protrayed, as in Diagram 3.12.

The benefit to industry α due to extra pollution is also simple to describe. As firms are identically treated let each firm pollute at a level e. Total pollution is $E = Ne$. Write

$$B(E) = \sum_{i=1}^{N} \pi_\alpha^i(e) = N\pi_\alpha(e) = N\pi_\alpha\left(\frac{E}{N}\right)$$

for total profit for industry α when the total pollution level is Ne, and by

$$M_B = B'(E) = \frac{d}{dE}\left\{N\pi_\alpha\left(\frac{E}{N}\right)\right\}$$

the marginal profit to industry α. From Diagram 3.7 it is readily checked that this last is monotonically decreasing and equals zero at the level of pollution $N\hat{e}$.

In Diagram 3.12 the points E_4, E_5 and E_6 denote three levels of pollution, E, at which the curves M_B and $N|M_L|$ intersect. In

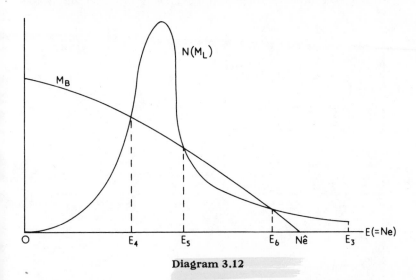

Diagram 3.12

Diagram 3.13 they denote the corresponding 'turning' points of the resulting net benefit curve $B-N|L|$.[25] Plainly E_4, being the global maximum argument of the function $(B-N|L|)$, denotes the socially efficient level of pollution in the river, while E_5 is a local minimum

[25] We are assuming that net social benefit is merely the algebraic sum of the net profits of the two industries. Notice that in Diagram 3.13 we have drawn the curve so that $B-N|L|<0$ at $E=0$. Thus it is supposed that the fixed cost, NA, for industry α is 'large'. In such a situation it would be silly to clamour for a zero pollution level. One might wish to argue that industry α should not have been allowed to be located upstream in the first place. But without knowing the nature of industry α one can make no such claims. Perhaps transport costs for the inputs and outputs of industry are low at this geographical location.

and E_6 is a local maximum without being globally so. Each one of them is a tax equilibrium but, of course, E_4 is the desirable one.[26] Now suppose that in the absence of any social management of the problem the market equilibrium has resulted in a level of pollution, E, that is in excess of E_5 (because, say, the law ascribes rights to the pollutor so that the market equilibrium level of pollution is $N\hat{e}$ ($> E_5$)). If now an attempt is made to manage the level of pollution via a sequence of marginal cost–benefit analyses, then the system will eventually find itself a resting place at E_6, since each move in the sequence is made with a view of climbing the 'local hill' whose

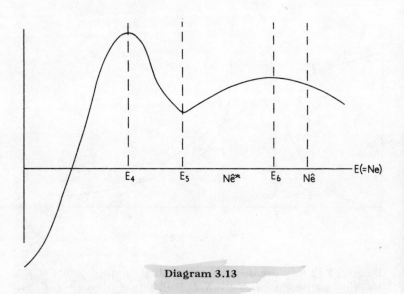

Diagram 3.13

peak is at E_6. It follows that social management via marginal social benefit–cost analysis will lead the economy to the local maximum E_6 which, while plainly better than the market equilibrium level of pollution, is still far removed from E_4. There is consequently a definite sense in which there is over-pollution at E_6, but one would typically not know that this is so. The reason is that at E_6 whether

---

[26] Actually the point $E=0$ is a tax equilibrium as well where industry α is taxed at such a prohibitive rate for the effluent it discharges that it is forced to close down entirely.

at the margin one increases or decreases the level of pollution there is a drop in net benefit. The problem really concerns the availability of global information. If the government really knew the technological and economic possibilities in their entirety, so that the entire net benefit curve $B-N|L|$ was known, there would be no problem. The authorities would merely glance at the curve, pick out E_4, and legislate it, or equivalently, choose that rate of taxation on industry which would support E_4. The crux of the problem lies in that typically the net benefit schedule over the entire non-negative range of the level of pollution is not known to the government. The regulator picks up the problem at the market equilibrium point. Typically it contemplates marginal moves (it obtains only local information about $B-N|L|$ from the firms) and continues supporting these moves so long as net benefit $B-N|L|$ is increasing at each move. If the market equilibrium level of pollution happens to lie to the left of the point E_5 (say because the benchmark level of pollution e^* is small) there is no problem, since social management via cost–benefit analysis will unerringly take the system to E_4. But as we have seen, if the market equilibrium level of pollution E happens to lie to the right of E_5 this procedure merely takes the system to E_6 which, while superior to the market equilibrium, still supports too much pollution.

The upshot of this discussion is that Pigouvian taxes for socially managing externalities are not necessarily reliable. There may be multiple tax equilibria. Likewise, a simple 'gradient process' for locating the optimal level of pollution will not necessarily work because the net benefit curve can on occasion have multiple peaks. The source of the problem that has arisen here lies in a sense in the fact that external diseconomies, like pollution, often imply non-convexities in technological possibilities. But we do emphasize that this is so only in a sense. For recall that in the problem of the common, while individual firms inflict diseconomies on one another, the symmetric nature of such infliction resulted in the net benefit curve being single peaked (see Diagram 3.6). For external diseconomies in general the case that we have just analysed is more likely to be the rule than an exception. The problem of pollution control is a difficult one to solve.[27]

[27] Recently some attempts have been made to devise search procedures that will locate the global optimum even in the face of non-convexities in technological possibilities (see in particular Heal (1973)).

7. Conclusions

The examples analysed in this chapter appear to suggest the following conclusions.[28]

(1) In the presence of externalities a market equilibrium may well be Pareto inefficient.

(2) External diseconomies in production often imply non-convexities in the space of named commodities, and this *can* ensure that a competitive equilibrium with markets for externalities simply does not exist.

(3) A competitive equilibrium with markets for externalities, when it exists, is Pareto efficient.

(4) If a competitive equilibrium with markets for externalities exists, so does a tax equilibrium exist. Moreover, every competitive equilibrium allocation with markets for externalities can as well be established as an appropriate tax equilibrium.

(5) There are cases (e.g. the problem of the common) where even though a competitive equilibrium with markets for externalities may not exist, there exists a unique tax equilibrium which is Pareto efficient.

(6) Even ignoring income effects, both the size of total net benefits and its distribution among different agents at a market equilibrium depend on the specification of legal rights for generating externalities.

(7) Even ignoring income effects, different schemes designed to produce the optimum levels of externalities have different distributional implications.

(8) In general when production possibility sets are non-convex in the space of named commodities a tax equilibrium is not unique, and each local minimum and each local maximum of the net benefit function will be supported by a tax equilibrium. In such situations the government will need to conduct *global* cost–benefit analysis to

---

[28] We emphasize that with the exception of 3, 4, 6, 7 and 9 the conclusions are all qualified by an existential quantifier. And yet such qualified conclusions—which our examples support—are worth stating explicitly because they indicate the general tendencies for 'plausible' economies with externalities. One can certainly construct examples where these general tendencies are violated. For example, 10 is surely not an implication of 9 because, for example, income effects may be 'perverse'. But even in the absence of income effects 10 can be untrue without further qualifications (see, for example, Buchanan and Karfoglis (1963) and Diamond and Mirrlees (1973)). For general arguments leading to conclusions 2 and 5 see Foley (1970), Starrett (1971, 1973) and Bergstrom (1974).

compute the optimal allocation and thus calculate the tax structure that will support it.

(9) If there is a presumption that competitive markets for externalities will not be established, the production of external economies ought to be subsidized and the production of external diseconomies ought to be taxed.

(10) An implication of (9) is the presumption that at a market equilibrium with externalities there is an under-production of external economies and an over-production of external diseconomies.

Notes on Chapter 3

The literature on externalities is simply huge. It would be almost impossible to give even a reasonably complete bibliography for it. Our account of the problem of externalities in general and Pigouvian taxes in particular is based on the writings of Pigou (1932), Meade (1952), Samuelson (1954), Musgrave (1954), Arrow (1969), Foley (1970) and Starrett (1972, 1974). For a more detailed exposition of the subject see Maler (1974), Meade (1973), and Baumol and Oates (1975). An excellent treatment of common property problems is in Dales (1972) and Christy Jr. and Scott (1972). The terminology 'named' goods is taken from Hahn (1971) who used it in a different context.

The problem of the common was brought to the attention of non-economists in a widely cited article by Hardin (1968). The article is vigorously written and is characterized as much by loose analyses as by incorrect conclusions.

So far as we know our *presentation* of the problem of the common is new. The literature usually deals with the case when there is *free entry* to the common property by potential firms (see, for example, Gordon (1954). Firms are assumed to continue to enter so long as there are positive profits to be made. In equilibrium, therefore, firms make no profit, and the average product of vessels is equal to the rental price. We have, instead, kept the number of firms fixed at N and have investigated the notion of an equilibrium when the common property resource (i.e. the fishing ground) is free to each of them. Stating it another way, in the conventional treatment of the problem the number of firms exploiting the common property resource is endogenous to the analysis. In our presentation it is given exogenously. Given a fixed number of firms, N, we have shown that firms make a positive profit at the market equilibrium. but that the size of the profit is small if N is large. Positive profit for each firm is implied at the market equilibrium for our problem so long as in deciding how many vessels to introduce, each firm i takes into account the effect of its fleet of vessels, x_i, on the average product of vessels on the fishing ground (equation 3.27). Suppose instead, that even though N is finite each firm i *pretends* that the average product $F(X)/X$ is independent of the number of vessels, x_i, that it introduces. Instead of equation 3.28 the symmetric market equilibrium condition will then read as $F(Nx)/Nx=p$ and, therefore, that in equilibrium there are no profits to be made by firms. This last is a sensible notion of an equilibrium so long as it is sensible for each firm to suppose that it cannot influence the average product of vessels. But presumably this will be a reasonable position for a firm to take so long as N is large. It is for this reason that we have analysed the more general condition of equilibrium as embodied in equation 3.28 and have obtained the zero profit case as a limiting one when N tends to infinity.

As we have remarked, there are a number of ways one can present the problem of the common. For a full general equilibrium treatment of the problem (i.e. where the input price—in our case, p—is determined within the system), see Cohen and Weitzman (1975). Unlike Cohen and Weitzman, who are concerned with modelling an entire economy in which the single fixed factor (land) is communally owned, we have been concerned with a common property resource that appears in only one sector of the economy. A partial equilibrium approach with the number of firms given exogenously seems best suited for this purpose. It enables us to handle the diverse examples discussed in section 5.

An important question that we have not touched on in our discussion of optimal regulation of externalities is the one regarding incentives designed to make agents reveal their true preferences regarding the supply of externalities. We have tacitly supposed that the true preferences are revealed. For firms this is not an absurd assumption, given that the externalities are of a technological nature. Their effects can, in principle, be determined. But the assumption that the government can elicit the true preferences of consumers (e.g. the example in section 3) needs justification. We have not provided one. For a discussion of this range of questions see, for example, the recent contributions of Groves and Ledyard (1977), Green and Lafont (1977) and Maskin (1977).

Our discussion of externalities—though not our definition of the concept—has focused attention on what is usually, but somewhat misleadingly, called non-pecuniary externalities. A sharp distinction between pecuinary and non-pecuniary externalities is difficult to make. For discussions on this point see Scitovsky (1954) and Starrett (1974).

CHAPTER 4

INTERTEMPORAL EQUILIBRIUM

1. A Basic Result

It is clear that in developing the economics of exhaustible resources time must be brought explicitly into the construction. It is equally clear that the problems concern the allocation of a fixed stock of a commodity, perhaps unknown in size, between competing uses at different dates. In developing the theory it is as well to discuss the simplest considerations first. We shall add complications as we go along.

Assume for the moment that time is discrete. In what follows we shall always regard the 'present' instant as $t=0$. Since the past is past, choice affects the present and future only. Given this, we can without loss of generality consider the case where time assumes the non-negative integer values, $t=0, 1, 2 \ldots$ Imagine, to begin with, an individual concerned simply with three instants of time, $t=0, 1, 2$. Imagine also that there is a single commodity whose stock at $t=0$ is known by him to be S_0. The commodity does not deteriorate over time (unlike ice-cream on a hot day). Nor does it grow (unlike forest resources). Nor indeed does it provide a constant flow of service over the three dates (unlike land). In fact, assume that there is no production in this world. But assume that storage is possible costlessly. In effect the commodity is much like a non-deteriorating piece of cake, or a quantity of hard-tack. It has to be divided for consumption over three dates.

The individual has title to the entire stock, S_0, and is concerned with dividing it for consumption at the three dates. Despite the fact that we are postulating a single individual and an absence of production the example does pose an economic problem: namely the problem of 'exchange' over time. The more the individual consumes at $t=0$, the less he will inherit at a future date. The more he wants to inherit at a future date the less he can consume at $t=0$. Let us denote by x_0, x_1 and x_2 his consumption levels at the three dates $t=0, 1, 2$. Assume next that his preferences, $at\ t=0$, over consumption levels at these dates can be represented by a strictly concave, everywhere differentiable, and monotone increasing function, u, where

4.1 $$u = u(x_0, x_1, x_2).$$

There is no uncertainty. A consumption plan for the individual is a non-negative vector $x = (x_0, x_1, x_2)$. By assumption, the function u reflects at $t = 0$ the manner in which he evaluates different consumption plans.[1] The individual is concerned at $t = 0$ with choosing a consumption plan from among the set of feasible consumption plans. By the nature of the commodity we have postulated a feasible plan x is one for which

4.2 $$x_0 + x_1 + x_2 \leqslant S_0 \quad \text{with} \quad x_0, x_1, x_2 \geqslant 0.$$

We suppose that the individual chooses that consumption plan which maximizes 4.1 subject to the constraint 4.2. Let $x^* = (x_2^*, x_1^*, x_2^*)$ denote the chosen policy. The first point to note is that since by assumption u is monotonically increasing (i.e. there is no satiation) the chosen consumption plan will exhaust the resource stock; that is $x_0^* + x_1^* + x_0^* = S_0$. The second point to note is that if $x^* \gg O$ (i.e. each component of x^* is strictly positive) then

4.3 $$u_{x_0}(x^*) = u_{x_1}(x^*) = u_{x_2}(x^*) \quad \text{where} \quad u_{x_{t0}} = \frac{\partial u}{\partial x_t}.$$

This condition, which is eminently congenial to common sense, is a basic result in the economics of exhaustible resources. The condition expresses the requirement that if the chosen plan consists of positive consumption at each date, the marginal utility of consumption at each date, viewed from date $t = 0$, must be the same along the plan. Or to state it slightly differently, the marginal rate of indifferent substitution between consumption at any two dates must be equal to unity along the chosen path. The necessity of this condition is immediate. If it were not met, there would be two adjacent dates with differing marginal utilities along the plan. This in turn would imply that a marginal reallocation of consumption of the resource from the date at which marginal utility is lower to the date at which marginal utility is higher would yield higher utility to the individual. The plan would then not be his chosen plan. Sufficiency follows, of

[1] Questions bearing on the notion of an equitable allocation of exhaustible resources over time, and possible biases that market imperfections lead to, will be discussed in Chapter 6–14.

course, from the fact that u is strictly concave and that the constraint set 4.2 is convex.

Condition 4.3 is valid only when $x^* \gg O$ (i.e. consumption at each date is positive). The foregoing argument will obviously not work if, say, some consumption plan x^* that just exhausts the stock has the property that $x_0^* = 0$ and $u_{x0}(x^*) < u_{x1}(x^*) = u_{x2}(x^*)$. Since $x_0^* = 0$, obviously $u_{x0}(x^*)$ cannot be further increased. It is entirely possible that there simply does not exist a consumption plan that just exhausts the stock and which at the same time satisfies condition 4.3. The basic result in its general form is, therefore, as follows: viewed from $t = 0$, the marginal utility of consumption along the

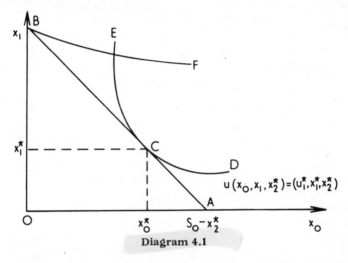

Diagram 4.1

chosen plan at each date at which there is positive consumption, is the same (say λ) and, furthermore, the marginal utility of consumption at those dates at which there is no consumption is no greater than λ.[2]

---

[2] Formally, the problem is to maximize $u(x_0, x_1, x_2)$ by choosing x_0, x_1 and x_2 subject to the constraints $x_0, x_1, x_2 \geqslant 0$ and $x_0 + x_1 + x_2 \leqslant S_0$. A necessary and sufficient condition for x^* to be the chosen policy, is that there exist Lagrange multipliers, μ_0, μ_1, μ_2 and λ that satisfy the conditions

4.3′ $\qquad u_{x0}(x^*) + \mu_0 = u_{x1}(x^*) + \mu_1 = u_{x2}(x^*) + \mu_2 = \lambda$

and

$$\mu_t \geqslant 0, \quad \text{and} \quad \mu_t x_t^* = 0 \qquad (t = 0, 1, 2);$$
$$\lambda \geqslant 0, \quad \text{and} \quad (S_0 - x_0^* - x_1 - x_2^*) = 0$$

If $x^* > > 0$ then obviously $\mu_t = 0$ and consequently the condition 4.3′ reduces to 4.3.

It is worthwhile presenting the argument diagrammatically as well. Holding the consumption level at $t=2$ fixed at x_2^* the individual selects x_0 and x_1 to maximize $u(x_0, x_1, x_2^*)$ subject to the constraint $x_0 + x_1 \leqslant S_0 - x_2^*$. Diagram 4.1 portrays the situation. The isosceles triangle OAB (with OA = OB) represents the feasible set. Given that u is by assumption an increasing function, the individual will choose a point on AB. If DE is an indifference curve generated by the function $u(x_0, x_1, x_2^*)$ he will select C, the unique point at which the indifference curve is tangential to AB. It is, of course, obvious why the marginal rate of indifferent substitution between consumption at dates $t=0$ and $t=1$ must be unity at C. AB is defined by the equation $x_0 + x_1 = S_0 - x_2^*$. The marginal rate of transformation along AB is precisely unity. The characteristics of the resource are such that an act of saving (i.e. refraining from current consumption) any given amount of the resource yields no physical return over and above the amount saved. If, on the other hand, BF is an indifference curve, he will select B, which is characterized by $x_0 = 0$ and $x_1 = S_0 - x_2^*$. The slope of the curve BF at B is not necessarily equal to the slope of AB, and the more general condition 4.3' holds.

While shockingly simple, the foregoing result is basic to the theory of exhaustible resources. We shall note in what follows that it will appear repeatedly in various guises.

2. Consistent Preferences: A Mild Digression

The individual selects the consumption plan x^* at $t=0$. He consumes x_0^* at $t=0$. Comes the next date. The total stock remaining at $t=1$ is then $S_0 - x_0^*$. The question arises whether he will now wish to consume x_1^* or whether he will revise his plan. In what follows we shall take it that the individual has *intertemporally consistent preferences*, in the sense that at $t=1$ his preferences are still reflected by the utility function 4.1. By $t=1$ he will have already consumed x_0^*. Thus, were he to attempt at $t=1$ to recompute his optimal plan he would wish to choose x_1 and x_2 with a view to maximizing $u(x_0^*, x_1, x_2)$, subject to the constraint $x_1 + x_2 \leqslant S_0 - x_0^*$. It is, of course, immediate that his recomputed consumption plan at $t=1$ is still x_1^* and x_2^*. With intertemporally consistent preferences he will not wish to revise his original consumption plan. Putting it slightly differently, endowed with consistent preferences over time the individual's chosen plan is consistent over time. In effect, to say that the individual has a consistent set of preferences over time is to say that a single utility function (e.g. 4.1) can be ascribed to him.

But it is important to bear in mind that intertemporally consisteht *preferences* and intertemporally consistent *plans* are distinct notions. Our example demonstrates that the former implies that the chosen plan is intertemporally consistent. To say that an individual's preferences are inconsistent over time is to say that his preferences will *change* as time rolls on. This may be due to a variety of reasons. Habit formation is a typical case. Getting 'hooked' on, say, drugs and labour-saving devices are oft-cited examples. Under such circumstances the individual cannot be said to have a single preference ordering over time. A single utility function cannot be ascribed to him over time. Under perfect certainty the individual will, of course, know in advance exactly how his preferences will change. Nevertheless, even with inconsistent preferences the individual may, by making use of his knowledge of the manner in which his preferences will change, wish to search for a consistent plan; which is, in our sense, a plan that he does not find necessary to revise. It is clear enough then, that to assume an intertemporally consistent preference ordering for the individual (and thereby to ascribe him a single utility function over time) affords considerable analytical advantages. Under such an assumption the individual will choose his optimal plan, as viewed from the vantage of the initial date, and find no reason to alter his plan as time unfolds.[3]

3. The Basic Result: An Interpretation

We have described in some detail the individual's choice problem and his chosen consumption plan x^*. Let us now attempt a different interpretation. Suppose we were to regard a consumption plan $x = (x_0, x_1, x_2)$ as a commodity bundle, where commodities are distinguished by the date at which they are made available for consumption. While in our present example there is a single physically distinguishable commodity, there would in effect be three distinct commodities under this interpretation. It is very natural to extend the notion of a commodity and to characterize it not merely in terms of its physical attributes and location, but also by the date at which it is made available for consumption (or production). A barrel of oil is, no doubt, a barrel of oil. But its economic value presumably does depend on when it is made available. From the point of view of a consumer and a producer the date at which a

[3] Endogenous taste changes have been discussed in recent years by, among others, Hammond (1976) and Yaari (1976, 1977). On consistent preferences, see also Heal (1973).

given commodity is made available is an important feature. Dated commodities are a very intuitive notion. But with this extension of the notion of a commodity we are in familiar territory, for 4.2 could now be regarded as a conventional budget constraint imposed on the individual. To begin with, we could imagine that the individual possesses an income, S_0, measured in terms of the resource, dated $t=0$, and that he is to select a commodity bundle x. But what of prices under this interpretation? We have already selected as our numeraire the resource, dated $t=0$. The price p_t, for commodity x_t, is under this interpretation, the quantity of x_0 that has to be paid (at $t=0$), for delivery of a unit of the resource at t. In short, we suppose that there are *forward markets*. In our example there are two forward markets. They are the markets, established at $t=0$, for the dated goods x_1 and x_2. It is usual to refer to p_t as a *present value price*, since it is a price that has to be paid at $t=0$ for future delivery (i.e. delivery at t). Our simple example can now be given the following interpretation. One can imagine the individual concluding all his transactions at $t=0$. He 'sells' his entire endowment S_0 at the initial date to 'purchase' the consumption bundle x^*. It follows that under this interpretation his budget constraint will read $p_0 x_0 + p_1 x_1 + p_2 x_2 \leqslant p_0 S_0$. Now, we have already normalized and set $p_0 = 1$. If in fact $p_1 = p_2 = 1$ as well then this budget constraint is none other than the constraint 4.2. It follows that under this interpretation a crucial feature of the budget constraint 4.2 is that the present value prices of commodities x_1 and x_2 are each equal to unity. We shall repeatedly have occasion to note this particular price structure implied by exhaustible resources under competitive conditions.

4. Time Dated Commodities and Forward Markets: A General Account

While our simple example was of a single individual, it should have made it apparent how this natural extension of the notion of commodities (i.e. time dated commodities) allows one to incorporate time into the theory of competitive equilibrium of a private owner-ship economy. Ignoring locational issues, and for the moment uncertainty, if there are l physically distinguishable goods and services, and if we are interested in analysing an economy over T dates $(t=0, 1, \ldots, T-1)$, then formally we could regard the economy as consisting of lT commodities and services. With this interpretation we are on home ground. The entire framework developed in Chapter 2 can now be invoked. In particular, we can discuss coherently the notion of a competitive equilibrium of private ownership economy, conditions for its existence, and its Pareto-efficiency properties. On the other side of the coin, we can consider Pareto-efficient allocations and analyse the structure of prices and lump sum transfers that could sustain such allocations in a decentralized planned economy. We need to emphasize that with dated goods the notion of a competitive equilibrium of a private ownership economy presupposes the existence of lT markets at $t=0$. Of these, $l(T-1)$ are, by definition, *forward markets*. At an equilibrium all transactions (i.e. sales and purchases) are carried out at the market date $t=0$. As time unfolds, individuals and firms merely carry out their commitments undertaken at $t=0$. There is no need for markets to be re-established at $t \geqslant 1$. We shall call such an equilibrium an *intertemporal competitive equilibrium*.

A consumer's endowment vector in this construction is an lT vector (with some components possibly zero) of dated goods. One should bear in mind that such an endowment vector will consist not merely of commodities dated $t=0$, but also of goods and services that will be available to him in the future (e.g. his own future labour services). A feasible production plan for producers (firms) in the construction will consist of an lT vector (with some components possibly zero) of dated inputs and outputs. The typical producer will study the present values of net profits associated with feasible production plans and will be concerned with maximizing his present value profit. He can calculate such present values with unerring accuracy because the present value prices are all quoted at the market date $t=0$. It should be emphasized that in this construction each consumer faces a *single* budget constraint which expresses the condition that the present value of his purchases does not exceed his wealth, where the latter is by definition the sum of the present values of his endowment and the present value profits to which he is entitled from the firms. Condition 4.2 was a simple example of such a single budget constraint. If there are constant returns to scale in production, producers make no profit in equilibrium. But we hasten to emphasize that it is the *present value* of profits that is nil in this situation. This is perfectly consistent with the present value of transactions being positive at certain dates (known in advance, of course), and the present value of transactions being negative in others (again, known in advance). It is consistent with the notion of earning a positive return on investment. Since this last may not be entirely obvious we shall illustrate it formally in the examples in the subsequent sections.

The notion of present value prices is simple enough. But what does one mean by spot prices in this framework? Imagine two adjacent dates t and $t+1$, and two physically distinguishable commodities i and j. Denote by p_i^t, p_j^t, p_i^{t+1}, and p_j^{t+1} the present value prices in unit of account of the four dated goods, i and j dated t and $t+1$. Assume that they are all strictly positive. Now it is often convenient to choose a single physically distinguishable commodity (e.g. gold) as a numeraire, with a view to looking at the structure of relative prices as time unfolds. In short, if i is the numeraire, it is often convenient to consider the relative prices p_j^t/p_i^t and p_j^{t+1}/p_i^{t+1}. These latter two prices are known as the *spot prices* of commodity j at dates t and $t+1$. The terminology is self-explanatory, for if an individual desires to receive a unit of commodity j *at date* t, then p_j^t/p_i^t is the quantity of commodity i that has to be paid by him if he makes the payment at date t. Similarly for p_j^{t+1}/p_i^{t+1}. Needless to say, unless further structure is imposed on the economy there is in general no way of telling how p_j^t/p_i^t is related to p_j^{t+1}/p_i^{t+1}. Consequently, in order to facilitate economic analysis it is useful to consider circumstances where one has reasons for believing that relative prices remain constant over time, i.e. those situations where $p_j^t/p_i^t = p_j^{t+1}/p_i^{t+1}$. An intertemporal equilibrium is usually said to sustain a *steady state* if *all* relative spot prices remain constant over time.[4]

Finally we can define another notion which will play a key role in our subsequent analysis. Define r_j^t

$$4.4 \qquad\qquad r_j^t = \frac{p_j^t}{p_j^{t+1}} - 1.$$

It is usual to refer to r_j^t as the *own rate of interest* (or the *own rate of return*) on commodity j over the interval $(t, t+1)$. The terminology can be explained as follows. Suppose that at $t=0$, an individual proposes to deliver one unit of commodity j at date t. He receives p_j^t units of account which he can use to purchase p_j^t/p_j^{t+1} units of j for delivery at $t+1$. Consequently the net gain in j is given by the RHS of 4.4. Since in fact the individual gives up one unit of j at t the RHS is the rate of return in good j. The important point to note is that this own rate of interest defined by competitive prices depends

---

[4] The massive literature on capital and growth theory is much concerned with such steady states. For excellent expositions, see Hahn and Matthews (1964), Solow (1970), Bliss (1975) and Dixit (1976).

on not only t and $t+1$, but as well on the commodity in question. In general then, it makes no sense to talk of *the* rate of interest along an intertemporal competitive equilibrium.[5] In general there are as many rates of interest as there are physically distinguishable commodities and time intervals. It is only along a steady state (as we have defined it) that it is legitimate to refer to a unique rate of interest over time. A glance at 4.4 will make it clear that r_j^t is independent of its indices along a steady state. It is also clear that $r_j^t \geqslant -1$. In fact, for a large class of examples that we shall have reason to be interested in analysing it will transpire that $r_j > 0$.

Now $p_j^t/p_i^t = (p_j^t/p_i^0)(p_i^0/p_i^1) \ldots (p_i^{t-1}/p_i^t)$. Using 4.4 in this yields

$$4.5 \qquad \frac{p_j^t}{p_i^t(1+r_i^0)(1+r_i^1)\ldots(1+r_i^{t-1})} = \frac{p_j^t}{p_i^0}$$

It is then clear that p_j^t/p_i^0 is the *discounted* value of the spot price (p_j^t/p_i^t) of j at t. The *discount factor*, $1/(1+r_i^0)(1+r_i^1) \ldots (1+r_i^{t-1})$, has been obtained from the set of own rates of interest on i, the numeraire good. This is why it is customary to refer to p_j^t/p_i^0 as the present value price in numeraire of j, dated t.

5. Durables

The treatment of durable commodities is simple enough in principle. The idea is to regard the flow of services made available by a durable good as a sequence of dated commodities. Let us suppose that j is a durable good. Normalize, and set $p_i^0 = 1$. Let p_j^t denote the present value price of a unit of the *service* provided by the commodity at t. Likewise for p_j^{t+1}. One refers to p_j^t and p_j^{t+1} as the present value *rental* prices of the durable good j, and to p_j^t/p_i^t and p_j^{t+1}/p_i^{t+1} as the spot rental prices of j in terms of numeraire. If an individual in this economy wishes to purchase a unit of the service of commodity j at each of these two dates t and $t+1$, then should he wish to make the payment (in numeraire good i) at $t=0$, he would be required to pay $(p_j^t + p_j^{t+1})$. How does all this relate to the price of the durable good itself? Suppose, to fix ideas, a given durable good (j) has the property of providing one unit of services at each date for precisely $\tau + 1$ dates, at the end of which period it simply breaks down and can serve no purpose. Let us

---

[5] The classic paper on efficiency prices and own rates of interest is Malinvaud (1953). For an equally well-known expository piece, see Koopmans (1957). The most detailed treatment is in Bliss (1975).

suppose that the commodity is manufactured at $t=0$. Then the competitive price P_j^0 of this brand new durable good will be $\sum_{t=0}^{\tau} p_j^t$. If an owner of this commodity were to rent it out at $t=0$ for one period he would require a rental price p_j^0 at $t=0$. If he contracts to sell it at $t=1$ (the one period old durable) he is assured $\sum_{t=1}^{\tau} p_j^t$ at $t=0$. His gross receipt is

$$p_j^0 + \sum_{t=1}^{\tau} p_j^t = \sum_{t=0}^{\tau} p_j^t,$$

which is the price of the durable good itself. In terms of receipts he is indifferent between selling the durable good at $t=0$ and renting it out for one period and selling the one period old durable at $t=1$. In short, the present value price of a durable good is the sum of the present value rentals that accrue to it over its economic lifetime. The competitive price of a durable good is the capitalized value of the competitive rentals that can be charged for it.

All this is really rather obvious. But it does suggest that a durable commodity is characterized by the flow of services it can provide. For durables like land, the flow of services is more or less constant. But not entirely so. Excessive cultivation can ruin a piece of land. The time flow of the services provided by a given quantity of a durable good is not really given, but can be controlled. At one extreme of this are exhaustible resources, whose time flow of services is entirely endogenous. Indeed, we can define the quantity of such a commodity (e.g. oil) by the intertemporal sum of the services (i.e. rates of extraction and utilization) provided by it. But we can obviously vary this time flow any way we like, so long as they sum to the same quantity (see constraint 4.2). This is one way of viewing exhaustible resources.

It should now be clear what we mean by the expression 'capital gains' (or 'losses') on durables. To revert to our example suppose that the durable good, j, is manufactured at $t=1$. Then the spot price in terms of the numeraire i at $t=1$, of this brand new durable good will be $\sum_{t=1}^{\tau+1} p_j^t / p_i^1$. One says that this durable enjoys *capital gains* (*losses*) between dates 0 and 1 if

$$\sum_{t=0}^{\tau} p_j^t / p_i^0 < (>) \sum_{t=1}^{\tau+1} p_j^t / p_i^1.$$

The notion of capital gains and losses relates to the behaviour of the spot price of durable goods.

Depreciation, while in practice extremely difficult to calculate, is simple enough as a concept. The idea is that a commodity changes its physical characteristics with the passage of time and use. A used machine has different capabilities from a brand new one of the same make. Now if one knows precisely the physical alterations a commodity undergoes with the passage of time and use, then there is no problem in handling depreciation. But in fact one does not usually know this. A simple approach is often to suppose that a given commodity depreciates at a given proportional rate over time. If μ is the rate then it is as though a unit quantity of a commodity at t becomes $(1-\mu)$ units of the commodity (with the *same* physical characteristics) at $t+1$.[6]

Given this it is easy enough to see that the own rate of return on a durable good during an interval is closely related to the competitive rental earned by the good in the interval and as well to its rate of depreciation. Suppose that j is a durable good. Let P_j^t and P_j^{t+1} denote the present value prices of j dated t and $t+1$, and let p_j^t denote the present value price of the service provided by it during $(t, t+1)$, that is, the rental earned by it during the interval. Finally, let μ_j be the rate of depreciation. From our preceding discussion it follows that

$$P_j = p_j^t + (1-\mu_j)P_j^{t+1}$$

which, on rearranging, yields

4.6 $$P_j^t/P_j^{t+1} - 1 = p_j^t/P_j^{t+1} - \mu_j$$

Notice that now the LHS of 4.6 is by definition the own rate of interest r_j^t on the *durable* j (see equation 4.4 and its interpretation).

6. The Arbitrage Equation

After this elaborate discussion of competitive prices it is time to deduce an important property that the prices of durables must necessarily satisfy. Since for technical reasons we shall wish presently to consider time as a continuous variable let us ease the way by supposing that while time is regarded as being discrete, each interval

---

[6] While proportional depreciation is very often assumed in the construction of growth models it has mostly convenience to recommend it. The convenience it provides is that the value of a stock at t can be calculated from the value of the stock at $t-1$ and gross investment at $t-1$. One does not need to know the age composition of the durables in existence. It is the only survival function with this property. It is difficult to over-emphasize how strong such an assumption is.

is of length θ (and not unity). During an interval all economic variables are assumed to remain constant. By convention we shall speak of the *rate* of consumption of a commodity at t. If this is x_t then we shall say that during the interval $(t, t+\theta)$ total consumption is $x_t\theta$. Likewise $p_t\theta$ will denote the price paid for a unit rate of consumption during $(t, t+\theta)$. Suppose now that both i and j are durable commodities. Now denote by P_i^t and P_j^t the present value prices in the unit of account of the durables i and j, dated t. As earlier, we are for the moment continuing to denote these last two prices by capital letters because they refer to the price of the durable goods themselves and not to the service flows made available by them. Suppose there is an equilibrium where the durables i and j are held in positive amounts. Then it cannot be the case that holding one of these is less profitable than exchanging it for the other and holding the latter. Consider then an individual endowed at t with one unit of good j and consider his position at $t+\theta$.

Let p_j^t be the rate of rental (in unit of account) for one unit of good j during $(t, t+\theta)$. So holding one unit of j during this interval yields $p_j^t\theta$. Let μ_j be the rate of depreciation, so that at $t+\theta$ the agent has $(1-\mu_j\theta)$ units of j. Consequently, at $t+\theta$ he can purchase

4.7
$$P_j^{t+\theta}\{(1-\mu_j\theta)+p_j^t\theta/P_j^{t+\theta}\}/P_i^{t+\theta}$$

units of good i.

Alternatively the individual could exchange one unit of j at t for P_j^t/P_i^t units of good i. Let p_i^t be the rate of rental (in unit of account) for one unit of i during $(t, t+\theta)$ and let μ_i be i's rate of depreciation. Then by holding P_j^t/P_i^t units of commodity i the individual would, at $t+\theta$, have

4.8
$$P_j^t\{(1-\mu_i\theta)+p_i^t\theta/P_i^{t+\theta}\}/P_i^t$$

units of good i.

At an equilibrium the individual will obviously be indifferent between these two options. Consequently 4.7 must equal 4.8. For notational ease write $q_j^t=P_j^t/P_i^t$ for the spot price of durables j at t relative to durable i. And assume for simplicity that $\mu_i=0$. Then setting 4.7 equal to 4.8 and rearranging slightly yields

4.9
$$q_j^{t+\theta}p_j^t/q_j^tP_j^{t+\theta}-\mu q_j^{t+\theta}/q_j^t+(q_j^{t+\theta}-q_j^t)/\theta q_j^t=p_i^t/P_i^{t+\theta}$$

Despite its mildly cumbersome form, it is difficult to over-emphasize the importance of equation 4.9. Repeatedly we shall have to make use of it. It is widely referred to in the literature as the *arbitrage equation*. It is also referred to occasionally as the *myopic rule*. The former terminology is plain enough. Under competitive conditions individuals are allowed to arbitrage freely at the quoted prices. If the LHS of equation 4.9 were to exceed its RHS then no individual would wish to own the durable good i. As between i and j everyone would prefer to hold j as an asset. Owners of i would wish to sell their entire holdings of i but no one will wish to purchase it. The market for i at t would, consequently, not equilibrate. The reverse would be the case if the LHS of equation 4.9 were to fall short of its RHS. For a price structure to support an intertemporal competitive equilibrium it is necessary that equation 4.9 holds at each date. But is it sufficient? Not quite: we shall investigate this subsequently.

It is technically convenient to analyse many problems under continuous time. In doing this we shall suppose, without justifying it here, that all the variables are continuous functions of time. What remains then is to take the limit as $\theta \to 0$. It is then immediate that equation 4.9 reduces to the form

$$4.10 \qquad \frac{p_j^t}{P_j^t} - \mu_j^t + \frac{\dfrac{dq_j^t}{dt}}{q_j^t} = \frac{p_i^t}{P_i^t}$$

Equation 4.10 is a particularly convenient form of the arbitrage equation. The RHS represents the competitive rental rate of a unit quantity of the durable i at t. Since by assumption i does not depreciate this is also the rate of return (r_i^t) on holding i at t (see equation 4.6). The first term on the LHS represents the competitive rental rate of a unit quantity of durable j at t and the second term denotes the percentage rate of depreciation. Their algebraic sum yields the rate of return on holding j at t (see equation 4.6). Finally, the third term denotes the capital gains; the percentage rate at which the spot price of j relative to i changes at t. We need not repeat why the LHS must necessarily equal the RHS under fully competitive conditions.

7. Commentary on Intertemporal Equilibrium

One does not need to be particularly perceptive to recognize that chances are slight that, as a descriptive device, the notion of an intertemporal competitive equilibrium of a private ownership economy will be adequate for the world as we know it. There are three interrelated features that are particularly worth emphasizing here.[7] The first is the supposition that there is a complete set of forward markets at $t=0$ on which goods and services can be bought and sold for delivery at any future date. The second bears on the fact that, if T (the horizon contemplated for the economy) is even moderately large, a great many of the agents in the economy are ones who, while they will exist in the future, do not do so now. The third is the fact that the only budget constraint faced by transactors in this construction is the requirement that the present value of the flow of receipts minus that of purchases be non-negative; in other words, that each agent faces a single budget constraint. We shall take up each of these points in turn.

(1) An absence of forward markets is, by the convention we have adopted, an absence of markets for a number of time dated commodities. What will be the consequence of this? Consider a situation where there is a known unaugmentable stock of resource such as iron ore at $t=0$. This can be converted into ore at any future date by simply incurring the costs of storage. Now suppose that the ore is marketable at $t=0$, whereas ore in the future is not currently marketable. Then any seller who decides to convert some of his current ore into future ore takes a risk; selling present resource of course involves no risk. The only exceptions to this would be when the prices that will rule at future dates are currently known with certainty, or when traders believe they can predict such prices accurately. It is difficult to see how in general the former situation could arise without a well-developed set of forward markets. In the latter case one might say that there is no subjective risk, in that the trader feels certain about the results of his acts, but nevertheless he may in an objective sense be bearing a risk, as his belief is unlikely to be correct. The point is that in the absence of forward markets, spot markets clear on the basis of expectations about future prices that may be incompatible. Later on, when the future has become the present, the market will clear as a spot market, and at prices which, had they been anticipated earlier, would have led to decisions different from those that in fact took place. This is obviously a source of inefficiency. We shall analyse such possibilities in Chapter 8 section 3.

Another approach to the same problem is to consider the co-ordinating role of the price system. In a single period economy, with which we were much concerned in Chapters 2 and 3, prices

---

[7] We have already noted the inadequacy of several other features in Chapter 2.

influence decisions to buy and sell in such a way that the potentially vast number of independent decisions are compatible in the sense that all plans to buy or to sell are realizable. However, in a dynamic framework one has to realize that current consumers and producers are not only making decisions about current supplies and demands, but are also making decisions influencing these variables in the future. Thus, for example, the investment plans of the steel industry will influence the future demand for iron ore, while the investment plans of the ore industry will influence future supply. The current price of ore on the spot market will presumably ensure that current supply and demand are matched. But what of the compatibility of future supplies and demands? It is here that forward markets play a decisive role.

In the absence of these forward markets there is a tendency for a number of institutions to develop that are partial substitutes. For example, in the present case there would be clear incentive for both parties to merge into a vertically integrated ore supplier-cum-steel producer, eliminating for the supplier some of the demand uncertainty and for the user some of the supply uncertainty. A similar but less dramatic move would be for the two to sign a long-term contract in which the ore supplier agrees to provide, and the steelmaker to accept, specified quantities at specified prices for a number of years into the future. Such a contract is of course similar to that which would result from trading on a set of forward markets, but in the absence of market institutions it will occur as the result of bilateral bargaining. In practice one does often observe both vertical integration and long-term contracts.[8]

(2) We shall take up this point at length in Chapter 9, but a brief discussion at this stage would not be out of place. The point to note is that the theory of competitive equilibrium of a private ownership economy presupposes a well-defined set of consumers (households). It is of some significance that a number of such households will not yet exist at the market date $t=0$. What is necessary is that each household's 'pound votes', as the popular jargon would have it, are cast on market day. In other words what is required is that unborn generations are adequately represented at $t=0$. Conceptually this is a subtler issue than might appear at first sight. For one thing, how is the future individual's current 'agent' to know what the individual's preferences will be? The agent can but conjecture future

[8] An absence of forward markets is by no means the sole reason for vertical integration. See, for example, Arrow (1975).

preferences. For another, the notion of initial endowment vectors of yet unborn individuals is not readily transparent since a part, at least, of the endowments are gifts, which are current decisions made by individuals alive today.

One way to face these issues would be to regard a household in this construct as a family line (or a commune line) where the current decision makers of the household choose for the future as well. If the current decision makers seriously misjudge the preferences of their progeny in this characterization, the plans will not be intertemporally consistent.

Now in a rough sense this interpretation does not violate observation unduly. Heads of families do often make current decisions having taken into account their impact on their offspring and potential offspring. To the extent that future generations are inadequately represented in the current market the issue bears on the intertemporal *distribution* of goods and services. We have already noted that in so far as distributional judgements are concerned, the private ownership economy may well perform very badly. The point that we are discussing here concerns the adequacy with which the free market allocates resources for the future.

(3) Intimately related to (1) is the characteristic that the only budget constraint faced by transactors is the one requiring that the present value of the differences between receipts and purchases be non-negative. To see the significance of this it is useful to realize what it is ruling out. It is ruling out situations where transactors have to balance their books at each date separately, or over any subgroup of dates. It allows a trader to make a substantial loss for an initial number of dates so long as the present value for his net profits is not negative. It is therefore being assumed that there are perfect capital markets on which it is possible to borrow against future earnings.[9]

Given all this, why might we still be interested in this construction? For a number of reasons. Consider, for example, the claim:

[9] In recent years there have been a number of contributions that have avoided this unpalatable assumption and that have been concerned with developing the notion of competitive equilibria in the absence of a complete set of forward markets. The resulting construction is necessarily a 'sequence' economy. One approach has been to postulate agents with point expectations about future spot prices and in addition that these expectations are 'rational', in the sense that the expectations are fulfilled by the sequence of equilibrium prices. On this, see Hahn (1971, 1973b), Starrett (1973), Radner (1972), Guesnerie and Jaffray (1974) and Hart (1975). We shall analyse a simple sequence economy in Chapter 6 section 1 and also in Chapter 8.

'The forces of supply and demand will ensure that natural resources are utilized efficiently over time'. It is undoubtedly the case that there are many who will make this claim (or some variant of it) and will at the same time be totally innocent of what precisely the claim is, or at the very least, be ignorant of the conditions under which such a claim can be defended. There must be many whose faith in the market mechanism is abiding, but who would be surprised if they were to learn of the features that need to be instituted for that faith to be justified. There are positive reasons as well. An understanding of this theory enables one often to locate *biases* in resource allocation when it is recognized that some central feature of the construction is being violated in the world as we know it. This is valuable information, particularly for natural resources, since much concern is often expressed about the possibly over-rapid rates at which such resources are being extracted currently. One would presumably like to know the direction of the bias (over-rapid extraction or insufficient extraction of an exhaustible resource) under different kinds of market failure. This is not the kind of information that is easy to obtain. Nevertheless, for a number of situations the qualitative nature of the biases can be described. We shall, naturally, be much concerned with such issues in what follows. Finally, looking at the other side of the coin, it is valuable to have an understanding of the nature of the price system that can sustain a given efficient policy. Much of our discussion will be directed towards this issue.

CHAPTER 5

RENEWABLE RESOURCES: SOME ECOLOGICAL AND ENVIRONMENTAL MODELS

1. Population Growth Curves

Some of the most interesting questions that arise in the context of intertemporal resource allocation concern the rate of utilization of those resources that are at the same time self-renewable and *in principle* exhaustible. Resources such as minerals and fossil fuels, with which we shall be much concerned in the forthcoming chapters, do not fall into this category, for they are not renewable. They are a prime example of exhaustible resources. The act of extracting and utilizing a unit of such a resource reduces the total stock by precisely that amount. There are no means by which the total stock can be increased. Improvement in technology (e.g. enabling one to mine deeper layers) can, of course, increase the quantity that can be *extracted*. But that is a different matter. Then again, discoveries of new deposits will increase the *known* available stock. But this too is a different matter.

Durable commodities like buildings and automobiles are also not in this category. Even if the entire stock of such a commodity were to be destroyed at a stroke, at least a part of the original stock could presumably be replaced in time. To the extent that such durables require exhaustible resources in their production, the possibilities of replenishing them will presumably be circumscribed by the availability of these exhaustible resources. But this again is a different matter. Indeed, production possibilities through the interplay of reproducible commodities and exhaustible resources will be the focus of attention in Chapter 7. Here we shall be concerned with resources of a different kind. Our concern will be with those resources that are capable of regenerating themselves so long as the environment in which they are nurtured remains favourable. Animal, bird and fish populations are typical examples of such resources. Arable and grazing land are yet another class of examples, though they may not appear so at first sight. So long as a piece of agricultural land is utilized carefully and so long as there are no natural calamities, it regenerates itself over the annual cycle. But if utilized in excess over a period of time the quality of the soil will deteriorate. Indeed, if such a period of excessive utilization is long enough the piece of land can become valueless for agricultural purposes, having been reduced to barren wasteland.

A variety of other environmental problems are as well best analysed in the context of self-renewable resources. Both water and the atmosphere generally undergo a natural self-cleansing process as pollutants are deposited in them. But the effectiveness of such natural cleansing processes (i.e. the rate at which the pollution disappears) often depends on the rate at which such pollutants are deposited. If the rate of deposits is unduly high over a period of years it may take a long time for the resource to regenerate itself.

In this chapter we shall determine the rate of exploitation of such self-renewable natural resources under alternative institutional arrangements. In the process of doing so we shall analyse in an intertemporal setting a number of problems discussed in Chapter 3. Consequently, for continuity of interpretation we shall regard the resource in question as a specific species, and suppose that it inhabits its natural environment undisturbed by human predators. Denote its population size at time t by Z_t.[1] Let θ represent a short interval of time. The population size, $Z_{t+\theta}$, will generally depend on a whole host of factors. One supposes, quite naturally, that it will depend on Z_t and on the length of the interval θ. It will depend on a variety of other factors as well, such as the age structure at t, the availability and quality of its means of sustenance, the impact of non-human predators and its own biological characteristics.[2] We denote these other factors generically by λ which may, in turn, depend on t as well. Symbolically we express by G a function defined over all the factors we have enumerated and express the demographic progress of the species as

5.1 $$Z_{t+\theta} = G(Z_t, \lambda, \theta).$$

---

[1] We refer to Z_t as the population size at t though in the biological literature the equations pertaining to Z that we shall develop are concerned with the total mass of the species. Here we are regarding the population size and the total mass of a given species as synonymous. We are identifying a species by its location as well. Thus we are treating cod off the coast of Iceland as a different species from cod off the coast of Newfoundland.

[2] We are considering deterministic models only. Thus we ignore what would otherwise be regarded as chance factors such as the alteration in the natural environment. These, to take only one example, were at least partly responsible for the recent anchovy crisis off the coast of Peru (on this see Idyll (1973)).

A simple form of G that has been much studied is the case where λ is regarded as constant and where G can be expressed as

$$G = Z_t + H(Z_t)\theta,$$

and, consequently, that

5.2 $$Z_{t+\theta} - Z_t = H(Z_t)\theta.$$

It is therefore being supposed in 5.2 that at any given value of Z_t the increment in the population size during the short interval $(t, t+\theta)$ is simply proportional to θ.[3]

Most often it will prove convenient to regard time as a continuous variable. In this case divide both sides of equation 5.2 by θ and, taking the limit as $\theta \to 0$, we obtain the ecological balance between this species and its natural environment as

5.3 $$\dot{Z}_t = H(Z_t), \quad \text{with } Z_t \geqslant 0.$$

Certain special forms of H may now be mentioned.

(a) When $H(Z) = 0$ the species is assumed to have a constant population size. It is undoubtedly best exemplified by exhaustible resources such as fossil fuels and minerals, though the term 'species' to characterize such resources is no doubt somewhat odd.

(b) The case where $H(Z) = \lambda Z$ ($\lambda > 0$) is presumably appropriate for 'small' enough population sizes, for it would seem plausible that, at levels of Z at which there is an abundance of the means of sustenance, the exponential growth curve is a reasonable first approximation.

(c) An appealing set of considerations for many animal, bird and fish populations is captured by the function form of H depicted in Diagram 5.1.[4]

Since we shall make use of this functional form it will prove useful to characterize this formally:

5.4 $H''(Z) < 0$ for all $Z \geqslant 0$. Furthermore, there are two values, $\bar{Z}$ and $\underline{Z}$ (with $\bar{Z} > \underline{Z} \geqslant 0$) at which $H(\underline{Z}) = H(\bar{Z}) = 0$. Consequently there is a unique $\hat{Z}$ at which $H'(\hat{Z}) = 0$.

---

[3] In equation 5.1 we have suppressed λ since it is being assumed constant for the species in question. It is supposed as well that H is a twice differentiable function of Z.

[4] It is in fact a plausible functional form for the stock of fresh water in an underground reservoir as well. But see Brown and McGuire (1968).

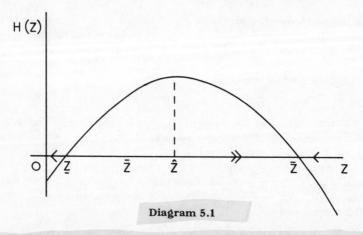

Diagram 5.1

It follows immediately from equation 5.3 that $\dot{Z}_t=0$ if either $Z_t=\underline{Z}$ or $Z_t=\bar{Z}$. These are the two stationary points of 5.3. Of these, $\underline{Z}$ is unstable, while $\bar{Z}$ is stable. The intuitive idea behind 5.4 is as follows. For very small population sizes the chance that the species will become extinct is rather large since mating encounters are low given the thinness of the population. As we are considering deterministic models the idea is caught sharply by specifying a threshold value of Z (here $\underline{Z}$), such that if the species population size ever gets below $\underline{Z}$ it will eventually become extinct. For various land animals the biotic potential is 'low'. For such species $\underline{Z}$ would be 'large'. Unlike these, various species of fish have a 'high' biotic potential. For them $\underline{Z}$ would be 'low'; and indeed for all practical purposes it may be convenient to regard $\underline{Z}=0$ for them.

In the demographic interval $(\underline{Z}, \hat{Z})$ conditions for the species are really favourable. The population increment $H(Z)$ is increasing in the range (i.e. $H'(Z)>0$) as there is ample food for its sustenance. But the rate of increase is decreasing (i.e. $H''(Z)<0$) because of the constancy of the food supply. In the range $(\hat{Z}, \bar{Z})$ the constant food supply has really begun to bite. While $H(Z)$ is still positive it is declining at an increasing rate (i.e. $H''(Z)<0$) so that each marginal increase in the population size imposes an accelerating pressure on the reduction in population increment. For $Z>\bar{Z}$ the population size relative to the constant food supply is too large and the net reproduction rate is negative.

All this is, of course, very stylized. In essence we are supposing that the species inhabits a stable environment. The general form of the integral of equation 5.3 and thus the time profile of the population size of the species is simple to determine, and it is represented in Diagram 5.2. The population profile Z_t depends critically on the initial population size Z_0. If $\underline{Z} > 0$ and $Z_0 < \underline{Z}$ the species is doomed, for one has $\lim_{t \to \infty} Z_t = 0$. But even if $\underline{Z} < Z_0 < \bar{Z}$ there are two broad cases. If $\underline{Z} < Z_0 < \hat{Z}$ the population curve assumes the well-known S-shaped curve AB, where the point of inflexion is that value of t at which $Z_t = \hat{Z}$. If $\hat{Z} < Z_0 < \bar{Z}$ the population curve has no point of inflexion. The critical thing to notice, however, is that if $Z_0 > \underline{Z}$

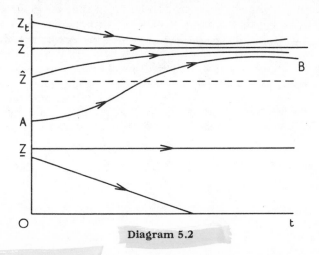

Diagram 5.2

then $\lim_{t \to \infty} Z_t = \bar{Z}$. Thus there is a ceiling to the population size that is imposed by the constant environment, in the sense that the size cannot remain indefinitely above $\bar{Z}$ by a fixed positive amount. One would regard $\bar{Z}$ as the largest sustainable population size.

Unquestionably the most famous special form of this general class of bell-shaped curves, $H(Z)$, is the case where H is quadratic in Z, that is, where

$$5.5 \qquad H(Z) = -\alpha + \beta Z - \gamma Z^2, \quad \text{with } \alpha \geqslant 0;\ \beta,\ \gamma > 0 \quad \text{and } \beta^2 > 4\alpha\gamma.[5]$$

A yet more special case is where $\alpha = 0$ and, therefore, $\underline{Z} = 0$. Equation 5.5 then reduces to

[5] One may note that if it is possible to expand $H(Z)$ as a Taylor series cases (a), (b) and equation 5.5 are simply cases that one obtains by stopping with the zeroeth, first and second degree terms.

5.6 $$\dot{Z} = \beta Z - \gamma Z^2.$$

This is simple to integrate explicitly, yielding as its solution

5.7 $$Z_t = \frac{\beta Z_0}{\gamma Z_0 + (\beta - \gamma Z_0) \exp(-\beta t)}$$

Equation 5.7 denotes the classic logistic curve.[6]

2. The Own Rate of Return

Recall the discrete time formulation 5.1 of the growth equation. If Z_t is the population size at t we know that the size at $t + \theta$ will be $Z_t + H(Z_t)\theta$. Suppose instead that at t the size is not Z_t but $Z_t + \Delta Z_t$, where ΔZ_t is a small positive number. The question is: what will be the size of the population at $t + \theta$? Let us denote it by $Z_{t+\theta} + \Delta Z_{t+\theta}$. Diagram 5.3 depicts the situation where a stock of size Z_t gives rise to an *addition* to the stock of OA over the next time period θ, and a stock of size $Z_t + \Delta Z_t$ given an addition of size OB. An increase in the stock by ΔZ_t therefore leads to an increase

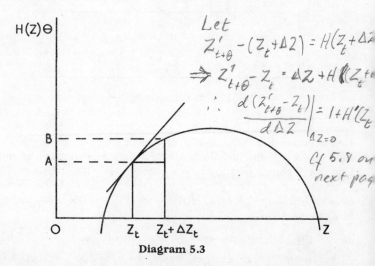

Let
$$Z'_{t+\theta} - (Z_t + \Delta Z) = H(Z_t + \Delta Z)$$
$$\Rightarrow Z'_{t+\theta} - Z_t = \Delta Z + H(Z_t + \theta)$$
$$\therefore \left.\frac{d(Z'_{t+\theta} - Z_t)}{d\Delta Z}\right|_{\Delta Z = 0} = 1 + H''(Z_t)$$

Cf 5.8 on next page

Diagram 5.3

[6] On this see, for example, Lotka (1956, pp. 64–7). The logistic curve has been used to describe the growth equation for halibut in the Pacific. See Crutchfield and Zellner (1962) It has been used as well to fit data concerning the rate of diffusion of new technical knowledge among firms in a given industry. On this see Griliches (1957) and Mansfield (1961).

in the addition to the stock by AB. Since by assumption ΔZ_t is small, $AB/\Delta Z_t$ is approximately equal to $H'(Z_t)\theta$. In other words

$$5.8 \qquad \frac{\Delta Z_{t+\theta}}{\Delta Z_t} - 1 \cong H'(Z_t)\theta.$$

But equation 5.8 expresses the fact that $H'(Z_t)$ is the per period percentage change in the population size in the period $(t, t+\theta)$ if the population size at t were to be increased from Z_t to $Z_t + \Delta Z_t$. It is this latter that is referred to as the *own rate of return* on the species at the population size Z_t. It is worth emphasizing that by definition the own rate of return is the *marginal* rate of return on the species. This is to be distinguished from the average rate of return, which is obviously $H(Z)/Z$. Indeed, such a model of population growth bears a striking resemblance to the more familiar models of capital accumulation.[7]

If this were all there would not be much purpose in discussing such a population model. Indeed it is not yet clear why one would be interested in the own rate of return on such a species. The interesting questions arise when we introduce into its natural environment a second species, the human population, that preys on this one. In the remainder of this chapter we shall explore the implications of such interactions when the population growth function H satisfies 5.4.

3. Exploitation in the Absence of Regulations

Denote by Y_t ($\geqslant 0$) the total rate of catch at t. It follows that the growth equation 5.3 then reads as

$$5.9 \qquad \dot{Z}_t = H(Z_t) - Y_t.$$

Questions of economic interest arise when Y_t can be controlled. If $\underline{Z} > 0$ and if past exploitations had gone on at such massive scales that $Z_0 < \underline{Z}$, there is not much to say. Since $Y_t \geqslant 0$ the species is doomed in any case. But plainly various possibilities are open if $Z_0 > \underline{Z}$. Notice that if $\underline{Z} < Z_0 < \bar{Z}$, then one can always choose $Y_t = H(Z_0)$ for all $t \geqslant 0$ so that $Z_t = Z_0$ for all $t \geqslant 0$. This would be the policy of creaming off precisely the net addition to the population at every instant so as to keep the population size constant over time. One naturally calls such a course of action a *stationary policy*.

[7] See, for example, Solow (1963). See also Chapter 7.

Notice that among the stationary policies the maximum rate of catch is attained when $Z = \hat{Z}$, so that $Y = H(\hat{Z})$. This maximum sustainable yield is analogous to the Golden Rule in the literature on capital accumulation.[8] Notice as well that if $Z_0 > \underline{Z}$ then provided one is willing to wait long enough, the population size can reach any prescribed level so long as it is not greater than $\bar{Z}$. If $\underline{Z} < Z_0 < \bar{Z}$ and if $\dot{Z}$ (where $Z_0 < \tilde{Z} < Z$) is the target population size one is for some reason aiming for, then the policy that would enable the population size to attain this target in the shortest possible time would consist of setting $Y_t = 0$ until Z_t attains the level $\tilde{Z}$. One would call such a course of action the *time minimizing policy* for attaining $\tilde{Z}$.

For illustrating the problem of the common in Chapter 3 we recognized that the catch is the output of a productive process. There we focused attention on the problems of external diseconomy that may occur among a given number of firms exploiting a common property natural resource such as a small catchment area containing a species of fish. We recognized there that the source of the problem of over-exploitation of such a resource in an unregulated economy lies in the fact that the common property has a positive value for society as a whole. The only cost borne by a firm is the cost of the inputs required to obtain the catch. The firm is not required to pay any fee for tapping the resource. In what follows we shall continue to make the assumption that the catchment area (fixed in size), and the species within it are a common property resource. There is, therefore, no licence fee levied for introducing the inputs into the catchment area, nor a fee for removing the catch from its natural environment.[9] But here we shall be concerned with the inter-temporal aspects of the problem of exploitation of such a common property resource. And once we introduce time into the analysis it seems rather plain that over-exploitation, with the possible eventual extinction of the species, can arise under a wide variety of circumstances. For example we do not necessarily have to suppose that a well-defined set of firms goes on a rampage because there is no guarantee that other firms will not have depleted the species in the immediate future. A gentler scenario would see firms entering or leaving the catchment area, depending on what is the

---

[8] For a thorough discussion of the Golden Rule in a single commodity economy see Phelps (1961), or Heal (1973).

[9] In Chapter 3 we had analysed the structure of the optimal licence fee on the single input for the one period profit maximization problem.

profitable course of action. Consequently here we do not specify the number of firms exploiting the common property resource in advance. We postulate instead that there is *free entry* into the catchment area. It is in fact rather simple to show that under such circumstances a species may well be depleted in finite time.

Consider an economic environment where the catch is valued in the market at a price q, which is independent of time and independent of the size of the catch. It may be simplest to think of there being many schools of such species differing only in their location and that we are analysing the consequence of free entry into a given catchment area. Alternatively it may be supposed that while there are only a few catchment areas the value of the catch is derived from its immediate product (say oil, if whale is the species in question) which has perfect substitutes in the market. Thus q is independent of the size of the catch. Similarly we assume, for expository ease, that it is constant over time. Our account of the technology of catching the species will be a generalization of the technology described in Chapter 3, section 4. As earlier let X denote the total number of units of the variable input which, to be specific, we shall refer to as fishing vessels. Let y denote the size of the catch per vessel, and let Y denote the total catch. We take it that

5.10 $y = f(Z, X)$, where $f_Z \geqslant 0$ and $f_X \leqslant 0$. $\left.\begin{array}{l} \\ \\ \\ \end{array}\right]^{10}$
        $Y = Xf(Z, X) \equiv F(Z, X)$, where $F_X > 0$, $F_{XX} \leqslant 0$,
           $F_{ZX} \geqslant 0$, $F(Z, 0) = 0$, and $F(0, X) = 0$.

Notice that 5.10 does not rule out the possibility that F shows increasing returns to scale in Z and X. Moreover, the only significant feature in which the production function F, as caught in 5.10, differs from the technology of Chapter 3, section 4 is the explicit introduction of the total stock in 5.10. Since the problem was posed in the context of a single period in Chapter 3, section 4 this population size, Z, was merely an implicit parameter in the production function there. But in our analysis here Z may well vary over time, and if the stock size affects the ease with which the catch can be made it needs to be introduced in the production function. One supposes that generally a larger population size makes the catch easier to obtain. This explains why one would wish to suppose $f_Z \geqslant 0$. If $f_X < 0$,

---

[10] As it stands 5.10 is a very loose specification of the production technology. In order to keep the argument simple, we shall subsequently consider some very special cases of 5.10.

there is crowding among vessels as well. This was a central assumption in our discussion of the common's problem in Chapter 3. In fact, for the single period problem analysed there, crowding was precisely the source of the inefficiency of the market equilibrium. For certain activities, however, crowding may well be a negligible problem for relevant input sizes. This may be so in the case of hunting for a species in the large plains, or indeed for certain fish populations located over a wide area. In such instances $f_X = 0$. The other assumptions regarding F are, of course, self-explanatory.

For simplicity we take it that firms enter or depart from the fishing ground depending on what is instantaneously the profitable thing to do. To simplify yet further we identify each vessel with a different firm. Consequently, the aim is to study the adjustment of the total number of vessels in the catchment area as a response to instantaneous profit. Denote by p the rental price of a single vessel. Assume that p is constant. It follows that net profit, π_t, accruing to each vessel (and hence each firm) is $qf(Z_t, X_t) - p$. Imagine then that the adjustment mechanism can be expressed as

5.11 $$\dot{X}_t = \mu\pi_t = \mu\{qf(Z_t, X_t) - p\}, \quad \text{where } \mu > 0.$$

In other words it is being supposed that the rate of change of the total number of vessels is simply proportional to π_t. It follows that the adjustment is adaptive, for the tendency is for X to increase so as to wipe out π_t if it is positive and to decrease so as to raise π_t to zero if it is negative. But the adjustment does not necessarily occur instantaneously. μ is the speed of adjustment, given the way time is measured.

Recall now that equation 5.9 can be expressed as

5.12 $$\dot{Z}_t = H(Z_t) - F(Z_t, X_t).$$

Equations 5.11 and 5.12 are a pair of non-linear differential equations in X and Z and we are interested in their solutions. In fact the solutions can be described qualitatively without much difficulty.[11] But for our purposes here we shall simplify a good deal further so as to provide the flavour of the kinds of problem that can arise with the minimum of technical considerations. The quickest route to a simplification of the pair of equations is to consider the special

[11] See, for example, Smith (1968).
[12] Compare this with free access equilibrium condition 3.36 for the case of a large number of firms and, more pertinently, with the comments in the Notes on Chapter 3.

case where $\mu = \infty$ (i.e. the adjustment is instantaneous). It transpires that this special case is not misleading, in that *qualitatively* most of the features of interest that emerge when μ is assumed finite emerge as well when μ is assumed infinite.

Since the adjustment is assumed to be instantaneous (i.e. $\mu = \infty$) one has $\pi_t = 0$ for all t. It follows, then, that

5.13 $$qf(Z_t, X_t) = p.^{12}$$

The ecological system is now described by equations 5.12 and 5.13. Let us then eliminate X_t between these two equations and, thereby, reduce the system to a single first-order differential equation in Z. In order to achieve this elimination most easily assume further that the catch function 5.10 is of the form

5.14 $$F(Z, X) = Z^a X^b, \qquad 0 < a, b < 1.$$

Using 5.13 and 5.14 it follows that $qZ_t^a X_t^{b-1} = p$. So $X_t = (q/p)^{1/(1-b)}$ $Z_t^{a/(1-b)}$ and therefore $Z_t^a X_t^b = (q/p)^{b/(1-b)} Z_t^{a/(1-b)}$. But $f = F/X$. Therefore equation 5.12 becomes

5.15 $$\dot{Z}_t = H(Z_t) - \left(\frac{q}{p}\right)^{b/(1-b)} Z_t^{a/(1-b)}.$$

The problem has been reduced to analysing the single first-order differential equation 5.15.

Diagrams 5.4 and 5.5 describe the two broad cases that arise.[13] In Diagram 5.4 it is assumed that q/p is sufficiently 'small' compared to the other parameters of the system so that in fact there are two stationary points of the equation 5.15 (i.e. points at which $\dot{Z} = 0$). They are denoted by Z_e and Z^e, the intersections of the curves $H(Z)$ and $(q/p)^{b/(1-b)} Z^{a/(1-b)}$. The solution path of Z depends on Z_0, its initial value. The natural initial value is $\bar{Z}$, the long run population size of the species in its natural environment; that is, prior to the encroachment by the human population. In this event the population size tends in the long run to Z^e, as one can confirm from Diagram 5.4. The species certainly survives under this adjustment mechanism with the given parameter values: indeed, the species survives so long as $Z_0 \geqslant Z_e$.[14]

But now consider Diagram 5.5, where q/p is assumed sufficiently 'large' compared to the other parameters of the system that so there

---

[13] Without any loss in generality both the diagrams have been drawn on the assumption that $a < 1 - b$.

[14] Notice that $Z^e > \hat{Z}$. Consequently the own rate of return on the species in the long run is *negative*. This feature by itself should *not* be regarded as an indictment of the absence of regulations on catching the species.

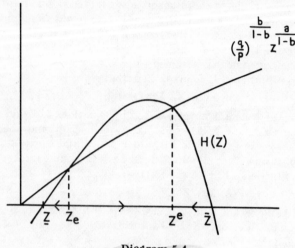

Diagram 5.4

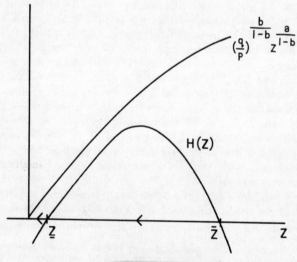

Diagram 5.5

is no stationary value of Z. The problem is that the curves $H(Z)$ and $(q/p)^{b/(1-b)}Z^{a/(1-b)}$ simply do not intersect. In this event the solution Z_t of equation 5.15 declines monotonically and in *finite* time attains the value zero irrespective of what its initial value is.

It is interesting to see why the price ratio, q/p, matters with regard to the existence of a positive equilibrium point of equation (5.15). If q/p is 'small' then the industry's profit is nil at a 'low' value of X (see equation 5.13). It follows that the total catch F is 'low'. Consequently the species survives indefinitely. If q/p is 'large' then the industry's profit is nil only at a 'large' value of X. It follows that the size of the total catch, F, is 'high'. Consequently the species is simply not allowed to regenerate itself. Notice as well that for 'large' q/p, so long as the instability of the system—i.e. the impending extinction of the species—is detected before Z_t attains the value $\underline{Z}$, regulatory measures can be contemplated in order to allow the species to survive. But once $Z_t < \underline{Z}$ the species is doomed. No subsequent regulations can rescue it from extinction. But the question can be asked why the firms do not see the impending extinction of the species. The answer is that it is possible that firms know nothing of the growth function H. Indeed, if H is not known with much accuracy there is no way to tell that $Z_t < \underline{Z}$. So long as $Z_t > 0$ the species is still in existence. So long as $\underline{Z} > 0$ there is no natural signal from the species to suggest that the species is doomed. This is one major difference between replenishable natural resources and genuinely exhaustible resources like minerals and fossil fuels. It is a simple matter of arithmetic that the rate of exploitation of the latter kind of resource must necessarily tend to zero in the long run. But this does not have to happen with a resource of the former kind. Replenishable natural resources can be exploited in finite quantity almost indefinitely as long, of course, as one husbands the resource and the stock is not allowed to get below $\underline{Z}$. But suppose no one has really made a careful estimation of the growth function H. Unregulated exploitation can, as we have just seen, bring the stock size to a level below $\underline{Z}$ without anyone recognizing that the species' fate has been sealed. Even if government regulation is brought to bear on the rate of exploitation now, it is simply too late. The species is as good as extinct.[15]

---

[15] We are supposing, of course, that $\underline{Z}$ is not itself controllable. That is, it is not possible to nurture the species under special conditions so as to lower $\underline{Z}$. One should note that our argument is not affected by such possibilities.

The complete destruction of an unregulated common property resource is not an entirely rare phenomenon. On occasion the problem is recognized a little before total destruction has been achieved. If there is sufficient public interest in the matter regulations are brought to bear on the problem. In Chapter 3 we noted a number of such examples. However, the chief deficiency in the formal model of the common's problem there lay in the fact that it concerned a single period and such processes that generally lead to the extinction of a potentially renewable species take time to make their presence felt. In order to avoid strategic elements in the behaviour of firms we have, by way of contrast with the formal model of Chapter 3, section 4, considered the situation where the number of firms exploiting the common property resource is not fixed and given but, rather, where there is free entry by potential firms into the catchment area. Often one hears the remark that such and such unregulated process of exploitation has 'irreversibly destroyed a replenishable species', be it an animal or fish population, an underground reservoir or, indeed, a common grazing land. The simple adjustment mechanism that we have analysed here is an articulation of what such an unregulated process might be.

4. Present Value Profit Maximizing Catch Policy 1: Catch Obtained Costlessly

We have noted that the absence of regulation can easily have serious implications for the future of a potentially renewable resource. The question arises as to what kinds of regulations are worth introducing. Let us, by way of fixing ideas, suppose that the government (regulator) has recognized that an absence of regulations in the past has brought the species' size to a dangerously low level. Let us also take it that the government identifies the social benefit of a catch policy with the size of the industry's surplus. We shall justify such an identification *for this problem* subsequently.[16] It follows that in order to locate those regulations that ought to be introduced we need to answer the following question, namely: what catch policy maximizes the present value of the industry's profits?

To get a flavour of the problem let us first consider the simple case where the species can be caught costlessly. In other words, no resources are required in catching the species. As before, denote the

[16] We shall see later in what way this particular assumption will affect the kind of regulation that might be worth contemplating.

industry's total catch at t by Y_t. Let r denote the competitive market interest rate, assumed positive and constant, and assume furthermore that it is also the rate that the regulator regards as being appropriate for discounting purposes. Since in this simple case gross revenue at each instant measures net profit at that instant, we can express the present value of the industry's flow of profits as

$$5.16 \qquad \int_0^\infty \exp(-rt)\, q\, Y_t\, \mathrm{d}t.$$

It follows that the industry's policy should be to choose a feasible time profile of Y_t that would maximize 5.16. But a feasible time profile of Y_t is simply a non-negative schedule that satisfies the population growth equation 5.9. Now recall Diagram 5.1. Denote by $\tilde{Z}$ the solution of the equation $H'(Z) = r$. That is, the population size at which the own rate of return on the species equals the competitive market rate of interest. Since $r > 0$ it follows that $\tilde{Z} < \hat{Z}$. To have an interesting problem we shall wish to suppose as well that $\underline{Z} < \tilde{Z}$. This last assumption, quite apart from being realistic for many species, is the interesting one analytically since otherwise it is simple to see that in terms of pure profits the species is not worth preserving.

Denote by Z_0 the stock size of the species at $t=0$, the date at which the industry's entire future catch policy is to be decided. Assume that $\underline{Z} < Z_0 < \tilde{Z}$. Plainly $H'(Z_0) > H'(\tilde{Z}) = r$. Consider now an interval $(0, \theta)$ of sufficiently small duration. The question is whether Y should be chosen positive during this interval. The answer is 'no', since given that q is constant, setting $Y=0$ during $(0, \theta)$ and creaming off from a larger population in the future would enable the industry to earn a higher return $\{H'(Z_0)\theta\}$ than $r\theta$. This implies that the industry's present value of profits would be higher. But this argument continues to hold so long as $Z_t < \tilde{Z}$. It follows that there is an initial period during which the industry ought to set $Y_t = 0$. Meanwhile the population size of the species grows. With $Y_t = 0$ the population size will reach $\tilde{Z}$ in finite time. Should the industry allow the population size to grow beyond $\tilde{Z}$? No, since at a higher population level the own rate of return on the species falls below r and an exactly reverse argument would be called into play. At $\tilde{Z}$, we have $H'(\tilde{Z}) = r$. At the margin the industry will be indifferent between holding the stock of the species as an asset, or holding the numeraire asset earning r. It follows that from the instant when $Z_t = \tilde{Z}$ the industry ought, in the interest of profits, to allow the population size to stay put at $\tilde{Z}$ and simply cream off the net addition to the stock. It ought to set $Y_t = H(\tilde{Z})$ from this instant onwards.

We sum up: If $\underline{Z} < Z_0 < \tilde{Z}$, and if the species can be caught costlessly, then the industry's present value of profits is maximized by setting $Y_t = 0$ until $Z_t = \tilde{Z}$. That is, the industry's policy should be to aim at a target stock $\tilde{Z}$ (where $H'(\tilde{Z}) = r$) and to achieve this target via the time minimizing policy. The optimal policy subsequent to achieving the target is to pursue the stationary programme.[17] Since $r > 0$ it is also the case that the rate of catch, $H(\tilde{Z})$, along the stationary programme is less than the rate of catch along the Golden Rule ($H(\hat{Z})$). That is, the optimal long run rate of catch is less than the maximum sustainable rate of catch (see Diagram 5.6).

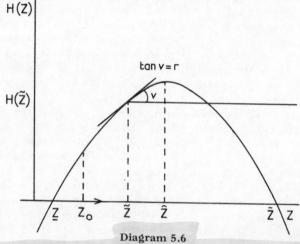

Diagram 5.6

($\dot{Z} = H(Z)$ i.e. $Y = 0$) until $Z_t = \tilde{Z}$. Subsequently $\dot{Z} = 0$, i.e. $Y = H(\tilde{Z})$).

---

[17] Such discontinous programmes (viz. $Y_t = 0$ for a period followed by $Y_t = H(\tilde{Z})$) are often referred to in the literature as 'bang-bang' policies. They have arisen in the literature on optimum economic growth where, as in the present context, the integrand has been assumed linear in the control variable. See, for example, Uzawa (1966). All this is, of course, on the assumption that $Z_0 < \tilde{Z}$ which is, presumably the interesting case. If $Z_0 > \tilde{Z}$ the optimal policy consists in obtaining an infinite rate of catch at $t = 0$ so as to bring down the stock size instantaneously to $\tilde{Z}$. This is possible given that the catch is costless to obtain. If resources are required to obtain the catch obviously the optimum policy will be to arrive at $\tilde{Z}$ more gradually from above.

This result, which will cause no surprise to the economist, is instructive for at least three reasons. It implies (1) that the goal of intertemporal profit maximization is not necessarily inconsistent with the conservationist's aims and in particular (2) that a total temporary ban on the exploitation of a seriously depleted species could be advocated not merely by a conservationist but by a hard-headed profit maximizer as well, and (3) that there is no sanctity about the maximum sustainable rate of catch as a long-run policy.

The first two points are particularly telling given that we have analysed the problem solely in terms of what would loosely be called the 'economic value' of the species. The species has been valued solely in terms of the potential catch it will yield. Indeed, if there were a competitive market for the entire fishing ground *inclusive* of the stock at $t = 0$ its total value would be the present value of profits generated by the present value maximization catch policy. The total market value, V_0, would be

$$5.17 \qquad V_0 = \exp(-rT) \int_T^\infty \exp\{-r(t-T)\}\, qH(\tilde{Z})\, \mathrm{d}t = qH(\tilde{Z})\, \frac{\exp(-rT)}{r},$$

where $T\ (>0)$ is the date at which the stock size attains the figure $\tilde{Z}$ under the time minimizing policy. That is,

$$5.18 \qquad T = \int_{Z_0}^{\tilde{z}} \frac{\mathrm{d}Z}{H(Z)}.$$

If someone had a legal right to the catchment area inclusive of the species stock, V_0 would be the price he would charge for the entire fishing ground and the stock as a freehold property. Indeed, if we denote by s_0 the (imputed) price at $t = 0$ of a unit of the species in its natural environment, then

$$5.19 \qquad s_0 = \frac{\mathrm{d}V_0}{\mathrm{d}Z_0} = \frac{qH(\tilde{Z})}{r}\ \frac{\mathrm{d}\{\exp(-rT)\}}{\mathrm{d}Z_0}.$$

It is the maximum quantity of the numeraire asset that one would be willing to pay at $t = 0$ for one more unit of the species in its natural environment at that date.

From 5.19 it follows that

$$s_0 = -qH(\tilde{Z})\exp(-rT)\, \frac{\mathrm{d}T}{\mathrm{d}Z_0},$$

which, on using 5.18, reduces to

Derives

5.20
$$s_0 = \frac{qH(\tilde{Z})\exp(-rT)}{H(Z_0)} > 0.$$

where s_0 is the imputed price of a unit of Z in the natural environment.

Combining 5.17 and 5.20 one obtains the fact that

5.21
$$s_0 H(Z_0) = r V_0.$$

Equation 5.21 is a useful result to bear in mind, for the RHS denotes the (imputed) *rental* value of the catchment area inclusive of the stock at $t=0$, and the LHS denotes the (imputed) value of the 'output' yielded by this total capital asset at $t=0$. They must be equal in equilibrium. In fact it is worth bearing in mind that there are *two* distinct capital assets, namely the catchment area (i.e. the fishery), and the stock of the species. Since the imputed value of the stock at $t=0$ is $s_0 Z_0$, the imputed value of the catchment area at $t=0$ is merely $V_0 - s_0 Z_0$. Now if $\underline{Z} = 0$, then given that by assumption $H(Z)$ is strictly concave (see 5.4), we have $H(Z_0) > H'(\tilde{Z})Z_0 = rZ_0$ and, therefore, on using 5.21, that $V_0 - s_0 Z_0 > 0$.[18]

Now in fact the equality between the rental value of the catchment area inclusive of the stock and the imputed value of the output yielded by the capital assets must hold for all t along the profit maximizing catch policy. Thus, denote by Z_t^* the time profile of the stock size along the profit maximizing catch policy. Let V_t denote the present value, *evaluated at t*, for the flow of profits accrued over all time *subsequent* to t along this policy. Finally, let s_t denote the imputed *spot* price of the species in its natural environment at t.[19] Then the generalization of equation 5.21 reads as

5.22
$$s_t H(Z_t^*) = r V_t.$$

Consider first an instant t, when $0 \leqslant t < T$; that is, an instant at which no catch is made. We assume that the imputed price, s_t, is differentiable at t.

Differentiating 5.22 with respect to time yields

5.23
$$\dot{s}_t H(Z_t^*) + s_t H'(Z_t^*)\dot{Z}_t^* = \frac{r\,\mathrm{d}V_t}{dZ^*}\dot{Z}_t^*.$$

---

[18] This last will not be necessarily true if $\underline{Z} > 0$. In this case for Z a little in excess of $\underline{Z}$ the average rate of return on the species falls short of the marginal rate of return. We are then in the realm of 'increasing returns to scale'.

[19] This is most often referred to as a 'shadow price'.

But $s_t = dV_t/dZ_t^*$. Furthermore, since $Y_t = 0$ one has $\dot{Z}_t^* = H(Z_t^*)$. Consequently equation 5.23 reduces to

$$5.24 \qquad \frac{\dot{s}_t}{s_t} + H'(Z_t^*) = r,$$

which is the arbitrage equation (or the myopic rule) discussed in Chapter 4. Had there been property rights to the catchment area inclusive of the species and were there to be competitive markets for the stock of the species in its natural environment for all t, equation 5.24 would have emerged as an equilibrium condition in the asset market. As it is, one would wish to regard equation 5.24 as describing the intertemporal behaviour of the *imputed* price, s_t, of the stock in its natural environment. Given that for $0 \leqslant t < T$, one has $Z_t^* < \tilde{Z}$, it is the case that $H'(Z_t^*) > H'(\tilde{Z}) = r$. Consequently, for $t < T$ we have

$$5.25 \qquad \frac{\dot{s}_t}{s_t} < 0.$$

Thus, since the own rate of return $\{H'(Z_t^*)\}$ on the species exceeds the rate of interest for $t < T$ there are imputed capital losses in holding assets in the form of the species stock. All this is, of course, very intuitive. For $t \geqslant T$ the myopic rule 5.24 takes on a simpler form. Recall that $Z_t^* = \tilde{Z}$ for $t \geqslant T$. Thus

$$5.26 \qquad V_t \equiv \int_t^\infty qH(\tilde{Z})\exp\{-r(\tau - t)\}\, d\tau = \frac{qH(\tilde{Z})}{r}; \qquad t \geqslant T.$$

Moreover $s_t = dV_t/dZ_t^*$. Consequently from 5.26 one has

$$5.27 \qquad s_t = \frac{qH'(\tilde{Z})}{r} = q, \qquad \text{for } t \geqslant T.$$

In other words, once the long-run stationary target stock, $\tilde{Z}$, is attained the (imputed) spot price s_t of the species in its natural environment, is equal to the market price for the catch, q. This is intuitively obvious, given that by assumption there are no costs in catching the species. Consequently so long as the species is being caught at a positive rate, one would not expect a wedge between the price of the catch and the price of the species in its natural environment. The myopic rule 5.24, therefore takes on the form

$$H'(Z_t^*) = r \qquad \text{for } t \geqslant T,$$

which is another way of saying that $Z_t^* = \tilde{Z}$ for $t \geqslant T$.

It is possible to show that dV_t/dZ_t^* is a continuous function of time at $t=T$, despite the fact that there is a discontinuity in the catch policy at this precise instant. Since $s_t = dV_t/dZ_t^*$, this means that the imputed spot price of the species in its natural environment is also continuous at $t=T$. Using 5.25 and 5.27 it follows that $s_t > q$ for $0 \leqslant t < T$.

If one were to imagine the profit maximizing catch policy to be guided by an imputed price system then the fact that $s_t > q$ for $0 \leqslant t < T$ would ensure that no catch is made during this initial interval. The species is judged more valuable in its natural environment than at the market place. It would not be profitable for the 'owner' of the stock to undertake any fishing activity during this period (see Diagram 5.7).

We have analysed at some length the catch policy that would be followed if the industry's present value of profits were to be maximized. In fact, if we ignore the conservationist's goals and questions of income distribution, the profit maximization catch policy that we have just obtained is also what social cost–benefit analysis would

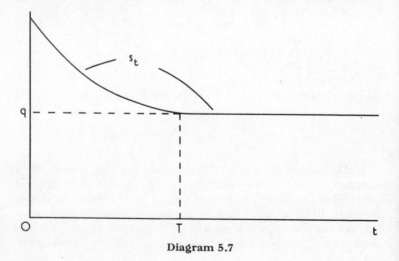

Diagram 5.7

dictate. Since q has been assumed independent of the size of the catch there is no consumer's surplus to be reckoned in an exercise in cost–benefit analysis. If we were to include as well the conservationist's goal, then of course we would wish to value the stock not only in terms of the market value of its potential catch but also in terms of the benefit of contemplating and, in many cases, viewing the stock itself. In this instance it is simple to see that social cost–benefit analysis would dictate a long run stationary stock size in excess of $\tilde{Z}$. But given that by our assumption $\tilde{Z} > \underline{Z}$, so that the species survives, there seems little point in adding the analytical complications of introducing other goals.

The conservationist's goals make a telling point on social cost–benefit analysis, however, if $H'(\underline{Z}) < r$. In this event the industry's interest would be to run down the species to extinction unless it were compensated for preserving it. For certain animal species there is a well-developed market for viewing the stock itself. In this instance, if the revenue acquired from having the stock on view is large enough it would be in the industry's interest to preserve the species even if $H'(\underline{Z}) < r$. Game parks owned by private individuals presumably are an example of there being a market for viewing the stock. Mostly, though, the market for viewing the stock may simply not be large enough. If, as we have continued to suppose, the catchment area is a common property and a co-ordinated policy by the different firms is unlikely to be attained, or if it is suspected that $H'(\underline{Z}) < r$, then government regulation will generally be required for the species to survive. Today, regulations for protecting a species simply abound for fisheries and forests located within a national boundary, although such regulations are usually not arrived at on the basis of any explicit optimization exercise. Unhappily though, international regulations are harder to come by. The most notorious recent case is, of course, the whale population, and in particular, the blue whale species. Such species cannot be viewed. Consequently they derive their economic value solely from the immediate products obtained from the catch; for example, oil or ingredients for pet food in the case of the whale.

The optimal catch policy that we have obtained in this section has a remarkably simple structure. But the simplicity has been purchased at a price, namely that we have supposed the catch to be costlessly obtainable. It is time to relax this assumption. In the following section we analyse the consequence of introducing a technology for obtaining the catch.

5. Present Value Profit Maximizing Catch Policy, 2: Catch Requires Resources

It transpires that the problem of characterizing an optimal catch policy is considerably harder to solve when we introduce a technology for obtaining the catch.[20] But it can be shown that for an entire class of catch functions the most important features of the earlier solution carry over.[21] The feature that is particularly worth emphasizing consists in the existence of a unique long-run stationary catch policy preceded by a period when the industry refrains from catching the species. Such a feature, of course, would emerge only if the initial stock size, Z_0, is assumed 'low' (though greater than the threshold level, $\underline{Z}$). Since this is undoubtedly the interesting initial condition for the population size we shall continue to make this assumption in what follows. As in the previous section we shall not attempt to be rigorous in our argument here. Instead, we shall take it that the optimum consists in aiming at a long-run stationary catch policy. But we shall explore the kinds of arguments that are required to *locate* the stationary policy. Towards this recall 5.10. Continue to suppose that the rental price of a vessel is fixed at p. Thus if X_t is the total number of vessels introduced by the industry at t, the net profit, π_t at time t is,

$$\pi_t = qF(Z_t, X_t) - pX_t.$$

It follows that the industry's problem is to determine a time profile of the size of the active fleet, X_t, which will maximize

5.28
$$\int_0^\infty \{qF(Z_t, X_t) - pX_t\}\exp(-rt)\,\mathrm{d}t$$

subject to the constraint 5.12. Note that as in the earlier case, Z_0 is given as a datum.

Assume $\underline{Z} < Z_0 < \tilde{Z}$, where $\tilde{Z}$ is defined as before (i.e. $H'(\tilde{Z}) = r$). To be specific, and unless we state otherwise, suppose $F_Z > 0$ (and therefore $f_Z > 0$). The point to notice now is that other things being equal, a larger population size is always favoured by the industry because average catch per vessel is higher, implying therefore that profits are higher. Let us denote by X_t^* the size of the industry's

[20] See Gardener Brown, Jr (1974), Spence (1975) and Spence and Starrett (1975).
[21] See Spence and Starrett (1975).

active fleet of vessels along the profit maximizing catch policy (i.e. the policy that maximizes 5.28 subject to the constraint 5.12). Denote as Z_t^* the time profile of the species stock implied by this policy. Thus

$$\dot{Z}^* = H(Z_t^*) - F(Z_t^*, X_t^*),$$

with $Z_0^* = Z_0$. Let us assume, without providing any justification, that the profit maximizing catch policy consists of attaining in the long run a target stock Z^* and that the policy subsequent to attaining it consists of the stationary programme at Z^*. Assume also, again without providing any justification, that along the profit maximizing catch policy the target is reached at some *finite* date T (> 0). Thus $Z_t^* = Z^*$ for $t \geqslant T$. In the previous section, where the catch was assumed to be achievable costlessly, we were able to locate the target by an elementary sequence of heuristic arguments. Here, matters are more complex. Nevertheless, our aim is to describe the formal arguments that will enable us to locate the target stock for our present problem. Denote by X^* the number of vessels used at each instant along the long-run stationary programme. It follows from equation 5.12 that

5.29 $$H(Z^*) = F(Z^*, X^*) \qquad \text{for } t \geqslant T.$$

Given Z^* and the restrictions on the production function F (see 5.10) one notes that X^* is uniquely specified by 5.29. Thus write by $X^* = M(Z^*)$ the solution of equation 5.29. Net profit at each instant subsequent to T is therefore given by

5.30 $$\pi(Z^*) = qH(Z^*) - pM(Z^*), \qquad t \geqslant T.$$

Since we are concerned with locating the long-run stationary catch policy let us place ourselves at the vantage point of an instant t' ($\geqslant T$); that is an instant t' at which the stock size is Z^* and at which the stationary catch size is indeed being pursued. In short, by t' the transition phase is over and the long-run stationary programme is under way. If, as in the previous section, we denote by $V_{t'}$ the present value, evaluated at t', of the flow of profits for all $t \geqslant t'$ we have from 5.30 that

$$V_{t'} = \int_{t'}^{\infty} \{qH(Z^*) - pM(Z^*)\} \exp\{-r(t-t')\}\, dt$$

or,

5.31 $$V_{t'} = \frac{qH(Z^*) - pM(Z^*)}{r}, \qquad t' \geqslant T.$$

Again, as before, denote by $s_{t'}$ the imputed spot price of the species in its natural environment at t'. Then $s_{t'} = dV_{t'}/dZ^*$, which on using 5.31, yields

5.32 $$s_{t'} \equiv s^* = \frac{qH'(Z^*) - pM'(Z^*)}{r}, \qquad t' \geqslant T.$$

Since the RHS of 5.32 is independent of time it follows that the spot price, $s_{t'}$, is constant for $t' \geqslant T$, and we have denoted it by s^* in 5.32. The fact that $s_{t'}$ is constant for $t' \geqslant T$ is, of course, very intuitive, given that we are analysing a stationary catch policy. Notice now that the cost of catching the species can really be regarded as a transport cost involved in moving the species from its natural environment to the market place. This would imply that, so long as the species is caught at a positive rate, the price of the catch (q) is greater than the imputed price of the species in its natural environment, the difference being simply the cost of catching a unit of the species at the margin. But the cost of catching a unit of the species at the margin is simply p/F_X. It follows that for $t' \geqslant T$

5.33 $$p = (q - s^*)F_X(Z^*, X^*).$$

Equations 5.29, 5.32 and 5.33 are three in number and there are three unknowns, Z^*, X^* and s^*, to solve for. If a meaningful solution (i.e. non-negative values for each of the unknowns) does not exist, then our original supposition that intertemporal profit maximization entails a long-run stationary catch programme is wrong. Let us then suppose that a meaningful solution exists. This will certainly be true for a large class of catch functions F and growth functions H. The problem is not so much whether a meaningful solution exists, but rather that there may be multiple solutions. This last certainly does cause complications in computing the profit maximizing catch policy and is very similar to the possibility of multiple Pigouvian tax equilibria discussed in Chapter 3 section 6.[22] In what follows, for expository ease we shall assume that the solution is unique. This will enable us to speak of *the* long-run stationary catch policy. Later we shall demonstrate that for a specific parametrization of

[22] For details see Spence and Starrett (1975).

H and F that we have reasons for being interested in, this assumption will in fact be correct.

As it stands, equation 5.32 is not in a convenient form. We can re-express it. In order to do this, write equation 5.29 as $H(Z^*) = F\{Z^*, M(Z^*)\}$. Differentiating this yields

$$H'(Z^*) = F_Z(Z^*, X^*) + F_X(Z^*, X^*)M'(Z^*),$$

which in conjunction with 5.33 reduces equation 5.32 to the form

5.34 $$r = \frac{(q - s^*)}{s^*} F_Z(Z^*, X^*) + H'(Z^*).$$

Equation 5.34 is of course the familiar myopic rule along the stationary programme and is a direct counterpart of equation 5.27 for the case where the catch is costlessly obtainable. Notice at once that since $q > s^*$ (equation 5.33) we have $r > H'(Z^*)$. This is so because we have supposed that $F_Z > 0$. Consequently $Z^* > \tilde{Z}$, where $H'(\tilde{Z}) = r$. It is in fact rather simple to see why this must be so. Introducing 'transport' costs and, in particular, supposing $F_Z > 0$, implies that the return to leaving a marginal unit of the species in its natural environment is composed of two parts. The first consists of the own rate of return which appeared as well in the case where transport costs were assumed to be nil. But there is a second part, which consists of a reduction in future transport costs, given that $F_Z > 0$. It follows that the introduction of a cost in catching the species increases the target population size from $\tilde{Z}$ to a higher value. In fact it is strictly an increase only if $F_Z > 0$. Otherwise the target remains the same.

A striking feature of the system of equations we are analysing here is that it is entirely possible that $Z^* > \hat{Z}$ (where $H'(\hat{Z}) = 0$). In other words, if $F_Z(Z^*, X^*)$ is large enough it may well be worth aiming at a target stock size at which the own rate of return on the species is negative. When this is so this negative rate of return is more than made up by the return due to a reduction in the cost of catching the species. We shall illustrate this possibility subsequently.

It would be instructive at this stage to compare the equations governing the long-run stationary catch policy derived here with the equation (viz. equation 3.32) governing the optimum social management of the common's problem discussed in Chapter 3, section 4. Recall that the analysis in Chapter 3 was conducted in the context of profit maximization for the industry at a single period. Even so one would suppose that the optimal long-run stationary policy discussed here will bear a relationship to the conclusions arrived at in Chapter 3. But equation 5.33 looks suspiciously different from the profit maximizing condition 3.32 and, of course, nothing like equation 5.34 appeared in our analysis of the single period problem of the common. The latter is no mystery. The species stock size was assumed given in our discussion of the problem in Chapter 3. It was not a variable there. In our present dynamic model the stock size is very much a variable—at least in the long run—and it is the long-run stationary policy that we are discussing now. Consequently it is not surprising that no counterpart of equation 5.34 appeared in our discussion of the common's problem. But what of the seeming difference between equations 3.32 and 5.33? In fact even this difference can readily be accounted for. Recall that the size of the stock was given in the single period problem and that the profit maximizing catch policy consisted of a total catch size which fell short of the total stock. Hence the imputed value of the species in its natural environment (as opposed to the value of the fishing ground) was simply zero there. The total profit $\tilde{R}$ at the social optimum (see equations 3.32 and 3.45) was the rent attributable to the catchment area, assumed fixed in size. But the species *stock*, being in excess supply for the single period problem, was socially valueless. In other words, what appears as s^* in equation 5.33 was simply nil for the single period problem; which brings us back to our earlier observation that one needs to draw a distinction between the social value of the stock in its natural environment and the social value of the fishing ground. This latter was certainly positive in our account of the single period problem of the common. Indeed, it was precisely because the fishing ground was free for the individual firm that the free access equilibrium emerged as being inefficient. But there the implicit price of the stock was nil because the species was not captured in its entirety at the social optimum. Here the problem is different. We do have a constraint on the size of the catch and this is reflected in the fact that $H(Z^*) = F(Z^*, X^*)$ (equation 5.29). In fact there is no slack in 'capacity' since precisely $H(Z^*)$ units are allowed to be caught. Consequently, the imputed price of the species in its natural environment is positive. In fact subsequent to the stationary stock level Z^* being attained (i.e. $t \geqslant T$) the imputed spot price of the entire stock is s^*Z^*. The imputed *rental* on this stock is consequently rs^*Z^*. It follows from 5.30 that the imputed rent per unit of time, R^*, on the catchment area (i.e. the fishery) can be expressed as

5.35 $\qquad R^* = qF(Z^*, X^*) - pX^* - rs^*Z^* = qH(Z^*) - pM(Z^*) - rs^*Z^*.$

It will be instructive to explore the conditions under which it is assured that $R^* \geqslant 0$. Towards this one can use equations 5.29, 5.33 and 5.34 in equation 5.35 to express R^* in the more convenient form

5.36 $\qquad R^* = (q - s^*)[F(Z^*, X^*) - \{X^* F_X(Z^*, X^*) + Z^* F_Z(Z^*, X^*)\}]$
$\qquad\qquad\qquad + s^*\{H(Z^*) - Z^* H'(Z^*)\}.$

Now recall that by assumption 5.4 $H(Z)$ is strictly concave. Furthermore, from 5.33 one has $q > s^*$. Consequently $R^* > 0$ is certainly assured so long as $F(Z, X)$ shows no tendencies towards increasing returns to scale in Z and X and so long as $\underline{Z} = 0$ (see footnote 18). In fact 5.36 is a particularly illuminating expression for R^*, because it brings out clearly the fact that the rent attributable to the catchment area is composed of two parts. One component arises from the catchment area (fixed in size) being an implicit factor in the catch function, F, and the other from it being an implicit factor in the growth function for the species. Notice that if F exhibits constant returns to scale in Z and X and at the same time were the growth function $H(Z)$ simply proportional to Z (the latter, thereby, violating 5.4), then $R^* = 0$. This is precisely what intuition would suggest, since in this event the catchment area would not be a fixed factor in either of its roles.

It would, however, be difficult to justify a total absence of increasing returns to scale for F. If the catchment area is reasonably large in size, it may be plausible to argue the absence of any crowding among vessels, and consequently that $F(Z, X) = f(Z)X$, with $f(0) = 0$, $f'(Z) > 0$ and $f''(Z) < 0$. Such a catch function exhibits increasing returns to scale in Z and X. Then again, consider the following parametrization of F and H.

5.37 $\qquad F(Z, X) = AZ^{\alpha}\{1 - \exp(-\nu X)\},$ where $\quad 1 > \alpha > 0, \ \nu > 0.$
5.38 $\qquad\qquad H(Z) = Z^{\alpha}(A - Z^{1-\alpha}),$ and $\quad A > 1.$

We shall subsequently point out the reasons why we shall be interested in these functional forms. But for the moment notice that 5.38 satisfies the assumptions embodied in 5.4 but where the threshold level of population, $\underline{Z}$, is zero. Notice also that while 5.37 certainly satisfies the assumptions embodied in 5.10, the catch function exhibits decreasing returns to scale in Z and X at 'large' values of X but that it exhibits increasing returns at 'small' values of X.

In what follows we shall describe for this special case the entire catch policy that maximizes the present value of the industry's flow of profits. First consider the long-run stationary policy. Suppressing the asterisks from the variables, equations 5.29, 5.33 and 5.34 reduce respectively to the forms,

5.39 $$Z^{1-\alpha} = A\exp(-\nu X).$$
5.40 $$A\nu(q-s)Z^{\alpha}\exp(-\nu X) = p.$$
5.41 $$sr = A(q-s)\alpha Z^{\alpha-1}\{1-\exp(-\nu X)\} + s(\alpha AZ^{\alpha-1}-1).$$

Eliminating X from equations 5.39 and 5.41 yields

5.42 $$s = \frac{q\alpha(AZ^{\alpha-1}-1)}{1+r-\alpha}.$$

In Diagram 5.8 the curve BC denotes the functional relation between s and Z represented in (5.42). Notice that $Z = A^{1/(1-\alpha)}$ at $s = 0$. Now eliminate X from equations 5.39 and 5.40 to obtain

5.43 $$AZ = \frac{p}{\nu(q-s)}$$

In Diagram 5.8 the curve DE portrays the functional relation between s and Z represented in 5.43. From the shapes of the curves BC and DE notice that if they intersect they do so at a *unique* point. But notice also from 5.43 that if $p/\nu q$ is 'large' then the two curves will simply not intersect. This is the situation where there is no non-trivial stationary catch policy. In fact it can be shown that in this situation it is not profitable to catch the species in the long run. Diagram 5.8 portrays the more interesting situation where the two curves intersect at a point at which both s and Z have positive values. Denote them by s^* and Z^*. Using the value Z^* in equation 5.39 yields the value of the remaining unknown, X^*. It follows that there is a unique stationary catch policy. Notice as well from equation 5.38 that the own rate of return on the species is zero at $\hat{Z} = (\alpha A)^{1}/(1-\alpha)$. It follows that if p is large (but not too large!) $Z^* > \hat{Z}$, and therefore that the own rate of return on the species is negative along the long-run stationary catch policy. The remaining questions are the characteristics of the catch policy prior to the long-run stationary stock, Z^*, being achieved. We limit our exposition to the more interesting situation where $Z_0 < Z^*$, that is, past exploitations of the species have seriously depleted the stock, in the sense that the stock size at $t = 0$ falls short of the desired target stock Z^*. It can, in fact, be shown by utilizing an argument similar to (but somewhat more involved than) the one we employed in the previous section, that the initial policy should be to refrain from catching the species.[23] In other words, the broad characteristics of the profit maximizing catch policy for this case are no different from those that we obtained for the case where the catch can be

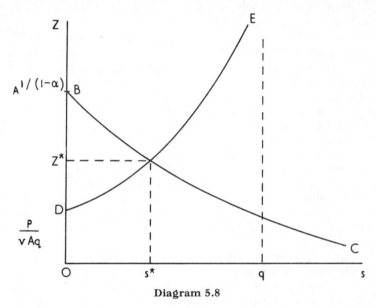

Diagram 5.8

obtained costlessly. Specifically, these characteristics are (i) that there is a unique long-run target stationary catch policy preceded by (ii) a finite period during which the species is not caught at all. That is, the long-run stationary stock ought to be achieved via the time minimizing policy.

6. Optimal Regulatory Policy

In the previous section we discussed the present value profit maximizing catch policy for an entire industry involved in capturing

[23] See Spence (1975).

a given species. With the usual provisos we take it that this is also the socially desirable catch policy. Let us, by way of fixing our ideas, continue to suppose that there is a unique long-run target stock, Z^*; that $\underline{Z} < Z_0 < Z^*$; and that the *initial* optimal course of action is the time minimizing one (i.e. that the industry refrains from catching the species until $Z = Z^*$). Let T denote the date at which the target is attained. Recall that, by assumption, both the catchment area and the stock are a common property for the firms in the industry in question. What we are concerned with here is the structure of taxes which, if they are introduced by the government, will ensure that the individual firms will operate at levels consistent with the industry's profit maximizing catch policy. Stated another way, we are concerned with the structure of taxation that will enable the industry's profit maximizing catch policy to be decentralized. We analysed such an issue at length in the context of the single period problem of the common in Chapter 3. Not surprisingly the matter, though related to the analysis there, is somewhat more complicated here. The regulatory policy during the initial period $(0, T)$ is not of great interest; for plainly the government would wish to impose a prohibitive tax on fishing to keep firms out of the catchment area during $(0, T)$. The interesting questions concern the tax schedules that will sustain the long-run optimum stationary policy. In other words, we assume that $Z = Z^*$ and that we are interested in the tax policy that will ensure that precisely X^* vessels will be introduced into the catchment area at each instant.

Consider first the case where the number of firms in the industry is endogenous to the problem. There is then *free* entry into the catchment area by potential firms. As in section 3 let us identify each vessel with a different firm. The question then is: what structure of taxation will ensure that precisely X^* firms will be involved in exploiting the species? Now from equation 5.33 we know at once that the government ought to impose a fee of s^* dollars per unit of the species captured by the firms. It follows that the *net* price that firms face for the species is $(q - s^*)$. But this is not necessarily enough to ensure the desired result, since at an *equilibrium* with free entry, each firm makes zero profit (see equation 5.13). Consequently the *average* catch per vessel will equal $p/(q - s^*)$ in equilibrium and this will not necessarily square with equation 5.33. Thus, suppose that the government, in addition, were to levy a licence fee, τ^*, per vessel (i.e. per firm), where

5.44 $\qquad \tau^* = (q - s^*) \left\{ \dfrac{F(Z^*, X^*)}{X^*} - F_X(Z^*, X^*) \right\}.$

The rental price of a vessel in effect, then, is $p + \tau^*$. Consequently, at an equilibrium with free entry we have

$$(q - s^*) \frac{F(Z^*, X)}{X} = p + \tau^*$$

5.45

$$= p + (q - s^*) \left\{ \frac{F(Z^*, X^*)}{X^*} - F_X(Z^*, X^*) \right\}.$$

Given our assumptions regarding F, there is a unique solution, X^*, of equation 5.45. But with $X = X^*$, the equation reduces to the form

$$(q - s^*) F_X(Z^*, X^*) = p,$$

which is none other than equation 5.33.

The problem is somewhat different if we supposed that the catchment area is partially restricted and that there are N identical firms involved in exploiting the common property fishery. Here N is given exogenously and the optimal stationary catch policy is analogous to our treatment of the single period problem of the common. We shall exploit this analogy to derive the structure of optimal regulations for the present problem. As in the case of free entry that we have just analysed, we know that the government ought to levy a fee of s^* dollars per unit of the species captured by a firm. Consequently the net price that firms face for the species is $(q - s^*)$. Recall equation 3.29, which denoted the market equilibrium for the single period problem with N firms. Recall also equation 3.43, which denoted the optimal licence fee per vessel for this problem. It is then immediate that equation 5.33 would be sustained as a stationary state tax equilibrium if the government, in addition, were to levy a licence fee, $\hat{\tau}$, per *vessel*, where

5.46 $\qquad \hat{\tau} = \dfrac{(N-1)}{N} (q - s^*) \left\{ \dfrac{F(Z^*, X^*)}{X^*} - F_X(Z^*, X^*) \right\}.$

Each firm would then introduce precisely X^*/N vessels at the market equilibrium. Notice that it is only in the special case when $F(Z, X)/X$

is independent of X, that $\tau^* = \hat{\tau} = 0$. This is the situation where there is no crowding. In this situation it is plain that there should be no tax on vessels. But when $F_{XX} < 0$ at the optimum, one has $\tau^* > \hat{\tau} > 0$. Note also from 5.45 and 5.46 that $\tau^* \simeq \hat{\tau}$ if N is large. This is, of course, in line with one's intuition.

The general nature of the regulatory policy, then, is pretty clear when the catchment area and the species in it are a common property. There are two regulatory measures that the government needs to introduce. The first is a tax on each unit of the species that is removed from the catchment area. The second (provided there are diminishing returns to the number of vessels at the optimum) is a tax on each vessel that is introduced into the catchment area. The former corrects for the fact that the species in its natural environment has a positive imputed price which firms do not have to pay when the catchment area is a common property. The second corrects for the fact that so long as the catchment area is common property, firms do not bear the damage that they cause on other firms where there is a crowding of vessels.

7. Blue Whales: An Application[24]

In recent years much concern has been expressed about the possibly excessive rates at which certain whale species have been hunted. Indeed, in the early 1960s it was thought that the blue and the right whales were near to extinction.[25] In sections 4 and 5 we analysed in qualitative terms the nature of an optimal catch policy of a renewable resource when the stock size is judged as being seriously low. It would prove fruitful to apply the theory that we developed earlier to a specific example, conduct a case-study, and see what orders of magnitude are involved for an optimal policy. We do this here in the context of blue whales.

It is not surprising that while annual data on the size of the catch and on the number of vessels used in hunting for blue whales can be collected, data on the size of the whale population are unavailable. Table 5.1 presents the data on the number of boats and the size of catch for the period 1909–60. The golden age of whale hunting would appear to have been the decade of 1929–38. In fact we shall note presently that the rate of catch during this period

[24] This section is based on Spence (1975).
[25] For an excellent account of the difficulties in arriving at international regulations on whale hunting, see McVay (1966). This article did much to generate public interest on this issue.

was well in excess of the maximum sustainable rate of catch of blue whales. The population undoubtedly was seriously depleted during this decade.

The functional forms for both the catch function and the population growth function that were used for estimation were the discrete analogues of the forms 5.37 and 5.38. Thus, allowing time to take the integral values (a unit interval being a year) it is supposed that

5.44
$$Z_{t+1} - Z_t = Z_t^\alpha (A - Z^{1-\alpha}_t),$$

and

5.45
$$Y_t = F(Z_t, X_t) = AZ_t^\alpha \{1 - \exp(-\nu X_t)\}.$$

We shall not go into the estimation procedure here.[26] However, on using the data in Table 5.1 it transpires that

5.46
$$\nu \simeq 0 \cdot 0019; \quad \alpha \simeq 0 \cdot 8204 \quad \text{and} \quad A \simeq 8 \cdot 356.$$

Using these figures it is simple to confirm that the maximum sustainable catch (the Golden Rule catch) is 9890 blue whales per year and that the population size which can sustain this yield (i.e. $\hat{Z}$ in Diagram 5.1) is 45 177 blue whales. However we have noted that the Golden Rule is by no means necessarily the long-run optimal policy. Indeed, we know from equations 5.39–5.41 that the long-run stationary optimal policy depends, among other things, on the rate of discount, r, and the ratio q/p of the price of the catch and the rental on boats.

Now, the final year for which data is presented in Table 5.1 is 1960. We shall therefore conduct the optimization exercise from 1960 as the initial year. Towards this we need first to estimate the whale population for 1960. Using equations 5.44 and 5.45 it is plain that

5.47
$$Z_{t+1} = \frac{Y_t}{1 - \exp(-\nu X_t)}.$$

Using the data for 1960 and the estimate for ν from 5.46 it emerges that the model implies a population size of 1639 whales in 1960. For illustrative purposes suppose that $r = 0 \cdot 05$ per year. A problem arises with obtaining figures for q and p. One estimate of the market value of a blue whale is about \$6000. A rough figure for the rental of a fully manned boat would be \$400 000. In this case $p/q = 66$. Using these figures in equations 5.39–5.41 suggests that the stationary optimum population is $Z^* = 67\,000$ whales and that the number

[26] For details, see Spence (1975).

Table 5.1. Data on boats and catches 1909–60[27]

Year	Number of boats	Size of catch
1909	149	316
1910	178	704
1911	251	1739
1912	246	2417
1913	254	2968
1914	182	4527
1915	151	5302
1916	94	4351
1917	130	2502
1918	141	1993
1919	154	2274
1920	112	2987
1921	142	5275
1922	174	6869
1923	194	4845
1924	234	7548
1925	235	7229
1926	233	8722
1927	222	9676
1928	242	13792
1929	337	18755
1930	280	26649
1931	100	6705
1932	186	19067
1933	199	17486
1934	242	16834
1935	312	18108
1936	254	14636
1937	357	15035
1938	362	14152
1945	158	3675
1946	246	9302
1947	307	7157
1948	348	7781
1949	382	6313
1950	468	7278
1951	430	5436
1952	379	4218
1953	368	3009
1954	386	2495
1955	419	1987
1956	395	1775
1957	417	1995
1958	420	1442
1959	399	1465
1960	418	1987

[27] This data was originally taken from *International Whaling Statistics* published in Oslo, Norway, by the Committee for Whaling Statistics.

of vessels to be employed annually along the stationary optimum is $X^*=63$. It follows from 5.45 that the optimum stationary catch is about 9000 annually. Since the estimated population size of 1639 for the year 1960 falls short of the target population size (67 000), we know from the theory developed in the previous section that it is optimal to cease catching blue whales until the target population size is reached. The question then is: what is the waiting time? Using equation 5.44 it is simple to confirm that with an initial stock of 1639 whales this waiting time is about nine years. An interesting point to note about these figures is that the target stock, 67 000, exceeds the stock size which supports the Golden Rule. It follows that at $Z^*=67\,000$ the own rate of return on blue whales is *negative*. The point is that boats are sufficiently expensive relative to the catch ($p/q=66$) to make it worthwhile to aim at a target population level in excess of the Golden Rule level $\hat{Z}$. For recall that by assumption a larger population size makes the catch easier to obtain (see equation 5.34).

Now the illustrative figures of $q=\$6000$ and $p=\$400\,000$ are most certainly suspect. In such a situation it is always worthwhile conducting a sensitivity analysis with different figures for these parameters. Table 5.2 brings together the various figures of interest for different values of p/q. The first row assumes that $p/q=0$. This pertains to our analysis of section 4. Despite the fact that one knows in advance that $p>0$, the figures in this row are worth bearing in mind if only to note that if $r=0\cdot05$ is judged a reasonable discount rate, $p=0$ implies that $Z^*=34\,400$ blue whales. Now this is well in excess of any estimate of today's population size of the species. Moreover, we know that if $p>0$, the optimum target stock is greater than 34 400 whales. It follows that a figure of around 34 400 is a minimum that the whaling industry ought to aim at.

Table 5.2.[28] Sample calculation for the optimal path ($r=0\cdot05$, $Z_0=1639$, $q=\$6000$).

p/q	Z^* (thousands)	Y^* catch	X^* boats	Profit/year at Z^* (millions)	Number of years with no catch	Present value profits (millions)
0	34·4	9635	129	57·8	5	906
28	50	9845	95	57·4	7	806·5
124	90	6930	39	41·5	12	462·7
209	120	2732	12	16·4	17	343·9

[28] Table reproduced from Spence (1975).

8. Revocable and Irrevocable Processes

The study of ecological issues leads one often to draw a distinction between revocable and irrevocable processes. In fact the distinction is not always clear-cut. Even when it is, it is not immediate whether the notions are particularly illuminating for categorizing economic processes. Nevertheless, the distinction is well established in common parlance. We need, therefore, to discuss it.

Consider once again a species inhabiting its natural environment. It is usual to regard its population size as the 'state' of the 'system' and to regard the ecological balance condition 5.3 as the underlying process governing the system. If, instead, the species is caught at a rate Y_t the underlying process would be altered and would be represented by equation 5.9. Since Y_t can be controlled, the process that the ecological system is subject to, is a controlled one. To fix ideas, imagine that we are analysing the system at $t=0$. Assume that $Z_0 > \underline{Z}$. Then provided we are prepared to wait long enough there is a feasible policy that will enable the population size to attain any level between $\underline{Z}$ and $\bar{Z}$. It is then appropriate to say that the catch policy of the past (i.e. prior to $t=0$), was one that constituted a *revocable* process, since there are population size levels attained in the past which can also be attained in the future provided we are prepared to wait long enough. Not so if $Z_0 < \underline{Z}$. By assumption 5.3 the species will become extinct in finite time. There are no feasible means by which the population size can be made to attain some previously attained level. One would say under these circumstances that past policies were such as to have resulted in an *irrevocable* process. For this example, then, the notions are straightforward and at the same time have a certain amount of cutting power. If the species is judged to be worth preserving and if unregulated catch policies of the past resulted in an irrevocable process, one can, without much pause, pronounce past policies as having been disastrous. Matters are slightly more perplexing if past policies were in fact revocable. While one might not pronounce past catch policies as an unmitigated disaster, the situation need not be exactly rosy. For suppose Z_0 is only barely in excess of $\underline{Z}$. Suppose further that present value profit maximization at $t=0$ entails the policy of refraining from catching the species until such time as the stock level reaches the size $\tilde{Z}$ ($> Z_0$). As our numerical example of the previous section suggested, the wait can easily be a long one. Consequently the observation that the process was a revocable one is, while undoubtedly true, not exactly comforting. One's concern is often not with whether past policies are revocable, but with the options open to the present decision maker as a result of past policies. There are cases where past policies may well have been revocable, but where such policies have severely restricted the options open to the decision maker today. Long drawn out wars, resulting in a massive destruction of fixed capital are, of course, a dramatic example of this.

On the face of it then, the idea of irrevocable processes is simple enough. A process is irrevocable if it prevents a system from ever returning to a previously attained state. Otherwise it is revocable. The problem is that for economic systems there is often a good deal of ambiguity about what constitutes their 'states'. Consider, for example, an economy where, among other things, production possibilities are circumscribed by an interplay of exhaustible resources and stocks of reproducible capital goods. There is an obvious temptation to include the stock figures in the description of the 'state' of the economy. But if we pursue this approach, the act of extracting a resource and using it in production necessarily constitutes an irrevocable process. One might just wonder whether the notion of irrevocability possesses any cutting power in the description of economic policies bearing on exhaustible resources. The immediate question then is: are the total stock figures the appropriate indices to look at when describing the state of the economy? Granted that positive extraction rates reduce the stocks of exhaustible resources, how does this mere fact harm future generations if at the same time there is accumulation of capital, leading to a sufficient increase in the stocks of the reproducible capital goods.[29] Given that it is consumption possibilities that are of relevance, it would seem sensible that one's notion of the state of an economy ought to reflect the consumption possibilities open to it. For whether or not economic policies pursued at any moment 'short-change' future generations depends on the dent that such policies make on future consumption possibilities. Figures for the asset levels by themselves do not provide any guidance in judging this issue. What is required is information regarding the asset levels coupled with the technological possibilities open to the economy in question. Needless to say, there are several ways in which one can generate this coupling. It would seem then that there is no sure-fire method of denoting the 'state' of an economic system. This is

[29] We shall analyse this range of questions in Chapters 7–10.

unavoidable. For what is a purely descriptive notion for a physical system takes on at the same time an evaluative complexion for an economic one. And much depends on the purpose to which the notion of an 'economic state' is put.

Irrevocability of a decision (or a sequence of decisions) by itself does not offer a ground for evaluating the decision. It is a descriptive feature of a decision which must, of course, be taken into account when choosing from feasible economic policies. It is likely to be a particularly telling feature if there is considerable uncertainty about future possibilities or future needs. But in this case the uncertainty ought to be very much a part of the building block of one's criterion for evaluating different policies.[30] If a particular set of decisions (such as, say, a massive increase in industrial activity in a particular locality, leading to increased deposits of effluent) is judged to be worth avoiding, the judgement, possibly a sound one, cannot be defended solely on the ground that the resulting process (i.e. increased contamination of the environment) is, at least in the medium run, irrevocable. Rather, a serious defence would be based on the argument that it is desirable to hedge against the possibility that these irrevocable decisions have damaging consequences (e.g. the possible genetic effects of industrial effluence).[31]

Where have the foregoing considerations led us? We began by noting that the notion of an irrevocable process governing an economic system is by no means always unambiguous, and that this is so for the simple reason that there is a good deal of ambiguity in the notion of an economic 'state' itself. Furthermore we noted that, even when we have defined it suitably to serve our purpose, the mere fact that an action (or a sequence of actions) is irrevocable is not an argument for not undertaking it. The issues that must be brought under consideration in defending an intertemporal policy are considerably more complex in nature than the question of whether or not the decisions undertaken to implement the policy are irrevocable.

9. Conclusions

The examples analysed in this chapter suggest the following conclusions.

[30] See Chapter 13, and also Henry (1974).
[31] For specific examples of the possibility of genetic effects of chemical effluent, see, for example, Legator (1972). In Chapter 13 we shall analyse certain complications for decision under uncertainty when the decision in question is irrevocable.

(1) Free entry by firms into a common property, such as a fishery, can lead to an exhaustion of the resource in finite time even when it is in the industry's interest to maintain the resource indefinitely. This is so if, other things being equal, the resource is valuable. If it is not, free entry does not necessarily imply that the resource is doomed.

(2) Commercial profitability as a criterion for exploiting a renewable resource is not necessarily inconsistent with the conservationists' goals. Under quite general circumstances an industry's profits are maximized by a policy which maintains the resource indefinitely.

(3) Under a wide set of circumstances the maximization of the present value of net profits of an industry will dictate the total temporary ban on the exploitation of a seriously depleted renewable resource.

(4) There is no sanctity about the maximum sustainable rate of exploitation of a renewable resource (i.e. the Golden Rule) as a long-run policy. So long as a larger stock makes the catch easier to obtain, the long-run optimal stationary catch policy will be at a stock size at which the own rate of return on the resource falls short of the rate of interest. Indeed the optimal long-run stock may well be at a point where the own rate of return is negative.

(5) An implication of (1) and (2) is that a renewable resource may often be seriously depleted not because of the profit motive *per se*, but because of the profit motive in conjunction with free entry into the common property that nurtures the resource.

(6) Optimal regulatory policy bearing on the exploitation of a common property resource can, in the absence of quantity regulations, be thought of as being: (a) a tax on each unit of the resource removed from the catchment area, and (b) a tax on the variable inputs introduced by firms in extracting the resource (if there are diminishing returns to these inputs at the optimum).

(7) An important feature bearing on a number of resource problems is the fact that certain decisions are irrevocable. But the fact that an act is irrevocable is not in itself an argument for not undertaking it.

Notes to Chapter 5

There has been a rapidly growing literature on environmental issues over the past decade or so. If past evidence is anything to go by, it should prove to be one of the most fruitful areas for interdisciplinary collaborative research. In this chapter we have focused attention on what appears to us to be among the more interesting economic issues that arise in such contexts. For an excellent discussion of some specific environmental problems (with empirical applications), see Krutilla and Fisher (1975). For a discussion of world fishery problems, emphasizing the institutional issues, see Christy, Jr. and Scott (1972). For a survey with an extensive bibliography see Fisher and Peterson (1975).

Sections 1–7 have been based essentially on the writing of Smith (1968, 1975), Brown (1974) and Spence (1975). The model presented in section 3 is a special case of the one in Smith (1968). The assumption of $F_Z > 0$ (see assumption 5.10) is referred to by Smith as a *stock externality*. He refers to the assumption, $F_{XX} < 0$ as a *crowding externality*. While our special case (equation 5.13) generates the basic implications of free entry into a common property, the reader should read Smith (1968) to appreciate the different possibilities that exist under more general conditions. The exposition of this chapter has been based on Dasgupta (1977b).

CHAPTER 6

EXHAUSTIBLE RESOURCES: AN INTRODUCTION

1. Extraction from a Single Competitive Industry: The Pure Royalty Case

(i) *Formal characterization of exhaustible resources:* It is not difficult to be precise about the definition of an exhaustible resource. If we ignore the act of extraction as a production activity, such a resource is among the class of non-produced goods (i.e. it is a primary commodity). But then, so is agricultural land, and we do not usually regard land as being exhaustible in the same way as fossil fuels are. The distinguishing feature of an exhaustible resource is that it is used up when used as an input in production and at the same time its undisturbed rate of growth is nil. In short, the intertemporal sum of the *services* provided by a given stock of an exhaustible resource is finite. Land, if carefully tilled, can in principle provide an unbounded sum of services over time. This is the difference. And this remains true even if one contemplates the possibility of recycling an exhaustible resource; for it is not possible, even in principle, to recover the entire quantity used. One will never be able to recover an entire ton of secondary ore from a ton of primary ore in use, or an entire ton of tertiary ore from a ton of secondary ore in use. There will be a leakage at every round of recycling. Moreover this leakage rate is bounded away from zero. Consequently, the integral of services provided by a given initial stock of such a resource is bounded.[1]

We have defined an exhaustible resource in terms of the service it is capable of providing over time. This is, of course, not to be confused with the *value* of the service it is capable of providing. We shall presently distinguish between the two. Let t denote time, and, in what follows, we follow the usual convention of regarding 'the present' as $t = 0$. Then denote by S_0 the initial stock of an exhaustible

[1] It is for such reasons that we shall ignore recycling possibilities in what follows. This is not to say that questions of economic interest do not arise in the context of recycling possibilities. For a detailed analysis of this, see Weinstein and Zeckhauser (1974).

resource (i.e. the stock at $t=0$).[2] We ignore uncertainty here. Hence S_0 is known. Let $R_t(t \geqslant 0)$ denote the rate of extraction at time t. In what follows, we shall, for simplicity, identify the service that the resource provides at t with the rate of extraction at t. Among other things, we are by this device identifying the rate of extraction of the resource with its rate of *utilization*. Taking time as a continous variable, the stock of the resource at $t(t > 0)$ is then given by

6.1
$$S_t = S_0 - \int_0^t R_\tau \, d\tau.[3]$$

Feasibility implies that $S_t \geqslant 0$ for $t \geqslant 0$. Consequently

6.2
$$\int_0^\infty R_t \, dt \leqslant S_0.$$

This is the precise sense in which the 'sum' of possible services provided by the exhaustible resource is finite. If a proposed extraction policy R_t is a continuous function of time then we can differentiate equation 6.1 and obtain an equivalent statement concerning the relationship between the stock of such a resource and its rate of utilization:

6.3
$$\dot{S}_t = -R_t, \quad S_0 \text{ given}; \qquad R_t, \quad S_t \geqslant 0.$$

Obviously equation 6.1 is somewhat more general than equation 6.3. But since we shall, for much of the time, be concerned with continuous extraction functions R_t we shall regard the two equations as being identical.

Now a glance at 6.2 suggests that $\lim_{t \to \infty} R_t = 0$. Feasibility dictates

[2] Measured in its 'natural' units, e.g. barrels of crude oil, or tons of coal, etc.
[3] We are avoiding important complications here. The *recoverable* stock S_t, in many cases (e.g. in the case of oil and natural gas) depends in a complicated way on the rates of extraction up to t. Thus if the rates of extraction R_t, are unduly high, some of the remaining stock may simply not be recoverable given the current technology of extraction. In general then equation 6.1 will be replaced by

$$S_t = S_0 - H\{(R_\tau)_{\tau=0}^t\}$$

where H is some well-defined functional of the extraction policy from 0 to t. In equation 6.1 we are identifying total stock with the total recoverable stock and hence H is merely the integral form.

that the flow of services obtainable from an exhaustible resource must necessarily decline to zero in the long run. This much is pretty plain, and also goes a long way towards explaining why the fact that certain resources are exhaustible has been the cause of much concern in recent years. But this does not mean that the concern is necessarily well founded. We shall go into this in Chapter 7. Here we propose to analyse the behaviour of the competitive price of an exhaustible resource with the simplest of examples. But before we can do that there is a technical matter to be taken into account. We have already mentioned that in analysing a variety of resource allocation problems it is often convenient to assume that time is a continuous variable. But if we assume this even if the time horizon facing the economy is assumed to be finite, the number of time dated commodities is infinite. In fact the theory of competitive equilibrium of a private ownership economy can be extended to handle an infinity of commodities.[4] We shall, naturally, verify this for the examples that follow. A question that arises is: what is the appropriate time horizon to impose on an economy under study? So far we have limited it to a finite date (though possibly far away into the future). But in the absence of any evidence indicating that an economy will terminate at some given future date it would seem to be an illegitimate imposition. The temptation to take all future dates explicitly into account is then logically irresistible.[5]

(ii) *The arbitrage equation again:* Let us begin by concentrating attention on a given exhaustible resource. To simplify we shall consider a partial equilibrium framework in this chapter. Assume to begin with that time is discretely measured in equal intervals of length θ. For the moment assume too that there are no costs of extraction. Suppose that our numeraire is an asset, the rate of return on which during the interval $(t, t+\theta)$ is $r_t(>0)$. Denote by p_t the competitive spot price per unit of the resource at t. Let us construct the arbitrage equation linking the two assets. Consider an individual who owns p_t units of the numeraire asset at t. If he holds on to this he is assured $(1+r_t\theta)p_t$ units of numeraire at $(t+\theta)$.[6] This is one option that he has. Alternatively he can purchase a unit of the resource

---

[4] See, for example, Bewley (1973).

[5] Of course, it would be rational to take into account the possibility that the world will end at some future date. That is a different matter and we shall explore these issues subsequently. See also Heal (1973, Ch. 11).

[6] If the asset is a durable that physically depreciates then by assumption $r_t\theta$ is the rental, net of depreciation, accruing to the asset during $(t, t+\theta)$ (see equation 4.7).

stock at t and sell it at $(t + \theta)$. In this event he will receive $p_{t+\theta}$ units of numeraire at $(t + \theta)$. Under competitive conditions he will be indifferent between these options. By assumption we take it that at t the individual knows the spot price $p_{t+\theta}$ that will prevail at $(t + \theta)$. If a complete set of forward markets exist this will certainly be the case. But even if a complete set of forward markets were not to exist, one could imagine that at each date t there is a single period forward market, so that the spot price $p_{t+\theta}$ is known at t. As a description of the world this latter assumption may well be a great deal nearer the mark. We can now express the arbitrage condition as

$$6.4 \qquad\qquad p_{t+\theta} = (1 + r_t \theta) p_t.$$

It is simple to confirm that equation 6.4 is a special case of equation 4.9 in that the resource does not earn any rental while lying underground. Putting it another way, there are no dividends to be had in holding a stock of the resource. Consequently, $r_j^t = 0$ in equation 4.9.[7] The stock does not deteriorate in quality either. Consequently, $\mu_j = 0$. What remains of equation 4.9 is precisely equation 6.4. Now rearranging equation 6.4 and taking the limit as $\theta \to 0$, we obtain the movement of the spot price of an exhaustible resource as

$$6.5 \qquad\qquad \frac{\dot{p}_t}{p_t} = r_t.\text{[8]}$$

It would not be an exaggeration to regard equation 6.5 as the fundamental principle of exhaustible resources. In what follows we shall refer to it as the Hotelling Rule.[9] The only way that a given unextracted stock of such a resource can yield a return to its owner is by appreciating in value.[10] It follows that under competitive conditions it is the rate of capital gains enjoyed by the resource that must equal the rate of return earned in holding any other asset (in equation 6.5 the other asset is the numeraire good). This is precisely what equation 6.5 describes. The equation also draws attention to the following important feature. Even if r_t were constant

---

[7] We are assuming that j is the exhaustible resource.

[8] Again, equation 6.5 is a special case of equation 4.10 and it characterizes the arbitrage condition for exhaustible resources.

[9] In honour of Harold Hotelling who noted this condition in his classic paper of 1931.

[10] We should emphasize that we are assuming extraction costs to be nil. We shall consider the influence of extraction costs presently.

over time, so long as it is not nil, the spot price of the exhaustible resource cannot remain constant over time. Consequently, so long as an economy possesses exhaustible resources, as well as resources that earn rentals, and so long as competitive conditions hold, one cannot have steady states in the sense in which we have defined the term. Spot prices cannot remain constant over time under competitive conditions. The observation may appear as a trivial one. It is. Nevertheless, since much of our economic intuition would appear to be founded upon a comparison of steady-state configurations, the observation does warn us to be wary of relying unduly on our trained intuition when analysing economic issues bearing on exhaustible resources.

We have defined the arbitrage equation 6.5 as a condition describing stock equilibrium in the market for assets. It will prove instructive to define it as well as a condition of flow equilibrium for the market for the exhaustible resource. For simplicity continue to assume away extraction costs. Let p_t^R denote the spot price of a unit flow of the resourcei at t and let p_t continue to denote the price of a unit of stock at t. Assume that there are competitive markets for both the flows of the resource and its stocks. Suppose an individual owns S_t units of the stock at t. Then the spot value of his asset at t is $p_t S_t$. Under competitive conditions this must be equal to the maximum present value, calculated at t, that he can earn by extracting the resource over time. If it were greater, no one would wish to extract. If it were less, no one would wish to hold on to the stock at all. Let R_τ ($\tau \geqslant t$) denote an extraction policy. For simplicity suppose that the return to holding the numeraire asset is constant ($r > 0$). Given the price paths p_t and p_t^R the owner will wish to select that time profile of extraction $R\tau$ which will maximise his present value of profits. It follows then that

6.6
$$p_t S_t = \max_{(R_\tau)} \int_t^\infty p_t^R R_\tau \exp\{-r(\tau - t)\} \, \mathrm{d}t,$$

subject to the condition

6.7
$$\int_t^\infty R\tau \, \mathrm{d}\tau = S_t.$$

Let R_τ^* $(\tau \geqslant t)$ be the solution to the maximization problem 6.6. Then differentiating both side of equation 6.6 with respect to t one obtains

6.8 $$\dot{p}_t S_t + p_t \dot{S}_t = r p_t S_t - p_t^R R_t^*.$$

From 6.7 we have that $\dot{S}_t = -R_t^*$. Using this in equation 6.8 yields

6.9 $$(\dot{p}_t - r p_t) = (p_t - p_t^R)\frac{R_t^*}{S_t}.$$

But under competitive conditions the stock price must equal the flow price. For, with no extraction costs, a unit of oil in the ground is equal to a unit sold in the market. Thus $p_t = p_t^R$. It follows from equation 6.9 that $\dot{p}_t / p_t = r$ which is precisely the Hotelling Rule. But it is also clear that with the price of the resource rising like compound interest at the rate r the value of the stock (and, therefore, the maximum present value of sales) is independent of the actual extraction policy; so long, of course, as the entire stock is exhausted over the future. In other words R_t^* is not uniquely given. To see this, given that $\dot{p}_t / p_t = r$, we have on integration that $p_\tau = p_t \exp\{r(\tau - t)\} = p_t^R \exp\{r(\tau - t)\}$. Using this in the RHS of equation 6.6 reduces the equation to

$$p_t S_t = p_t \int_t^\infty R_\tau \, d\tau.$$

All this is merely a roundabout method of saying that if the price of the resource rises at the compound rate r, owners of the resource stocks will be indifferent at the margin between extracting (and selling the resource flow) and holding at each instant. It is then possible to imagine the overall rate of extraction of the resource just equal to the competitive demand at the current price, with the result that the market for the resource flow clears at each instant. We shall confirm this presently. But before undertaking to do this there are two observations that need to be made. First, an inspection of equation 6.5 suggests that, even if the entire time profile of r_t is known, the arbitrage condition merely dictates the percentage rate at which the spot price of the resource must change; it does not provide any instruction for determining the price level at which to commence. In other words, we are in need of an initial condition.

Second, even though we have assumed extraction costs to be nil, p_t is not nil. That is to say, if the resource is of use its competitive price will be positive (and rising at the percentage rate r_t) even though 'production' costs are nil. Stating it another way, with extraction costs assumed away, the entire value of a stock of the resource is composed of the flow of services it can provide. This is why the competitive value of a pool of oil or a deposit of coal is often referred to in the literature as its *royalty* value. It is worth re-emphasizing this point, and in particular the fact that under competitive conditions the spot price of the exhaustible resource rises at the compound rate r_t. This tilt in the competitive price path is an inescapable feature of an exhaustible resource with negligible extraction costs, and to look at the matter from another point of view, a necessary condition for an efficient utilization of the resource. The fact that the spot price is rising over time is *in itself* no evidence of a growing monopoly power of the owners of the resource.

(OPEC supporters) . . . seem to be rejecting the play of free market forces in determining prices. In such a market the price of a product is closely related to the cost of producing the last unit of supply that is demanded by a buyer. No one anywhere in the world is pumping oil that cost $10 a bbl. to 'produce'. The cost of bringing up a barrel ranges from 10¢ in Saudi Arabia to 60¢ in Venezuela to $3 or so in the US. OPEC's defenders seem to have the notion that somehow market forces have never properly recognized the value of oil, that its price always should have been higher. This tosses rational economic analysis out of the window.[11]

As we have already remarked, exhaustible resources present several special features that are often overlooked. The foregoing quotation is an apt example of the kind of argument that one must avoid. There is much to learn.

(iii) *Demand for the resource and a sequence of momentary equilibria*: Let us now introduce the demand side of the picture. Suppose that the market demand curve for the flow of resource (R_t) at t is given by the function $D(p_t, t)$. If the resource is a factor of production, like ores and fossil fuels, then D is a derived demand curve. To conduct this analysis in the simplest possible manner, suppose that the demand curve does not shift over time and, in particular, that

6.10 $$R_t = D(p_t, t) = p_t^{-1/\alpha} \quad \text{where } \alpha > 0.$$

[11] *Time* magazine, October 14, 1974, p. 36.

That is, demand is iso-elastic.[12] Let r be constant (>0). Then integrating equation 6.5 yields

6.11 $$p_t = p_0 \exp(rt)$$

Notice that 6.11 describes the movement of the spot price of the resource. Since the rate of return to holding the numeraire asset is by assumption r, the present value price of the exhaustible resource is $p_t \exp(-rt) = p_0$ (see equation 4.5). It is constant over time. We remarked on this feature when discussing the single consumer in Chapter 4, section 1. Let us commence at $t = 0$, when the total stock of the resource is S_0. Competitive conditions prevail and the resource flow market is assumed to clear at each date. Using 6.11 in equation 6.10 then yields,

6.12 $$R_t = p_0^{-1/\alpha} \exp(-\frac{r}{\alpha}t).$$

The rate of utilization of the resource falls at a constant percentage rate r/α. This is so because as the market price rises the current rate of utilization falls along the demand curve. Now what we are aiming to describe here is a *sequence of momentary equilibria* where at each instant the market for the resource flow equilibriates and where the asset market equilibriates as well (equations 6.10–6.12). If we were to postulate the existence of a complete set of competitive forward markets (i.e. an *intertemporal competitive equilibrium*) then the equilibrium price system would certainly satisfy equations 6.10–6.12. But the arguments leading to equations 6.10–6.12 have not depended on the existence of a complete set of forward markets. We have supposed merely that at each date both the asset market and the market for the flow of the resource equilibriate. This observation alone should warn us that such a competitive process may well misbehave. We can confirm this.

In formal terms we should notice that none of the arguments establishing the conditions for momentary equilibrium allows us to determine the initial price p_0. It is as yet an unknown of the problem. And it will remain so unless we impose further structure on the construction, e.g. the assumption of a complete set of forward markets. But given that in the world as we know it, such a complete set of markets does not exist, it is essential to see the implications

---

[12] Production possibilities that generate such a derived demand function are discussed in Chapter 11.

of this indeterminacy of p_0. Towards this let us integrate 6.12 to yield

6.13
$$\int_0^\infty R_t \, dt = \int_0^\infty p_0^{-1}\alpha \exp\left(-\frac{r}{\alpha}t\right) dt = \frac{\alpha}{r}\, p_0 - 1/\alpha$$

The total stock initially is by assumption S_0. Define p_0^* as

6.14
$$p_0^* = \left(\frac{rS_0}{\alpha}\right)^{-\alpha}.$$

It is then immediate from equation 6.13 that if $p_0 = p_0^*$ the competitive process will ensure that total extraction of the resource over time will be precisely equal to the initial stock. The rate of extraction will be $R_t = (rS_0/\alpha)\exp(-rt/\alpha)$ (see Diagrams 6.1 and 6.2). But suppose the initial price is 'wrongly' set. In particular, suppose that $p_0 > p_0^*$. In this case the price will be 'too high' at each date (Diagram 6.1) and consequently the flow of extraction will be 'too low' at each date; 'too low' in the sense that the integral of sales will fall short of the total stock, S_0. One could extract a little more without ever exhausting the stock. Such an outcome is patently inefficient. A marginally lower initial price would allow the process to yield a higher rate of extraction at each instant, without the resource being ever exhausted. But what would be the economic motivation for certain owners of the resource to refrain forever from extracting? It is this. Since any given stock appreciates in value at the rate r a typical resource owner is indifferent between storing and extracting. Furthermore, if there is no terminal date for the economy there is no end to the process. It is then possible to imagine some resource owners never actually extracting. It follows that if $p_0 > p_0^*$, then for the sequence of momentary equilibria to be sustained, there will always be some part of the stock that is never extracted.[13] Notice that this feature would not occur if resource owners were far-sighted, and in particular if a complete set of forward markets were to exist. It is arising because we are postulating a competitive process in which agents are myopic. Resource owners expect the price of the

[13] The possibility of inefficiency along a competitive process with no terminal date was originally noted in Malinvaud (1953), Koopmans (1957) and Samuelson (1958). In a different context, the point was raised also by Hahn (1966). We shall analyse the 'Hahn problem' in Chapter 8.

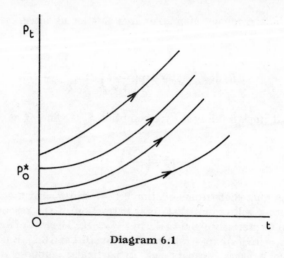

Diagram 6.1

resource to rise at the rate r at each instant, and their expectations are indeed fulfilled at each instant. We have, therefore, been postulating rational expectations (see footnote 8 in Chapter 4). This is why the arbitrage equation is often termed the myopic rule.

What if $p_0 < p_0^*$? The situation here is different. The spot price is 'too low' (Diagram 6.1) and the rate of extraction is 'too high' (Diagram 6.2). Clearly then, were the process to persist, the resource

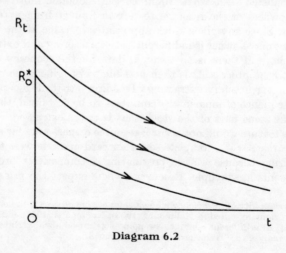

Diagram 6.2

would be exhausted in finite time. The question is whether the process could persist. Probably not. If resource owners see the exhaustion of the resource in sight (i.e. they realize that the resource will be exhausted in finite time), there will be tremendous gains to be had from hoarding the resource until the date of exhaustion and selling after this date. But as soon as traders attempt to buy up stocks the spot price of the resource would jump in value in order to restore the asset market equilibrium. Such a disequilibrium behaviour should get the economy off any path that has $p_0 < p_0^*$. This, if course, is not a conclusive argument; merely a belief that traders act on the basis not only of price signals but other signals as well. In particular one would imagine that if traders recognized that there is positive demand for the resource flow even at very high prices, that the current price is not very high and that the stock is very nearly depleted, they would use these pieces of information in making decisions. But as we have remarked, the reverse case (i.e. when $p_0 > p_0^*$) could easily persist. Resource owners would recognize that there will be no 'shortages' under the process in the near future. But unless they are very far-sighted, they would not know that a certain portion of the original stock will never be extracted, and indeed might well have an instinctive aversion to an unsolicited price reduction, the measure needed to restore efficiency.

Although extremely simple, the foregoing example has brought out an important form of market failure. In the absence of a complete set of forward markets an indefinite sequence of momentary equilibria with fulfilled expectations could rather readily lead to an unpalatable outcome, one where the outcome results in too much conservation, not too little. The result should not be surprising. In order to calculate the correct price today one needs to know where the economy ought to move to in the long run. In the absence of an announced target it should not be surprising that there are errors all along the way. One way for the entire set of future possibilities to be taken into account at the initial date is for there to be a complete set of forward markets. Another is to have a planning board, announcing *notional* prices (or *shadow* prices) to guide the pace of extraction. Let us look into this now.

2. A Socially Managed Exhaustible Resource

Let $R = D(p)$ be the market demand curve for the resource flow. Since by assumption $D'(p) < 0$, we can invert the function. Thus $p = D^{-1}(R)$. Write this as $B(R)$. The gross rate of consumers' surplus at R is by definition $\int_0^R B(R')dR'$. The rate of return on the numeraire asset is by assumption $r(>0)$. We shall imagine that the planning board is concerned with the pace of extraction of the resource (of size S_0 at $t=0$) with a view to maximizing the present discounted value of the flow of gross consumer's surplus.[14] We are, then, supposing for vividness that the resource is socially managed. The planning problem is this:

Choose an extraction path R_t $(t \geqslant 0)$ with a view to maximizing

6.15

$$\int_0^\infty \exp(-rt) \left\{ \int_0^{R_t} B(R') \, dR' \right\} dt$$

subject to the constraints

$$S_t = S_0 - \int_0^t R_\tau \, d\tau \quad \text{and } R_t, S_t \geqslant 0 \text{ for } t \geqslant 0$$

Write $u(R) = \int_0^R B(R') \, dR'$. We can now express the objective function in 6.15 as

$$\int_0^\infty \exp(-rt)u(R_t) \, dt.$$

In strictly formal terms the only difference between the problem expressed in 6.15 and the problem faced by our single consumer in Chapter 4, section 1 is that time is assumed here to be continuous and that the horizon is infinite. Consequently we can bring our earlier analysis to bear on the present problem. Now suppose, for ease of exposition, that there is a different set of consumers at each date. The market demand curve performs a particular form of aggregation over the set of consumers at each date.[15] Problem 6.15 in this

---

[14] A full defence of such a government objective will be postponed until Chapter 9. Among other things one is supposing that r is judged by the planners to be the appropriate rate of discount. Were the resource to be privately owned the objective could still be defended. Since extraction costs are nil, producer profits at each date equal consumer expenditures for the resource at each date. Thus gross consumers' surplus equals the sum of the net surpluses accruing to producers and consumers. In what follows we suppose that the elasticity of demand tends to a finite limit as demand goes to zero. Otherwise a 'best' extraction policy will not exist. On this see Chapter 9.

[15] One may not like such an aggregation procedure on distributional grounds. But we are ignoring intratemporal distributional questions here.

interpretation would be one concerning the optimum method of dividing a given stock over an infinite set of people living at different instants of time.

Since $B(R) > 0$ for $R > 0$ we have $u'(R) > 0$ for $R > 0$. Under this interpretation, then, it is trivial to define a Pareto efficient extraction policy. First, a definition of an *inefficient* extraction policy. For simplicity suppose that we are concerned solely with the class of all *continuous* extraction paths. By a *feasible* extraction policy R_t we shall mean one which satisfies the constraints in 6.15. It is then natural to say that a feasible policy R'_t is *inefficient* if there is a feasible policy R_t such that $R_t \geqslant R'_t$ for all $t \geqslant 0$ and such that for some positive interval of time $R_t > R'_t$. It is equally natural to regard a policy R_t as *efficient* if it is *not* inefficient. The motivation of this definition of an efficient extraction policy stems directly from our discussion of Pareto efficiency in Chapter 2. But for our present problem, identifying efficient and inefficient policies is a trivial matter. Given our definition it follows immediately that a feasible extraction policy $R_t (\geqslant 0)$ is efficient if and only if $S_0 = \int_0^\infty R_t \, \mathrm{d}t$.[16] But problem 6.15 is not concerned with only efficient extraction policies, but rather with determining the best policy. Given that $u'(R) > 0$ we know at once that the optimum extraction policy (if one exists) will in fact be efficient.[17]

Locating the condition which the optimum extraction policy must satisfy is a simple enough matter. It is the obvious analogue of condition 4.3. Let us simplify matters and suppose that along the optimal policy the rate of extraction is always positive, i.e. that it is not optimal to exhaust the resource in finite time.[18] Then the condition we shall get is the the analogue of 4.3 which states that along the optimal path the marginal social valuation of resource utilization at each date is constant when looked at from date $t = 0$.

6.16 $$\exp(-rt)\, u'(R_t) = \lambda \qquad (> 0).$$

By definition of u, if R is the rate of extraction, $u'(R)$ is the market clearing spot price for the resource flow. If the planners call for a rate of extraction R_t, the flow will be sold in the market at the price

[16] This is the sense in which the competitive process analysed in the previous section was found to lead rather readily to inefficient outcomes.

[17] In what follows we shall not bother with the question of the existence of a solution to problem 6.15. Needless to say our examples will be chosen, in such a way as to ensure existence.

[18] The reader will realize that this can be ensured by supposing, for example, that $u'(R) \to \infty$ as $R \to 0$,.

$u'(R_t)$. It follows that the present value price of the resource must remain constant along the optimum extraction path. We are now home. For writing $p_t = u'(R_t)$ and differentiating equation 6.16 with respect to time yields the condition $\dot{p}_t/p_t = r$, which is all very familiar. The remaining bits of the analysis are not worth repeating. Since the optimum policy must be efficient it must satisfy both equation 6.16 and the condition $\int_0^\infty R_t \, dt = S_0$. There is no indeterminancy in the initial price level (or equivalently the initial rate of extraction). This brings us back to our earlier observation. A complete set of forward markets or, alternatively, the conscious efforts of a planning board could in principle be relied upon to co-ordinate flows and stocks of an exhaustible resource in such a manner as to result in an efficient outcome. But in the absence of either, a competitive process, even if it were to sustain an equilibrium at each instant in time, cannot be relied upon to achieve this result. Perhaps we should not have expected anything else.

3. Resource Exhaustion in Finite Time

It is merely for the sake of ease of exposition that in the previous two sections we supposed demand for resource flow to be positive irrespective of the price. As a consequence it was noted that along an intertemporal competitive equilibrium (or, for that matter, along the socially managed path) the resource was never exhausted. One would suppose that for most resources demand would fall to zero at high enough prices. One needs to have an account for this case. This is simple enough to construct.

Suppose, for simplicity, a linear demand function. That is, $p_t = A - BR_t$, with $A, B > 0$. Now, so long as stocks are positive, the arbitrage equation will hold and the spot price will be given by equation 6.11. Furthermore, given the demand function and the assumption that the resource flow market clears at each date, we must then have

$$R_t = \frac{A}{B} - \frac{p_0 \exp(rt)}{B}, \quad \text{with } R_t = 0 \text{ for } p_t \geqslant A.$$

In short, the resource will be exhausted in finite time along an intertemporal competitive equilibrium. Along such an equilibrium the date of exhaustion (T) and the initial price, p_0^*, will be determined by the condition that the spot price of the resource at T will equal A, at which level demand falls to zero. That is, p_0^* and T will be given by the conditions

$$p_0^* \exp(rT) = A$$

and

$$\int_0^T R_t \, \mathrm{d}t = \int_0^T \left\{ \frac{A}{B} - \frac{p_0^* \exp(rt)}{B} \right\} \mathrm{d}t$$

$$= \frac{AT}{B} + \frac{p_0^*}{Br} \{1 - \exp(+rT)\} = S_0.$$

To state it more vividly, as long as stocks are positive the price of the resource will rise at the percentage rate r. Consequently the current rate of utilization will fall along the demand curve until the price reaches the level A at which demand is precisely nil. Along an intertemporal competitive equilibrium the initial price will be so chosen that the date at which demand for the resource flow falls to zero is also the date at which the resource is exhausted. This is exactly what intuition would lead one to expect.

4. Extraction from a Single Competitive Industry: The Presence of Extraction Costs

(i) *Some general observations:* It is time to introduce extraction costs into the picture. Any reasonable account of the economics of exhaustible resources must allow for the fact that resources are utilized in the process of extraction. There are several features to be considered. The first is particularly relevant for resources such as oil and natural gas, where the *recoverable* stock depends on the rates of extraction. If the rates of extraction from a given field are unduly high, a certain portion of the stock is dissipated and cannot be recovered. This would appear to have occurred in several of the oil fields in the eastern states of the USA until recently. It is plain enough that this aspect of extraction costs is difficult to formalize in a simple manner. A loose approach would be to suppose that the average cost of extraction is an increasing function of the rate of extraction. Second, extraction technology would appear to improve with time. Third, the average cost of extraction from a given deposit would seem to be dependent on the stock remaining. In particular, one would suppose that *ceteris paribus* the marginal cost of extraction would increase as the stock diminishes, given that one is, as it were, digging deeper into the ground with less of the stock left.

We shall analyse the influence of extraction costs in what is otherwise the model presented in the previous section. For simplicity of exposition, assume that there is a single pool of the resource. Let C denote the cost of extracting the resource at the rate R when the stock size is S. A simple form of such a cost function would then be

6.17 $C = f(t)R_t g(R_t)G(S_t)$ where $f'(t) < 0$, $g'(R) > 0$ and $G'(S) < 0$.

Such a cost function captures the features that we have enumerated.

It is simplest to regard extraction costs as 'transport' costs involved in moving the resource from the source to the market. This alone suggests that the effect of extraction costs is to drive a wedge between the price of the unextracted resource and the price of the extracted resource, and in particular that the latter price is higher. It is then immediate that under competitive conditions the difference between these two prices is the marginal cost of extraction. Let p_t continue to denote the competitive spot price of the unextracted resource and let q_t be the competitive spot price of the extracted resource. Then

6.18 $$q_t = p_t + \frac{\partial C}{\partial \overline{R}_t}$$

and it is q_t that determines the volume of the resource flow that clears the market. Consider now the arbitrage equation. As before, let r be the rate of return on holding the numeraire good. Under competitive conditions the rate of return on holding the marginal unit of the stock consists of two components. The first consists of the capital gains that the stock enjoys. This in fact constituted the entire return in the model of the previous section. The second consists of the *reduction* in extraction costs due to the fact that this marginal unit has been stored, and not extracted. The arbitrage condition is a statement regarding the equality of these two rates of return at each instant. Thus, supposing time to be measured in discrete units, consider an individual who owns p_t units of the numeraire asset at t. If he holds on to this he is assured $(1 + \theta r)p_t$ units of numeraire at $t + \theta$. Alternatively he can purchase a unit of the unextracted resource stock at t and sell it at $t + \theta$. The maximum he will receive at $t + \theta$ in this case is not $p_{t+\theta}$ units of the numeraire. He will receive $p_{t+\theta}$ and in addition $(\Delta C)\theta$ units of the numeraire, where ΔC denotes the *reduction* in the rate of extraction cost during $(t, t + \theta)$ due to the fact that an additional unit of the resource has remained unextracted during this interval. Under competitive conditions he will be indifferent between these two options. Consequently

$$p_{t+\theta} + (\Delta C)\theta = (1 + r\theta)p_t.$$

Rearranging these terms and letting $\theta \to 0$ then yields

6.19
$$\frac{\dot{p}_t}{p_t} - \frac{\overline{\dfrac{\partial C}{\partial S_t}}}{p_t} = r.$$

Using 6.17 in equation 6.19 one obtains

6.20
$$\frac{\dot{p}_t}{p_t} - \frac{f(t)R_t g(R_t)G'(S_t)}{p_t} = r.$$

Condition 6.20 describes the equilibrium in the asset market. If demand for the extracted resources is unchanging and iso-elastic (see 6.10), then on using 6.17 and 6.18 one obtains the equilibrium condition for the extracted resource flow as

$$R_t = \{p_t + f(t)g(R_t)G(S_t) + f(t)R_t g'(R_t)G(S_t)\}^{-1/\alpha}.$$

The competitive price path (q_t) of the extracted resource is extremely complicated. Since $G'(S) < 0$, it is clear that $\dot{p}_t/p_t < r$, and also clear why it must be so. There are gains to be had in storing over and above capital appreciation.[19] Furthermore, equation 6.18 suggests that if the marginal cost of extraction declines rapidly over time, because of innovations in the technology of extraction, it is possible for q_t to decline over time for a while. But it does bring out clearly that the price of the extracted resource consists of two components: the marginal cost of extraction and the royalty price. Thus, while it is true that '. . . the price of (an exhaustible good) is closely related to the cost of producing the last unit of supply that is demanded by the buyer',[20] this 'close' relationship is in fact an extremely complicated one and not much can be asserted without solving these foregoing equations. In the absence of extraction costs obtaining the explicit price trajectory was an easy enough matter, but this is not so when extraction cost functions assume complicated forms.

[19] One should, perhaps, point out that by 'storage' we mean 'not extracting'. So long as there are costs of extraction it never pays under competitive conditions to extract and to store above ground. This is so because $r > 0$. For further details see Heal (1976) and Solow and Wan (1976).

[20] Cf. footnote 11.

(ii) *Single ore with constant average cost of extraction:* In order to analyse the behaviour of the competitive price with extraction costs we shall obviously have to simplify a good deal. Imagine then that the average cost of extraction is a constant, $b(>0)$. From equation 6.20 it is then immediate that

6.21
$$\frac{\dot{p}_t}{p_t} = r,$$

and from equation 6.18 that

6.22
$$q_t = p_t + b.$$

From 6.21 we have $p_t = p_0 \exp(rt)$ and consequently

6.23
$$q_t = b + p_0 \exp(rt).$$

We need to estimate the 'correct' initial royalty price p_0^*. Continuing to assume an unchanging iso-elastic demand curve it follows that
$$q_t = b + p_0 \exp(rt) = R_t^{-\alpha},$$
and therefore,
$$R_t = \{b + p_0 \exp(rt)\}^{-1/\alpha}$$

For this extraction path to exhaust the resource completely it is required that

6.24
$$S_0 = \int_0^\infty R_t \, dt = \int_0^\infty \{b + p_0 \exp(rt)\}^{-1/\alpha} \, dt.$$

The 'correct' initial price p_0^* is the solution of equation 6.24. Let us, by way of illustration, assume $\alpha = 1$ (the elasticity of demand is unity). Then integrating 6.24 yields
$$S_0 = \frac{1}{br} \log \left(\frac{b + p_0^*}{p_0^*} \right).$$

Therefore

6.25
$$p_0^* = \frac{b}{\{\exp(brS_0) - 1\}}.$$

Using 6.23 and 6.25 one obtains

6.26
$$q_t = b + p_0^* \exp(rt) = b + \frac{b \exp(rt)}{\{\exp(brS_0) - 1\}}.$$

Equation 6.26 exposes the two components of the competitive price of the extracted resource in an extremely tidy manner. Analytically, the interesting situation is one where S_0 is 'large'. In this case p_0^* is 'small' and consequently $q_t \simeq b$ initially. The price of the unextracted resource (p_t) rises exponentially at the rate r, but the price of the extracted resource (q_t) does not. In fact, q_t rises at a variable rate less than r, for $\dot{q}_t/q_t = r p_0^* \exp(rt)/(b + p_0^* \exp(rt)) < r$. In other words, q_t does grow, but given that by assumption p_0^* is 'small' the royalty component is negligible during the early years, and the extraction cost component dominates. This makes good intuitive sense. If the stock is large the fact that the resource is exhaustible is not of much concern. It is much like a conventional commodity whose unit cost of production is b. But with time the royalty component begins to dominate, since $q_t = b \exp(rt)/\{\exp(brS_0) - 1\}$ for large t. With time the fact that the resource is exhaustible begins to bite, and the production cost becomes a negligible part of its price. Indeed, in the long run $q_t \simeq p_t$ and the spot price of the extracted resource grows at the rate r (see Diagram 6.3). In short, it all depends on how large the initial stock is. But how 'large' is large? To get a feel for this note that since $p_0^*/b = 1/\{\exp(brS_0) - 1\}$ (equation 6.25) if, say, $brS_0 > 6$ then $p_0^*/b < 0\cdot01$; that is, the initial price of the unextracted resource ought to be less than 1% of the marginal cost of extraction. Suppose by way of illustration that $r = 0\cdot05$ per annum and that by normalization $b = 1$. Consider the case where p_0^* is small, and $R = (b + p_0^*)^{-1/\alpha}$. If $\alpha \simeq 1$ then $R_0 \simeq b + p_0^* \simeq b \simeq 1$. Suppose

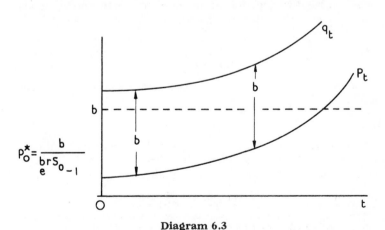

Diagram 6.3

$S_0 = 250$ (i.e. the initial stock is 250 times the initial rate of consumption of the resource). In this case $brS_0 = 12 \cdot 5$. Using equations 6.23, 6.25 and 6.26 it can be then computed that it will be about 130 years until brS_t falls to a value as low as 6.[21] The equilibrium price, q_t, will roughly equal b until the remaining stock is less than forty times the current annual rate of extraction.

Now it must be admitted that unchanging demand conditions (as caught in 6.10) are unlikely. One could imagine that if anything, demand will grow. This will work against the orders of magnitude we have just presented, in the sense that for a given initial stock q_t will diverge away from b at a faster rate if demand for the resource is assumed to increase, rather than stay constant.[22] This brings us back to our earlier observation that the relationship between q_t and the marginal cost of extraction depends on a number of complicated features. Roughly speaking, q_t hovers near this cost of extraction so long as the stock is large in some sense. This is not so otherwise.

(iii) *Deposits of different quality:* Let us complicate matters somewhat and suppose that there are different deposits of the same resource, the difference being in unit extraction costs. In particular suppose there are two deposits with unit extraction costs b_1 and b_2 $(b_2 > b_1)$.[23] Let p_{1t} and p_{2t} be the spot prices of the unextracted resource at these two deposits, and let q_{1t} and q_{2t} denote their extracted spot price. The first point to note now is that under competitive conditions the two deposits will not be mined simultaneously over any interval of time. For suppose they were. Then owners of the two deposits will be indifferent between storing and extracting over this interval. Consequently

6.27
$$\frac{\dot{p}_{1t}}{p_{1t}} = \frac{\dot{p}_{2t}}{p_{2t}} = r.$$

But since the two deposits contain identical products, $q_{1t} = q_{2t}$. This implies that

6.28
$$b_1 + p_{1t} = b_2 + p_{2t}$$

Now equations 6.27 and 6.28 are patently inconsistent with one another. Therefore the two deposits will not be mined simultaneously but instead will be mined sequentially. The precise sequence is

[21] These figures are taken from Kay and Mirrlees (1975).

[22] We shall leave it to the reader to verify this claim.

[23] One might wish to suppose that the second deposit is less accessible; or some geological difference makes extraction cheaper at the first deposit.

exactly as one would imagine: the better quality deposit will be mined first until it is exhausted, and the lower quality deposit will be mined subsequently. This is precisely what considerations of efficiency dictate. Given that $r > 0$ it makes sense to delay mining the higher cost deposit. Formally, the argument runs as follows. So long as stocks of both deposits are positive, equation 6.27 will hold in order that the asset market clears. For an initial period (T) the second deposit will be found unprofitable to mine. That is,

6.29 $q_t = b_1 + p_{1t} < b_2 + p_{2t}$ for $0 \leqslant t < T$.

During this period the owners of the first deposit undercut the price of the second one. The owners of the second deposit store, and do not

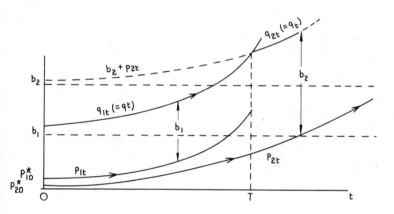

Diagram 6.4

find it profitable to extract, since the market price of the extracted resource does not cover the higher cost of extraction (b_2). Meanwhile q_t grows continuously (this follows from 6.27 and 6.29), and the extraction rate falls.[24] At T the first deposit is exhausted and there is a switch to the second deposit. The point to note now is that q_t must be continuous at T. For suppose that at T the extracted price were to jump to a higher value. Then since we are supposing that resource owners would know of this jump at T, owners of the first

[24] This last follows directly from our assumption of an unchanging downward sloping demand curve.

deposit could increase their profits by ceasing production just before T, and producing after T. But by hypothesis they cease operating after T. Consequently there cannot be a discontinuous increase in the price at T. Nor can there be a discontinuous fall at T since otherwise owners of the second deposit would find it profitable to enter production before T. This establishes the continuity of q_t at T. From date T the second deposit takes over and it is as though there is a single deposit. The story from then on is the same as the one we have already constructed for competitive extraction from a single quality deposit. In particular for $t \geqslant T$ one will have $q_t = q_{2t} = b_2 + p_{2t}$.

The continuity of the market price for the extracted resource (q_t) at T is an extremely valuable piece of information. Diagram 6.4 portrays the precise price trajectories. An important point to bear in mind is that during $(0, T)$ while the prices of a unit stock in both deposits rise at the same rate (equation 6.27), the price *levels* are by no means the same. Even common sense suggests that unit price of the second deposit will be lower during $(0, T)$. It is less valuable given that it is costlier to mine. It follows then that formally there are three unknowns to our problem; namely the initial prices p_{10}^* and p_{20}^*, and the switching date T. How are they determined under ideal circumstances? If there is a complete set of forward markets these equilibrium values will be determined by feasibility requirements. Suppose the initial stocks in these two deposits are $S_0^{(1)}$ and $S_0^{(2)}$. Let $D(q)$ be the market demand for the flow of the extracted resource at the price q. Then we must have

6.30
$$\int_0^T D(q_t)\, dt = \int_0^T D\{b_1 + p_{10}^* \exp(rt)\}\, dt = S_0^{(1)}$$

and

6.31
$$\int_T^\infty D(q_t)\, dt = \int_T^\infty D\{b_2 + p_{20}^* \exp(rt)\} dt = S_0^{(2)}$$

and finally,

6.32
$$\{b_1 + p_{10}^* \exp(rT)\} = \{b_2 + p_{20}^* \exp(rT)\}$$

Equation 6.32 expresses the continuity of q_t at T. Now equations 6.30–6.32 will in general determine uniquely the three unknowns.[25] Given that q_t is continuous, the flow of extraction, R_t, is continuous. Since demand conditions are by assumption unchanging, the rate of extraction under competitive conditions is a declining function of time. Diagram 6.5 portrays this.[26]

(iv) *Extraction in the presence of a 'backstop technology'*: There is a limiting case of the preceding model which is of considerable interest. Suppose that the lower grade deposit contains in effect an unlimited stock (i.e. $S_0^{(2)} = \infty$). Controlled nuclear fusion would provide a

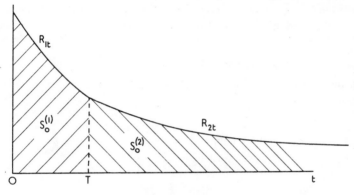

Diagram 6.5

[25] The remaining feature of Diagram 6.4 that needs explanation is the kink in the trajectory for q_t at T. But this is simple enough to explain. From equation 6.27 we know that

$$\lim_{t \to T-} \left[\frac{\dot{p}_{1t}}{p_{1t}} \right] = \lim_{t \to T+} \left[\frac{\dot{p}_{2t}}{p_{2t}} \right] = r.$$

Consequently,

$$\lim_{t \to T-} \left[\frac{\dot{q}_{1t}}{q_{1t} - b_1} \right] = \lim_{t \to T+} \left[\frac{\dot{q}_{2t}}{q_{2t} - b_2} \right].$$

Since $b_2 > b_1$ it follows directly that

$$\lim_{t \to T-} (\dot{q}_{1t}) > \lim_{t \to T+} (\dot{q}_{2t}).$$

[26] The generalization to more than two grades of deposit is simple enough. With a complete set of future markets the sequence of extraction will be from the cheapest to the most expensive deposit in precisely the manner we have described above for the case of two grades of deposit.

motivation for our being interested in such a model. Until this comes about, a reasonable approximation would be provided by the availability of shale oil. In other words, suppose that in addition to a given deposit of an exhaustible resource (with unit extraction cost at b_1) there is a known technology for producing a substitute product whose unit cost of production is b_2. It has become customary to refer to this as a *backstop technology*. Since the substitute is by assumption a conventional produced good, its market price under competitive conditions is precisely b_2.[27] Our earlier discussion will have made it clear what the price movement under competitive conditions will be. Let p_t denote the price of the unextracted resource and q_t its price after extraction. Given that $b_1 < b_2$ the deposit will be mined for an initial period $(0, T)$ while the substitute product will not be profitable. Thus equation 6.21 will hold during $(0, T)$. Furthermore

6.33 $$q_t = b_1 + p_0^* \exp(rt) < b_2 \quad \text{for} \quad 0 \leqslant t < T.$$

As one would expect, the two unknowns p_0^* and T will be determined by the conditions

6.34 $$\int_0^T D\{b_1 + p_0^* \exp(rt)\} \mathrm{d}t = S_0^{(1)}$$

and

6.35 $$\lim_{t \to T} \{b_1 + p_0^* \exp(rt)\} = b_2.$$

Diagrams 6.6 and 6.7 depict the time profiles of the competitive price and the rate of production of the resource and its substitute.

While exceedingly intuitive, the foregoing result is important to bear in mind. It reminds us that if the unit cost of extraction is less than the unit cost of producing a product that is more or less a perfect substitute, then the substitute ought not to be manufactured initially.[28] The backstop technology ought to be held in reserve until the resource is completely depleted. Of course, under competitive conditions the backstop technology *will* be held in reserve until the resource runs out, because so long as stocks are not depleted

[27] In order to check that this fits in with our discussion so far, note from equation 6.26 that $q_t \to b$ if $S_0 \to \infty$.

[28] We are now making use of the efficiency properties of the intertemporal competitive equilibrium. Hence the term 'ought' in the sentence.

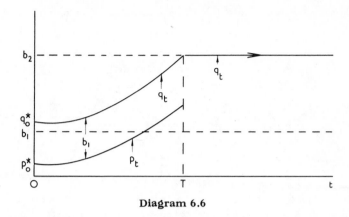

Diagram 6.6

resource owners will be able to undercut the competitive price of the substitute product. The result is of importance for another reason: it provides us with well-defined bounds for the competitive price of the extracted resource. For, $b_1 < q_t \leqslant b_2$. The larger is the initial stock the longer will q_t hover near b_1 (see 6.33) and consequently the longer will it be before the backstop technology makes its appearance.

Let us, by way of illustration, see what orders of magnitude may be involved. Suppose demand is unchanging and iso-elastic and that the price elasticity is unity. Then during $(0, T)$ we shall have $b_1 < b_1 + p_0^* \exp(rt) < b_2$, and consequently, using the demand assumption,

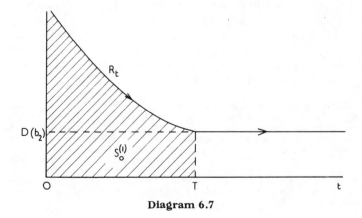

Diagram 6.7

that $R_t = \{b_1 + p_0^* \exp(rt)\}^{-1}$. From equations 6.34 and 6.35 we have then

$$6.36 \qquad S_0^{(1)} = \int_0^T \frac{dt}{\{b_1 + p_0^* \exp(rt)\}}$$

$$= \frac{1}{b_1 r} \left[\log\left(\frac{b_1 + p_0^*}{p_0^*}\right) - \log\left(\frac{b_1 + p_0^* \exp(rT)}{p_0^* \exp(rT)}\right) \right]$$

and

$$6.37 \qquad b_2 = b_1 + p_0^* \exp(rT).$$

By normalization set $b_1 = 1$ and suppose $b_2 = 10$.[29] Suppose that $S_0^{(1)} = 50$ (i.e. total stock is 50 times current rates of extraction) and $r = 0.05$ per annum. It is then simple to confirm that $p_0^* \simeq 0.03$ and that $T \simeq 100$ years. If, on the other hand, $S_0^{(1)} = 100$, then $p_0^* \simeq 0.0001$ and $T \simeq 275$ years. Of course, these conclusions cannot be taken seriously. If nothing else, demand is expected to grow, and the numerical results will not be as striking then. But they do suggest that the royalty component of the price of many exhaustible resources may well be rather small in initial years.

It is occasionally claimed that the competitive price of using an exhaustible resource is the cost of producing a substitute product. In a widely read popular report on the recent four-fold price increase of Arab oil, this view was attributed to OPEC defenders:

> Nearly every OPEC member . . . rejects the notion that the price of oil is now too high. 'What do they mean by high?' asks Iran's Minister of the Interior . . . incredulously. He reasons that the price is about equal to what it would cost to obtain an alternative form of energy, such as gas produced from coal. Thus he . . . insist(s) that \$9.70 per bl is a fair price.[30]

[29] This is not an entirely fictitious figure. \$2.00 a bl is a rough average figure for extraction of crude oil and it is occasionally said that the cost of producing shale oil is the equivalent of \$20.00 per bl of crude. Oil shale, while not exactly unlimited in quantity, is pretty much like a backstop technology. For alternative assumptions see Nordhaus (1973).

[30] *Time* magazine, October 14, 1974, p. 36. The two quotations in this chapter would seem to suggest that on occasion buyers of a resource believe in one economic logic, and the sellers in another. Presumably each picks the one that is comforting to it. In this instance both would seem to be using incorrect *arguments*.

In the long run, when the resource is near exhaustion, the argument would seem reasonable, but not until then. So long as there is a considerable gap between b_1 and b_2, and so long as the stock is large, the competitive price of an exhaustible resource is well below the cost of producing the substitute. Any attempt to set the price of an exhaustible resource roughly equal to the cost of producing a substitute product would result in excessive conservation.

(v) *Variable cost of substitute product:* Perhaps the most questionable feature of the conception of a backstop technology put forward above is that b_2 is independent of time. One would suppose that with the passage of time the cost of, say, providing energy from an alternative source (e.g. shale rock) would fall. Thus, suppose that b_2 is a continuous and monotonically decreasing function of time and

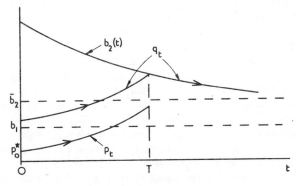

Diagram 6.8

that $b_2 \to \bar{b}_2 > b_1$ (see Diagram 6.8). It is clear enough what the price movement along an intertemporal competitive equilibrium will be. The deposit will be mined during an initial interval $(0, T)$ during which the backstop technology will be held in abeyance. Both equations 6.21 and 6.33 will hold during $(0, T)$. Moreover, the initial royalty price, p_0^*, and the exhaustion date T will be obtained from (a) the requirement that at T the resource is entirely depleted and (b) the condition that $q_T = b_1 + p_0^* \exp(rT) = b_2(T)$. From date T onwards, when the backstop technology is in use, $q_t = b_2(t)$ (see Diagram 6.8).

A limiting form of the above picture of technical advance that has been much discussed in the recent literature is one in which it is supposed that while the backstop technology will exist in the future it is unavailable currently.[31] Controlled nuclear fusion, or a 'clean' breeder technology would provide the obvious examples. No doubt one should postulate uncertainty in the date of discovery of the technical innovation.[32] Here we ignore such problems and suppose that it is known that the backstop technology (of constant unit cost b_2) will make its appearance at T^*. The question is: what will be the pace of extraction along an intertemporal competitive equilibrium?

In order to provide the answer recall the construction in section 4(iv) (see Diagrams 6.6 and 6.7). There we supposed that the backstop technology is currently available and we denoted by T the date at which the switch is made from the resource to the backstop. Quite obviously, if $T^* \leqslant T$ the same analysis goes through here. If society chooses to introduce the backstop in thirty years' time even when it is currently available, it will choose to introduce it in thirty years' time if instead it is currently unavailable but it is known that it will be discovered in twenty-five years' time Nothing is affected so long as $T^* \leqslant T$. But, of course, matters are different if $T^* > T$. There is now a precise sense in which society would prefer to have the backstop made available earlier.[33] But by hypothesis there is nothing society can do to alter T^*. What happens instead is that the pace of extraction and the price path take on a different form. The precise pattern is simple enough. For ease of exposition suppose that there is positive demand for the resource flow no matter what the price. Quite obviously then the initial royalty price of the resource will exceed p_0^* in Diagram 6.6 for if not the resource will be exhausted by date T (since equation 6.21 must hold so long as the resource is not exhausted), and nothing will be available from then until date T^*. We need now hardly point out why this cannot be sustained along an intertemporal competitive equilibrium. In fact the initial royalty price (which we write as p_0^{**}) takes on that value which will entail that the entire stock is depleted precisely at T^*; p_0^{**} being larger, the greater is T^*. During $(0, T^*)$ the price of the extracted resource is $q_t = b_1 + p_0^{**} \exp(rt)$. Quite obviously $q_{T^*} = b_1 + p_0^{**} \exp(rT^*) > b_2$. There is therefore a discontinuous fall in the

---

[31] See, for example, Dasgupta and Heal (1974), Manne (1974), Dasgupta and Stiglitz (1976) Kamien and Schwartz (1978) and Davison (1978).

[32] This is done in the references cited in the previous footnote. See also Chapters 14 and 16.

[33] This is of course a 'cet. par.' statement. We are ignoring the costs incurred in speeding up research. Questions bearing on research and development are explored in Section 5.

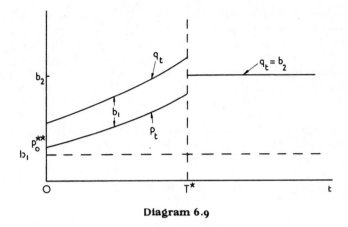

Diagram 6.9

price at T^*. This is shown in Diagram 6.9. As we have remarked, the farther away is T^* the greater is the initial royalty price p_0^{**}. In the limit, if $T^* \to \infty$ the present construction assumes a form identical to the one discussed in section 4(ii).

5. Resources Depletion and Research and Development

(i) *Introduction:* Thus far we have supposed that the date of invention of the backstop technology, T^*, is not a decision variable. In fact of course a good portion of investment in modern industrial economies is channelled towards research and development (R and D). This means that T^* is endogenous. In Chapters 13, 14 and 16 we shall go into some of the more difficult problems associated with the modelling of R and D. In this section we construct a simple model of R and D, one which is a direct generalization of the previous construction, and see what the basic ideas are.[34]

Continue to assume an absence of uncertainty. The economy possesses a given stock S_0, of an exhaustible resource at the initial date $t=0$. For simplicity of exposition suppose that extraction costs are nil. We hypothesize goal oriented research, where the invention consists in the discovery of a backstop technology whose unit cost of production is b (> 0). Suppose that for the research to be successfully carried out a sequence of well defined problems needs to be solved. By investing more in R and D one can speed up research and therefore ensure that the problems are solved earlier. This in

[34] This section is based on Dasgupta, Gilbert and Sitglitz (1977).

turn means that the date of invention can be brought forward by increasing R and D expenditure. Thus the model hypothesizes that a choice variable is the *date* of invention. Let the technology of R and D be characterized by a function $T(x)$, where T is the date of invention if x is R and D investment undertaken at $t=0$.[35] Quite naturally, we shall suppose that $T'(x)<0$. We assume in addition that $T''(x)>0$; i.e. that there are diminishing returns in R and D technology (see Diagram 6.10).

For simplicity of exposition we shall often take it that social benefit from consumption of the commodity in question is given by

$$6.38 \qquad\qquad u(R)=R^{1-a} \qquad (0<a<1).$$

Thus market demand is of the form

$$6.39 \qquad\qquad p(R)=(1-a)R^{-a}.$$

Demand is therefore iso-elastic, and the elasticity of demand is $1/a$, (>1).

(ii) *The Socially Managed Economy:* To begin with, recall the discussion in section 4(iv). There we had supposed that the invention had already occurred. We know from equations 6.34 and 6.35 that the *innovation* date is a function of the initial stock. Let $T(S_0)$ denote the date of innovation (Diagram 6.6). As equations 6.34 and 6.35 make clear, $T'(S_0)>0$; i.e. the greater is initial stock the longer would society wish to hold the backstop in abeyance.

Return now to the R and D and resource depletion problem. The planner is required to choose R and D investment (and hence the date of invention), the date of technological innovation, and the rates of resource depletion. All this is to be chosen at $t=0$. For simplicity of exposition suppose $T(0)=\infty$ (see Diagram 6.10). That is, if R and D expenditure is nil the substitute product will not be found. Let $x^*(\geq0)$ denote optimal R and D expenditure (to be determined of course). Then we know in advance that $T(x^*)\geq T(S_0)$. Since the cost of advancing the date of invention is positive there is no point in having the invention before $T(S_0)$ if we are not, in any case, prepared to innovate prior to this date. Thus the welfare trade-off the planner must consider is the gain in advancing the date of invention nearer $T(S_0)$ and the gain in postponing it by saving on R and D expenditure. Therefore it is clear that excepting for some

[35] We are cutting through many problems here by supposing the date of invention to depend only on the present value of R and D expenditure.

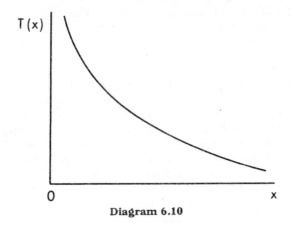

Diagram 6.10

unusual circumstances, $T(x^*) > T(S_0)$. Which means that we can appeal to the analysis in section 4(v) (Diagram 6.9). But we know from that analysis that the socially optimal spot price of the resource rises exponentially at the rate of interest during the interval $0 \leq t < T(x^*)$. The initial price is so chosen that the last unit of the resource is exhausted at $T(x^*)$, and innovation occurs at the date of invention. This means of course that there is a discontinuous fall in the social price at the date of invention (see Diagram 6.9). This is in the event $T(x^*) > T(S_0)$. If in fact $T(x^*) = T(S_0)$ price is a continuous function of time (Diagram 6.6).

We have obtained the optimum rate of depletion for a given date of invention. What remains is to obtain the optimal date of invention; or, in other words, the optimal level of R and D expenditure. Let us write by $W(S_0, T(x))$ the capitalized value of social benefits (gross of R and D expenditure) along the optimal programme of resource depletion when S_0 is the initial stock and $T(x)$ is the date of invention (innovation). It is simple to confirm that when $T(x) \geq T(S_0)$, and $u(R)$ satisfies (6.38), then

6.40 $$W(S_0, T(x)) = S_0^{1-a}(a/r)^a \, (1 - \exp(-rT(x)/a))^a + (a/r)(1-a)^{(1-a)/a} \, b^{-(1-a)/a} \exp(-rT(x))$$

(The first term in the RHS of 6.40 is the present value of social benefits of optimal resource consumption during $(0, T(x))$, and the second term is the present value of the flow of per period net social surplus for the post-innovation economy, $t \geq T(x)$). But the planning problem in general is one of

6.41 $$\text{maximizing } W(S_0, T(x)) - x.$$
$$x \geqslant 0$$

A glance at 6.40 tells us that W is not in general a concave function of x. This, as our discussion in Chapter 3, section 6 has made clear, means that social cost-benefit analysis of R and D expenditure is a difficult exercise, even in the simplest of models. In Chapter 14 we shall note that such non-concavities in the social benefit function when R and D is a decision variable is a pervasive feature.

Let x^* denote the solution of 6.41. It is clear that $x^* = x^*(S_0)$ and quite obviously, $x^{*\prime}(S_0) \leq 0$. Moreover, we know from 6.41 that if the optimum value, x^*, is greater than zero, then

$$T'(x) \ \partial W / \partial T = 1 \text{ at } x^*,$$

and if $T'(x) \ \partial W / \partial T < 1$ for all $x > 0$, then $x^* = 0$. Continue to suppose that W satisfies 6.40. It is then immediate that $\partial^2 W / \partial S_0 \partial x < 0$: i.e. the marginal social benefit of R and D expenditure is a decreasing function of resource stock. It is also easy to check that $x^* = 0$ if S_0 exceeds a finite size S. That is, there exists a level of stock, $\bar{S}$, such that if the initial stock exceeds this level no R and D expenditure ought to be undertaken. This does not mean that R and D expenditure ought *never* to be undertaken! It means simply that the research programme ought to be initiated only when the stock declines to the level $\bar{S}$. All this is congenial to common sense. If an economy is well-endowed with natural resources there is no point in its initiating research programmes designed to produce substitute products. It is better simply to wait until the need for substitutes is sufficiently high.

(iii) *The Competitive Economy:* We turn now to the case of competitive search for the backstop technology. For simplicity we suppose that all firms face the same R and D technology, $T(x)$. Thus, if a firm invests x at $t = 0$ it makes the invention at $T(x)$. The incentive to invent arises out of potential monopoly power. Therefore we take it that the first firm to invent is awarded the patent. If more than one firm are first to invent then they share the patent. With these assumptions we may now discuss informally the payoff to a firm that is considering the amount of R and D activity it ought to undertake. To begin with, it depends on the length of the patent. Moreover, it depends not only on how much *it* invests in R and D, but also on the levels of investment carried out by others; (for example, if any other firm invests more, the gross return on the given firm's R and D expenditure is nil, since it will not be awarded the patent. By assumption there is a severe cost in *not* being the first to invent in this model.) Finally, it depends on the size of the stock and the ownership pattern of the exhaustible resource (e.g. whether it is competitively owned or whether it is owned by a monopoly (cartel)). These considerations suggest that the problem at hand is a good deal more complicated than the one we have already analysed in this section. For, unlike the realm of the socially managed economy which is characterized by a *single* decision maker, the environment under consideration here results in a *game*, as there are several decision makers interacting with one another. In what follows, let us, as in Chapters 3 and 5, suppose that potential inventors play a Nash game with one another. That is, each firm i chooses x_i, taking the choice of x_j $(j \neq i)$ as given. But this is by no means the end of the matter. The payoff to the first inventor depends on the stock of the exhaustible resource at the date of invention and also on the ownership pattern of this resource. To the extent stocks are large at the date of invention the present value of profits to the first inventor is low, since the resource owner(s) will be able to undercut the patent holder for that long a while. While intuitively obvious, it is difficult to overemphasize this point. For it implies that the fact that the current price of an exhaustible resource is 'high' (e.g. because the owners have formed a cartel) does not mean that the return to R and D is 'high'. Quite the contrary: to the extent the current price is high, current rates of extraction are 'low', and therefore the remaining stocks at a given date of invention will be 'high'. There will be more scope for resource owner(s) to undercut the inventor. Potential inventors will have less incentives for undertaking R and D activity.

These foregoing considerations may suggest that the problem at hand is analytically intractable. Not quite – for irrespective of the 'game' that is to be played between there source owner(s) and the patent holder(s), yielding the form of the payoff function to the patent holder(s)), the equilibrium outcome is characterized by the following property: With free entry into R and D activity at most one firm is involved in R and D at an equilibrium, and its net present value of profits is zero.

The proof of this proposition, which does not depend on firms facing identical R and D technologies, is really rather simple. Notice first that at an equilibrium only winners will be engaged in R and D activity. Notice as well that if more than one firm undertakes R and D activity at a potential equilibrium, any one of them is in a position to increase its expenditure by ever so little and thereby ensure that it is the sole winner (assuming that others do not alter their R and D expenditures). Its expenditure by this move remains more or less what it was, but the present value of profits is increased by a discrete amount, since it knows that it will be awarded the exclusive right to produce. If the length of the patent is too short (e.g. zero) no firm will engage in R and D. Thus an equilibrium is characterized by at most one firm engaged in R and D. Furthermore, free entry into R and D activity ensures that the present value of profits to the firm engaged in R and D is nil.

The simplification afforded by this result is considerable. But there remains the problem of computing the post-invention payoff to this single firm undertaking R and D activity. For instance, if the exhaustible resource is owned by a few large firms (countries) we are in the realm of an intertemporal oligopoly game (between the resource owners and the single inventor) and each agent has to take into account the others' actions in order to choose best its own action.[36]

We consider the case where the resource is owned competitively. Suppose then that T^* is the date of invention. For the moment we suppose it to be exogenously given. We take it that a single firm will be awarded the patent at T^*. For simplicity suppose that the patent is of infinite duration. All this is known at $t = 0$. We are interested in characterizing a dynamic game equilibrium outcome, one where there are forward markets. Notice that the future patent holder enjoys a market power not shared by the competitive resource owners. The greater the resource stock remaining at T^* the smaller is the patent holder's market power, for competitive resource owners will be able to undercut it for just that much longer. Ideally, the patent holder would like to see complete resource depletion by T^* so that he may exercise his full monopoly power from the date of invention, But he may be unable to ensure this outcome since there are forward markets, and by hypothesis the asset market is perfectly arbitraged. *Given* T^* the future patent holder's aim is to maximise the present value of his profits. Now, he can influence the price path (and therefore the rates of depletion) of the exhaustible resource by buying up the entire stock from the

[36] We shall analyse such intertemporal oligopoly equilibria in Chapter 11.

competitive market and then controlling the rates of extraction, and also by announcing his post-invention production plans. But he is subject to one important market constraint; viz. that price cannot ever rise at a rate greater than the rate of interest. Now it is clear that even if he were to purchase the entire stock at $t=0$ and then proceed to deplete the stock he will sell in such a manner that the market price rises precisely at the rate of interest; for if it were ever less than this he would make a loss in this transaction, in present value terms. Thus we may as well suppose that the competitive resource owners supply the market so long as the stock lasts, but that the initial price, p_0, is influenced by the future patent holder's

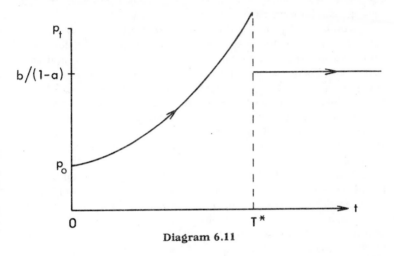

Diagram 6.11

announced production policy for $t \geq T^*$. In what follows we provide a description of the game equilibrium outcome without supplying formal proofs.[37] For simplicity continue to suppose that market demand for the product satisfies 6.39.

There are two cases to consider. Suppose first that T^* is 'large' (which is to say that S_0 is 'small'). Then the market price along the game equilibrium outcome is as depicted in Diagram 6.11.

During $(0, T^*)$ the resource is marketed and the price rises at a percentage rate equal to r. The initial price so gets chosen that at T^* (the date of invention) the resource is exhausted. Innovation occurs at T^* and the patent holder markets the commodity at the pure

[37] For details see Dasgupta and Sitglitz (1976).

monopoly price $b/(1-a)$. The key points are (i) that the innovation date coincides with the date of invention, (ii) that there is a discontinuous fall in price at the date of invention and (iii) that the patent holder begins to exploit his full monopoly power from the date of invention.

We have just noted that if T^* is 'large' the future patent holder can exercise his market power completely so as to drive his competitive rivals out of business by the date he wishes to assume control (viz. the date of invention). It is this he cannot do if T^* is 'small' (i.e. if S_0 is 'large'). Let T denote the date he chooses to innovate (i.e. begin exploiting the backstop technology). Quite obviously $T \geq T^*$. Quite obviously also he will never wish to share the market with his competitive rivals, for this will delay exhaustion. He can always do better by driving the initial price down and hastening the date of exhaustion by announcing his production plans for $t \geq T$. Now we know that so long as the resource lasts, $\dot{p}_t/p_t = r$, and that there cannot be a discontinuous rise in the price (there are forward markets). Thus if the patent holder wishes to innovate at T^* (i.e. set $T = T^*$) then in order to ensure that the resource is exhausted at T^* he will have to drive down the initial price so low that $p_{T^*} = p_0 e^{rT^*} < b$. But in this case the monopolist will sustain a loss for an initial period subsequent to innovation. He will clearly wish to avoid this and ensure that at the date of innovation the market price is no less than b. But he can ensure this only by not forcing the initial price too low a level. He can do this by announcing an innovation date T in excess of T^*. But he does not wish to delay entry unduly, for he will thereby be postponing the collection of profits. In particular he does not wish to postpone entry until the market price reaches the long run monopoly price of $b/(1-a)$. He does best by entering when the market price is somewhere between b and $b/(1-a)$.

The complete characteristics of the game equilibrium outcome when T^* is 'small' is shown in Diagram 6.12. The initial price gets so chosen that at T^* the resource is not yet exhausted. Price continues to rise at the rate of interest and the resource is exhausted at $\hat{T}$, where $b < p_0 e^{r\hat{T}} < b/(1-a)$. The patent holder enters the market at $\hat{T}$ and so controls the rate of production that the market price rises at the rate of interest. This continues until $\tilde{T}$, where $p_0 e^{r\tilde{T}} = b/(1-a)$. For $t \geq \tilde{T}$ the patent holder produces at the classical monopoly rate by charging the full monopoly price $b/(1-a)$. Therefore during $(\hat{T}, \tilde{T})$ the patent holder earns less than full monopoly profits.

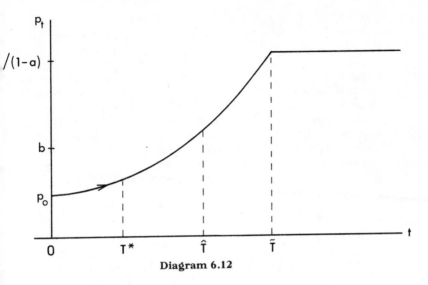

Diagram 6.12

Holding T^* fixed it is clear that $\tilde{T}$ is a function of S_0, and $\tilde{T}'(S_0) \geq 0$. Our analysis has in particular confirmed the intuitive feeling that for large enough S_0 the greater the value of S_0 the less the market power of the patent holder, but that below a level of initial stock monopoly power of the future patent holder is complete.

We now turn to the R and D problem and let T^* be endogenous. Let $V(S_0, T^*)$ be present value of profits accruing to the future patent holder along the game equilibrium outcome. It is immediate that $\partial V/\partial T^* < 0$. We return to a consideration of the R and D technology introduced earlier, and suppose $T^* = T(x)$, (see Diagram 6.10). It is clear that for all x, $W(S_0, T(x)) > V(S_0, T(x))$. Assume now that $T(0) = \infty$ and that $T(\infty) = 0$. We know therefore that with free entry into R and D activity there is at most one firm engaged in R and D and that its present value of profits is nil. If $\hat{x}$ is the equilibrium level of R and D expenditure, then it is the largest solution of

6.42 $$V(S_0, T(x)) = x.$$

(If $V(S_0, T(x)) < x$ for all $x > 0$, then $x = 0$ is the unique equilibrium).

The first point to note is that it is entirely possible that $\hat{x} > x^*$, where x^* is the socially optimal level of R and D expenditure. When this is the case, competition in R and D results in excessive speed of research. The invention is made too early, and the firm which engages in excessive R and D does so in order to forestall entry by rival firms. One should bear in mind that for the model at hand the social waste is not due to a duplication of research effort in the market economy, for only one firm is so engaged. The second point to note is that if S_0 is large it is entirely possible that $\hat{T} > T(\hat{x})$, so that pressure of competition in R and D activity forces this single firm to invent at a date earlier than when he plans to innovate. During $(T(\hat{x}), \hat{T})$ this firm holds an unused patent and, what is interesting, is that it knows that it will sit on an unused patent when investing $\hat{x}$ at $t = 0$. This feature too, as we noted in section 5 (ii), is not socially desirable.

6. Conclusions

Let us sum up:

(1)   The competitive (efficiency) price of an extracted exhaustible resource is the sum of the marginal cost of extraction and the price of the unextracted resource (the royalty price). In particular, the extracted price exceeds the marginal cost of extraction and is not equal to it.

(2)   If the cost of extraction of the resource is independent of the stock, the royalty price will, under competitive conditions, grow at a compound rate. This rate of increase will equal the rate of return on holding the numeraire good.

(3)   An implication of (2) is that the present value royalty price of a resource is constant over time.

(4)   An implication of (1) and (2) is that the price of the extracted resource will grow at a lower rate than the rate of increase in the royalty price (and may fall initially). But in the long run the two prices will grow at the same rate.

(5)   If the marginal cost of extraction is a declining function of the stock, the percentage rate of change in the competitive royalty price of a resource is less than the rate of return on holding the numeraire, the difference being the reduction in future extraction costs as a result of storing the marginal unit of stock.

(6)   A sequence of momentary equilibria (one along which at each date both the asset market and the market for the extracted resource are in competitive equilibrium) cannot be relied upon to ensure an efficient utilization of an exhaustible resource. In particular, if the initial royalty price is set 'too high' there will be excessive conservation.

A fraction of the initial stock will never be extracted. But the 'market' may never discover its erroneous ways.

(7) If there is a complete set of future markets, or if there is a planning board looking far into the future, such a market failure need not arise and in principle can be circumvented.

(8) An implication of (1) is that if the stock is large an extracted resource is much like a conventional produced commodity, in that its price roughly equals the marginal cost of extraction (i.e. the royalty price is negligible). As the stock diminishes, if there are no substitutes in sight, the fact that the resource is exhaustible becomes important. At this stage the price of the extracted resource roughly equals the royalty price, which is far in excess of the cost of extraction.

(9) The existence of a substitute product for an exhaustible resource does not imply that the competitive (efficiency) price of the extracted resource is the cost of producing the substitute. Indeed if the cost of extraction is less than the cost of producing the substitute product the competitive price of the extracted resource lies between these cost figures. If the stock is large the price will be roughly equal to the cost of extraction (i.e. the royalty price is negligible). It is only when the resource is near exhaustion that the price rises to the cost of producing the substitute.

(10) An implication of (9) is that the fact that a substitute has been discovered does not provide an argument for producing it initially. As long as the production cost of the substitute exceeds the extraction cost of the exhaustible resource the substitute ought not to make its appearance initially, and under fully competitive conditions it will not make its appearance initially. The resource and the substitute will not be utilized simultaneously, but sequentially.

(11) So long as there is no uncertainty, if advancing the date of invention of a backstop technology entails positive costs society ought so to plan its R and D expenditure that invention occurs at the date it wishes to make the transition to the new technology.

(12) If current stocks are large, R and D activity ought to be postponed.

(13) Under free entry into R and D activity, competitive search for a backstop technology may well result in excessive R and D expenditure. In particular, the invention may occur too soon and the transition to the new technology may occur at a subsequent date; which is to say, the inventor may find it profitable to hold an unused patent for a period.

Notes to Chapter 6

The classic articles on the economics of exhaustible resources are by Gray (1914) and Hotelling (1931). The subject was created in these contributions. Hotelling was concerned with the intertemporal price behaviour and the pace of extraction for both a competitive extractive industry and for one that is a private monopoly. We shall study the latter in Chapter 11. It would appear that the contribution did not receive much attention, since very little work was done on the subject until the mid-1960s. Some of the best contributions to the subject during the 1960s are in Gaffney (1967). The article by Herfindahl in this collection is particularly noteworthy. He extended the Hotelling results to include different grades of an ore and the consequent sequencing of their exploitation along a competitive process.

Since the beginning of this decade a considerable amount of work has been done on the subject, but mostly in the context of aggregate growth models with exhaustible resources. For a brilliant exposition of this subject as it appeared at the end of 1973, see Solow (1974a).

The problem of incorporating a substitute product into the analysis was a focus of attention in Nordhaus (1973), Dasgupta and Heal (1974), and more recently extended considerably by Dasgupta and Stiglitz (1978a) and Gilbert (1978) to include mixed market structures. Our exposition has relied heavily on all of these contributions. Where our exposition differs from earlier ones, perhaps, is in our relatively greater emphasis on the connection between models of resource extraction under competitive conditions and the intertemporal general equilibrium models of Malinvaud (1953) and others. For splendid expositions of intertemporal general equilibrium models, see Koopmans (1957) and the recent contribution of Bliss (1975).

It is worth mentioning that an alternative approach to discussing exhaustible resources is to postulate an infinite resource base, but with unit cost of extraction increasing indefinitely with cumulative extraction. Thus, on using the notation introduced in this chapter if one were to denote cumulative extraction as Z_t (i.e. $Z_t = \int_{-\infty}^{t} R\tau \, d\tau$) one could postulate an infinite resource base (i.e. $S_t = \infty$) and, for example, a cost function $C = R_t H(Z_t)$, where $H(Z_t) \to \infty$ as $Z_t \to \infty$. It is immediate then that R_t must tend to zero in the long run. It does not, of course, follow immediately that Z_t will be bounded above. This last requires further arguments for its demonstration. The general principles that we have obtained in this chapter can be arrived at via this alternative approach to studying exhaustible resources. On this, see Heal (1976). The approach followed in this book—namely, to assume in advance that the integral of resource utilization is bounded above—appears to be simpler and possibly more intuitive.

CHAPTER 7

PRODUCTION WITH EXHAUSTIBLE RESOURCES

1. Production Possibilities and Intertemporal Programmes

Exhaustible resources are normally inputs in production, not final consumption goods. It is then important to introduce production possibilities with exhaustible resources directly into our construction. This is the purpose of this chapter.

Begin with the simplest case. There is no uncertainty. The stocks of exhaustible resources are all known at the starting date. In addition, assume away the possibility of discovering substitute products in the future (e.g. harnessing solar energy which is, to all intents and purposes, inexhaustible). Presumably, then, an exhaustible resource would pose a 'problem' if it is, in some sense, *essential* in the production of final consumption goods, and not otherwise. The earth abounds with resources that, with current technology, have little or no use. No one would seem to lose any sleep over the fact that many such resources are exhaustible.[1] So the question is whether one can make this intuitive notion of essentiality precise. It will transpire that one can. Nevertheless, it is not an easy matter to judge under what circumstances a given resource is in fact essential. The matter depends in a complex way on the production possibilities open to the economy.

We concern ourselves with production possibilities facing an economy as a whole. To fix ideas, assume that the economy is closed to trade with the rest of the world. As we are concentrating on the entire economy we need not consider intermediate goods. They will net out from our formulation. Consider then the simplest laboratory in which to analyse production possibilities over time. Imagine that there is a single durable produced commodity whose

---

[1] This does not mean that they will not prove useful in the future. Presumably the Iron Age ushered in the usefulness of iron ore. Likewise, copper found use with the advent of the Bronze Age. Moreover, fossil fuels began replacing timber as a source of energy only rather recently.

total stock at time t is K_t.[2] We take it that this composite commodity serves as the single consumption good as well. The output flow of this commodity can therefore be used indifferently between consumption and investment, where by investment we refer to the act of augmenting the stock of the composite good.

Depreciation is normally difficult to handle analytically unless it is assumed that the capital good depreciates at a fixed proportional rate. But this is an unsatisfactory method of dealing with depreciation. In any event, it is important to bear in mind that depreciation acts as a 'drag' on production possibilities. So long as the percentage rate of depreciation is bounded above one knows in advance the maximum extent of this drag. We are concerned here with the constraints on production possibilities due to the presence of exhaustible resources. It will not be unduly misleading then to ignore the depreciation of the augmentable capital good, and we take it that the composite commodity does not deteriorate.

While land has often been reclaimed in the past, it is usually thought of as being fixed in size. We can take this simplifying route and suppose a constant flow of service from land. Alternatively, if we are envisaging industrial production only, we may feel that land is of negligible importance and therefore simply ignore it. In what follows we shall, for expository ease, suppose that land is of no importance.

Labour produces the severest difficulties in many ways, not only because there are many kinds of labour services but also because there is no suitable demographic theory predicting the course of labour availability. It is usual in constructing growth models to cut through such problems and to postulate an exponentially increasing population size.[3] For our purpose this will not quite do. Our concern is in the main with the implications of a finite earth for the growth possibilities open to an economy. In this context the assumption of an exponentially rising population size is an absurdity, if only for reasons of space. The simplest plausible assumption is a constant population profile. In what follows we shall suppose this. In effect this supposes that the objective of ZPG (zero population growth) has

[2] For our purpose here nothing is lost conceptually by our assumption of a single produced commodity. We could easily carry out the subsequent analysis by regarding lathes and blast furnaces, factory buildings and computers, refrigerators and shoes as distinct commodities. This would complicate the exposition without providing any additional insights.

[3] For surveys, see Hahn and Mathews (1964), Solow (1970), Wan (1973) and Burmeister and Dobell (1972).

been accepted and achieved. We denote this constant population size by L. It is clear that we may as well identify L with the actual labour force, since this latter is a constant fraction of the population size (the age structure being constant over time by our assumption).[4]

This assumption of an exogenously given population size poses its own interpretative problems, since one has to assume away the existence of a level of consumption below which life cannot be sustained. We shall, of course, by suitable assumptions be able to avoid zero consumption. But the assumption of an exogenously given population size is tantamount to the supposition that the subsistence level of consumption is nil.

It remains to introduce an exhaustible resource in production. Nothing at all is lost in our supposing that there is a single exhaustible resource. Consequently, we suppose this to be the case. As before S_t denotes its stock and R_t denotes its rate of extraction (and utilization in production).

Imagine next that the composite commodity can, in conjunction with labour service and the *flow* of the exhaustible resource in production, reproduce itself. Let Y_t and C_t denote the output flow and the consumption flow of this composite good. Net investment (equal by assumption to gross investment) in fixed capital is $\dot{K}_t$. We can then ask ourselves the following question: *given* a pair of values for K_t and R_t (and knowing L) and given the technological possibilities at t, what is the maximum output Y_t obtainable? Suppose that the question has an answer and, in particular, that this maximum level defines a non-negative twice continuously differentiable function G which is increasing in K_t, R_t and L. Thus the production set is

7.1 $$0 \leqslant Y_t \leqslant G(K_t, R_t, L, t); \quad K_t, R_t \geqslant 0.$$

The notion of *static* efficiency, with which we were much concerned in Chapters 2 and 3, would then require that:

7.2 $$Y_t = G(K_t, R_t, L, t); \quad K_t, R_t \geqslant 0.$$

In what follows we shall, for expository ease, always postulate static efficiency and assume 7.2 to hold. The explicit dependence of the production function, G, on time in 7.2 captures the possibility

---

[4] For an analysis of growth possibilities open to an economy possessing exhaustible resources and an exponentially growing labour force see Stiglitz (1974a).

that technical knowledge changes with time, and indeed changes costlessly. Since we are postulating a world of certainty at this stage this change in knowledge, is by assumption, predictable. If there is an improvement in knowledge (i.e. technical progress) it is captured here by the condition $\partial G/\partial t > 0$. But it must be emphasized that we are at this stage postulating a very special form of technical change; one which is *disembodied*. The formulation in equation 7.2 does not allow us to distinguish between machines of old and new vintages. New knowledge can by assumption be applied on an equal footing on the entire stock of the composite commodity. Indeed, that is why we are entitled to discuss production possibilities in terms of the entire stock of the composite commodity.[5]

By assumption, net output Y_t can be used indifferently between consumption and capital accumulation.[6] Gross national expenditure is then $C_t + \dot{K}_t$, and on the assumption that none of the output is thrown away, we have

7.3 $\qquad C_t + \dot{K}_t = G(K_t, R_t, L, t); \qquad \text{with } K_t, R_t, C_t \geqslant 0$

and K_0 given, where $G(K_t, R_t, L, t)$ is the gross national product.

Now recall as well that

7.4 $\qquad\qquad S_t = S_0 - \int_0^t R_\tau \, d\tau; \qquad S_t, R_t \geqslant 0.$

At $t = 0$ the economy will have stocks K_0 and S_0 of its two physical assets as an inheritance from the past. Thus equations 7.3 and 7.4 describe the complete production possibilities open to the economy for all $t \geqslant 0$. We shall refer to the future evolution of the four variables, K_t, S_t, R_t and C_t (for $t \geqslant 0$) as a *programme* and we shall denote a programme as $[K_t, S_t, R_t, C_t]_{t=0}^\infty$. Given K_0 and S_0, a programme $[K_t, S_t, R_t, C_t]_{t=0}^\infty$ will be called *feasible* if it satisfies equations 7.3 and 7.4.

2. Essential and Inessential Exhaustible Resources

(i) *A definition:* We examine the output and consumption possibilities open to the economy in question. It is clear that exhaustible

[5] For a thorough discussion of these issues bearing on technical progress, the distinction between embodied and disembodied technical progress, see Hahn and Mathews (1964) and Solow (1970).

[6] 'Net' output, because resources may be required to extract the natural resource. For simplicity we shall take it that extraction costs are nil. This will allow us to identify Y with gross output.

resources would not pose a fundamental problem if output in the absence of such resources were not merely positive, but large enough for the entire population to enjoy a reasonable standard of living. Thus, if in fact $G(K, O, L, t) > 0$ for $K > 0$, and in addition, $G(K_0, O, L, t)$ is large enough, there is no problem. This much is immediate. The interesting case is another extreme; the case where the resource is necessary for production, i.e. $G(K, O, L, t) = 0$. Now it may be tempting to argue that it is surely appropriate to regard the exhaustible resource as being essential if this is the case (i.e. if output is nil in the absence of the resource). But this would be a mistake. A finite quantity of a resource can be spread thinly over the distant future. What one needs to know is whether one can pursue a programme along which consumption never falls below the rate that is judged as representing a reasonable standard of living. Now, this may be possible even if output in the absence of the resource is nil. In other words, the existence of a finite stock of a resource that is necessary for production does not imply that the economy must eventually stagnate and decline. If there is continual resource augmenting technical progress (see section 2(iii)), it is possible that a reasonable standard of living can be guaranteed for all time. But even if we postulate an absence of technical progress we must not overlook substitution possibilities. If there are reasonable substitution possibilities between exhaustible resources and reproducible capital, it is possible that capital accumulation could offset the constraints on production possibilities due to exhaustible resources. We shall explore these issues.[7] But our discussion does suggest that when we ask whether an exhaustible resource is essential we are not asking whether the resource is necessary for production. Rather, we are asking whether feasible consumption must eventually fall below the rate that is judged as representing a reasonable standard of living. One aspect of the worry expressed by the original world modellers must surely have originated from this question.[8] Now, it is plain that in certain situations the answer to this question does not depend on the size of the initial stocks, K_0 and S_0. For example, if technical progress is firmly expected not to occur and if, at the same time, it is judged that there are no substitution possibilities whatsoever between

[7] Presumably, increasing returns to scale in production can also offset the limitations imposed by natural resources. Here we shall make the moderately pessimistic assumption of an absence of increasing returns. There remains substitution possibilities and technical progress.

[8] See, for example, Forrester (1971), Meadows et al. (1972). For a lucid account of these models see Cole et al. (1973).

reproducible capital, exhaustible resources and labour, then doom cannot be avoided, no matter how large the initial stocks. Confronted with such a gloomy picture, there is not an awful lot one can discuss except, of course, the question of how best to prepare to meet our doom. Equally plainly, there are technological environments where the answer does depend on the size of the initial stocks; where for large initial stocks it is possible to maintain consumption above a level judged reasonable, but not otherwise. If this is in fact an appropriate description of the world, then it is surely legitimate to ask whether current and projected rates of consumption and resource extraction for the near future are not unduly profligate in the sense that, if pursued, consumption must fall below the stipulated level in the not too distant future. The question acquires a bite for such a world if it is shown as well that current stocks are large enough for this decline to be avoidable.

Interpreted generously, we would judge that it is this question that motivated the construction of the original World Models. And what reasoned criticisms there are of these models are really a demonstration that the answers to this question provided by the models are unwarranted.[9]

The purpose of this chapter is to discuss the conceptual issues that arise when exhaustible resources are incorporated in production possibilities. The motivation behind the construction of the specific examples in this volume is quite different from the motivation behind the construction of complex World Models. Part of our aim is to keep a check on our intuition, as well as to see how one might go about formulating certain questions. It is then reasonable to avoid specifying in advance the level of consumption that is judged as representing a reasonable standard of living. For if we were not to avoid it the actual size of the initial stocks could well play a decisive role in the discussion of whether doom is inevitable. Analytically this would add virtually nothing and would make the exposition awkward. It is better simply to avoid it. We shall therefore regard an exhaustible resource as being *inessential* if there is a feasible programme along which consumption is bounded away from zero; or in other words, if a positive sustainable level of consumption is feasible. Likewise, regard a resource as *essential* if feasible consumption must necessarily decline to zero in the long run. In short, doom cannot be

---

[9] We have in mind the critical assessments of Cole *et al.* (1973), Nordhaus (1973) and Kay and Mirrlees (1975).

avoided in the long run if there are exhaustible resources that are essential.

(ii) *Examples of essential and inessential resources: no technical change:* Perpetual technical progress, while unlikely, is not an absurd notion. But it is important to investigate the growth potentials of an economy under the pessimistic assumption of no technical change. Technical progress can then merely help matters. Let $G(K_t, R_t, L, t) = F(K_t, R_t, L)$. As in earlier chapters, we take it that F is strictly concave and homogeneous of degree one. That is, constant returns to scale prevail over all and there are diminishing returns to each factor. Since L is by assumption a constant we may as well suppress it and write $F(K, R)$, where F is homogeneous of degree less than unity in K and R. It will be helpful to impose some further structure on F in order to discuss consumption possibilities open to the economy. As we remarked earlier, the question really centres on the substitution possibilities between reproducible capital goods and exhaustible resources. Loosely speaking, the greater is the ease with which reproducible capital goods can substitute for exhaustible resources in production, the less worrying are exhaustible resources as a problem. The natural index capturing the notion of substitution possibilities is the *elasticity of substitution* between K and R.[10] And the simplest laboratory in which to explore such questions is the class of production functions F for which the elasticity of substitution between K and R is constant (i.e. independent of K and R); in short, the CES production functions.[11]

Let σ (>0) denote the elasticity of substitution between reproducible capital and the exhaustible resource. Normalize and write $L=1$. The CES production function is then given as

$$7.5 \quad Y = F(K, R) = \{\alpha_1 K^{(\sigma-1)/\sigma} + \alpha_2 R^{(\sigma-1)/\sigma} + (1 - \alpha_1 - \alpha_2)\}^{\sigma/(\sigma-1)}$$

$$\alpha_1, \alpha_2, 1 - \alpha_1 - \alpha_2 > 0 \quad \text{and} \quad \sigma > 0, \sigma \neq 1.$$

The case $\sigma = 1$ corresponds to the Cobb–Douglas form, where

$$7.6 \quad Y = F(K, R) = K^{\alpha_1} R^{\alpha_2} \quad \text{with} \quad \alpha_1, \alpha_2 > 0 \quad \text{and} \quad \alpha_1 + \alpha_2 < 1.[12]$$

Most of the cases can be disposed of rather rapidly. From 7.5 it is immediate that $F(K, O) > 0$ if $\sigma > 1$. The resource is not necessary

---

[10] For a good intuitive discussion of the concept see Hicks (1935).

[11] See Arrow, Chenery, Minhas and Solow (1961).

[12] The case $\sigma = 0$ corresponds to the Leontief technology, one where, with suitable choice of units, $F(K, R) = \min (K, R.)$ It is, of course, not a strictly increasing function.

for production. Its exhaustibility does not pose a problem. It is trivially inessential.

The case $\sigma < 1$ is also not interesting analytically. For notice first that given decreasing returns to scale in K and R the average product per unit of the resource in use, F/R, is a declining function of R. Notice as well that on dividing 7.5 through by R we can re-express it as

$$\{F(K, R)/R\}^{(\sigma-1)/\sigma} = \alpha_1(R/K)^{(1-\sigma)/\sigma} + \alpha_2 + (1 - \alpha_1 - \alpha_2)R^{(1-\sigma)/\sigma}.$$

Taking limits on both sides as $R \to 0$

$$\lim_{R \to 0} F(K, R)/R = \alpha_2^{\sigma/(\sigma-1)}, \qquad \text{for } 0 < \sigma < 1.$$

The average product per unit of the resource in use is bounded above. Given 7.4 (i.e. the fact that there is only a finite resource base), it implies that total output (i.e. the integral of output) the economy is capable of generating is finite. This follows from the fact that

$$\int_0^\infty Y_t \, \mathrm{d}t = \int_0^\infty F(K_t, R_t) \, \mathrm{d}t < \alpha_2^{\sigma/(\sigma-1)} \int_0^\infty R_t \, \mathrm{d}t = S_0 \alpha_2^{\sigma/(\sigma-1)}.$$

This in turn implies that output must eventually decline to zero. Consequently consumption must decline to zero. The point is that if $\sigma < 1$ there are severe limitations to substitution possibilities, with the result that capital accumulation cannot hope to compensate for the eventual decline in resource utilization. The economy is doomed.[13]

There remains the Cobb–Douglas case. A glance at 7.6 indicates that the resource is necessary for production. But the average product per unit of the resource in use is unbounded. It is then not immediate whether the resource is essential or not. We look into this.

It transpires that the crucial question is whether or not $\alpha_1 > \alpha_2$. This should not be entirely surprising. For these two parameters represent the elasticities of output with respect to reproducible capital and the exhaustible resource. Roughly speaking, if $\alpha_1 > \alpha_2$ fixed capital is sufficiently important in production to allow for the possibility of a permanently maintainable output level despite the

[13] It should be emphasized that we are postulating an absence of technical progress here.

declining availability of the natural resource. The idea is to accumu-
late capital at a sufficiently fast rate to make this feasible. We begin
by demonstrating that the condition $\alpha_1 > \alpha_2$ allows for the possibility
of a permanently maintainable output (and consumption) level.

To do this we show that there is a programme of accumulation and
extraction which allows constant positive consumption for all time
and which does not exhaust the resource. For this we experiment
with a programme along which K_t increases linearly in t. Thus
consider

7.7 $$K_t = K_0 + mt, \qquad m > 0.$$

Let us see whether this is consistent with $C_t = \bar{C} > 0$ for all $t \geqslant 0$,
and the non-exhaustion of the exhaustible resource. Now it follows
from 7.7 that $\ddot{K}_t = 0$. Moreover from 7.3 it follows that if $C_t = \bar{C}$, then
$\dot{Y}_t = \ddot{K}_t = 0$. From the production function 7.6 we then have

$$\dot{Y}_t / Y_t = 0 = \alpha_1 \dot{K}_t / K_t + \alpha_2 \dot{R}_t / R_t = \alpha_1 m / (K_0 + mt) + \alpha_2 \dot{R}_t / R_t.$$

Consequently

7.8 $$\dot{R}_t / R_t = -\alpha_1 m / \alpha_2 (K_0 + mt).$$

Integrating equation 7.8 yields

7.9 $$R_t = (A + m)^{1/\alpha_2} (K_0 + mt)^{-\alpha_1/\alpha_2}$$

where A is the constant of integration. Now if we use 7.6, 7.7 and
7.9 in equation 7.3 it follows immediately that $A = \bar{C}$, the arbitrarily
chosen constant consumption level. Thus

7.10 $$R_t = (\bar{C} + m)^{1/\alpha_2} (K_0 + mt)^{-\alpha_1/\alpha_2}.$$

What remains is to confirm that the extraction path 7.10 is feasible.
In fact let us insist on the condition that the entire stock is depleted
in infinite time.

We require then that

$$S_0 = \int_0^\infty R_t \, dt = \int_0^\infty (\bar{C} + m)^{1/\alpha_2} (K_0 + mt)^{-\alpha_1/\alpha_2} dt.$$

For this integral to exist it is necessary and sufficient that $\alpha_1 > \alpha_2$
We begin by supposing this to be the case. It follows then on integrating that

7.11 $$\bar{C} + m = m^{\alpha_2} \left(\frac{\alpha_1 - \alpha_2}{\alpha_2} \right)^{\alpha_2} S_0^{\alpha_2} K_0^{\alpha_1 - \alpha_2}.$$

From equation 7.11 it follows that we can eliminate one of the two unknowns (say m). This leaves us with the unknown $\bar{C}$. But the point about 7.11 is that it implies that it is possible to choose positive values of $\bar{C}$ and m (see Diagram 7.1). Moreover, the larger S_0 and K_0 the larger is the range of $\bar{C}$ that one can select. This last is, of course, intuitively obvious.

In what follows we shall have several occasions to refer to the class of constant consumption programmes that we have constructed. It will then prove convenient to bring equations 7.7, 7.10

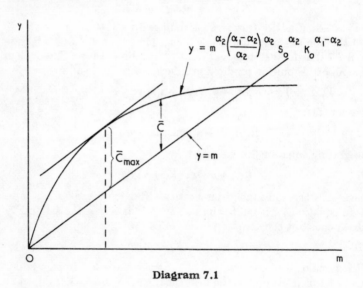

Diagram 7.1

and 7.11 together and denote such constant consumption programmes as

$$7.12 \quad \left.\begin{array}{l} K_t = K_0 + mt, \qquad m > 0 \\[4pt] R_t = (\bar{C} + m)^{1/\alpha_2}\,(K_0 + mt)^{-\alpha_1/\alpha_2} \\[4pt] C_t = \bar{C} > 0 \\[4pt] \text{and} \\[4pt] m + \bar{C} = m^{\alpha_2}\left(\dfrac{\alpha_1 - \alpha_2}{\alpha_2}\right)^{\alpha_2} S_0^{\,\alpha_2}\,K_0^{\,\alpha_1 - \alpha_2}. \end{array}\right\}$$

We have seen that a programme defined by 7.12 implies a constant output level ($Y_t = \bar{C} + m$) and a constant consumption level ($C_t = \bar{C}$). We still have a degree of freedom left in choosing $\bar{C}$. The question arises as to the maximum value of $\bar{C}$ obtainable from 7.12. The question is of importance because it will transpire that the programmes defined by 7.12 are of rather general interest. Differentiating equation 7.11 with respect to m and setting $d\bar{C}/dm = 0$, shows that $\bar{C}$ is maximized at the value of m given by [14]

7.13 $$m^{1-\alpha_2} = \alpha_2 \left(\frac{\alpha_1 - \alpha_2}{\alpha_2} \right)^{\alpha_2} S_0{}^{\alpha_2} K_0{}^{\alpha_1 - \alpha_2}.$$

If we now multiply equation 7.13 by $m\alpha_2$ and use equation 7.11 it follows that

$$m = \alpha_2(m + \bar{C}) = \alpha_2 Y.$$

Let us define by $s_t = (Y_t - C_t)/Y_t$ the *net* rate of savings along a given programme. From feasibility it is clear that $s_t \leqslant 1$. It also follows from equation 7.3 that $s_t = \dot{K}_t/Y_t$ (the net investment output ratio). Now a programme defined by 7.12 is sustained by a constant savings rate (since $Y_t = \bar{C} + m$ and $C_t = \bar{C}$). It is given by $s = m/(\bar{C} + m)$. We can then ask: what is the value of s that will sustain the maximum feasible $\bar{C}$ implied by a programme 7.12? The answer is now immediate. $\bar{C}$ is maximized when $s = \alpha_2$.

This is a useful result to have. Since α_2 is the elasticity of output with respect to the resource input, it is probably quite small in value, around 0.05 say. The foregoing argument implies that a net rate of savings of about 5% per annum associated with a programme 7.12 will ensure the maximum constant consumption level that such a programme can sustain. Such a rate of savings allows fixed capital to be accumulated at a sufficiently fast rate so as to maintain output and consumption constant in the face of vanishing resource input.

Let us, by way of completeness, characterize explicitly the maximum feasible value of $\bar{C}$, which we shall denote as $\bar{C}_{\max}$. Using equation 7.13 in equation 7.11 yields

7.14 $$\bar{C}_{\max} = (\alpha_2{}^{\alpha_2/(1-\alpha_2)} - \alpha_2{}^{1/(1-\alpha_2)})$$
$$\left(\frac{\alpha_1 - \alpha_2}{\alpha_2} \right)^{\alpha_2/(1-\alpha_2)} S_0{}^{\alpha_2/(1-\alpha_2)} K_0{}^{(\alpha_1-\alpha_2)/(1-\alpha_2)} > 0.$$

(see Diagram 7.1).

[14] It is readily checked from 7.11 that $\bar{C}$ is a strictly concave function of m. See also Diagram 7.1.

What we have demonstrated so far is that if $\alpha_1 > \alpha_2$ the exhaustible resource is inessential. We have yet to determine consumption possibilities open to the economy if $\alpha_2 \geqslant \alpha_1$. This can be done with little extra effort. What we shall demonstrate is that if $\alpha_2 \geqslant \alpha_1$ then the requirement that output remains at a positive constant level cannot be met with a finite resource base even if all output is saved at all times. This will in turn mean that output must eventually tend to zero no matter what the rate of savings is, and therefore that feasible consumption must tend to zero.

Suppose then that $s = 1$ and that $\dot{Y}_t / Y_t = 0$. In what follows we shall express by $g_z = \dot{z}_t / z_t$ the percentage rate of change of any variable z. Given the Cobb–Douglas form of the production function we have

$$g_Y = \alpha_1 g_K + \alpha_2 g_R = 0$$

and hence

7.15
$$g_K = -\frac{\alpha_2}{\alpha_1} g_R.$$

Write $x = Y/K$ for the average output–capital ratio. Then $g_K = \dot{K}_t / K_t = Y_t / K_t = x_t$, and consequently 7.15 can be expressed as

7.16
$$\alpha_1 x_t + \alpha_2 g_R = 0.$$

Differentiating equation 7.16 with respect to time we obtain

7.17
$$\alpha_1 \dot{x}_t + \alpha_2 \dot{g}_R = 0.$$

But since $x = Y/K$, it follows that $g_x = g_Y - g_K$. Given that by assumption $g_Y = 0$ along the programme, $g_x = -g_K = -x_t$. Using this in equation 7.17 yields

7.18
$$\alpha_2 \dot{g}_R - \alpha_1 (x_t)^2 = 0.$$

Now use 7.16 in 7.18 to obtain

7.19
$$\dot{g}_R = \frac{\alpha_2}{\alpha_1} g_R^2.$$

Equation 7.19 can be integrated, yielding

7.20
$$g_R = -m\alpha_1 / \alpha_2 (K_0 + mt), \qquad m > 0$$

where m is a constant of integration. But equation 7.20 is precisely equation 7.8. We are, therefore, back where we began. We can now integrate 7.20 to obtain, as before,

7.21
$$R_t = (A + m)^{1/\alpha_2} (K_0 + mt)^{-\alpha_1/\alpha_2},$$

which is equation 7.9. This extraction path, as was noted earlier, is not integrable if $\alpha_2 \geqslant \alpha_1$, for $\int_0^T R_t \, dt \to \infty$ as $T \to \infty$. Therefore, with a finite resource base the percentage rate of change in output must eventually be negative and must eventually be bounded away from zero even when all output is saved. Thus, if $s = 1$ and $\alpha_2 \geqslant \alpha_1$ then $\lim_{t \to \infty} Y_t = 0$. But if $\lim_{t \to \infty} Y_t = 0$ when $s = 1$, then *a fortiori*, $\lim_{t \to \infty} Y_t = 0$ when $s_t \leqslant 1$ (i.e. even if the savings rate is allowed to vary). Moreover, one cannot have $\lim_{t \to \infty} C_t > \lim_{t \to \infty} Y_t$. Hence $\lim_{t \to \infty} C_t = 0$. We conclude that if $\alpha_2 \geqslant \alpha_1$ the exhaustible resource is essential. Doom cannot be averted.

We sum up: if the elasticity of substitution between reproducible capital and exhaustible resources exceeds unity exhaustible resources do not pose a fundamental problem, since they are not even necessary in production. If the elasticity of substitution is less than unity the economy cannot avoid decay. Output (and hence consumption) must eventually decline to zero. The critical form is then the Cobb-Douglas one. The exhaustible resource is necessary for production. But if the elasticity of output with respect to reproducible capital (α_1) exceeds that with respect to the resource input (α_2), the economy can maintain a consumption level that is bounded away from zero by a judicious choice of policy. If, on the other hand, $\alpha_2 \geqslant \alpha_1$, output must eventually decline to zero. The natural resource is therefore essential if $\alpha_2 \geqslant \alpha_1$. It is inessential if $\alpha_1 > \alpha_2$.

This result bearing on consumption possibilities open to an economy with a Cobb–Douglas technology is a striking one.[15] It suggests why, among the class of CES production functions, we ought to be interested in analysing the possibilities offered by the Cobb–Douglas form. It implies that, even in the absence of any technical progress, exhaustible resources do not pose a fundamental problem if $\alpha_1 > \alpha_2$ which is presumably the best educated guess today. From the evidence of factor shares alone one would imagine α_1 to be about four times of α_2.[16]

If a permanently sustainable consumption level is possible it may seem plausible that unbounded consumption is possible as well; provided of course the pace of capital accumulation is sufficiently stiff to begin with. One would suppose that if consumption were to

[15] It was originally established by Solow (1974b).
[16] See the estimates in Nordhaus and Tobin (1972). One would suppose that $\alpha_2 \simeq 0.05$ and $\alpha_1 \simeq 0.20$ from data on factor shares. See Chapter 8 section 1.

be held below $\bar{C}_{max}$ for an initial number of years during which capital is accumulated at a sufficiently fast pace, later generations could enjoy ever-increasing levels of consumption. This is indeed the case. Since this will be demonstrated in Chapter 10, we shall not present such an example here. But it is important to keep such a possibility in mind. For it implies that if $\alpha_1 > \alpha_2$ unlimited growth in output and consumption are a possibility.

There are reasons for supposing that the elasticity of substitution between natural resources and a labour–capital composite exceeds unity (and) or possibly that there has been rather rapid resource saving technical progress in the past.[17] While we have not as yet analysed growth possibilities in the presence of resource-saving technical progress, it is plain that either possibility ensures that exhaustible resources do not pose a fundamental problem.[18] But such empirical estimates must be treated with considerable caution. Rapid resource saving technical progress in the past does not imply that we shall continue to enjoy such technical progress in the future. Certainly, the pace of technical progress over the past has been uneven. One would suppose that a disproportionate fraction of technological improvements during the past 5000 years has been concentrated over the last 300 years or so. Even so it is unwise to rule out the possibility of technical improvements occurring continually over the future. It is certainly dangerous to use past evidence and merely extrapolate into the future. It is at least equally dangerous to ignore past evidence totally and to rule out technical change.[19]

Estimates bearing on substitution possibilities between exhaustible resources and reproducible capital are a good deal harder to make use of. The main analytical novelty that exhaustible resources present in the analysis of growth possibilities open to an economy is that one has to be particularly conscious about the properties of production functions at the 'corners'. The banality of this observation is matched only by the problems this poses in obtaining empirical estimates. Certainly it is possibly that we live in a world where for 'moderate' values of the capital–resource ratio the elasticity of substitution exceeds unity.[20] The point of concern, of course, is its

[17] For such estimates see Nordhaus and Tobin (1972).
[18] We shall analyse production possibilities in the presence of continual technical progress in section (iii) and Chapter 8.
[19] This is, presumably, one of the central criticisms that can be levelled against predictions of the Doomsday writers (e.g. Meadows et al., 1972).
[20] As we noted earlier, these are the indications obtained by Nordhaus and Tobin (1972).

behaviour for large values of the capital–resource ratio (K/R) given that large values cannot be avoided in the long run.[21] In particular, the assumption that the elasticity of substitution is independent of the capital–resource ratio may well be a treacherous one to make. Past evidence may not be a good guide for judging substitution possibilities for large values of K/R.

(iii) *Resource augmenting technical progress:* Disembodied technical progress, the kind that was postulated in section 7(i), is useful for heuristic purposes. The construct is a 'first approximation', so to speak, to capturing the notion of technological discoveries. At first sight the construction is overwhelmingly naive. This is not to say though that empirically we are likely to obtain significantly biased results due to such a postulate.[22] We shall discuss certain aspects of the question of new discoveries in Chapter 16. For the moment it will be useful to analyse formally the effect of continual technical progress on production possibilities. Recall that we began by postulating a production function of the form, $G(K_t, R_t, L, t)$. Suppose, in particular, that one can express the function in the form $G(K_t, R_t f(t), L)$, with $df/dt > 0$. It is customary to say in this case that the economy is enjoying resource augmenting technical progress at the rate $(df/dt)/f(t)$.[23] Suppose for example that $f(t) = \exp(\lambda t)$, $\lambda > 0$. There is, then, continual resource augmenting technical progress at a constant rate. It is clear that the exhaustible resource is inessential. For in this case $Y_t = G(K_t, R_t \exp(\lambda t), L)$ and even though R_t must decline to zero eventually, one can so regulate its decline that $R_t \exp(\lambda t)$ is bounded away from zero. Constant positive consumption is feasible, and this is so even if substitution possibilities are nil.

The Cobb–Douglas economy merits special mention. The point to note is that it is not possible to distinguish between capital, resource, and labour augmenting technical progress. To illustrate this suppose λ_K, λ_R and λ_L are the rates of technical progress associated with each of these factors of production. Then we may write

$$F = \{K_t \exp(\lambda_K t)\}^{\alpha_1} \{R_t \exp(\lambda_R t)\}^{\alpha_2} \{L \exp(\lambda_L t)\}^{1-\alpha_1-\alpha_2}$$

$$= \exp[\{\alpha_1 \lambda_K + \alpha_2 \lambda_R + (1-\alpha_1-\alpha_2)\lambda_L\}_t] K_t^{\alpha_1} R_t^{\alpha_2} L^{1-\alpha_1-\alpha_2}$$

[21] Either this, or one runs down capital sufficiently rapidly as well, in which event consumption trivially goes to zero in the absence of technical progress.

[22] On this, see Solow (1957, 1963).

[23] One can analogously define capital and labour augmenting technical progress. On this, see for example, Hahn and Mathews (1964).

Writing $\lambda = \alpha_1 \lambda_K + \alpha_2 \lambda_R + (1 - \alpha_1 - \alpha_2) \lambda_L$ and, as usual normalizing by setting $L = 1$ we obtain

7.22 $$F = \exp(\lambda t) K_t{}^{\alpha_1} R_t{}^{\alpha_2}.$$

3. Static Efficiency—Economic and Thermodynamic

(i) *Introduction:* Before using the output possibilities formulated in equation 7.2 to develop ideas of dynamic efficiency, it will be instructive to devote a little time to discussing the form that the function $G(.)$ might take in certain cases. Of particular interest is the case when the exhaustible resource under discussion is an energy source. So that the analysis can be conducted diagramatically, let us abstract from the dependence of G on L and t, and write, as earlier,

$$Y_t = G(K_t, R_t)$$

so that output at any date is a function of the available capital stock and the rate of energy input—for this is how we shall interpret R_t here. In this case, thermodynamic considerations can tell us a little about the form that the function $G(.)$ must take. In particular, they tell us that to achieve any given output level, a certain minimum energy input is required. This requirement is determined by the difference between the thermodynamic potential of the finished product, and that of the inputs: under no circumstances can the energy consumed by the process be less than this difference, and indeed it could equal this difference only under highly idealized conditions involving *inter alia* perfect insulation and indefinitely slow transformation of materials.[24] The existence of a minimum energy input needed to achieve a given output level conveys important information about the shape of the isoquants of the function G. In particular, it implies that any isoquant must have an asymptote parallel to the K axis at this minimum value. Diagram 7.2 depicts such a situation: $R_m(Y_i)$ is the minimum energy requirement of output level Y_i, and no amount of capital–energy substitution can take the energy input below this.

The rather precise structure of the isoquant map makes it possible to develop some insights into the relationship between the economic and thermodynamic concepts of efficiency in the use of energy resources, a relationship which has often been the source of confusion. Resources are used efficiently in the thermodynamic sense

[24] For details, see Berry, Heal and Salamon (1978).

if any given output is produced with the minimum possible expenditure of energy. A slightly weaker and more practical concept is that of ε–effectiveness: a broad pattern of resource use is ε–effective in the thermodynamic sense if an output of Y is produced from an energy input that does not exceed $R_m(Y) + \varepsilon$. In terms of Diagram 7.2 an input combination is ε–effective in the thermodynamic sense if it lies at a point on an isoquant whose horizontal distance from the asymptote does not exceed ε. In Diagram 7.3 the regions that are ε-effective for some preassigned ε are shown shaded.

It is now natural to enquire into the circumstances under which economic forces will ensure ε-effective use of energy resources. The answer should be clear from the diagram, which also includes two

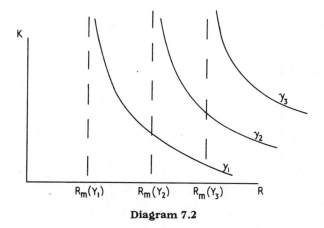

Diagram 7.2

factor-price lines, one (P_1) corresponding to a relatively low, and the other (P_2) to a relatively high, price of energy. Obviously, all that is needed for ε-effectiveness is that the price of energy be 'high enough', in the sense of producing a factor-price line whose slope is at least equal to slope of the relevant isoquant when it enters the region within ε of the asymptote. Of course, this is a very appealing result. The attainment of pure thermodynamic efficiency requires in effect that the production process should be chosen so as to minimize the energy input associated with any output level, without any weight being given to the minimization of the inputs of other factors. Cost minimization will achieve this outcome only if all inputs other than energy are free: but it will almost achieve this outcome (i.e.

attain ε-effectiveness) if the price of energy is 'very high' relative to other prices, so that it is 'more important' to economize on the use of energy than of other factors.

The above analysis makes it extremely easy to draw certain conclusions about the relationship between economic and thermodynamic concepts of efficiency. Of course, by economic efficiency here we mean static Pareto efficiency (see equations 7.1 and 7.2) and a necessary condition for the attainment of Pareto efficiency in a market economy, is that firms are competitive profit maximizers (see Chapter 2). This in turn requires that the cost of any given output be minimized—and this will imply ε-effectiveness in the thermodynamic sense if the price of energy relative to the price of

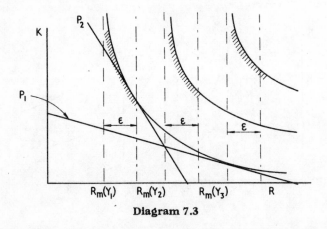

Diagram 7.3

fixed capital is sufficiently high. So economic efficiency implies that energy resources are used ε-effectively in thermodynamic terms provided that the price of energy is sufficiently high. We have already noted that if energy is provided by an exhaustible resource with no substitutes, then its price will rise exponentially over time, and so will eventually exceed any preassigned number, and in particular will become 'sufficiently high' in the above sense. So in the long run a competitive economic system will use energy resources efficiently from the thermodynamic point of view if those resources are limited and irreplaceable.

(ii) *Production functions:* It is natural to enquire into the extent to which the production functions discussed in earlier sections conform to the picture just presented. It is relatively easy to confirm that for $\sigma < 1$, the isoquants of a CES production function in K and R have strictly positive asymptotes in both directions, so that irreducible minimum input levels are specified for any output level. Of course, when one recognizes that for $\sigma = 0$, the CES function has right-angled isoquants, which obviously associate minimum input levels with any output level, this fact is not surprising. The formal analysis is as follows. We have

$$Y = \{\alpha_1 K^{(\sigma-1)/\sigma} + \alpha_2 R^{(\sigma-1)/\sigma} + (1-\alpha_1-\alpha_2)\}^{\sigma/(\sigma-1)}, \quad \text{with } 0 \leqq \sigma < 1.$$

Rearranging,

$$\alpha_2 R^{(\sigma-1)/\sigma} = Y^{(\sigma-1)/\sigma} - (1-\alpha_1-\alpha_2) - \alpha_1 K^{(\sigma-1)/\sigma}$$

Clearly $(\sigma-1)\sigma < 0$, so that as K tends to infinity, the term in K vanishes and the limiting value of R is

$$R_m(Y) = \left\{ \frac{Y^{(\sigma-1)/\sigma}}{\alpha_2} - \frac{(1-\alpha_1-\alpha_2)}{\alpha_2} \right\}^{\sigma/(\sigma-1)}.$$

This defines the R-asymptote for the Y-isoquant, and is strictly positive for $\sigma < 1$. For $\sigma \geqq 1$, however, the isoquants of the CES function have as their asymptotes the axes, so that if amongst the listed inputs is an energy source, the function violates the thermodynamic principles enunciated above.

An interesting consequence of this analysis is the following. Rather obviously, if one uses a two-factor CES production function with energy as one factor, then the elasticity must be less than one. And if one works with a variable elasticity two-factor production function with energy as one factor and if, as seems most likely, the elasticity tends to a limit as the capital–resource ratio increases, then this limit must be less than one. So that even in the variable elasticity case, the economy will behave in the long run as if it were governed by a CES function with $\sigma < 1$. In either case, it is clear that a strictly positive consumption level is not sustainable in the absence of resource-augmenting technical change.

What are the implications of this analysis for the production function $Y = K^{\alpha_1} R^{\alpha_2}$ with which we have chosen to work? Clearly, if K is regarded as capital and R an energy flow, it is unsatisfactory because it violates the thermodynamic constraints outlined. Fortunately, we shall rarely need to interpret K and R as capital and energy: we will usually be prepared to argue that the flow of capital services symbolized by K embodies energy either in the sense that, energy having been used to construct the capital equipment, this is a source of potential energy, or in the sense that a flow of energy is needed to run the equipment so that the provision of a certain energy flow is implied by the provision of a flow of capital services. Interpretations such as these imply that one cannot make deductions about the minimum energy input requirements implied by the production function simply by inspecting its isoquants, even if one of its arguments is a flow of energy additional to that implied by K.

(iii) *Recycling:* While discussing the efficiency of resource use it is worth discussing explicitly, albeit briefly, the possibility of recycling. The impact of this is of course to increase the effective resource base and, although we shall not explicitly mention recycling possibilities after this section, we shall always assume that stocks of exhaustible resources that feature in subsequent analyses are measured in such a way as to include the possibility of augmentation via recycling. It is not difficult to see how recycling expands the effective resource base. Let S be the available resource stock, and suppose that of every unit used a fraction, β, is eventually recycled to form an input into resource-using processes. Then if R_t units are used as inputs in period t, the net resource usage is only $(1-\beta)R_t$ and the resource constraint takes the form

$$\sum_{t=0}^{\infty} (1-\beta)R_t \leqq S \quad \text{or} \quad \sum_{t=0}^{\infty} R_t \leqq S(1-\beta)$$

The effective resource base is thus increased by a factor $1/1-\beta$, and could be made very large by effective recycling policies. As a matter of interest, typical values of β for industrial countries are at present about 0·45 for ferrous metals, and about 0·30 for non-ferrous metals.

The main problem encountered with recycling activities seems to have been the great instability of the price of recycled materials, which has acted as a disincentive to the establishment of recycling capacity. There seem to be several reasons for this instability; partly it is just a reflection of the potential instability of a market system with exhaustible resources discussed in Chapter 6, in this case made slightly more complex by the fact that the range of alternative assets, previously capital goods and resources, is now augmented by the existence of scrap. But there are also problems which are more specific to the nature of the recycling activity—in particular, that the demand for recycled resources is often more volatile than the demand for resources in general, and that the supply of recycled resources is usually rather inelastic. The volatility of demand is usually ascribed to the fact that producers of, for example, steel or paper, who use both new and recycled inputs, tend to buy their new inputs on long-term contracts which oblige them to accept a certain minimum input each month, whatever their needs might be. This practice has developed largely as a response to the uncertainties and absence of markets referred to in Chapters 4 and 6, and in so far as it compensates for these is obviously to be welcomed. However, it does have the unfortunate side-effect of forcing the markets for recycled resources to bear the brunt of the fluctuations in input demand caused by variations in demand for output. As recycled inputs are usually a minority of inputs, this concentration can amplify the fluctuations.

We have now seen why demand for recycled inputs may be unusually volatile: it was also mentioned earlier that their supply is typically inelastic, so that there is little market stabilization by supply responses to price changes. This inelasticity arises because recycled inputs are produced from scrap and their supply is thus governed by the rate of scrapping, which in turn is a function of factors largely distinct from those influencing final demand for the products of the resource using industry.

4. Efficient and Inefficient Programmes

(i) *Definition:* Thus far we have merely investigated production possibilities open to the economy in question. We have been concerned with the class of feasible programmes. But as in the analysis of single period economies (Chapter 2 and 3) not all feasible programmes are of interest. One would like to focus attention on some subset of feasible programmes that command particular attention. This brings us to the notion of efficient programmes.

The issue here is more complicated than it was in Chapter 6. The exhaustible resource is an input in production here. Presumably we are interested in the time profile of final consumption along a given programme. Unlike the account of the matter in Chapter 6, it will not do to look merely at the integral of resource utilization along a programme to judge whether it is intertemporally efficient. Towards this we shall assume, for expository ease, that we are comparing feasible programmes along which C_t is a continuous function of time. In this case it is natural to regard a feasible programme

$[K_t, S_t, R_t, C_t]_0^\infty$ as being intertemporally *inefficient*, if there exists a feasible programme $[\bar{K}_t, \bar{S}_t, \bar{R}_t, \bar{C}_t]_0^\infty$ such that $\bar{C}_t \geqslant C_t$ for all $t \geqslant 0$ and $\bar{C}_t > C_t$ for some t. In such a case we shall say that $[\bar{K}_t, \bar{S}_t, \bar{R}_t, \bar{C}_t]_0^\infty$ *dominates* $[K_t, S_t, R_t, C_t]_0^\infty$. It is then natural to say that a feasible programme is intertemporally *efficient* if it is not inefficient. In general there will be an infinity of efficient programmes (and an infinity of inefficient programmes as well). Like the notion of static efficiency the concept of intertemporal efficiency defines a partial ordering over feasible programmes.

Diagram 7.4 depicts three feasible consumption profiles, christened α, β, γ. Of these, it is supposed that α and β are both efficient.

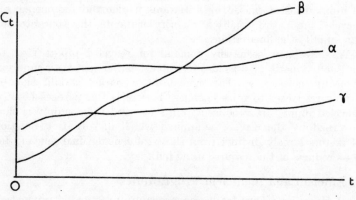

Diagram 7.4

Consequently they intersect at least once. β and γ have been constructed in such a way that they cross each other at least once. Consequently neither dominates the other. But α dominates γ. It follows that γ is intertemporally inefficient.

Since $\partial G/\partial R > 0$ it is clear enough that for a programme to be efficient it is nessary that $\lim_{t \to \infty} S_t = 0$. It is also clear that one can have $S_t \to 0$ along an inefficient programme. The condition, $\lim_{t \to \infty} S_t = 0$, is a necessary but is not a sufficient condition for intertemporal efficiency To see this trivially consider a programme along which $C_t = 0$ for all $t \geqslant 0$ and $\lim_{t \to \infty} S_t = 0$. This is one along which all output is always invested in capital accumulation. Since the economy is capable of positive output (i.e. $G > 0$ for $K, R > 0$) the programme is plainly inefficient. Identifying efficient programmes is no easy matter.[25] It is also worth bearing in mind that the notion of intertemporal efficiency concerns the characteristics of an entire programme. It is a global notion, and one needs to know the entire path and the production possibilities open to the economy in order to judge whether the programme is efficient. This means peering into the distant future. Information about current rates of resource depletion and capital accumulation will not be enough to identify an efficient path though, as we shall see subsequently, they will on occasion be enough to identify inefficient programmes.

These points may appear to be a trifle esoteric. In fact they are not. When we ask whether the formation of a cartel by a group of resource owners leads to too slow a pace of resource extraction (a presumption borrowed from the static theory of pure monopoly), we must have some such notion as intertemporal efficiency in mind. As we shall see subsequently, we usually have something more in mind than mere efficiency. But the point remains that in order to assess current rates of resource depletion and capital accumulation, we are required to peer into the future. Perhaps we should not have expected otherwise.

(ii) *The characterization of efficient programmes:* It was easy enough to define the notion of an efficient programme. It is a different matter altogether to locate conditions that will enable one to judge whether a programme is efficient or not. We noted that intertemporal efficiency is a global notion. The current rates of extraction and capital accumulation do not provide sufficient information to say if the programme being pursued is intertemporally efficient. This is hardly surprising. We are discussing the property of an entire programme. It would be amazing indeed if one could identify the property by looking merely at a single time component of it.

It would be convenient to have a set of simple conditions that are both necessary and sufficient for a programme to be intertemporally efficient. We shall present such a set of conditions here for a simple economy and sketch the arguments that go towards constituting the proof.

[25] The literature discussing conditions that will enable one to identify efficient programmes is gigantic, and was initiated in a classic paper by Malinvaud (1953). For a lucid discussion of the problem see Koopmans (1957) and Bliss (1975). For our purposes here the relevant recent contributions are those of Phelps (1965), Cass (1972) and Majumdar (1974). Conditions characterizing efficient programmes are presented in section 4 (ii).

We take it that a programme $[K_t, S_t, R_t, C_t]_0^\infty$ is feasible if it satisfies equations 7.3 and 7.4. As usual, we shall assume that G is strictly increasing, strictly concave in K, R and L and that it is twice continuously differentiable. To present the conditions in a simple manner it will prove useful to suppose in addition that $\lim_{K \to 0} G_K = \lim_{R \to 0} G_R = \infty$. This is certainly satisfied by a Cobb–Douglas form. It is also satisfied if G is of the form 7.5 and $\sigma > 1$. As usual, we take it that $L = 1$. Finally, for ease of exposition we shall restrict our attention to programmes along which K_t, R_t, $C_t > 0$ for all $t > 0$.

Imagine to begin with that time is measured in discrete intervals of length θ. Subsequently we shall take the limit as $\theta \to 0$. Along a programme $[K_t, S_t, R_t, C_t]_0^\infty$, $C_t\theta$ and $R_t\theta$ by convention represent the levels of consumption and resource utilization during the interval $(t, t+\theta)$. Let $[\bar{K}_t, \bar{S}_t, \bar{R}_t, \bar{C}_t]_0^\infty$ denote a feasible programme where $\bar{K}_t$, $\bar{R}_t$, $\bar{C}_t > 0$ for all $t \geqslant 0$. Consider two adjacent intervals of time, $(t, t+\theta)$ and $(t+\theta, t+2\theta)$. The idea now is to see if, by keeping the programme entirely unchanged at all intervals other than these two, one cannot reap a higher level of consumption during $(t, t+\theta)$ without reducing the level of consumption during $(t+\theta, t+2\theta)$. If one can, the original programme must be inefficient. Since we are contemplating a possible resource reallocation over the two adjacent time intervals only, we need to limit ourselves to the discrete time analogue of equation 7.3 only at these intervals.

They read as

7.23
$$\begin{cases} C_t\theta + K_{t+\theta} - K_t = G(K_t, R_t, t)\theta \\ C_{t+\theta}\theta + K_{t+2\theta} - K_{t+\theta} = G(K_{t+\theta}, R_{t+\theta}, t+\theta)\theta. \end{cases}$$

Write $I_t\theta = K_{t+\theta} - K_t$ and $I_{t+\theta}\theta = K_{t+2\theta} - K_{t+\theta}$ for the investment carried out during the two adjacent intervals. If $[\bar{K}_t, \bar{S}_t, \bar{R}_t, \bar{C}_t]_0^\infty$ is intertemporally efficient it will not be possible to increase C_t while holding $\bar{C}_{t+\theta}$, $\bar{K}_t$, $\bar{K}_{t+2\theta}$, $\bar{S}_t$ and $\bar{S}_{t+2\theta}$ fixed in 7.23. Thus, conducting a variation on the first equation in 7.23 gives

7.24
$$\Delta C_t + \Delta I_t = G_{R_t}\Delta R_t.$$

Similarly conducting a variation on the second equation in 7.23 yields

7.25
$$\Delta I_{t+\theta} = G_{K_{t+\theta}}\Delta K_{t+\theta} + G_{R_{t+\theta}}\Delta R_{t+\theta}.$$

Since $\bar{K}_t$ and $\bar{K}_{t+2\theta}$ are held fixed in this variation, $\Delta I_t + \Delta I_{t+\theta} = 0$. Likewise, since $\bar{S}_t$ and $\bar{S}_{t+2\theta}$ are held fixed, $\Delta R_t + \Delta R_{t+\theta} = 0$. Adding equations 7.24 and 7.25 then yields

$$7.26 \qquad \Delta C_t = (G_{R_t} - G_{R_{t+\theta}})\Delta R_t + G_{K_{t+\theta}}\Delta K_{t+\theta}.$$

Since by assumption $[\bar{K}_t, \bar{S}_t, \bar{R}_t, \bar{C}_t]_0^\infty$ is efficient, the proposed variation can yield no extra consumption during $(t, t+\theta)$. Hence $\Delta C_t = 0$. Since $\bar{K}_t$ is given, one has $\theta\Delta I_t = \Delta K_{t+\theta}$. Using these two facts and equation 7.24 in equation 7.26 then implies

$$7.27 \qquad G_{K_{t+\theta}} = (G_{R_{t+\theta}} - G_{R_t})/G_{R_t}\theta.$$

Now in order that $[K_t, S_t, R_t, C_t]_0^\infty$ is intertemporally efficient it is necessary that it satisfies equation 7.27 for every adjacent pair of intervals. For the foregoing argument has shown that, if it fails to satisfy the condition at any adjacent pair of intervals, it is possible to alter the rates of capital accumulation and resource depletion in such a manner that consumption is increased at one of the intervals, leaving unchanged the level of consumption at all the other intervals. If we now take the limit as $\theta \to 0$ equation 7.27 reduces to the form:

$$7.28 \qquad G_{K_t} = \frac{\dfrac{\mathrm{d}}{\mathrm{d}t}(G_{R_t})}{G_{R_t}} \qquad \text{for all } t \geqslant 0.$$

This looks suspiciously familiar. It is. Even though the equation has been arrived at from purely technological considerations it can be given a ready interpretation. Let the stock of the composite commodity serve as the numeraire. Under competitive conditions G_{K_t} denotes the spot rental rate earned by owners of the capital stock. Since by assumption the composite good does not deteriorate G_{K_t} is also the own rate of return on this good (see equation 4.7). Furthermore, under competitive conditions G_{R_t} is the spot price of the exhaustible resource. Consequently under such conditions 7.28 is the arbitrage equation 4.16, an identification that goes a long way towards establishing the manner in which an efficient programme can be decentralized. This is a matter that was discussed at length in the timeless worlds of Chapters 2 and 3 and is one that will be taken up again in Chapters 8 and 10.

It has been established that for a programme to be intertemporally efficient it must satisfy the Hotelling Rule. It is not a sufficient condition though, for one problem is that it is possible for condition 7.28 to be satisfied along a programme that does not exhaust the entire stock of the resource, and we have already argued that this would be inefficient.

It is worthwhile discussing more formally how this can come about despite the implicit optimization undertaken in arriving at equation 7.28. The critical point to note is that the condition has been arrived at by making a *local* perturbation on the base programme $[\bar{K}_t, \bar{S}_t, \bar{R}_t, \bar{C}_t]_0^\infty$; in particular, perturbing only two adjacent intervals at a time. But for each pair of intervals $(t, t+\theta)$ and $(t+\theta, t+2\theta)$, and t no matter how large, there is an infinity of future to come. Given this, one cannot tell from the fact that 7.28 holds whether all the resource stock will be utilized in infinite time. To put it more vividly, suppose a fraction of the initial stock, S_0, is thrown away. Now consider an intertemporally efficient programme with the reduced initial stock. It will satisfy equation 7.28. But in terms of the original stock, S_0, the programme is not intertemporally efficient. Consequently, equation 7.28 does not represent a condition sufficient for efficiency. The argument that has been used in arriving at equation 7.28 demonstrates that a feasible programme satisfying it is not dominated by any feasible programme that is identical to it for large enough t. In other words, a feasible programme satisfying 7.28 is efficient with respect to the set of all feasible programmes that are eventually identical to it. We shall refer to such a programme as *locally efficient*; 'local', because the comparison is being made among programmes that are eventually identical to one another. Equation 7.28 is necessary and sufficient for local efficiency. Plainly, an efficient programme is locally efficient. Moreover, we have argued that a locally efficient programme can be intertemporally *in*efficient since, for example, it is consistent with a fraction of the resource stock never being utilized.

Therefore we need something in addition to condition 7.28 to guarantee intertemporal efficiency. We have laboured these points at some length here because it suggests that at least for some simple economies this 'something' is the condition

7.29
$$\lim_{t \to \infty} S_t = 0.$$

This, in fact, can be shown to be the case for the Cobb–Douglas economy. If the production function is of the form 7.22 (with $\lambda \geqslant 0$) then a necessary *and* sufficient set of conditions for a programme to be intertemporally efficient is that it satisfies conditions 7.28 and 7.29.

This is an extremely convenient characterization of efficient programmes. It is intuitively appealing and easy to use. It differs somewhat from the characterization of efficient programmes for economies with durable capital goods and no exhaustible resources. For such economies it is legitimate to identify intertemporal inefficiency with a systematic 'over-accumulation' of capital assets.[26] Roughly speaking, inefficiency is such economies is due to too high a rate of investment in the long run; in the sense that the high rate of consumption made possible by such accumulation are never taken advantage of. For our Cobb–Douglas economy the story can be told in the following manner: if a feasible programme satisfying 7.28 is intertemporally inefficient, it is due to an *under-utilization* of the exhaustible resource. If a programme satisfying 7.28 in addition fully utilizes the resource, it is intertemporally efficient. Capital over-accumulation cannot take place along a programme satisfying conditions 7.28 and 7.29.[27]

It will prove instructive, by way of illustration, to use the characterization we have discussed on a programme defined by 7.12. Recall that we postulated an absence of technical progress there. Assume $\alpha_1 > \alpha_2$. Recall as well that programmes defined by 7.12 satisfy condition 7.29. Finally, recall that $G_K = \alpha_1 G/K$ and $G_R = \alpha_2 G/R$. Now

$$\frac{\dot{G}_{R_t}}{G_{R_t}} = \frac{\dot{G}_t}{G_t} - \frac{\dot{R}_t}{R_t}.$$

[26] See for example, Koopmans (1957), Phelps (1965), Cass and Yaari (1966) Cass (1972) and Majumdar (1974).

[27] If the production function is not Cobb–Douglas, conditions 7.28 and 7.29 will not in general prove sufficient for intertemporal efficiency, since the two together do not rule out capital over-accumulation. It is ruled out if the present value of the durable capital stock tends to zero in the long run. Formally, the condition reads

7.29' $\lim\limits_{t \to \infty} K_t \exp\left(- \int\limits_0^t F_{K\tau}\, d\tau \right) = 0.$

Here $F_{K\tau}$ is the shadow interest rate at τ (see section 4). Condition 7.29' is a technical one and we shall not go into it here. (See the references in the previous footnote.) But intuitively it ensures that the capital stock is not accumulated 'unnecessarily'. The point about the Cobb–Douglas economy is that if the programme satisfies 7.28 it necessarily satisfies 7.29' as well. Therefore we need not use 7.29'. On all this, see Mitra (1978).

Since $G = Y_t = \bar{C} + m$, it follows that $\dot{G}_{Rt}/G_{Rt} = -\dot{R}_t/R_t$. Using equation 7.8 one has;

7.30
$$\frac{\dot{G}_{R_t}}{G_{R_t}} = \frac{m\alpha_1(K_0 + mt)^{-1}}{\alpha_2}.$$

Furthermore, on using 7.12 again one obtains

7.31
$$G_K = \alpha_1(\bar{C} + m)(K_0 + mt)^{-1}.$$

In order that equation 7.28 is satisfied one has from equation 7.30 and 7.31 that

7.32
$$\alpha_2 = \frac{m}{\bar{C} + m}$$

But $m/(\bar{C} + m)$ is the savings ratio along the programme defined by 7.12. What condition 7.32 states is that in order that a programme defined by 7.12 is intertemporally efficient it is necessary that this constant savings ratio be equal to α_2. It follows that the programme sustaining the constant consumption flow $\bar{C}_{\max}$ (equation 7.14) is intertemporally efficient. In fact of all the programmes defined by 7.12 this is the only one that satisfies the Hotelling Rule.

5. The Social Rate of Return on Investment

(i) *Definition:* A central organizing idea in capital theory is the notion of the *social rate of return on investment*.[28] As we shall see presently it is intimately related to the notion of own rates of interest (Chapter 4, section 3) and consequently to the structure of intertemporal prices. However, the merit of working with the concept is that one does not need to presuppose a price guided economy It is founded directly on technological possibilities. In what follows we shall find it immensely useful. We define it first. The concept can be readily generalized and most emphatically does not rely on the simple characterization of the economy presented in section 1. For smooth technologies the idea, in more general settings, is to consider the marginal rates of transformation between various consumption goods over adjacent intervals of time. The concept attains a sharpness if one postulates a single *consumption* good. Heterogeneity of capital goods presents no problems. For continuity of exposition,

[28] For a powerful demonstration of the usefulness of the concept, see Solow (1963). See also Koopmans (1965) and Arrow and Kurz (1970).

however, we persist in studying the simple economy described in section 1 (see equations 7.3, 7.4). Let $(K_t, S_t, R_t, C_t)_0^\infty$ denote an intertemporally efficient programme, where $K_t, C_t, R_t > 0$ for all $t \geq 0$. Call this the base programme. The idea is to look at a feasible neighbouring programme with a view to determining the return yielded by a unit of extra investment along the base programme. For ease of exposition suppose that time is measured in discrete intervals, of length θ. Consider two adjacent intervals of time, $(t, t+\theta)$ and $(t+\theta, t+2\theta)$. Formally, the aim is to keep the programme unchanged at all intervals other than these two and to calculate the maximum increase in consumption obtainable during $(t+\theta, t+2\theta)$ if the rate of consumption during $(t, t+\theta)$ is reduced by a unit.[29] Thus denote by $\theta \Delta C_t$ the decrease in consumption undertaken during $(t, t+\theta)$ and by $\theta \Delta C_{t+\theta}$ the maximum feasible increase in consumption during the next period. By assumption, $\Delta C_t < 0$ and $\Delta C_{t+\theta} \geq 0$. One then defines *the social rate of return on investment* as

$$\frac{1}{\theta}\left(-\frac{\Delta C_{t+\theta}}{\Delta C_t} - 1\right).$$

It is the own rate of return on the homogeneous commodity. This certainly squares with one's intuitive notion of the rate of return of investment. If by saving at an extra rate of £1 of consumption during $(t, t+\theta)$ the economy can be provided with at most an *extra* £1.25 rate of consumption during $(t+\theta, t+2\theta)$ without altering the rate of consumption during any other interval one would like to say that between $(t, t+\theta)$ and $(t+\theta, t+2\theta)$ the society can earn a per period return of 25% on its marginal investment.[30] Stating it in more traditional terminology, the social return on investment between $(t, t+\theta)$ and $(t+\theta, t+2\theta)$ is the marginal rate of transformation between consumption during the two intervals less unity.

Several points need to be emphasized. First, the rate of return on investment is a pure number per unit of time. Second, it is defined via a variation on a base programme, so that in discussing the notion one must specify the efficient programme along which the variation is being contemplated. Third, there is no reason for supposing that the rate of return is independent of time, and in fact

[29] Readers will note that the programme can be kept unchanged at all intervals other than these two because of the smoothness of the technology postulated here.
[30] Such a figure is not entirely hypothetical. See, for example, Solow (1963, Chapter III).

there is every reason for supposing that it will depend on t. Fourth, if the base programme chosen is not an efficient one (a case we have ruled out by definition) the 'social rate of return on investment' is, strictly speaking, infinity. This is so because one can choose ΔC_t vanishingly small without correspondingly having to reduce $\Delta C_{t+\theta}$ to zero. This too makes sense. If society is pursuing an inefficient programme, one can enjoy an increase in consumption at some date without having to sacrifice any consumption at any other date. In such a situation there is no 'trade-off' between consumption at two dates. The notion of such a trade-off arises only for perturbations around an efficient programme. It is this trade-off that is central to the notion of the rate of return on investment.

This is about as far as one can usefully go without specifying the technological possibilities in some detail. It would prove very useful if we could obtain a simple characterization of the notion in terms of technological parameters. We turn to this now.

(ii) *A characterization*: Let $[K_t, S_t, R_t, C_t]_0^\infty$ be an intertemporally efficient programme. As we are contemplating a possible resource reallocation over two adjacent time intervals only, we need only to limit ourselves to the two equations designated 7.23. Thus K_t, $K_{t+2\theta}, S_t, S_{t+2\theta}$ are held fixed for this perturbation. As earlier, denote by $I_t\theta = K_{t+\theta} - K_t$ and $I_{t+\theta}\theta = K_{t+2\theta} - K_{t+\theta}$ the levels of investment carried out during the two adjacent intervals. Consequently $\Delta I_t + \Delta I_{t+\theta} = 0$. Furthermore $\Delta R_t + \Delta R_{t+\theta} = 0$. Now conduct a variation on the two equations in 7.23 to obtain

7.33 $$\Delta C_t + \Delta I_t = G_{R_t}\Delta R_t$$

and

7.34 $$\Delta C_{t+\theta} + \Delta I_{t+\theta} = G_{K_{t+\theta}}\Delta K_{t+\theta} + G_{R_{t+\theta}}\Delta R_{t+\theta}.$$

Adding equations 7.33 and 7.34 yields

7.35 $$\Delta C_t + \Delta C_{t+\theta} = (G_{R_t} - G_{R_{t+\theta}})\Delta R_t + G_{R_{t+\theta}}\Delta K_{t+\theta}.$$

Since K_t is by assumption held fixed, $\theta\Delta I_t = \Delta K_{t+\theta}$. Using this and equation 7.33 in equation 7.35 implies that

7.36 $$\frac{(\Delta C_t + \Delta C_{t+\theta})}{\theta} = (G_{R_t} - G_{R_{t+\theta}})\Delta R_t/\theta + G_{K_{t+\theta}}(G_{R_t}\Delta R_t - \Delta C_t).$$

Since the base programme is by assumption intertemporally efficient equation 7.27 must hold. Therefore equation 7.36 reduces to

$$7.37 \qquad -\left(\frac{\Delta C_{t+\theta}}{\Delta C_t}+1\right)\!\Big/\theta = G_{K_{t+\theta}}$$

It follows that the social return on investment between the periods $(t, t+\theta)$ and $(t+\theta, t+2\theta)$ along the base programme $[K_t, S_t, R_t, C_t]_0^\infty$ is $G_{K_{t+\theta}}$, the marginal product of the durable capital good at $t+\theta$. If we now move to continuous time by taking the limit $\theta \to 0$ and denote by r_t the social rate of return on investment at t, then 7.37 reduces to the form

$$7.38 \qquad r_t = G_{K_t}.$$

This is not really a surprising result. But it is a very useful result to have. It implies that the social rate of return on investment does not depend in a complicated way on the entire base programme. Specifically, it implies that if a programme $[K_t, S_t, R_t, C_t]_0^\infty$ is intertemporally efficient, the rate of return at t during the pursuit of this programme requires our knowledge only of K_t and R_t. We do not require the knowledge of the level of the reproducible asset and the rate of resource utilization at any other instant. In short, the structure of production postulated in our model is simple enough to allow us to calculate the social rate of return at any date t by using only 'local' information—that is, values of K and R at t only.

There is, finally, a small point to be disposed of. The identification of the social rate of return on investment with the marginal product of the stock of the durable composite commodity (equation 7.38) holds only when the base programme is intertemporally efficient. As we have remarked, given our smooth technology the social rate of return on investment is strictly speaking infinity if the perturbation is undertaken around an inefficient programme, even though the marginal product of the stock of the durable asset is a well-defined, finite number (G_k). Now if, as we shall see, under certain institutional environments (specifically, under competitive conditions) G_{K_t} is in fact the return that private owners earn on the stock of the durable asset it implies that, if a programme is intertemporally inefficient, there is a divergence between the social rate of return and the private rate of return. But in our simple model with disembodied technical change, if a programme is intertemporally efficient there will be no divergence between the private and the social rates of return—provided, of course, competitive conditions hold.[31]

Let us now perform an illustrative calculation. Suppose that for some reason or other society chooses the constant consumption programme given in equation 7.14.[32] We have already established that this consumption path is intertemporally efficient. Since $Y_t = K_t^{\alpha_1} R_t^{\alpha_2}$, it follows that

7.39
$$\frac{\partial Y_t}{\partial K_t} = \alpha_1 K_t^{\alpha_1 - 1} R_t^{\alpha_2}$$

Using 7.12 in equation 7.39 now implies that

7.40
$$\frac{\partial Y_t}{\partial K_t} = F_{Kt} = \alpha_1 (\bar{C}_{\max} + m)(K_0 + mt)^{-1}$$

where $\bar{C}_{\max}$ is given in 7.14. But the point about 7.40 is that it demonstrates that the social rate of return on investment during the pursuit of this programme is falling over time, and that it tends to zero in the very long run. This is not too surprising. By assumption there is no technical progress. The supply of labour is by assumption held constant. The rate of resource utilization, as a matter of plain arithmetic, declines to zero. The stock of reproducible capital along the programme goes to infinity. There is therefore continual capital deepening, both in terms of the capital-labour ratio, and the capital-resource ratio. It ought then to be expected that the rate of return will decline over time.

6. Conclusions

To sum up:

(1) The fact that certain exhaustible resources are necessary for production is in itself not a reason for alarm. Two offsetting forces come readily to mind: capital accumulation and technical progress. But even in the absence of technical progress it is possible to sustain

[31] In certain models of technical progress, e.g. one where there is 'learning by doing' (see Arrow, 1962), there are genuine externalities driving a wedge between private and social rates of return. Here, no such complication arises.

[32] In Chapters 9 and 10 we shall discuss the kinds of argument that may be brought to bear in justifying a programme such as 7.14.

a positive level of aggregate output and consumption if there are sufficient substitution possibilities between reproducible capital goods and exhaustible resources.

(2) An example of (1) is the case of an economy with constant population and a Cobb–Douglas technology. If the elasticity of output with respect to reproducible capital (α_1), exceeds the elasticity of output with respect to exhaustible resources (α_2), the economy is capable of a sustained level of output and consumption per head. If, on the other hand, $\alpha_2 \geqslant \alpha_1$, consumption per head must necessarily decline to zero in the long run in the absence of technical progress.

(3) If the elasticity of substitution between reproducible capital and exhaustible resources exceeds unity such resources are not necessary for production. Resources do not pose any essential problem. If the elasticity of substitution is less than unity, then in the absence of technical progress output and consumption must necessarily decline to zero.

(4) If there is a constant positive rate of resource augmenting technical progress (no matter how slow the rate) the qualifications in (2) and (3) do not apply. The economy is capable of sustained consumption even if the elasticity of substitution between reproducible capital goods and exhaustible resources is nil.

(5) Characterizing intertemporally efficient programmes is a difficult task. For the simple Cobb–Douglas economy a set of necessary and sufficient conditions for a feasible programme to be intertemporally efficient is (i) that the percentage rate of change of the marginal product of the exhaustible resource equals the marginal product of the reproducible capital good and (ii) that the stock of the resource is fully utilized.

Notes on Chapter 7

The re-examination of capital theory with the inclusion of exhaustible natural resources is of surprisingly recent origin. It is this task that was undertaken in Dasgupta and Heal (1974), Solow (1974b), Stiglitz (1974a, b), Ingham and Simmonds (1974), Dasgupta (1974a), Weinstein and Zeckhauser (1974) and Mitra (1978). Our discussion of the issues raised in this and the following chapter has relied heavily on each of these contributions.

It is perhaps surprising on reflection that a vigorous debate over the World Models (as presented by, say, Forrester (1971)) could have been undertaken in the absence of an exploration of the kinds of circumstances in which a sustained level of output and consumption is possible. One strand of objections that have been raised against the technological possibilities envisaged by the various World Models is precisely this (see, for example, Nordhaus (1973) and

Kay and Mirrlees (1975)). Nevertheless, it is probably true that until very recently we did not possess a categorization of simple technological environments in which exhaustible resources are essential. One would have supposed that this would be a necessary preliminary investigation. It is for this reason that we have given prominence to this range of questions (see section 2). Our presentation of the subject has relied especially on the contributions of Solow (1974b).

The reader may well question the relevance of our discussion of consumption possibilities; given that we have made three highly simplifying assumptions, viz. (i) that fixed capital does not depreciate, (ii) that there are no extraction costs; and (iii) that the production function is of the CES variety. We comment on each in turn.

Consider the Cobb–Douglas economy, with $\alpha_1 > \alpha_2$. It is simple to show that if depreciation follows the radioactive law (i.e. a fixed fraction of existing stock of fixed capital falls apart at each instant) the exhaustible resource is essential. Consumption must eventually fall to zero (this is assuming no technical change). Radioactive decay is therefore a positive embarrassment to our discussion in the text. But then it is highly unrealistic as well. Economists continually postulate it in theoretical models because of the analytical advantages it affords. There is little else to commend it.

If instead, fixed capital decays linearly in time (the straight-line method of depreciation) all the claims in the text regarding essential and inessential resources go through. As another variant, suppose depreciation is proportional to gross output, Y. Again, our claims go through. The exposition would have been a more awkward had we assumed either of the latter two. We have therefore avoided depreciation.

For the purposes of this chapter, postulating an absence of extraction costs proves not to be an embarrassment. A pretty general formulation is one where the resource stock is assumed to be spread over different fields, and where a field is characterized by a constant unit cost of extraction. Only a little reflection is required to realize that this will not affect our claims regarding production conditions in which resources are essential (or inessential). On this, see Solow and Wan, Jr. (1976).

Our having restricted the discussion to CES production functions may well cause disquiet among readers. But it is useful to see first what the discussion illuminates. Suppose in fact that the elasticity of substitution is a function of the resource–capital. ratio Thus, $\sigma = \sigma(R/K)$. We are interested in those programmes along which $R_t/K_t \to 0$. Write $z_t = R_t/K_t$. Now suppose that $\lim_{z \to 0} \inf \sigma(z) > 1$. Then obviously the resource is inessential. Likewise (in the absence of technical progress), the resource is essential if $\lim_{z \to 0} \sup \sigma(z) < 1$. If, on the other hand, $\lim_{z \to 0} \inf \sigma(z) = 1$, and $\alpha_1 > \alpha_2$ the resource is inessential. Very roughly speaking, it is the asymptotic property of the elasticity of substitution (as $z \to 0$) that is of concern. Restriction to the CES is therefore not misleading for our purposes here.

CHAPTER 8

RESOURCE DEPLETION AND CAPITAL ACCUMULATION IN A COMPETITIVE ECONOMY

1. The Perfect Myopic Foresight Case

(i) *Formulation of the problem:* The discussion in the previous chapter was designed to explore the consumption possibilities open to a closed economy making use of exhaustible natural resources as inputs in production. It is time that we imposed a specific institutional structure on the economy and analysed its implications. The environment most thoroughly explored is undoubtedly the competitive case. We shall analyse such an economy here.

A difficulty that arises in tracking down the implications of a competitive private ownership economy is the ambiguity in its definition when time is introduced explicitly into the construct and the horizon is assumed to be infinite. We noted an important feature of this in Chapter 6 section 3. There we found that it was possible to have a sequence (in our continuous time example, a continuum) of momentary equilibria along which price expectations are fulfilled at each instant despite an absence of a complete set of forward markets.[1] Further modifications suggest themselves. For example, an absence of forward markets may result in price expectations not being realized. The story is difficult to unravel even when it is assumed that all individuals at a given date are identical and have the same 'point expectations'—viz. that expectations about future prices are held with certainty. This is so since there are various accounts that one can offer about how expectations are formed.

Let us suppose for the moment that efficient instantaneous output is given by equation 7.2: (i.e. $Y_t = G(K_t, R_t, L, t)$). We continue to

---

[1] That is, such a sequence of momentary equilibria was found not necessarily to be an intertemporal competitive equilibrium. It came as no surprise, then, that for our example excepting for one (i.e. the one that represented the unique intertemporal competitive equilibrium) such sequences were either intertemporally inefficient or not feasible.

assume that G is strictly concave and homogeneous of degree unity in K, R and L. Furthermore, assume that G is twice continuously differentiable in all its variables. We shall find it convenient to work with spot prices. Towards this choose the price of unit stock of the composite commodity as the numeraire at each instant. For our model economy this leaves one with three spot prices: the rental rate on the durable capital good, the price of the exhaustible resource, and the wage rate. Denote these by r_t, p_t and w_t. We take it that each of these three factor markets is perfectly competitive at each date. At time t, K_t is the stock of the durable commodity and L is the quantity of labour, both of which we shall assume are inelastically supplied. At an equilibrium allocation at t the exhaustible resource will be extracted and supplied up to the rate R_t where

8.1 $$\frac{\partial G}{\partial K_t}=r_t; \quad \frac{\partial G}{\partial R_t}=p_t; \quad \text{and} \quad \frac{\partial G}{\partial L}=w_t.$$

Given 8.1 and the fact that G is homogeneous of degree unity in K_t, R_t, and L one notes that

8.2 $$G(K_t, R_t, L, t)=r_t K_t+p_t R_t+w_t L.$$

All this is straightforward. That under competitive conditions the marginal product of the durable capital good is the private rate of return (the rental rate on the capital good) is surely an expected result. But the discussion in Chapter 7 section 5(ii) tells us that, if competitive conditions yield an efficient programme, this rental rate is also the social rate of return on investment.

Now, the LHS of equation 8.2 represents the gross national product at t. The RHS denotes the gross national income. We need now to give an account of the composition of gross national expenditure—that is, the allocation of output between consumption and investment. Towards this, we shall make the simplest of hypotheses, that at each date a constant proportion $s(0<s<1)$ of gross output is invested in fixed capital. Let I_t denote gross investment in fixed capital.[2] Using equation 7.3 one has then that

8.3 $$I_t=\dot{K}_t=sY_t=sG(K_t, R_t, L, t)$$

---

[2] Since the composite good does not deteriorate it denotes net investment in fixed capital as well.

and consequently, that

8.4 $$C_t = (1-s)G(K_t, R_t, L, t).$$

Such a consumption function as 8.4 has been widely used in descriptive models of economic growth. It has also been questioned seriously as an appropriate hypothesis for the economies one knows.[3] We shall make the assumption embodied in 8.4 not because of its plausibility, but because it will allow us to discuss, in the simplest manner possible, the issues that we shall wish to raise.

We have not completed our description of the economy. There are two physical assets: the exhaustible resource and the durable composite commodity. We have postulated that they are privately owned. Assume for simplicity that extraction costs are nil. The market value of the physical assets at t is then $K_t + p_t S_t$. We have yet to determine the condition that describes the equilibrium in the asset market. Suppose then that this asset market is competitive at each date. Then individuals must expect to receive the same return from holding their wealth in the form of the durable capital good as in the form of the natural resource.[4] Suppose now that individuals at a given date have identical beliefs. At t individuals observe the price of the resource to be p_t. Suppose finally that the representative individual at t expects the price to change at the percentage rate $\dot{p}_t^e/p_t$. This then is the universally expected rate of return on holding wealth in the form of the natural resource.[5] Now the private rate of return on holding wealth in the form of the durable capital good is r_t. This is known at t. It follows then that for the asset market to equilibriate

8.5 $$\dot{p}_t^e/p_t = r_t.[6]$$

Let us first analyse a sequence of momentary equilibria along which expectations are realized at each instant. Now, expectations will certainly be realized at each instant if the sequence of momentary equilibria is established by means of a complete set of forward

---

[3] For reasoned assessments of such questions see Farrell (1959). For alternative hypotheses about savings behaviour in the literature on economic growth see, for example, Kaldor (1957), Passinetti (1962), Uzawa (1960) and Shell *et al.* (1969).

[4] By assumption there is no uncertainty. Expectations are firmly believed in.

[5] Cf. Chapter 6 section 1(ii).

[6] Cf. equation 6.5. This is the arbitrage equation.

markets (i.e. if the sequence is an intertemporal competitive equilibrium). As in Chapter 6 section 1(ii) we are postulating something
'weaker' here; that individuals have correct beliefs at each instant
about the rate of capital gains enjoyed by a natural resource,
despite the possible absence of a complete set of forward markets.
This distinction is worth recalling; the distinction between a *sequence
of momentary equilibria with perfect foresight* and an *intertemporal
competitive equilibrium*. We have argued that the latter implies the
former and we shall note again presently that the former does not
imply the latter. Now, since $\dot{p}_t/p_t$ is by definition the realized rate
of return on holding the natural resource as an asset, and since we
are hypothesizing that individuals have correct expectations at
each date,

8.6 $$\dot{p}_t^e/p_t = \dot{p}_t/p_t.^7$$

Our description of a momentary equilibrium (short period
equilibrium) at t is now complete. It is defined by equations 8.1–8.4
and equations 8.5 and 8.6. It remains for us to trace out the implications of a sequence (continuum) of such momentary equilibria.
Now a glance at the conditions describing a momentary equilibrium
tells one that the initial price–rental ratio, p_0/r_0, is indeterminate in
our construction. Presumably the initial price–rental ratio is a
consequence of the past history of the economy. But the construction by itself cannot tell us whether one price–rental ratio is more
likely than another. This suggests that the long-run behaviour of
the economy may well be indeterminate. And indeed, in analysing
the behaviour of a sequence of momentary equilibria in Chapter 6,
we noted this to be the case. There it was supposed that the competitive rental rate earned on the numeraire asset, r, was constant
and given exogenously. It was then easy enough to show that if the
initial price–rental ratio is 'high' such a sequence of momentary
equilibria traces out a programme along which a fraction of the
original stock of the resource never gets extracted. Likewise, if the
initial price–rental ratio is 'low' the programme is in fact not
feasible, in that the resource gets depleted in finite time even though
there is positive demand for it at the quoted price. In other words,
there is a precise sense in which almost all of the programmes that
fulfil myopic expectations are either intertemporally inefficient or
are not feasible.

[7] In short, we are postulating rational expectations; exactly as in Chapter
6 section 1(ii).

In our earlier example it was an easy enough matter to see intuitively why it is so likely that such a sequence of self-fulfilling motions leads the economy astray, i.e. why market failure is so likely a possibility. Matters are a good deal more complicated for the present example. Here, the rental rate, r_t, is endogenous to the system. Nevertheless the behaviour of a sequence of momentary equilibria with perfect foresight is similar to the behaviour that we observed in the earlier example. Since the intuitive reasoning is similar, we shall not repeat it. But a formal demonstration is required. This will enable us to check that the result arrived at in Chapter 6 did not depend in some way on the partial equilibrium nature of the analysis conducted there.

(ii) *The formal argument*:[8] In order to carry out the analysis it will prove helpful to impose some further structure on production possibilities. The analysis is particularly simple if we were to suppose that the production function is Cobb–Douglas in form. This is just as well. The discussion in Chapter 7 section 2 above made it clear as to why the Cobb–Douglas form is of particular interest for the natural resource problem.

To contrast production possibilities with those available in the economy analysed in Chapter 7 section 2 we shall postulate the existence of continual technical progress. Suppose then that

$$8.7 \qquad \left. \begin{array}{c} Y_t = G(K_t, R_t, L, t) = \exp(\lambda t) K_t{}^{\alpha_1} R_t{}^{\alpha_2} L^{1-\alpha_1-\alpha_2} \\ \text{where } \lambda > 0,\ \alpha_1,\ \alpha_2,\ 1-\alpha_1-\alpha_2 > 0. \end{array} \right\}$$

Using 8.7 in 8.1 implies that

$$8.8 \qquad\qquad\qquad r_t K_t / Y_t = \alpha_1$$

$$8.9 \qquad\qquad\qquad p_t R_t / Y_t = \alpha_2$$

$$8.10 \qquad\qquad\qquad w_t L / Y_t = 1 - \alpha_1 - \alpha_2.$$

This is obvious. α_1, α_2 and $1-\alpha_1-\alpha_2$ represent the elasticities of output with respect to the three factors of production, K_t, R_t and L respectively. Consequently, they represent the share of national income accruing to the factors under competitive conditions. For the Cobb–Douglas case these shares are constant.

As usual, we may as well normalize and set $L=1$. It remains to make use of 8.7 in the conditions representing momentary equilibrium. In fact, in order to investigate the dynamics of the economy

---

[8] The reader ought to be warned that this section is more technical than the others.

under review it will prove useful to work with the output–capital ratio Y_t/K_t and the 'resource–utilization ratio', R_t/S_t.

As before, let $x_t = Y_t/K_t$. Write $y_t = R_t/S_t$. And as before let g_z denote the percentage rate of change $\dot{z}_t/z_t$ of any variable z_t. Our strategy will be to obtain equations describing the intertemporal behaviour of x_t and y_t. Now clearly

8.11 $$g_x = g_Y - g_K,$$

and

8.12 $$g_y = g_R - g_S = g_R + y_t$$

(since $g_S = \dot{S}_t/S_t = -R_t/S_t$). From equation 8.3 one has

8.13 $$g_K = s Y_t/K_t = s x_t$$

Now differentiate 8.7 logarithmically to obtain

8.14 $$g_Y = \lambda + \alpha_1 g_K + \alpha_2 g_R .$$

From 8.8 and 8.9 it follows that

8.15 $$p_t = \frac{\alpha_2 Y_t}{R_t}$$

and that

8.16 $$r_t = \alpha_1 x_t.$$

Using equations 8.15 and 8.16 and combining equations 8.5 and 8.6 then yields

8.17 $$\dot{p}_t/p_t = g_p = g_Y - g_R = \alpha_1 x_t$$

Now use equation 8.13 in equation 8.14 and solve equations 8.15 and 8.17 for g_Y and g_R to obtain

8.18 $$g_Y = \frac{\lambda + \alpha_1 x_t(s - \alpha_2)}{1 - \alpha_2}$$

and

8.19 $$g_R = \frac{\lambda - \alpha_1 x_t(1 - s)}{1 - \alpha_2}.$$

As a final step use equations 8.13, 8.18 and 8.19 in equations 8.11 and 8.12 to obtain

8.20
$$\dot{x}_t = x_t \left[\frac{\lambda}{1-\alpha_2} - \left\{ \frac{\alpha_1\alpha_2 + s(1-\alpha_1-\alpha_2)}{1-\alpha_2} \right\} x_t \right],$$

8.21
$$\dot{y}_t = y_t \left\{ y_t - \frac{\alpha_1(1-s)}{1-\alpha_2} x_t + \frac{\lambda}{1-\alpha_2} \right\}.$$

8.20 and 8.21 are a pair of autonomous non-linear differential equations in x_t and y_t, and our task is to describe in general terms their solution paths.[9] Notice first that feasibility requires that x_t, $y_t \geqslant 0$.[10] We can then restrict our attention to the non-negative orthant defined by x and y. A point $(\bar{x}, \bar{y})$ on the non-negative orthant at which $\dot{x}_t = \dot{y}_t = 0$ is referred to as a *stationary point*. The terminology is obvious. If $x_t = \bar{x}$ and $y_t = \bar{y}$ then x_t and y_t do not change in value over time. A glance at equations 8.20 and 8.21 suggests that $x_t = y_t = 0$ is such a stationary point. We shall see presently that we have no reason to be interested in this stationary point. It is one at which $R_t = 0$ (and hence output, $Y_t = 0$). For the moment we restrict our attention to points at which x_t, $y_t > 0$.

Equation 8.20 is rather simple to analyse, for y_t does not enter into it. Quite clearly

$$\dot{x}_t \gtreqless 0 \text{ as } x_t \lesseqgtr \frac{\lambda}{\alpha_1\alpha_2 + s(1-\alpha_1-\alpha_2)}.$$

In short, along any feasible path, x_t converges to the value x^*, where

8.23
$$x^* = \frac{\lambda}{\alpha_1\alpha_2 + s(1-\alpha_1-\alpha_2)} > 0.^{[11]}$$

Equation 8.21 is more complicated, because the intertemporal behaviour of y_t depends on both x_t and y_t. It does not look as though it is amenable to an explicit integration. But for our purpose this

[9] For an excellent introductory treatment of such differential equations, see Hurewicz (1958) and Hirsch and Smale (1974).

[10] It is also not feasible for the economy to have $x_t > 0$ and $y_t = 0$.

[11] Indeed this can be seen rather readily if we were to integrate equation 8.20 directly.

does not really matter. We are interested in the qualitative properties of the solutions of equations 8.20 and 8.21. This we can investigate successfully without recourse to an explicit integration. Now it is obvious that

8.24 $$\dot{y}_t \gtreqless 0 \text{ as } y_t \gtreqless \frac{\alpha_1(1-s)x_t}{1-\alpha_2} - \frac{\lambda}{1-\alpha_2}.$$

In particular, $\dot{y}_t = 0$ along the locus

8.25 $$y = \frac{\alpha_1(1-s)x - \lambda}{1-\alpha_2}.$$

Diagram 8.1 brings together the various possible solution paths of the pair of equations 8.20 and 8.21. It should be noted that time is not explicitly depicted in the diagram.[12] It follows that from the diagram alone we shall be unable to discuss the 'speed' with which each of the two variables is changing with time. But here we are not concerned with the speed with which these variables change in their values, but rather with their general characteristics. In Diagram 8.1 a typical 'phase path' is the locus that is followed by the pair (x_t, y_t) if the economy were to commence on the path. At any point (x_t, y_t) at which either $\dot{x}_t \neq 0$ or $\dot{y}_t \neq 0$, the slope of the phase path passing through the point is given by $dy/dx = \dot{y}_t/\dot{x}_t$, where the numerator and the denominator of the RHS are given by equations 8.20 and 8.21. It is clear that only one phase path can pass through such a point. It is also immediate that there is a phase path passing through each point. The arrow associated with a given path shows the direction of movement along the path.

The first question to ask is whether the vertical straight line given by equation 8.23 intersects the straight line given by equation 8.25 on the non-negative orthant. It is readily checked that the answer is 'yes' if, and only if, $s \leqslant \alpha_1$. We shall not be concerned with describing the dynamics of our economy for every conceivable set of parametric values. The interesting case is certainly the one where $s \leqslant \alpha_1$.[13] In fact we suppose that $s < \alpha_1$. In Diagram 8.1 the straight

---

[12] The diagram depicts what is referred to as the phase portrait of the pair of equations. It is called a *phase diagram*. See, for example, Hurewicz (1958) and Hirsch and Smale (1974).

[13] It is also the plausible case. From estimates of factor shares one would imagine that $\alpha_1 \simeq 0.20$. An average net savings rate less than 20% seems a reasonable hypothesis.

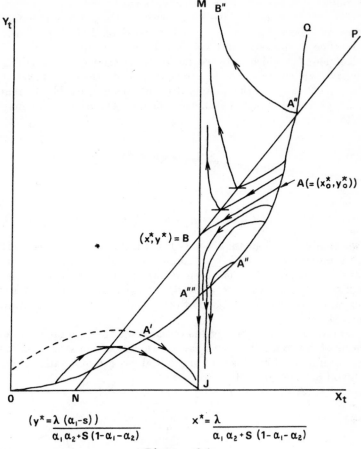

$$\left(y^* = \frac{\lambda\,(\alpha_1 - s)}{\alpha_1 \alpha_2 + S(1 - \alpha_1 - \alpha_2)}\right) \qquad x^* = \frac{\lambda}{\alpha_1 \alpha_2 + S(1 - \alpha_1 - \alpha_2)}$$

Diagram 8.1

line NP depicts equation 8.25 and the vertical line JM depicts equation 8.23. They intersect at B at which

$$x^* = \frac{\lambda}{\alpha_1 \alpha_2 + s(1 - \alpha_1 - \alpha_2)}$$

and

$$y^* = \frac{\lambda(\alpha_1 - s)}{\alpha_1 \alpha_2 + s(1 - \alpha_1 - \alpha_2)}.$$

It follows that $B = (x^*, y^*)$ is also a stationary point of the system.

Consider Diagram 8.1. To begin with, recall that the economy possesses stocks K_0 and S_0 at the initial date. But they do not determine x_0 uniquely, since this last depends on the initial rate of extraction, R_0, which is by no means predetermined by anything we have said so far about the economy. But it does mean that not every point (x, y) on the non-negative orthant is a feasible starting point for the economy. We confirm this now. On using 8.7 we may write

$$8.26 \qquad x_0 = \frac{Y_0}{K_0} = K_0^{\alpha_1-1}R_0^{\alpha_2} = K_0^{\alpha_1-1}S_0^{\alpha_2}y_0^{\alpha_2}.$$

In other words,

$$8.27 \qquad y_0 = x_0^{1/\alpha_1}K_0^{(1-\alpha_1)/\alpha_2}S_0^{-1}.$$

Equation 8.27 defines the locus OQ in Diagram 8.1. The economy must initiate from some point on it. Various configurations are possible. Diagram 8.1 has been drawn on the assumption that $K_0^{(1-\alpha_1)/\alpha_2}S_0^{-1}$ is 'small' so that OQ intersects NP at two distinct points, one of which is to the north-east and the other to the south-west of B.[14]

So far, the arbitrariness of the initial point has been discussed in terms of real quantities. One can as well make the same point in terms of the arbitrariness of the initial price–rental ratio. From 8.8 and 8.9 one can write

$$8.28 \qquad p_0/r_0 = \frac{\alpha_2 K_0}{\alpha_1 R_0}$$

Equation 8.28 is important. It makes the point that while the initial price–rental ratio is arbitrary for the economy under review, once it is given the future of the economy is determined. A given value of p_0/r_0 implies a unique value of R_0 (equation 8.28) and hence a unique value of x_0 (equation 8.26) and, consequently, a unique value of y_0 (equation 8.27). In short, an initial value of the price–rental 'determines' the initial point on the locus OQ in Diagram 8.1, and

---

[14] The reader can easily construct the remaining configurations and describe the possible outcomes, all of which are similar to the possibilities that we shall describe.

the economy subsequently follows the phase path emanating from this point.[15]

Now suppose that $x_0 > x^*$ but that the initial point, A″, lies to the south-east of B. Since $x_0 > x^*$ we have $\dot{x}_0 < 0$. Since by assumption A″ lies 'below' NP we have $\dot{y}_0 < 0$. Thus $dy_0/dx_0 > 0$. Indeed, so long as the economy lies to the south-east of B we shall have $\dot{x}_t < 0$ and $\dot{y}_t < 0$. But the path emanating from A″ will always remain to the south-east of B, because as the economy approaches JM, $\dot{x}_t$ tends to zero; moreover the economy will never reach the horizontal axis OX, since $\dot{y}_t \to 0$ as $y_t \to 0$ (equation 8.21). The general shape will then be A″J. We have now noted that the point $J = (x^*, 0)$ is also a stationary point of the system. But unlike the other two stationary points, it is not a feasible point of the system. Indeed, no point on the horizontal axis, with the exception of the origin, is feasible. For $y = 0$ implies that $R = 0$. But if $R = 0$ then $Y = 0$; in which case $x = 0$. Nevertheless, the point J, while not feasible, is a stationary point and, in fact, locally stable. A phase path such as A″J will tend asymptotically to J, but the economy will never get there.

Next suppose that the economy initiates at A′ (with $x_0 < x^*$) and lying 'below' NP). Then $\dot{x}_0 > 0$ and $\dot{y}_0 < 0$ so that $dy_0/dx_0 < 0$, and indeed $\dot{x}_t > 0$ and $\dot{y}_t < 0$ throughout such a path for the reason that the economy will always remain within the triangle NBJ. The general shape will be as A′J. The economy will tend asymptotically to J, but will never actually get there. The dashed curve leading to A′ is the backward continuation of the phase path through A′. It would have been a feasible path had the economy not been constrained to initiate on OQ. It still merits attention. Since phase paths cannot intersect at any non-stationary point the shape of the dashed curve implies that all initial points to the south-west of A′ on OQ will eventually lead the economy asymptotically to J.

Suppose finally that the economy initiates at a point such as A‴. Since $x_0 > x^*$ we have $\dot{x}_0 < 0$ (see 8.22 and 8.21), and since A‴ lies 'above' NP we have $\dot{y}_0 > 0$ (see 8.24). Consequently $dy_0/dx_0 < 0$. Moreover, so long as the economy lies within the region enclosed by BM and BP, $dy_t/dx_t < 0$ with $\dot{x}_t < 0$ and $\dot{y}_t > 0$. Furthermore, as the

---

[15] We are qualifying the word 'determines' advisedly. There is no causal implication here. We are describing the initial momentary equilibrium at which certain economic variables are related to one another in a certain way. It is as legitimate to say that the initial capital–output ratio (x_0^{-1}) 'determines' the initial price–rental ratio (via equations 8.26 and 8.28) as it is to say that the initial price–rental ratio 'determines' the initial capital–output ratio. In fact both are illegitimate expressions. Hence the qualification.

economy approaches JM the absolute value of $\dot{x}_t$ gets smaller, so that $|dy_t/dx_t| \to \infty$. This explains the shape of the phase path A″B″.

We have established that if x_0 is 'large' the phase path emanating from OQ will have the property $x_t \to x^*$ and $y_t \to \infty$. We have also argued that if $x_0 \leqslant x^*$ the phase path will have the property $x_t \to x^*$ and $y_t \to 0$. In the former case the economy tends in the long run to diverge away from B and move 'upwards'; and in the latter the economy diverges away from B and moves 'downwards'. If we were now to use the fact that phase paths are continuously distributed on the phase plane it would follow that there is a point $A(=(x_0^*, y_0^*))$ on OQ with the property that the phase path emanating from A tends to B, with $\dot{x}_t, \dot{y}_t < 0$ all along the path. It is a technical matter to demonstrate that there is in fact only one such point A with this property. This can be demonstrated, though we shall not go into it here.[16]

To sum up: if the initial point is A the economy will tend in the long run to the stationary point $(x^*, y^*) = B$. If the initial point is 'below' A the economy will tend asymptotically to the stationary point J. If the initial point lies 'above' A the economy will pursue a path along which $x_t \to x^*$ and $y_t \to \infty$.

The foregoing conclusion looks suspiciously like the conclusion that we arrived at earlier (Chapter 6 section 1(iii)) regarding the evolution of a sequence of momentary equilibria along which agents have perfect foresight in the short run. It will now come as no surprise to note that phase paths emanating from points 'below' A support programmes which, although locally efficient, are intertemporally inefficient; and that phase paths emanating from points 'above' A support programmes that are feasible only for a finite period.

Consider the latter case first. Along such a path $x_t \to x^*$ and $y_t \to \infty$.

It then follows from equation 8.21 that for any positive ε, no matter how small, there is a large enough t for which

8.29
$$\dot{y}_t/y_t \geqslant (y_t - a + \varepsilon) > 0,$$

where

$$a = \frac{\alpha_1(1-s)x^* - \lambda}{(1-\alpha_2)}.$$

[16] See Dasgupta (1974a) and Stiglitz (1974a).

But condition 8.29 implies that we may as well analyse the solution of the equation

8.30
$$\frac{\dot{y}_t}{y_t} = y_t - a > 0.$$

Integrating equation 8.30 yields $y_t = a\{1 - b \exp(at)\}$, with $b > 0$. But then y_t becomes infinite in finite time. Since by definition $y_t = R_t/S_t$ this implies that the resource stock is exhausted in finite time. This contradicts the condition $x_t \to x^* > 0$. Such a path is inconsistent with feasibility requirements in the long run. The initial price–rental ratio can equilibriate the initial date's factor market only if the rate of extraction, R_0, is 'too high' (relative to its value at A). Subsequently, the workings of the arbitrage condition ensures that the price–rental ratio is always too low. There is nothing in the dynamics of the economy to 'correct' the initial under-pricing of the natural resource. The rate of extraction is too rapid. The resource is exhausted in finite time.

But this cannot be the entire story. As the resource stock nears exhaustion at a rapid rate along such an errant path, one would presume that resource owners will see the exhaustion coming and will come to realize that their asset will become very valuable in the near future, given its impending exhaustion. Presumably then they will wish to restrict the rate of extraction and wish to hoard, bidding up the flow price of the resource as a consequence. In other words, one imagines that there must be some such corrective mechanism swerving the economy away from the original errant path that we have been analysing. But such a corrective mechanism supposes that price expectations are based on stocks of the natural resource— a supposition which, while being highly plausible, is nevertheless far removed from the short-run perfect foresight story we have been investigating.

Paths initiating from a point above A are inconsistent with the hypotheses of our construction. What of paths that initiate at A or at points 'below' A. Recall that $x_t \to x^*$. The path originating at A tends to B; while the remaining paths tend to J. Such paths are of course feasible. Moreover both output and consumption along such paths increase without limit. To confirm this, note that since $x_t > 0$ one has $y_t > 0$. From equation 8.3 this implies that $\dot{K}_t > 0$. Therefore either K_t tends to a finite positive limit or is unbounded. In fact a finite limit is not possible. If it were, then by 8.3 one will have

$Y_t \to 0$. But this would imply that $x_t \to 0$. This contradicts the fact that $x_t \to x^* > 0$. Hence $K_t \to \infty$ along such a path. This implies that $Y_t \to \infty$. From equation 8.4 this means that $C_t \to \infty$. There is an unlimited increase in consumption along such paths despite the presence of an exhaustible resource which is necessary for production. But unlike the account of Chapter 7 section 2 we have not assumed that $\alpha_1 > \alpha_2$. We have not needed to, because unlike the technology analysed there we have postulated continual technical progress. The existence of a positive exponential rate of technical progress, no matter how small the rate, is sufficient to allow output and consumption to increase without bound even if $\alpha_2 \geqslant \alpha_1$.

If the economy were to initiate at A or at a point on OQ below A consumption is unbounded in the long run. There is no doomsday. The world survives. How then do we distinguish between the characteristics of the path AB and the remaining paths such as A″J? The feature that distinguishes them is that along AB the economy utilizes fully its resource stock while along a path such as A″J a fraction of the stock is never utilized.[17] In short, a path such as A″J although locally efficient, is intertemporally inefficient. The point is that the initial price–rental ratio associated with a point on OQ below A is 'too high' (relative to its value at A). The fact that the arbitrage equation ensures that the price rises at the rate of interest implies in effect that the price of the resource always remains 'too high'. A high initial price of the resource leads traders to expect the price to be still higher in the near future, an expectation that is fulfilled. At each date then the demand for the flow of the resource into production is 'too low'. There are always some resource owners who continue to delay extracting the resource and merely enjoy the capital gains associated with it. This delay goes on endlessly; a part of the stock never gets extracted. There is nothing in the workings of the economy that will 'correct' the initial excessive price.

[17] Along AB we know $y_t \to y^* > 0$. Since $R_t \to 0$, it follows that $S_t \to 0$. To show that paths initiating at points below A are inefficient is more difficult. As an example, let the point on OQ lie to the south-east of B, for example the point A″. Denote by an asterisk values of variables along AB and by a caret, values of variables along A″J. One wants to show that $R_t^* > \hat{R}_t$ for all $t \geqslant 0$. Now $y_0^* > \hat{y}_0$. And by construction $\hat{y}_t < y^*$ for all t. Clearly then $R_0^* > \hat{R}_0$. Suppose that at some date T, $R_T^* < \hat{R}_T$. This implies that there is a date t, with $0 < t < T$ such that $R_t^* = \hat{R}_t$ and $\hat{g}_{Rt} > g_{Rt}^*$. Let τ be the first such date. From equation 8.19 note that $g_{R\tau}^* < \hat{g}_{R\tau}$ implies $x_\tau^* > \hat{x}_\tau$. But if $R_t^* > \hat{R}_t$ for $0 < t < \tau$, then $K_\tau^* \geqslant \hat{K}_\tau$. Consequently $x_\tau^* \leqslant \hat{x}_\tau$. This is a contradiction. It follows that τ does not exist. In other words, $R_t^* > \hat{R}_t$ for all $t > 0$. Since $S_t^* \to 0$, this implies that $\hat{S}_t$ tends to a positive limit.

The foregoing arguments suggest that we should be particularly interested in the path AB and, consequently, the unstable long-run stationary point $B = (x^*, y^*)$. It is appropriate to refer to it as being unstable because the slightest disturbance to the economy during its passage along AB will cause it to diverge away from B in the long run. We have yet to argue that AB supports an intertemporal competitive equilibrium. We do this here in a rough and ready manner. To begin with, the single feature that distinguishes the private ownership economy being analysed here from the private ownership economy of Chapter 2 is that in the present construct the number of agents and the number of commodities is infinite. This is not a trivial difference. But despite it one can show that an intertemporal competitive equilibrium exists for the economy under review here, and that it is efficient.[18] Now, an intertemporal competitive equilibrium, we have argued earlier, must be a sequence (here a continuum) of momentary equilibria along which expectations are always fulfilled. Its evolution must then be one of the paths in Diagram 8.1. It cannot obviously be a path such as A‴B‴ since the latter is not feasible. It cannot be a path such as A″J since the latter is intertemporally inefficient. There remains AB which must, therefore, support an intertemporal equilibrium. Consequently, AB supports an efficient programme. We conclude that there is a unique intertemporal competitive equilibrium for the private ownership economy that we have been analysing.[19]

The reason why one ought to be interested in the behaviour of 'sequence economies' such as the one we have just analysed stems from the observation that a complete set of forward markets does not exist in the world as we know it. In order not to prejudice the arguments in advance we have supposed a 'frictionless' economy; one along which factor markets are always perfectly competitive and where there is perfect foresight in the short run. Moreover, the capital market is assumed competitive at each date, so that the arbitrage condition (equation 8.5) holds at all times. Despite these assumptions (or perhaps *because* of them!) the long-run outcome is indeterminate. It is indeterminate because, to put it one way, the initial price–rental ratio (p_0/r_0) is indeterminate in our construct. The myopic rule (i.e. the arbitrage equation) cannot on its own

[18] On this see, for example, Bewley (1973).
[19] For examples of a multiplicity of intertemporal competitive equilibria (literally a continuum of them in fact) for models of economic growth, see Shell *et al.* (1969) and Mirrlees (1975).

specify this. Now as we remarked earlier, presumably the initial price–rental ratio is a consequence of the past history of the economy. But an analysis of past history can at most 'explain' why the initial price–rental ratio is what it is. There is nothing in the construction to tell us whether one initial price–rental ratio is more likely than another.

What moral is to be drawn from this? The moral, or so it would seem, is that the claim that a decentralized competitive environment will ensure an efficient utilization of natural resources is a very tenuous one. To make the claim true one will need to hypothesize the existence of a complete set of forward markets, from the initial date to infinity. Alternatively, one will need to move away from advocating a completely decentralized environment and to establish an agency or unit calculating the intertemporal price structure supporting the path AB and legislating such a price structure.[20] Short of this there is no guarantee whatsoever that a competitive environment will not result in the economy pursuing an errant programme.

(iii) *Long-run characteristics of the intertemporal competitive equilibrium:* Since the path AB supports an intertemporal competitive equilibrium it is worth discussing the behaviour of economic variables along it. Recall that by construction $\dot{x}_t < 0$ and $\dot{y}_t < 0$ along AB. Both the output–capital ratio and the resource-utilization ratio decline monotonically to their long-run values x^*, y^*. Using 8.16 it follows that r_t declines monotonically to $\alpha_1 x^*$. The rate of return on investment tends to a positive value. This is so despite continual capital deepening, both in terms of the capital–resource ratio and the capital–labour ratio. The reason why the rate of return does not tend to zero despite this is the presence of technical progress. Unlimited technical progress ensures that investment is always productive. Furthermore, on using 8.9 and 8.10 it is seen that both the price–rental ratio and the wage–rental ratio increase without bound; which is to say that $p_t \to \infty$ and $w_t \to \infty$. To be more precise, p_t increases in the long run at the constant percentage rate $\alpha_1 x^*$.[21] Now p_t is the spot price of the resource. Since the own rate of interest on the composite good is F_{Kt}, the present value price of the resource is $p_t \exp(-\int_0^t F_{K\tau} d\tau)$ (see equation 4.6). But $F_{Kt} = \dot{p}_t / p_t$. Hence the

[20] This last is often referred to as 'indicative planning'. For a lucid exposition of the logic of indicative planning, see Meade (1971).

[21] The analysis of Chapter 6 section 1(iii) can then be viewed as a special case of the present analysis; one where $r = \alpha_1 x^*$.

present value price is $p_t \exp(\log p_0/p_t) = p_0$, which, as we noted earlier, is another way of expressing Hotelling's Rule (see Chapter 4 section 1).

What of the long-run rate of growth of output and consumption? Since $x_t \to x^* > 0$, $g_K \simeq g_Y$ for large enough t. Moreover, since $y_t \to y^* > 0$, $g_y \to 0$ and hence $g_R \simeq g_S = -y^*$ for large t. Now use equation 8.14 to deduce that

$$g_Y \to \frac{\lambda - \alpha_2 y^*}{1 - \alpha_1} = \frac{\lambda s (1 - \alpha_1)}{\{\alpha_1 \alpha_2 + s(1 - \alpha_1 - \alpha_2)\}^2}.$$

Since the savings rate is constant this is also the long-run rate of growth of consumption and investment.

Let us use some illustrative numbers to investigate the orders of magnitude involved. Let the rate of technical progress be 1.5% per unit of time (annum), i.e. $\lambda = .015$.[22] Furthermore, assume that $\alpha_1 = 0.20$, $\alpha_2 = 0.05$. It follows that the share of national income accruing to labour $(1 - \alpha_1 - \alpha_2)$ is 75%. Finally suppose $s = 0.10$. It follows that $x^* \simeq 0.17$ and $y^* \simeq 0.017$. Consequently $r_t \to 0.034$ and $g_Y = g_C \to 0.015$. In other words, the long-run output–capital ratio is 0.17 and the rate of return on investment declines to about 3.4%. The long-run rate of resource utilization is 0.017. Along the path 1.7% of the existing stock will be extracted at each date in the distant future, with output and consumption both growing approximately at the rate of 1.5% per annum.

(iv) *The terms of trade along an intertemporal equilibrium:* Our analysis of both this section and that of Chapter 6 section 1(ii) has confirmed that if extraction costs are negligible and there is no uncertainty, the price of exhaustible resources will rise under competitive conditions at the rate of interest. This implies that along an intertemporal competitive equilibrium (AB) the price of exhaustible resources (e.g. minerals and fossil fuels) will not maintain parity with the price of manufactured goods (e.g. machinery). To put it another way, the 'terms of trade' will move against manufactured commodities. An absence of such declining terms of trade should alert us to the possibility of market failure. All this has, of course, a bearing on practical matters. Consider, for example, the claim that the terms of trade have over a period of years gone against nations that are much involved in the supply of primary

[22] Such a figure is by no means arbitrary. This is an estimate arrived at for the US economy during the period 1909–49 in a classic paper by Solow (1957).

products, and the implied complaint of serious market failure.[23] In order to counter this complaint it will not do merely to analyse the statistics carefully and show that the claim is wrong, that in fact the prices of primary commodities have maintained parity with the price of manufactured goods. The maintenance of parity is itself an indication of market failure, unless it is shown that extraction costs have fallen dramatically during this period, or that reserves are very large.[24] Of course, it is perfectly in order to analyse the statistics, demonstrate that the prices of primary commodities have maintained parity with those of manufactured goods, and to say that if this is an evidence of market failure then so much the worse for competitive markets. However, quite often those who wish to demonstrate the maintenance of parity with a view to countering the charges of market failure are precisely those who at the same time desire to defend the market mechanism. Our formal analysis has shown that it is this last position that is illegitimate.

2. The Measurement of Net National Product

The gross national product (GNP) of the economy we have been analysing is Y_t. Along AB, $Y_t \to \infty$. But what of net national product (NNP)? It has been supposed that the durable composite commodity does not deteriorate. This might suggest that in such a world there is no difference between GNP and NNP. And indeed, if one follows the procedures usually pursued by national income statisticians in computing NNP there *will* be no difference. But this would seem to be a mistake. The natural exhaustible resource is also an asset which is 'depreciated' as the resource is extracted and utilized in production. The concept of NNP in a closed economy, or so it would appear, is designed to capture the sum of the value of consumption flow and the value of the change in the stocks of assets that the economy possesses. Since the output flow of the composite commodity is the numeraire and since by assumption it can be used indifferently between consumption and investment, the NNP in our economy at t is $C_t + \dot{K}_t + p_t \dot{S}_t$. It follows then that

$$\text{NNP} = Y_t - p_t R_t.$$

Using equation 8.15 it follows that $\text{NNP} = (1 - \alpha_2) Y_t$. Consequently $\text{NNP} \to \infty$ along AB. But the point is that if the value of the annual

[23] 'Market failure' is, of course, a soft way of describing the complaint that is often levelled.

[24] See Chapter 6 section 4 for these two qualifications, and the discussion in Chapter 15.

rate of depletion is not deducted from Y_t, annual NNP will be over-estimated by $\alpha_2/(1-\alpha_2)$ per cent. Likewise, for the notion of net national income (NNI). Gross national income (GNI) in our economy is, as we noted in equation 7.2, $r_tK_t+p_tR_t+w_tL$. By our foregoing argument NNI $= r_tK_t+w_tL$. In other words, the *net* income accruing to owners of the natural resource is nil. Their gross income is of course the value of the rate of extraction. But they lose as much by depreciating their stock by just that amount. To put it another way, in computing the NNI it would be appropriate to ignore the earnings of the owners of exhaustible resources.

This raises several issues. At this point we shall not delve into the question of whether the notion of NNP captures in some sense the 'well-being' of an economy; nor indeed into the question of what precisely NNI figures are designed to illuminate. We shall go into such questions in Chapters 9 and 10. Here we shall present a stark example to indicate that NNI, if appropriately measured, can give seemingly paradoxical results.

Imagine a society whose sole asset is an exhaustible resource which serves as the single consumption good.[25] As there is no production we shall refer to this as a 'cake-eating' society. To show that such an economy is a special case of our general production economy introduced in Chapter 7 section 1 we need to remind ourselves that a cake-eating economy can be depicted as one in which $Y_t = G(K_t, R_t, L, t) = R_t$. From equation 7.3 one obtains then that

$$8.31 \qquad\qquad C_t + \dot{K}_t = R_t$$

Since there is no difference between the two assets K_t and S_t in this economy, we may as well suppose $K_t = 0$. From equation 8.31 it then follows that GNP $= C_t$, and of course $p_t = \partial G/\partial R_t = 1$. Thus NNP $= C_t + \dot{S}_t = C_t - R_t = 0$. Now C_t may be very high for a time. But in the international NNI league table this economy will look ghastly. It will be the 'poorest' of nations, despite its current affluence.

The moral of this example would appear to be as follows. Consumption in the cake-eating society must eventually decline to zero. It is then just possible that the appropriate measure of NNP at any given date is designed to indicate something about long-run possibilities open to the economy.[26] But this is not how NNP

---

[25] A small oil-rich country purchasing consumer goods from abroad could provide such an example. For illuminating discussions of the notion of NNP in a dynamic context see Samuelson (1965) and Weitzman (1976).

[26] On this, see Samuelson (1965) and Weitzman (1976).

figures are usually interpreted. One tends often to remark that a nation is currently poor if its NNP is low. This last is obviously a mistake if NNP is correctly measured. Our cake-eating society, by consuming its wealth, may well be doing very well for itself currently despite a zero level of NNP. Or to put it another way, the fact that the current rate of consumption of an economy is high is not an evidence of a high rate of NNP. For production economies with no exhaustible resources such as identification is not too misleading since, after all, one cannot 'consume' factories. But the point takes on a sharp form when exhaustible resources enter into the picture.

3. Imperfect Short-run Foresight

(i) *Introduction:* The analysis in section 1 was concerned with the evolution of a competitive economy in which agents forecast immediate future prices accurately. In our continuous time formulation it was tantamount to forecasting accurately the rate of change of the price of natural resources (condition 8.6). As a description of the world as we know it this will obviously not do. In the absence of forward markets, price predictions do go wrong. Indeed, in our complete capital model where the rate of return on investment is not constant over time and is endogenous to the system, such price predictions can easily go awry. Unlike the economy of Chapter 6 section 1(iii) there is no constant exogenous interest rate to which the rate of capital gains on exhaustible resources can be anchored. It is then important to dispense with the assumption of short-run perfect foresight. This is not an easy matter. Any reasonable construction will take into account the fact that the future is uncertain, and that different agents view the future differently. Indeed, it is by no means clear what one means when one says that 'traders' expect the future prices of resources to be one thing rather than another. To state it in another way, it is not clear how one aggregates individual expectations. Here we shall side-step this entire range of problems and suppose that agents have identical expectations and in particular that they have 'point expectations'; which is to say that they believe that there is no uncertainty about future prices. They are fully confident of their forecast. Consequently they act on that belief. If the belief is not realized they revise their beliefs and again act on them. But it is supposed at each stage that the current belief is held with certainty. What remains then is to find plausible hypotheses of such revision of expectations. Various possibilities suggest themselves, and we shall discuss two such hypotheses. Modelling imperfect foresight is not for the weak-hearted.

(ii) *Adaptive expectations with price signals*: Write $g_p = \dot{p}_t/p_t$ and $g_p^e = \dot{p}_t^e/p_t$ as the realized and expected rates of capital gains on the exhaustible resource. If expectations are not fulfilled the two will not be the same. A formulation that has been much discussed in the literature regarding the manner in which expectations are revised goes by the name *adaptive expectations.*[27] For our problem, adaptive expectations on the rate of change of p_t reads as

$$8.32 \qquad \dot{g}_p^e = \mu(g_p - g_p^e), \qquad \mu > 0.$$

μ, a constant, can be regarded as the speed of adjustment. Notice that the assumption embodied in 8.32 is that the expected rate and growth of price is an exponentially weighted average of past realized growth rates of prices. The idea is simple enough: if the realized rate of capital gains exceeds (falls short of) the expected rate of capital gains the expected rate of capital gains is revised upwards (downwards). Indeed, the assumption of short-run perfect foresight (condition 8.6) could be regarded as a limiting case of condition 8.32; the case where $\mu = \infty$ (i.e. the speed of adjustment is infinite).

We replace condition 8.6 by 8.32 and suppose that otherwise the economic environment is the same as the one presented in section 1; that is, the asset market and the factor markets are always in equilibrium. Let us continue to work with the output–capital ratio, x, and the resource utilization ratio, y. Routine calculation then yields

$$8.33 \qquad \dot{x}_t = x_t \left\{ \frac{\lambda - (\alpha_1\alpha_2 + s(1 - \alpha_1 - \alpha_2))x_t}{1 - \alpha_2 + \alpha_1\alpha_2 x_t/\mu} \right\}$$

and

$$8.34 \qquad \dot{y}_t = y_t \left\{ y_t - \frac{\alpha_1(1 - s)x_t + \{\alpha_1 s x_t^2(\alpha_1 - s)\}\mu - \lambda(1 - \alpha_1 x_t)/\mu}{1 - \alpha_2 + \alpha_1\alpha_2 x_t/\mu} \right\}^{28}$$

An analysis of equations 8.33 and 8.34 is similar to the analysis of equations 8.20 and 8.21. As in that earlier analysis we shall take

[27] See, for example, Nerlove and Arrow (1958). The discussion on adaptive expectation that follows is based on Dasgupta (1974a) and Stiglitz (1974a). For an analysis of the logic underlying adaptive expectations, see Burmeister and Turnovsky (1976).

[28] The derivation of equations 8.33 and 8.34 parallels that of the equations 8.20 and 8.21. Consequently we omit it here. Note that 8.33 and 8.34 reduce to 8.20 and 8.21 if $\mu = \infty$.

it that $s < \alpha_1$. In this case, it is readily checked that other than the origin there are two stationary points of equations 8.33 and 8.34; the points B and J of Diagram 8.1. Diagram 8.2 presents the phase portrait of the pair of differential equations. It differs from Diagram 8.1 in one important respect; the locus (NP) of points along which $\dot{y} = 0$ is not a straight line but has the general shape depicted in

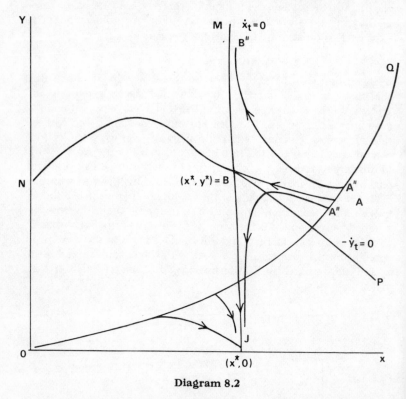

Diagram 8.2

Diagram 8.2. Other than this the diagram is self-explanatory and the properties of the programme along the various phase paths parallel the properties of the programmes along the paths of Diagram 8.1; except in one manner. And it is this. Since μ is by assumption finite none of the programmes under consideration here satisfies equation 8.6 and hence the Hotelling Rule 8.17. Consequently none of the programmes is locally efficient. This is true even for the programme supported by the phase path AB, even though expectations are nearly fulfilled as the economy approaches B. It appears then that the present construction has not yielded any significant alterations in the qualitative behaviour of a sequence of momentary equilibria. But while relatively simple to analyse it is vulnerable to a number of criticisms, chief among which arises out of the observation that expectations are based not only on price signals, but quantity signals as well. Let us investigate the possible implications of this.

(iii) *Adaptive expectations with quantity signals:* The simplest departure from the model of the previous section is to suppose that only quantity signals matter. But it is not the stock figure that imparts information to traders; rather, it is the rate at which it is being depleted. The resource–utilization ratio, y, would seem the appropriate index. A variety of possibilities suggest themselves. But, if we suppose that traders are myopic, it would seem reasonable to suppose that they would be particularly conscious of the current resource-utilization ratio and would regard it as being somewhat sacrosanct. If they find it increasing they become anxious about future resource availability and think that the rate of capital gains will increase so as to counteract this trend towards excessive extraction. Likewise, if they find y_t to be declining they imagine undue hoarding and expect the rate of capital gains to fall, thereby coaxing a higher resource–utilization ratio. No doubt this is somewhat of a caricature. But it is useful to analyse simple formulations to see what they imply. Let μ denote the speed of adjustment. We take it then that

$$8.35 \qquad \dot{g}_p^e / g_p^e = \mu(\dot{y}_t / y_t); \qquad \mu > 0.$$

If the current resource–utilization ratio increases (decreases) it is expected that the rate of capital gains will increase (decrease).

In what follows we replace equation 8.6 by equation 8.35 and suppose that the economic environment is otherwise the same as in section 1. From equation 8.7 we have $\dot{g}_p^e / g_p^e = \dot{r}_t / r_t$, and from equation 8.16 that $\dot{r}_t / r_t = \dot{x}_t / x_t$. Hence we can express equation 8.35 as

$$8.36 \qquad \dot{g}_p^e / g_p^e = \mu(\dot{y}_t / y_t) = \dot{r}_t / r_t = \frac{\dot{x}_t}{x_t} = \mu(g_R + y_t).$$

Using equations 8.11, 8.13 and 8.14 it follows that

$$8.37 \qquad \frac{\dot{x}_t}{x_t} = \lambda - s x_t (1 - \alpha_1) + \alpha_2 g_R,$$

and from equations 8.36 and 8.37 that

$$g_R = \frac{\lambda - sx_t(1-\alpha_1) - \mu y_t}{\mu - \alpha_2}.$$

Consequently

8.38 $$g_x = \frac{\dot{x}_t}{x_t} = \frac{\mu\{\lambda - sx_t(1-\alpha_1) - \alpha_2 y_t\}}{\mu - \alpha_2}.$$

The interesting situation is one where $\mu > \alpha_2$. Diagram 8.3 portrays the phase diagram for the pair of equations 8.36 and 8.38.

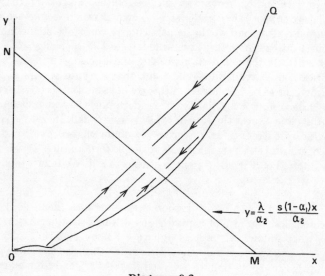

Diagram 8.3

As usual, the economy must initiate on the curve OQ given by equation 8.27. The straight line MN is the locus along which both x and y remain constant (note that $g_x = \mu g_y$). MN denotes the set of stationary points of the system of equations. There is a continuum of stationary points. If the economy initiates at a point on OQ to the north-east of MN then $\dot{x}_t, \dot{y}_t < 0$. Likewise, if it initiates at a point to the south-west of MN then $\dot{x}_t, \dot{y}_t > 0$. In either event the system is stable, in the sense that $\dot{x}_t \to 0$ and $\dot{y}_t \to 0$ provided, of course, the initial price–rental ratio is not too low.[29] But it must be admitted that it is not the usual variety of stability we are faced with here. There is a continuum of stationary points (MN) and the initial point on OQ determines the one to which the system travels.[30] But it needs to be pointed out that stationary points of this present construction display totally different features from the stationary points of the previous one. A point on MN is characterized by the condition $\dot{x}=\dot{y}=0$. But if x and y are constant then in order that expectations are realized these two variables must be related by the condition $y(1-\alpha_1-\alpha_2)=\alpha_1(1-\alpha_1)x=\lambda$.[31] MN intersects this locus at only one point when $s<\alpha_1$ and does not intersect it if $s>\alpha_1$. Therefore, while the expected rate of change of capital gains is nil in the long run, there are circumstances (as in Diagram 8.3) where the realized rate of capital gains does not equal the expected rate even asymptotically. Expectations are never fulfilled in such circumstances, even in the long run. It is a hopelessly inefficient economy.

That a decentralized economy will perform inefficiently if expectations are not realized is a trite observation. The reason why the results of this section are disturbing is not because they reiterate this simple truth. It is because they suggest how sensitive the behaviour of an economy is likely to be to the precise manner in which expectations are formed and revised. We began this section by suspecting that modelling imperfect foresight is a treacherous exercise. The examples of this section have rather confirmed this suspicion. The moral may well be to go out and observe the actual behaviour of the realized prices of natural resources and to assess what theory it conforms to. This will be attempted in Chapter 15.

(iv) *Disequilibrium in the asset market:* Before concluding this chapter we must emphasize that there is an important class of questions that we have not addressed. Although we have analysed the dynamics of resource depletion and capital accumulation under a variety of different assumptions about the nature of expectations

[29] Otherwise the initial point will lie far up along OQ, with the result that the phase path emanating from it will not asymptote on to MN.

[30] Formally, what we have here is an example of a quasi-stable system.

[31] To see this, note that with x and y assumed constant and expectations being fulfilled we must have $\dot{F}_{R/F_R}=r=\alpha_1 x$. Moreover, $\dot{F}_{R/F_R}=g_Y-g_R=g_Y+y$. Hence $\alpha_1 x=g_Y+y$. But $g_Y=\lambda+\alpha_1 g_K+\alpha_2 g_R$, and $g_Y=g_K$. Therefore $(1-\alpha_1)g_Y=\lambda-\alpha_2 y$. Hence $\alpha_1 x=(\lambda-\alpha_2 y)/(1-\alpha_1)+y$; which is the condition stated. Notice that the point (x^*, y^*) (Diagrams 8.1 and 8.2) lies on this locus.

about resource price movements, it has always been assumed that the asset market is in equilibrium, in the sense that the expected return to holding resource stocks always equals the return on capital. Formally, equation 8.5 has been assumed to hold. It is, however, quite conceivable that circumstances might arise under which expected returns are not equal—because, for example, a major technological development changes the profitability of capital or the productivity of resources, or because of some unexpected shock to the economy. Given this possibility, it is obviously important to enquire whether or not a discrepancy between these expected rates of return is likely to be self-correcting. We have avoided this issue so far simply because answering this question is very difficult; there are many possibilities, and little that is clear-cut emerges from the analysis.

Consider by way of illustration a situation where for some reason the expected return to the resource is less than the return available on capital, i.e.

$$\dot{p}_t^e/p_t < r_t.$$

What consequences will flow from this? One would expect the supply of the resource on to the market to rise as holders move into the higher-earning asset. This will lower the actual price of the resource, presumably confirming the original expectation. If capital and resources are complementary, it will also tend to raise the return on capital, again reinforcing the original discrepancy. Thus far no corrective forces have emerged. There may in fact be some, though their importance is difficult to evaluate. As the relative price of the resource falls, there may be a tendency to substitute it for other inputs (such as labour and produced goods), and this will reduce the rate of price decrease. It may also be the case that if people's expectations about the future price depend in some measure on the rate of resource use (as suggested in 8.35), then the increase in resource depletion rates associated with a decline in the return to holding resources will eventually lead to expectations of sharp price increases, which will of course be equilibrating. This chain of effects is depicted in Diagram 8.4. As a final comment on this general area, it is worth noting that the forces shown in this diagram correspond closely to the factors which we claim in Chapter 15 to have been influential in the oil market in the 1950s and 1960s.

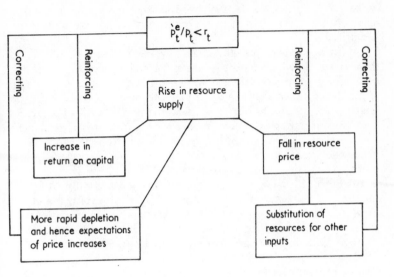

Diagram 8.4

4. Conclusions

We sum up the main results as follows:

(1) If a constant proportion of aggregate output is invested at each instant, a sequence of momentary equilibria with perfect short-run foresight can readily yield an intertemporally inefficient programme. For many plausible technological circumstances there is only one initial price–rental ratio that will result in an efficient outcome. Any other value of the initial price–rental ratio will result in the economy pursuing an errant path.

(2) An implication of (1) is that, in the absence of a complete set of forward markets, an apparently smooth-functioning market economy can very well be under-utilizing its stock of exhaustible natural resources continually. At each instant the price of exhaustible resources is 'too high'.

(3) In the absence of extraction costs, a programme supported by an intertemporal competitive equilibrium is one along which the percentage rate of change of the price of exhaustible resources equals the rate of return on investment. While the latter in a complete capital model is not constant, it is positive. In consequence the price of exhaustible resources will not maintain parity with the

price of produced goods. Being supported by an intertemporal competitive equilibrium such a programme is also intertemporally efficient.

(4) In a complete capital model, where the rate of return on investment is endogenous, it is reasonable to postulate a sequence of momentary equilibria along which short-run expectations remain unfulfilled. If expectations regarding the rate of capital gains on exhaustible natural resources are adapted on the basis of a divergence between expected and realized rates of capital gains, the behaviour of such a sequence does not appear to be much different from the behaviour of a sequence along which expectations are always realized.

(5) Such sequence economies display substantially different features if expectations regarding the rate of capital gains on exhaustible resources are adapted on the basis of quantity signals, such as the divergence between the realized resource-utilization ratio and a long-run expected resource–utilization ratio.

Notes on Chapter 8

This chapter has been based on Dasgupta (1974a), Solow (1974a) and Stiglitz (1974a). The central result of section 1, namely, the likely misbehaviour of a sequence of momentary equilibria (with perfect myopic foresight) in complete capital models of economic growth was demonstrated in a remarkable paper by Hahn (1966). The literature built around Hahn's article is simply huge. For lucid discussions of the issues involved here see, for example, Shell and Stiglitz (1967), Samuelson (1967), Hahn (1968), Cass and Shell (1975) and Mirrlees (1975). As we have tried to argue in this section and also in Chapter 6 section 5, the 'Hahn problem' is closely related to the possible inefficient outcomes of decentralized competitive environments that have no terminal date. This latter possibility was the centre of attention in the classic contribution of Malinvaud (1953), Koopmans (1957) and Samuelson (1958). The literature stemming from this source is not merely huge, it is gigantic. Among the important contributions in this area are Phelps (1965), Cass and Yaari (1966), Radner (1967), Kurz and Starrett (1970), Starrett (1970), Peleg and Yaari (1970), Cass (1972), McFadden (1973), Majumder (1973) and McFadden et al. (1976). Much of the motivation behind these contributions has been the attempt at providing characterizations of efficient programmes in terms of 'efficiency' prices. In terms of terminology adopted in this and the previous chapter, the aim has been to explore the nature of price systems that support intertemporal competitive equilibria. However, the environments in which these investigations were carried out contained no exhaustible resources. It is for this reason that we have discussed such issues at length, both in section 5 of the previous chapter and in section 1 of this chapter.

The question of what are appropriate models of expectation formation in the absence of forward markets is a sensitive one. Again, the literature discussing this is vast. For assessments, see Hahn (1970) and Burmeister and Turnovsky (1976). The formations discussed in section 3 are designed to illustrate the kinds of issues that are typically involved in such discussions. They are drawn from Dasgupta (1974a) and Stiglitz (1974a).

CHAPTER 9

MEASURABILITY, COMPARABILITY AND THE AGGREGATION OF INTERGENERATIONAL WELFARES

1. Market Mechanism and Intergenerational Distribution of Welfare

It was noted in Chapter 2 that while a competitive equilibrium of a private ownership economy has several virtues (e.g. that under certain conditions it is Pareto efficient), ensuring a reasonable distribution of welfare among individuals is not one of them. This should hardly be surprising. The equilibrium is contingent on the distribution of initial endowments in the private ownership economy. There is nothing in the construction to rule out a distribution of initial endowments which leads to an undesirable distribution of welfare at an equilibrium. Although a commonplace, this observation immediately invites a few clarificatory remarks. The issue that we are concerned with here is the distribution of *welfare*. To the extent that the consumption of goods and services affect individual welfare we are, by implication, concerned with the distribution of goods and services. But this raises several points. A *diverse* pattern of consumption within a population is not an evidence of an undesirable welfare distribution. Man 1 may prefer wine to beer and man 2 may have the opposite preference. If we now observe man 1 consuming wine and man 2 beer, the pattern of consumption is no doubt diverse. But one would be inclined to say that this is a superior state of affairs to one where the two persons share the wine and beer equally. This suggests that diversity of consumption patterns can be justified on the ground that preferences differ among individuals. But *needs* may differ as well, and one may wish to prescribe an unambiguous inequality in the consumption of goods and services because of this. And societies on occasion do subscribe to this view. It is tacitly subscribed to when a society expends greater resources on the education of a handicapped child than on that of a child who is not, or on the services provided to a disabled person than those provided to a person who is not. There is no doubt, of course, that the notion of needs is an unusually complex one and that the term assumes a variety of complexions in different contexts. In what follows we shall go into this range of questions.

If a desirable distribution of welfare cannot be assured at a competitive equilibrium for a timeless economy, it may seem plausible that chances are no better that a decentralized economy will ensure a defensible distribution of welfare among generations over time. In Chapters 4 and 8 we noted how stringent the conditions have to be in order that a decentralized competitive environment sustains an intertemporally efficient programme. A central problem, or so we noted, is that one requires a complete set of competitive forward markets. In addition, one must bear in mind that most of the postulated agents of the economy are those who, while they are taken to exist sometimes in the future, do not exist at the market date (i.e. $t=0$). Their 'votes' have therefore to be cast by proxy. This in turn means that existing individuals have to guess the preferences and needs of their descendants. Let us see if we can observe any correlates of these notions in the economies we know.

Now of course one always observes exchanges between generations. In all societies parents support their young, and in some the young reciprocate later by supporting the parents in their old age. Social sanctions against deviant behaviour help ensure that such implicit contracts are not violated.

The notion of initial endowments takes on an interesting form for the intertemporal economy. A typical individual may be said to be born with an endowment of potential raw labour and native wit. The act of acquiring an education with eventual repayment for it is merely an intertemporal exchange between the individual and the agent who finances the education. This is as true for a world where education is used as a 'screening' device as it is for one where education creates 'human capital'.[1] In fact, of course, a good deal of intergenerational transfer takes place in the form of pure gifts. So long as the present value of expenditure by a parent on his offspring exceeds the present value of receipts from them the parent will have made a net gift to his children.

Now in many cultures it would seem odd to regard a net transfer of wealth from one generation to the next as a gift. Parents possess

[1] See, for example, Spence (1974) and Becker (1964) for these alternative models.

such a marked natural concern for their children that to describe the transfer thus would prove too ritualistic a characterization. After all, one does not usually describe a purchase for oneself as a gift. This feature, that a parent's welfare is strongly influenced by the welfare of his children, is obviously one that can readily be accommodated in the theory of intertemporal equilibrium. It is on occasion caught in the literature in a rough and ready manner by way of a 'bequest function' which is included in the normal utility function of an individual.[2] Anticipating matters somewhat, the point to note here is that, as long as the mutual concern that each of every two successive generations displays towards the other is adequate, a competitive environment can in principle handle the issue of intergenerational distribution of welfare adequately. To take an example, the concern that a parent has for his far off descendants may be very weak indeed. But if his concern for his offspring is adequate this need not matter, since his offspring in turn will bear a concern for their offspring, and so on, down the generations.[3]

There is no question, however, that there are many reasons why a decentralized economy may sustain an unpalatable distribution of welfare among generations. We have gone into this at length in the earlier chapters and shall go into it again later.[4] But so far we have explored reasons why a decentralized environment may fail to sustain an intertemporally efficient programme. The problem we are concerned with here and in the next chapter stems from the observation that a programme can be intertemporally efficient and yet be perfectly ghastly. One may be tempted to argue, nevertheless, that an intertemporal competitive equilibrium cannot but sustain a desirable distribution of welfare among generations because parents display a natural concern for their offspring, a concern that one does not normally display towards one's contemporaries. In fact this is a verbal compromise; for surely it is legitimate to ask whether this natural concern that is shown by one generation towards the next is adequate.[5] In this chapter we shall discuss the kinds of

[2] See, for example, Meade (1966, 1969) and Yaari (1964).

[3] These issues have been discussed lucidly in the important contributions of Meade (1964, 1966, 1969) and Cass and Yaari (1967).

[4] A particularly interesting form of intergenerational externality has been noted in the literature which casts additional doubts on the efficacy of the market mechanism to cope adequately with the problem of intergenerational welfare distribution. On this, see Sen (1960, 1966) and Marglin (1963).

[5] Or indeed, whether the concern is excessive. We have friends who feel that the rate of investment in Britain and the United States during the nineteenth century was too high. They would have preferred to record a more gradual rise in consumption levels.

consideration that have been found relevant when considering this question.

2. The Setting

Assume that time is measured in discrete intervals of unit length ($t=0, 1, 2, \ldots$). As usual we take it that the population size is constant, L. But of course people die and new ones are born. At the level of aggregation that we shall be concerned with here, it will be reasonable to ignore the life-cycles of individuals explicitly. Indeed it will be of help to regard a person a period hence as a different person. Therefore we shall be able to refer to the L persons at t as the generation at t. Let C_t denote aggregate consumption at t. For most of the time we shall suppose that C_t is divided equally among the L persons at t. Such a rule can of course be justified. For the moment we postulate it without offering any justification. As usual, $[C_t]$ denotes an infinite consumption sequence. Let $\mathfrak{O}$ denote the set of all feasible consumption sequences. The problem that we are concerned with is the question of ordering the elements of this set in a manner that is ethically defensible. The aim ultimately will be to choose that programme which is judged best in terms of this ordering.[6]

Before we can proceed further, there are two points that need to be discussed. The first concerns the fact that in the above framework the only aspect of an intertemporal economic programme that has come up for scrutiny is consumption. But in fact choice of an economic programme is usually dictated in reality by not merely the rates of consumption at different dates but also by such items as stocks of capital that serve to establish national prestige and strength. In fact, however, it is natural to evaluate different programmes by looking at their consumption profiles. The value of investment ultimately lies in the potential consumption it represents and not in itself. And this last is caught by our interest in entire intertemporal consumption sequences. Furthermore, to the extent that the manufacture of machinery for warfare can be defended on security grounds, they would presumably represent 'consumption' goods.

The second point concerns the fact that we are considering infinite consumption sequences and are therefore supposing that there is no terminal date to the planning horizon for the economy.

---

[6] One may not be able to do this always, of course. We shall come up against such possibilities later in this chapter.

More than anything else it is this feature that is likely to appear fanciful at first sight; especially since it runs so counter to the manner in which national plans are actually constructed. If it is known with certainty that the world will cease to exist by some future date, then that would be the end of the matter. Obviously we would not be interested in 'consumption' beyond that date. The problem is that there is some chance that the world will survive. Granted that the chance is remote that generations in the far distant future will exist. But it will then be granted that the burden that they will have to bear would also be great should they in fact exist and if no provisions were left for them.[7] An alternative to infinite time horizon planning, or so it might appear, is to consider a finite horizon (say five or ten or fifteen years) and to set a target capital stock that must be accumulated at the end of the horizon. In fact this is the manner in which national plans are often constructed. But this route is not really an *alternative*. For presumably the planner would be asked to provide a justification for the choice of the target capital stock. Since the justification will be on the basis of the potential consumption levels beyond the horizon made possible by the target, this approach is merely a shorthand for infinite time horizon planning. But leaving aside the possibility of extinction, planning over an infinite future may still appear fatuous, given the uncertainties in future technological possibilities. The set of feasible consumption sequences, $\supset$, cannot possibly be known at the initial date. In fact of course, uncertainty about the future does not provide an argument for not considering all future periods. Rather, it invites us to take explicit account of the nature and extent of this uncertainty.[8] The feasible set $\supset$ has to be accordingly redefined. At any event, an interesting point that will emerge in the following chapter is that an explicit inclusion of all future periods does not involve making sensitive decisions far away in the future. But it does affect sensitively consumption levels at the initial date and the immediate future.[9]

[7] Pascal, as the reader will no doubt recall, proposed a similar argument for the consideration of those who feel that the possibility that God exists is remote.

[8] The technical problems can be severe though. We shall discuss some of the simpler issues in Chapters 13 and 14.

[9] The matter has been put very nicely by Gale (1967, p. 2); 'To describe the situation figuratively, one is guiding a ship on a long journey by keeping it lined up with a point on the horizon even though one knows that long before that point is reached the weather will change (but in an unpredictable way) and it will be necessary to pick a new course with a new reference point, again on the horizon rather than just a short distance ahead'.

The planner is concerned with ranking the set of all feasible consumption sequences, ℭ. Suppose for the moment that this welfare ranking is complete and that in particular it can be represented by a function $V([C_t])$. Following traditional terminology we shall refer to V as a *social welfare function*.

In what follows we shall suppose throughout that individuals prefer more consumption to less and that the welfare ranking of feasible consumption programmes respects this preference. Consequently the chosen plan from ℭ will necessarily be intertemporally efficient. But presumably there are very many consumption sequences in ℭ that are intertemporally efficient. The social welfare function ranks these as well. The question arises: how are the conflicting needs of different generations to be weighed and balanced off against one another so as to give rise to this ranking? Quite obviously, there can be no resolution to this problem. What one can do though is to articulate in a precise manner the various considerations that may appear morally relevant in answering it. This in turn leads to different ethical frameworks that are each, in its own way, quite appealing. No single framework is likely to be found compelling by all who are concerned with this moral exercise. We turn now to some of these frameworks.

3. Classical Utilitarianism

During the past hundred years or so the most influential of the secular moral doctrines has unquestionably been Classical Utilitarianism. It is remarkable the extent to which people are given to using some variants of Utilitarian arguments without acknowledging it or indeed in many instances being aware of it. Despite the seemingly endless debates that have been conducted on what does or does not constitute a Utilitarian argument, the statement of the doctrine itself is unambiguous. We quote here from the last of the great Classical Utilitarians, from a passage that reflects one of his rare lapses from eloquence.

'By Utilitarianism is . . . meant the ethical theory, that the conduct which, under any given circumstances, is objectively right, is that which will produce the greatest amount of happiness on the whole; that is, taking into account all whose happiness is affected by the conduct'[10].

Two pages later Sidgwick expounds on the theory in unambiguous terms: 'We shall understand, then, that by Greatest Happiness is

[10] Sidgwick (1890), p. 409.

meant the greatest possible surplus of pleasure over pain, the pain being conceived as balanced against an equal amount of pleasure, so that the two contrasted amounts annihilate each other for purposes of ethical calculation. And of course, here as before, the assumption is involved that all pleasures included in our calculation are capable of being compared quantitatively with one another and with all pains; that every such feeling has a certain intensive quantity, positive or negative (or, perhaps, zero) in respect of its desirableness, and that this quantity may be to some extent known: so that each may be at least roughly weighed in ideal scales against any other.'[11]

Let u_t^i be the utility level of individual i in generation t. Total utility, from the present ($t=0$) to the indefinite future, is then given by the expression

$$9.1 \qquad W = \sum_{t=0}^{\infty} \left(\sum_{i=1}^{L} u_t^i \right).$$

A central feature of the formulation, as caught in 9.1, is that future utilities are not being discounted at positive rates: and, indeed, several Utilitarians have judged the discounting of future utilities morally objectionable. Thus, for example, Ramsey regarded the practice, '. . . ethically indefensible . . .' and thought it '. . . arises merely from the weakness of the imagination'[12]. More recently Harrod has judged it as '. . . a polite expression for rapacity and the conquest of reason by passion'.[13]

There is at least one major defect with *ex cathedra* pronouncements such as Harrod's. It is injudicious to comment on a moral doctrine without having, as a first step, undertaken an analysis of its implications under various plausible circumstances. Explorations in the theory of optimum economic growth with positive utility discounting have suggested that in many circumstances positive utility discounting implies consumption rates in the early years that are not remotely rapacious.[14]

But quite apart from this, the Ramsey–Harrod position overlooks an important point: that there is a positive chance that life on earth

[11] Sidgwick, p. 411.
[12] Ramsey (1928, p. 543).
[13] Harrod (1948, p. 40).
[14] If anything it is *future* consumption claims that are rapacious. For such calculations, see Cass (1965), Koopmans (1965), Mirrlees (1967) and Chakravarty (1969). However, in the following chapter we shall note that Harrod's worry may well be justified for economies with exhaustible resources.

will cease to exist at some future date. As physical theories stand, if nothing else, the gradual cooling of the sun will eventually spell doom for us all. There is of course the chance, however remote the chance may be, that this eventual extinction date will be farther away than any date that we care to mention. This, as we noted earlier, is precisely the reason why morally we are compelled to take all future generations into account. But this is not to say that it carries with it the moral implication that the *utilities* of all generations be given the same weight. The point then is that one might find it ethically reasonable to discount future utilities at positive rates, not because one is myopic, but because there is a positive chance that future generations will not exist. Sidgwick, as usual, is unambiguous on what the Utilitarian stand is:

'It seems . . . clear that the time at which a man exists cannot affect the value of his happiness from a universal point of view; and that the interests of posterity must concern a Utilitarian as much as those of his contemporaries, except in so far as the effect of his actions on posterity—*and even the existence of human beings to be affected*—must necessarily be more uncertain'[15].

Let $\gamma_t(>0)$ denote the utility discount factor applied to generation t. Discounting future utilities at positive rates implies that $\gamma_t > \gamma_{t+1}$ for all $t \geqslant 0$. Total discounted utility is then

9.2
$$W = \sum_{t=0}^{\infty} \gamma_t \left(\sum_{i=1}^{L} u_t^i \right).$$

In what follows we shall abstract from all items other than consumption that affect an individual's utility level: not because other features of one's existence do not affect one, but because it may be a reasonable approximation to suppose that such other features are independent of the levels of consumption and consequently do not affect the arguments involved here. For the problem at hand it would be distinctly odd to postulate the precise manner in which the utility *function* varies from person to person across generations. At this level of aggregation it is easiest to suppose identical utility functions. Thus $u_t^i(\cdot) = u(\cdot)$. If now $u(\cdot)$ is strictly concave in its arguments then it follows immediately that a Utilitarian would regard an equal division of a *generation's* total consumption level among its members as the optimum distribution of this total

---

[15] Sidgwick (1890), p. 412; our italics.

consumption level.[16] This being so, we may as well normalize and suppose $L=1$. Presumably the utility level of a given generation is influenced by the postulated future consumption level.[17] There is some evidence that past consumption matters as well.[18] In this event $u_t = u([C_t])$. But our aim here is to articulate the Classical Utilitarian notion of intergenerational justice. If too much inter-generational concern is built into individual utility functions there is a danger that we shall have included into these personal utility functions the individual's sense of justice. In this case a Utilitarian exercise based on such functions will involve double counting. This danger will certainly be avoided were we to postulate totally selfish individuals. Each generation is then concerned with its own consumption level. Thus $u_t = u(C_t)$.[19]

Using this in 9.2 yields total (discounted) utility as

$$9.3 \qquad W = \sum_{t=0}^{\infty} \gamma_t u(C_t); \qquad \gamma_t \geqslant \gamma_{t+1} \ldots > 0, \quad \text{and} \quad u(\cdot)$$

a continuous and increasing function of C_t.

Since γ_t is the utility discount factor, one can now define the *utility discount rate* between t and $t+1$ as $(\gamma_t - \gamma_{t+1})/\gamma_{t+1}$. It is also occasionally referred to as the *rate of pure time preference* and sometimes as the *rate of impatience*. A simple form of the discount factor that has been much used in recent years is the one for which $\gamma_t = 1/(1+\delta)^t$, with $\delta \geqslant 0$. The discount rate is then a constant δ. This would seem an appropriate procedure if it is felt that the probability of extinction in the next T years is approximately the same as the probability of extinction during the interval t to $t+T$ should the world survive till t and that this is true no matter what t and T are (i.e. the stochastic process generating the possibility of extinction is a Poisson one). In this case we have

$$9.4 \qquad W = \sum_{t=0}^{\infty} u(C_t)/(1+\delta)^t, \qquad \delta \geqslant 0.$$

[16] We should emphasize here that individuals are assumed not only to possess identical utility functions but that all members of a given generation possess the same skills. If skills varied, a Utilitarian optimum would not prescribe identical treatment. On this, see for example, Allingham (1973).

[17] See, for example, Phelps and Pollak (1968), Rawls (1972), Arrow (1973a) and Dasgupta (1974, 1974c).

[18] See, for example, Wan, Jr. (1970), Samuelson (1971) and Ryder and Heal (1973).

[19] There is the danger with such utility function that there will be 'under counting'. This simplification is, of course, not crucial to Classical Utilitarianism. We are making the assumption here for conceptual simplicity.

The Utilitarian would wish to select that feasible consumption profile $[C_t]$ which maximizes W. But note that if $[C_t^*]$ is an optimum consumption programme when $u(\cdot)$ is the utility function, it remains an optimum consumption programme if instead the utility function is $au(\cdot)$, where $a > 0$. One does not require an absolute scale in which to measure utility. A Utilitarian prescription is invariant to the *same* positive homogeneous transformation applied to all utility functions. This restriction—that the utility functions be unique up to a positive proportional transformation and that, if such a transformation is used on one individual's utility function, then the same transformation must be used on all other utility functions—defines the sense in which interpersonal comparisons of welfare are made by Utilitarianism for our particular problem.[20]

All very well, one might say. But how is this interpersonal comparison to be made in principle? One strand of Utilitarianism, as exemplified in the writings of Sidgwick, has faced the question in a remarkably interesting manner. The idea lies in postulating a rational and impartial spectator who in effect empathizes with the needs and aspirations of all individuals. The moral calculation is then done on the basis of this empathy. This particular Utilitarian exercise has been described eloquently by today's leading anti-Utilitarian.

'A rational and impartial sympathetic spectator is a person who takes up a general perspective: he assumes a position where his own interests are not at stake and he possesses all the requisite information and powers of reasoning. So situated he is equally responsive and sympathetic to the desires and satisfactions of everyone affected by the social system. His own interests do not thwart his natural sympathy for the aspirations of others and he has perfect knowledge of these endeavours and what they mean for those who have them. Responding to the interests of each person in the same way, an impartial spectator gives free reign to his capacity for sympathetic identification by viewing each person's situation as it affects that person. *Thus he imagines himself in the place of each person in turn, and when he has done this for everyone, the strength of his approval is determined by the balance of satisfaction to which he has sympathetically responded.* When he has made the round of all the affected parties,

---

[20] For a detailed discussion of different types of interpersonal comparison see Sen (1970, 1977a). If the time horizon were finite a Utilitarian prescription would be invariant to transformations of the form $au_t + b_t (a > 0,$ and b_t a function of t). For the problem at hand we have in general to suppose $b_t = 0$. The reason why this is so will become apparent in section 4.

so to speak, his approval expresses the total result. Sympathetically imagined pains cancel out sympathetically imagined pleasures, and the final intensity of approval corresponds to the net sum of positive feeling'.[21]

The moral exercise seems clear enough. Each one of us, or so the argument goes, should assume the mantle of this rational and impartial sympathetic spectator. Having conducted this introspective utility comparison each of us will then be led to seek the happiness of all.

4. The Existence of a Utilitarian Optimum

The Classical Utilitarian prescription would appear to be clear enough. Or is it? Even leaving aside the problem of making interpersonal comparisons, the injunction: 'Choose that policy which maximizes the sum of the individual utility levels', is not of much help if a maximum does not exist.

How may this happen? There are several possibilities. To see this it is helpful to look at the mathematical structure of the problem. Recall that a real valued function $f(x)$ defined on a set X attains a maximum value on X if (a) f is continuous on X and (b) X is nonempty and compact. This is Weierstrass's theorem.[22] If either of these conditions fails to hold it is possible that no maximum exists on X. Now, the non-existence of a maximum value on X would be characterized by one of two possibilities: (i) $\sup_{x \varepsilon X} f(x)$ exists, but it is not attained at any point in X; and (ii) $\sup_{x \varepsilon X} f(x)$ does not exist.[23] Since we are taking all future generations explicitly into account, it is plain that under Classical Utilitarianism it is possible that we may not be able to appeal to Weierstrass's theorem, since the (discounted) sum of an infinite number of utility levels may not converge. It may diverge to plus or minus infinity; or indeed, it may oscillate. If it does, then the Classical Utilitarian rule does not define a real valued function on the set of utility sequences. There is no real valued function to be maximized. This possibility, which has been a centre of attention among optimum growth theorists in

[21] Rawls (1972), pp. 186–7; our italics.
[22] Recall as well that if X is a subset of a metric space then to say that X is compact is to say that every infinite subset of X has a limit point in X.
[23] By $\sup_{x \epsilon X} f(x)$ we mean the least upper bound of f on X (i) is exemplified by the case $f(x) = x$ for $0 \leqslant x < \frac{1}{2}$ and $f(x) = 0$ for $1 \geqslant x \geqslant \frac{1}{2}$ and X is the closed interval $[0, 1]$, and (ii) is exemplified by the case $f(x) = 1/x$ in the open interval $(0, 1)$.

recent years, is one that the Classical Utilitarians appear to have overlooked when elaborating on their moral theory.

Recognition of this possibility suggests an extension of the Classical Utilitarian Rule which, at the same time, retains the spirit of Utilitarianism. After all, it may be argued, what does it matter if several feasible (discounted) utility sums refuse to converge so long as there is a feasible utility sequence that reaches a greater (discounted) utility sum than any other feasible utility sequence for large enough t? This motivates the following definition: a utility sequence $[u_t]$ is said to *overtake* (*strictly overtake*) the utility sequence $[\hat{u}_t]$ if there exists a $T \geqslant 0$ such that

$$\sum_{t=0}^{\tau} \gamma_t(u_t - \hat{u}_t) \geqslant (>)0 \quad \text{for all} \quad \tau \geqslant T.$$

Furthermore, we say that a feasible utility sequence is optimal according to this criterion of comparison if it overtakes all other feasible utility sequences.[24] We shall refer to the welfare rule based on the overtaking criterion as the Overtaking Utilitarian Rule. Clearly, the criterion defines a partial ordering over utility sequences since it is possible that, given two infinite utility sequences, neither overtakes the other; as in the case of the undiscounted sums of the two sequences $[\tilde{u}_t] = (2, -2, 2, -2, 2, \ldots)[\tilde{u}_t] = (1, \frac{1}{3}, (\frac{1}{3})^2, (\frac{1}{3})^3, \ldots)$. Clearly also, if a Classical Utilitarian optimum exists then this optimum overtakes all feasible utility sequences and is, therefore, an optimum in terms of the Overtaking Utilitarian Rule. The reverse, of course, need not hold, as can be seen in the case of the sequences $[\hat{u}_t] = (1, 1, 1, \ldots)$ and $[\hat{\hat{u}}_t] = (2, \frac{1}{2}, 2, \frac{1}{2}, \ldots)$. Since the undiscounted utility sum of each sequence tends to infinity, Classical Utilitarianism (with no discounting) does not provide a rule for distinguishing between them, though it is clear that $[\hat{\hat{u}}_t]$ strictly overtakes $[\hat{u}_t]$.

Nevertheless, it may be thought that in demanding that the sum of the per-period utility differences between two sequences be of unambiguous sign for large enough t one is demanding too much. This suggests the following weaker criterion of comparison. We shall say that a utility sequence $[u_t]$ *catches up* with (*strictly surpasses*)

[24] The overtaking criterion was introduced by Koopmans (1965) and in Weizsacker (1965). For a critique of the overtaking criterion, see Guha (1974). Notice that an Overtaking Utilitarian prescription remains unchanged if u_t is replaced by $au_t + b_t (a > 0)$.

the utility sequence $[\hat{u}_t]$ if for all $\varepsilon > 0$, there exist $T(\varepsilon) \geqslant 0$ such that

$$\sum_{t=0}^{\tau} \gamma_t(u_t - \hat{u}_t) \geqslant (>) - \varepsilon \quad \text{for} \quad \tau > T(\varepsilon).$$

A feasible utility sequence is said to be optimal according to this criterion of comparison if it catches up with all other feasible utility sequences.[25] We shall refer to the welfare rule based on this criterion of comparison as the Extended Utilitarian Rule.

It is of course immediate that, if a utility sequence overtakes another, it catches up with the other as well. Therefore, if an Overtaking Utilitarian optimum exists, then so does an Extended Utilitarian optimum. The reverse need not hold. We conclude then that if an Extended Utilitarian optimum does not exist then an Overtaking Utilitarian optimum does not exist, and therefore a Classical Utilitarian optimum does not exist. Of the three criteria we have discussed so far Extended Utilitarianism is the weakest. Unfortunately even an Extended Utilitarian optimum does not exist in certain simple economic environments. In what follows we shall illustrate this by means of the simplest planning problem involving exhaustible resources.[26]

Consider once again a cake-eating economy (see Chapter 6 section 2 and Chapter 8 section 2). A feasible consumption profile is a non-negative sequence satisfying the constraint $\sum_{t=0}^{\infty} C_t \leq 1$. Generations have identical utility functions. Let the utility of generation t be given by an increasing and strictly concave function of its consumption level, C_t. There is no possibility of extinction, so that future utilities are not discounted. We demonstrate that an Extended Utilitarian optimum does not exist.[27] To see this, note first that in the cake-eating economy the only feasible consumption profile with equal consumption for all generations is the one where each generation consumes nothing. But since $u(\cdot)$ is by assumption an increasing function, an indefinite refrainment from consumption is obviously the 'worst' possible policy in terms of the Extended Utilitarian rule. Therefore we look at other feasible policies. Any other feasible consumption sequence will display different consumption levels for

[25] This notion of optimality was introduced by Gale (1967) and McFadden (1967).
[26] This example was discussed originally in Gale (1967).
[27] In the discussion in Chapter 6 section 2 a positive rate of utility discount, (r), was used. This, in conjunction with the assumption that the elasticity of marginal utility tends to a finite limit with vanishing consumption ensured that the problem that we shall encounter below did not arise there.

at least two adjacent generations, say T and $T+1$. Let $[C_t]$ be such a feasible policy with $C_T \neq C_{T+1}$. Since by assumption $u(\cdot)$ is strictly concave we have

$$u\{(C_T + C_{T+1})/2\} + u\{(C_T + C_{T+1})/2\} > u(C_T) + u(C_{T+1}).$$

Therefore, by keeping the levels of consumption for all generations other than T and $T+1$ the same as in $[C_t]$ we can increase the utility sum over the two generations T and $T+1$ by getting them to share equally their total allotment $C_T + C_{T+1}$. It follows that given any feasible $[C_t]$ there is another feasible consumption sequence along which the utility sum over at least two generations is higher and along which the utility levels of all other generations remain unchanged. The latter consumption sequence therefore strictly surpasses $[C_t]$. In short, for every feasible policy there is another which strictly surpasses it, and is therefore judged better under Extended Utilitarianism. It follows that an optimum does not exist according to this rule, and consequently no optimum exists under Classical Utilitarianism either. What remains to be shown is that for certain classes of utility functions the non-existence of a Classical Utilitarian optimum is characterized by the fact that, while the least upper bound of the utility sum exists, it is not attained and that for certain classes of functions it is characterized by the non-existence of the least upper bound of the utility sum.

Consider, to begin with, the class of iso-elastic utility functions of the form

$$u(C) = C^\eta, \qquad 1 > \eta > 0$$

(i.e. the absolute value of the elasticity of marginal utility is less than unity). It is simple to show that $\sup_{[C_t]} \sum_{t=0}^{\infty} C_t^\eta$ does not exist. For consider the sequence $C_t = 1/T$ for $t = 0, 1, \ldots, T-1$ and $C_t = 0$ for $t \geq T$. The utility sum is $\sum_{t=0}^{T-1} T^{-\eta} = T^{1-\eta}$, and this tends to infinity as $T \to \infty$.

The reverse situation arises with the class of iso-elastic utility functions of the form

9.4
$$\left. \begin{array}{l} u(C) = -C^{-(\eta-1)}, \qquad \eta > 1 \\ \text{or} \\ u(C) = \log C \end{array} \right\}$$

(i.e. the absolute value of the elasticity of marginal utility is greater than or equal to unity). Since along any feasible consumption sequence $C_t \to 0$, we must have $u(C_t) \to -\infty$, with the form 9.4. It follows that $\sum_{t=0}^{T} u(C_t) \to -\infty$ for all feasible policies. Once again $\sup_{[C_t]} \sum_{t=0}^{\infty} u(C_t)$ does not exist.

It is useful to have an example where the non-existence of an optimum is characterized by the fact that while the least upper bound exists it is not attained. Towards this suppose

9.5 $$u(C) = 1 - \exp(-aC), \qquad a > 0.$$

With this function the utility sum converges for all feasible programmes. Now consider once again the feasible policy $C_t = 1/T$ for $t = 0, 1, \ldots, T-1$ and $C_t = 0$ for $t \geqslant T$. With 9.5 as the utility function we have

$$\sum_{t=0}^{T-1} u(C_t) = \sum_{t=0}^{T-1} \left\{ 1 - \exp\left(-\frac{a}{T} \right) \right\} = T\left\{ 1 - \exp\left(-\frac{a}{T} \right) \right\} \to a$$

as $T \to \infty$. It is trivial to confirm that $\sup_{[C_t]} \sum_{t=0}^{\infty} \{1 - \exp(-aC_t)\} = a$. It exists. The problem is that it is not attained along any feasible programme.

5. Choice Behind the Veil of Ignorance

We have noted that at least one variant of Classical Utilitarianism envisages interpersonal comparison of utilities as being arrived at through pure introspection. Postulating a rational and impartial spectator that makes the rounds, so to speak, is merely an articulation of the idea that an assertion such as the gain to one person due to a policy exceeds the loss suffered by another, is a statement of fact; a statement that can be confirmed by introspection. The Utilitarian prescription that these gains and losses be *added* is given coherence by supposing this spectator to respond sympathetically to each such gain and loss.

An alternative conception of distributive justice that has been recently advanced is founded on the social contract doctrine.[28] The idea here consists of the claim that the principles of justice are to be conceived as those that free and rational persons concerned to further their own interests would agree should govern their social life and institutions if they had to *choose* such principles from behind a 'veil of ignorance'; that is, in ignorance of their own abilities, of

[28] See Rawls (1972).

their psychological propensities, and of their status and position in society and the level of development of the society of which they are to be members. This position of primordial equality of the choosing parties has been named by Rawls 'the original position'. The veil of ignorance is designed to '. . . ensure(s) that no one is advantaged or disadvantaged in the choice of principles by the outcome of natural chance or the contingency of social circumstances. Since all are similarly situated and no one is able to design principles to form his particular condition, the principles of justice are the result of a fair agreement or bargain'.[29]

It will be out of place here to attempt to describe the richness of the Rawlsian framework and the detailed differences between its implications and those of Classical Utilitarianism. Here we are concerned only with its implications for intergenerational distribution of consumption. On this Rawls supposes that '. . . The (choosing) parties do not know which generation they belong to . . . They have no way of telling whether it is poor or relatively wealthy, largely agricultural or already industrialized . . . The veil of ignorance is complete in these respects . . . *Since no one knows to which generation he belongs, the question is viewed from the standpoint of each and a fair accommodation is expressed by the principle adopted.* All generations are virtually represented in the original position, since the same principle would always be represented . . .'[30]

The critical point to note is that the conception of justice advanced above, when stripped down to its bones, is built on the problem of individual choice under uncertainty. But merely noting this does not get us very far; we still have to provide an account of how an individual will choose under uncertainty.[31] In fact there is some ambiguity about the manner in which Rawls envisages the parties in the original position to choose among *intertemporal* consumption programmes.[32] Here we take a route that is an extension of the one advanced originally by Harsanyi (1955).

For simplicity of exposition we continue to normalize and suppose that each generation consists of precisely one individual (i.e. $L=1$), and again, to make the moral calculation simple, suppose that

[29] Rawls (1972), p. 12.

[30] Rawls (1972), pp. 287–8; our italics.

[31] For different formalizations, see for example, von Neumann and Morgenstern (1944), Milnor (1954), Luce and Raiffa (1957), Chapters 2 and 11, Harsanyi (1955) and Rawls (1972).

[32] On this, see Rawls (1972), Arrow (1973a), Dasgupta (1974) and Solow (1974b).

generations are all identical in terms of their preferences. A party in the original position has to choose from among the set of feasible consumption programmes. Suppose for simplicity that the chooser is concerned with ordering the set of all consumption sequences bounded between zero and (some) $\underline{C}$ (>0). Thus $0 \leq C_t \leq \underline{C}$, for all $t \geq 0$. We have already supposed that each generation prefers more consumption to less. Thus each generation's preferences can be represented by *any* increasing function, $w_t(C_t)$. But in the Harsanyi framework each generation is invited to present its preference ordering over *lotteries* defined on its own consumption; (i.e. it is invited to present its preference ordering over probability measures defined on $[0, \underline{C}]$). But by hypothesis generations have identical preferences. This means that their preferences over such lotteries are identical. We now suppose that the choosing party knows this preference ordering. Moreover we suppose that the representative generation's preference ranking over these lotteries satisfies the von-Neumann–Morgenstern axioms. Then we know that generation t's preference ordering over *sure* consumption levels can be represented by a function that is unique up to a positive linear transformation. Thus we have

9.6 $$w_t(C_t) = a_t u(C_t) + b_t, \qquad a_t > 0 [33]$$

where $u(\cdot)$ is an increasing and continuous function, and a_t and b_t are arbitrary constants. We note as well that $u(\cdot)$ defines the representative generation's attitude to risk. Thus, for example, if it is risk-averse, then $u(\cdot)$ is strictly concave.[34] By hypothesis the choosing party in the original position knows $u(\cdot)$. But we have already noted that a knowledge of $u(\cdot)$ merely restrict the admissible set of utility functions for generation t to the (infinite) family defined by equation 9.6. In ranking alternative consumption sequences, therefore, it is not enough for the choosing party in the original position to know $u(\cdot)$. This is so because in order to aggregate intergenerational welfares, the choosing party needs to have a rule by which to select a member from each set in 9.6. We are therefore back with the problem of intergenerational welfare comparisons, a problem that we noted earlier in our discussion of Classical Utilitarianism. Now, the manner in which intergenerational welfare comparisons is conducted in the Harsanyi–Rawls framework is similar to the one discussed earlier in section 3. The choosing party

[33] For axioms on preferences over lotteries that can be represented by 9.6, see Luce and Raiffa (1957).
[34] See Chapter 13.

is assumed to make the rounds from generation to generation, so to speak, and having empathized with the needs and aspirations of each and every generation it arrives at a 'normalization', one for each generation's utility function $w_t(\cdot)$ (i.e. it chooses a_t and b_t in 9.6); one pair for each generation).[35] Again, for expository simplicity suppose that generations are 'identical' in every respect. Then the choosing party will use the same normalization for all generations, and we shall have $w_t(C_t) = w(C_t) = u(C_t)$ (say). Given this normalization the choosing party can associate with each consumption sequence $[C_t]$ a corresponding utility sequence $[w(C_t)]$. Since behind the veil of ignorance the choosing party does not know which generation it belongs to, it would regard each $[C_t]$ as an unknown lottery.[36] The original ethical problem with which we began this Chapter is thereby reduced, in the Harsanyi–Rawls framework, to a classical decision problem under uncertainty. But the point to reiterate is that the choice problem is given its moral dimension by the assumption that the party is behind the veil of ignorance and therefore does not know to which generation it belongs. Its vested interests are removed by this device. It will rank consumption programmes in an impartial manner, taking into account the interests of all generations, since it may end up as a member of any generation. Moreover, as we have been supposing that more consumption is preferred to less by all generations, $w(\cdot)$ is an increasing function. Indeed, this framework provides one with one of the most powerful defences of the demand that we should be interested in intertemporally efficient programmes. If more consumption is preferred to less by all generations and the chooser does not know to which generation he belongs he will not choose an intertemporally inefficient consumption programme.

The question arises what decision rule the choosing party ought to follow behind the veil of ignorance. In his pioneering work on social welfare functions, Harsanyi supposed that the choosing party's preference over hypothetical lotteries satisfy the von-Neumann–Morgenstern axioms as well. Assume now that behind the veil of ignorance the party faces a (subjective) probability π_t of being a

---

[35] To be accurate the Harsanyi framework does not require intergenerational comparison of utility levels; i.e. the choosing party does not require to normalize the b_t's. But for expository ease we shall suppose that it does. Moreover, we shall need to assume this in our discussion of maxi-min below.

[36] 'Unknown lottery', because thus far in the exposition there is no presumption that the party knows what probability distribution to impute to its uncertainty about which generation it will belong to.

member of generation t. It will follow then that as between two programmes $[C_t]$ and $[C_t^1]$ it will choose on the basis of the expected utility associated with the programmes; i.e. according to whether

$$9.7 \qquad V([C_t]) \equiv \sum_{t=0}^{\infty} \pi_t w(C_t) \gtreqless V([C_t^1]) \equiv \sum_{t=0}^{\infty} \pi_t w(C_t^1)$$

It is important to recognize that despite the *formal* similarity between the functions 9.3 and 9.7, their interpretations are different. While $w(\cdot)$ in 9.7 is usually called the utility function of generation t it is not a utility function in the sense of Classical Utilitarianism. Generation t's attitude to risk determines the form of $w(\cdot)$, whereas $u(\cdot)$ in 9.3 is a measure of the quantity of happiness of a given generation. $u(\cdot)$ and $w(\cdot)$ have different geneses.

9.7 is still not a decision rule, because the question arises what probability distribution the choosing party ought to base its decision on. If the number of generations is finite one route is to have the party assume an equal chance of being a member of any generation. This may be justified by an appeal to the principle of insufficient reason.[37] Alternatively, as in the Harsanyi framework, the assumption of equi-probability could be intrinsic to the meaning of 'impersonal choice' for the choosing party.

'. . . an individual's preferences satisfy this requirement of impersonality if they indicate what social situation he would choose if he did not know what his personal position would be in the new situation chosen (and in any of its alternatives) but rather had an equal *chance* of obtaining any of the social positions . . .'[38]

But for our problem matters are different. One cannot have a uniform probability distribution defined over the integers (i.e. $t = 0, 1, 2, \ldots$).[39] But presumably there is a chance that the world will be extinct at some date. Let λ_t denote the (subjective) probability on the part of the choosing party at $t = 0$ that the world will terminate at a date *beyond* t. Then the natural analogue of the principle of insufficient reason, or indeed Harsanyi's condition

[37] See Harsanyi (1955, 1974). The principle of insufficient reason is discussed at length in Luce and Raiffa (1957).
[38] Harsanyi (1955), p. 316.
[39] Notice the formal similarity between this last statement and the reasons why the cake-eating problem presented difficulties in the previous subsection.

characterizing impersonal choice, is one that leads the choosing party to maximize

$$9.8 \qquad V([C_t]) = \sum_{t=0}^{\infty} \lambda_t w(C_t), \qquad \lambda_t > 0.^{40}$$

Since by definition $\lambda_t > \lambda_{t+1}$ for all t, λ_t is formally akin to the discount factor introduced in our discussion of Classical Utilitarianism. For example, if it is thought that the probability of extinction is generated by a Poisson process, then

$$\lambda_t = (1+\delta)^{-t}, \qquad (\delta > 0).$$

The Harsanyi framework postulates that the choosing party's preferences over lotteries satisfy the von-Neumann–Morgenstern axioms and, in particular that behind the veil of ignorance it chooses on the supposition that it has an 'equal' chance of being a member of any generation. In developing the contract doctrine Rawls conceived of the veil of ignorance in a different manner. In the Rawlsian framework ignorance behind the veil is 'complete', in the sense that the choosing party has no basis for imputing any probability distribution to the uncertainty it faces. In particular, it is supposed that the decision rule which the choosing party obeys is the 'maxi–min' criterion. Using this criterion for the problem at hand the party ranks two programmes $[C_t]$ and $[C_t^1]$ according as

$$\inf [w(C_t)] \gtreqless \inf [w(C_t^1)].^{41}$$

Since by our hypothesis generations are identical and $w(\cdot)$ is increasing, the party ranks the two programmes $[C_t]$ and $[C_t^1]$ according as

$$9.9 \qquad \inf [C_t] \gtreqless \inf [C_t^1]$$

In fact the criterion embodied in 9.9 would emerge from the Harsanyi framework as well if it were the case that each *generation* is infinitely risk averse. To see this, suppose by way of illustration that

$$w(C_t) = - \frac{C_t^{-(\eta-1)}}{(\eta-1)}, \qquad \eta > 0.$$

---

[40] On this, see for example, Yaari (1965) and Dasgupta and Heal (1974).

[41] 'inf' means 'greatest lower bound' of the sequence in question. If the 'inf' is attained then 'inf' == 'min'. For an axiomitization of the maxi-min decision rule, see Luce and Raiffa (1957), chapter 13.

In Chapter 13 we shall show that the larger is the value of the parameter η the greater is the extent to which the representative generation is risk-averse. But using this utility function in 9.8 we have

9.10 $\qquad V([C_t]) = -\sum_{t=0}^{\infty} \lambda_t C_t^{-(\eta-1)}/(\eta-1), \qquad \eta > 0, \qquad \lambda_t > 0.$

What happens when $\eta \to \infty$? To answer this consider two consumption sequences $[C_t]$ and $[C_t^1]$. Suppose that each sequence has a minimum term. It can then be shown that if the choosing party ranks $[C_t]$ and $[C_t^1]$ according to the function 9.10, then in the limit as $\eta \to \infty$ it chooses that programme whose minimum term is the larger.[42] This should not be overly surprising. The larger is η the more risk averse is the representative generation. Therefore, with larger and larger values of η those dates at which consumption is relatively low loom larger and larger in the choosing party's eye. In the limit it is obsessed with the dates at which consumption is lowest. Its choice conforms to the maxi–min strategy.

Our interest in this criterion is not because Rawls, in his well known work, has argued that the choosing party will obey it when choosing an intertemporal consumption sequence. In fact he has not.[43] But it is eminently worth considering such extreme cases. They enable one to see sharply the implications of different hypotheses.

6. Intuitionist Conceptions

Quite possibly the most common position that welfare economists have held on the nature of interpersonal welfare comparisons is to regard them as normative judgements.[44] This contrasts sharply with the variant of Classical Utilitarianism that was discussed earlier.

[42] See Hardy, Littlewood and Polya (1943), Chapter 5.

[43] Cf. Rawls (1972). It can be argued though that he ought to postulate extreme risk aversion here, given that he postulates it elsewhere in his book. On this, see Arrow (1973b).

[44] Welfare principles bearing on the choice of intertemporal programmes based on this interpretation have been explored in a remarkable set of papers by Koopmans (1960, 1972, 1972a), Koopmans, Diamond and Williamson (1964), Diamond (1965) and Gorman (1968). This section is based on these works. For further explorations along intuitionist lines, see Hammond (1976a), d'Aspremont and Gevers (1977), Sen (1977a), Maskin (1978) and Roberts (1978). Of these more recent contributions the axiomatic structure explored by Maskin (1978) is, in some sense, closest to the structure that we shall be discussing here.

It is to be contrasted as well with the notion arising out of choice behind the veil of ignorance. In this third view the precise nature of the welfare comparisons is so severely related to the manner in which it is judged appropriate to aggregate individual welfares that it is often difficult to disentangle these two distinct issues. Let us see what the approach is.

As before, $\supset$ denotes the set of feasible consumption sequences. In order to endow the framework with some degree of generality one would want $\supset$ to be a sufficiently rich set.[45] Let $\supset_u$ denote the resulting set of utility sequences. In what follows we suppose that $\supset_u$ consists of the set of all sequences bounded between zero and one.[46] That is, $\supset_u$ consists of the set of all $[u_t]$, such that $0 \leq u_t \leq 1$ for all t. Now this may be because, say, $\supset$ consists of the set of all sequences bounded between zero and (some) $\bar{C}$ (>0), and the utility function, measured in some ideal scale, is given by the form

$$u(C_t) = A\{1 - \exp(-aC_t)\}, \qquad \text{where } a > 0 \text{ and } A = 1/\{1 - \exp(a\bar{C})\}.$$

Alternatively (and the more likely cause) it may be because, while there is no ideal scale, the person conducting the moral exercise has so chosen to scale the utility functions that the set of feasible utility sequences consists of all those that are bounded between zero and one. Now if this last is the case then the choice of the scale reflects the precise ethical judgement about the manner in which interpersonal welfare comparisons ought to be made.

Associated with each consumption sequence $[C_t]$ there is then a utility sequence $[u(C_t)]$. We now need a notion of 'distance' between two utility sequences. In what follows we suppose that the distance between two sequences $[u_t]$ and $[\hat{u}_t]$ is $\sup_{t \geq 0} [|u_t - \hat{u}_t|]$.

The person conducting the moral exercise is concerned with the manner in which the members of $\supset_u$ ought to be ranked. In the intuitionist approach the person appeals neither to an impartial and sympathetic spectator, nor to hypothetical choice behind the veil of ignorance. Instead, he appeals to his moral intuition. Suppose that his ranking of these utility sequences can be represented by a continuous function $W([u_t])$.[47] W is the person's social welfare function.

---

[45] As compared to, say, the $\supset$ associated with the cake-eating economy.

[46] There is nothing sacrosanct about either zero or one. In fact, any pair of bounds will do.

[47] In Diamond (1965) and Koopmans (1972a) the existence of W is established from the more 'primitive' postulate of a continuous ordering over $\supset_u$.

Now all this has not got us very far, since wo do not know the form of W, i.e. the manner in which the utilities ought to be aggregated. It is at this point that an appeal is made to some further moral precepts.

In performing such ethical exercises it is best to begin by appealing to what may be felt to be very general precepts, and calculate the extent to which they restrict the form of W.

One can begin by appealing to the Paretian precept: if two utility sequences $[u_t]$ and $[\hat{u}_t]$ have the property that $u_t \geqslant \hat{u}_t$ for all $t \geqslant 0$ and $u_t > \hat{u}_t$ for some t then $W([u_t]) > W([\hat{u}_t])$. As this is widely appealed to, we shall assume that this is accepted.[48]

What else may one appeal to? If one is persuaded by the Ramsey–Harrod view of the undesirability of favouring the states of early generations over the later ones, one will wish to postulate an 'equal treatment principle' and subscribe to it. The most natural formulation of this idea is as follows: for all $t \geqslant 0$ and all feasible $[u_t]$,

$$W(u_0, u_1, \ldots, u_{t-1}, u_t, u_{t+1}, \ldots) = W(u_t, u_1, \ldots, u_{t-1}, u_0, u_{t+1}, \ldots);$$

i.e. an interchange of u_0 and u_t ought not to matter.[49]

But now we are in trouble: we have asked for too much. There is no W defined in $\mathfrak{I}_u$ that is at the same time continuous, Paretian and satisfies the 'equal treatment principle'.[50]

To prove this consider the utility sequence

$$[u_t] \equiv (0, 1, 0, \tfrac{1}{2}, 1, \ldots, 0, 1/2^k, 2/2^k, \ldots, (2^k - 1)/2^k, 1, 0, \ldots).$$

This is clearly feasible. Now consider the utility sequence

$$[u_t^k] \equiv (1, 1, 0, \tfrac{1}{2}, 1, \ldots, 0, 0, 1/2^k, \ldots, (2^k - 2)/2^k, (2^k - 1)/2^k, 0, \ldots).$$

This too is feasible, and it will be noted that $[u_t^k]$ has been obtained from $[u_t]$ by interchanging the initial 0 with the $(k+1)$st 1 appearing in $[u_t]$ and then interchanging the sequence $(1/2^k, 2/2^k, \ldots, (2^k-1)/2^k, 0)$ with $(0, 1/2^k, 2/2^k, \ldots, (2^k-2)/2^k, (2^k-1)/2^k)$. This involves a

---

[48] Notice that $W([u_t]) \equiv \inf\limits_{t \geqslant 0} [u_t]$ is not Paretian in the sense that we have just defined the term. In other words, the 'maxi-min' principle is not Paretian. In the next chapter we shall note that this will not matter for our purpose.

[49] This could be called an intertemporal 'anonymity' principle. Compare this with the anonymity rule in May (1952), and the strong anonymity rule in Sen (1977).

[50] This result, attributed to M. Yaari, is in Diamond (1965).

finite number of interchanges. Therefore, by appealing to the equal treatment principle one has $W([u_t]) = W([u_t^k])$. Now define

$$[u_t^*] \equiv (1, 1, 0, \tfrac{1}{2}, 1, \ldots, 0, 1/2^k, 2/2^k, \ldots, (2^k-1)/2^k, 1, 0, \ldots).$$

Clearly, sup $[|u_t^k - u_t^*|] = 1/2^k$. But this is by definition the distance between $[u_t^k]$ and $[u_t^*]$. Therefore $\lim_{k \to \infty} [u_t^k] = [u_t^*]$. Since by assumption W is continuous we must have $W([u_t]) = W([u_t^*])$. However notice that $[u_t^*]$ is Pareto superior to $[u_t]$, and since W is by assumption Paretian, $W([u_t^*]) > W([u_t])$. We have, therefore, arrived at a contradiction. There is no social welfare function W that is (1) continuous, (2) Paretian, and (3) treats generations equally. Plainly something will have to give. But which one?

One escape clause would be to refrain from insisting that all utility sequences must be ethically comparable. In choosing between A, B and C what does it matter, after all, if B and C are non-comparable, so long as A is found superior to both? In short one may not wish to posit a social welfare function. In fact this is what we shall do in the exercises of the next chapter (see Chapter 10 section 3(iii)). But if W is not posited then it is difficult to know how to formulate the equal treatment principle.

An alternative route is to assume the existence of a continuous social welfare function and to continue to insist that it be Paretian— i.e. dispense with the equal treatment precept. This may seem reasonable, given the possibility of extinction. But then one needs to search for some other precepts. We come now to two moral considerations that have been much discussed in recent years. Interest in them lies not because they are necessarily compelling but, because taken in conjunction with the previous assumptions on W, they have an interesting implication on the form of W.

To begin with one may feel that it is desirable to treat the 'well-beings' of different generations independently of one another. Loosely speaking, this is to suppose that the rate at which it is desirable to 'exchange' utility of one generation with that of another is independent of any third generation. To give precision to this idea consider a feasible utility sequence $[\bar{u}_t] = (\bar{u}_0, \bar{u}_1, \bar{u}_2, \ldots, \bar{u}_t, \ldots)$, which we shall use as a reference. Consider now two other sequences

$$[u_t] = (u_0, u_1, u_2, \ldots, u_t, \ldots) \quad \text{and} \quad [\hat{u}_t] = (\hat{u}_0, \hat{u}_1, \hat{u}_2, \ldots, \hat{u}_t, \ldots).$$

A very weak form of the idea is to consider the conjunction of the following three requirements:

(a) If $W(u_0, \bar{u}_1, \bar{u}_2, \ldots, \bar{u}_t, \ldots) \geqslant W(\hat{u}_0, \bar{u}_1, \bar{u}_2, \ldots, \bar{u}_t, \ldots)$, then the inequality is independent of $[\bar{u}_t]$.

(b) If $W(u_0, u_1, \bar{u}_2, \ldots, \bar{u}_t, \ldots) \geqslant W(\hat{u}_0, \hat{u}_1, \bar{u}_2, \ldots, \bar{u}_t, \ldots)$, then the inequality is independent of $[\bar{u}_t]$.

(c) If $W(\bar{u}_0, u_1, u_2, \ldots, u_t, \ldots) \geqslant W(\bar{u}_0, \hat{u}_1, \hat{u}_2, \ldots, \hat{u}_t, \ldots)$, then the inequality is independent of $[\bar{u}_t]$.

Quite obviously, postulates (a)–(c) capture only very partially the idea of intergenerational independence that we are interested in. To get a full flavour of what we are after we need to be able to make repeated applications of the postulates. This and a good deal more is provided for by the following ethical consideration: if two utility sequences have identical utility levels at $t=0$, then the ranking of these sequences ought to be the same as the ranking of the two utility sequences obtained by advancing the timing of all subsequent utility levels by one period. In other words, the precept is that in the evaluation of two utility sequences the calendar date for the timing of the utility levels ought not matter.

More formally, consider two sequences $[u_t] \equiv (u_0^*, u_1, u_2, \ldots, u_t, \ldots)$ and $[\hat{u}_t] \equiv (u_0^*, \hat{u}_1, \hat{u}_2, \ldots, \hat{u}_t, \ldots)$. Then $W(u_0^*, \hat{u}_1, \hat{u}_2, \ldots, \hat{u}_t, \ldots) \geqslant W(u_0^*, u_1, u_2, \ldots, u_t, \ldots)$ if and only if $W(\hat{u}_1, \hat{u}_2, \ldots, \hat{u}_t, \ldots) \geqslant W(u_1, u_2, \ldots, u_t, \ldots)$.

This postulate, usually called the *stationarity* assumption, allows postulates (a)–(c) to be applied repeatedly. But it has a good deal more bite than just that. What is now possible to show is that if a continuous and Paretian W satisfies as well the independence and stationarity postulates, then it can be represented in the form[51]

9.11
$$W([u_t]) = \sum_{t=0}^{\infty} \psi(u_t)/(1+\delta)^t, \qquad \delta > 0,$$

and ψ an increasing and continuous function, unique up to a positive linear transformation.

[51] See, for example, Koopmans (1972a). Of course, any monotone increasing function of W will also reflect the same ranking. Notice that since $0 \leqslant u_t \leqslant 1$ and ψ is continuous $\psi(u_t)$ is bounded between two numbers, and hence the RHS of 9.11 is a convergent sum.

As we are supposing here that $u_t = u(C_t)$, and u continuous and increasing, it follows that 9.11 can be written as

9.12 $$V([C_t]) = \sum_{t=0}^{\infty} v(C_t)/(1+\delta)^t, \qquad \delta > 0,$$

and v a continuous and increasing function, unique up to a positive linear transformation.

At first sight this may appear a sleight of hand: and indeed in the absence of perusing a proof of the proposition one cannot fully appreciate the subtlety of the result. It is, of course, easy enough to verify that 9.11 satisfies each of the assumptions that have been made about W. The result we are referring to here says that 9.11 (and any continuous monotone increasing function of it) is the only form of W that will satisfy this set of assumptions.

Several points need to be noted now. First, note that ψ, (and therefore v) is not an explicit function of time. Second, 9.11 (and therefore 9.12) reflect what could be called a constant positive rate of discount δ applied to the planner's ethical assessment of the state of well-being of future generations. The key point is that generations cannot be treated identically. This has been stated in a succinct manner by Koopmans.[52]

'Somewhat fancifully, one may say that the real numbers appear to be a sufficiently rich set of labels to accommodate in a continuous manner all infinite sequences of consumption . . . *only* if one gradually or eventually decreases the weight given to the more distant (consumption levels) in the preference ordering to be represented.'

The axiom structure studied here implies that the inequality in treatment must be of an exceptionally simple form. Third, the postulates are not specific enough to yield the precise functional form of $\psi(\cdot)$ (and therefore, v) and the value of δ. Additional considerations are required to obtain the form of $\psi(\cdot)$ and the value of δ. Here there is a good deal of flexibility. Thus, for example, even when it is judged that $u(\cdot)$ is not strictly concave (because, say, individuals do not display risk-aversion throughout, and such evidence is brought to bear in introspecting the form of $u(\cdot)$) it may still be felt that the weight given to an addition of consumption going to a generation ought to decrease as the consumption level increases. If it is then possible to find an increasing ψ that yields $\psi\{u(\cdot)\}$ (and therefore $v(\cdot)$) strictly concave this consideration will

[52] Koopmans (1972a), p. 97.

have been reflected. In this sense the intuitionist conception is by far the most flexible of the frameworks we have discussed here. This, of course, is also one of its drawbacks.

7. Conclusion

We have now reached an interesting position: three conceptually distinct moral frameworks have, under certain circumstances, been shown to prescribe the same form for the social welfare function (viz. 9.4, 9.9 and 9.12). Their interpretations are, of course, quite different, and it is for this reason that we have gone into this range of questions at some length. The point is this: given the simplicity of the additive separable form for a social welfare function, an overwhelming majority of the exercises in the theory of optimum planning have been based on it. As the authors are normally silent about the moral framework they are appealing to, and as Classical Utilitarianism is the most well known of doctrines, it is on occasion thought it is to this doctrine they must be committed. Not so: our discussion suggests that several frameworks of thought are consistent with the additive separable form, with and without discounting.

Notes on Chapter 9

Our categorization of different ethical doctrines follows that given in the profound work of Rawls (1972), (especially Chapters 3 and 5); though, of course, our focus of attention is considerably narrower, being only on the question of distribution among generations.

Our interpretation of the Harsanyi framework (section 5) is different from the one given by Pattanaik (1968). For further discussion on the matter, see Harsanyi (1976).

Section 6 is based on the contributions of Diamond (1965) and Koopmans (1972a). The results proven in them are somewhat more general than the ones we have reported here. Moreover, as we have not presented all the proofs no attempt has been made to provide the most economic set of axioms. Thus, for example, our version of the stationarity assumption can be arrived at from a weaker version (viz. 'that there exists a u_0^* such that . . .') in conjunction with the independence assumption made earlier.

An issue of fundamental importance that we have not addressed ourselves to is the aggregation of individual *social* welfare functions. In the Classical Utilitarian view there is no problem at this level. Recourse to the impartial spectator ensures that all individuals will assent to the same objective, viz. the maximization of the utility sum. Our version of hypothetical choice behind the veil of ignorance does not resolve this problem, though since different choosing parties behind the veil of ignorance may normalize 9.6 differently. We have assumed the problem away by our assumption of identical generations. The intuitionist conception gives particular leeway to individual ethical beliefs, so that, again, 9.11 reflects the moral views of the person conducting the exercise. A different individual may agree to the *form* depicted in

9.11 though disagreeing with $\psi(\cdot)$ and δ. The issue that we have addressed ourselves to in this Chapter and which we shall discuss also in the next is the manner in which an individual may marshal the various arguments that he may find relevant in reconciling the conflicting demands of different generations. What we have called a social welfare function is an *individual's* social welfare function.

CHAPTER 10

THE OPTIMAL DEPLETION OF EXHAUSTIBLE RESOURCES

1. A General Argument

In the previous chapter we were much concerned with various frameworks that have been utilized in arriving at welfare judgements. We concentrated especially on the question of the manner in which one may evaluate the distribution of consumption across different generations. It is time that we applied those arguments to a specific class of economies and analysed their implications on the rate of capital accumulation and resource depletion.

The economy is the one described in Chapter 7 section 1. In particular, there is a single consumption good. For the moment assume that time is measured in discrete intervals of unit length. As usual, population is constant. A consumption profile is an infinite sequence $\{C_t\} = (C_0, C_1, C_2, \ldots, C_t, \ldots)$. A feasible programme $[K_t, S_t, R_t, C_t]_0^\infty$ is one which satisfies the equations

10.1

$$\left. \begin{array}{l} K_{t+1} - K_t = G(K_t, R_t, L, t) - C_t, \qquad K_0 \text{ given} \\ \text{and} \\ S_{t+1} = S_t - R_t, \qquad S_0 \text{ given} \\ \text{with } K_t, S_t, R_t, C_t \geq 0. \end{array} \right\} {}^1$$

As usual we take it that G is twice continuously differentiable, strictly increasing, strictly concave and linear homogeneous in K, R and L.

Let $V(\{C_t\}) = V(C_0, C_1, \ldots, C_t, \ldots)$ denote the social welfare function. We have already discussed the kinds of arguments that may be brought to bear in arriving at particular forms of V. At this stage we shall not specify its exact form. We take it, however, that it is Paretian (i.e. it is strictly increasing in each of its arguments). We shall also suppose that it is 'smooth' in a sense that will

---

[1] It should be noted that 10.1 is the discrete time analogue of equations 7.3 and 7.4.

be made precise subsequently. In what follows all welfare judgements will be made on the basis of V.

The goal is to find, if they exist, those consumption profiles from among the set of feasible profiles which will maximize V. This is the planning problem. As we noted in the previous chapter it is also a difficult problem. Seemingly innocuous forms of V may possess no maxima in the simplest of economic environments (see Chapter 9 section 4). We ignore such problems for the moment and merely suppose that a maximum exists. Since V is Paretian this maximum is attained along an intertemporally efficient programme. For if the programme were not efficient one could find a feasible programme dominating the sequence. The consumption profile along this dominating programme would yield a higher value for V. Efficiency is a necessary condition for optimality. It is, of course, not a sufficient condition, since there is an infinity of efficient programmes. The social welfare function, V, provides a ranking of these efficient programmes. In Chapter 7 we learnt a great deal about the properties of efficient programmes; and we shall return to them. We now need a condition which, in conjunction with the requirement of efficiency, will enable us to locate the optimal programme. We turn to this. In undertaking this task it will be useful to define a new term.

Let $\{C_t\}$ be a feasible consumption profile. We shall call that rate at which it is found just *desirable* to substitute consumption at some period t for that in the next period $(t+1)$, *the social rate of time preference* between t and $t+1$. We denote it by ρ_t. It is also occasionally referred to as *the consumption rate of interest* and often as *the social rate of discount*.[2] It is a welfare term. It is useful to reconsider the factors that might influence it. One might argue that ρ_t should be positive if $C_{t+1} > C_t$; the argument being that an extra bit of consumption at t is more valuable than the same *extra* bit at $t+1$, since individuals will, in any case, have more consumption at $t+1$. One might then wish to have ρ_t roughly proportional to the rate of growth of consumption, or at any rate, an increasing function of it. One may feel that ρ_t ought to depend on the level of consumption at t as well. On the other hand it may not seem reasonable to have ρ_t depend significantly on consumption rates at times far away from t. This last observation is a mild variant of the independence axiom discussed in the last chapter (see section 6).

[2] See, for example, Arrow and Kurz (1970), Little and Mirrlees (1969) and Dasgupta, Marglin and Sen (1972).

There is a second reason why ρ_t may be positive. We might under-value consumption at $t+1$ as compared to consumption at t simply because $t+1 > t$. We have already noted that, myopia apart, we may wish to take into account the possibility of extinction. It was noted in the previous chapter that this component of ρ_t is usually referred to as the *rate of pure time preference*, or alternatively, as the *rate of impatience*. It was found that a positive rate of impatience is an implication of some particular axioms regarding preferences defined over certain classes of feasible consumption programme.

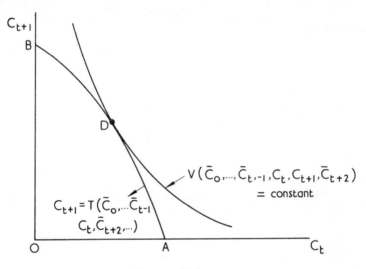

Diagram 10.1

ρ_t is a pure number per unit of time. In terms of traditional terminology it is the marginal rate of indifferent substitution between consumption at t and consumption at $t+1$ less unity. More formally, consider $V(\bar{C}_0, \bar{C}_1, \ldots, \bar{C}_{t-1}, C_t, C_{t+1}, \bar{C}_{t+2}, \ldots)$, where the bar denotes that these quantities are kept fixed. Now, as in Diagram 10.1 we can plot in the (C_t, C_{t+1}) plane the social indifference curve,

10.2 $V(\bar{C}_0, \bar{C}_1, \ldots, \bar{C}_{t-1}, C_t, C_{t+1}, \bar{C}_{t+2}, \ldots) = \text{constant}.$

If V is strictly concave, 10.2 defines a nice (strictly) convex curve.

Its slope minus one we have called ρ_t. Thus, from 10.2 we have

$$\frac{\partial V(\{C_t\})}{\partial C_t}\, dC_t + \frac{\partial V(\{C_t\})}{\partial C_{t+1}}\, dC_{t+1} = 0,$$

yielding

10.3 $\qquad \rho_t \equiv -\dfrac{dC_{t+1}}{dC_t} - 1 = \dfrac{\partial V(\{C_t\})/\partial C_t}{\partial V(\{C_t\})/\partial C_{t+1}} - 1.$

Notice at once that in general ρ_t depends on all the arguments of V. But as we have argued earlier it may appear appropriate to have ρ_t depend only on C_t and C_{t+1}. This will be the case if V assumes the 'Utilitarian' form discussed in the previous chapter. Thus suppose

10.4 $\qquad V(\{C_t\}) = \sum_{t=0}^{\infty} u(C_t)/(1+\delta)^t, \qquad \delta \geqslant 0$

(We are assuming here that the infinite sum exists.) Then since $\partial V(\{C_t\})/\partial C_t = u'(C_t)/(1+\delta)^t$, we have

10.5 $\qquad \rho_t = \dfrac{u'(C_t) - u'(C_{t+1})/(1+\delta)}{u'(C_{t+1})/(1+\delta)}.$

When we come to discussing the 'Utilitarian' optimum in section 3 we shall make use of equation 10.5. But for the moment we concentrate on the more general form 10.3. Since an optimum programme is intertemporally efficient we are concerned with only efficient consumption programmes expressed as

$$C_{t+1} = T(\bar{C}_0, \ldots, \bar{C}_{t-1}, C_t, \bar{C}_{t+2} \ldots),$$

where again, the bar denotes that these quantities are being kept fixed. Given the assumption that we have made earlier in this section about the production function in 10.1, T is a concave curve. It has been drawn as AB in Diagram 10.1. It will be recalled from the account in Chapter 7 section 5(i) that the social rate of return on investment at t, r_t, is the slope of the curve AB less unity at the point at which the rate is being computed. Thus

$$r_t = -\partial T/\partial C_t - 1.$$

Diagram 10.1 now indicates that if consumption at all dates other than t and $t+1$ are held fixed at their 'barred' values, then in

choosing between points on AB one cannot do better than to choose
D, the point at which $\rho_t = r_t$. In traditional terminology the condition tells us that the marginal rate of transformation between
consumption at dates t and $t+1$ must equal their marginal rate of
indifferent substitution.[3]

Let us now generalize the above argument. Begin by making the
rather innocuous assumption that consumption along an optimal
programme is positive throughout (though possibly tailing off to
zero in the long run). Continue to assume that V is strictly concave.
Let $[K_t, S_t, R_t, C_t]_0^\infty$ denote an efficient programme, and let r_t
denote the social rate of return on investment along it. Then a
necessary and sufficient condition for this programme to be optimal
is that

10.6 $r_t = \rho_t$ for all t.

It will be useful to restate condition 10.6 explicitly in the language
of social cost–benefit analysis, since the latter is so familiar. Suppose
that the LHS of equation 10.6 were to fall short of the RHS at any
date. Now one marginal unit of consumption at t can be transformed
into $1 + r_t$ units at $t+1$. But this will fall short of $1 + \rho_t$, the number
of units of extra consumption at $t+1$ that will compensate for the
loss of a unit of consumption at t. It follows that social welfare
could be increased by consuming somewhat more at that date
and consequently investing just that much less. In the language of
cost–benefit analysis, the return on marginal investment (r_t), being
less than the rate (ρ_t) at which it is socially desirable to discount
next period's consumption, makes this alteration an improvement.
When this marginal adjustment is made (i.e. a neighbouring programme is chosen) presumably r_t is increased (since G is strictly
concave) and ρ_t reduced (since V is strictly concave). One makes
these marginal adjustments until the two are brought into equality.
Similarly, if the LHS of equation 10.6 exceeds its RHS at any date
along an efficient programme a reverse argument comes into play
and so social welfare could be improved by consuming somewhat
less at that date. In the language of cost–benefit analysis this

[3] This conclusion is correct if, as in Diagram 10.1, the optimum is a point
at which $C_t, C_{t+1} > 0$. It will not necessarily be correct if in fact the optimum
is at A or B. We ignore such 'corner' solutions in our exposition. The
reader will note that precisely this condition (i.e. $\rho_t = r_t$) was depicted in
Diagram 4.1. Since OA = OB in Diagram 4.1, the rate of return on investment
is strictly zero in that example. Consequently at C, the point of tangency,
$\rho = r = 0$. Not at all surprising. We had been describing a *pure storage* problem
there.

marginal investment is worth carrying out, since the return on the investment exceeds the rate at which it is judged desirable to discount next period's consumption. If this marginal investment is made (i.e. a neighbouring programme is chosen) r_t decreases and ρ_t increases. One makes these marginal adjustments until the two are brought into equality.

The necessity of condition 10.6 for a programme to be optimal is therefore clear enough. The fact that for an efficient programme 10.6 is also sufficient is a good deal harder to prove.[4] But the result is probably not altogether surprising.

This is about as far as one can go in general terms. In the next two sections we shall analyse optimal programmes in the light of differing ethical beliefs.

2. The Maxi-min Programme

Generations have identical tastes and needs. Each generation is concerned solely with its own consumption level. We may as well then analyse the maxi-min consumption profile and not bother about writing down utility levels at all. We have, however, two simple points to dispose of. The first is a point that has already been raised in the last chapter, namely that the maxi-min criterion is not Paretian in the sense that the term has been used throughout this book. This will in fact cause no embarrassment, because obviously we shall wish to search from among the set of intertemporally efficient programmes. So that loosely speaking, the maxi-min policy from this set will be the 'correct' maxi-min policy. The second point is that with maxi-min ethical preferences condition 10.6 cannot be given any meaning. This is because along an optimum programme the social rate of time preference, ρ_t, cannot be defined. One can demonstrate this very simply. Diagram 10.2 below is similar to Diagram 10.1 in all respects excepting for the shape of the social indifference curves. A typical indifference curve is JDH. D is obviously the maxi-min policy over the two periods t and $t+1$. And indeed so long as the boundary points of the production set are all efficient the maxi-min policy will always lie on the 45° line ODE. But at points such as D the indifference curves have 'corners'. The marginal rate of indifferent substitution between consumption at these two dates cannot be defined.

[4] For such demonstrations see the references in the notes to Chapter 10, and especially Arrow and Kurz (1970).

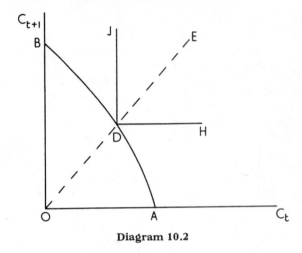

Diagram 10.2

Condition 10.6 has then to be dispensed with. But this is no cause for worry. Diagram 10.2 shows that with the maxi-min criterion we choose from among the set of feasible pairs of consumption (C_t, C_{t+1}) the one with the highest constant consumption for the two periods (i.e. the point D). It is now obvious that the criterion will choose from among the set of all feasible consumption programmes $\{C_t\}$ the one with the highest constant consumption for all periods; the maximum constant consumption programme.

Let us now illustrate this by means of an example.

For expository ease suppose time to be continuous. The economy is described by equations 7.3 and 7.4. The production function is Cobb–Douglas, and there is no technical change (i.e. $F(K_t, R_t, L) = K_t^{\alpha_1} R_t^{\alpha_2}$). Suppose $\alpha_1 > \alpha_2 > 0$, and as usual that $1 - \alpha_1 - \alpha_2 > 0$. Now recall the programmes defined by equations 7.12. In particular, recall the maximum constant consumption path $C_t = \bar{C}_{\max}$ (see equation 7.14). For convenience let us rewrite the programme as

10.7
$$
\left.
\begin{aligned}
&K_t = K_0 + mt, \\
&R_t = (\bar{C}_{\max} + m)^{1/\alpha_2}(K_0 + mt)^{-\alpha_1/\alpha_2} \\
&C_t = \bar{C}_{\max} > 0 \\
&\text{and} \\
&m^{1-\alpha_2} = \alpha_2 \left(\frac{\alpha_1 - \alpha_2}{\alpha_2}\right)^{\alpha_2} S_0{}^{\alpha_2} K_0{}^{\alpha_1 - \alpha_2}
\end{aligned}
\right\}.
$$

The last equation of 10.7 yields the rate of investment, $\dot{K}_t (=m)$

along the programme. It is constant. Moreover, the larger are S_0 and/or K_0 the larger is the volume of investment per instant. One recalls as well that the savings ratio sustaining this programme is α_2, the share of royalty to national income.

In Chapter 7 section 3(ii) it was noted that the programme is intertemporally efficient. It must then be the optimum consumption policy under the maxi-min criterion. Any other (continuous) feasible programme must have consumption less than $\bar{C}_{\max}$ during some interval and must therefore be judged inferior to the consumption path $C_t = \bar{C}_{\max}$.

We have already discussed several features of the programme yielding $C_t = \bar{C}_{\max}$. The resource utilization ratio has not, however, been analysed. Using equation 10.7 it is readily checked that R_t/S_t is proportional to $(K_0 + mt)^{-1}$. Now, $S_t \to 0$. It follows that a vanishing fraction of this vanishing stock is all that is required in the long run to maintain consumption at the level $\bar{C}_{\max}$. A constant savings ratio of α_2 implies a sufficiently high rate of capital accumulation to overcome this dwindling resource use.

It remains to discuss some institutional settings in which the optimum programme is set in motion. Suppose first that we are postulating a socially managed economy. Both the assets are owned socially and the rate of consumption is determined and legislated socially. Let the homogeneous reproducible asset be the numeraire. It follows then that the government could decentralize the pace of capital accumulation and resource extraction by announcing complete intertemporal profiles of the social rate of return and the shadow price of the exhaustible resource. One can then imagine the government production managers (by maximizing shadow profits) demanding, and the government resource owners supplying, precisely equal amounts so that the 'shadow market' for the flow of the resource is cleared at each date. At the same time the announcement of the intertemporal profile of the social rate of return r_t will in principle ensure that the optimum investment decisions are made. The marginal investment project along the optimum programme will have zero present value when discounted at the rates r_t. In Chapter 7 (section 5(ii)) we looked at the profile of r_t along the maxi-min programme. The question remains: what does the spot shadow price of the resource look like along the maxi-min programme? Let p_t denote this price. Then

10.8 $$p_t = F_{Rt} = \alpha_2 K_t^{\alpha_1} R_t^{\alpha_2 - 1}.$$

Using 10.7 in 10.8 yields

10.9 $\quad p_t = \alpha_2 m^{\alpha_2 - 1} \left(\dfrac{\alpha_1 - \alpha_2}{\alpha_2} \right)^{\alpha_2 - 1} S_0^{\alpha_2 - 1} K_0^{(\alpha_2 - 1)(\alpha_1 - \alpha_2)/\alpha_2} (K_0 + mt)^{\alpha_1/\alpha_2}$

where m is determined from the last equation in 10.7. It follows from equation 10.9 that p_t rises ultimately like t^{α_1/α_2}. But it ought to be borne in mind that since the programme is intertemporally efficient, it satisfies the Hotelling Rule ($F_K = \dot{F}_R/F_R$). The present value shadow price of the exhaustible resource is therefore constant.

Suppose now a different institutional setting, one where the government can legislate the price of the resource, even though the resource is owned privately by price taking individuals. Suppose next that individuals save a fixed fraction, s, of their disposable income. The government desires to steer the economy along the optimum. To make the problem interesting one must suppose that $s \neq \alpha_2$ (otherwise the government needs only to facilitate the establishment of a complete set of forward markets). We next take it that the government can tax the citizens and use the tax for investment purposes. Moreover, assume that private capital and public capital are indistinguishable. Let T_t be the total tax receipt at t. Then gross investment is equal to the sum of personal savings and taxes. Hence

10.10 $\qquad\qquad \dot{K}_t = s(Y_t - T_t) + T_t,$

where Y_t is, as usual, total output. Now along the optimum programme

$$Y_t = \bar{C} + m = \frac{\bar{C}_{\max}}{(1 - \alpha_2)}$$

(see equation 10.7), and

$$\dot{K}_t = m = \frac{\alpha_2 \bar{C}_{\max}}{1 - \alpha_2}.$$

It follows from equation 10.10 that

$$T_t = T = \frac{(\alpha_2 - s)\bar{C}_{\max}}{(1 - \alpha_2)(1 - s)}.$$

To steer the economy along the optimum the governments needs to introduce a constant rate of taxation on income. This procedure will certainly work if $s < \alpha_2$, since in this case $T > 0$. If $s > \alpha_2$ (the citizens are over-saving) then $T < 0$, and the tax is in fact a subsidy. But this will be impossible for the government to impose unless it owns some capital of its own. So a somewhat different policy suggests itself. The idea now is for the government to tax income at a rate T_t and to have the proceeds consumed. Total consumption is then $C_t = (1-s)(Y_t - T_t) + T_t$, and the rate of capital accumulation is

10.11 $$\dot{K}_t = s(Y_t - T_t).$$

It follows from equation 10.11 that in order to pursue the maxi-min programme the government needs to set

$$T_t = \frac{(s - \alpha_2)}{s(1 - \alpha_2)} \, \bar{C}_{max} > 0.$$

But in each case (i.e. $s \lessgtr \alpha_2$), with the government having announced T_t and with the forward markets having established r_t and p_t, private and social profitability calculations will steer the economy along the optimum programme. Private (and in the case $s < \alpha_2$, social) cost–benefit analysis will ensure that aggregate investment demand at t is precisely equal to the RHS of 10.10 or 10.11 (depending on the case at hand). With p_t and r_t known the marginal investment project will show zero present value of profits along the optimal programme. At the same time the demand for the resource flow for production will be precisely that which is optimal. Since the present value of the resource price is constant suppliers may as well bring forth the required amounts at each date.

3. The 'Utilitarian' Optimum

(i) *General characteristics:* For technical reasons it will be convenient to work with continuous time. Thus we take it that

10.12
$$\left. \begin{array}{l} V = \int\limits_0^\infty \exp(-\delta t) u(C_t) dt \\[2mm] \text{where} \\ \delta \geq 0, \quad \text{and} \quad u'(C) > 0, \; u''(C) < 0 \\ \lim_{C \to 0} u'(C) = \infty \quad \text{and} \quad \lim_{C \to \infty} u(C) = 0 \end{array} \right\}.$$

In 10.12 the social welfare function is the continuous time analogue of 10.4. In what follows we shall refer to $u(C_t)$ as the *felicity* of consuming C_t, since, as we noted in the previous chapter, V may merely reflect an individual's ethical views, which may or may not conform with Utilitarianism.[5] If in fact V is founded on Utilitarianism, then what we are calling the felicity function is the traditional utility function.

In the above formulation δ is the constant rate of impatience. It is the percentage rate at which the felicity discount factor, $\exp(-\delta t)$, changes. The strict concavity of $u(\cdot)$ is an important assumption. It ensures that V is strictly concave over the set of feasible consumption profiles. The fact that V is Paretian on consumption sequences is caught by the assumption that $u' > 0$. The two limit conditions are, for our purposes, innocuous. The first will ensure that consumption is always positive along an optimum programme. The second is to ensure that V is bounded above. If one were to work with a felicity function for which $\lim_{C \to \infty} u(C) = B < \infty$ one could as well express the social welfare function as $V = \int_0^\infty \exp(-\delta t)\{u(C_t) - B\}\, dt = \int_0^\infty \exp(-\delta t)\, v(C_t)\, dt$, and thereby obtain $\lim_{C \to \infty} v(C) = 0$. Matters can be quite different if $u(c)$ is unbounded above. We shall ignore this case in what follows.[6]

It is clear from 10.12 that if V is well defined (i.e. the infinite integral exists) it is smooth enough for the social rate of time preference (ρ_t) to be definable.[7]

Earlier we obtained the expression for it under the discrete-time formulation (see equation 10.5). We now need the continuous-time formulation of the RHS of equation 10.5. In order to do this the dates t and $t+1$ in 10.5 are replaced by t and $t+\epsilon$, where ϵ is an arbitrarily small number. Also replace $1/(1+\delta)^t$ by $\exp(-\delta t)$ and $1/(1+\delta)^{t+1}$ by $\exp\{-\delta(t+\epsilon)\}$. Thus the RHS of 10.5 becomes $[\exp(-\delta t)\, u'(C_t) - \exp\{-\delta(t+\epsilon)\}\, u'(C_{t+\epsilon})]/\exp\{-\delta(t+\epsilon)\}\, u'(C_{t+\epsilon})$, On taking the limit of the above expression as $\epsilon \to 0$ we obtain

$$
\left.
\begin{aligned}
\rho_t &= -\frac{d}{dt}\{\exp(-\delta t)\, u'(C_t)\}/\exp(-\delta t)\, u'(C_t) \\[2mm]
\text{or} & \\[2mm]
\rho_t &= \delta - \frac{u''(C_t)\dot{C}_t}{u'(\bar{C}_t)}
\end{aligned}
\right\}.
$$

10.13

[5] The terminology is due to Gorman (1957).

[6] For details of this case see Dasgupta and Heal (1974).

[7] In fact it is definable even if the felicity sum is non-convergent but where, say, an extended Utilitarian optimum exists. We are ignoring such problems here because we are supposing that a maximum value of V exists.

Equation 10.13 tells us that the social rate of time preference at t is the percentage rate at which discounted marginal felicity decreases at t.

Write

$$\eta(C) = - \frac{u''(C)C}{u'(C)} \qquad (>0)$$

as the elasticity of marginal felicity. Then 10.13 can be expressed as

10.14 $$\rho_t = \delta + \eta(C_t) \frac{\dot{C}_t}{C_t}.$$

The two terms in the RHS of 10.14 bring out clearly the two sets of considerations that we argued may well be relevant when considering the appropriate value of ρ_t along a given programme. Since $u''(C) < 0$, we have $\eta(C) > 0$. Consequently, if $\dot{C}_t > 0$ the second term is positive. Thus in fact strict concavity of $u(\cdot)$ captures the view that there is a case for discounting future consumption if future generations are going to be better off. This component of the social rate of discount at any given date depends solely on the percentage rate of change in consumption and the elasticity of marginal felicity at that date, and that too in a multiplicative way. The higher is $\dot{C}_t/C_t$ and/or the larger is the value of $\eta(C_t)$ the greater is the social rate of discount at t. δ reflects the second component of ρ_t that we discussed earlier on. Even if $\dot{C}_t = 0$, one may wish to discount future consumption simply because it is in the future and there is a possibility of extinction. Moreover, we noted earlier that $\delta > 0$ is indeed an implication of certain postulates on preferences defined over infinite consumption profiles. But there would be many who would find no justification for discounting future felicity. For this reason one must also consider the case $\delta = 0$. But even if the felicity rate of discount is chosen to be zero the consumption rate of interest (ρ_t) will throughout be positive along a rising consumption programme. Let us see what the orders of magnitude might be. Suppose $\delta = 0$, $\dot{C}_t/C_t = 0 \cdot 03$ and $\eta(C_t) = \eta = 2$. Then $\rho_t = 0 \cdot 06$ (i.e. the social rate of discount is 6% per unit time at t). If, on the other hand, $\delta = 0 \cdot 02$ (roughly speaking a generation thirty-five years hence is given half the felicity weight of the current generation), then $\rho_t = 0 \cdot 08$. But, being 'if then' statements they are not a direct guide to policy. The task we have set ourselves is to locate the optimum consumption programme (and therefore the optimum time profile of the social rate of discount). Let us now conduct this planning exercise We take it that technological possibilities are given by the continuous-time formulation of 10.1. For the moment assume no technical change. A programme $[K_t, S_t, R_t, C_t]_0^\infty$ is feasible if it satisfies the equations

10.15
$$\left.\begin{array}{l}\dot{K}_t = F(K_t, R_t) - C_t, \qquad K_0 \text{ given} \\ \text{and} \\ \dot{S}_t = -R_t, \qquad S_0 \text{ given}, \quad \text{and} \quad K_t, R_t, S_t, C_t > 0\end{array}\right\}.$$

The planning problem consists in obtaining that feasible programme that will maximize 10.12. One may regard the situation as being one where the government chooses two functions C_t and R_t. The rates of consumption and resource extraction could then be regarded as the *control variables*. The time profiles of the stocks of the composite commodity and the exhaustible resource would then follow from equations 10.15. K_t and S_t are usually referred to as *state variables* in this formulation. At this stage we shall not enquire into the conditions under which an optimum programme exists. It will become clearer later that we shall need further assumptions to ensure that the planning problem that we have posed has an answer.

Assume then that an optimum programme exists. A question of interest is whether along an optimum the resource is exhausted in finite time or whether it is spread out thinly over the indefinite future. It transpires that it is not desirable to exhaust the resource in finite time if *either* (a) the resource is necessary for production (i.e. $F(K, 0) = 0$) *or* (b) the marginal product of the resource (or equivalently, its average product), is unbounded for vanishing resource use (i.e. $\lim_{R \to 0} F_R(K, R) = \infty$).[8] To economists, condition (b) would be really rather obvious. If the resource at the *margin* is infinitely valuable for zero rate of use it would clearly be suboptimal to exhaust it in finite time and have no resource left for use subsequent to the exhaustion date. It would prove desirable to spread the resource thinly over the indefinite future. However, if condition (a) is satisfied, but not (b), the result is not so obvious, though perhaps to non-economists it is the more transparent condition. But recall that by assumption the durable capital good can be eaten into. By assumption gross investment in fixed capital can be negative. Therefore, one can have positive consumption at all times

[8] This is proved in Dasgupta and Heal (1974) under somewhat different technological conditions.

despite an absence of the resource. This is why condition (a) on its own is not readily transparent. But one can see why the result comes out the way it does. Suppose (a) holds. If the resource is exhausted in finite time there is no production subsequent to the date of exhaustion. Subsequent generations will be forced to consume out of the remaining stock of the durable commodity. It would be a cake-eating economy, and the social rate of return on investment would be nil. Savings will have no productivity. It is this feature that can be avoided were the resource not to be exhausted in finite time. By assumption investment is productive ($F_K > 0$) so long as production is kept ticking along. But if (a) holds one can have production only if $R > 0$.

If, however, *neither* (a) *nor* (b) holds it can be shown that along an optimum programme the resource is exhausted in finite time.[9] The resource is neither necessary for production nor is it infinitely valuable at the margin at vanishing rates of use. The idea roughly is to use up the resource early in the planning horizon to raise the levels of consumption during the initial years while fixed capital is accumulated. Production is then maintained even after the resource is exhausted.

We have now at hand a necessary and sufficient condition under which it is desirable to spread the resource over the indefinite future. Along an optimal programme $R_t > 0$ if, and only if, either (a) or (b) holds. Since this is obviously the interesting case we shall assume, in what follows, that the production function satisfies either condition (a) or condition (b).

Since an optimum programme is intertemporally efficient it must satisfy the conditions

10.16 $$F_K = \dot{F}_R / F_R \qquad \text{for all } t \geqslant 0$$

and

10.17 $$\lim_{t \to \infty} S_t = 0.^{[10]}$$

Now we know that along an efficient programme $r_t = F_{Kt}$ (see Chapter 7 section 4(ii)). Using this fact and equation 10.14 in the optimality condition 10.6 yields

10.18 $$\frac{\eta(C_t)\dot{C}_t}{C_t} + \delta = F_{Kt}.$$

[9] See Dasgupta and Heal (1974).
[10] See conditions 7.28 and 7.29 in Chapter 7 section 3.

Equation 10.18 is widely referred to in the literature as the Ramsey Rule.[11] It is a special case of the rather general optimality condition 10.6. Its virtue lies in its simplicity. The condition brings out in the simplest manner possible the various considerations that may appear to being morally relevant in deciding on the optimum rate of accumulation. We now analyse the set of conditions that has been obtained.

Equations 10.16 and 10.18 together imply

$$F_{Kt} + \frac{u''(C_t)C_t}{u'(C_t)} \frac{\dot{C}_t}{C_t} - \delta = \frac{\dot{F}_{Rt}}{F_{Rt}} + \frac{u''(C_t)C_t}{u'(C_t)} \frac{\dot{C}_t}{C_t} - \delta = 0.$$

Integrating this yields

10.19 $\quad\quad \exp(-\delta t)\, u'(C_t)F_{Rt} = \lambda \quad\quad (>0), \ldots$

where λ is a constant.[12] This is familiar matter. The economy being discussed in this section possesses three 'commodities': felicity, aggregate output, and the exhaustible resource. Let felicity be the numeraire. Then in the language of shadow prices $u'(C_t)$ is the spot price of output (consumption). Consequently $u'(C_t)F_{Rt}$ is the spot price of the resource. It follows that $\exp(-\delta t)\, u'(C_t)F_{Rt}$ is the present value price of the resource (δ is the own rate of interest on felicity; see Chapter 4 section 2). It should by now be obvious that this must be constant along an optimum programme. But the shadow spot price of the resource in terms of output is F_R and this rises to infinity at the percentage rate F_K.

As we have mentioned earlier, equation 10.16 holds throughout an optimal programme if, and only if, either condition (a) or condition (b) holds. At least one of these conditions is met by the class of all CES production functions; so long, of course, as the elasticity of substitution is finite (see equations 7.5 and 7.6); that is, if

$$F(K, R) = \{\alpha_1 K^{(\sigma-1)/\sigma} + \alpha_2 R^{(\sigma-1)/\sigma} + (1 - \alpha_1 - \alpha_2)\}^{\sigma/(\sigma-1)}$$

for $0 < \sigma < \infty$ $(\sigma \neq 1)$. $\sigma = 1$ corresponds to the Cobb–Douglas form $F(K, R) = K^{\alpha_1}R^{\alpha_2}$ $(\alpha_1, \alpha_2, 1 - \alpha_1 - \alpha_2 > 0)$. If $\sigma > 1$, the resource is not necessary for production (i.e. condition (a) is not satisfied) but condition (b) is met.[13] If $0 < \sigma < 1$, then while condition (b) is not

[11] In honour of Frank Ramsey, who pioneered the theory of optimum intertemporal planning in an article published in 1928.

[12] As with earlier analyses (e.g. that in Chapter 4 section 4) the numerical value of λ is chosen so as to satisfy the resource constraint, 10.17.

[13] The resource is infinitely valuable at the margin for vanishing rate of utilization.

satisfied, the resource is necessary for production (i.e. condition (a) is met). For the Cobb–Douglas case $(\sigma=1)$ both (a) and (b) are satisfied. In what follows we shall work with the Cobb–Douglas form. As we argued in Chapter 7, for the resource problem this provides the most interesting possibilities.

A necessary and sufficient pair of conditions for a feasible programme to be optimal is that it is efficient and that it satisfies the Ramsey Rule. For a programme to be efficient it is necessary that conditions 10.16 and 10.17 are satisfied. Moreover, we noted in Chapter 7 section 3(ii) that if the production function is of the Cobb–Douglas form conditions 10.16 and 10.17 are together also sufficient for a programme to be intertemporally efficient. It follows that in a world with a Cobb–Douglas technology equations 10.16–10.18 form a set of necessary and sufficient conditions for a feasible programme to be optimal. If an optimal programme exists, it will be characterized by these equations. If an optimal programme does not exist, no feasible programme will at the same time satisfy them. The three equations will be inconsistent with the requirement that the programme be feasible.

It will prove immensely helpful to specialize further and suppose that η, the elasticity of marginal felicity, is a constant. The greater the value of η the more 'concave' is the felicity function. This will imply in turn what could, in some sense, be termed a more 'egalitarian' intertemporal consumption policy. This is typically how intuition would go. This turns out to be correct.

Let $F(K_t, R_t) = K_t^{\alpha_1} R_t^{\alpha_2}$. To have an interesting problem we take it, as usual, that $\alpha_1 > \alpha_2 > 0$. Naturally, $1-\alpha_1-\alpha_2 > 0$. By assumption $\lim_{C\to\infty} u(C) = 0$. Consequently $\eta > 1$, and so

$$u(C) = -C^{-(\eta-1)}.$$

(ii) *Positive felicity discounting* $\delta > 0$: It may seem plausible that an optimal programme exists if $\delta > 0$. This is in fact the case.[14] Here we shall characterize it in broad terms.

Rewrite equation 10.18 for the present model as

10.20
$$\dot{C}_t/C_t = \frac{\alpha_1 K_t^{\alpha_1-1} R_t^{\alpha_2} - \delta}{\eta}.$$

Feasibility dictates that $R_t \to 0$. Since $\delta > 0$, the only way one can ensure that $\dot{C}_t/C_t$ is non-negative in the long run is that $K_t \to 0$ as

[14] See Dasgupta and Heal (1974).

well. But if $K_t \to 0$ then $Y_t \to 0$, and hence $C_t \to 0$. Consequently an implication of equation 10.20 is that $C_t \to 0$. A positive rate of impatience, no matter how small, implies that it is judged optimal to allow the economy to decay in the long run, even although it is feasible to avoid decay. This is so no matter how large a value of η we choose to express our values. A positive rate of pure time preference tilts the balance overwhelmingly against generations in the distant future. This alone is a powerful result; it indicates that 'Utilitarianism' with a positive rate of impatience can recommend what can be regarded as ethically questionable policies. The welfare criterion does not recommend sufficient capital accumulation in the early years to offset the declining resource use inevitable in later years. Since the optimum is efficient, consumption at some interval must exceed $\bar{C}_{max}$. It can be shown that the consumption profile will have at most one peak (at $T \geqslant 0$); the lower is δ the further away

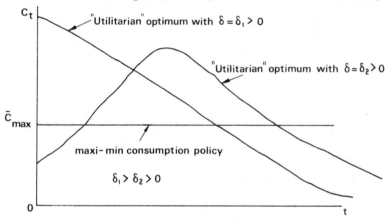

Diagram 10.3

in the future is the peak. In Diagram 10.3 a typical optimum consumption path (with $\delta > 0$) is contrasted with the intergenerational maxi-min policy. Of course, later generations (should they exist) suffer incredibly as a result of the initial profligacy under the Utilitarian programme. They are far worse off than they would be under the maxi-min policy.[15]

[15] To put the matter rather dramatically, notice that $u(C_t) \to -\infty$ as $C_t \to 0$. Nevertheless, the implication of $\delta > 0$ is that, *viewed from the present* instant (i.e. $t = 0$) this is not only not disastrous, but desirable! But if δ reflects the possibility of future extinction the probability that generations far off in the distant future will exist will also tend to zero!

A casual inspection of the Ramsey Rule 10.20 suggests that the effect of a large value of η is to flatten the consumption path somewhat, the dive towards zero consumption being that much postponed. It is interesting to note that the two parameters reflecting ethical values, η and δ, play somewhat dissimilar roles. In a loose sense, the larger is η the more 'egalitarian' is the distribution of consumption (and felicities) across generations.[16] This makes good sense if one recollects that the effect of a large η on the felicity function is to impose more curvature on it, as Diagram 10.4 demonstrates. There are benefits to be had in keeping consumption for a

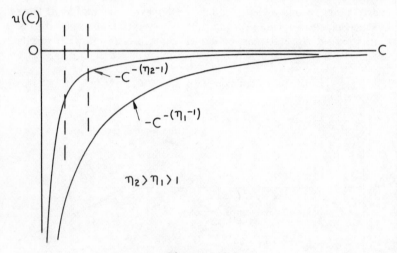

Diagram 10.4

long while within the region in which the felicity function makes a sharp turn. The effect of δ is quite different and its consequence is a discrimination against future felicities. Here the consequence is dramatic: a positive δ results in generations a long way away receiving very little capital. Their consumption rates are nearly zero.

Much of our attention has been focused on the way augmentable capital can substitute for exhaustible resources in production. With this in mind the Hotelling condition 10.16 can be written in an unusually simple form. It will enable us to interpret the manner in

[16] The precise sense in which this is true has been discussed well in Atkinson (1970). See also Mirrlees and Stern (1972).

which fixed capital ought to substitute for resource use along optimal programmes in general. Towards this define $\tilde{R}_t$ as $\tilde{R}_t = R_t^{(1-\alpha_2)/\alpha_1}$. One is then merely measuring the resource use in terms of a new system of units (for $\tilde{R}_t$ is a monotonically increasing function of R, and $\tilde{R}=0$ when $R=0$; $\tilde{R}=\infty$ when $R=\infty$). Now $F_R = \alpha_2 K^{\alpha_1} R^{\alpha_2-1} = \alpha_2 K^{\alpha_1} \tilde{R}^{-\alpha_1}$. Moreover, $F_K = \alpha_1 K^{\alpha_1-1} R^{\alpha_2} = \alpha_1(Y/K)$. On using this in equation 10.16 yields

$$\alpha_1(\dot{K}_t/K_t - \dot{\tilde{R}}_t/\tilde{R}_t) = \alpha_1 \frac{Y}{K},$$

Let $Z_t = K_t/\tilde{R}_t$, and let $x_t = Y_t/K_t$ denote the output capital ratio. Then the above reduces to

10.21 $$\dot{Z}_t/Z_t = x_t.$$

This is an appealing condition. It says that the greater is the output–capital ratio the faster is the percentage rate at which it is desirable to substitute fixed capital for the resource in use. Stating it another way, the more valuable is fixed capital in production (at the margin or on average, it does not matter), the greater is the speed with which fixed capital ought to substitute for resource in use. It ought to be emphasized that equation 10.21 is a condition that efficient paths must satisfy. Its validity does not rest on the Utilitarian formulation of the optimality criterion that we have been analysing in this section.[17]

We are interested in the optimum rate of resource depletion. Return once again to our general optimality condition 10.19. It is that $\exp(-\delta t)u'(C_t)F_{Rt} = (\lambda > 0)$. For the special case at hand (i.e. iso-elastic felicity function $u(C_t) = -C_t^{-(\eta-1)}$, $\eta > 1$, and Cobb–Douglas production function) this becomes

$$(\eta-1)\alpha_2 \exp(-\delta t)C_t^{-\eta}R_t^{-(1-\alpha_2)}K^{\alpha_1} = \lambda.\text{[18]}$$

This is written more conveniently as

10.22 $$C_t/K_t = \exp\{-(\delta/\eta)t\}\{(\eta-1)\alpha_2/\lambda\}^{1/\eta}K_t^{-(1-\alpha_1)/\eta}R_t^{-(1-\alpha_2/\eta)}.$$

---

[17] One can in fact cast equation 10.16 into a form similar to equation 10.21 for the class of CES production functions in general. The elasticity of substitution plays a key role in such an equation. For details, see Dasgupta and Heal (1974).

[18] For $u'(C_t) = (\eta-1)C_t^{-\eta}$ and $F_R = \alpha_2 K^{\alpha_1} R^{\alpha_2-1}$.

But observe that equation 10.21 and the fact that $\tilde{R}_t = R_t^{(1-\alpha_2)/\alpha_1}$ implies

10.23 $$C_t/K_t = Y_t/K_t - \dot{K}_t/K_t = -\frac{(1-\alpha_2)\dot{R}_t}{\alpha_1 R_t}.\,^{19}$$

From equations 10.22 and 10.23 we now obtain

10.24 $$\left(\frac{1-\alpha_2}{\alpha_1}\right)\dot{R}_t/R_t$$
$$= -\{(\eta-1)\alpha_2/\lambda\}^{1/\eta}\exp\{-(\delta/\eta)t\}K_t^{(\alpha_1/\eta)-1}R_t^{-(1-\alpha_2)/\eta} < 0.$$

It follows that R_t declines monotonically along the optimal programme.

Equation 10.24 is an equation in $\dot{R}_t$. We can now express the equation for capital accumulation, 10.15, as

$$\dot{K}_t = K_t^{\alpha_1} R_t^{\alpha_2} - C_t.$$

Now use equation 10.22 in this to obtain

10.25 $$\dot{K}_t = K^{\alpha_1} R_t^{\alpha_2}$$
$$-\exp\{-(\delta/\eta)t\}\{(\eta-1)\alpha_2/\lambda\}^{1/\eta}K_t^{\alpha_1/\eta}R_t^{-(1-\alpha_2)/\eta}.$$

Equations 10.24 and 10 25 are a pair of equations in $\dot{K}_t$ and $\dot{R}_t$. With $\delta > 0$ the pair is non-autonomous in time. This is what makes them difficult to dissect in detail. But it is possible to say a good deal about the long run behaviour of an optimum programme. We have argued that both $C_t \to 0$ and $K_t \to 0$. And of course $R_t \to 0$. Consequently $Y_t \to 0$. The economy is allowed to decay in the long run. It can in fact be shown that $F_K \to \delta\alpha_2/\{1-\alpha_1+\alpha_2(\eta-1)\} < \delta$. Consequently, $g_C \equiv \dot{C}_t/C_t \to -(\delta/\eta)(1-\alpha_2)/(1-\alpha_1-\alpha_2+\eta\alpha_2) < 0$. It is also possible to demonstrate that $g_S \equiv \dot{S}_t/S_t \to -\delta(1-\alpha_1)/\{1-\alpha_1+\alpha_2(\eta-1)\}$.[20] Consequently $R_t/S_t \to \delta(1-\alpha_1)/\{1-\alpha_1+\alpha_2(\eta-1)\}$. Suppose then that $\eta = 2$ and $\delta = 0.02$. Suppose also, by way of illustration, that $\alpha_1 = 0.25$ and $\alpha_2 = 0.05$. Then $R_t/S_t \to 0.02$; about 2% of the then existing stock ought to be extracted in the long run. To state it equivalently, about fifty years of resource supply at the then current rates of extraction ought to be available in the long run.

[19] 10.21 says that $\dot{K}_t/K_t - \dot{\tilde{R}}_t/\tilde{R}_t = Y_t/K_t$. But $\dot{\tilde{R}}_t/\tilde{R}_t = (1-\alpha_2)/\alpha_1\dot{R}_t/R_t$ and $C_t = Y_t - \dot{K}_t$. These yield 10.23.
[20] For proofs of all these assertions, see Dasgupta and Heal (1974) and Stiglitz (1974b).

Moreover, the optimum rate of consumption will be declining in the long run at about $1\cdot2\%$ per annum, while the consumption rate of interest, $\rho_t(=F_K)$ will approach the figure of about $0\cdot1\%$ per annum.

(iii) *No felicity discounting:* $\delta=0$: The interesting special case is $\delta=0$. The consequences are quite different if we assume this. Let us now do so. Equations 10.24 and 10.25 are then autonomous differential equations. Diagram 10.5 depicts their phase paths. GH is the locus of points at which $\dot K_t=0$. It is obtained from equation 10.25 by setting $\delta=0$ and $\dot K_t=0$. Its equation is

$$10.26 \qquad K=\{(\eta-1)\alpha_2/\eta\}^{1/\alpha_1(\eta-1)}R^{-\{1+\alpha_2(\eta-1)\}/\alpha_1(\eta-1)}.$$

Anywhere to the north-east of GH, $\dot K_t>0$. Anywhere to the south-west of GH, $\dot K_t<0$. As equation 10.24 makes clear, there is no corresponding locus along which $\dot R_t=0$. $\dot R_t<0$ at all points. Now recall that K_0 and S_0 are given as initial conditions; but R_0 has to be chosen optimally. If R_0 is chosen too low (say the initial point lies to the south-west of GH) both $\dot K_t<0$ and $\dot R_t<0$. Capital will be decumulated and, as R_t gets lower the rate of decumulation will get higher (see equation 10.25). The entire stock of fixed capital will be consumed in finite time. The programme will not be feasible. Indeed, as Diagram 10.5 makes clear, if the initial point chosen lies 'slightly' to the north-east of GH (say, the path A'B') the corresponding trajectory A'B' will reach a maximum value for the capital stock, and will then turn down. Capital will be decumulated from then on, and, as R_t gets lower, the rate of decumulation gets higher. Fixed capital will be consumed in finite time. There is then a 'critical' phase path AB that asymptotes to GH as $R\to0$. Any path to the left of AB eventually turns down and runs out of capital in finite time. But along AB, $K_t\to\infty$ as $t\to\infty$. If an optimum exists, one suspects it is this path.[21] If R_0 is chosen too high (i.e. the initial point chosen lies to the north-east of AB; say on A"B"), R_t remains too large always, in the sense that the integral of resource usage will exceed the initial stock. Such a path is not feasible.

It remains to confirm that AB is the optimal path. In order to do this it would prove convenient if we were able to obtain the equation representing AB in an explicit form. Now, for very low values of R, AB has the same functional form as GH, since it asymptotes to GH. Let us conduct an experiment and suppose that AB has the functional form

---

[21] We say 'if' because we are now considering the case $\delta=0$.

10.27 $$K = \Pi R^{-(1+\alpha_2(\eta-1))/\alpha_1(\eta-1)}, \qquad \text{with } \Pi > 0.$$

We now need to verify that this equation satisfies the optimality conditions 10.16–10.18 for some value of Π. If it does, it will yield the value of Π as well. Towards this differentiate equation 10.27 with respect to time. This yields

10.28 $$\dot{K}_t = - \frac{\Pi\{1+\alpha_2(\eta-1)\}}{\alpha_1(\eta-1)} R_t^{-\{1+(\alpha_1+\alpha_2)(\eta-1)\}/\alpha_1(\eta-1)}\dot{R}_t.$$

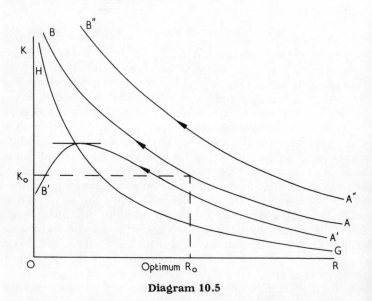

Diagram 10.5

Now use 10.27 and 10.28 to eliminate K_t and $\dot{K}_t$ from equation 10.25. This gives us an equation in $\dot{R}_t$. Now eliminate $\dot{R}_t$ between this and equation 10.24. This yields

10.29 $$\Pi = \{\eta/(\eta-1)(1-\alpha_2)\}^{\eta/\alpha_1(\eta-1)}\{(\eta-1)\alpha_2/\lambda\}^{1/\alpha_1(\eta-1)}.$$

We have thus shown that the trajectory defined by 10.27 and 10.29 satisfies the optimality conditions. Our hunch was correct. Equation 10.27 does indeed denote AB, with the value of Π being given by 10.29. We can now use equation 10.27 in equation 10.24 to eliminate K_t and reduce it to a differential equation depending solely on R_t.

This in turn is readily integrable. We omit details here. But it can
be checked that the integral is:

10.30 $$R_t = (R_0^{1-\mu} + Mt)^{1/(1-\mu)}$$

where $M > 0$ and

10.31 $$\mu = \frac{(\alpha_1 + \alpha_2)(\eta-1)^2 + (1+\alpha_2)(\eta-1) + (1-\alpha_1)}{\alpha_1(\eta-1)\eta} > 1.^{22}$$

From this it follows that

$$\frac{1}{1-\mu} = -\frac{\alpha_1(\eta-1)\eta}{\alpha_2(\eta-1)^2 + (\eta-1)(1+\alpha_2-\alpha_1) + (1-\alpha_1)} < 0.$$

If the integral of the extraction function 10.30 is to converge it is
necessary and sufficient that $1/(1-\mu) < -1$; or $\mu < 2$. From 10.31 it
follows that this is so if, and only if, $\eta > (1-\alpha_2)/(\alpha_1-\alpha_2)$ (>1). We
have therefore demonstrated by actual construction that if $\eta >
(1-\alpha_2)/(\alpha_1-\alpha_2)$, there is a feasible programme which satisfies the
optimality conditions 10.16–10.18, even though $\delta = 0$. Therefore
this programme is optimal. We have yet to describe the movement
of consumption along the optimum. This is simple. Using 10.27 in
equation 10.22 yields

10.32 $$C_t = \Pi^{\alpha_1/\eta} R_t^{-1/(\eta-1)} \{(\eta-1)\alpha_2/\lambda\}^{1/\eta}.$$

Since R_t is monotonically declining (equation 10.30) consumption
along the optimal path is monotonically increasing. Moreover, since
$R_t \to 0$ it follows that $C_t \to \infty$. As a final check, notice that $C_t^{-(\eta-1)}$ is
proportional to R_t (equation 10.32). Therefore the felicity integral
along this programme does indeed converge. Notice further that
since $K_t \to \infty$, $F_K \to 0$. It follows from equation 10.20 that $g_C \to 0$
(i.e. while consumption increases to infinity, its long-run rate of
growth declines to zero). We shall confirm presently that optimum
consumption is a fixed proportion of optimum GNP. Therefore the
long-run rate of growth of optimum GNP is also zero. The behaviour
of the long-run resource utilization ratio is similar to that along the
maxi-min programme, for 10.30 implies that R_t/S_t is proportional
to $(R_0^{1-\eta} + Mt)^{-1}$. Consequently $R_t/S_t \to 0$. A vanishing fraction of

²² Simple manipulation shows that $\mu > 1$ if, and only if, $(\alpha_1-\alpha_2) + (1-\alpha_1-\alpha_2)\eta + \alpha_2\eta^1 > 0$; which is true by assumption.

a vanishing resource stock is all that is required to sustain the unbounded increase in output and consumption. When $\alpha_1 > \alpha_2$ exhaustible resources pose no threat whatsoever.

We can as well describe the optimal programme in terms of the savings ratio required to sustain it. Using equation 10.27 in the production function implies that aggregate output (GNP) along the optimum is given by

$$Y_t = \Pi^{\alpha_1} R_t^{-1/(\eta-1)},$$

and, consequently, on using 10.32 that

$$C_t/Y_t = (\eta-1)\alpha_2^{1/\eta}\Pi^{-(\eta-1)\alpha_1/\eta} = \frac{(\eta-1)(1-\alpha_2)}{\eta} < 1-\alpha_2$$

or, to state it another way

10.33 $$s_t = \dot{K}_t/Y_t = 1 - C_t/Y_t = \frac{1+\alpha_2(\eta-1)}{\eta} > \alpha_2.$$

The savings ratio along the optimal programme is constant and exceeds α_2.

It is tempting to see what orders of magnitude may reasonably be involved. Let $\alpha_1 = 0 \cdot 25$ and $\alpha_2 = 0 \cdot 05$. Then we need $\eta > 95/20$. Suppose in fact that $\eta = 5$. In which case $s_t = 24\%$. This is a high rate of savings, though not unduly high.

We can characterize fully the optimal programme for different values of η. We have argued that for $\delta = 0$ it is required that $\eta > (1-\alpha_2)/(\alpha_1-\alpha_2)$. Now $(d/d\eta)\{1+\alpha_2(\eta-1)\}/\eta < 0$,

$$\lim_{\eta \to \infty} \frac{\{1+\alpha_2(\eta-1)\}}{\eta} = \alpha_2,$$

and

$$\lim_{\eta \to \frac{1-\alpha_2}{\alpha_1-\alpha_2}} \frac{\{1+\alpha_2(\eta-1)\}}{\eta} = \alpha_1.$$

Equation 10.33 tells us then that if we ignore the case $\eta = (1-\alpha_2)/(\alpha_1-\alpha_2)$ from our description, the optimal savings ratio falls from α_1 to α_2 as η rises from $(1-\alpha_2)/(\alpha_1-\alpha_2)$ to ∞. All this squares with one's intuition and merges rather beautifully with the maxi-min policy. As we remarked earlier, the larger is η the more egalitarian is the underlying preference ordering. If $(1-\alpha_2)/(\alpha_1-\alpha_2) < \eta < \infty$ the 'Utilitarian' optimum does entail unbounded consumption in the long run. But the larger is η the more 'delayed' is the rise in consumption to 'infinity'. Earlier generations consume less than $\bar{C}_{max}$ (so that later generations may benefit from the higher rate of capital accumulation); but the greater is η the closer are the initial rates of consumption to $\bar{C}_{max}$, and consequently, the further delayed is the date at which consumption under Utilitarianism reaches the level

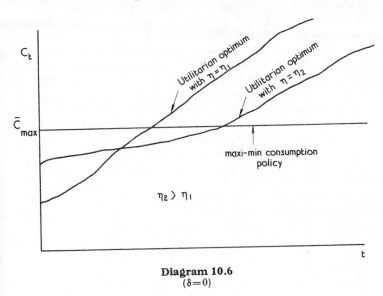

Diagram 10.6
($\delta = 0$)

$\bar{C}_{max}$. That is, the Utilitarian optimum consumption path becomes 'flatter' as η is raised in value (see Diagram 10.6). In the limiting case, $\eta = \infty$, the Utilitarian solution merges with the maxi-min programme. This last should be no surprise at all.

The arguments leading to the characterization of the Utilitarian optimum suggest strongly that for $\delta = 0$ an optimum does not exist if $\eta \leq (1-\alpha_2)/(\alpha_1-\alpha_2)$. This is indeed the case. The point is that, even although the economy is capable of unbounded consumption, it is not productive enough to allow consumption to rise to infinity at a rate fast enough for the felicity integral to converge to a finite

number. All feasible programmes yield consumption paths that lead
the felicity integral to diverge to $-\infty$. No optimum policy exists.[23]
To state it equivalently, no feasible programme satisfies the three
optimality conditions 10.16–10.18 simultaneously.

4. Commentary on the Implications of 'Utilitarian' and Maxi-min Criteria

While we have commented rather extensively on the implications
of differing ethical views on the rates of capital accumulation and
resource depletion, it is as well to sum up our findings of the previous
two sections and comment on some of the grander issues.

If $\delta > 0$ and $\eta > 1$ a Utilitarian optimum exists. Consumption and
output along the optimum decline to zero in the long run. The larger
is the value of η (or, correspondingly, the smaller is δ) the more
delayed it is before consumption is allowed to approach zero. The
optimum consumption path can have at most one peak in the future.
If δ is 'large' optimum consumption is monotonically declining;
there is no peak in the future. If δ is 'small' consumption rises
initially, attains a peak, and then declines to zero in the long run.
If $\delta = 0$ a Utilitarian optimum exists if and only if $\eta > (1 - \alpha_2)/(\alpha_1 - \alpha_2)$.
Output and consumption increase monotonically without bound
along the optimum programme. Earlier generations consume less
than $\bar{C}_{max}$ with a view to allowing later generations to enjoy high
rates of consumption. The savings ratio along the optimum is
throughout constant. The larger is the value of η the 'flatter' is the
optimum consumption path. In the limiting case $\eta = \infty$ the Utilitarian optimum coincides with the maxi-min (constant consumption)
programme. If $\eta \leqslant (1 - \alpha_2)/(\alpha_1 - \alpha_2)$ and $\delta = 0$ no Utilitarian optimum
exists (see Diagrams 10.5 and 10.6).

Despite their simplicity the constructions of the previous two
sections have laid bare the various considerations that would typically be found relevant; they have also brought out the differing
implications of such considerations. All this may, nevertheless,
appear as being altogether too abstract and too esoteric. Abstract it
certainly is; but the recognition that the world as we know it is a
good deal more complicated and messy, while undoubtedly true,
does not in itself provide an argument against analysing abstract
models of the kind that we have been analysing. One will need to
indicate the precise features of the world which, being violated by

[23] One should note the similarity between this and the case discussed in
Chapter 9 section 4 with the utility function satisfying 9.4.

our abstract models, make our general conclusions misleading. Highly aggregative models, such as ours, cannot of course provide any guidance for detailed *intersectoral* planning.[24] But we have not been concerned with such questions. The aim here has been to obtain the implications of differing ethical norms on the behaviour of aggregate consumption and resource utilization. Simplification is in fact desirable here. It enables us to see sharply the relevant issues that are involved. Complications merely clutter up matters. They usually hamper one in judging why certain results come out the way they do. Experience in studying world models should have settled this point once and for all.

The questions that we have been studying here are, of course, by no means esoteric. Governments of most countries and of most political inclinations have in the past been concerned with the rate of investment and, more recently, with the rate of utilization of the world's exhaustible resources. The key point here is in striking an appropriate balance between the competing claims of different generations. The social welfare function approach to the problem is merely a formal way of articulating such competing claims. If it is judged appropriate to contemplate a 'Utilitarian' welfare function one is entitled to refer to 'the felicity function' of a given future generation without having to admit that utilities can be measured and summed. The extensive discussion in the previous chapter on such issues should have made this obvious. Nor indeed, as we have argued, does the fact that future tastes and needs and technology are uncertain provide an argument for avoiding the question of optimum accumulation and resource depletion. Uncertainty about such matters has not restrained governments from choosing one policy rather than another. If there is uncertainty about such matters, as there surely is, uncertainty should be built directly into the construction. Many such questions in the face of uncertainty are rather hard to answer. We shall broach a number of them in Chapters 13 and 14. But it is crucial to ask whether ignoring uncertainty and replacing random variables by their expected values lead to wildly inaccurate policies. The limited experience that has been accumulated on such matters suggests strongly that the error will often be very small.[25]

The conclusions that have emerged from the analyses of the previous two sections are striking. Even within the Utilitarian

---

[24] For this, see, for example, Chakravarty (1969).
[25] For an elegant demonstration of this see Mirrlees (1974).

framework the characteristics of the optimal policy are highly sensitive to the decision of whether or not future felicities should be discounted. In this sense δ is a crucial parameter. Whether or not it is positive matters a great deal to the consumption levels of future generations. It is a parameter to which a good deal of thought needs to be given.[26]

A Utilitarian formulation of the problem of optimum planning has been shown to imply the desirability of a varying consumption level over time. This contrasts sharply with the dictates of the maxi-min criterion on the present model. Here the maxi-min criterion calls for a boosting of consumption for an initial period relative to the Utilitarian optimum with no utility discounting; and this at the expense of forgoing higher consumption levels that could be achieved thereafter. One requires a rigidly 'egalitarian' objective to reject such a trade-off. Any system of values that makes it permissible to accept less for some generations provided that this is accompanied by substantial increases to others, will lead a society to choose a varying consumption stream of the Utilitarian type.

Another way of identifying the difference between the maxi-min formulation and the Utilitarian one with no discounting is to note that for the model presented here the former is a criterion that denies the optimality of 'economic development'. It recommends that there be no growth in output and consumption (though there is a growth in capital stock).[27] Obviously, for a given resource endowment, the lower is the economy's initial capital stock the lower will be the maximum consumption level ($\bar{C}_{max}$) that it can sustain. Consequently, if all countries were to adopt the maxi-min criterion, capital poor countries would forever have lower levels of consumption per head than those that were initially capital rich. It is in this sense that in our model here the maxi-min criterion is at the mercy of initial conditions. An economy wedded to it is imprisoned in poverty should it have been unfortunate to have inherited low stocks of capital and resources from the past. One of the stated aims in desiring economic development is the achievement of a suitable trade-off between present and future consumption levels. The

[26] This contrasts greatly with the Utilitarian consequences for simple technologies with no exhaustible resource. Whether δ is zero or whether it is chosen positive does not seem to matter much in such economies. On this see Koopmans (1965) and Mirrlees (1967).

[27] This is not invariably an implication of the maxi-min principle. The sharp result that we have obtained is a consequence of our assumption that a generation's welfare depends solely on *its* consumption level. On this see Arrow (1973a), Dasgupta (1974b).

'Utilitarian' approach to the problem appears to possess the flexibility in striking this balance, and for this reason may appear more attractive to capital-poor countries. The maxi-min criterion may, however, seem attractive to members of a rich community where the need may be less acutely felt for accumulating capital with a view to raising the standard of living of future generations still further. Such a view may appear at first sight to smack of a naturalistic fallacy—the view that one can obtain ethical norms solely from factual matters. Not at all. It is prudent to give expression to one's underlying ethical preferences in terms of simple criteria. But it would seem that such seemingly simple formulations as Utilitarianism and the maxi-min criterion are in fact much too opaque in the absence of a demonstration of what they imply. It is here that exercises in optimal planning prove to be really valuable. They enable us to see in what way the implications of various ethical norms differ. It is in this sense that it is a legitimate exercise to revise or criticize ethical norms in the light of their implications.

Such exercises serve other functions as well. It was rather natural to pose a planning problem by looking at feasible consumption profiles and to give expression to differing ethical preferences in terms of simple norms based on them. Indices such as the growth rate of GNP did not appear to be the natural ones on which to rest one's ethical beliefs. One can, of course, obtain the optimum rates of growth of GNP from the exercises that we have performed. In fact we have done this. But the rate of growth of GNP cannot function well as a primitive ethical norm. In fact, the rate of growth of GNP along the maxi-min programme was found to be strictly zero. As the sole guide for judging the 'performance' of an economy growth rate of GNP must be rejected. And yet it is very often so used. Worse still are primitive prescriptions, such as that GNP ought to grow at a steady rate.[28] The rate of growth of GNP and consumption along the Utilitarian optimum was found not to be constant; except of course in the long run, when it is zero if $\delta = 0$.

There are several other general prescriptions that have often been offered which merit attention at this stage. It is worth relating the implications of our exercises to the idea of a *stationary economy*, the realization of which is often described as the only way of solving

---

[28] We are using the expression 'primitive prescription' in the sense of the prescription being not derived from some more basic ethical norm, such as, say, a welfare function founded on the distribution of consumption across generations.

the problems posed by the existence of finite resources and pollution.[29] A precise description of a stationary economy with exhaustible resources is not readily found in the literature; but it is possible that what is contemplated is a situation where population and consumption levels are both constant and where net capital accumulation is nil. We have assumed the first of these characteristics; and the extensive discussions of production possibilities in Chapter 7 led us to recognize that, if exhaustible resources are inessential, then constant consumption and an absence of capital accumulation are possible only when the resource is not necessary for production. Otherwise, in order to maintain consumption at a given level, capital must be accumulated as the resource is depleted.

There is a less exacting definition of a stationary economy to be found in some of the literature. It describes such an economy as involving 'the maximum possible substitution of stocks for flows', together with the acceptance of an objective function that 'maximizes the benefits for those living today subject, . . ., to the constraint that it should in no way decrease the economic and social options of those who will inherit this globe'.[30] The rationalization normally given for the desirability of substitution of stocks for flows is that it is the flow of exhaustible resources that normally produce outputs of pollutants. In the long run it is then in our interest to reduce these flows, with the adoption of technologies and life-styles that involve placing greater reliance on stocks of wealth. Now, this idea of stock-flow substitution, though phrased differently, is very similar to the recommendations that have emerged from a study of optimal growth paths. We have seen that both the maxi-min objective and the Utilitarian one recommend a continuing substitution of fixed capital (stock) for resource use (flow). Indeed, it is worth emphasizing that a continual increase in the prices of exhaustible resources that results from the efficient operation of a market system would provide a strong incentive for profit-orientated traders to adopt precisely this stock-flow substitution. This is, of course, without our having introduced the output of pollutants into the construction.

The second part of the quote is not easy to interpret. If by 'economic options' available at a given date one means the set of all consumption paths feasible from that date onwards it is a point of view we have discussed in Chapter 5 (section 8). Suppose instead

[29] See, for example, Daly (1973).
[30] Randers and Meadows (1973, p. 301).

that it is interpreted as our being required not to choose any policy that will imply a decline in welfare levels over time. Then the maximin consumption criterion would seem to be what is involved. We have analysed this at length.

The moral would seem to be this. Welfare judgements about the distribution of benefits across generations involve considerations that cannot be caught in simple and catchy phrases. Even the simplest expressions of such judgements appear to be much too opaque. It is treacherous to rely on them without having, as a first step, conducted an analysis of their implications.

5. Extension to an Open Economy

The results of the previous sections have all been derived in the context of a closed economy—i.e. an economy in which no explicit account is taken of the possibility of trading in the resource, or of investing (or borrowing) abroad. An alternative to interpreting the results as applying to a closed economy, would be to interpret them as applying to the world as a whole—the world viewed as a single unit clearly has no scope for foreign trade or investment. At the level of the individual country, however, engaging in foreign trade and investment are obviously relevant options: oil-rich countries typically export oil, investing the proceeds abroad, and oil-poor countries import oil, often borrowing from oil-producing countries to finance their imports. It is then important to know whether the addition of these policy options changes our conclusions. In fact, this addition makes some important and substantial differences. In particular, we can show that under certain circumstances the optimal rate of resource depletion is independent of the felicity discount rate and the parameters of the felicity function—a major change from the results in previous sections. In practical terms this is an important result, because the felicity function and the felicity discount rate are both difficult to agree on and any argument which reduces the sensitivity of an optimal policy choice to them will be welcomed by policy-makers.

A relatively simple argument will establish conditions for the independence of an optimal depletion policy from the felicity discount rate and parameters representing the felicity function. Assume domestic output Y to be a function of the domestic capital stock K and resources used in domestic production R, with an exogenous rate of technical progress so that Y also depends explicitly on time:

$$Y = F(K, R, t).$$

In addition to the output from production, there are two other sources of domestic income: revenue from the sale of resources abroad, and interest earned on assets owned abroad. This total income may be consumed, used to augment the domestic capital stock, or used to purchase foreign assets and augment the economy's holdings of these. Thus the overall balance equation is

10.34 $$C + \dot{W} = F(K, R, t) + r(W - K) + p(E)E$$

where W is the country's total wealth, r the rate of interest on foreign investment, E the level of export sales and $p(E)$ the price these earn. In assuming p to depend on E we are of course assuming the country to be a price-maker on world markets. It is implicit in this formulation that capital is malleable, in that domestic capital can be instantly and costlessly transformed into foreign capital, and vice versa. In short, we are supposing a small resource-rich country trading with a capital-rich world.

A country whose operations are described by 10.34 is in the position of an investor who may hold his wealth in any of three assets —domestic capital, foreign capital, or the unextracted resource. The returns available on these investments take different forms: clearly the rate of return on foreign investment is simply r, the extra income generated by holding one more unit, and the rate of return on domestic investment is F_K, the marginal product of domestic capital. The return to holding the unextracted resource is equal to the rate of increase in the amount that can be earned by using an extra unit: if that unit is exported, this amount is the marginal revenue, $m(E) = p'(E)E + p(E)$, and if it is used domestically, it is just the marginal product, F_R. Of course, if the country is running its affairs efficiently, these two will be equal:

10.35 $$F_R = m(E) = p'(E)E + p(E)$$

since, if the earnings in one activity exceeded those in the other, it would pay to expand the more remunerative one and contract the less remunerative one until the returns were brought into equality (or one activity was phased out altogether). As the two magnitudes in 10.35 give the 'effective price' of the unextracted resource, the rate of return to this is the rate at which these grow, or

10.36 $$\frac{\frac{d}{dt}(F_R)}{F_R} = \frac{\frac{d}{dt}\{p'(E)E + p(E)\}}{p'(E)E + p(E)}.$$

The returns to the three different forms of investment have now been identified as r, F_K, and the magnitudes in 10.36. Of these, r is given by forces ruling in world capital markets, while the others are determined by domestic policy: F_K depends on the domestic factor proportions, as does F_R, while $p(E)$ is determined by export policies. How should the available investable funds be spread between the three investment media giving rise to these returns? The answer, not surprisingly, is that an optimal investment policy will be one along which the rates of return on all these are equal— i.e. an optimal investment policy will satisfy

$$10.37 \qquad r = F_K = \frac{\dfrac{d}{dt}(F_R)}{F_R} = \frac{\dfrac{d}{dt}\{p'(E)E + p(E)\}}{p'(E)E + p(E)}.$$

As with equation 10.35, a formal proof is hardly necessary; it is intuitively clear that, if one asset had a higher return than another, it would pay to shift resources into that asset until returns were equalized.

The conditions in equation 10.37 characterize an *efficient* pro-gramme for the economy we are studying; we are interested in optimal paths, paths which maximize a felicity integral

$$\int_0^\infty u(C_t) \exp(-\delta t)\, dt$$

subject to the production and accounting constraints described above. Efficiency is necessary for optimality, but for a complete statement of the conditions necessary for optimality one must supplement 10.37 with a condition equating the social rate of time preference to the rate of return.[31] The former is, as before,

$$\rho_t = \delta - \frac{u''(C_t)\dot{C}_t}{u'(C_t)}$$

so that this condition implies

$$10.38 \qquad \delta - \frac{u''(C_t)\dot{C}_t}{u'(C_t)} = r.$$

[31] See equation 10.6.

This condition, together with the efficiency conditions 10.37, initial conditions, and the integral constraint on resource use, is sufficient to describe completely an optimal path. Below we analyse such a path for particular functional forms: specifically, let us assume

10.39
$$\frac{-u''(C)C}{u'(C)} = \eta, \qquad \text{constant.}$$

10.40
$$p(E) = \gamma E^{\gamma - 1}, \qquad 0 < \gamma < 1.$$

10.41
$$F(K, R, t) = \exp(\beta t) K^{\alpha_1} R^{\alpha_2}, \qquad \alpha_1 + \alpha_2 < 1.$$

World demand for the resource is thus taken to be iso-elastic, and the production function Cobb–Douglas with diminishing returns to capital and resources and technical progress at rate β. These are familiar assumptions.

From 10.38 and 10.39 it is clear that

10.42
$$C_t = C_0 \exp\left\{\left(\frac{r - \delta}{\eta}\right)t\right\}$$

and similarly 10.35, 10.37 and 10.40 imply

10.43
$$E_t = E_0 \exp\left\{\left(\frac{r}{\gamma - 1}\right)t\right\}.$$

From 10.37 it is obvious that

$$F_R(t) = F_R(0) \exp(rt)$$

so that, using 10.41,

10.44
$$K_t^{\alpha_1} R_t^{\alpha_2 - 1} = K_0^{\alpha_1} R_0^{\alpha_2 - 1} \exp\{(r - \beta)t\}.$$

The equality of F_K with r gives

10.45
$$K_t = \left(\frac{\alpha_1}{r}\right)^{1/(1 - \alpha_1)} R_t^{\alpha_2/(1 - \alpha_1)} \exp\left\{\left(\frac{\beta}{1 - \alpha_1}\right)t\right\}.$$

From 10.44 and 10.45, it is simple to confirm that R_t and K_t both grow exponentially at rates given by

10.46
$$\frac{\dot{R}}{R} = \frac{\beta - (1 - \alpha_1)r}{1 - \alpha_1 - \alpha_2}$$

10.47
$$\frac{\dot{K}}{K} = \frac{\beta - \alpha_2 r}{1 - \alpha_1 - \alpha_2}.$$

From equation 10.46 one obtains that

10.48 $R_t = R_0 \exp(-mt)$,   where $m \equiv \dfrac{(1-\alpha_1)r - \beta}{1-\alpha_1-\alpha_2}$

and from equation 10.47 that

10.49 $K_t = K_0 \exp(-nt)$,   where $n \equiv \dfrac{\alpha_2 r - \beta}{1-\alpha_1-\alpha_2}.$

From equation 10.48 it is immediate that for the extraction policy to be feasible we shall need to suppose that

$$\beta < (1-\alpha_1)r.$$

Let us suppose this to be the case. Now recall that by assumption only W_0 and S_0 are given as initial conditions. R_0, K_0, E_0 and C_0 are all unknowns. Now equations 10.43 and 10.48 imply

10.50
$$\int_0^\infty (R_t + E_t)\, dt = \frac{R_0}{m} + \frac{E_0}{r}(1-\gamma) = S_0.$$

Equation 10.50 relates optimal E_0 to optimal R_0. The point to note is that neither δ nor η enters this equation. Notice next that equation 10.45 implies

10.51
$$K_0 = \left(\frac{\alpha_1}{r}\right)^{1/(1-\alpha_1)} R_0^{\alpha_2/(1-\alpha_1)}.$$

This relates optimal K_0 to optimal R_0, again without involving either δ or η. Finally note that equation 10.35 implies that

10.52
$$\alpha_2 K_0^{\alpha_1} R_0^{\alpha_2 - 1} = \gamma^2 E_0^{\gamma - 1}.$$

This is yet another equation relating optimal K_0, E_0 and R_0 without invoking either δ or η. These three optimal initial values are obtained from equations 10.50–10.52 and their values are independent of the parameters of the valuation function. From equations 10.43, 10.48

and 10.49 it follows then that optimal E_t, K_t and R_t are all independent of δ and η, i.e. independent of social preferences. This in turn implies that optimal domestic output, Y_t, is independent of social preferences. What is influenced by δ and η is C_t (see 10.42) and W_t (see equation 10.34).

The conclusion that optimal Y_t is independent of social preferences is similar to a standard result in static trade theory, to the effect that an open economy's production point is independent of its preference function and is determined entirely by world prices. Diagram 10.7 illustrates this. The production point is that point on

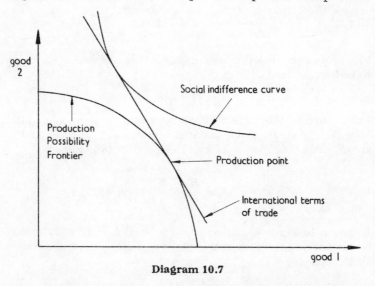

Diagram 10.7

the production possibility frontier where this has a slope equal to the world terms of trade, and is thus determined entirely by this frontier and international prices. In fact the present result is stronger than the static result, in that the static result implies that domestic production, but not of course the volume of trade, is independent of preferences. What has been shown above is that both domestic production and trade (that is, E_t) are independent of preferences. The reason is that export policy is determined entirely by the efficiency conditions 10.35 and 10.37.

It will be recalled that we have had to suppose that

$$\beta < (1 - \alpha_1)r.$$

One notices that if this condition is not satisfied, no optimum exists. While the 'sup' of the valuation integral exists it is not attained. The next point to note is that

$$10.53 \qquad \dot{K} \geqq 0 \quad \text{if and only if} \quad \beta \geqq \alpha_2 r.$$

In words, if the rate of domestic technical progress is too low relative to the return abroad, the optimal policy involves the gradual phasing-out of domestic industry. This slightly surprising result is in fact easily explained. The dynamic efficiency condition 10.37 implies

$$F_K = r.$$

Now, F_K is a declining function of K/R: on any feasible path, R tends to zero, so that to maintain F_K constant, K must fall. But if technical progress is introduced, F_K has an exogenous upward trend which may be sufficiently great to permit F_K to remain constant even when K is non-decreasing. Hence we find an inequality such as 10.53.

Before concluding this section, we should certainly enquire which, if any, of our simplifying assumptions are essential to the results obtained.[32] One such is that the future is known with certainty. If for example future demand conditions are unknown, price becomes a random variable, so that the return on the resource contains a stochastic element. Efficiency now requires that the expected return, plus a risk premium, be equated to the certain returns available elsewhere (see Chapter 13). The complication is that the size of the risk premium will depend on the elasticity of the marginal felicity function which, as we shall see (in Chapter 13 section 1) is a measure of risk-aversion. Hence preferences necessarily affect the choice of a depletion policy.

Another assumption which was important to our conclusions, was that the rate of return on foreign assets is exogenous, i.e. intertemporal terms of trade are given. Allowing this to depend on the volume of foreign assets held by the domestic country makes the problem considerably more complex, and in particular destroys the independence results established for the simple case. One can

[32] For a more detailed discussion of the following points, see Dasgupta, Eastwood and Heal (1978).

see why fairly easily: write the return on foreign assets as $r(W-K)$. Then 10.37 has to be replaced by

$$r'(W-K)(W-K)+r=F_K = \frac{\frac{d}{dt}(F_R)}{F_R} = \frac{\frac{d}{dt}\{P'(E)E+P(E)\}}{P'(E)E+P(E)}$$

because the average and marginal returns on foreign investment now differ, and it is of course the latter that is relevant here. The facts that r is now endogenous, and that W appears in this equation, mean that the whole system of equations is more interdependent than before, and the earlier simple solutions are no longer valid. In intuitive terms, one can say that with r exogenous (i.e. the resource rich country being small) foreign investment was a qualitatively different activity from domestic investment, being immune, for example, from diminishing terms. But as soon as r is endogenized, this qualitative distinction disappears, foreign investment is no longer so sharply distinct from domestic, and one would expect the results to conform more closely to those for the closed economy.

Notes to Chapter 10

The concern of this chapter could be described in summary form as an application of the theory of optimal economic growth to economies with exhaustible natural resources. The theory of optimum intertemporal planning was initiated in the classic paper by Ramsey (1928). The same techniques were employed by Hotelling (1931) to analyse problems relating to resource depletion. After nearly three decades of lull the subject was vigorously explored during the 1960s. Among the most notable contributions to it in the context of aggregate models of economic growth were Chakravarty (1962), Koopmans (1965), von Weizsacker (1965), Mirrlees (1967) and Arrow and Kurz (1970). Two important collections of papers on the matter appear in Shell (1967) and the *Review of Economic Studies* (January 1967). A good overview of the basic concerns of this theory and of the relevant mathematical techniques can be found in Intriligator (1969). For less technical surveys, see Koopmans (1967), Phelps (1966) and Heal (1973). For a lucid account of the application of Ramsey to multi-sector models of economic growth see Chakravarty (1969). The literature of the 1960s extended the original Ramsey analysis to models far more complex than that which he used, and also addressed itself to the question of the existence of a solution to an optimal 'growth' problem; a question that we have touched on here and in the previous chapter (section 4).

A notable feature of the literature of the 1960s is the absence of exhaustible resources in the technological possibilities open to the economies under investigation. In recent years a number of authors have attempted to remedy this deficiency and to extend the original Hotelling analysis in various directions. A collection of these papers have appeared in the *Review of Economic Studies* (Symposium 1974). It transpires in fact that the characteristics of optimum programmes are quite different if exhaustible natural resources are introduced into production possibilities. The purpose of this chapter was to provide an account of these characteristics. Sections 2 and 3 have relied on Dasgupta and Heal (1974), and in particular, Solow (1974b). The exposition is based on Dasgupta (1977a). Optimal planning with exhaustible resources for an open economy has been analysed in Dasgupta et al. (1978). Section 5 has been based on this.

There are four important issues that have been discussed in the recent literature and into which we have not gone here. Stiglitz (1974b) and Ingham and Simmons (1975) have investigated the circumstances where population grows at a constant rate, and Dasgupta and Heal (1974), Dasgupta et al. (1977), Kamien and Schwartz (1978), Dasgupta and Stiglitz (1976), Gilbert (1976) and Loury (1976) have considered the effects of uncertainty about future technology. Intuitively it is clear that uncertainty must play a major role in the formulation of decisions relating to resource depletion, because such decisions must be influenced by the possibility that new technologies not based on these resources will be developed, or that new deposits of resources will be discovered. Dasgupta and Heal (1974) show that under certain conditions such possibilities can adequately be incorporated into the decision-making process by raising the felicity discount rate in a simple manner. Dasgupta et al. (1977) and Kamien and Schwartz (1978) extend this analysis to a model which allows for the possibility that expenditure on research may influence the probability that a new, resource-independent technology will be developed. The issues raised by these contributions will be discussed briefly in Chapters 14 and 16.

The third issue that we have neglected to discuss here is the question of optimum population policies. This is a particularly difficult topic, not only because it usually poses mathematical difficulties but also because the welfare basis of judgements on population policies is often obscure. The problem has been discussed in general terms by Meade (1955), Dasgupta (1969, 1974), Pitchford (1974), Lane (1977) and Koopmans (1974a). The problem has been discussed in the context of exhaustible resources by Koopmans (1974a, b), Lane (1977) and Khalatbari (1976).

The fourth and unquestionably the most thoroughly explored set of issues that we have not discussed here concerns the problem of various 'second-best' intertemporal programmes. In the text we have supposed all *technologically* feasible intertemporal programmes to be *institutionally* feasible, either through direct legislation, or through the imposition of taxes. An implication of this, as we noted in equation 10.2, is that the appropriate discount rates to use in investment decisions are the social rates of return of the economy. But in general one would suppose that the aggregate level of investment is constrained by special considerations (e.g. limited fiscal powers of the government), so that not all technologically feasible intertemporal programmes are in fact feasible. The theory of optimum intertemporal planning, in the face of such added constraints, was pioneered by Arrow (1966) and Marglin (1966), and the appropriate discount rates to use in investment decisions are no longer necessarily the (unconstrained) rates of return. The implications of such added constraints on social cost–benefit analysis have been analysed subsequently by Dixit (1968), Little and Mirrlees (1969, 1974), Arrow and Kurz (1970), Dasgupta et al. (1972), Stern (1972) and Marglin (1976), among others.

CHAPTER 11

IMPERFECT COMPETITION AND EXHAUSTIBLE RESOURCES

Introduction

In earlier chapters we have discussed, among other matters, the behaviour of perfect resource markets. In fact, of course, many of these markets are substantially imperfect. In this chapter, therefore, we shall analyse the consequences of some of these imperfections. But before doing this it will be useful to make precise the sense in which the issues to be dealt with here differ from those in Chapters 3 and 5. There the focus of attention was the implication of the *non-existence* of certain markets. Here, matters will be different. We shall take it, in what follows, that all relevant markets exist; but that for various reasons they function wrongly. In short, we shall be concerned here with what is traditionally called imperfect competition.

Even in a timeless setting imperfect competition is difficult to model, with no widely accepted framework for the analysis. The difficulties, if anything, are compounded when one moves to an intertemporal setting that is essential for an analysis of resource depletion problems. We shall begin with the case that is the least controversial: the case of a single owner of a resource. This will lead the way for an exploration of the theory of dynamic oligopoly.

1. Monopoly: The Basic Issues

Consider the case of a monopolist with a stock, S_0, of a resource, facing a downward sloping market demand function, $p(R_t, t)$ where p is the price at which the flow R_t is sold at time t. As we are concerned with imperfections in the market for the exhaustible resource it is simplest to assume away market imperfections in the rest of the economy. Suppose then that the numeraire asset earns a competitive rate of interest, $r(>0)$. The monopolist is concerned with maximizing the present discounted value of the flow of profits derived from selling the resource. Assume for the moment that the resource can be extracted costlessly. His problem then is to choose an extraction policy, R_t, so as to maximize

$$\int_0^\infty p(R_t, t)R_t \exp(-rt) \, \mathrm{d}t$$

subject to the constraints $\int_0^\infty R_t \, \mathrm{d}t \leqslant S_0$ and $R_t \geqslant 0$.

Just as in the static theory of pure monopoly we suppose that the instantaneous net profit function is strictly concave in R. This means that instantaneous net marginal revenue decreases as output flow increases. With zero extraction cost this means that the market demand curve satisfies the property $(\partial^2/\partial R^2)\{p(R, t)R\} < 0$. Let m_t denote marginal revenue at t; i.e. $m_t = (\partial/\mathrm{d}R)\{p(R, t)R\}$. It is then immediate that so long as it is found profitable to extract (and therefore to sell), the monopolist will extract at a rate at which net marginal revenue accruing to him increases at a percentage rate equal to r. Formally

11.1 $$\dot{m}_t/m_t = r, \qquad (R_t > 0).$$

Such a result should now be familiar matter. One might, for example, note that if equation 11.1 holds, the present discounted value of the net marginal revenue is constant. If it were not satisfied, then some marginal reallocation of the extraction rate between dates with different present value of net marginal revenues would increase the present value of profits.

An alternative argument leading to equation 11.1 is obtained by viewing the resource stock as an asset. Suppose that at t the monopolist is wondering whether to extract (and sell) one extra unit, or to delay its sale for a short period of time θ. If he sells at t he increases his net profit by m_t. This is therefore the opportunity cost of delaying the sale. The return to such a delay is the difference between the gain of selling at $t + \theta$ and selling at t as a proportion of the opportunity cost, i.e.

$$(m_{t+\theta} - m_t)/\theta m_t.$$

Letting θ tend to zero, this becomes $\dot{m}_t/m_t$ and 11.1 then states that the monopolist should manage his resource stock so that it earns him a rate of return just equal to the competitive market interest rate. It thus emerges that, as is standard in this field, 11.1 is both a flow and a stock equilibrium condition (see Chapter 6 section 1(ii) for the analogous argument for the competitive extractor).

In what follows we shall analyse equation 11.1 in some detail. Now

$$m_t = \frac{\partial}{\partial R_t} \{p(R_t, t)R_t\} = p(R_t, t) + R_t \frac{\partial p}{\partial R_t}.$$

For simplicity we shall suppose throughout that the demand curve shifts uniformly over time. Thus $p_t = f(t)p(R_t)$. Let

$$\eta(R) = \frac{p(R)}{R}\frac{\mathrm{d}R}{\mathrm{d}p} \leq 0$$

denote the price elasticity of demand for the resource flow. (By assumption this is not an explicit function of time.) Then

11.2 $$m_t = p_t(1 + 1/\eta(R_t)).$$

Write $\gamma(R_t) = 1 + 1/\eta(R_t)$. Then on differentiating equation 11.2 we obtain

11.3 $$\dot{m}_t/m_t = \dot{p}_t/p_t + \dot{\gamma}_t/\gamma_t.$$

Using equation 11.3 in equation 11.1 yields

11.4 $$\dot{p}_t/p_t = r - \dot{\gamma}_t/\gamma_t.$$

It will be recalled that, under the assumptions made here, the competitive price of the resource will satisfy the condition

11.5 $$\dot{p}_t/p_t = r \qquad (R_t > 0)$$

(see Chapter 6 sections 1(ii), and 2). Our first task is to compare the monopolist's extraction policy with that sustained along an inter-temporal competitive equilibrium. In order to do this we need to compare equations 11.4 and 11.5. Moreover, in order to make the comparison meaningful we need to suppose that the demand curve that the monopolist faces is identical to the demand curve of the competitive industry. This last is an assumption that we shall make throughout the rest of this chapter when comparing outcomes under different market structures.

2. The Role of Elasticity of Demand

(i) *Constant elasticity of demand:* In comparing equations 11.4 and 11.5 we shall consider various possible cases. The simplest is that of the constant elasticity demand function,

11.6 $\qquad p = \beta R^{-\alpha} f(t), \quad \beta f(t) > 0 \quad \text{and} \quad 1 > \alpha > 0$

(cf. equation 6.10).

In this case $\eta = -1/\alpha < -1$ and γ is a constant (i.e. $\dot{\gamma} = 0$)[1]. Consequently equations 11.4 and 11.5 are identical.

We conclude that the depletion policy pursued by a pure monopolist facing an iso-elastic demand function (with the absolute value of the elasticity greater than one) and zero extraction costs is identical to the outcome realized along an intertemporal competitive equilibrium if the competitive industry faces the same demand function. There is a simple explanation of this. Along an intertemporal competitive equilibrium the resource price rises at the rate of interest; and under pure monopoly it is net marginal revenue that rises at this rate. But with an iso-elastic demand function 11.6 and zero extraction cost, price is proportional to net marginal revenue, so that the two conditions are in fact identical. If, in particular, r is the social rate of discount, monopoly extraction is optimal.

This foregoing result, perhaps surprising at first sight, runs counter to the presumption based on the static theory of pure monopoly that a monopoly producer restricts output and sells at a price higher than efficiency considerations would dictate. But the point to note is that in postulating a single resource owner we are postulating a monopolist over a *stock*; whereas the traditional monopolist of the textbook is the single producer of the *flow* of an output. The result provides yet another example of the fact that it is treacherous to rely unduly on intuition based on analyses of the latter in studying the former. The result also alerts us to the possibility that there are circumstances in which the monopolist extracts at a rate *faster* than would be the case under competitive

---

[1] Note that we need to insist that $\eta < -1$. If $0 > \eta > -1$ along the entire demand curve the monopolist's problem has no solution. This is familiar matter, and to have a well-defined problem we need to postulate an elastic demand curve. But since exhaustible resources are usually inputs in production their market demand curves are derived demand curves. The question arises what kinds of technological possibilities imply 11.6 as a derived demand curve for a resource. The answer, not surprisingly, is the Cobb–Douglas one. To see this, note that with 11.6, price is proportional to marginal revenue. In particular, $p = m/(1-\alpha)$. If $F = K^{\alpha_1} R^{\alpha_2}$ (cf. equation 7.6) and output is numeraire, then $p = F_R = \alpha_2 \cdot K^{\alpha_1} R^{\alpha_2 - 1}$, and $m = \mathrm{d}/\mathrm{d}R(RF_R) = \alpha_2^2 K^{\alpha_1} R^{\alpha_2 - 1}$ and so $p = m/\alpha_2$. Thus $\alpha_2 = 1 - \alpha$. Since by assumption $1 > \alpha_2 > 0$ (see Chapter 7) we have $0 < \alpha < 1$, which is what is assumed in 11.6. Thus, if $\alpha_2 = 0.05$ then $|\eta| = 1.05$. But this is the elasticity of the long-run derived demand curve. The short-run elasticity would be expected to be lower than unity. On this see Chapter 15.

conditions; and circumstances in which the reverse is the case. Let us look into this.

(ii) *Variable elasticity of demand:* For more general demand functions γ is not independent of R and so equations 11.4 and 11.5 differ. To characterize the difference, we need to investigate the behaviour of γ more closely. Now $\dot{\gamma}_t = (\mathrm{d}\gamma/\mathrm{d}R)\dot{R}_t$. Consequently $\dot{\gamma}_t = -(\mathrm{d}\eta/\mathrm{d}R_t)\dot{R}_t/\eta^2$. Recall that we have needed to suppose that marginal revenue decreases with output (i.e. $m'(R) < 0$). It follows that so long as equation 11.1 holds (i.e. so long as the resource lasts) the quantity supplied to the market must decline over time in order to ensure rising marginal revenue. Hence $\dot{R}_t < 0$ and

$$\text{Sign } \dot{\gamma} = \text{Sign } \frac{\mathrm{d}\eta}{\mathrm{d}R}.$$

Taken in conjunction with 11.4, this establishes that:

$$\text{(i)} \quad \text{If } \frac{\mathrm{d}\eta}{\mathrm{d}R} > 0, \qquad \dot{p}/p < r$$

11.7

$$\text{(ii)} \quad \text{If } \frac{\mathrm{d}\eta}{\mathrm{d}R} < 0, \qquad \dot{p}/p > r.\text{[2]}$$

The manner in which the monopolistic outcome differs from the competitive one thus depends entirely on the way in which the elasticity varies along the demand function. We therefore consider the possibilities here.

One could argue that as the monopolist lowers his price and his market expands, this brings him increasingly into competition with substitutes for his product and that this raises the absolute value of the elasticity of his demand. For the example of oil this argument would run as follows. As the price is lowered, oil cuts increasingly into markets which, by virtue of some particular technological or geographical characteristic, had traditionally been the preserve of other fuels (e.g. electricity plants situated near coalfields might switch to oil). In such case, oil's advantage is marginal and easily

[2] We should point out that for an extraction policy to satisfy condition 11.7(ii), we have to disallow competitive speculators purchasing the resource from the monopolist, hoarding the resource, and making large capital gains (since $\dot{p}/p > r$). This will be discussed below.

lost by small price changes, and the demand elasticity would be large in absolute terms.

Although the above is plausible, there is an equally cogent argument leading to the opposite conclusion. The above argument depends on the existence of a substitute with which the resource seller comes increasingly into competition as the price is lowered. The alternative case rests on the fact that as the price is raised, this increases the incentive to invent substitutes that did not previously exist, or to proceed with development work on potential substitutes whose development had been held in abeyance while the resource price was low. Again illustrating the general point with the particular case of oil, the argument would run in terms of higher oil prices encouraging the development of shale oil, of dual-firing systems in boilers, and a variety of other changes which would increase the elasticity facing oil sellers. Thus according to this argument the absolute value of the elasticity facing a resource supplier is likely to be an increasing, rather than a decreasing, function of his price.

It is clear from this that there are convincing reasons for expecting the demand elasticity facing a monopolistic resource supplier to vary with output, but that this variation need not be of any particular simple type. But in order to facilitate analysis, we shall begin by considering the two simple possibilities presented in 11.7, and analyse first the case where the absolute value of the elasticity increases as R falls: this is the case where $d\eta/dR > 0$, and an increase in price (fall in supply) increases the availability of substitutes.[3] In this case, $\dot{p}_t/p_t < r$ and the monopoly price path is flatter than the competitive price path. Assume that market demand for the resource is positive no matter how high the price. In this event it is clear that the monopolist will not find it profitable to exhaust the resource in finite time (why?). His present-value profit maximizing extraction (and sales) will always be positive, and the corresponding price path will satisfy equation 11.4. Moreover, we know from the discussion in Chapter 6 (section 1(iii)) that with such a market demand curve the resource will never be exhausted along an intertemporal competitive equilibrium. Along such an equilibrium the competitive industry will also never exhaust the resource and, in particular, industry sales will fall along the demand curve, with the price rising at the rate of interest (equation 11.5). Moreover, the

[3] A linear demand curve will have this property. Suppose $p = A - BR$ $(A, B > 0)$. Then $d\eta/dR = A/BR^2 > 0$.

integral of sales over the infinite future will equal the initial stock. Now, we have just argued that for the case under study the monopoly price path is flatter than the competitive one. It must, therefore, either lie entirely below, or cross it once from above. But the former would imply that the monopoly extraction path is not feasible (why?). Hence the price paths must cross. This is depicted in Diagram 11.1.

It is clearly from this that relative to the competitive outcome, the monopolistic outcome involves too much conservation of the resource—because for an initial interval, price is higher and so extraction is lower. This accords with conventional wisdom. We expect a monopolist to supply less, and at a higher price, than a

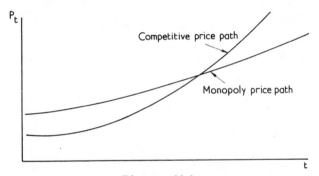

Diagram 11.1

competitive industry, and such a move promotes conservation— hence the adage that 'the monopolist is the conservationist's best friend'. Of course, this is not a completely accurate description of the effect of monopoly because in the long run the monopolist charges a lower price than the competitive industry. This last is because he has, in the long run, to sell the same amount as the competitors; so if he sells at a lower rate initially, he must reach a higher rate to compensate in the long run. This flattening of the price trajectory does of course have the advantage of avoiding for long high prices at which, by assumption, demand facing the monopolist becomes very elastic.

We turn next to the alternative case, where $d\eta/dR < 0$ and the absolute value of the demand elasticity increases with increasing output and increasing penetration of the markets of competing products. In this case, $\dot{p}_t/p_t > r$ and the monopoly price path is steeper than the competitive one. Suppose again that market demand is positive no matter how high the price. The monopoly price path must then either intersect the competitive path once from below, or lie entirely above. As in the previous case, one confirms that it must intersect it. This is depicted in Diagram 11.2. In this case, the reverse of the previous one, the monopoly outcome leads initially to excessively rapid depletion of the resource (relative to the competitive case), because price is initially lower and consumption higher than in the competitive case. There is, however, an important qualification that has to be made: it is not altogether

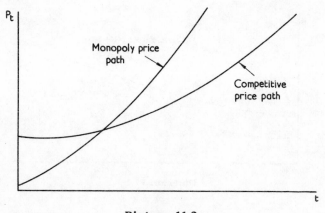

Diagram 11.2

clear that a price path along which $\dot{p}/p > r$ can be sustained as a dynamic equilibrium. With $\dot{p}/p > r$ the resource will appear to a potential buyer to offer an abnormally high rate of return, and this will generate a large investment or speculative demand, in addition to the demand $R(p)$ indicated by the demand curve at the ruling price. Indeed, in principle investors would be willing to buy unlimited quantities and the market would not clear. How important such a phenomenon is in practice would depend on the extent to which investors could finance large speculative holdings of the resource—there is empirical evidence that such operations have been limited because of lack of finance. However, if this effect is important, we should probably add to the constraints facing the monopolist another, to the effect that $\dot{p}/p \leq r$. When $d\eta/dR < 0$ for all output levels, such a constraint would always be binding. In this case, the monopoly outcome would be identical with the competitive outcome.

Our earlier deliberations suggest, however, that neither of the simple cases just considered is entirely plausible. Probably both of the effects mentioned will be operative, so that the absolute value of the demand elasticity increases as output rises, but also increases as price rises, assuring a minimum at some intermediate values.

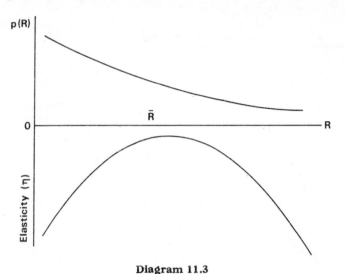

Diagram 11.3

Diagram 11.3 shows such a situation. A demand function with these properties is

$$p = \alpha \exp\left(\frac{1}{B+R}\right), \qquad \alpha > 0, \quad B \geqslant \tfrac{1}{2}.$$

In this case demand elasticity is

$$\eta(R) = -\left(\frac{B^2}{R} + 2B + R\right),$$

which is minus infinity at $R=0$ and $R=+\infty$, and reaches a maximum of $-4B$ when $R=B$. Notice that with such a market demand curve, demand is nil for sufficiently high prices. This makes the analysis somewhat more complicated. In what follows we merely sketch the argument.

In general, let $\bar{R}$ be the output level at which the elasticity reaches its maximum (the absolute value its minimum). Then for $R > \bar{R}$, we have the second of the two cases discussed earlier with $\dot{p}_t/p_t > r$, and for $R < \bar{R}$, the reverse is true. If the constraint $\dot{p}_t/p_t \leq r$ is inoperative, the resulting price path will be as in Diagram 11.4. Price initially rises faster than the competitive rate, and eventually slower. The two price paths intersect once or twice; by the final

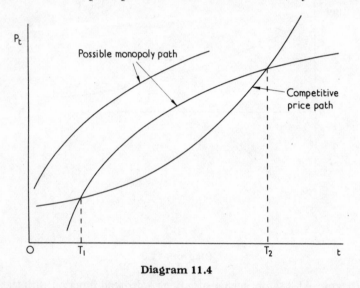

Diagram 11.4

intersection, cumulative consumption on the monopolistic path is less than that on the competitive path, though if there are two intersections there may be an initial interval during which the monopolist achieves excessively high depletion rates.

Of course, if the constraint $\dot{p}_t/p_t \leq r$ is operative, we have

$$\frac{\dot{p}_t}{p_t} = r \quad \text{for} \quad R \geqslant \bar{R}$$

$$\frac{\dot{p}_t}{p_t} < r \quad \text{for} \quad R < \bar{R}.$$

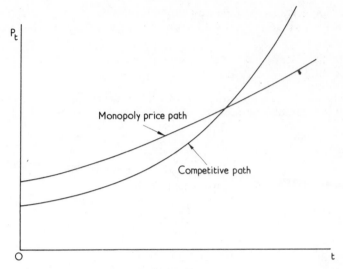

P_t

Monopoly price path

Competitive path

O   t

Diagram 11.5

Such a situation is depicted in Diagram 11.5. The earlier arguments
can be used to show that the monopoly path now lies initially above
the competitive one, intersecting once. Quite obviously monopoly
leads to too much conservation in this case.

3. Extraction Costs and Monopoly

The introduction of extraction cost reinforces the general presumption that we have obtained earlier that monopoly ownership
of a resource stock results in excessive conservation relative to the
competitive outcome. It will be recalled that we argued that in order
to maximize the present value of the flow of profits the monopolist
will extract at a rate along which his marginal revenue, net of
extraction cost, rises over time at the rate of interest. Suppose then
that the marginal extraction cost is b (>0), and in order to keep the
notation consistent with that in Chapter 6 let q denote the price of
the extracted resource. The monopolist will then ensure that

11.8
$$\frac{\dfrac{d}{dt}\left\{\dfrac{\partial}{\partial R_t}(R_t q_t)\right\}}{\dfrac{\partial}{\partial R_t}\left\{(R_t q_t)-bR_t\right\}}=r \quad \text{for} \quad R_t>0.$$

For simplicity suppose demand to be iso-elastic. Thus $q_t = \beta R_t^{-\alpha} f(t)$, with $1 > \alpha > 0$ and $f(t)\beta > 0$. Equation 11.8 then reduces to the form

$$11.9 \qquad \frac{\gamma \dot{q}_t}{\gamma q_t - b} = r, \quad \text{for} \quad t > 0,$$

where $\gamma = 1 + 1/\eta$ ($\equiv 1 - \alpha$). Now $0 < \gamma < 1$. Since the LHS of equation 11.9 is a diminishing function of γ, it follows that

$$11.10 \qquad \frac{\dot{q}_t}{q_t - b} < r.$$

Now recall that for a competitive industry

$$11.11 \qquad \frac{\dot{q}_t}{q_t - b} = r$$

(see equations 6.21 and 6.22).

On comparing equations 11.10 and 11.11 one concludes immediately that the initial price of the extracted resource is higher under monopoly than under a competitive extraction programme (see Diagram 11.5). There is excessive conservation under monopoly.[4]

4. Monopsony

We now switch to consideration of the polar case, that of a single buyer of a resource who faces many competing sellers. Such a situation is by no means without descriptive power. If they acted in collusion, the major international oil companies could clearly form a dominant buyer of oil, and indeed were widely regarded as being such and exploiting their buying power in the 1950s and 1960s. A similar statement could be made of the market for bauxite, where the number of buyers is again small, so that an effective monopsony is certainly a possibility. Of course, there is also a possibility of collusion and hence of effective monopoly on the supply side, so that the most compelling theoretical formulation would be one of bilateral monopoly. However, in the dynamic as in the static case, it is impossible to make any precise statement about

---

[4] For a thorough discussion of this issue and in particular those circumstances where a monopolist is overly profligate see Khalatbari (1976), Stiglitz (1976) and Sweeney (1977).

the outcome in such a case, except of course that it lies between the cases of monopoly and monopsony. By studying the extreme of this range with which we are not yet familiar, namely monopsony, we make a move towards an understanding of bilateral monopoly, as well as analysing a configuration which may be of interest in its own right.

In the conventional static analysis, monopoly and monopsony are opposite cases, in that a monopoly produces too little at too high a price, and a monopsony buys too little at too low a price. The formal analyses are almost identical. A very distinctive feature of monopsony in the resource depletion context is that it does not display this polarity with the monopoly case. To see this, consider a situation where there are a large number of competing owners of an exhaustible resource, and a single buyer. In this situation, what price will the buyer offer? The key point to note is that there is no reason for him to offer a price for the unextracted resource which is more than 'infinitesimal'. The owners are by hypothesis price takers, and so have only two options open to them—to hold on to their stocks, or to sell at the going price. If the buyer is a monopsonist, they cannot sell to anyone else, and in particular cannot except by selling to him generate funds which can be invested at the going interest rate. This of course implies that there is no reason for the price offered by the monopsonist to rise over time. Returning to the main theme, the owners' options are to hold their stocks, earning no return, or to sell at a price slightly in excess of zero and invest the proceeds. Clearly the latter is preferable, so that the monopsonist will be able to buy as much of the resource as he chooses at a price just above zero. To be precise, an equilibrium will be characterized by the monopsonist purchasing the entire stock at a price equal to zero.

The implications that this rather striking result has for the efficiency of resource-use depend on the assumptions made about the structure of the remainder of the market. We shall consider a case, clearly typical and persuasive, where the monopsonist is buying a resource in order to process it in some way and distribute it to a retail market. Oil majors, aluminium companies and many others clearly come near to this category. In this case, the monopsonist's behaviour will be that of a seller with a fixed stock and a given extraction and processing cost structure, and will be determined by the nature of competition in the retail market. Given that the monopsonist is a single buyer of the resource, he is presumably a single seller of it and its derivatives in the retail market, in which case the bias relative to an efficient outcome is identical to that introduced by a monopolist with positive extraction costs, the case considered in the previous section. Another interesting possibility is that there is a form of imperfect competition in the retail market, with the monopsonist the sole supplier of resource-based products, but with substitute products not derived from the resource whose production becomes profitable above a certain price. These would provide at least potential competition and limit the prices the monopsonist would feel free to charge: this is precisely the market structure that will be discussed in section 7 of this chapter.

In conclusion, we can see that monopsony adds no complications to our analysis of the types and sources of market inefficiency, and *is in fact identical to monopoly*. What does emerge very clearly is that resource suppliers facing a monopsonist are extremely weakly placed, and clearly have an immense incentive to form a cartel and change the market structure to one of bilateral monopoly. Although a very simple point, this does seem to yield valuable insights into events of recent years.

5. Imperfect Competition

(i) *Motivation:* As we noted in the previous sections the pure monopoly case is simple to analyse. We discussed it in detail so as to fix ideas. But as an approximate description of the world as we know it, this will obviously not do for many resources. Granted that resource owners have been known to form cartels. Often though, as in the case of oil, not all resource owners join the cartel. What we are then faced with is a mixed market structure, one which in some sense lies in between the polar forms of perfect competition and pure monopoly. But as we recognized in Chapter 2, mixed market structures are hard to analyse, since it is relatively easy to question any given notion of a viable outcome. In the remainder of this chapter we shall analyse some simple equilibrium notions that were introduced in Chapter 2.

It is as well to emphasize that in what follows we shall be exploring intertemporal equilibrium notions. In effect each of the actors will be assumed to 'announce' his entire plan of action in the light of his own interests, as he sees them. The idea will be to see if such intended plans can give rise to a coherent realization. This is not, of course, to say that such a realization is in any sense socially 'optimal', and indeed, part of the investigation is to locate the direction of bias in extraction patterns along such equilibria. But as we are continuing to assume here an absence of environmental uncertainty, we shall in effect be supposing that the entire sequence of future prices will be 'announced' at the initial date in order that the intertemporal equilibrium is sustained. Stating it another way, we shall be postulating rational expectations.[5] Since the inter-temporal equilibria that we shall analyse will usually not sustain a steady state, the assumption of rational expectations may be particularly difficult to accept. And yet it is doubtful if such an assumption is worse than its alternatives. Clearly, long-term decisions by an agent are made on the basis of his expectations about the future, and in particular, expectations about the actions of others. Past experience is but one element in the formation of such expectations. But for certain markets (e.g. the post-1973 oil market) past prices may well be poor indicators of future prices. Moreover, we had an indication in Chapter 8 (section 3) of the ease with which it is possible to postulate a myriad of hypotheses regarding the formation of expectations with wildly differing consequences. The fact, of course, is that we simply do not know how expectations are formed. But we do know that rational expectations yield tidy formulations. These are easy to work with. This forms the motivation for the constructions that follow.[6] But it is worth bearing in mind that as a description the rational expectations hypothesis is likely to be way off the mark here.

(ii) *The duopoly case:* Suppose there to be two resource owners. It may appear at first sight that such an economy would be simple to analyse—not at all. For what is at issue is an appropriate notion of an equilibrium outcome. Each owner can presumably influence the market price. But neither has complete control over it. If they form a cartel and maximize the present value of the flow of their joint profits we are back to the pure monopoly case. Therefore we suppose that they do not co-operate. Now if the duopolists are more or less equally placed an outcome that is worth exploring is an intertemporal Nash equilibrium. We look into this.

Let r be the competitive rate of interest and let R_{1t} and R_{2t} be rates of extraction of the duopolists. Then $R_t = R_{1t} + R_{2t}$ is total extraction at t. Assume extraction to be costless and for notational ease suppose that the demand curve does not shift. Let $p(R_t)$ denote the market demand function. In computing an intertemporal Nash

[5] See Chapter 8.
[6] But see Chapter 15 for an analysis of the pre-1973 oil market.

equilibrium we take it that each duopolist chooses that extraction programme for himself which will maximize his present value of profits *given* the extraction policy of the other. Thus suppose $\hat{R}_{2t}$ to be the extraction policy of the second duopolist. The first will then choose that extraction (and sales) path which will keep constant the present value of its net marginal revenue.[7] Formally this means that

11.12
$$R_{1t}\frac{\mathrm{d}}{\mathrm{d}R_{1t}}\{p(R_{1t}+\hat{R}_{2t})\}+p(R_{1t}+\hat{R}_{2t})=\lambda_1\exp(rt)$$
$$(\lambda_1>0),\quad \text{for}\quad R_{1t}>0$$

Likewise, if the second duopolist supposes that the first will choose the policy $\hat{R}_{1t}$ then it will choose R_{2t} in such a way that

11.13
$$R_{2t}\frac{\mathrm{d}}{\mathrm{d}R_{2t}}\{p(\hat{R}_{1t}+R_{2t})\}+p(\hat{R}_{1t}+R_{2t})=\lambda_2\exp(rt)$$
$$(\lambda_2>0),\quad \text{for}\quad R_{2t}>0$$

If $\hat{R}_{1t}$ and $\hat{R}_{2t}$ sustain an intertemporal Nash equilibrium they must, respectively, be solutions of equations 11.12 and 11.13. If we sum these equations we obtain

11.14
$$\hat{R}_t p'(\hat{R}_t)+2p(\hat{R}_t)=(\lambda_1+\lambda_2)\exp(rt)\equiv\lambda\exp(rt)$$
$$\text{for}\quad \hat{R}_{1t},\hat{R}_{2t}>0.$$

Suppose for ease of exposition that there is positive demand for the resource no matter how high the price. Then equations 11.12 and 11.13 (and therefore 11.14) will hold for all t.

Now let us define

11.15
$$\gamma(R)=2+\frac{1}{\eta(R)},$$

[7] This is another way of saying that, given the extraction policy of the other, each duopolist will choose that extraction policy which will ensure that (so long as it is profitable to extract) his net marginal revenue grows at the rate r.

where η is the elasticity of market demand. Then equation 11.14 can be expressed as

$$p(\hat{R}_t)\gamma(\hat{R}_t) = \lambda \exp(rt).$$

Differentiating this with respect to time yields

11.16 $$\frac{\dot{p}_t}{p_t} = r - \frac{\dot{\gamma}_t}{\gamma_t},$$

where, as earlier, sign $\dot{\gamma}_t = $ sign $d\eta/dR$.

Equation 11.16 is analogous to equation 11.4 which we obtained for the pure monopolist, the difference being that the definition of γ is different here. Nevertheless, we can repeat virtually verbatim the analysis of section 2. If the demand function is iso-elastic, then $\dot{\gamma} = 0$, and so we can conclude that for this case the dynamic Nash equilibrium outcome is identical to the competitive one. If on the other hand the elasticity varies along the demand curve, then the biases in extraction along the Nash equilibrium outcome are qualitatively identical with those associated with the monopoly solution. But what one observes is that the bias is likely to be less along the Nash outcome than in the case of the monopolist because for a given value of R_t, γ_t as defined for the duopoly case is greater than it is for the pure monopoly case (compare equations 11.4 and 11.16). What the analysis does indicate is that in general there is excessive conservation along the Nash duopoly outcome.

(iii) *Similarly placed oligopolists*: If instead there are $N(N > 2)$ identically placed resource owners, the symmetric Nash equilibrium outcome is as easy to analyse as the duopoly case was. We shall not present the argument in any detail. Suppose that other than the number of resource owners the construction is exactly that of the previous subsection. We assume that each resource owner selects that extraction path which will maximize the present value of his profits given the extraction policies of the others. It is then simple to verify that along the symmetric Nash equilibrium path the market price for the resource will satisfy equation 11.16, with the single difference that with N resource owners, $\gamma \equiv N + 1/\eta(R)$. Since sign $\dot{\gamma} = $ sign $(d\eta/dR)$, the biases in the overall rate of depletion along the symmetric Nash equilibrium are the same as before. Nevertheless, with large N the *magnitude* of the bias becomes small. This is to be expected, for one would suppose in advance that with large N the Nash outcome would tend to the competitive solution.[8]

6. Asymmetrically Placed Oligopolists: The Phenomenon of Limit Pricing

For many resources the assumption of symmetrically placed oligopolists is a dubious one. Certainly much of the recent concern with the structure of resource markets was prompted by the 1973 action of the Organization of the Petroleum Exporting Countries (OPEC). Roughly speaking, what one observes in a number of such situations is the presence of a dominant resource owner (e.g. a cartel) surrounded by a number of relatively independent producers (i.e. a competitive fringe). In such a situation a Nash outcome is unlikely to be viable. Rather one would suppose the dominant resource owner to 'announce' his policies, having taken into account the response of the competitive fringe and the fringe responding passively. As we noted in Chapter 2 a simple notion capturing this situation is the equilibrium concept of von Stackelberg. We begin by analysing such outcomes in the context of the simplest of economic environments.

Imagine a single owner of a resource that can be extracted at negligible cost. One might suppose that the monopoly represents a cartel of all the resource owners, where by a cartel we mean a set of producers who explicitly consider the effects of their co-ordinated supply decisions on the resource price. Suppose in addition that there is in existence a perfect substitute product that can be produced at a price $\bar{p}$. As in Chapter 6 we shall refer to this as a backstop technology. There is no patent on the backstop technology.

The producers with access to the backstop therefore form a competitive fringe. In what follows we shall suppose an absence of collusion between firms that have an access to the backstop technology. Given this, our task is to describe an outcome that can be thought of as representing an intertemporal equilibrium.

Consider first the resource owner. He is concerned with the present discounted value of the flow of his profits. But his flow of profits depends on the actions of the competitive firms exploiting the backstop technology. As they are competitive they can be assumed

---

[8] This is not to be confused with the limiting case for large N in the problem of the common discussed in Chapter 3. The reader should work out for himself why the limiting cases for these two different examples should display totally different features.

to be passive price-takers. If the cartel agrees to sell the resource at a price lower than $\bar{p}$ it faces no competition; the competitive firms will not produce. If it sets a price in excess of $\bar{p}$ it will find no buyer, since the competitive firms will undercut it. $\bar{p}$ is then obviously the upper limit to the price which the cartel can charge. Consequently the demand curve that it faces has the shape given in Diagram 11.6.

For simplicity, consider the case of a demand function which is iso-elastic for prices below $\bar{p}$. Assume to begin with that the elasticity exceeds unity in absolute value. It is obvious then from equation 11.4 and the discussion of section 2(i) that if the cartel finds it optimal to set the price below $\bar{p}$ during an interval, it will ensure that the price rises at the rate of interest. But it is forced to observe

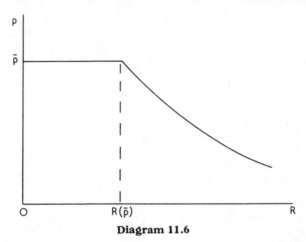

Diagram 11.6

the constraint $p_t \leq \bar{p}$. Now this might suggest that the initial price will be so chosen by the cartel that at the date the price rises to $\bar{p}$, reserves will just get depleted—implying thereby that the cartel's profit maximizing extraction policy is identical to the competitive outcome (see Chapter 6 section 4(iv))—not so. If the cartel insists on exhausting its resource at the date p_t reaches $\bar{p}$, it will have to set a 'low' initial price. But in fact it can increase the present value of its profits if the initial price were set somewhat higher. But this would imply that the cartel will have some reserve left at the date p_t attains the value $\bar{p}$. It would ideally like to allow the price to rise beyond $\bar{p}$ at the interest rate. But it is unable, of course, to do this, since $p_t \leq \bar{p}$. The remaining reserves will be sold at the price $\bar{p}$. The backstop technology will make its appearance once reserves are entirely depleted. In general then, the oligopoly equilibrium will have the following characteristic. During an initial interval $(0, T_1)$, the price will be below $\bar{p}$ and rising at the rate of interest. The cartel will therefore undercut the competitive fringe. At T_1, price will reach $\bar{p}$. During an interval (T_1, T_2) the cartel will sell its resource at the price $\bar{p}$. Since the fringe makes zero profit they may as well not produce. The cartel is therefore the sole supplier. At T_2 the resource is just exhausted. From this date the fringe supplies. Since these competitive suppliers make no profit, they may as well produce to satisfy the market demand at $\bar{p}$.[9] The price trajectory is shown in Diagram 11.7.

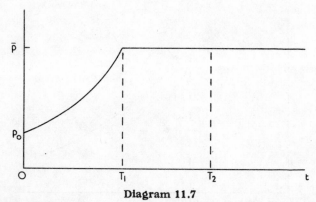

Diagram 11.7

(Equation 11.5 holds during $(0, T_1)$ and cartel is sole supplier. During (T_1, T_2), $p_t = \bar{p}$ and cartel is sole supplier. For $t \geqslant T_2$ the backstop supplies the market and $p_t = \bar{p}$.)

Since $T_2 > T_1$, the initial price along this oligopoly equilibrium exceeds the initial price along an intertemporal competitive equilibrium. Suppose r is the social rate of discount as well. The oligopoly equilibrium is therefore characterized by an *under*-utilization of the resource initially, with the result that the backstop technology makes its appearance at a date later than is socially desirable. The equilibrium also displays a form of limit pricing behaviour on the part of the cartel. During (T_1, T_2) the cartel sets the highest price compatible with keeping its competitors out of the market. So long as $T_1 > 0$

_____
[9] If S_0 is 'small', $T_1 = 0$ and the first interval is degenerate. For proofs of these statements, see Dasgupta and Stiglitz (1976) and Hoel (1978).

this limit pricing phenomenon does not occur immediately, but only at a future date.

The phenomenon of limit pricing appears in a sharp form for the case where the elasticity of demand, η, is less than unity in absolute value (i.e. demand is inelastic). As marginal revenue $m_t = p_t(1 + 1/\eta)$, this is negative and, in the absence of the constraints imposed by the presence of a competitively owned backstop technology the cartel would wish to supply infinitesimal amounts of the resource at an unlimited price. Given a competitively owned backstop technology, it is obviously not free to do this.

The cartel cannot find a buyer at a price in excess of $\bar{p}$, but it would presumably wish to set a price as high as possible subject to this constraint. Loosely speaking, the cartel's optimal policy will be to charge a price 'marginally less' than $\bar{p}$, thus positioning itself just below the kink in the demand curve that it faces (Diagram 11.6). This amounts to a form of limit pricing, or entry deterrent pricing; the monopolist chooses the highest price compatible with keeping the potential competitors out of the market.

To be precise, the equilibrium outcome is characterized by the following: the cartel sets the price equal to $\bar{p}$. Since the competitive firms make zero profit at this price they may as well not produce, and indeed, initially we suppose that they do not. The cartel therefore supplies the entire market. The price remains at $\bar{p}$ and it supplies the market demand $R(\bar{p}, t)$ at each instant until stocks are exhausted. From this date the competitive fringe supplies the market at the

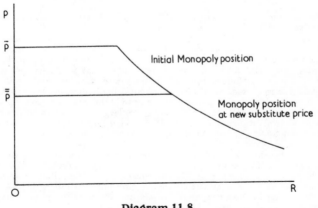

Diagram 11.8

price $\bar{p}$. They make zero profit, but they may as well produce. The equilibrium outcome is therefore characterized by the price equalling $\bar{p}$ throughout. The cartel's pricing policy is therefore independent of the size of its stock.

Obviously, the outcome described above is very different from an optimal one (see Chapter 6 section 4(iv) for the latter), when the market rate of interest, r, is the social rate of discount. In particular, (1) the equilibrium involves an excessive conservation of the resource; an observation that can be stated alternatively as (2) the date of the introduction of the substitute product (i.e. the timing of the introduction of the innovation) is farther away in the future than is socially desirable.[10]

The limit-pricing policy has interesting implications for the incentives that suppliers of the substitute have to undertake development expenditures designed to reduce its price. The point is that if the price of the substitute is reduced from $\bar{p}$ to $\bar{\bar{p}}$, the cartel simply establishes a new price 'just below' $\bar{\bar{p}}$, on the kink of the modified demand curve, as in Diagram 11.8. Reducing their price thus gains the suppliers of the substitute nothing in the immediate future—they will still be undercut as long as resource supplies last—and they may have little incentive to allocate resources to achieving such reductions. However, although they would not benefit from the reduction of the limit from $\bar{p}$ to $\bar{\bar{p}}$, consumers of the resource clearly would: they would be saved $\bar{p} - \bar{\bar{p}}$ on each unit purchased. It is thus the case that the benefits of development expenditures intended to reduce the price of the substitute accrue to consumers, and not

---

[10] For a simulation exercise based on a somewhat more complex model, see Pindyck (1976). In the context of the market for bauxite Pindyck treats members of the International Bauxite Association (IBA) as the cartel. In fact the IBA members produce about 75% of the non-Communist world bauxite production, but it emerges from Pindyck's simulation work that the remaining producers do not matter. It is thought that $\tilde{p} = \$15.60$ per metric ton at 1973 prices (at higher prices it becomes economical to produce alumina from other sources, e.g. aluminite, dawsonite, high-alumina clay, etc.). The long-run price elasticity of demand for bauxite is thought to be low—perhaps as low as -0.08. Initial reserve estimates are large (for IBA members about 225 years of production at current levels of production) and current production cost is about $5.00 per ton. Pindyck calculates that at 5% interest rate the IBA's optimal pricing policy is between $12.50 and $13.00 per ton in 1973 prices for the next twenty-five years, and increasing gradually to the limit price thereafter. The *competitive* price, however, would have risen from $6.40 to $9.00 during the same period. The cartelization of the bauxite market results in a 60% increase in the sum of discounted profits for members of IBA. How does the simulation result bear up to the facts? In 1973 prices bauxite is currently selling in the range $12.00 to $14.00 per ton.

initially to the suppliers of the substitute. Such development expenditures have a positive social return but little private return. It is a recognition of this possibility that lies behind many of the arguments advanced in support of the establishment of a minimum price of oil: the worry is that in the absence of such a price floor, investors might not be willing to commit funds to the development of alternative energy sources because of the risk of the final product being undercut by low-cost oil producers. The earlier analysis suggests that in the case of an elasticity less than unity in absolute value (apparently the case for oil, at least over short periods), this fear may well be justifiable. However, the foregoing arguments are by no means conclusive. The analysis of Chapter 6, section 5 taught us that a careful modelling of the incentives for innovation requires several subtle considerations and that it is by no means clear what the direction of bias is in R and D investment in market economies. The problem is a formidable one.

7. Resource-owning Cartel and Resource-owning Fringe

(i) *A simple construction:* The construction of the previous section was designed to highlight the phenomenon of limit pricing; a phenomenon that has been observed in some resource markets (see footnote 10). But it is undoubtedly not a widespread phenomenon in markets for exhaustible resources, even in those where cartels have been formed. Now, one would conjecture that this is due not so much to the magnitude of the elasticity of demand for the resource as to the fact that cartels usually do not own the entire resource stock. Rather, they control a sizable chunk of the reserve, the remainder being owned by a fringe. In this section we shall begin by characterizing the oligopoly equilibrium for the simplest of such situations and then proceed to introduce considerations that have to be taken into account in describing actual markets. We shall note rapidly that exact characterizations of dynamic oligopoly equilibria are analytically difficult to come by when such complications are introduced. This will then pave the way for a simulation exercise that will be described in section 8 of this chapter.

Let S_t^f and S_t^m denote the stocks of the exhaustible resource that are owned at time t by the competitive fringe and the cartel respectively. Assume for the moment that extraction is costless both for the cartel and the fringe. Suppose as well the presence of a backstop technology available at a price $\bar{p}$ for unit flow. We take it that the backstop is competitively owned. To fix ideas we assume an unshifting demand curve with the property that the elasticity of demand increases with decreasing flow of the resource. This will be the case, say, for a linear demand curve. As usual, r will denote the competitive rate of interest.

Let p_t denote the spot price of the resource flow. The idea underlying the intertemporal oligopoly equilibrium is exactly as it was in the previous section. Each member of the competitive fringe (whether owning a bit of the resource or producing with the backstop technology) is a present value profit maximizer, taking the intertemporal profile of p_t as given. The cartel knows that the fringe behaves thus. It chooses that price path p_t which will maximize the present value of *its* flow of profits. A dynamic oligopoly equilibrium is one along which the price profile p_t allows the market to clear at each date.

Three features of the equilibrium price path can be immediately written down. First, $p_t \leq \overline{p}$ for all t. As we have gone into this feature in the previous section we need not repeat why this must be so.

Secondly, p_t can never display a discontinuous increase at any t. For if this were announced in advance (and remember we are supposing rational expectations and a perfect capital market) demand for the resource 'just before' t would be infinite, since individuals will be able to enjoy huge capital gains associated with this jump. In particular, the presence of speculators will ensure that $\dot{p}_t/p_t \leq r$, a point that we have discussed earlier.

Thirdly, so long as $S_t^f > 0$ (i.e. the fringe stock is positive), $\dot{p}_t/p_t = r$. For suppose $\dot{p}_t/p_t < r$ at some t at which $S_t^f > 0$. The fringe owners, knowing this, will sell their entire stock 'just before' t and purchase the numeraire asset earning a return r. This implies that the resource flow is infinite for that instant (remember that there are no extraction costs). In short, the supply response of the fringe will force the price down to zero.

This third point illustrates how the presence of a competitive fringe owning part of the resource stock imposes severe constraints on the monopoly power of the cartel. For suppose, by way of illustration, that below $\overline{p}$ demand is inelastic. Then in the absence of the resource owning fringe we would observe the limit price phenomenon that was discussed in the previous section. The presence of the fringe will prohibit this from occurring; the price must rise so long as the fringe stock is positive. Observe that it is in the interest of the cartel to set a low price for the resource initially so as to encourage rapid

depletion of the fringe stock. The fringe stands in the way of monopoly profits. But since $\dot{p}_t/p_t \leq r$ even after the fringe stock is exhausted, the cartel stands to lose profits in the short and medium
run if it sets p_0 too low. It is a balance of these two considerations
that will determine the correct initial price from the cartel's point
of view.

We can now describe the general characteristics of the oligopoly
equilibrium. Let R_t^f and R_t^m denote the rate of extraction at t by
the competitive fringe and the cartel, respectively.

Now, so long as $p_t < \bar{p}$, total supply R_t is $R_t = R_t^f + R_t^m$. Moreover,
we know from our earlier analysis that if $p_t < \bar{p}$ and $R_t^m > 0$ then
marginal revenue accruing to the cartel must grow at the percentage
rate r. For simplicity of exposition let market demand be elastic at
$\bar{p}$. The general characteristics of the oligopoly price are as follows.
During an initial interval, say $(0, T_1)$,

11.17 $$\dot{p}_t/p_t = r \qquad \text{(and } S_t^f > 0 \text{)}.$$

During this phase both the cartel and the fringe supply the market,
i.e. R_t^m, $R_t^f > 0$. The point is that even although we have assumed the
elasticity of *market* demand to be rising with falling consumption,
the cartel will wish to supply so long as marginal revenue accruing
to *it* rises at the rate of interest. Provided that fringe supply is
adjusting appropriately, it is perfectly possible for both equation
11.17 to hold and for the marginal revenue accruing to the cartel to
rise at the rate of interest. For the model at hand this will indeed be
the case. Therefore, during $(0, T_1)$ both the cartel and the fringe will
supply the market. At T_1 fringe stock will be exhausted and the
cartel becomes the sole supplier. During an interval (T_1, T_2) the
cartel will be the sole supplier, with $p_t < \bar{p}$ and the price equation
will be 11.4 which, for completeness we rewrite as

11.18 $$\dot{p}_t/p_t + \dot{\gamma}_t/\gamma_t = r.$$

Since by assumption $\dot{\gamma}_t > 0$, during (T_1, T_2) we have $\dot{p}_t/p_t < r$. This
last causes no disequilibrium tendencies, since the fringe stock is
exhausted at T_1. At T_2 the price reaches $\bar{p}$ and stays there. The price
trajectory is shown in Diagram 11.9. The point to note now is that
the equilibrium is not usually characterized by the fact that the
cartel will have just exhausted its stock at T_2. If it wants to exhaust
its stock at the date when price reaches the value $\bar{p}$ it will have to
set a 'low' value for p_0. But if it does so it will receive a 'low' price

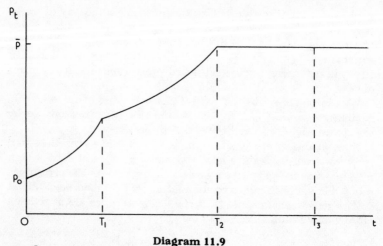

Diagram 11.9

($R_t = \bar{R}'_t - R^m_t$ for $0 \leq t \leq T_1$ and $R_t = R^m_t$ for $T_1 < t \leq T_3$. Back stop supplies for $t < T_3$).

when it enters the market. It is this balancing of low profits earlier and large profits later that yields p_0. If, as generally would be the case, the cartel stock is positive at T_2, the equilibrium is characterized by the cartel being the sole supplier during (T_2, T_3) at the price $\bar{p}$. At T_3 the cartel stock is exhausted and the backstop supplies take over.

We have noted how the existence of a fringe stock constrains the cartel's behaviour. It is equally worthwhile to look at the effect of the cartel on the competitive fringe. To do this, compare the dynamic oligopoly equilibrium analysed here with the intertemporal competitive equilibrium discussed in Chapter 6 (see section 4). If the cartel had not formed—i.e. the entire stock of the resource were competitively owned—the equilibrium outcome would have been characterized by the price rising at the rate of interest, r, until reaching $\bar{p}$; at which instant the entire stock would have just been exhausted. Consequently the initial price would have been lower than the initial price in Diagram 11.9. The formation of the cartel causes the initial price to be higher than considerations of intertemporal efficiency would dictate. It follows that the formation of the cartel results initially in an *under*-utilization of the exhaustible resource. Resource *users* bear the burden due to the cartelization. Cartel members, of course, enjoy higher profits. But interestingly enough, so do fringe owners of the resource stock. The cartel's action raises the value of the fringe stock. Fringe owners are free riders—having made no moves themselves. They can afford to extol the virtues of free competition in public and frown on the activities of the cartel. In private they applaud the formation of the cartel.

(ii) *Some complications:* A feature of the oligopoly equilibrium studied above which is worth emphasizing is that both the cartel and the fringe supply the market during an initial period, and that this is followed by a period when the cartel is the sole supplier. If the initial stock at the disposal of the fringe is not negligible, one would suppose that the cartel would supply a small fraction of the total market supply during initial years.[11] Indeed, one supposes that there are circumstances where the cartel finds it most profitable to allow the fringe to supply the entire market during an initial period. Nevertheless, it is clear that the foregoing construction is of very little use for the purposes of analysing resource markets in the world we know. First, the assumption of rational expectations is pretty hard to swallow. Secondly, the absence of extraction costs flies against the face of evidence. It is tempting to retain the former assumption since, as we argued earlier, it is difficult to know what to replace it by. But there is a good deal of empirical evidence which tells one how to remove the latter assumption. We look into the consequences of extraction costs.

A little reflection suggests that positive extraction costs could indeed make quite a dent on the equilibrium outcome. For example, it is widely believed that OPEC would not have raised the price of its crude oil fourfold in 1973 to over $9 per barrel if non-OPEC producers had unlimited capacity to extract. But capacity constraints (an extreme form of extraction cost curve) exist and this will cause an alteration in the structure of the oligopoly equilibrium.

Consider the simplest such construction. The model is the same as in the previous subsection except that now there is a capacity constraint (a function of time) operating on the competitive fringe resource owners. Thus let $\bar{R}_t^f$ denote the maximum rate of extraction feasible by the fringe at t. Then $R_t^f \leq \bar{R}_t^f$.[12] We have already noted that along an equilibrium $\dot{p}_t/p_t = r$ if $0 < R_t^f < \bar{R}_t^f$. But the equilibrium can be sustained by $\dot{p}_t/p_t < r$ if $R_t^f = \bar{R}_t^f$. With $\dot{p}_t/p_t < r$ the fringe

[11] For a confirmation of this claim see section 8.

[12] i.e. extraction costs are nil for the cartel. They are nil for the fringe so long as $R_t^f \leq \bar{R}_t^f$. Extraction costs are infinite for a fringe rate of extraction exceeding $\bar{R}_t^f$.

would like to extract at a higher rate and convert to holding the numeraire asset. Alas, it cannot, given the capacity constraint. In short, if $R_t^f > 0$, the pair of conditions

11.19 and
$$\left.\begin{array}{c} \dot{p}_t/p_t \leq r \\[2mm] R_t^f \leq \bar{R}_t^f \end{array}\right\}$$

come with 'complementary slackness' (i.e. if one is a strict inequality, the other is an equality). But this suggests that if fringe capacity is 'small', it will be biting, and the cartel may find it in its interest to dominate the market at once. In fact, of course, the smaller is fringe capacity, the greater is the cartel's monopoly power.[13] Thus, with fringe capacity biting, the first part of 11.19 is a strict *inequality*, and so, during an initial interval, $R_t^f = \bar{R}_t^f > 0$ and $R_t^m > 0$, i.e. both the fringe and the cartel supply the market at the same time, as in the previous sub-section.

Typically one would expect fringe capacity to be controllable by the fringe (e.g. accelerating the development of North Sea or Alaskan oil). Here we shall suppose $\bar{R}_t^f$ to be exogenously given and to make matters realistic, suppose it to increase with time. Assume for simplicity that demand is elastic at $\bar{p}$. The following is a possible equilibrium if $\bar{R}_t^f$ is low initially. During an initial interval $(0, T_1)$, fringe capacity is a binding constraint. Equation 11.19 holds and $R_t^f = \bar{R}_t^f$ and $R_t^m > 0$. Moreover $p_t < \bar{p}$. During a second interval $(T_1 T_2)$ fringe capacity is an unbinding constraint and fringe stock is still positive. Thus equation 11.17 holds, and R_t^f, $R_t^m > 0$. Moreover $p_t < \bar{p}$. At T_2 the fringe stock is just exhausted and during (T_2, T_3) equation 11.18 holds and $p_t < \bar{p}$. Moreover $p_{T_3} = \bar{p}$. During (T_3, T_4) the cartel is still the sole supplier, selling at the price $\bar{p}$. At T_4 the cartel stock is just exhausted and the backstop technology takes over. Diagram 11.10 illustrates this possibility.

This is about as far as one can go in providing analytical characterizations of oligopoly equilibria. It must be remembered that we have so far assumed the cartel to be able to extract costlessly and that up to the capacity constraint fringe extraction cost is nil as well.[14] Both these assumptions need to be removed.

---

[13] The cartel's powers are weakest with unlimited fringe capacity—the case discussed in the previous subsection.
[14] To be accurate, we have supposed that the cartel capacity constraint—even if it exists—is never binding.

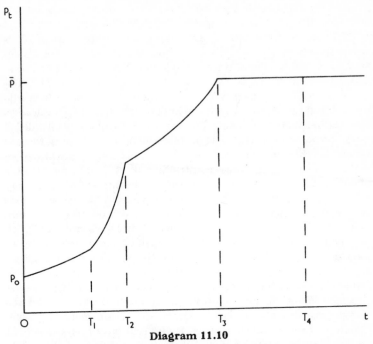

Diagram 11.10

$(R_t' = \bar{R}_t' > 0$, and $R_t^m > 0$ for $0 \leq t \leq T_1$; $0 < R_t' < \bar{R}_t'$ and $R_t^m = 0$, for $T_1 \leq t \leq T_2$; $R_t' = 0$, and $R_t = R_t^m > 0$ for $T_2 \leq t \leq T_4$. Backstop technology supplies the market for $t > T_4$.)

But once we introduce realistic extraction cost functions, exact solutions are impossible to read. In the following section we report on a simulation exercise based on the theory developed so far.

8. Oligopolistic Resource Markets: An Application to OPEC and the Oil Market[15]

In 1973 the price of crude oil from member states of OPEC increased fourfold to about $9 per barrel. Today it is nearly $15 per barrel. The dramatic price increase of 1973 is unquestionably one of the main reasons for the renewed interest in the structure of resource markets in general and the oil market in particular. Given that currently the cost of extraction in OPEC fields is a little over $1 per barrel and given that proven world reserves are not really negligible,

[15] This section is based on Cremer and Weitzman (1976).

it is widely thought that a price of $15 per barrel of crude oil is a good deal higher than its 'efficiency price'.[16] This carries with it the implication that the rate of extraction (and utilization) of oil is currently *too low*. This would seem plausible. But it is sometimes thought that the current price is too high not only from the point of view of overall efficiency but also from OPEC's point of view. The claim is that it is in OPEC's own economic interest to lower its price.[17] And this carries with it the implication that, if OPEC leadership realizes its true economic interest, the price of crude oil will fall in the future. Now it is this claim that is not at all obvious, for it is immediate that such a claim cannot be discussed in the absence of an explicit reference to some construction that builds on OPEC's oligopolistic behaviour. Moreover, the suspicion that the claim may well be false is given credence by an appeal to the constructions discussed in sections 6 and 7 where we noted a number of circumstances in which the price of an exhaustible resource along an oligopolistic equilibrium is a good deal higher than its price along an intertemporal competitive equilibrium. But we hasten to emphasize that a question such as whether OPEC has set a price too high in terms of its own interests cannot really be resolved. The answer depends on the manner in which it is judged best to model the oligopolistic structure of the oil market. It is all the more surprising, therefore, that several simulation studies that have been carried out on different formulations of the oil market have yielded not widely dissimilar results regarding the movement of the price of crude oil.[18] In what follows we shall outline the implication of a model very similar to the one discussed in the previous section when used to describe the oil market.

It is supposed that OPEC is the cartel and that the remaining oil producers in the world form a competitive fringe. There is no backstop technology in the foreseeable future and world demand for oil is assumed linear. At $10 per bl (in 1975 prices), world demand was approximately 15 bbl/year.[19] At $10 per bl a long run demand

[16] The efficiency price of an exhaustible resource and its relation to its extraction cost and total reserve (i.e. initial stock), was the subject matter of Chapter 6.

[17] This claim has been made by many, but especially by economic journalists. See, for example, Cairncross (1973).

[18] Among the most notable ones are those of Cremer and Weitzman (1976) and Pindyck (1976). The Pindyck study is much the more ambitious one. Here we shall follow the Cremer–Weitzman route because it is the simpler.

[19] In what follows bl stands for a barrel; and bbl denotes one billion (10^9) barrels.

elasticity of -0.4 is assumed. This last would appear to be in line with current opinion on the matter.[20] Suppose next that world demand will grow at the rate g. Denoting by $R(q_t, t)$ world demand for oil flow at t when the price is q_t, these specifications imply that

$$R(q_t, t) = (21 - 0.6q_t)\exp(gt).$$

It will be noticed that this supposes that demand is nil at the choke-off price of \$35 per bl (in 1975 prices).

It is supposed that fringe capacity will grow at the rate of α. Thus $R_t^f \leq \bar{R}_o^f \exp(\alpha t)$. In 1975, production by non-OPEC countries was about 11 bbl. Thus we set $\bar{R}_o^f \simeq 11$ bbl/year. Assume that both g and α equal 3% per year. As in the analysis of the previous section, we take it that plausible capacity constraint for OPEC members will be non-binding.

A central problem in calculating extraction costs is in estimating the cost of capital. In some recent works it has been suggested that capital costs are inversely proportional to the quantity of unexploited reserves.[21] Indeed, this is a special case of the rather general cost function that was discussed in Chapter 6 (see section 4).

Let K_t^i denote the capital cost for 1 bl capacity per unit time, S_o^i the initial stock (reserve) and R_t^i the rate of extraction in the ith 'field'. It is supposed that

11.20
$$K_t^i = \frac{K_o^i S_o^i}{S_o^i - \int_o^t R_\tau^i \, d\tau}.$$

We take it that capital costs for 1 bl *daily* capacity in 1975 were about \$7000 in the USA and Western Europe; about \$500 in the Persian Gulf and North Africa and about \$1500 in the rest of the world. These foregoing figures represent K_o^i. Assuming a rate of depreciation of 8% per year and a discount rate of 5% per year these correspond to a stationary state capital cost per bl of about \$3 in the USA and Eastern Europe, \$0.18 in the Persian Gulf and North Africa, and \$0.70 in the rest of the world.

'Proven recoverable reserves' have always in the past been revised upwards, as new fields are discovered. Moreover, published estimates of such reserves are based on the amount that is *profitable* to extract. Therefore, as the price of oil rises and extraction costs decline due to technological improvements, so do the estimates of recoverable reserves. An authoritative source is the British Petroleum statistical

[20] See, for example, Berndt and Wood (1974).
[21] The classic source is Hubbert (1962).

review of the world oil industry. For simplicity it is supposed that total reserves are precisely twice the proven recoverable reserves as given in their 1974 estimates. Thus we take it that $S_o = 944$ bbl for the Persian Gulf and North Africa, 53 bbl for Western Europe, 81 bbl for the USA and 364 bbl for the rest of the world. It will be noted from the theory that was developed in the previous section that, to the extent that such reserve estimates are too high, the oligopoly price based on such estimates will be biased *downwards*.

What remains is to consider transport and current costs. As earlier, all prices are expressed at the 1975 price level. The specification followed here is one where they total about $1·00 per bl for OPEC, $0·80 per bl in Western Europe, $0·95 per bl in the USA and $1·55 per bl in the rest of the world.

These figures imply a marginal extraction cost ranging from $0·18 + $1·00 = $1·18 per bl for OPEC to $3·00 + $0·95 = $3·95 per bl in the USA. But these are *current* marginal extraction costs. The model supposes extraction costs to increase as reserves are depleted and capital costs rise according to 11.20.

Before reporting on the simulation results regarding the movement of oil price along a von Stackelberg oligopoly equilibrium based on the above specification, let us consider a simple *static* example. This will help in understanding the results of the intertemporal model. In this static model the cartel (OPEC) might wish to assume that the competitive fringe produces at full capacity and subject to this constraint the cartel maximizes its single period profit. If q is the price of extracted crude oil, world demand is $(21 - 0·6q)$. Non-OPEC output of oil was about 11 bbl in 1975. Assume this is the capacity of the competitive fringe. Moreover, extraction cost for OPEC is about $1·18 per bl. Therefore OPEC profit, π, is given as

$$\pi(q) = (21 - 0·6q - 11)(q - 1·18),$$

and this is maximized at $q \simeq \$8·9$. Thus, taking a totally myopic view it is in OPEC's interest to set the price of oil at $8·9 per bl if it were to suppose that the competitive fringe will wish to produce at full capacity and that this capacity is 11 bbl. Notice that OPEC's pure monopoly price in this static world would be about $18 per bl. Thus the greater is fringe capacity, the lower is OPEC's monopoly power. All this is very intuitive, but it is revealing as well. For it suggests that as fringe capacity increases OPEC's monopoly power will be eroded, and therefore this intertemporal consideration will lead

OPEC to raise its initial (1975) price to a figure higher than $8·9 per bl. This is borne out by the simulation result that we now tabulate.

In running the simulation, time was measured in intervals of ten years (starting 1975) to focus attention on the long run aspect of the model.[22] And as we have already mentioned, all prices are constant prices, in 1975 dollars. The result that we shall tabulate was based on the assumption that the competitive fringe discounts at 8% per year but that OPEC discounts at 5% (to take into account less productive possibilities open to OPEC). While this wedge between the discount rates used by the various producers introduces complications for the theory of oligopoly discussed in the previous section, it will be noticed that the complication is very mild.

Table 11.1 below describes the oligopoly outcome with the above specification.

Table 11.1

	1975–85	1985–95	1995–2005	2005–15
Price of crude oil per bl	$9·8	$10·3	$14·7	$20·8
Annual OPEC production	5 bbl	6 bbl	14 bbl	21 bbl
Annual non-OPEC production	13 bbl[a]	17 bbl[a]	12 bbl	4 bbl

[a]Indicates that the competitive fringe is producing at full capacity.

The crucial points that Table 11.1 yields are three in number. First, note that the oligopoly price of oil hardly rises during the first twenty years (implying that we should not expect the real price of OPEC oil to grow much in the next two decades) and then rises sharply until it is nearly $21 per bl in the period 2005–15. Secondly, OPEC's share of the world oil market is about a third during the first twenty years but then it rises dramatically in the third period until by the fourth it is virtually a pure monopoly. The third point to note is that the price during the first twenty years is not much greater than the figure of $8·9 per bl which is the short-run optimum price for OPEC, given an 11 bbl capacity for the competitive fringe. This suggests that fringe capacity during the first twenty years has a good deal of bite, in that the capacity to respond on the part of the fringe is sharply limited. One expects that in this model OPEC would

[22] Note that no distinction has been made between long-run and short-run demand curves. The short-run demand curve would be more inelastic.

ideally like to set the initial price low so as to allow the fringe to deplete its reserves rapidly and run up its extraction cost before entering the market in a serious way. Alas, it cannot, given the fringe's capacity constraint. Certainly, the theory developed in the previous section indicates strongly that this would be the case. And indeed it is, if one considers Table 11.2, which tabulates the result of a simulation run based on the same specifications as before, except for one alteration: namely, that now it is assumed that there is no capacity constraint facing the competitive fringe.

As the table indicates, with no capacity constraint on the part of the fringe, OPEC finds it profitable to allow the fringe to dominate the market in initial years. The price is 'low', about $6 per bl. In the second period OPEC controls nearly half the market, considerably more than its share in the same period in Table 11.1. But the two tables display similar features for the third and fourth decades. This is not surprising. During these two decades the capacity constraint on the fringe does not bite anyway. An absence of such a constraint will then make little difference.

We shall not report here the results of a sensitivity analysis that was carried out on the foregoing model.[23] Plausible variations in the various parameters suggest that a key parameter is the capacity constraint faced by the fringe. As Table 11.2 shows removal of this constraint implies a 'low' initial price of about $6 per bl along the equilibrium. Even this figure is probably a good deal higher than the initial competitive price of oil. For, the most remarkable feature of Table 11.2 is that in the first period OPEC does not produce at all— a possibility that we noted at the beginning of section 7(ii) in this chapter. But recall that from the specification that has been followed, OPEC enjoys considerable initial cost advantages over the fringe members; so that as the theory developed in Chapter 6 implied, it is the *fringe* that ought not to produce initially if the pace of world

Table 11.2

	1975–85	1985–95	1995–2005	2005–15
Price of crude oil per bl	$6·1	$9·9	$15·6	$21·1
Annual OPEC production	0	10 bbl	15 bbl	21 bbl
Annual non-OPEC production	20 bbl	13 bbl	10 bbl	3 bbl

[23] For a detailed commentary, see Cremer and Weitzman (1976).

extraction is to be efficient. Under fully competitive conditions this is precisely what would have happened.

The results of the simulation model suggest that cartelization has resulted in the price of crude oil being a good deal higher than the competitive price. There is no presumption, however, that OPEC has set a price that is too high in terms of its own economic interest.

9. Conclusions

Our analysis of oligopolistic resource markets has shown that, if demand for the resource is iso-elastic (with the absolute value of the elasticity exceeding unity) and extraction costs are negligible, the oligopoly price of an exhaustible resource equals its competitive price (sections 2(i), 4(ii) and 4(iii) of this chapter). If either of the two assumptions is removed, the price (and hence the pace of extraction) in an oligopolistic market differs from that of a competitive one; and, in particular, there is a presumption that the bias is towards a higher initial price, and therefore excessive initial conservation. It is this last that runs counter to the fear expressed in recent years that resources are being depleted too rapidly. Our foregoing analysis suggests that if this fear is well founded, it ought not to be due to the oligopolistic nature of the market. It ought to be for other reasons. Moreover, the bias resulting from such other reasons must more than counteract the bias towards excessive conservation due to oligopoly. Among such other reasons is the oft-expressed view that in a decentralized economy the market rate of interest exceeds the social rate of discount,[24] and therefore, that the competitive rate of interest, r, used throughout this chapter, is higher than the socially desirable discount rate. This may be so. But there are equally cogent reasons for supposing that the rate of interest in a decentralized economy falls short of the social rate of discount.[25] Suppose, for the sake of argument, that the market rate of interest exceeds the social rate of discount. The analysis of Chapter 10 (section 1) would then suggest that the rate of capital accumulation ought to be stepped up. It is this observation, among others, that leads to the view that the interests of future generations will be better served if the current generation leaves them capital equipment rather than minerals and fossil fuels in the ground.[26] Chapter 10 was concerned with the mix

[24] See, for example, Sen (1960) and Marglin (1963).
[25] See, for example, Bevan (1974). We shall discuss some of these issues in Chapters 13 and 14.
[26] See, for example, Kay and Mirrlees (1975).

of capital equipment and depletable reserves that ought to be left for future generations. In this chapter we have analysed a set of reasons why the optimal mix might not be achieved. Two reasons we have identified consist in the market rate of interest being 'wrong' and the resource market being oligopolistic. There are other reasons, of course, chief among them being the presence of uncertainty and government tax policy. The remainder of this book will be taken up with these issues.

Notes on Chapter 11

The analysis of mixed market structures, old as it is, has been conducted vigorously by many in recent years. Two important technical monographs are Nikaido (1975) and Marschak and Selton (1973). For an introduction to the subject matter, see Malinvaud (1972), Chapter 6.

The study of extraction patterns under monopoly ownership of an exhaustible resource and an analysis of the direction of the resulting bias have been undertaken in Khalatbari (1976), Heal (1976), Stiglitz (1976) and Sweeney (1977). Again, the *locus classicus* of these ideas is Hotelling (1931).

Resource extraction in mixed market structures has been analysed by several authors recently. Dasgupta and Stiglitz (1976) considered various forms of competition between resource suppliers and the suppliers of a substitute product, and in particular analysed intertemporal Nash and von Stackelberg equilibria under various circumstances that include a random date of arrival of the substitute product. Salant (1976) and Khalatbari (1976) have analysed Nash outcomes among several resource owners, and Gilbert (1978) has studied the intertemporal von Stackelberg solution that results from an interaction between a resource cartel that controls a sizable chunk of the resource stock and a competitive fringe that owns the rest. Sections 5–7 of this chapter are based on these studies. Our analysis of resource depletion in the presence of a monopsonist (section 4) was prompted by the suggestive remarks in Dasgupta (1977).

The theory of dynamic limit pricing has been examined under various conditions by Gaskins (1971), and Phelps and Winter (1971). The treatment here is based on Dasgupta and Stiglitz (1976) and Hoel (1978).

In addition to these theoretical works there have been several simulation studies of the oil market using intertemporal equilibrium notions developed in section 7. Section 8 was based on the study by Cremer and Weitzman (1976). In a more ambitious study Pindyck (1976) has simulated the world oil market, again with OPEC as a cartel and other producers acting as a competitive fringe. Pindyck builds in adjustment lags and distinguishes between short- and long-run demand elasticities. His preferred specifications are quite different from those of Cremer and Weitzman (e.g. the reserve estimates are lower in Pindyck's study). At a 5% discount rate applied to both OPEC and the fringe Pindyck's simulation runs yield a 1975 oligopoly price of oil of about $13.25 per bl *falling* to a little under $10.00 per bl during 1978–80 and then *rising* gradually to a little over $20 per bl in the year 2010. Total world demand stays remarkably close to about 17.50 bbl per year during these thirty-five years (a result expected due to the very low short- and long-run elasticities of demand assumed in the model) and OPEC's share of this market remains a little over 50% until 1980, then rising gradually until the year 2010 when the share exceeds 70%. Pindyck computes the *competitive* price under the same specification. It rises steadily from a figure of about $4.62 per bl in

1975 to about \$25.50 per bl in the year 2010. During this period total competitive sales remain within the range 15.50 bbl and about 20 bbl per year. Pindyck also calculates that with his preferred specification, cartelization of the oil market results in a 55% increase in the present value of profits accruing to members of OPEC—which indicates that the incentive for the cartel to remain cohesive is strong.

A problem of considerable interest is the manner in which members of a cartel would decide on sharing the gains resulting from cartelization. Various possibilities suggest themselves. For an application of the Nash bargaining solution (see, for example, Luce and Raiffa (1957), Chapter 4) to this problem, see Hynilicza and Pindyck (1976).

CHAPTER 12

TAXATION OF EXHAUSTIBLE RESOURCES

Introduction

Resource-based industries are typically subject to substantial taxation. In addition to conventional profits or corporation taxes, they are typically required to pay royalties, revenue taxes, excess profits taxes, and are subject as well to a variety of other forms of taxation. It is not coincidental that they are so burdened. As we have seen in earlier chapters, a large part of their profit may be pure rent, and this is obviously a tempting target for taxation. Indeed, it is well known that under certain circumstances one can tax away pure rents with no loss of allocative efficiency and, as we shall see, there are certain forms of tax which can be levied on an extractive industry without distortion. However, it is certainly not the case that all conceivable taxes on extractive industries produce no deadweight loss, and in the ensuing sections we consider the impact of some of the most widely used taxes. We also return once again to the problem of the commons, discussed in Chapter 3 and, making use of techniques and results from the last chapter, analyse the dynamic version of this problem. It is of particular interest in the present context because a resolution of this problem requires the introduction of a fairly complex dynamic tax scheme, and provides an interesting example of taxes as a corrective force, rather than as potentially distortionary revenue raisers.

The first of our tasks, in what follows, is to consider the effects of various revenue-raising taxes, and in particular, the extent to which the imposition of such taxes changes the patterns of resource use. We shall refer to this as the *bias* (or *distortion*) introduced by the tax, and will always measure this as a deviation from the intertemporal competitive equilibrium allocation, using this latter as an ideal benchmark since, for simplicity, we shall suppose in what follows that the competitive interest rate is identified with the social rate of discount. Such an approach, while hallowed by tradition, is nevertheless of limited appeal. The correct question to ask is: what is the best set of biases (distortions) to have, if you must have them? The

361

government may wish to resort to taxation with a view to removing existing distortions (e.g. the Pigouvian taxes in Chapters 3 and 5). It may wish to resort to taxation on distributional grounds, or for the supply of public goods. As regards distributional issues we noted in Chapter 2 (section 4) and Chapter 10 (section 2) that one can in principle think of taxes and subsidies that are non-distortionary, the imposition of which enables the full optimum to be realized (see in particular, the closing remarks in the Notes to Chapter 10). This full optimum is often called the first-best. But one recognizes that in the economies that one knows the first-best is much like the Holy Grail. The inability of governments to rely entirely on non-distortionary taxes and subsidies forces one to enquire into the optimum structure of distortionary ones.[1] This is a particularly difficult exercise, bringing together, as it does, welfare economics, taxation theory and the analysis of public investment criteria. The subject is particularly murky, since the structure of optimum taxes often depends sensitively on the constraints that the government faces in wielding the various controls available to it.

In fact we shall not pursue this approach here. Much of the time we shall instead analyse the bias in extraction patterns introduced by various types of taxes. Excepting for the analysis in section 8 we shall suppose throughout that the government is resorting to taxation of the extractive industry with a view to raising revenue.

It is, however, important to realize that in any particular institutional situation it is most unlikely that the allocation of resources would be fully optimal in the absence of the taxes we are about to consider. There would typically be many other distorting taxes in existence, and it is important to recognize that the introduction of a further distortion does not necessarily imply a loss in welfare.[2] Therefore, the relevant question is: in terms of social welfare what are the best set of taxes to impose if it is found necessary to impose them? The answer to this question depends obviously on the pre-

[1] Such optima are usually called 'second-best' ones. In recent years they have been explored extensively. See, for example, Boiteux (1958), Lipsey and Lancaster (1956), Diamond and Mirrlees (1971), Stiglitz and Dasgupta (1971), Atkinson and Stiglitz (1976) and Stern (1976).

[2] As we cannot go deeply into the modern theory of public finance here, we shall not elaborate on this proposition. But it is quite often appealed to in practice. The April 1977 suggestion in the United States that the gasoline sales tax ought to be raised substantially in order to counter existing distortions so that consumption of petroleum is reduced is presumably based on such a view.

existing circumstances, though the mode of analysis in the following sections should be of value in reaching the answer.

These foregoing points are worth bearing in mind, particularly so because we shall avoid the general equilibrium effects of taxation and shall instead focus attention on a given extractive industry in isolation. The analysis will be 'partial equilibrium' in nature. In this sense the analysis will be similar in spirit to those conducted in Chapters 6 and 11. The idea then is to study the effect of various types of taxes on the intertemporal allocation of an exhaustible resource. Moreover, we suppose in what follows that the government announces its entire intertemporal tax policy, so that expectations are throughout realized.

Three final preliminary points should be noted. We shall be comparing intertemporal competitive equilibria with and without the tax in question. In other words, we shall avoid the problem noted in Chapter 6 section 1(iii) regarding the likely misbehaviour of a sequence of momentary equilibria. It is sensible to avoid it since, if we allow the initial price to be indeterminate, the direction of the biases resulting from a tax will also be indeterminate. There is thus not much scope for discussion. Moreover, it will be assumed throughout that demand for the resource flow is positive no matter how high the price. This last, as we noted in the previous chapter, greatly simplifies the search for biases in extraction patterns. Finally, it is obvious that government tax policy affects not only the pace at which known deposits are exhausted but it affects also the pace at which new deposits are searched for. In this chapter we suppose that the total stock is known. In Chapter 14 we shall look briefly at the effect of taxation on exploration.

1. A Sales Tax

Much discussed in recent years is the implication of a sales tax on an exhaustible resource. Let us analyse it. Let p_t be the competitive price of a unit of unextracted resource (i.e. royalty price) and let q_t denote the consumer price of a unit of extracted resource. For simplicity of exposition we suppose that average extraction cost is a constant b. Let r denote the competitive rate of interest, assumed equal to the social rate of discount. Suppose the government were to announce and levy a specific tax τ_t^s on the sale of the resource. Then we know that the following two conditions must hold (see Chapter 6 section 4(ii)):

12.1 $$\dot{p}_t/p_t = r$$

and

12.2 $$q_t = p_t + b + \tau_t^s$$

In Chapter 6, section 4 (ii) we analysed the pattern of extraction when $\tau_t^s = 0$. The question is: how is this pattern altered when $\tau_t^s > 0$? To see this we shall consider two special forms of τ_t^s.

To begin with let p_o^* denote the initial price of the unextracted resource if $\tau_t^s = 0$ for all t. We discussed this in Chapter 6, section 4(ii). Now suppose the government were to announce a tax schedule of the form $\tau_t^s = \tau_0^s \exp(rt)$ (i.e. it sets an initial tax τ_0^s and allows the specific tax to grow at the rate of interest). Suppose, furthermore (and it will become clear why), that $0 < \tau_o^s < p_o^*$. Then, from equation 12.1 we have $p_t = p_0 \exp(rt)$ and, therefore, from equation 12.2 that

12.3 $$q_t = (p_0 + \tau_0^s) \exp(rt) + b.$$

As we are considering an intertemporal competitive equilibrium with the tax, the value of p_0 will be that which will allow the integral of sales over time to equal the total initial stock. Now, in the absence of the tax we would have had

12.4 $$q_t^* = p_o^* \exp(rt) + b.$$

A comparison of equations 12.3 and 12.4 tells us immediately that an exponentially rising tax schedule introduces no alteration in the pattern of extraction, since the consumer price schedule remains the same (i.e. $q_t = q_t^*$). p_0 adjusts, so that

12.5 $$p_0 + \tau_0^s = p_o^*.$$

The higher is τ_0^s (subject to $\tau_0^s < p_o^*$) the lower is p_0 and therefore the value of the deposit.[3] To put the matter differently, the entire tax is absorbed by the resource owners. Such a sales tax introduces no distortions, and is equivalent to a proportional tax on the value of the deposit.[4]

---

[3] We leave it to the reader to consider what will happen if $\tau_0^s \geqslant p_0^*$.

[4] If these competitive resource owners are foreign owners then τ_t^s is in effect an import tariff. An exponentially increasing specific tariff is then a means by which a government can expropriate foreign deposits without causing any bias in extraction. But this supposes a single importing nation. Interesting problems can arise if there are many importing countries; see, Newbery (1976).

Suppose instead a constant specific sales tax, i.e. $\tau_t^s = \tau^s > 0$. Then from equation 12.2 we have

12.6 $$q_t = p_t + b + \tau^s,$$

and therefore, it is as though the cost of extraction were to rise from b to $b + \tau^s$. It is simple to see that the tax is distortionary. To see this most sharply suppose the elasticity of demand for the resource flow is unity. As earlier, let p_o^* denote the initial royalty price of the resource in the absence of the tax and p_0 the initial price with the tax in force. Then we know from the analysis of Chapter 6, section 4(ii)—equation 6.25—that

12.7 $$p_o^* = b/\{\exp(brS_0) - 1\}$$
and
12.8 $$p_0 = (b + \tau^s)/[\exp\{(b + \tau^s)rS_0\} - 1],$$

where S_0 is the initial stock. It is then immediate that $p_0 < p_o^*$ and, therefore, that the value of the deposit is reduced by the imposition of the tax. But unlike the previous case there is a distortion now, since, in the obvious notation, $q_0 > q_o^*$.[5] The effect of the tax is to increase the initial price to consumers. This in turn means that initial demand is less. The tax results in lower initial extraction rates. In traditional language, only a fraction of the tax is absorbed by the owners of the resource. The remainder is passed on to consumers in higher prices during an initial interval.[6]

2. A Profits Tax

Of the many forms of taxation that affect the pace of resource depletion, by far the most widespread is the profits tax—a form of taxation impinging on almost all resource-owner industries. In principle it may as well be called a 'rent' or royalty' tax, since it is just that. Let τ_t be the rate of tax on the rent accruing to a resource

---

[5] i.e. on using 12.7 and 12.8, $p_0 + b + \tau^s > p_0^* + b$ despite the fact that $p_0 < p_o^*$.

[6] Since the exponentially rising specific sales tax studied above is non-distortionary it is the optimal tax. Formally, let $D(q_t, t)$ be the demand curve for the resource flow, and $\bar{R}$ the revenue requirement of the government, and $u,(D_t, t)$ the flow of consumer surplus (i.e. $q_t = \partial u/\partial D_t$). If the government is concerned with the present discounted sum of net consumer's surplus, its problem is to choose a schedule $\tau_t^s (0 \leqslant t \leqslant \infty)$, which maximizes $\int_0^\infty [u\{D(q_t,t)\} - bD(q_t,t)]\exp(-rt)dt$, subject to the constraints, $p_t = p_0\exp(rt), q_t = p_t + b - \tau_t^s$, $\int_0^\infty \tau_t^s D(q_t,t)\exp(-rt)\,dt = R$, and $\int_0^\infty D(q_t, t)\,dt = S_0$. It can be shown that if an optimum exists it is of the form $\tau_0^s = \tau_0^s\exp(rt)$.

owner. Then the after-tax price per unit of the resource accruing to an owner is

12.9 $$p_t = (q_t - b)(1 - \tau_t).$$

Along an intertemporal competitive equilibrium equation 12.1 must be satisfied as well. Thus

12.10 $$\frac{\dot{q}_t(1 - \tau_t) - (q_t - b)\dot{\tau}_t}{(q_t - b)(1 - \tau_t)} = r.$$

It follows that if the tax rate is constant (i.e. $\dot{\tau}_t = 0$) the intertemporal allocation of the resources is no different from the competitive allocation in the absence of taxation. There is no distortion. The effect of the tax is simply to reduce the competitive value of the deposit to a fraction $(1 - \tau)$ of its original value. Thus, in the obvious notation, $p_0 = (1 - \tau)p_o^*$; the consumer price schedule remains unaffected. The constant profit tax is identical to a specific sales tax growing at the rate of interest.

Usually, however, taxes are imposed on interest earnings as well as profits. If a constant tax rate $\tau(0 < \tau < 1)$ is levied on both profits and interests we have, from equations 12.9 and 12.1, that

12.11 $$\frac{\dot{q}_t}{q_t - b} = r(1 - \tau).$$

Integrating equation 12.11 yields

12.12 $$q_t = (q_0 - b) \exp\{r(1 - \tau)t\} + b,$$

where q_0 is that value which will ensure that the integral of sales over the indefinite future equals the initial stock, S_0. If we continue to denote by starred prices those that sustain an intertemporal competitive equilibrium in the absence of taxation, then

12.13 $$q_t^* = (q_o^* - b) \exp(rt) + b,$$

and since for large t, $\dot{q}_t^*/q_t^* = r > r(1 - \tau) = \dot{q}_t/q_t$, we note that $q_0 > q_o^*$ and therefore that during an initial interval of time the tax results in a higher consumer price and consequently in a lower pace of extraction.

3. Royalties

Almost as ubiquitous as profits taxation is the requirement that extractive companies pay a royalty to the government of the country in which they operate. This is typically a payment of a certain percentage of the value of the resources extracted—for example, oil companies operating in the United Kingdom currently have to pay a royalty equal to $12\frac{1}{2}\%$ of the value of the petroleum 'won and saved' from UK fields in each half-year. This is essentially a tax on the gross revenue from resource sales (but must not be confused with the so-called revenue tax, to be discussed later). If τ is the rate at which such a tax (or royalty) is levied we have

$$p_t = q_t(1-\tau) - b,$$

and therefore, from equation 12.1 that

12.14 $$\dot{q}_t = rq_t - \frac{br}{(1-\tau)}.$$

Integrating equation 12.14 yields

12.15 $$q_t = \left(q_0 - \frac{b}{(1-\tau)}\right)\exp(rt) + \frac{b}{1-\tau}.$$

A glance at equation 12.15 suggests that the effect of the tax is formally identical to the effect of a once for all increase in average extraction cost. It is therefore identical to a constant specific sales tax. The tax certainly introduces a distortion, and in particular, results in higher initial consumer prices and consequently greater conservation. It is also clear that the effect of a royalty is to reduce the value of the deposit, since $p_0 < p_0^*$ (see for example equations 12.7 and 12.8.)

There is in fact a simple verbal argument which makes the impact of a royalty clear. The revenue produced by a one-unit depletion is just the price, so that the tax liability incurred as a result is proportional to the price. But with positive extraction costs, price minus cost rise over time at the interest rate, so that price rises more slowly than the interest rate. Hence the present value of the price falls over time, as therefore does the present value of the tax liability resulting from depletion. A firm concerned to minimize its tax liability has in consequence an incentive to postpone depletion.

4. A Capital Gains Tax

The return from holding an exhaustible resource comes entirely in the form of capital gains. Many countries levy taxes on such gains. Let us investigate the impact of such a tax here. Let τ^c be the rate of tax on capital gains and let τ be the rate of taxation on interest income. It follows that the arbitrage equation now reads as

12.16 $$(1-\tau^c)\dot{p}_t/p_t=r(1-\tau).$$

In the absence of any other taxation on the resource $q_t=p_t+b$. Therefore, if $\tau^c=\tau$ there is no distortion at all. Indeed the value of the deposit remains unaltered (i.e. $p_0=p_o^*$). Thus the distortion arising out of an interest income tax (section 3 above) can be thought of as resulting from a failure to treat capital gains properly; a point that we shall explore further in the next section.

If $1>\tau^c>\tau>0$ then $\dot{p}_t/p_t>r$ and consequently the intertemporal equilibrium will involve excessive depletion during an initial period. The reverse is the case if $\tau>\tau^c$.

While discussing the impact of a capital gains tax, it is important to note that the taxation of capital gains on resource stocks may sometimes be implied by the provisions of other taxes, even though there is formally no capital gains tax in existence. The point is that in most countries, companies trading in extractive resources face a corporate profits tax and, under the provisions of such taxes, it is, or has been, common for increases in the value of stocks of a resource held to be included in the definition of taxable profits. In general the provision has applied only to stocks of the resource already extracted, so that its impact on patterns of resource-allocation over time may have been minimal—but it is nevertheless an important illustration of the point that a tax is not always identical with its legislative designation.

5. The Depletion Allowance

Under United States tax law, the tax liability of an oil company is based on its trading profits minus an amount known as the depletion allowance. This allowance is proportional to the depletion of the company's oil reserves during the year under consideration. Its justification is on the grounds that depletion of these reserves amounts to depreciation of the company's capital assets, and thus should be tax deductible, as with any other form of depreciation.[7]

[7] See also the discussion on the treatment of resource depletion in correct NNP calculations (Chapter 8 section 8.)

But the point is that the value of the quantity of oil extracted during an interval does not represent the true economic depreciation of the asset and so one can argue that the allowance is based on an incorrect figure. Let us look into this.

To begin with we may note that a constant rate of depletion allowance introduces no distortion in the pace of extraction if the price of unextracted resource is used to value the depletion. Let τ be the rate of profit taxation and let α $(0 \leq \alpha \leq 1)$ denote the percentage of depletion allowance, where 'depletion' is computed as the market value of the rate of extraction using the unextracted resource price to compute this value. Then in the usual notation,

12.17 $$p_t = (q_t - b)(1 - \tau) + \alpha \tau p_t$$

and therefore

12.18 $$p_t = (q_t - b)(1 - \tau)/(1 - \alpha \tau).$$

But by the arbitrage equation 12.1 we have, on using 12.18, that

$$\dot{p}_t/p_t = \dot{q}_t/(q_t - b) = r.$$

The allowance introduces no bias. With $\alpha < 1$ it merely reduces the value of the well.

It does introduce a bias if instead the depletion is computed by using the post-extraction price. In this case

12.19 $$p_t = (q_t - b)(1 - \tau) + \alpha \tau q_t.$$

On using equations 12.1 and 12.19 we obtain

$$\frac{\dot{q}_t(1 - \tau + \alpha \tau)}{q_t(1 - \tau + \alpha \tau) - b(1 - \tau)} = r,$$

which, on integration, yields

12.20 $$q_t = \{q_0 - b(1 - \tau)/(1 - \tau + \alpha \tau)\} \exp(rt) + b(1 - \tau)/(1 - \tau + \alpha \tau).$$

It is immediate from equation 12.20 that the effect of this constant percentage depletion allowance is equivalent to a once for all *reduction* in the average cost of extraction. It follows that the effect of the allowance is to reduce the consumer price of oil during an initial interval. This implies that the rate of extraction is higher during this initial interval.

The impact of such depletion allowance can be given a simple intuitive explanation. The value of such an allowance to the producing firms varies as the price of the resource changes, and in particular rises with price over time. But with positive extraction costs, consumer price rises less rapidly than the rate of interest, and in consequence the present value of the depletion allowance falls. The tax saved by a one-unit depletion today has a greater present value than that saved by a one-unit depletion in the future, providing a clear incentive to deplete sooner rather than later.

6. True Depletion Allowance

We can now bring together the analysis of sections 3, 5 and 6 above to discuss the effect of a tax allowance on 'true economic depletion'.[8] The point is that the change in the value of a well during an interval consists not only of the value of the resource depleted during this interval but also of the appreciation in the value of the remaining stock due to capital gains. This latter term is of particular importance for exhaustible assets since their competitive prices rise at the after-tax rate of interest. In section 2 we noted that a constant rate of profit taxation (the tax being imposed on interest income as well), introduces a bias towards insufficient initial depletion. As the analysis of the first part of section 5 makes clear, this will continue to be so if a constant exemption rate is allowed on the value of the un-extracted resource. But if capital gains are excluded from this exemption there is no bias. To see this, let τ be the rate of tax on profits (including interest income) and τ^c the rate of taxation of capital gains. Then we have (see equation 12.17)

12.21 $$p_t = (q_t - b)(1 - \tau) + \alpha \tau p_t$$

and

12.22 $$(1 - \tau^c)\dot{p}_t/p_t = (1 - \tau)r.[9]$$

If $\tau^c = \tau$ then equations 12.21 and 12.22 imply that there is no alteration in the rate of extraction along an intertemporal competitive equilibrium, since they imply that

$$\dot{p}_t/p_t = \dot{q}_t/(q_t - b) = r.$$

But if $\tau^c = \tau$, then the tax structure is one in which even though a part of the loss in the value of the well due to depletion is exempt from corporate taxation, the capital gains realized by resource owners is not. In other words, the tax allowance (exemption) is on

---

[8] The concept of true economic depreciation is thoroughly analysed in Samuelson (1964).
[9] This is equation 12.16.

the true economic depreciation of the deposit and the foregoing analysis has shown that there is no bias in extraction pattern in this case. So long as $\alpha < 1$, $p_t = (q_t - b)(1 - \tau)/(1 - \alpha\tau)$, and the affect of the tax structure is a reduction in the value of the wells. If $\alpha = 1$ (i.e. full depletion allowance) the value of the wells remains unaltered as well, but in this case the government earns no revenue.

7. The UK Petroleum Revenue Tax

Companies operating oil and gas fields within the jurisdiction of the UK government are, in addition to profits taxes and royalties, liable to the Petroleum Revenue Tax. A striking feature of this tax is the misleading nature of its title; it is not, as one might suppose, similar to a royalty and levied on revenues. It is essentially an excess profits tax, and is levied on revenue net of certain operating and exploration costs, and net of royalty payments. Not all operating and exploration costs are allowable against tax—thus interest on loans is not deductible (providing an incentive to hire plant rather than buy it with borrowed capital), nor is any expenditure depending wholly or partly on the quantity, value, proceeds or profits from oil won from the field. A further complication is that the incidence of the tax is to be limited so that liability to this tax in any year does not exceed 80% of the amount by which 'adjusted profits' exceed 30% of accumulated capital expenditure at the end of that year. Although the rationale of many of the details of the tax is unclear, this last provision makes it clear that it is basically an excess profits tax. The effect of its various provisions is that a graph depicting a petroleum revenue tax liability against gross revenue from an oil field might, for a typical structure of costs, look as in Diagram 12.1. Liability is zero below a certain revenue level: tax is then paid at a marginal rate that may start at 80% if the constraint that the tax should not exceed 80% of the excess of adjusted profits over a 30% return on capital is binding, and which decreases to 45% once revenue is sufficiently high that this does not bind.

Although the effects of such a complex tax are difficult to establish analytically, there is a simple intuitive argument that makes a part of this clear. The fact that there is a certain level of revenues below which no tax is payable provides an incentive to keep revenues below this level and avoid the tax—and this clearly means slowing the rate of depletion. Indeed, the fact that the average tax rate can be shown to be monotonically increasing once tax starts to be paid, obviously reinforces such an effect. We thus see that though in name

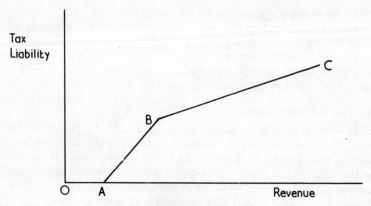

Diagram 12.1

AB has slope 0·80 from equation
$$\text{Tax} = 0\cdot8\{(R-C) - 0\cdot3K\}$$
BC has slope 0·45 from equation
$$\text{Tax} = 0\cdot45(R-C)$$
where R = revenue, C = current costs, K = accumulated investment.

a revenue tax and in structure a profits tax, what we have in effect is similar to a royalty. Now, we have already noted in section 3 that the imposition of a royalty is analytically identical to a once for all increase in the average cost of extraction, reducing the value of the well. To the extent that the imposition of this royalty makes the cost of extraction (as faced by resource owners) from UK fields a good deal more costly than from fields elsewhere in the world the effect of the UK tax will be to delay extraction from its fields.[10] Although many would find this a very satisfactory conclusion—and argue, for example, that it is an appropriate counterbalance to the use of excessively high discount rates by the private sector—it is never-theless somewhat paradoxical. An explicit aim of much of the rele-vant legislation was in fact designed to encourage rapid development of these fields!

8. A Dynamic Version of the Problem of the Common

We have had several occasions to refer to the problem of the common in a static context (see Chapter 3) and have analysed the problem in a dynamic context with free entry (Chapter 5). There are

[10] We discussed the sequence of extraction from different fields under different market structures in Chapters 6 and 11.

some special features that arise with resources like oil and natural
gas which we shall analyse here. The aim then will be to study the
appropriate corrective tax policy to meet the difficulty. For clarity
we consider a situation with just two firms, and we shall suppose that
they own adjacent oil concessions, with half of an initial stock of S_0
under each concession when the analysis begins. However, the stock
S_0 really forms a single underground pool and can migrate freely from
one concession to the other—hence the 'problem of the common'.
In particular, we suppose that at any instant of time the rate of
migration of oil from one concession to another is proportional to the
difference between the stocks under the two concessions: one could
think of this as diffusion through a porous membrane in response to
pressure differences. This implies that the differential equation
governing the adjustment of the stock is

12.23 $\qquad \dot{S}_{it} = -R_{it} + \alpha(S_{jt} - S_{it}), \qquad j, i = 1, 2 \quad \text{and} \quad i \neq j, \alpha > 0.$

where S_{it} is the stock under concession i at time t, and R_{it} is the rate
of extraction from the ith concession. For simplicity suppose there
are no extraction costs.

We again consider a Cournot–Nash equilibrium in which each
firm takes the other's time-profile of output as given, and maximizes
subject to this and equation 12.23. Routine arguments (see Chapter
11, section 4(ii)) lead to the conclusion that each will choose his output to satisfy

12.24 $\qquad R_{it}p'(R_t) + p(R_t) = \lambda_i \exp\{(r+\alpha)t\}, \qquad i = 1, 2,$

where $R_t = R_{1t} + R_{2t}$. As before, each firm seeks to make marginal
revenue grow over time, though no longer at the discount rate; the
growth rate of marginal revenue now equals the discount rate plus
the rate of migration of oil between the two concessions. It is intuitively clear that introducing migration at a rate α acts like an
increase in the discount rate, because it implies that for a zero own
extraction rate and a constant stock under the other concession, a
firm's stock declines exponentially at rate α:

$$\dot{S}_{it} = -\alpha S_{it} + \alpha S_{jt}$$
$$= -\alpha S_{it} + \beta$$
where $\beta = \alpha S_{jt}$, a constant. Hence
$$S_{it} = \gamma \exp(-\alpha t) + \delta$$

where γ and δ are constants, if S_{jt} is constant (a reasonable assumption over a short period). Hence delay in extracting the oil is penalized at a rate α, which thus acts just like a discount rate.

Summing equation 12.24 yields

12.25 $$p(R_t)\gamma(R_t) = \lambda \exp\{(r+\alpha)t\}$$

where $\gamma(R) \equiv 2 + 1/\eta(R)$, with $\eta(R)$ being the elasticity of market demand (see equations 11.14–11.15). It follows that

12.26 $$\dot{p}_t/p_t = r + \alpha - \dot{\gamma}_t/\gamma_t$$

where

$$\text{sign } \dot{\gamma} = \text{sign } \frac{d\eta}{dQ} \quad \text{(see equation 11.16).}$$

It is thus clear that the existence of a common pool with internal migration rate α increases the rate of price appreciation by α, and consequently increases the initial rate of consumption of the resource. This is just what one would expect.

Let us now turn to an analysis of the type of tax policy that could offset this bias. We suppose for this purpose that the elasticity of demand is constant, so that $\dot{\gamma}_t = 0$. In this case the bias present is due solely to the fugacious nature of oil reserves, in conjunction with the rule of capture prevailing. As the analysis of Chapter 11, section 4(ii) made clear there is no bias due to the duopoly nature of ownership of the resource. As the extensive discussion of Pigouvian taxes in Chapters 3 and 5 made clear, in designing a corrective tax it is sensible to go directly to the heart of the matter and locate the source of the bias. Under our present assumption the intertemporal Nash equilibrium price path is given as

12.27 $$\dot{p}_t/p_t = r + \alpha.$$

Clearly the problem is that the effective interest rate is too high. Consider then an *ad valorem* tax levied on resource sales at the rate τ_t at t. Let q_t be the consumer price of the resource. Then $p_t = q_t(1-\tau_t)$. Replacing this in equation 12.24 yields

12.28 $$R_i q'(R_t)(1-\tau_t) + q(R_t)(1-\tau_t) = \lambda_i \exp\{(r+\alpha)t\}, \qquad i = 1, 2.$$

That is, after-tax marginal revenue grows at the rate $r + \alpha$, so that the present value of net marginal revenue is the same at all dates, at the effective rate of interest $r + \alpha$. Summing equations 12.28 leads to the counterpart of equation 12.25 as

12.29 $$q(R_t)(1-\tau_t)\gamma(R_t) = \lambda\exp\{(r+\alpha)t\}.$$

Differentiating equation 12.29 now yields (since $\dot{\gamma}_t = 0$)

12.30 $$\dot{q}_t/q_t = r + \alpha + \dot{\tau}_t/(1-\tau_t).$$

The aim of the corrective tax is to ensure that the consumer price, q_t, rises at the rate of interest (recall that by assumption extraction costs are nil). Therefore must have

$$\frac{\dot{\tau}_t}{1-\tau_t} = -\alpha,$$

or

12.31 $$\tau_t = 1 - (1-\tau_0)\exp(\alpha t).$$

Since $\tau_0 < 1$, equation 12.31 implies that at least in the long run $\tau_t < 0$ and therefore the government needs to *subsidize* the sale of the resource. This may appear paradoxical since, in the absence of any government intervention, there is excessive extraction in initial years along a Nash equilibrium. But this suggests that $\tau_0 > 0$, so that $\tau_t > 0$ initially and declining continuously. The point is that since underground migration of oil results in the effective interest rate being increased, the apparent profitability of future sales is decreased relative to the present. It is then entirely natural to introduce a tax which, by decreasing over time, exactly offsets this effect.

Although the dynamic commons problem could in principle be overcome by taxation, to the best of our knowledge such an approach has never been used. The problem has invariably been tackled by unitization, or by regulations controlling well-spacing and enforcing pro-rationing of the outputs from individual wells. Regulatory authorities have thus displayed their customary preference for working via quantitative controls rather than via prices. It will become clear in the discussions of Chapter 13 that uncertainty may sometimes justify this preference, though it is certainly not clear whether such a factor is operative in the present case.

Notes to Chapter 12

There is really very little further literature on this topic—a surprising fact. Something of a classic is Gaffney (1967). A more recent contribution is Brannon (1975), and in particular the paper by Stiglitz in that volume. Considerable institutional detail for the USA can be found in the paper by McDonald in Kalter and Vogely (eds.) (1976). Our analysis of the problem of the common (section 9) is drawn from Khalatbari (1977).

CHAPTER 13

UNCERTAINTY, INFORMATION AND THE
ALLOCATION OF RISK

Introduction

Our earlier discussion has on several occasions alluded to the impact of uncertainty on allocations involving exhaustible resources. But we have not gone into such issues in any detail. Instead, we have supposed an absence of uncertainty, or at the very least, that one would not go far wrong if all random variables were replaced by sure values (e.g. their expected values). It is time to remedy this. The need for such an exploration is plain. Uncertainty about future possibilities looms rather large, and this may have a telling impact on the rates at which we ought today to deplete our stocks of exhaustible resources. Thus, for example, any appraisal of the rates at which fossil fuels are depleted today must surely be based on an assessment of the likelihood of major technological discoveries in energy generation in the future—such as 'clean' breeder reactors or controlled nuclear fusion. Likewise, an appraisal of the depletion rate for iron ore reserves must depend *inter alia* on a view of the likelihood of alternatives to steel being found in many uses. Then again, new reserves of extractive resources are continually being discovered. But such discoveries cannot be predicted with certainty.

A discussion of uncertainty and its effects on natural resource allocation readily invites one to consider the production and transmission of information. Seismic surveys and laboratory experiments designed to help control nuclear fusion are both aimed at producing information. In this and the following chapter we study the effect of uncertainty and the problems of information in relation to natural resources. Our account will be incomplete because the theory of these matters is incomplete. This is particularly so for the problems associated with the acquisition and transmission of information. None the less we hope to answer some questions and we shall indicate where the unsolved problems are.

In this chapter we shall, in the main, study the problem of individual decision-making under uncertainty in the context of natural resource use. The following chapter will be concerned with resource and information allocation in a decentralized economy. In keeping with our earlier approach, we shall investigate the nature of the market structure that needs to exist in order that one can claim with confidence that a market equilibrium under uncertainty sustains an efficient allocation of resources. Such an investigation then leads rather naturally to one's asking whether one can identify 'biases' in resource extraction if, for one reason or another, a given market structure does not sustain an efficient outcome. An identification of such biases goes some way towards identifying the kind of public policy measures that may be needed. Again, except for some simple examples, our conclusions will be pessimistic. It is not clear as a general rule in what way an equilibrium allocation in a decentralized environment, even when it exists, is inefficient.

1. Risk Sharing, Fair Insurance Contracts and the Law of Large Numbers

(i) *General considerations:* In order to sort out some preliminary ideas it will prove convenient to abstract from time. Imagine then a timeless world or, equivalently, a world in which the focus of attention is on a single period. Imagine next a sample space consisting of S elements θ_s $(s = 1, \ldots, S)$. In what follows we shall refer to θ as a *state of nature*.[1] There are thus S states of nature. Assume for the moment that there is a known probability distribution, π_s $(=\pi(\theta_s))$, defined over θ_s. Thus $\pi_s \geq 0$ $(s = 1, \ldots, S)$ and $\sum_{s=1}^{S} \pi_s = 1$. We take it for simplicity that there is a single commodity in this world which, for brevity, we shall refer to as income, y. We now introduce an individual into this world. By a *prospect* (or *lottery*) $\bar{y}$, we shall mean a vector $\mathbf{y} = (y_1, \ldots, y_s)$, where y_s is an amount of income that the individual receives if, and only if, θ_s occurs. We would now wish to endow the individual with a preference ordering over different prospects. The critical point is the fact that the individual must make a choice before the state of nature is revealed.

For vividness one might wish to think that there are two instants of time $(t = 0, 1)$ where the decision has to be made at $t = 0$ regarding which prospect to choose and where the state of nature is revealed at $t = 1$. The precise sense in which we are none the less in a timeless

---

[1] We are using the expression 'state of nature' in the manner in which it is used in statistical decision theory. A state of nature is '. . . a description of the world so complete that, if true and known, the consequence of every action would be known' Arrow (1971, p. 45).

world is that the individual has no choice over the income he receives at $t=0$. Let us suppose that the individual's preferences over prospects can be represented by an increasing, strictly concave and indefinitely differentiable utility function, U, where

13.1 $$U = U(y_1, y_2, \ldots, y_s).$$

In fact, for much of the time we shall suppose that U is of the special form

13.2 $$U = \sum_{s=1}^{S} \pi_s u_s(y_s)$$

where $u_s(\cdot)$ is an increasing, strictly concave, and indefinitely differentiable function defined over income.[2] Notice that 13.2 stipulates that the utility function $u_s(\cdot)$ in state θ_s depends on s. This would appear to be a reasonable requirement. But for expository ease we shall often consider a special case of 13.2, one where $u_s(\cdot)$ is independent of s. Thus

13.3 $$U = \sum_{s=1}^{S} \pi_s u(y_s).$$

A glance at 13.1–13.3 suggests at once that formally we can regard a prospect, y, as a commodity bundle and, consequently, pretend that there are S commodities in the world we are describing. Choosing a commodity bundle y implies a claim to 'commodity' y_s if, and only if, θ_s occurs as a state of nature. Following traditional terminology we shall refer to these as *contingent commodities*.[3] That is to say, we can add a further dimension to the characteristics of a commodity. A commodity, in this view, will be characterized not only in terms of its physical attributes, its location and the date at which it is made available, but as well by the state of nature at which it appears. Looked at in this light we shall be able to exploit the standard theory of the consumer. This is precisely what we shall now do.

[2] Equation 13.2 represents the 'expected utility' hypothesis of von Neumann and Morgenstern. The conditions on preferences over lotteries that ensure that 13.1 can be expressed as 13.2 are so well known that we shall not go into them here. For an excellent account of this, see Luce and Raifa (1957, Chapter 3) and the discussion on Hirschleifer (1965). Recall that we have already appealed to this framework in Chapter 9 section 4.

[3] See Arrow (1964).

Let $\bar{y} = \sum_{s=1}^{S} \pi_s y_s$ denote the expected value of the prospect y, and let us suppose that the variance of y is positive. Assume that U takes the form 13.3. Then given that $u(\cdot)$ is strictly concave, one has

13.4
$$\sum_{s=1}^{S} \pi_s u(\bar{y}) = u(\bar{y}) > \sum_{s=1}^{S} \pi_s u(y_s).$$

(We illustrate this for the case $S = 2$ in Diagram 13.1.) The consumer would prefer a contingent commodity bundle in which he is provided precisely with $\bar{y}$ units of income in each state of nature. In short, the consumer is *risk-averse*. He prefers a sure income $\bar{y}$ to an uncertain income with mean value $\bar{y}$.

In much of what follows we shall suppose that individuals are risk averse. We do this because, despite the fact that individuals on occasion engage in gambling, their dominant behaviour in facing risky situations appears to be characterized by risk-aversion, as an analysis of the implications of risk-aversion makes clear.

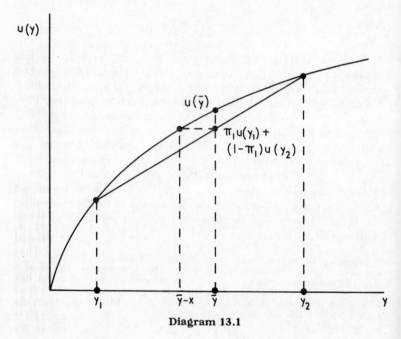

Diagram 13.1

Now given 13.4 we know that there is some positive number, x, such that

13.5 $$\sum_{s=1}^{S} \pi_s u(\bar{y} - x) = u(\bar{y} - x) = \sum_{s=1}^{S} \pi_s u(y_s),$$

(see Diagram 13.1). Stated in words, the individual is indifferent between the commodity bundle y and the commodity bundle which consists of a sure income somewhat less than the mean of y. It is then natural to refer to x as the *cost of risk-bearing* associated with the consumption bundle y. Were the individual risk-neutral (i.e. u were linear in y) then one notes from 13.5 that $x = 0$ (i.e. the individual is indifferent between prospects with the same expected return). In our example we have postulated risk-aversion on the part of the individual by the assumption of *strict* concavity of u. It follows that $x > 0$. One should note that the actual value of x depend on y. It seems reasonable that the cost of risk bearing, x, should somehow be related to the variance of y: the larger the variance, the larger the cost of risk-bearing. This is not usually true.[4] But it is sometimes true and since, for expository ease, we shall often wish to identify 'risk' with variance it will prove worthwhile to locate circumstances in which this identification is correct. This will also enable us to see why in general it may not be correct. Towards this, write $E\{u(y_s)\} \equiv \sum_{s=1}^{S} \pi_s u(y_s)$, and rewrite equation 13.5 as

13.6 $$u(\bar{y} - x) - u(\bar{y}) \equiv E\{u(y_s)\} - u(\bar{y}).$$

We can now expand the RHS of equation 13.6 as a Taylor series. Suppose that the commodity bundle y is sufficiently concentrated so that terms in the series consisting of moments greater than two can be ignored. In this case equation 13.6 can be expressed as

$$u(\bar{y} - x) - u(\bar{y}) \simeq u'(\bar{y}) \sum_{s=1}^{S} \pi_s (y_s - \bar{y}) + \frac{u''(\bar{y})}{2} \sum_{s=1}^{S} \pi_s (y_s - \bar{y})^2$$

13.7
$$\simeq \frac{u''(\bar{y})}{2} \sigma^2(y),$$

where $\sigma^2(y)$ is the variance of y.[5]

[4] On this, see Rothschild and Stiglitz (1970).

[5] Equation 13.7 is an approximate result. It is exact if $u(\cdot)$ were a quadratic function, since the third and higher derivatives of $u(\cdot)$ would then be nil. Since we have assumed $u(\cdot)$ to be strictly increasing and strictly concave we must rule out the quadratic form.

Similarly we may expand the LHS of 13.7 as a Taylor series. Since by assumption y is concentrated, x is 'small' and so we can ignore the second and higher powers of x. Therefore equation 13.7 reduces to

$$-xu'(\bar{y}) \simeq u''(\bar{y})\sigma^2(\mathbf{y})/2,$$

or

13.8

$$x \simeq \frac{-u''(\bar{y})\sigma^2(\mathbf{y})}{2u'(\bar{y})},$$

We conclude that for highly concentrated prospects with the same mean income, $\bar{y}$, the variance is a good measure of the cost of risk-bearing for the individual in question. Let us express by $\eta(y)$ the elasticity of marginal utility, $u'(y)$. That is, $\eta(y) = -\{yu''(y)\}/\{u'(y)\}$. Equation 13.8 can then be expressed as

13.9

$$x = \frac{\eta(\bar{y})}{2} \frac{\sigma^2}{\bar{y}}.$$

$\eta(y)$ is referred to in the literature as the index of *relative risk aversion*.[6] Given a prospect, the larger is $\eta(\bar{y})$ in value the greater is the cost of risk-bearing.[7]

Let us now do an exercise with this apparatus. Continuing to suppose a timeless world assume now that there are N identical individuals ($i=1, \ldots, N$), each of whom is faced with a random income y, with mean $\bar{y}$ and variance σ^2. We further suppose that these random variables are independent of one another. For vividness one might like to think of each individual as owning an oil tract and that the value of oil under each tract, net of drilling expenses, is a random variable with mean $\bar{y}$ and variance σ^2.[8] For simplicity suppose that each tract requires a fixed drilling expense and that the actual value of oil under the tract is known only after drilling takes place. Finally, let us suppose that were individual i to choose not to drill, he could invest elsewhere the fixed drilling expenses thus saved and earn a sure net income $\bar{z}$. In other words, the alternative venture is certain.

[6] See Arrow (1965) and Pratt (1964).

[7] If $\eta(y) = \eta$ (a constant), then the utility function is of the form $u(y) = -y^{-(\eta-1)}$ for $\eta > 1$; $u(y) = \log y$ for $\eta = 1$ and $u(y) = y^\eta$ for $0 < \eta < 1$. We exploited the case $\eta > 1$ a great deal in Chapter 10, and the case $\eta < 1$ in Chapter 11.

[8] We have to suppose that the tracts are sufficiently far removed from one another so as to make plausible the assumption of independence of random variables.

Consider now individual i deciding in isolation as to what to do. Given that he is risk-averse we know in advance that he will choose not to drill on his tract if $\bar{z} \geq \bar{y}$. Indeed, we know from equation 13.9 that to a first approximation he will choose not to drill so long as

13.10
$$\bar{z} + \frac{\eta(\bar{y})\sigma^2}{2\bar{y}} > \bar{y}.$$

Stated another way, this risk averse individual will compare the two investment opportunities not merely in terms of their expected returns, $\bar{z}$ and $\bar{y}$, but will discount the uncertain venture somewhat. Specifically, he will discount the uncertain prospect by a risk-premium, which is in fact the cost of risk-bearing.

To make the example interesting let us, to be precise, suppose that

13.11
$$\bar{y} = \bar{z} + m$$

where
$$0 < m < \frac{\eta(\bar{y})\sigma^2}{2\bar{y}}.$$

Thus both 13.10 and 13.11 hold. It follows then that none of the N individuals, acting in isolation, will drill. Each will invest in the sure prospect yielding an income $\bar{z}$. But there are gains to be had in sharing in risks. Given the complete symmetry of the model it is immediate that the agreed upon risk-sharing must be symmetrical. In other words, the N individuals should decide on sharing equally in the income from each tract. It would then be as though each individual were to own $1/N$ of every tract. Under this arrangement in risk-sharing, if each individual were to undertake to drill on his tract, his expected income from each tract will be $\bar{y}/N$ and the variance of his uncertain income from each tract will be σ^2/N^2. It follows that his expected income from this joint venture is $N(\bar{y}/N) = \bar{y}$. Moreover, given that the random incomes from the tracts are by assumption independent of one another, the variance of his income from this arrangement is $N(\sigma^2/N^2) = \sigma^2/N$. This rather natural arrangement of spreading one's risks enables an individual to reduce his risks dramatically, if N is large. Note that his expected income from this joint venture is still $\bar{y}$. Now if N is sufficiently large, one will have

13.12
$$m > \frac{\eta(\bar{y})\sigma^2}{2N\bar{y}}.$$

Using 13.11 and 13.12 it follows that, while in the absence of risk-sharing it is not worth anyone's while to undertake drilling activities, drilling is very much a worthwhile activity for everyone if the risks can be spread symmetrically. Indeed, under this risk-sharing arrangement the cost borne by each individual is $\eta(\bar{y})\sigma^2/2N\bar{y}$. And this is negligible if N is large. It is almost as though each individual is guaranteed a sure income from drilling activities. Everyone is better off, since

$$u\left\{\bar{y} - \frac{\eta(\bar{y})\sigma^2}{2N\bar{y}}\right\} > u(\bar{y} - m) = u(\bar{z}).$$

Indeed, this proposed arrangement yields the symmetric Pareto efficient allocation of risk bearing. All this makes good intuitive sense. Spreading one's risks over many independent tracts reduces risk. Failure in one tract will, on average, be matched by success in another. In fact, under this arrangement, since the cost of risk-bearing on the part of the representative individual is $\eta(\bar{y})\sigma^2/2N\bar{y}$, the total cost of risk-bearing for the N individuals, taken together, is $\eta(\bar{y})\sigma^2/2\bar{y}$. This is N times less than the total cost of risk-bearing for society as a whole were each to drill separately in the absence of any risk-sharing arrangement. Notice that even under this ideal risk-sharing arrangement the variance of the sum of the incomes from the N tracts for the economy as a whole is still $N\sigma^2$. Now this is large when N is large. So the question arises whether there was a sleight of hand in arriving at the claim that each individual reduces his risk to a negligible amount by this risk-sharing arrangement? Not at all. It is entirely correct that by arriving at this arrangement the representative individual reduces the variance in his income from σ^2 to σ^2/N. The point, however, is that under this arrangement the uncertain incomes faced by the individuals are not independent of one another. In fact they are perfectly correlated with one another, since everyone shares equally in whatever the total income is. Thus the total variance for the economy as a whole is not the sum of the variances of individual incomes.

The foregoing discussion has used what is in effect the law of large numbers to demonstrate how an ideal scheme of risk-sharing can, for all intents and purposes, allow individuals to rid themselves of risk. Looked at in a slightly different manner the ideal risk-sharing scheme can be interpreted in terms of the pure theory of ideal insurance coverage when there are a large number of independent risks. An insurance contract would consist of an insurance firm promising to 'pay' an individual $\bar{y} - y_s - \varepsilon$ $(\varepsilon > 0)$, if y_s is the actual income from his tract. If $y_s < \bar{y} - \varepsilon$ the insurance firm loses and if $y_s > \bar{y} - \varepsilon$, it gains. Meanwhile, the individual assures himself of a sure income of $\bar{y} - \varepsilon$ from drilling. The point to note now is that if N is large, ε can be negligible without the insurance firm fearing bankruptcy.[9]

There is a further point to be made. Suppose a new tract is discovered, once again yielding a net random income y with mean $\bar{y}$ and variance σ^2, and independent of the random incomes from the N previous tracts. It is like a marginal investment project. If the N individuals decide on sharing equally in this new drilling venture, the representative individual's expected income from the new venture will be $\bar{y}/N$ and the variance of this income will be σ^2/N^2. Given that in the absence of this new venture his expected income is $\bar{y}$ (from the ideal risk sharing arrangement over the N previous tracts), the cost of risk-bearing borne by him in this new marginal venture is $\eta(\bar{y})\sigma^2/2N^2\bar{y}$. It follows that the total cost of risk-bearing on the part of society as a whole is $\eta(\bar{y})\sigma^2/2N\bar{y}$, which is negligible if N is large. It follows that if the marginal project is shared equally by the individuals it ought to be assessed solely in terms of expected returns. The fact that its return is random should be ignored, even though individuals are risk-averse.[10]

The intuition behind the foregoing result is clear enough. Even a risk-averse individual treats a small risk in a risk-neutral manner if the risk is not correlated with the rest of his income. This is as it should be, since one can approximate his (curved) utility function by a straight line in this instance.

But while the foregoing result is of interest for industrial project appraisal in general, it is likely to be misleading for the energy sector. Consider, for example, an investment undertaken to discover a new deposit of oil or a research project designed to develop a substitute source of energy supply. Such investments have uncertain payoffs. But typically their payoffs are correlated with

[9] This is due to the fact that the coefficient of variation of the net income of the economy as a whole when everyone drills is $\sqrt{N\sigma^2}/N\bar{y} = \sigma/\sqrt{N}\bar{y}$, which tends to zero as N tends to infinity. We shall make use of this argument in calculating the return on investment in 'wildcat' oil drilling in section 1(ii). For a general theory of ideal insurance see Malinvaud (1972).

[10] This conclusion appears to have been alluded to in the literature for quite some time. The first rigorous proof of the proposition was presented in a more general setting by Arrow and Lind (1970). However, we shall note in section 4 that this proposition does not necessarily hold if investment has irrevocable consequences.

other income. For example, for an oil importing country the payoffs of such investments are high precisely in those states of nature where the price of oil is high (due, say, to an oil embargo) and, therefore, where the national income is low. Risk-aversion then implies that the cost of risk-bearing associated with such projects may well be *negative*, since such investments are an insurance against adverse states of nature. Other things being the same, a risk-averse society should prefer such a project to one whose return is positively correlated with national income (e.g. a project whose output is a complement to oil in production). It remains to formalize this intuitively plausible argument.

In doing this let y_s denote the random national income of the economy and let z_{1s} and z_{2s} denote two marginal projects. For simplicity of exposition we take it that all risks are small. Then just as we obtained the approximation 13.7 we now obtain

$$E\{u(y_s + z_{is})\} = u(\bar{y} + \bar{z}_i) + \frac{u''(\bar{y} + \bar{z}_i)}{2} \{\sigma_y^2 + \sigma_{z_i}^2 + 2 \text{ cov } (y_s, z_{is})\}$$

13.13   (for $i = 1, 2$).

Now suppose the two projects to have the same mean return (i.e. $\bar{z} = \bar{z}_1 = \bar{z}_2$). It then follows from 13.13 that

13.14
$$E\{u(y_s + z_{1s}) - u(y_s + z_{2s})\}$$
$$= \frac{u''(\bar{y} + \bar{z})}{2} \{\sigma_{z_1}^2 - \sigma_{z_2}^2 + 2 \text{ cov}(y_s, z_{1s}) - 2 \text{ cov}(y_s, z_{2s})\}.$$

Equation 13.14 implies that if the two projects have more or less the same variance as well, society should choose the project whose co-variance with national income is the smaller. This is a precise formulation of the conclusion we arrived at earlier.

In fact 13.14 allows us to compute the cost of risk-bearing as well. Suppose that the second project is devoid of any uncertainty. Then the equation reduces to the form

$$E\{u(y_s + z_{1s}) - u(y_s + \bar{z})\} = \frac{u''(\bar{y} + \bar{z})}{2} \{\sigma_{z_1}^2 + 2 \text{ cov}(y_s, z_{1s})\}.$$

From the definition of the cost of risk-bearing (equation 13.9) one concludes that, x, the cost of risk-bearing is

13.15 $$x = \frac{\eta(\bar{y} + \bar{z})}{2(\bar{y} + \bar{z})} \{\sigma_{z_1}^2 + 2 \text{ cov}(y_s, z_{1s})\}.$$

If $-2 \operatorname{cov}(y_s, z_{1s}) > \sigma_{z_1}^2$, then $x < 0$. The cost of risk-bearing associated with the uncertain project is negative. In this case a risk-averse society prefers an uncertain marginal project to a sure project with the same expected return. But this implies that society would prefer this uncertain project to a sure project even if its expected return is slightly less than the return from the sure project. One often hears the claim that projects concerned with oil exploration or research designed towards the discovery of oil substitutes carry with them an insurance value. The foregoing example makes precise what this claim is.[11]

(ii) *An application of the law of large numbers to 'wildcat' drilling:*[12] Imagine by way of illustration that investment in oil and gas production consists of drilling wildcat holes. We take it for simplicity that the success of such drilling is a random event occurring with a binomial distribution. In doing this we are, of course, supposing that the probability of success in one wildcat venture is independent of that in another.[13] The aim is then to estimate the expected value and the variance on the return on such investment.

Let N be the number of wildcats drilled by a firm and let $M(\leq N)$ be the number of those ventures that are successful. We take it that the probability of success for each wildcat is Π and that the cost of drilling each field is c. Finally, let p be the price of crude oil at the well-head, and S the average size of the deposit in each successful new field. It follows that the average value of crude oil discoveries for a successful wildcat is pS. The rate of return on investment is then

$$r = \frac{MpS}{Nc} - 1.$$

This is a random variable. Its expected value is given by

$$E(r) = \frac{pS}{c} E(M/N) - 1 = \frac{pS\Pi}{c} - 1$$

[11] In the literature on development planning it is often argued that irrigation projects possess this insurance value which fertilizer projects do not; the point being that an irrigation project has high yield precisely when the yield is 'needed' (i.e. when rainfall is low and hence national income is low), whereas fertilizers have high yields only when used with ample water. But when water is amply available presumably national income is high anyway. But one should bear in mind possible orders of magnitude. An inspection of 13.15 suggests that x is likely to be 'small' since $\bar{y}$ (expected national income) is likely to be 'large'.

[12] This is based on Stiglitz (1974).

[13] This is, of course, quite implausible, since the sites may be contiguous. For the implication of dependent probabilities, see Chapter 14.

and its variance is

$$\sigma^2(r) = \sigma^2(MpS/Nc) = (pS/Nc)^2\sigma^2(M) = (pS/c)^2\Pi(1 - \Pi)/N.^{14}$$

Suppose by way of illustration, that $\Pi = 0.13$, that $S = 418\,000$ barrels, and $p = \$2.90$ per barrel.[15] Data on drilling costs suggests an average cost for a productive well of \$78 500 in 1968.[16] Assuming that one-third of the revenue of the drilling firm is spent on average for overhead costs and royalties we have $c = \$1.5 \times 78\,500$. On using these figures we find that $E(r) = 0.39$ and that $\sigma^2(r) = 12/N$. This suggests that a firm with 1000 exploratory wells ($N = 1000$) will earn an average return of 33%, with variance $\cdot 012$ on the return. The coefficient of variations, $\sigma(r)/E(r)$ is about 0·3, which is rather small. To make this last point precise, one notes that with $N = 1000$ the probability is about 40%, that the rate of return on wildcat drilling will be inside the range (28%, 39%). The example brings out the manner how the law of large numbers can reduce risk in oil and gas drilling.

2. Information and Its Value

One way of reducing one's risks is to spread them by choosing one's actions appropriately. In section 1(i) we noted how a mutual insurance scheme enables one to do this. But the example was constructed on the assumption that individuals possess an identical attitude to risk and that they have identical judgements concerning the occurrence of the risks. It is clear that two additional reasons why individuals trade in risks (and thereby reduce their risks) are that individuals' attitudes to risk differ (i.e. $u(\cdot)$ in equation 13.3 differs from person to person) and that different individuals typically have different assessments of the probabilities of outcomes (e.g. two people are likely to impute different probabilities to the successful harnessing of fusion energy by the year AD 2000). The stock market and futures markets are two additional institutions that allow individuals to trade in risks, and in the next chapter we shall discuss the ideal scheme for trading in risks, a scheme that is

---

[14] Recall that $\sigma^2(r+1) = \sigma^2(r)$ and that for a binomial distribution with N trials and probability π of success the expected number of successes is $N\pi$ and the variance of the number of successes is $N\pi(1 - \pi)$.

[15] 0.13 is an estimate of the success rate of exploratory wells in the USA during 1960–67 and the figures for S and p are estimates based on the period 1955–67.

[16] See American Petroleum Institute (1971).

provided by what is usually referred to as a complete set of Arrow–Debreu contingent commodity markets.[17]

A second route that one can pursue in order to reduce the risks one faces is to obtain further information on the matters about which one is uncertain. Exploration activities consisting of seismic surveys and core drillings at a given location are undertaken precisely with the view to revising (i.e. obtaining better estimates of) the probability that it contains a commercially viable pool of oil. For recall that exploration activities are undertaken to obtain information about the size of the deposit in question, costs of extraction and degrees of impurity of different deposits, and as well the location of different deposits of the resource. Indeed, research activity in general is concerned with the acquisition of information. In particular, each step in a research programme is designed to yield information to the researcher. Like most things the acquisition of information requires resources to be spent, so that not all information is worth searching for. Nor in general does the acquisition of information *eliminate* uncertainty. But this does not provide one with the ground for not acquiring it. A thermometer that can measure temperature with 1°C accuracy is well worth purchasing in many situations. For really refined experiments it would be too crude an instrument to use. But the critical point to note is that, even when the acquisition of information does not eliminate uncertainty, it may alter the planned actions of the individual acquiring it. Therein lies its value. Improved knowledge of the total stocks of a resource allows one to choose current extraction rates which, in an expected-value sense, permit a better distribution of the rates of consumption of different generations. In the absence of such improved knowledge there may well be greater uncertainty about unexpected shortages in future supply.

What, then, is information and how do we measure its value? Here, we adopt the view advanced by statistical decision theorists and regard the acquisition of information as the observation of a *signal* (or a set of signals) that leads one to revise one's (subjective) probability of the occurrence of an *event*.[18] Since an event is by

[17] In honour of Arrow (1953) and Debreu (1959), who originated the theory of general equilibrium under uncertainty.
[18] For excellent accounts, see McGuire (1972) and Marschak and Radner (1971). This view does not cover the case where the knowledge acquired is totally new, in the sense that an event that was previously *unconceived* of is now describable. But then it is not possible to discuss such knowledge *prior* to its acquisition anyway.

definition a collection of states of nature, information acquisition results in an alteration of the (subjective) probabilities of the occurrence of the different states of nature. We now formalize these ideas.

As earlier, suppose there to be S states of nature, labelled, $\theta_1, \ldots,$ $\theta_s, \ldots, \theta_S$. For the moment we restrict our attention to a single decision maker. Let his (subjective) probability over state θ_s be $\Pi(\theta_s)$ (i.e. $\Pi(\theta_s) \geq 0$ and $\sum_{s=1}^{S} \Pi(\theta_s) = 1$). Ignoring the act of observing a signal for the moment let us suppose that the individual has a set of acts, A, to choose from. A denotes his feasible set of acts. As in Chapter 2, denote an act as $\boldsymbol{a}$. Let $u_s(\boldsymbol{a})$ be the utility to him of choosing $\boldsymbol{a}$ if θ_s is the state of nature.[19] For the moment suppose that the individual has to choose an act prior to knowing what is the true state of nature. That is what makes the decision problem that of one under uncertainty. Generally speaking, the point in undertaking exploration activities is to be able to rule out certain states of nature. Thus, suppose that there is a given set of signals, Y, such that the individual is entitled to make an observation from it at a cost (measured in utility numeraire) of $C(Y)$. Now, his feasible set of actions is, presumably, circumscribed by the set of signals Y. As we shall illustrate this at length in the following chapter we shall not elaborate on it here. But for the moment we note that $A = A(Y)$. Thus, for example, $A(Y)$ may consist of different extraction policies from a given deposit and Y may consist of various possible outcomes from a particular set of seismic surveys and core drillings at this location. In this instance, the different states of nature correspond to the different possible realizations of the various characteristics of the deposit (e.g. combinations of size and chemical composition of the deposit).

For simplicity, suppose Y is a finite set consisting of N elements, i.e. N signals, labelled, $y_1, \ldots, y_i, \ldots, y_N$. The individual in question is assumed to have a theory of his sampling process (i.e. the characteristics of Y). Thus we assume that he imputes a (subjective) prior probability $p_Y(y_i/\theta_s)$ that he will observe y_i conditional on θ_s being the true state of nature.[20] At the time the individual in question

---

[19] Since there is uncertainty about what the true state of nature is, the *consequence* of an action cannot be predicted. But it is assumed that each action has a *unique* consequence for each state of nature and since the states of nature can be described, so can these consequences. It is for this reason that, as in Chapter 2, we have defined utilities directly on actions and have not bothered to introduce consequences.

[20] It is important to recognize that such prior probabilities will typically differ from person to person, since different people typically hold different 'theories'. A man totally innocent of mineralogy will presumably hold different priors from those of an expert.

decides on whether or not to make an observation from Y (i.e. carry out the particular set of seismic surveys, etc.) he does not, of course, know which of the N possible signals he will actually receive. He can hardly expect to know the outcome of his seismic surveys prior to his carrying them out. But the point is that he can choose an action *after* receiving a signal from Y, should he decide to observe from Y. We can now use elementary probability theory to define by

$$13.16 \qquad \mu_Y(\theta_s/y_i) = \frac{\Pi(\theta_s)p_Y(y_i/\theta_s)}{\sum\limits_{s=1}^{S} \Pi(\theta_s)p_Y(y_i/\theta_s)}, \quad \text{for } \begin{matrix} i = 1, \ldots, N \\ s = 1, \ldots, S \end{matrix}$$

the probability he imputes to the occurrence of θ_s conditional on his observing the signal y_i. Such an $N \times S$ matrix of probabilities, $\mu_Y(\theta_s/y_i)$, is called the *information matrix* associated with Y for the individual in question, and in general one says that Y and its associated information matrix characterizes an *information structure*.

Certain special cases are now worth mentioning. If $p_Y(y_i/\theta_s)$ is independent of θ_s for all i and s, then from 13.16 we have

$$\mu_Y(\theta_s/\eta_i) = \frac{\Pi(\theta_s)p_Y(y_i/\theta_s)}{p_Y(y_i/\theta_s)\sum\limits_{s=1}^{S}\Pi(\theta_s)} = \Pi(\theta_s),$$

and, in purchasing Y the individual purchases *no* information, since his posterior probabilities are the same as the priors. In this instance Y is a completely *non-informative* information structure.

Consider now a case where $S \geq N$ and where the individual believes that for any given θ_s there is a *unique* $y_i \in Y$ that is generated as a signal. Then, according to him (or his theory!) the set of states of nature can be partitioned into N sets (say $S_1, \ldots, S_N$) such that $p_Y(y_i/\theta_s)=1$ for $\theta_s \in S_i$, and $p_Y(y_i/\theta_s)=0$ for $\theta_s \notin S_i$ (all $i=1, \ldots, N$).[21] In this case the purchase of Y enables the individual to possess a *finer* partition of the set of states of nature.[22] For, in this case we obtain from 13.16 the fact that

[21] $\{S_1, \ldots, S_i, \ldots, S_N\}$ is a *partition* of a set S if $\bigcup_i S_i = S$ and $S_i \cap S_j = \phi$ for $i \neq j$. We are supposing for ease of exposition and without loss of generality, that for all i, $p_y(y_i/\theta_s)$ is positive for *some* θs. Hence the partition above consists of N sets.

[22] A partition $P_1 \equiv \{S_1, \ldots, S_{N1}\}$ of a set S is said to be *finer* than the partition $P_2 \equiv \{S^*_1, \ldots, S^*_{N2}\}$ of S if $N_1 > N_2$ and for every $S_i \epsilon P_1$ there is $S^*_j \epsilon P_2$ such that $S_i c S^*_j$. Equivalently, one says that P_1 is *coarser* than P_2.

$$\mu_Y(\theta_s/y_i) = \frac{\Pi(\theta_s)}{\sum\limits_{s \epsilon S_i} \Pi(\theta_s) p_Y(y_i/\theta_s)} = \frac{\Pi(\theta_s)}{\sum\limits_{s \epsilon S_i} \Pi(\theta_s)} \quad \text{for } \theta_s \in S_i$$

13.17

and

$$\mu_Y(\theta_s/y_i) = 0 \quad \text{for } \theta s \notin S_i.$$

One then says that for the individual in question Y is a *deterministic* information structure. The terminology is really rather obvious. If he observes y_i he knows that the true state of nature lies in S_i. He is unambiguously better informed in this case than he was prior to his making the observation. But note from 13.17 that on observing y_i the *relative* probabilities of the states of nature in S_i remain as they were before. A special case of a deterministic information structure is one in which $N=S$. Consequently each set S_i in the partition consists of precisely one element. In this case observing a signal is equivalent to observing the true state of nature. He cannot hope to be better informed than that! It is called a *fully informative* structure. If an information structure is not deterministic it is called *noisy*.[23]

Return now to the decision problem. Suppose the individual purchases the right to observe a signal from Y. Recall that we have assumed $C(Y)$ to be the utility cost of making an observation from Y (i.e. the cost of exploration). *After* he observes a signal, say y_i, his expected utility is

13.18
$$U(Y) = \sum_{s=1}^{S} \mu_Y(\theta_s/y_i) u_s(\boldsymbol{a}) - C(Y).$$

He now chooses an action with a view to maximizing $U(Y)$. His optimal action is a function of the signal he receives.[24] Write this as $\mathrm{d}(y_i)$. Define

13.19
$$V\{\mathrm{d}(y_i), y_i : y_i \in Y\} = \max_{\boldsymbol{a} \in A(Y)} \sum_{s=1}^{S} \mu_Y(\theta_s/y_i) u_s(\boldsymbol{a}) - C(Y).$$

[23] In fact by a suitable redefining of the set of states of nature any problem with noisy information can be reformulated as a problem with a deterministic information structure. On this, see Radner (1972a).

[24] If it is a non-informative information structure this function will be a constant, i.e. his action will be independent of the signal received. But then he will be a fool to purchase it if $C(Y) > 0$. And he will not.

Now $\sum_{s=1}^{S} \Pi(\theta_s)p_Y(y_i/\theta_s)$ represents his prior probability of observing y_i. It follows that his expected utility, prior to making the observation (but subsequent to purchasing the *right* to make the observation) is

$$\sum_{i=1}^{N} V\{d(y_i), y_i : y_i \in Y\}\{\sum_{s=1}^{S} \Pi(\theta_s)p_Y(y_i/\theta_s)\},$$

which, on using 13.16 and 13.19, reduces to

13.20 $$\sum_{i=1}^{N} \max_{a \in A(Y)} \{\sum_{s=1}^{S} u_s(a)\Pi(\theta_s)p_Y(y_i/\theta_s)\} - C(Y).$$

The expression in 13.20 represents his maximum net expected utility in purchasing the right to observe from Y. To him it represents the *value* of the information structure Y.

It is often convenient to obtain an expression of the value of an information structure relative to some benchmark. Recall as well from the discussion in Chapter 9 that the von-Neumann–Morgenstern utility function $u_s(a)$ is unique up to a positive linear transformation, and one may wish to express the value of the information structure to an individual independent of the origin and the scale of $u_s(a)$. The natural benchmark is a non-informative structure. Denote this as Ω. This amounts to doing no research. It is then natural to suppose that $C(\Omega)=0$. For this information structure 13.20 assumes the form

$$\max_{a \in A(\Omega)} \{\sum_{s=1}^{S} u_s(a)\Pi(\theta_s)\}.$$

Without loss of generality assume that this is not nil. Then one can express the value of the information structure Y as

$$\frac{\sum_{i=1}^{N} \max_{a \in A(Y)} \left\{\sum_{s=1}^{S} u_s(a)\pi(\theta_s)p_Y(y_i/\theta_s)\right\} - C(Y) - \max_{a \in A(\Omega)} \sum_{s=1}^{S} u_s(a)\pi(\theta_s)}{\max_{a \in A(\Omega)} \sum_{s=1}^{S} u_s(a)\pi(\theta_s)}.$$

Typically, the individual is confronted with a family of information structures $Y_j (j=i, \ldots, M)$ to choose from. One supposes that Y_j consists of N_j possible signals. We have thus defined M research strategies. In the case of exploration activity they may involve more or less elaborate seismic surveys. The cost of purchasing the right to observe from Y_j is $C(Y_j)$. One wants to include in this family a non-informative information structure whose cost is nil. This amounts to the case where he undertakes no exploration. For each Y_j he maximizes 13.18 to arrive at 13.19. For each Y_j he computes the value of information as embodied in 13.20. He chooses that Y_j from the available family of information structures which maximizes 13.20.

Thus far the single decision maker, but it is clear enough in advance that to develop a general equilibrium theory with various types of information treated as commodities is no easy matter. Nor is there any reason for believing that the market for information is likely to work well. For surely, an individual's actions themselves directly convey information to others. The individual in question may not be able to prevent this. Thus, for example, if A has obtained specialized information about the reserves under a tract he may wish to sell the information to B. But in order for B to know what it is he is buying he will need to learn the information from A prior to purchase. But then B will have acquired the information. Information has, among other things, the attributes of a public good.[25] But even if A *can* sell the piece of information to B it is difficult for him to prevent resale. Matters are, however, a good deal subtler than just that. Even if resale can be prevented, A's actions based on this piece of information can usually be observed by others (e.g. that he is bidding furiously for the tract). And observant C will be able to infer *something* about the information that A possesses by observing his action (viz. that his surveys suggest a richly endowed tract). But even if A's actions cannot be observed, wily D, while innocent of the results of the seismic surveys conducted in that locality, will often be able to infer *some* of this information from the *consequences* of A's action (viz. that the price of the tract has been bid up).[26]

These are important matters, and they draw one's attention to the role that prices play in transmitting information among individuals, a role that is quite distinct from the one we have emphasized so far in this book: namely as a device for allocating resources efficiently under conditions of perfect certainty.[27]

[25] See Chapter 3.

[26] See, in particular, Green (1973), Grossman (1978), Grossman and Stiglitz (1976) and Radner (1976). We shall discuss these matters more formally in Chapter 14.

[27] Formally speaking, we have so far been viewing prices as Lagrange multipliers of some constrained optimization exercise.

3. Types of Uncertainty

There are two broad kinds of uncertainties that individuals face: (a) exogenous uncertainties and (b) institutionally induced uncertainties. The former would exist regardless of the institutional structure in which the individual lives. Uncertainty in the size and quality of reserves falls in this category. In Chapter 14 we shall study how certain institutions can cope with exogenous uncertainty. But for the moment it should be noted that uncertainty about the reserve size of, say, oil affects the rate at which society ought to extract it. If 'society' is risk-averse (i.e. if the social welfare function chosen implies risk-aversion), then under a wide class of circumstances it ought to extract more slowly at initial dates as a consequence of this uncertainty.[28] The reasons are the usual precautionary ones; the consequences of running out of oil, even if the prospect is remote, are unpleasant to the risk-averse individual.

Uncertainty about costs of extraction and in general the quality of reserves under different deposits affects not only the total rate of extraction, but also the timing of extraction from different fields. We noted in Chapter 6 that, in the absence of any uncertainty about costs of extraction, an efficient market will ensure that reserves are depleted from the cheapest to the most expensive deposit in a sequential manner. In the presence of uncertainty in extraction costs from different fields a poor grade field (i.e. high cost of extraction) may well be depleted before a rich grade one. Such are the penalties of ignorance.

These foregoing brief remarks alluded to current uncertainty. Of at least equal interest is future uncertainty regarding discovery of new reserves or the invention of substitute products (e.g. harnessing nuclear fusion). There is uncertainty both about the timing of such inventions and the costs of developing such new technologies (or carrying out explorations for new reserves). Each of these has important implications for the rate at which society ought today to deplete its known stock. Suppose, by way of illustration, the invention of a substitute product whose development costs are fixed and given. In Chapter 6 (section 4) we studied the manner in which the exhaustible resource would be depleted under efficient market conditions if the date at which the substitute will be invented is

---

[28] In particular, the net spot price of oil in such circumstances ought to grow at a rate less than the (sure) social rate of discount. This contrasts with the results in Chapter 6 (see section 6). On this, see Gilbert (1976), Kemp (1976), Loury (1976) and Heal (1978).

known in advance (see Diagram 6.9). Now suppose the invention
date is random, but with an expected value equal to the sure date
of the earlier case. What is the effect of such uncertainty on the
efficient rate of current extraction of the resource? The point to
note is that, to the extent that leaving a resource under ground
alleviates society from the risk of facing a resource 'scarcity' in the
near future, there is an incentive to postpone extraction. This
suggests that uncertainty in the arrival date of a substitute product
provides a risk-averse society with a reason for reducing the current
rate of extraction. But leaving the resource underground is risky,
because the invention will reduce its value.[29] This recognition
provides society with an incentive for increasing the rate of current
extraction. There is then an ambiguity in the implications of uncertainty about the invention date on socially efficient current
extraction rates. It transpires that whether such uncertainty ought
to lead the economy to extract it at a faster or slower rate depends
on the size of the initial stock.[30]

Of the various kinds of market induced uncertainties, those concerning investment, production and research and development
decisions of other agents are probably the most important that an
individual faces. In a completely centralized economy such uncertainty will not exist. In any decentralized environment such
uncertainty will be present. The aim of what goes by the title of
'indicative planning' is to lessen such market induced uncertainties.
In Chapters 2, 4, 6 and 10 we noted the role that prices can in
principle play in co-ordinating the myriad of decisions that are continually being made by individuals. In the following chapter we shall
analyse the nature of the price system which will enable individuals
to be unconcerned about uncertainties in the actions of others.

Speculative activity on the part of individuals, leading possibly
to increased fluctuations in the price of a mineral resource, is
another example of market-induced uncertainties. As new information is acquired by individuals about the mineral reserves and
development of substitute products, the market, presumably,
reflects some of it via the prices. One would suppose that the more
quickly the market responds to such information, the greater the

---

[29] In Chapter 6 (section 4(v)) we noted that the farther away in the future
is the arrival date of a substitute product, the greater is the value of the
current stock of a resource.
[30] The implications of such uncertainty on the rates of extraction under
various market structures have been analysed in Dasgupta and Stiglitz (1976,
1978b).

fluctuation in prices. But this kind of uncertainty is geared to the institution under study. In a society where such speculative activity is prohibited this kind of uncertainty would be absent.

4. Irrevocable Decisions and Option Values

We have already noted that one broad category of devices designed to reduce one's risks consists of mutual insurance schemes. In particular, it was noted that if the random returns of projects are uncorrelated it pays one to diversify his resources among them.[31] Examples of such diversification abound. In the context of natural resources, an economy simultaneously constructing nuclear and fossil fuel generators provides us with one. If the expected cost of a nuclear generator exceeds that of one using fossil fuels, then simultaneous constructions can still be justified on the ground that the future price of fossil fuels relative to that of nuclear fuels is uncertain.

A second device that is designed to reduce one's risk, we noted in section 2, is provided by the opportunity of purchasing information. The production of information (research and development and exploration activities) is a pristine form of this. From the discussion of section 2 it will be recalled that an individual, when choosing a particular information structure, does not know which signal he will in fact be receiving, but that he chooses his action after receiving the signal. In this section we shall analyse a very special case of this, a case provided by the passage of time. We are uncertain about tomorrow's weather at a given location. But tomorrow we shall know. How nice it would be, then, if we could delay until tomorrow a decision whose value is sensitive to tomorrow's weather condition. This is what one means when pointing to the desirability of keeping options open, and the general principle one is appealing to is the principle of flexibility. It is nice to keep one's plans flexible: that is, to take actions today which make it less costly to revise later, when new information is received. One knows that with the passage of time new information will be received.

Nowhere has the principle of flexibility been appealed to more than in the context of natural resources, whether it be the development of areas of scenic beauty, or the commercial exploitation of a species of uncertain threshold bio-mass, or over the closure of coal pits under conditions of low oil prices. There is a common property

---

[31] In section 1(i) we considered uncorrelated assets only. But the general principle of the desirability of diversification for a risk-averse individual holds for less than perfectly correlated assets. See Wilson (1977).

that each of these examples possesses, which is that the actions involved are irrevocable or revocable only at a high cost.[32] Since irrevocability is more or less the negation of flexibility, concern about such actions in the presence of uncertainty is understandable. In this and the following section we shall study two examples designed to capture different aspects of this issue. As we shall see, the example in the following section relates to the question of flexibility only indirectly and is designed to address the question of the relative advantages of regulations over taxation of natural resources in situations where the regulator possesses an information structure that is different from that of the individual agents exploiting the resource. The example in this section is directly concerned with the question of flexibility.[33]

Before presenting the example formally it is as well to point out its salient ingredients. Since we are concerned with the question of flexibility, the example is concerned with the possibility of a *sequence* of decisions over time. To keep matters simple we suppose as well that today's decision is irrevocable; that is, today's action cannot be 'undone' tomorrow. Finally, we suppose a risk-neutral decision maker. Since such an individual can replace random variables by their expected values without a blush, we shall be able to calculate easily the value to him of keeping his options open.

Imagine two instants $t = 0, 1$. There is a fixed quantity of land of size unity, entirely untarnished initially. The net benefit of developing a marginal unit of land at $t = 0$ is known with certainty to be b_0 (assumed independent of the amount developed). There are two states of nature θ_s ($s = 1, 2$). The state of nature is revealed at $t = 1$. If θ_1 prevails (the probability of this is π) then the *net* benefit of a unit of developed land is b_1 (assumed independent of the amount developed). If θ_2 prevails (the probability of this is, by definition, $1 - \pi$) the *net* benefit of a unit of developed land is b_2 (also assumed independent of the amount developed). In other words the uncertainty pertains to future benefits from land development.[34] We shall take it that when at $t = 1$ the state of nature is revealed there is further choice about how much land to develop at $t = 1$. Thus, decisions have to be made at both instants. Let D_0, denote the amount of land that is chosen to be developed at $t = 0$. And let D_1

[32] See Chapter 5 for a general discussion of irrevocable actions.
[33] Irrevocable investment and option values were discussed originally by Arrow and Fisher (1974) and Henry (1974a, b).
[34] The reader can readily reinterpret the example in terms of more familiar issues bearing on the emission of effluents.

and D_2 denote the size of developed land at $t=1$ under the two states of nature θ_1 and θ_2. Then expected net benefit can be represented as

13.21 $$b_0 D_0 + \pi b_1 D_1 + (1-\pi) b_2 D_2.$$

(We are supposing for simplicity a zero discount rate.) Notice that since expected net benefit is linear in D_0, D_1 and D_2 we are hypothesizing risk-neutrality. To have an interesting problem assume $b_1 < 0$, $b_2 > 0$ and $\pi b_1 + (1-\pi) b_2 > 0$. Thus in state θ_1 net benefit from land development is *negative*, but the expected net benefit from land development at $t=1$ is positive.

Let us first assume that land can be *un*developed costlessly, that is, the decision at $t=0$ is a revocable one. In this case the aim would be to maximize 13.21 by choosing D_0, D_1 and D_2, subject to the constraint $0 \le D_0$, D_1, $D_2 \le 1$. The optimal policy is clear enough. One chooses $D_1 = 0$ and $D_2 = 1$. The optimal value of D_0 depends on the value of b_0. If $b_0 < 0$ then one should set $D_0 = 0$. Likewise, if $b_0 > 0$ then one should set $D_0 = 1$. If $b_0 = 0$ then there is no unique optimal choice for D_0. But the central point is that the optimal decision at $t=0$ depends solely on the sign of b_0.

Now suppose that we pretend that the net benefit from land development at $t=1$ is known with certainty to be $\pi b_1 + (1-\pi) b_2$. For vividness one might like to suppose that a commitment is made at $t=0$ regarding the quantity of land to be developed at $t=1$ irrespective of what the state of nature is. The problem then is to choose D_0 and D (with $0 \le D_0$, $D \le 1$), with a view to maximizing

13.22 $$b_0 D_0 + \{\pi b_1 + (1-\pi) b_2\} D.$$

Plainly $D=1$, since $\pi b_1 + (1-\pi) b_2 > 0$ by assumption. But the optimal initial level of land development depends solely on the sign of b_0. No bias results in *current* decision as a result of replacing the random variable by its expected value in the objective function.

Suppose now that land development is irrevocable. If we continue to pretend that the net benefit from land development at $t=1$ is known with certainty to be $\pi b_1 + (1-\pi) b_2$, then the problem consists in maximizing 13.22 by choosing D_0 and D subject to the constraint $0 \le D_0 \le D \le 1$. Given that by assumption $\pi b_1 + (1-\pi) b_2 > 0$, one has $D=1$ at the optimum, and the optimal initial level of land development depends once again on the sign of b_0. Thus irrevocability of the act of developing makes no difference to the outcome. But the original problem consisted in choosing D_0, D_1 and D_2 with a view to maximizing 13.21. With the assumption of irrevocability the constraint is $0 \leq D_0 \leq D_1$, $D_2 \leq 1$. Let us compute the true optimum policy. If D_0 is the initial amount of land developed, then given that land development is irrevocable we shall wish to set $D_1 = D_0$, since further development will certainly not be desired if θ_1 is the state of nature. Plainly also one will desire to set $D_2 = 1$. Consequently 13.21 reduces to the form:

13.23 $$(b_0 + \pi b_1) D_0 + (1 - \pi) b_2,$$

and the planning problem is to maximize 13.23 by choosing D_0 subject to the constraint $0 \leq D_0 \leq 1$. It is clear that the condition for positive initial development is stiffer, it being that $b_0 + \pi b_1 \geq 0$. In other words, if $0 < b_0 < -\pi b_1$ then one should ideally set $D_0 = 0$ even though in the preceding analysis such a circumstance would dictate setting $D_0 = 1$. We conclude that, if investment is judged irrevocable, there may well be a tendency towards *over*-investment currently if the random future benefit is replaced by its expected value. That is to say, replacing random variables by their expected values is an incorrect move even for the risk-neutral decision maker if current decisions are irrevocable. For the example at hand he will require a rate of current benefits of at least the value $-\pi b_1$ (> 0) in order to foreclose his options.

5. Optimal Environmental Control Programmes Under Uncertainty

(i) *Effluent charges vs. licences:* Schemes for protecting the environment are usually devised in the face of uncertainty. More often than not the environmental effects of the emission of different sorts of pollutants are unknown. This is unavoidable. No doubt in many instances pilot studies can be conducted. But these take time, particularly so if the environmental effects are cumulative over time. Meanwhile decisions have to be taken about the appropriate control of pollution, even though the decision may be to introduce no regulations whatsoever. On the face of it, however, it would seem most unlikely that an absence of regulations is desirable. The extensive discussions in Chapters 3 and 5 have made it clear that, since property rights on the environment are usually impossible to devise, the social costs of the emission of pollutants are not reflected in private costs.

Uncertainty about the effects of different forms of pollution is one reason why debates on environmental issues are often so acrimonious.

Divergence of opinion about the form of the uncertainty is usually great even among experts. This is as true of the effect of, say, mercury deposits on marine life as it is of the effect of high altitude supersonic jets on the upper layers of the atmosphere.[35] But even if we were to ignore the divergence of opinion, it is an inescapable feature of environmental issues that decisions are required to be taken in the face of significant uncertainties. As new products are introduced and as new technologies are relied on to produce these products, new effluents are emitted into the environment. Even as information is acquired about the effects of existing types of effluents there are always additional forms introduced whose impact is unknown. To make matters worse, continuing emission of certain pollutants would be irrevocable if there are 'thresholds' of the kind that were discussed in Chapters 3 and 5.

All this is only one side of the picture—the social damage caused by pollutants. So far as regulatory agencies are concerned there is usually a good deal of uncertainty over the costs of pollution control programmes. Even if clean-up costs are known by the individual firms (who have the required expertise) they are unlikely to be known by the regulators. Again, we might argue that with time the regulatory agency can, by inviting expert opinion, obtain precise information of such costs. But pollution control programmes take time to plan and implement and the investment undertaken in such programmes are also largely irrevocable. A good deal of residual uncertainty on the part of the regulatory authorities will persist. Once this is recognized it is clear that one is up against a problem of 'moral hazard' as well. There will be a strong incentive on the part of private firms to overstate clean-up costs. The regulatory agency will not be able to confirm that the costs have been over-stated.

To sum up: environmental discussions need to be conducted in the face of a clear recognition that (a) the emission of pollutants usually display serious external diseconomies; (b) such processes may well be irrevocable; (c) the effect of pollutants on the environment is uncertain and that (d) the problem of moral hazard looms large which consequently constrains the kinds of regulations that might be envisaged. It is no wonder that environmental problems are formidable to solve.

In Chapter 3 we analysed a prototype environmental model in the form of the problem of the common and considered various

---

[35] The voluminous debate on the Anglo-French product, the Concorde, is a good example of this.

policies that may be considered for correcting for market failure. The discussion assumed away all uncertainty. It was noted that schemes as diverse as the optimal issue of licences and the optimal rate of taxation achieved the same outcome—namely the optimal rate of exploitation of the common property (see Chapter 3 section 4(iii)). In the face of uncertainty, however, the two schemes will not be identical in their consequences. It is interesting to see why. Now it has already been noted that environmental effects take time to make their presence felt. Therefore the uncertainty about the extent of social damage due to pollution will not be resolved until some time in the future. The regulatory scheme chosen today must then be independent of the resolution of this uncertainty. To give an example, suppose we are considering a policy to restrict the quantity of mercury discharged by a factory into a lake, and suppose that we are uncertain about the capacity of marine life to absorb this effluent without undue damage. Suppose as well that we shall gain this knowledge only in the future. Then today's decision about how much mercury the firm ought to be allowed to discharge must be independent of this knowledge. Formally, the point here is identical to the one raised earlier in this chapter that, if the state of nature is to be revealed to us in the future, today's decision cannot but be independent of the state of nature.

Turning next to the regulator's uncertainty about the cost of pollution control programmes the issue is similar. Such programmes take time to implement. Firms are unlikely to know today precisely what such clean-up costs are. The problem is compounded by the observation that 'moral hazard' is likely to be a feature in any such issue. It follows that the regulatory scheme introduced today must be independent of the resolution of the regulatory agency's uncertainty. It is now obvious why licences and pollution taxes are not identical in their effect. Recall that in the pure licensing scheme the regulator selects the total quantity of pollution to be emitted. In the pure tax scheme the regulator imposes an effluent charge and the individual firms decide how much to pollute. Thus, for any given realization of the social loss function, effluent taxes encourage too little clean-up if the private costs of clean-up are in fact higher than expected and they encourage too much clean-up if they are lower. The problem is reversed with the pure licensing scheme. Since the total quantity of pollution is decided by the regulator in advance it will be too little if private costs are lower than expected and too much if they are higher.

Given that they are different in their impact, it is important to ask which is superior. As one would expect, the answers depend on the curvatures of the benefit and cost function, and we shall presently confirm this by means of an example. But first it will be useful to obtain an intuitive feel for the proposition that it may well be desirable in general to rely on quantity restrictions for environmental control rather than effluent charges (i.e. taxes). Let x denote the total emission of a particular pollutant and let $L(x)$ be the social loss, in the sense of environmental damage due to this emission. For the moment we are supposing that this loss function is known with certainty. Now suppose that this function takes the shape described in Diagram 13.2. Such a form would seem plausible for a number of environmental problems, where X denotes a threshold level of pollution. As we have discussed this at length in Chapters 3 and 5 we need not justify it here again. Now suppose that clean-up costs as a function of the quantity of pollution is unknown by the regulatory agency and is a function of a random variable as well. Quantity controls (i.e. the issue of a fixed quantity of licences to pollute) would seem the better of the two schemes because the regulators can ensure by such controls that the level of pollution will be less than X—the level at which disaster strikes. Since the clean-up cost function is random, the only way to ensure against firms polluting beyond the level X via a pollution tax is to set a 'high' tax rate. But a 'high' tax rate may be undesirable if there is a good chance that clean-up costs are lower than expected, because in such circumstances the amount of clean-up will exceed the amount desirable. There will be too little pollution!

It remains to formalize these ideas.[36] For ease of exposition suppose there to be a single firm emitting the pollutant. By assumption it is a competitive firm. Denote by $B(x, \phi)$ the maximum profit accruing to it when x is the level of its emission, and ϕ is the value of the random variable reflecting the regulator's uncertainty about clean-up costs.[37] It is supposed that $B_{xx} < 0$ (see Diagram 3.7). Let us introduce uncertainty into the environmental damage function and denote the function as $L(x, \theta)$, where θ is a random variable. Specifically, L denotes the external diseconomy inflicted by the firm by way of damage to the environment. To keep the analysis tidy

[36] The example that follows is taken from Weitzman (1974).

[37] In Chapter 3 (section 6) it was shown how such a maximum profit function can be computed. See in particular equation 3.55 and Diagram 3.7. Note, however, that ϕ assumed a unique value there, as we supposed an absence of uncertainty.

we take it that L_x, $L_{xx} > 0$, (i.e. L is strictly convex in x, at least in the range that we are interested in). While this last assumption rules out functional forms such as the one displayed in Diagram 13.2 it will transpire that this does not matter. As is usual when discussing environmental issues we shall ignore distributional matters and take it that the regulator's objective function (i.e. net social benefit) is the expected value of $B(x, \phi) - L(x, \theta)$, which we denote by $E\{B(x, \phi) - L(x, \theta)\}$.[38] The idea is to maximize this. For simplicity we are limiting the enquiry here by restricting our attention to two modes of regulation: the pure effluent tax scheme and the pure

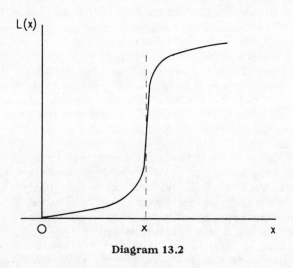

Diagram 13.2

quota scheme.[39] Our strategy will be to obtain the best of the pure pollution taxes and the most desirable level of quota and to compare the two in terms of the regulator's objective function.[40]

Turn first to the optimum quota. The idea is to maximize the objective function by choosing x. Let $\hat{x}$ be the optimum quota. It follows at once that $\hat{x}$ must be the solution of the equation

[38] The probability distribution defined jointly on ϕ and θ reflect the regulator's views on the uncertainty. A pair of values (θ, ϕ) represents a state of nature.

[39] On this see Dasgupta and Stiglitz (1975) and Roberts and Spence (1974).

[40] Since there is a single firm the pure quota and pure licence schemes are identical (see Chapter 3 section 4). In effect we have aggregated over different firms if in fact there is more than one firm.

13.24 $$E\{B_x(x, \phi)\} = E\{L_x(x, \theta)\},$$

and the regulator's objective function will attain the value

13.25 $$E\{B(\hat{x}, \phi) - L(\hat{x}, \theta)\}.$$

Calculating the optimum effluent charge is more complicated. Suppose that the regulator were to announce a tax rate t per unit of effluent discharged by the firm. By assumption the firm knows its maximum profit function with certainty: i.e. it knows the value attained by ϕ. Net profit for the firm would then be $B(x, \phi) - tx$ and it would choose x in order to maximize this. Thus, given a pair of values for ϕ and t the firm would set x at the level at which

13.26 $$B_x(x, \phi) = t.$$

Equation 13.26 can now be solved for x which we express as

13.27 $$x = g(t, \phi).$$

g could be called the firm's reaction function.

Now we have supposed that the regulatory agency knows the form of the function B, but that it does not know the value of ϕ with certainty. But it can calculate the function $g(t, \phi)$. Furthermore it knows that this is how the firm will respond to its choice of t. It follows that for a given choice of t the regulator's objective function assumes the value $E[B\{g(t, \phi), \phi\} - L\{g(t, \phi), \theta\}]$. The optimum effluent tax is one that maximizes this. Let $\tilde{t}$ be the optimum tax. It is immediate then that $\tilde{t}$ is the solution of the equation

13.28 $$E[g_t(t, \phi)B_x\{g(t, \phi), \phi\}] = E[g_t(t, \phi)L_x\{g(t, \phi), \theta\}].$$

Furthermore, the firm's response to the optimal tax will be given by the function $\tilde{x}(\phi) = g(\tilde{t}, \phi)$. Consequently the regulator's objective function will attain the value

13.29 $$E[B\{\tilde{x}(\phi), \phi\} - L\{\tilde{x}(\phi), \theta\}].$$

We need now to compare 13.25 and 13.29. Express the difference as Δ. That is

13.30 $$\Delta = E\{B(\hat{x}, \phi) - L(\hat{x}, \theta)\} - E[B\{\tilde{x}(\phi), \phi\} - L\{\tilde{x}(\phi), \theta\}].$$

If $\Delta > 0$ the pure quota scheme is superior to the pure tax scheme; the reverse if $\Delta < 0$.

We have elaborated the above formulation so as to display the formal structure of the problem that has been posed. As such equation 13.30 is of no help. We have learnt nothing of the sign of Δ. To learn this with relative ease requires of us to specify the functional forms in some detail. Let us then take it that the relevant uncertainties are small enough to justify taking quadratic approximations of B and L round the optimum quota level $\hat{x}$.[41] To be specific, assume that

13.31 $$B(x, \phi) = b(\phi) + \{B' + \beta(\phi)\}(x - \hat{x}) + (x - \hat{x})^2 B''/2$$

and

13 32 $$L(x, \theta) = a(\theta) + \{L' + \alpha(\theta)\}(x - \hat{x}) + (x - \hat{x})^2 L''/2$$

where a, b, α and β are functions of the random variables and B', L', B'' and L'' are constants, with B', L', $L'' > 0$ and $B'' < 0$. Since the considerations regarding production possibilities are quite separate from those bearing on the impact of effluents on the environment it is entirely reasonable to suppose that θ and ϕ are independent random variables. Consequently $\alpha(\theta)$ and $\beta(\phi)$ are independent. Therefore $E\{\alpha(\theta)\beta(\phi)\} = E\{\alpha(\theta)\}E.\{\beta(\phi)\}$. Without loss of generality suppose next that $E\{\alpha(\theta)\} = E\{\beta(\phi)\} = 0$. Let σ_α^2 and σ_β^2 denote the variances of the random variables α and β (i.e. $\sigma_\alpha^2 = E\{\alpha(\theta)^2\}$ and $\sigma_\beta^2 = E\{\beta(\phi)^2\}$). Retracing thé arguments used from equation 13.24 to equation 13.29 then implies that[42]

13.33 $$\Delta = \sigma_\beta^2 (B'' + L'')/2B''^2.$$

Equation 13.33 exposes in a remarkably simple manner the kinds of consideration that one supposes would be relevant when considering the relative merits of the two modes of regulation. Notice first that σ_α^2 does not appear in the equation. With quadratic approximations the uncertainty regarding the environmental damage function has the same effect on the choice of the two schemes and merely cancels out in the comparison. Notice next that if $\sigma_\beta^2 = 0$ then $\Delta = 0$. The two modes are identical. We noted this in Chapter 3. Notice finally that $\Delta > 0$ if $L'' > |B''|$; the reverse if $L'' < |B''|$. Licences are superior to pollution taxes as a regulatory scheme if the marginal damage function is steeper than the marginal profit function. This is an articulation of the qualitative conclusion that was offered earlier.

(ii) *Mixed schemes:* Thus far attention has been concentrated on two pure regulatory schemes. These are the ones that have traditionally been considered. One aspect of the old debate about whether

[41] Such a justification can be found in Samuelson (1970).
[42] For details, see Weitzman (1974).

to use prices or quantities in planning is based on the kinds of
consideration that have been raised here. In principle, however,
there is no reason to limit the enquiry to these two pure modes.
Mixed schemes can surely be devised. They will in general perform
better than either of the pure schemes and by definition cannot ever
perform worse. To see this, recall that a pure effluent tax consists
of a tax rate t (per unit of effluence) which is independent of the
quantity discharged. The pure quota can be viewed as a discontinuous tax schedule with $t=0$ for amounts discharged not in
excess of the quota level and a high enough t for any *additional* units
discharged so as to ensure that it is not profitable for the firm to
pollute beyond the quota.[43] Let $R(x)$ represent the revenue collected
by the regulatory agency when x is the level of pollution. Then
under the pure tax scheme $R(x)$ is a linear function, such as OA in
Diagram 13.3, while under the pure quota scheme $R(x)$ is a step

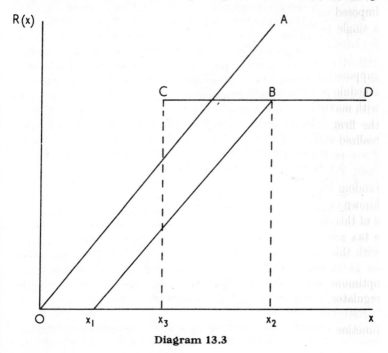

Diagram 13.3

[43] This supposes that $B_x(x, \phi) > 0$ and that $B(\hat{x}, \phi) > 0$ for all ϕ if $\hat{x}$ is the
quota level.

function such as Ox_3CD. A simple mixed scheme would be a function depicted as Ox_1BD. It consists of the imposition of a lower limit (x_1) and an upper limit (x_2) to the amount of pollution permitted by the firm, with a marginal tax rate, t, in between. If $x_1 = 0$ and $x_2 = \infty$ this reduces to the curve OA. If $x_1 = x_2 = x_3$ it reduces to Ox_3CD. In any event, the problem of the optimum mixed scheme of this simple form boils down to a choice of x_1, x_2 and the slope of the line x_1B. The problem of the optimum pure schemes, which we analysed earlier, were concerned in turn with the choice of x_3 and the slope of the line OA. The mixed scheme allows the regulator a greater range of choice. It follows that the optimum here cannot lead to lower expected social benefit than under the pure schemes. In general it will do better than both.

But it can be argued that such simple schemes as we have been considering are too limiting. In principle one would like to obtain the shape of the optimum tax schedule $T(x)$ (or, equivalently, the regulator's optimum revenue schedule $R(x) = -T(x)$) to be imposed on the firm without any restrictions of the kind that we have so far imposed on the class of feasible tax schedules. As we have assumed a single polluting firm the problem is simple to solve. Recall that we have supposed $B(x, \phi)$ to be the firm's benefit (profit) function and $L(x, \theta)$ to be the environmental damage function. We have also supposed that at the instant when the regulator announces the tax schedule it knows neither ϕ nor θ, and that he is concerned solely with maximizing $E(B(x, \phi) - L(x, \theta))$. Recall as well that at the time the firm selects its (net) profit maximizing output it knows the realized value of ϕ, but it does not know θ; (unless, of course, θ and ϕ are perfectly correlated, which we have assumed not to be the case). For simplicity of exposition suppose ϕ and θ are independent random variables. Then $E(L(x, \theta))$ is independent of whether ϕ is known or not. It follows immediately from our discussion in section 2 of this chapter that the regulator cannot do better than to impose a tax schedule $T^*(x)$ on the firm, where $T^*(x) = E(L(x, \theta))$. Faced with this tax schedule and knowledge of ϕ, the firm will choose x so as to maximize $B(x, \phi) - E(L(x, \theta))$. And this will be the optimum response of the firm from the point of view of the regulator.

Return now to the quadratic case. If the environmental damage function is of the form 13.32, then up to a constant we have

13.34 $$T^*(x) = E(L(x, \theta)) = L'(x - \hat{x}) + L''(x - \hat{x})^2/2$$

Recall that by assumption L', $L'' > 0$. Thus to the extent the slope of the marginal damage function is flat (i.e. L'' is small), 13.34 says that the optimum tax schedule approximates a pure tax. But to the extent L'' is large (i.e. the marginal damage function's slope is steep), the optimum schedule approximates the pure quota scheme; since 13.34 implies severe penalties to the firm for deviating from $\hat{x}$ if L'' is large. The point remains that 13.34 says that neither of the pure modes is optimal.

The title of section 5.(i) above is misleading. The question is not whether reliance ought to be placed on pure effluent charges or licences in controlling the level of environmental pollution. In general, reliance ought to be placed on neither on its own.

Notes on Chapter 13

Surprisingly enough, there are few textbooks on the economics of uncertainty, and none that can be recommended with unbridled enthusiasm. Until one is written the reader cannot do better than to read the collected essays in Arrow (1971) who pioneered some of the material in this chapter and much of the material in the next. For an excellent discussion of project choice under uncertainty, going well beyond the issues raised in section 1(i), see Wilson (1977).

The standard treatise on statistical decision theory is Pratt *et al.*(1964). Group action designed to achieve a common goal under conditions of uncertainty and differential information structures is the basis of the work of Marschak and Radner (1971). For an illuminating discussion of information structures and their comparisons, one should read this and McGuire (1972) and Radner (1972a).

The classic debate concerning the relative merits of taxation over regulations was placed firmly in the context of differential information structures by Meade (1973) and Weitzman (1974). A more general formulation of the problem, in the context of optimum income taxation, was discussed by Mirrlees (1971), and the formal similarity between these models and several others was noted in Dasgupta and Stiglitz (1975), who at the same time suggested the desirability of mixed modes. In fact, for the quadratic case (the one treated in the text) the general optimum had been obtained earlier by Marschak and Radner (1971). For further discussion of the Weitzman model, see Weitzman (1978). The eatlier models suppose a persistent information gap between the regulator and the individual agents. In the case where the regulator knows the damage function ($L(X)$) with precision but where there is more than one firm, mechanisms for getting the firms to reveal their benefit functions ($B(X, \theta)$) and, thereby, to close the information gap, have been discussed by Kwerel (1977), and Dasgupta and Maskin (1979).

CHAPTER 14

UNCERTAINTY AND THE ALLOCATION OF RESOURCES

1. The Arrow–Debreu Theory of Contingent Markets

In the previous chapter (see section 1) we noted how one may include the state of nature in the characteristics of a commodity. In this approach a commodity is characterized not merely by its physical attributes, but also the date and state of nature in which it is made available.[1] Using this device we developed some aspects of consumer-choice under uncertainty. We now extend the notion of an intertemporal competitive equilibrium to incorporate such environmental uncertainty.

For ease of exposition suppose time is discrete, and that there are precisely $(T+1)$ periods; $t=0, 1, \ldots, T$. Define a state of nature as, '. . . a description of the world . . .', from $t=0$ to $t=T$, '. . . so complete that, if true and known, the consequences of every action would be known'.[2] As earlier, let S be the number of states of nature ($s=1, \ldots, S$). At the initial date ($t=0$), no one knows what the true state of nature is. By hypothesis all uncertainty is resolved for everyone at $t=T$. Therefore, at T everyone will know precisely what the state of nature is.

It is assumed that with the passage of time all individuals continually receive information about the true state of nature. However, the point to emphasize is that this flow of information is costlessly obtained by all, and is not influenced by policy.

An *event* is a collection of states of nature. At $t=0$ the only operationally meaningful event is the entire set of states of nature. At date T, events that are singleton sets are also operationally meaningful. Therefore the partition of the set of states of nature is the coarsest at the initial date. It is the finest at the terminal date.[3] With the passage of time the partition of the set of states of nature

---

[1] Also its location. We ignore this last, since our concern is not with trade theory.

[2] Arrow (1970, p. 45).

[3] For definitions see footnotes 21 and 22 in Chapter 13.

becomes no coarser. A crucial assumption in the Arrow–Debreu theory is that at any given date all individuals have the *same* partition.[4]

An example would help. Suppose $T = 2$ and suppose that the only environmental uncertainty pertains to the weather at each date which may be either wet (W) or dry (D). At $t = 0$ there is uncertainty about weather at dates 1 and 2. There are, then, four states of nature, given by the sequences WW, WD, DW and DD. At the initial date no one knows what the true state of nature is. At $t = 1$ all individuals will be able to observe costlessly the weather for that date. It will be either W or D. If it is W they will all know that the true state of nature lies in the set (WW, WD). If it is D they will all know that

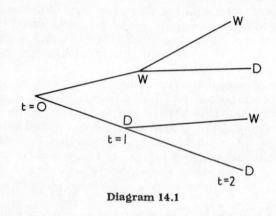

Diagram 14.1

it lies in the set (DD, DW). At $t = 2$ all individuals will be able to observe costlessly the weather once again. By this second observation they will all learn the true state of nature.

Diagram 14.1 portrays the *information tree* generated by this example. It is common to all individuals in the Arrow–Debreu theory. There is a single node at $t = 0$, two at $t = 1$, and four at $t = 2$. An event is a node in this information tree.

All decisions are made at the initial date, including those that will only be carried out at future dates. As we pointed out in the previous chapter, actions must be consistent with the information structure available at the date the action is to be carried out. But before elaborating on this there are two points to emphasize. The

[4] This is relaxed in Radner (1968). See the notes at the end of this chapter.

first is that while all individuals, by assumption, possess the same information tree, they do not necessarily impute the same probabilities to the occurrence of events. In general, people's views on such matters will differ and, indeed, this divergence of opinion will provide a reason for individuals to engage in trade. The second pertains to the structure of information that an individual possesses. At $t=0$ each individual knows that at $t=1$ he will observe a signal costlessly which will tell him which of the two nodes the world is at (see Diagram 14.1). Furthermore he knows at $t=0$ that at $t=2$ he will receive yet another signal conditional on the node the world was at the previous date and this will enable him to know precisely which node the world is finally at. In the terminology of Chapter 13 section 2 each individual obtains costlessly at each date a deterministic information structure, so that the observation of a signal from it enables him to refine his partition. Now recall equation 13.17, which defines the manner in which probabilities of states of nature are revised. It follows that the *relative* probabilities of the states of nature (say, WW and WD) emanating from a given node (W at $t=1$ in Diagram 14.1) are the same for an individual irrespective of whether he assesses them at the date–event pair defining the node in question (i.e. W at $t=1$) or whether he assesses them at a previous date from a node (the single node at $t=0$) which issues a branch leading to the node in question. But, of course, the probabilities of DW and DD are both zero conditional on W being the event (signal) at $t=1$.

Let l be the number of physically distinguishable goods and services. As there are $(T+1)$ dates and S states of nature, the number of dated contingent commodities is $l(T+1)S$. Let $X_{\kappa ls}$ ($\kappa=1, \ldots, l; t=0, \ldots, T; s=1, \ldots, S$) denote the quantity of such a commodity. We now come to the constraints on activities caused by imperfect information. To illustrate these, return to Diagram 14.1. By hypothesis all decisions (i.e. decisions to consume, produce, and trade at various date–event pairs) are made at $t=0$ when individuals have the least information about the true state of nature. The obvious point to recognize now is that all decisions must be contingent only on date–event pairs, i.e. nodes in the information tree. Thus, for example, consumption by án individual at $t=1$ if W is the event must be independent of whether the true state of nature is WD or whether it is WW; for at $t=1$ no one can distinguish between the two. All that individuals can distinguish at date $t=1$ is whether the event is W or D. Thus, numbering the four states of nature in Diagram 14.1 from top to bottom we must observe the constraints.

$$X_{\kappa 01} = X_{\kappa 02} = X_{\kappa 03} = X_{\kappa 04} \quad \text{for all } \kappa$$

14.1   and

$$X_{\kappa 11} = X_{\kappa 12} \quad \text{and} \quad X_{\kappa 13} = X_{\kappa 14} \quad \text{for all } \kappa$$

In short, commodities are defined by their physical characteristics and the date–event pair at which they are made available.

Having defined dated contingent commodities we turn to their prices. Let us choose a specific good at $t = 0$ as the numeraire. Let $p_{\kappa ts}$ be the competitive price of commodity $X_{\kappa ts}$. It is a present value contingent price. It is the price paid at $t = 0$ for delivery of commodity κ at date t if, and only if, s is the true state of nature, i.e. it is the present value price of commodity $X_{\kappa ts}$. But as emphasized earlier, transactions at any date are constrained by the common information available at that date. Thus the price for good κ to be delivered at $t = 0$ is $\sum_{s=1}^{S} p_{\kappa 0s}$. It is independent of the state of nature. Returning to our example, the price, to be paid at $t = 0$, for delivery of good κ at $t = 1$ if the event is W at $t = 1$ is $p_{\kappa 11} + p_{\kappa 12}$. Similarly, it is $p_{\kappa 13} + p_{\kappa 14}$ if the event at $t = 1$ is D. For sure delivery at $t = 1$ the price is $\sum_{s=1}^{4} p_{\kappa 1s}$.

As in Chapter 2 suppose consumers are n in number $(i = 1, \ldots, n)$. We may now define preferences and endowments on the space of dated contingent goods exactly as we did in Chapter 2, the single difference being that additional constraints, as captured in 14.1, must now be observed.

Let $u_i(\cdot)$ be the utility function representing individual i's preferences over these dated contingent goods and services. It may seem intuitively plausible that if u_i is strictly quasi-concave the individual is risk-averse. In fact this is not the case. But since the theory does not require anything stronger than quasi-concavity (and continuity!) we shall suppose this to be so. Let $\mathbf{w}_i$ be i's endowment vector of these dated contingent goods and services. Notice that there is no uncertainty about what his wealth is, since this last is, by definition, $p \cdot \mathbf{w}_i$. This is not to say that consumers bear no risk. They certainly do, because at $t = 0$ they do not know what the true state of nature is. In general, if they are risk-averse, they will wish to make provision for all states of nature (i.e. all branches in the information tree). But they will deliver, and will receive from, the market only those claims registered along the branch that the world actually follows with the passage of time.

The theory envisages production possibilities in a manner similar to the one described in Chapter 2. Let Y^j denote the production possibility set of producer j ($j = 1, \ldots, m$). It is defined on the space of all dated contingent goods and services. $y_j \in Y^j$ is a production plan and it must also satisfy constraints of the kind captured by 14.1 to represent the fact that inputs and outputs must be circumscribed by the information available. It is important to emphasize that there is no uncertainty about what the production *sets* are. A farmer will not know at the time of sowing seeds what size of crops he will be able to harvest. But if he knows his technology he will know what his output will be for every weather condition. In this example his production vector will consist of known inputs and contingent outputs, i.e. output for each state of nature. It is then immediate that producers bear no risk when there is a market for all dated contingent goods. For just as consumers can compute their wealths with perfect certainty, the producers can compute the present values of their profits, the net profit of the production plan y_j being $p.y_j$.

With these interpretations it is clear that we can bring to bear the entire apparatus developed in Chapter 2 (sections 3 and 4). We can define an intertemporal competitive equilibrium of a private ownership economy under uncertainty and we can establish its efficiency properties. Likewise, we may define Pareto efficient allocations of these dated contingent goods and discuss conditions under which such allocations can be achieved in a decentralized manner.[5] Since other than the matter of interpretation the analysis is identical to that in Chapters 2 and 4 we refer the reader to these earlier chapters.

Notice that in describing the Arrow–Debreu framework, we have postulated the existence of continuous and quasi-concave utility functions on the space of dated contingent commodities. The theory does not require that these utility functions are additive-separable. This last is obvious, because other than the matter of interpretation the model is formally identical to the one developed in Chapters 2 and 4, and no such assumption as additive separability was needed there. But it is possible to obtain particularly strong qualitative results if one supposes in addition that consumer preferences satisfy the von-Neumann–Morgenstern axioms. We noted an example of

---

[5] We are defining Pareto efficiency relative to the preferences at $t = 0$. It is on occasion called *ex-ante* efficiency. For a discussion of the limitations of this notion see Starr (1974) and Guesnerie and Montbrial (1974).

this in Chapter 13 section 1 while developing simple expressions for the cost of risk-bearing.[6] Let $\mathbf{X}_s^i$ be an $l(T+1)$ vector of dated goods consumed by individual i along that branch of the information tree which is associated with state of nature s. Let Π_s^i be the probability that i associates with the occurence of s (i.e. that the world will follow this branch). Then, for the model at hand, if the individual's preferences do satisfy the von-Neumann–Morgenstern axioms,

$$u^i(\mathbf{X}^i) = \sum_{s=1}^{S} \Pi_s^i V_s(\mathbf{X}_s^i),$$

with $\mathbf{X}^i$ satisfying constraints of the kind denoted by 14.1.

Several additional points bear emphasis here. First, the environmental risks considered by the theory need by no means be small ones. In particular, there is no presumption that the law of large numbers can be appealed to. Natural risks, such as the occurrence of earthquakes and droughts are ready examples. Secondly, the contingent commodity markets postulated in the theory enable consumers to shift their risks. Such markets allow consumers to lay bets on the occurrence of different states of nature. For recall that, by definition, $p_{\kappa ts}$ is the price to be paid at $t=0$ for a unit of commodity κ for delivery at t *if, and only if*, s is the state of nature. An equilibrium contingent price vector is a function of, among other things, the beliefs that consumers hold about the occurrence of the different states of nature (viz. Π_s^i; $i=1, \ldots, n$, and $s=1, \ldots, S$).[7] There is no presumption that consumers hold identical beliefs. It is for this reason that such contingent markets are often called competitive *risk* markets. It also provides a reason why the Pareto-efficiency property of such an equilibrium is called the efficient allocation of risk-bearing.

Thirdly, it should be noted that the risks that are considered in the model are exogenous risks, in the sense we used the term in Chapter 13 section 3. For note that by assumption the information

---

[6] Another example is the demonstration that an equilibrium with a complete set of competitive dated contingent markets is equivalent to an equilibrium with a complete set of competitive securities markets and spot markets for goods and services. We do not go into this here. For details, see Arrow (1964) and Guesnerie and Montbrial (1974).

[7] If the risks are personal (e.g. whether or not a given individual has an accident define two states of nature), and therefore small for the economy as a whole, the contingent prices assume a particularly simple structure. For, in such conditions an appeal can be made to the law of large numbers, provided of course the number of consumers is large. See Malinvaud (1972).

structure is the same for all individuals, and in particular, that it is exogenously given. It is not a decision variable. Furthermore, the existence of a complete set of competitive dated contingent prices ensures that there *are* no endogenous uncertainties, i.e. there are no market-induced uncertainties.

The distinction between exogenous and endogenous risks is by no means as clear-cut as it may appear from the expressions. Earthquakes and other such natural disasters are perhaps the pristine form of exogenous uncertainties. Price uncertainties due to an absence of a complete set of contingent markets are an example of the latter. Some of the more subtle examples, where the distinction is blurred, appear in the context of research and development. There is always a chance that a well-defined research project will prove to be unsuccessful; presumably also this chance is influenced by the zeal of the researcher. But a detailed monitoring of research effort is a wellnigh impossible task. The theory we are describing is concerned with the 'residual' uncertainty in the success of the project. But if research effort is not minutely observable by all, then of necessity there will be an incomplete set of markets, and in particular, the success or failure of the project will at least partially be influenced by decision—the decision by the researcher about how conscientious he is to be in his work. This phenomenon, which in the insurance literature is referred to as one of *moral hazard*, is widespread. Its presence explains why it is not possible in general to insure one's property for more than its nominal value. This in turn means that individuals are typically rationed on the amount of contingent goods they can buy which, of course, violates the hypothesis of the Arrow–Debreu construction that individuals face fixed dated-contingent prices, i.e. prices that are independent of the quantity purchased.

We emphasize these points so as to display the extent to which the theory is sensitive to the assumption of costless monitoring of states of nature, the likelihood of whose occurrence is not controllable. Paradoxically, these points also indicate the value of understanding the construction. The theory makes precise a sense in which the market mechanism can sustain an efficient allocation of resources. Our comments in Chapter 4 section 7 are relevant here. When all these considerations are taken into account it is difficult to see how one can persist in making claims about the virtues of the market of a kind that are often made. We shall return to these considerations in Chapter 16.

2. The Production of Information: Research and Development[8]

We have noted that individuals do not have choice over their information structures in the Arrow–Debreu model. Information structure does not appear as a decision variable. But in fact a great deal of resources are spent on both the production and dissemination of information in the world we know. It is then tempting to regard information as a commodity and to ask whether there are reasons for believing that decentralized economies are likely to produce the 'right' kinds of information, of 'right' amounts and have them disseminated to the 'right' extent. Only a little reflection is required, however, to persuade one that there are several major differences between 'knowledge' (the output of research and development) and conventional commodities, rendering the usual theorems on efficient and competitive allocations (see Chapter 2) inapplicable. These characteristics lead not only to the amount of information which would be produced and disseminated in a competitive situation being non-optimal, but they make it most unlikely that markets will be perfectly competitive. In this section we tabulate some of the more important of these characteristics. In the following sections we shall explore some of the immediate implications of these in the context of exploration activity.

(i) *Informational external economies:* Unlike private commodities, if one person gives another person a piece of information (viz. that he has observed signal y_i), it does not reduce the amount of information that the first person possesses. Thus, it is the cost of *transmitting* information, not the cost of *producing* information, which should determine how widely it ought to be disseminated. But often such transmission costs are negligible relative to their cost of production. In many such cases it is impossible for the producer to appropriate the benefits of information, and in some, the information acquired by the producer is transmitted *directly* to others free of cost, thereby conferring benefits on others. In such circumstances information is a public good, in the sense we used the term in Chapter 3. The entire discussion of Chapter 3 section 1 can be brought to bear on the problem. The presumption then is that a

[8] This section is based on Arrow (1970a), and Dasgupta and Stiglitz (1977) (1978c).

market equilibrium will usually lead to an *under*-production of such information.[9]

(ii) *Information and appropriability:* In many cases the returns from research and development (R and D) activity can be appropriated by the researcher, even though the cost of transmission of such information is negligible. But the appropriation of such returns through patent rights, secrecy, etc., is often associated with monopoly power and, although in such cases it is the expectation of future monopoly power which drives firms to incur R and D effort, it leads to insufficient utilization of the knowledge. That is, production based on this knowledge is restricted, and the knowledge is not allowed to be utilized by other firms. But it is important to emphasize that, while such monopoly power in production results in an insufficient utilization of knowledge, the expectation of this monopoly power may lead too many firms to engage in the original R and D activity, resulting in excessive expenditure on R and D.[10]

(iii) *Informational external diseconomies:* It is not difficult to think of cases where a piece of information can be appropriated by its producer but where the producer's action based on his information inflicts external diseconomies on others (e.g. through greater fluctuation in prices), so that while the information is of positive value to the *acquirer*, it is of negative value to others. But then each individual has an incentive to acquire the information for himself, since he does not take into account the external diseconomy that he inflicts on others. The situation is formally akin to the problem of the common (see Chapter 3 section 4), and here the presumption is that such a decentralized economy will acquire too much information.[11]

(iv) *The common pool property:* This is really a combination of the first three points but is nevertheless worth stressing. There is a sense in which all inventors draw upon a common pool of knowledge. Much invention consists of transforming basic ideas into marketable commodities, and some of the return, in a system in which basic ideas are not patentable but the produced commodities are, is really a rent on the basic ideas. Thus, individuals compete to produce

---

[9] The social value of such information is the sum of its private values and under ideal circumstances such information should be produced up to the amount where its marginal social cost of production equals its social value. See equation 3.16.

[10] For a demonstration of this, see Dasgupta and Stiglitz (1978c).

[11] For examples of such cases, see Hirschleifer (1970) and Wilson (1975). See also Green (1976) for a classification of informational externalities.

a marketable commodity to acquire a share in this common pool of rents. As in any common pool type situation, this may lead to excessive R and D activity (see Chapter 3 section 4). On the other hand, normally only a fraction of the returns can be appropriated, and thus most R and D activities contribute to the common pool, as well as take out from it, and to the extent this happens there may be not enough R and D investment (see Chapter 3 section 1). It is the net balance of these two effects which determines whether there is too much or too little research. This, in turn, is likely to depend on the nature of the research, the extent to which it is 'applied' or 'basic'.

(v) *Increasing returns in the use of information:* This is simply a restatement of the public goods nature of information, but emphasizing that, when the returns are appropriable, the return to conducting R and D will be larger, the larger the firm. The point is that the *same* piece of information can in principle be used at any scale of operation. There is no point in acquiring the same information more than once. Thus the cost of information per unit scale decreases as the scale increases. But the value of information per unit scale does not. This can easily lead to increasing returns to scale in the profitability of R and D expenditure.

The point can be illustrated without one having to invoke uncertainty.[12] We consider a single potential market, where Q denotes the quantity of the commodity in question. By assumption there are no income effects. We suppose that gross benefit of consuming Q is $u(Q)$, where $u'(Q)>0$ and $u''(Q)<0$. Thus, the competitive market price for the commodity is $p(Q)=u'(Q)$. Suppose that the market for this commodity is socially managed. If c is the (constant) average cost of production then the net social benefit of consuming Q is $u(Q)-cQ$. Define

14.2 $$V(c)=\max_{Q}\{u(Q)-cQ\}$$

as the indirect utility function. It is readily checked that $V(c)$ is a decreasing, convex function of c (see Diagram 14.2). We suppose that R and D expenditure is designed to reduce the cost of production. Thus if x is expenditure on R and D then $c(x)$ is the marginal (equal to average) cost of production. Naturally, we suppose that

[12] The example is taken from Dasgupta and Stiglitz (1978c).

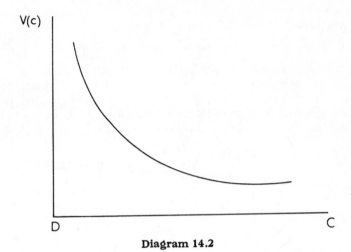

Diagram 14.2

$c'(x) < 0$.[13] Suppose in addition that $c''(x) > 0$ (i.e. decreasing returns in the technology of research—see Diagram 14.3).

Assume that the government can raise the funds for R and D expenditure from general taxation. Its problem then is to

14.3 $$\max_{x \geq 0} [V\{c(x)\} - x].$$

The point to note is that unless further structure is imposed on $c(x)$ one cannot guarantee that $V\{c(x)\}$ is a concave function of x. But if it is not concave then by definition there are increasing returns in the benefit of R and D expenditure—at least in some interval. To see this clearly, suppose

14.4 $$u(Q) = Q^\eta \qquad (1 > \eta > 0).$$

It is then simple to confirm from 14.2 that

14.5 $$V\{c(x)\} = \left(\frac{1-\eta}{\eta}\right) \eta^{1/(1-\eta)} / \{c(x)\}^{\eta/(1-\eta)}.$$

---

[13] It is as though Mother Nature has a patent on all techniques of production with average cost $c(x)$ for $x > 0$, and that society has to pay x to purchase the right to use the technique of production with average cost $c(x)$.

Suppose in addition that it is a new product under consideration. In particular, suppose $c(x)$ is iso-elastic, so that

14.6 $$c(x) = \beta x^{-\alpha} \qquad (\alpha,\ \beta > 0).$$

Notice that 14.4 supposes diminishing marginal utility of consumption, and 14.6 implies diminishing returns in the technology of research (see Diagram 14.3). But the two together do not, by any means, guarantee diminishing marginal utility of R and D expenditure. For, using 14.6 in 14.4 yields

14.7 $$V\{c(x)\} = \left(\frac{1-\eta}{\eta}\right)\eta^{1/(1-\eta)}x^{\alpha\eta/(1-\eta)}/\beta^{\eta/(1-\eta)}.$$

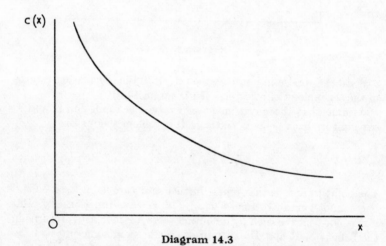

Diagram 14.3

We may now note that if $\alpha\eta > (1-\eta)$ then $V\{c(x)\}$ is strictly convex in x and, in particular, problem 14.3 does not possess a solution. There are unbounded increasing returns to scale. This is, of course, absurd, since we can hardly continue to suppose an absence of income effects as x is made larger and larger. But the point remains that *concavity* of V in x cannot, in general, be assumed.

We have noted throughout the book (see especially the discussion in Chapters 2 and 3) how important it is to assume an absence of increasing returns (i.e. an absence of non-convexities of certain sets) in guaranteeing the existence of a competitive equilibrium, and also in guaranteeing that an efficient allocation of resources can be decentralized by the use of appropriate shadow prices (see, for example, Chapters 6 and 10). The example that we have just discussed presents us with an additional reason for thinking that markets are likely to function badly if R and D activity is left exclusively in the private sector. In particular, the thrust of the example is that there is likely to be excessive specialization in terms of the *commodities* that are produced.[14]

(vi) *Set-up costs in the production of information:* It is often alleged that a little knowledge is a dangerous thing. Dangerous or not, it can certainly be shown to be of no use. If at the same time the acquisition of this little knowledge requires resources it is obviously better not to acquire it. We present a simple proof of this proposition.[15]

To do this, recall the formulation of information acquisition and its value in Chapter 13 section 2. In particular, recall the expression for the value of information—13.20. Suppose there is a continuum of information structures, Y_z, such that $z \geqslant 0$ and that $z = 0$ corresponds to the non-informative information structure. Let $c(z)$ be the cost of the information structure Y_z. We suppose without loss of generality, that $c'(z) > 0$ and that $c(0) = 0$. Let N be the number of potential signals in the information structure provided by the set Y_z. Since there is a continuum of information structures it is natural to suppose that $p_{Y_z}(y_i|\theta_s)$ is differentiable with respect to z. We assume in addition that $u_s(a)$ is differentiable in a and that the optimum action is differentiable in z.

Now consider the expression for the value of information, 13.20, which we rewrite here as

$$14.8 \qquad W(z) \equiv \sum_{i=1}^{N} \left[\max_{a \in A(Y_z)} \left\{ \sum_{s=1}^{S} u_s(a)\Pi(\theta_s)p_{Y_z}(y_i|\theta_s) \right\} \right] - c(z).$$

We wish to calculate $W'(z)$ at $z = 0$. What we shall show is that $W'(0) < 0$ and, therefore, that it is better to be uninformed than to be a little informed.

---

[14] For a more elaborate example of such informational economics of scale, see Wilson (1975).

[15] An example can be found in Wilson (1975), and for a general proof of the proposition, see Radner and Stiglitz (1975). The proof here is simpler, but the proposition proved here is less general than the one in the Radner–Stiglitz article.

To see this, differentiate 14.8 in the neighbourhood of $z=0$ to obtain

14.9 $$\frac{\mathrm{d}W}{\mathrm{d}z} = \sum_{i=1}^{N} \max_{\boldsymbol{a} \in A(Y_z)} \left[\sum_{s=1}^{S} u_s(\boldsymbol{a}) \Pi(\theta_s) \frac{\mathrm{d}}{\mathrm{d}z} \{p_{Yz}(y_i|\theta_s)\} \right] - c'(z).^{16}$$

Notice that at $z=0$ the optimum action is independent of the signal received, since Y_0 is non-informative.[17] Hence we can rewrite 14.9 as

14.10 $$\left(\frac{\mathrm{d}W}{\mathrm{d}z} \right)_{z=0} = \sum_{s=1}^{S} u_s(\boldsymbol{a}^0) \Pi(\theta_s) \left[\sum_{i=1}^{N} \frac{\mathrm{d}}{\mathrm{d}z} \{p_{Yz}(y_i|\theta_s)\} \right] - c'(0),$$

where $\boldsymbol{a}^0$ is the optimum action (independent of the signal) when Y^0 is the information structure. But by definition we know that for every state of nature θ_s and every information structure Y_z, $\sum_{i=1}^{N} p_{Yz}$

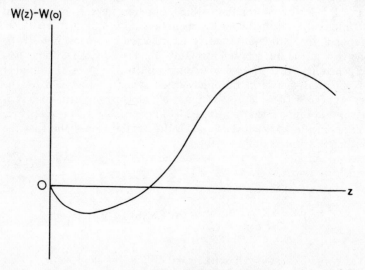

$W(z)-W(o)$

Diagram 14.4
(Information tree when T^* is the date of exploration.)

[16] The indirect effect on W via the change in *optimum action* due to a change in the information structure is, of course, nil precisely because the individual is optimizing for each signal. Hence this term does not appear in 14.9. It is the 'envelope' property we are appealing to here.
[17] See Chapter 13 section 2.

$(y_i|\theta_s)=1$. It follows that $\sum_{i=1}^{N} d/dz\{p_{Yz}(y_i|\theta_s)\}=0$. Thus equation 14.10 reduces to

14.11
$$\left(\frac{dW}{dz}\right)_{z=0} = -c'(0) < 0.$$

Thus for small positive z, $W(z) - W(0) < 0$, and if there are some values of z at which information is beneficial, then in general the net value of information, $W(z) - W(0)$, looks as in Diagram 14.4. In this case, there are increasing returns to scale in information acquisition, at least in some regions. This implies that the demand for information is not a continuous function of its price, raising doubts whether competitive markets for information can exist. In particular, the result implies that research will only be undertaken at a scale no smaller than some positive level, and that there will be specialization of *research strategies* (unlike the specialization in terms of commodities that was implied by point (v) in our list). To summarize, the result suggests that the private market for information is likely to be monopolistic rather than competitive.[18]

(vii) *Moral hazard:* It was noted in section 1 that the theorem establishing the efficiency of a competitive market allocation requires the assumption that there is a complete set of risk markets. But the risks associated with R and D activity in general are particularly difficult to insure against. For instance, whether the lack of success of a given research project is due solely to chance or whether it is at least partly to be explained by the researcher's slothfulness is not something that is easy to detect, and is in many cases impossible to detect. That is to say, many risk markets do not exist and even those that do are often not competitive.[19] As in the case with ordinary insurance, the moral hazard problem looms large in the market for R and D.

(viii) *Discovery of previously unthought of possibilities:* In discussing the issue of an optimal allocation of resources one needs to specify the various possible states of nature. This was implicit in the discussion of section 1. But it is not possible to *specify* (as opposed to being able to predict) an event (e.g. the control of

---

[18] This will be so if the 'non-convexity' in information value is not negligible relative to the size of the economy. It is an empirical matter if this is indeed the case.

[19] Thus, for example, cost-plus contracts that defence firms undertake with governments are, by their nature, not Arrow–Debreu contracts. On this, see Arrow (1970a).

nuclear fusion) before the idea (of atoms) has even been conceived of. The point is that R and D activity, as we have defined it, is designed to reduce uncertainty. Signals are usually obtained with a view to reducing the possible range of variation of the world (i.e. obtaining a finer partition of the states of nature). But truly basic research often leads to the recognition of states of nature which could not be described in the existing language prior to the research having been completed. On occasion these are called 'unexpected' discoveries. 'Unthought of' is a better description. This is more likely to be the case with 'basic' than with 'applied' research, since the latter often consists in translating basic research outputs into marketable products. But to the extent that the point does apply to basic research, it suggests that there are limits to the extent to which meaningful discussion can take place about the value of (future) basic research.[20]

These foregoing considerations suggest strongly that markets for information are unlikely to function well. 'Information' possesses a number of characteristics that conventional goods—like engineering equipments and consumer durables—do not possess. We have noted that informational externalities are more the rule than the exception, which implies (as we saw in Chapter 3) that, even if markets for information are competitive, they will not sustain an efficient allocation of resources. Furthermore, there often exist some fundamental increasing returns (non-convexities) in the value of information (points (v) and (vi) above) that make it unlikely that markets for information can be competitive.

We emphasize these points because it has often been claimed that fear on account of impending resource exhaustion (the Doomsday syndrome) is unfounded because as resources are depleted their prices rise, making the private search for substitutes more rewarding.[21] What we have argued above is that while the antecedent clause of the claim is correct the fear may none the less be well founded. There is every reason for supposing that the market cannot be relied upon to invest appropriately in the search for new deposits and substitute products.

[20] For an extreme such position, see Popper (1957). One does not have to take such a pessimistic position though. For example, we saw in Chapter 8 how one may be allowed to postulate a given rate of technical advance, without having to articulate the precise nature of this advance and debate fruitfully on economic issues on the basis of this postulate.

[21] See, for example, Nordhaus (1972), Maddox (1971) and Beckerman (1972).

UNCERTAINTY 427

In fact of course it has long been recognized that R and D ought not to be left exclusively in the hands of the private sector. Much basic research is conducted in government financed institutions, and our discussion provides a rationale for this. If a substantial portion of 'applied' research is carried out in the private sector in those economies where the production of goods and services is mainly in the private sector, the reason must be that much of such R and D expenditures form actual production activity. Designing, tooling, etc., involve learning and actual production simultaneously.[22]

Exploration activity, which is a special case of research, remains largely in the private sector. In the remainder of this chapter we look more carefully into the special problems that exploration, as an economic activity, raises. In the following section we consider a simple model of exploration and obtain the socially optimal policy. We shall note that there are severe difficulties in decentralizing such policies. In the final section, therefore, we discuss the private incentives for exploration.

3. Uncertainty in Reserves and the Social Value of Exploration

Exploration activity is undertaken with a view to obtaining information about reserves of exhaustible resources. We revert to the partial equilibrium framework of Chapter 6, and suppose, as in section 2 of that chapter, a socially managed resource. For simplicity we assume that once a reserve has been proven its extraction cost is nil. Moreover we suppose that there is no uncertainty about the location of deposits. The only source of uncertainty is the size of the reserves. Again, for simplicity, we shall suppose that the total stock at $t=0$ can only take one of two possible values, S_1 or S_2 ($S_2 > S_1$) and suppose *proven* reserves to be S_1. The probability that additional reserves, of amount $S_2 - S_1$, exist is agreed by all to be Π. $(1 - \Pi)$ is then the probability that no additional reserves exist. There are, then, two states of nature. The technology of exploration is simple in the world we are constructing here. One merely sinks a well at cost K to determine whether or not the additional reserve exists. In the terminology of Chapter 13 section 2, society can purchase a fully informative information structure at a cost K.

[22] This recognition forms the basis of models of technical progress in Arrow (1962a) and Kaldor and Mirrlees (1962).

Granted that, contrary to our assumption, exploration never eliminates uncertainty but merely reduces it, our simplification does nevertheless enable us to highlight two propositions of general validity, namely: (a) if known reserves are large, exploration ought not to be undertaken immediately, and (b) if the resource is sufficiently valuable at the margin when reserves are low, it is desirable for society to maintain a stock of known reserves at all times. For the simple model at hand the implication of (b) is that the exploration cost K ought to be incurred before known reserves, of size S_1, have been exhausted. We now proceed with the analysis.

Recall first the model presented in Chapter 6 section 2. As before, let R_t denote the resource flow at time t, and let $u(R_t)$ denote the gross consumer surplus of consuming R_t. The (compensated) demand function for the resource flow is then $p_t = u'(R_t) > 0$. We suppose, as usual, that $u''(\cdot) < 0$, and that the elasticity of $u'(R)$ tends to a finite limit as $R \to 0$. Finally, let $r(>0)$ be the (sure) rate of market interest, equal by hypothesis to the social rate of discount. We begin with some recapitulations. Suppose, as in Chapter 6 section 2, an absence of any uncertainty regarding the size of the stock. Let S be the initial stock. Then the planning problem consists in choosing that extraction policy R_t which

14.12
$$\left.\begin{array}{c} \text{maximizes } \int_0^\infty \exp(-rt)u(R_t)\,\mathrm{d}t \\[2em] \text{subject to} \quad R_t \geqslant 0 \quad \text{and} \quad \int_0^\infty R_t\,\mathrm{d}t \leqslant S \end{array}\right\}.$$

We have noted that the optimal policy dictates that for $R_t > 0$ the present value (shadow) price of the resource is constant; that is $\exp(-rt)u'(R_t) = \lambda$ (constant), where λ is chosen so as to satisfy the constraint $\int_0^\infty R_t\,\mathrm{d}t = S$. To keep the analysis simple we suppose, as earlier, that $\lim u'(R) = \infty$, $R \to 0$ so that it is never optimal to exhaust the resource. Now let $W(S)$ denote the value of the maximum and in 14.12 along the optimal programme. $W(S)$ is the maximum present value of consumer surplus when the initial stock is S.

Now suppose that society wishes to plan for precisely T years and does not care what happens thereafter. In this case the planning problem is to choose an extraction programme R_t with a view to

14.13
$$\left. \begin{array}{l} \text{maximizing} \int_0^T \exp(-rt)u(R_t)\,\mathrm{d}t \\[4mm] \text{subject to} \quad R_t \geqslant 0 \quad \text{and} \quad \int_0^T R_t\,\mathrm{d}t \leqslant S \end{array} \right\}.$$

In this case it is clear that the optimal policy will dictate that the present value (shadow) price of the resource is constant during $(0, T)$, i.e.

14.14
$$\exp(-rt)u'(R_t) = \lambda^* \qquad (0 \leqslant t \leqslant T)$$

where λ^* is now chosen so as to satisfy the integral constraint $\int_0^T R_t\,\mathrm{d}t = S$. Let $W(S, T)$ denote the value of the maximand in 14.13 along the finite time-horizon optimal programme. Armed with these recapitulations we can investigate the problem of the optimum timing of exploration under uncertainty, when society is concerned with maximizing the expected value of the discounted sum of net consumer surplus from the present to infinity.

But before doing this it is worth bringing out a familiar point. We have assumed that $u(\cdot)$ is strictly concave. It is then possible to show that $W(S)$ is strictly concave in S.[23] But this means that

14.15
$$W\{\Pi S_2 + (1 - \Pi)S_1\} > \Pi W(S_2) + (1 - \Pi)W(S_1),$$

and therefore that there is a positive cost borne by society due to this stock-uncertainty. Social welfare would increase if society were guaranteed the average stock $\Pi S_2 + (1 - \Pi)S_1$. This is a point we emphasized in Chapter 13 section 1. Society would be prepared, if it were possible, to spend at least some resources in removing this uncertainty before beginning to extract. By assumption it can. But it may be even better to begin extracting without resolving the

---

[23] It is easy to verify this by direct computation for the case where $u(\cdot)$ is iso-elastic. Thus, suppose, e.g. $u(R) = R^\eta$ $(1 > \eta > 0)$. In this case the optimal programme is

$$R_t = \left(\frac{rS}{1-\eta}\right)\exp\left(\frac{-rt}{1-\eta}\right)$$

and, therefore $W(S) = \{rS/(1-\eta)\}^\eta(1-\eta)/r$, which is, of course, strictly concave in S. We leave it to the reader to prove the general proposition. (Hint: the maximand in 14.12 is strictly concave in extraction programmes $\{R_t\}$ and the feasible set is convex).

uncertainty and to purchase the information at a later date—so that the present value of exploration costs are reduced. So the question arises as to when it ought to purchase the information and how it ought to extract from its known reserves until that time.

In fact the optimum extraction and exploration policy is easy to characterize. Suppose T is the date at which exploration is conducted, and suppose S $(0 \leqslant S \leqslant S_1)$ is the stock exhausted by then. Then for the interval $(0, T)$ the economy ought to pursue the programme implied by problem 14.13. During $(0, T)$ the *spot* price of the resource rises at the rate of interest (equation 14.14) and the initial price is so chosen that at T precisely S units of known reserves will have been exhausted. Since the uncertainty will not have been resolved until T, no one will be able to distinguish the two states of nature (characterized solely by the initial stock) until that date (see Diagram 14.5). The present value shadow price 14.14 is therefore independent of the state of nature. At T, K is spent on exploration and the uncertainty is resolved for every one. Given that by T the economy will have exhausted S units of known reserves, the probability that reserves are $(S_1 - S)$ is $(1 - \Pi)$ and that they are $(S_2 - S)$ is Π. At T the planners will begin pursuing the programme dictated by problem 14.12, with T being the then initial date. Since the uncertainty will have been resolved at T the planners will at that instant know precisely what figure for initial stock to impose in problem 14.12.

Given S and T the expected present value of net consumer surplus along this proposed contingent programme is

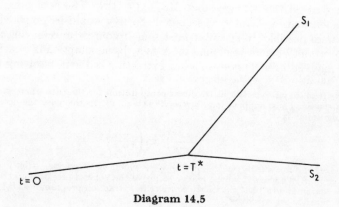

Diagram 14.5

14.16 $W(S, T) + \exp(-rT)\{(1-\Pi)W(S_1-S) + \Pi W(S_2-S) - K\}$

and the remaining problem is to choose S and T with a view to maximizing 14.16, bearing in mind that $T \geqslant 0$ and $0 \leqslant S \leqslant S_1$.

Since $\lim\limits_{R\to 0} u'(R) = \infty$ by assumption, it follows that $\lim\limits_{S\to 0} \partial W/\partial S$ $(S, T) = \infty$ for $T > 0$. It is then obvious that at an optimum $S < S_1$ (unless $T = \infty$). Suppose in fact optimum $T > 0$ and $\infty > T$ (and, therefore, that $S_1 > S > 0$).[24] In this case optimum choices of S and T must satisfy the conditions:

14.17 $\dfrac{\partial W(S, T)}{\partial S} = \exp(-rT)\{(1-\Pi)W'(S_1-S) + \Pi W'(S_2-S)\}$

and

14.18 $\dfrac{\partial W(S, T)}{\partial T} = r\exp(-rT)\{(1-\Pi)W(S_1-S) + \Pi W(S_2-S) - K\}.$

Let S^* and T^* be the solutions of equations 14.17 and 14.18. Equation 14.17 has a straightforward interpretation in terms of Arrow–Debreu contingent commodity prices. The LHS is the present value price (i.e. at $t = 0$) of a unit of the resource to be delivered at T^* irrespective of what the state of nature is. $\exp(-rT^*)(1-\Pi)$ $W'(S_1 - S^*)$ is the present value price of a unit of the resource to be delivered at T^* if, and only if, the new reserves are dry. Likewise, $\exp(-rT^*)\Pi W'(S_2 - S^*)$ is the present-value price for a unit of the resource to be delivered at T^* if and only if the new reserves have more of the resource.

We can express 14.17 in terms of spot prices as well. Now $p(T^*) \equiv \exp(rT^*)\partial W(S^*, T^*)/\partial S$ is the spot price of the resource at T^*. Clearly $p_1(T^*) \equiv W'(S_1 - S^*)$ is the spot price of the resource at T^* conditional on the discovery that the new reserves are dry (i.e. S_1 was the stock at $t = 0$), and $p_2(T^*) \equiv W'(S_2 - S^*)$ is the spot price at T^* conditional on the discovery that the new reserves contain deposits (i.e. S_2 was the stock at $t = 0$). Then 14.17 can be expressed as $p(T^*) = (1-\Pi)p_1(T^*) + \Pi p_2(T^*)$.

We can now depict the two sample paths of the spot price as in Diagram 14.6. At T^*, the date at which exploration is carried out

---

[24] This is true in general if K is large. The reader can confirm this easily for the case where $u(R) = R^\eta (1 > \eta > 0)$. If $W(S) > W(S, T) + \exp(-rt)\{(1-\Pi) W(S_1-S) + \Pi W(S_2-S) - K\}$ for all T $(\infty > T \geqslant 0)$ and all S, $0 \leqslant S \leqslant S_1$, then $T^* = \infty$. That is, it is never worth exploring.

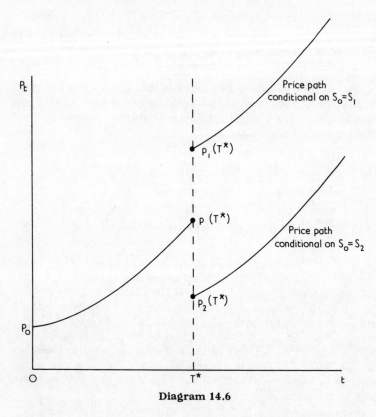

Diagram 14.6

and when the uncertainty is resolved, the economy enters a new regime and the spot price has a discontinuous change. By hypothesis there are two states of nature. If the state of nature is $S_0 = S_1$ (i.e. no additional reserves), the spot price jumps to $p_1(T^*)$. Otherwise it falls discontinuously to $p_2(T^*)$. The diagram is otherwise self-explanatory.

We sum up: the present value contingent resource prices that are implied by the optimum programme are as follows. For delivery of a unit of the resource at any t $(0 \leqslant t \leqslant T^*)$, it is $p_0 = p(T^*) \exp(-rT^*)$; for delivery of a unit of the resource at any t $(t \geqslant T^*)$, conditional on no additional reserves being found, it is $p_0' = (1 - \Pi)p_1(T^*) \exp(-rT^*)$; and for delivery of a unit of the resource at any t $(t \geqslant T^*)$, conditional on additional reserves being found, it is $p_0'' =$

$\Pi p_2(T^*) \exp(-rT^*)$. Therefore, for sure delivery of a unit of the resource at *any* date the present value price is p_0.[25] The structure of contingent prices for the exploration problem at hand is indeed very simple.

So far so good, and one might be led to suppose that this socially optimal programme of resource extraction and exploration can be decentralized by the government announcing that it will undertake exploration at T^* and then allowing individuals to trade at the present value contingent prices we have just analysed. In fact there are severe problems with such an attempt. The trouble is that the social optimum is extremely vulnerable to tampering by speculators. We look into this.

4. Private Incentives for Exploration

(i) *Speculative value of information, and the impossibility of fully informative price systems:* Suppose an attempt were made to sustain the optimum as an intertemporal equilibrium by the establishment of the above contingent resource prices. Consider a representative individual in this economy. He can, by incurring the exploration cost, carry out a private exploration of the unproven reserves at a date earlier than T^*. Assume that he can keep the acquired knowledge to himself. Then he will know for sure whether the initial stock was S_1 or whether it was S_2 before the others do. His information tree will be different from the others, with the node in Diagram 14.5 occurring earlier than T^*. Suppose he invests K and undertakes this private exploration at $t=0$. Assume that he discovers that the remaining tracts are barren, i.e. $S_0=S_1$. He can then undertake to deliver X units of the resource at a date t ($>T^*$) conditional on further deposits being discovered. For this undertaking he receives $\Pi p_0 X$ from the market. Likewise, if he discovers that there are additional reserves (i.e. $S_0=S_2$) he can undertake to deliver X units of the resource at a date $t(>T^*)$ conditional on the additional reserves proving to be barren. For this undertaking he receives $(1-\Pi)p_0 X$ from the market. In either case he knows that he will not actually have to deliver. Therefore he will not need to purchase these contingent goods. Prior to his exploration he does not, of course, know what its result is going to be. But this does not matter. By arguing as above he can guarantee for himself the lesser of the two figures $\Pi p_0 X$ and $(1-\Pi)p_0 X$. Since K is the cost of exploration,

[25] This is then a generalization of the Hotelling Rule for the problem at hand.

he can by this form of speculation guarantee for himself as large a profit as he likes by choosing a sufficiently large X.[26] But this cannot be, for presumably he will begin to influence the contingent commodity prices by his becoming a dominant supplier. In which case this speculator's action would drive the economy away from the optimum programme which these contingent commodity prices were designed to sustain.

What we have established is that the optimum cannot be sustained in a decentralized manner. What will actually happen in the economy we have been describing is hard to say. Obviously there cannot be a single price-taking speculator of the kind we have just described. What we have argued above is that in the case where there *is* a single speculator, he will by his action begin to influence the contingent prices. But the interesting point that arises from this possibility is not the fact that a monopoly element is thereby introduced into the economy. Rather it is that by his forcing certain contingent prices down (by his large promissory supplies), he will enable the other individuals to infer the true state of nature. Thus, for example, if he discovers S_1 to be the true state of nature he will, as we have argued above, wish to sell vast quantities of the resource contingent on S_2 being the state of nature at $t > T^*$, thereby lowering this contingent price. If the remaining individuals in the economy are astute enough, they will recognize that this lowering of the price means that someone has learnt that S_1 is the true state of nature. But in this case they will choose not to purchase the contingent resources the speculator wishes to sell. When this is so the speculator makes no gains out of his private information.

This kind of informational externality, transmitted via the price system, is extremely important to bear in mind.[27] If the speculator is astute enough, he may recognize the above possibility, that if he is overly greedy he will give his private information away via the price system. In which case he may decide to make a tidy profit— and not a killing!—so as not to influence the prices. This way, or so he may argue, he can keep his private information private. But then presumably there is more than one speculator. Each acts as a price taker and finds the acquisition of this private information profitable

[26] This point was raised by Hirschleifer (1970) to show that the private return on information can be great even in the absence of patents, since the inventor, prior to announcing his invention, can monopolize the factors of production that are important in the process that has just been invented.

[27] They have been discussed by Green (1973), Grossman (1977), Grossman and Stiglitz (1976) and Radner (1976).

provided no one else explores. But if, thereby, a sufficiently large number of speculators invest independently in exploration, their resulting actions will influence the contingent prices and thereby transmit the private information costlessly through the entire economy. When this happens the speculators are unable to reap any benefit from their exploration activities. Each will know this in advance. Therefore none will wish to undertake exploration. But if no one else does, a single speculator will argue that it is to his advantage to acquire the information; and so . . .

What we have argued above is that if the acquisition of information is not costless, a rational expectations equilibrium cannot exist if prices disseminate fully the information that is acquired by those who have invested in it.[28] For, cet. par., those who are 'uninformed' initially can do better than those who pay to become 'informed', since the uninformed can costlessly become informed by observing the implications of the informed group's action. In our example above, exploration activity reveals the full information about the state of nature to those carrying out explorations. The price system sustaining a rational expectations equilibrium is consequently fully informative. It follows that a rational expectations equilibrium does not exist for the example at hand.

Broadly speaking, there are two routes one can follow at this point. One is to dispense with the rational expectations hypothesis. The other is to recognize that the example is too simple: that exploration activity does not eliminate uncertainty but that exploration provides the speculator with noisy information.[29] If there is *sufficient* noise in the system, prices will not transmit as much information as that possessed by those conducting exploration. In such cases those who have purchased the information (i.e. conducted private exploration) may have just that much edge over those who are uninformed. But the former group have to spend resources to obtain the information (K per head). It is this cost that has to be weighed, in an expected sense, with the advantage of being 'informed'. If a rational expectations equilibrium exists in which only a fraction of the individual's undertake exploration activity it must be characterized by the property that individuals

---

[28] By 'rational expectations' here we mean, as in Chapter 8, that each individual predicts correctly the market price for each state of nature. For details, see Grossman (1975), Grossman and Stiglitz (1976) and Radner (1976).

[29] See Chapter 13 section 2 for a definition of noisy information.

are indifferent between becoming 'informed' and remaining 'uninformed'.[30]

As we remarked earlier, one route is to dispense with the rational expectations hypothesis. This is tempting because the hypothesis appears so far-fetched. Each individual is required to possess the correct theory of how the economy behaves in order to make the hypothesis credible. Such a requirement is, however, not credible. But if the rational expectations hypothesis is to be abandoned one has to postulate an alternative manner in which expectations are formed. As we noted in Chapter 8 it provides one with an open-ended subject.

All of this brings us back to the point we mentioned earlier. It is hard to judge what is the actual outcome of the economy we have been studying. But the point remains that if speculation is not prohibited, the social optimum discussed in the previous section cannot be decentralized. We should not have expected otherwise.

(ii) *Direct external economies in exploration:* It is treacherous to generalize from simple examples, but the previous discussion suggests that the speculative value of information may well lead to too early an exploration of tracts in a decentralized economy. In particular, one supposes that competition for leases leads to excessive exploration. This is one side of the coin. The other is the fact that exploration information is only partially appropriable—even if one ignores the externalities associated with the price system. If the returns from exploratory drillings at locations owned by different firms are correlated and if exploration information is not appropriable, exploration by one firm bestows direct benefits on others. Such direct informational externalities provide an incentive for firms to delay exploration, since each would ideally like the others to explore first. But even if such information is appropriable there may be a delay in exploration because it is possible that while joint exploration is profitable for the firms, independent exploration is not.

To make this last point specific, suppose the cost of exploration activity at each tract is K. Assume that each tract contains either a pool of oil of value V or nothing. There are two such tracts and the probability, in the absence of any exploration, that either tract has oil is Π. If exploration in either is successful, the conditional probability of the other tract containing oil is Π_d ($\Pi_d > \Pi$), and if it is unsuccessful the conditional probability is $\Pi_u (\Pi > \Pi_u)$. If we

---

[30] For details of such equilibria, see the references in footnote 28.

ignore time discounting, a *joint* exploration strategy would be a sequential one with expected profit.

$$W = (\Pi V - K) + \Pi[\Pi_d V - K] + (1 - \Pi) \max \{\Pi_d V - K, 0\}.$$

Now suppose that exploration information is fully appropriable. Then the expected profit to each firm from exploration is

$$W_i = \Pi V - K \qquad (i = 1, 2).$$

Since $\Pi_d > \Pi$ we can very well have $W_i < 0$ and $W > 0$.

Our extensive discussion of resource allocation with externalities in Chapter 3 suggests strongly, however, that the incentive for firms to delay exploration is greater when such information is not appropriable than it is when exploration information can be kept secret. But if information can be appropriated there may well be redundant exploration. This is reinforced if each firm engages in exploration in its own tracts with a view to obtaining information about the tracts of others and thereby undertaking speculation.

These foregoing considerations are inconclusive. We have noted several reasons why the market is likely to provide incorrect incentives for exploration activity. In this section we have paid particular attention to the public good aspect of exploration information and the speculative value of such information. These would tend to create opposing incentives. The latter encourages a rush towards exploration, and the former to delaying. There is no presumption that these opposing tendencies cancel each other.

Notes to Chapter 14

The theory of contingent commodity markets was developed by Arrow (1953) and Debreu (1959). For excellent surveys of the theory, see Radner (1970, 1974) and Guesnerie and Montbrial (1974).

Rational expectations equilibria with incomplete markets, but with fixed and identical information structures, were discussed by Hahn (1971) and Radner (1972). The optimality properties of the Radner (1972) equilibria have been explored in a definitive manner by Hart (1975), Grossman (1977) and Grossman and Hart (1978).

Radner (1968) was the first to draw attention to the structure of information assumed implicitly in the Arrow–Debreu theory. The formal part of the paper considered fixed although, unlike the Arrow–Debreu theory, non-identical information structures for the individuals postulated in the economy. The latter part discussed the problems general equilibrium theory was likely to face if information was allowed to assume the stature of commodities. This paper did much to generate interest in the economics of information in a general equilibrium context. Hahn (1973a) addressed himself to the question of what one may mean by an equilibrium when the structure of information is endogenous. Hahn's notion was formalized independently in a special context by Lucas and Prescott (1974).

In recent years explorations in the theory of general equilibrium with endogenous information structures have been pursued vigorously. The pioneering papers in this context are Lucas (1972) and Green (1973). Three collections of papers on the implications of endogenous information structures appear in symposia in the *Bell Journal of Economics* (Spring 1975), the *Quarterly Journal of Economics* (November 1976) and the *Review of Economic Studies* (October 1977). A disturbing feature of this literature has been the demonstration that seemingly innocuous economic environments often possess no non-co-operative (Nash) equilibria; see, for example, Rothschild and Stiglitz (1977), Wilson (1978), Grossman (1977) and Grossman and Stiglitz (1976). The mathematical structure of these examples has been analysed by Dasgupta and Maskin (1977). The discussion in section 4(i) of this chapter was designed to illustrate such problems in the context of exploration activity.

The literature on oil exploration is vast. For a good survey, see Grayson (1960), and more recently, the work of Gilbert (1976, 1976a). Price formation via competitive bidding is the focus of analysis in a series of papers by Robert Wilson (see, for example, Wilson (1977a)).

The economics of information is still in its infancy. Not only have the investigations merely unravelled *examples*, but we have as yet little account of the kind of optimality properties such equilibria—when they exist—possess. The discussion in sections 3 and 4(i) was designed to demonstrate these features.

CHAPTER 15

PRICE MOVEMENTS IN RESOURCE MARKETS

Introduction

The bias of this chapter is much more empirical and institutional than that of its predecessors. We hope to use it to provide illustrations of the practical importance of some of the phenomena referred to in previous chapters: many of our illustrations will be drawn from the oil industry because this is both an important industry and one that provides a very wide range of examples. However, we shall also discuss the validity of our observations in a wider context.

1. Externalities in a Dynamic Context

It was noted in Chapter 3 that the existence of external effects provides an important reason for querying whether the market mechanism would work efficiently. As we have already seen in Chapter 3, drilling for oil provides a very striking example of an externality, through what is referred to in the trade as the 'rule of capture'. Recall that the point involved here is a very simple one. Oil companies with neighbouring concessions may all drill their wells in the same reservoir, and of course the more oil is removed by anyone, the less remains for the others. Every company therefore has an incentive to remove oil as quickly as possible, and as it is expensive to store above ground, stocks are depleted, marketed and used more quickly than is desirable on grounds of economic efficiency. A well-known authority on the oil industry, M. A. Adelman (1972, p. 44) has gone so far as to say that 'given the rule of capture, therefore, and nothing more sweeping or pretentious in the way of economic assumption, the discovery of every field will mean a sudden and wasteful rush to over-produce'.

Obviously there is an important point at issue here: what is being alluded to is essentially a dynamic version of the problem of the commons that was discussed in a static context in Chapter 3, and formalized and analysed in a dynamic context in Chapter 12. There we analysed the nature of a corrective tax-and-subsidy policy, and commented that in fact such policies have rarely been adopted.

439

Of course, the importance of such a striking phenomenon has been widely recognized and, indeed, certain states in the USA have attempted to counteract this tendency towards too rapid depletion by passing laws requiring unit operation ('unitization') of oil fields—unit operation occurs when each reservoir is depleted by only one firm. With such a pattern of operation, the type of externality referred to above would cease to exist, and so therefore would the competitive scramble for rapid depletion. Adelman is somewhat sceptical about the effectiveness of unitization—remarking that 'the technical difficulties in reconciling unitization with private property in subsoil rights are admittedly very great. Even in the Soviet Union there has been slant drilling from one side of a republic's boundary into a pool on the other side: Texas cannot claim to be first here.' This last sentence certainly serves to emphasize the problems that may arise in implementing unit operation. In fact, the need to move from a situation of multiple ownership of an oil reservoir to unit operation seems to have been strongest in the USA; largely for historical reasons, oil concessions elsewhere are larger, with the result that a reservoir is more likely to be exploited by a single operator or a small number of operators.

There is another aspect of the 'rule of capture' problem which is worth mentioning. There is geological evidence to show that the total amount of oil that can be extracted from a field varies inversely with the rate at which that field is depleted. Hence competition between adjacent drilling rigs in the same oil field not only leads to an inefficiently high rate of depletion of a given stock, it also reduces the total recoverable stock. Petroleum geologists have introduced the concept of MER, or maximum efficient rate of recovery. This is a recovery rate such that up to this level, an increase in the depletion rate leads to no decline in the total ultimately recoverable, but an increase beyond this does reduce the total. Diagram 15.1 illustrates this idea by showing a typical relationship between ultimate oil recovery and the depletion rate: up to the MER, this relationship is relatively flat, but thereafter the cost of more rapid depletion, in terms of oil forgone, increases quite sharply.

2. Absence of Forward Markets

Another obvious respect in which oil markets differ from the ideal is that there are no forward markets in oil—and therefore no forward markets for contingent sales. Thus all of the issues raised in Chapters

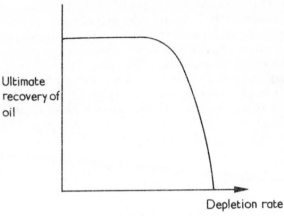

Diagram 15.1

8 and 14 become relevant; traders have to rely on their expectations of future prices in deciding how fast to deplete, and are faced with unavoidable uncertainty about future revenues.

The outcome of a situation where traders' decisions depend on their expectations of the relationship between present and future prices will, of course, depend on how those expectations are formed. We have earlier (Chapter 8) distinguished two possible ingredients of the expectation–formation process: the trend of past prices—which in the absence of a clear change in circumstances traders might reasonably extrapolate—and some index of the balance between the remaining stock of the resource and future demand for it. As a piece of casual and informal empiricism, we shall look briefly at data from the oil market in an attempt to see whether the factors we have referred to may have been amongst those operative. A more formal and rigorous test of some of the earlier models follows later.

Data on oil prices do seem compatible with the importance of the two 'ingredients' referred to above. Diagrams 15.2–15.4 show various time-series for the price of oil over the last two decades. These show that for the oils considered, which seem to be representative of those traded, prices measured in current US dollars rose to a local peak in the late 1950s, fell to a low level which they maintained during the 1960s, and in the early 1970s rose sharply. The fact that these prices are measured in current US dollars certainly deserves some comment, for during the early 1970s the dollar fell sharply in value relative to the currencies of most other industrial countries. If the prices are expressed in terms of current Deutsche marks, or current yen, then this rise seems much less sharp; much of the upward movement in the dollar price of oil in the early 1970s was simply compensation for a decline in the purchasing power of dollars. If the various time-series are expressed in constant rather than current prices, then this also has the effect of attenuating

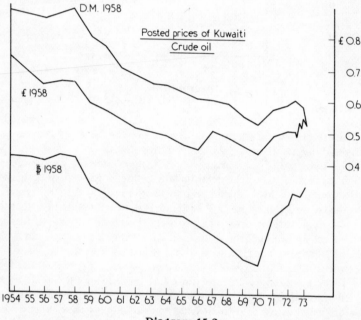

Diagram 15.2

price rises and emphasizing the falls. In many cases the February 1973 price measured in constant-purchasing-power units was actually below the price two decades earlier, substantially so in the case of prices measured in one of the stronger currencies. However, whatever adjustments one makes to allow for changes in the price level and in the values of currencies, it seems clear that there is a marked change in the behaviour of prices round about 1970. Prior to that date, prices were falling in both real and money terms, whereas

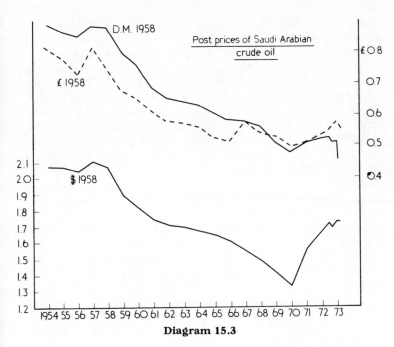

Diagram 15.3

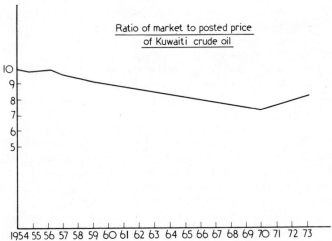

Diagram 15.4

subsequently there has been an upward trend, clearly discernible whatever adjustments are made to prices. Reference to the trade press of the oil industry confirms the idea that the advent of the 1970s marked a change in the attitude of the oil market. For example, Adelman, writing on 'The World Oil Outlook' in 1964, could start his survey with the words, 'The world oil market has and will continue to have great excess capacity', and roughly the same sentiments were expressed on many other occasions by other market analysts. A key problem of the 1960s was seen to be that of supporting the price of oil in the face of a surplus, as seen by allegations by the US Federal Trade Commission throughout the 1950s that oil companies were supporting the price of oil at an artificially high level, and by the formation of OPEC in 1960 as an organization intended to prevent the downward pressure on oil prices from being borne by producing countries. Since 1970, however, the emphasis has been entirely on the shortage of oil. The shortage of oil and the shortage of energy in general have provided the themes of a continuous stream of press comment in many different countries. Carried along no doubt by the pressure of public opinion thus created, the governments of both the USA and the UK have been moved to set up official enquiries into the possibility of serious energy shortages.

This abrupt transition from a regime where surpluses form the main source of concern, to one of an entirely opposite complexion, is a surprising phenomenon and one that repays close study. One important and interesting point is that this change in market behaviour does not seem to correspond to any similarly sharp change in the economic forces underlying the market. One might expect that it was the result of an increase in demand relative to supply, or of an increase in the growth rate of demand relative to that of supply. It is certainly true that the consumption of oil has been growing, but there does not seem to be any change in the trend in the 1970s. Nothing in the post-1970 experience seems inconsistent with the trend established in the period just before 1970. Nor has there been any fall in the rate at which additions to proven reserves have been discovered—though the exact significance of this point is open to question, as reserves are often known to exist before they are counted as proven reserves. One could regard the process of proving a reserve as simply confirming one's suspicions and making exact measurements of the parameters of the reserve. On this interpretation, it is not the amount of proven reserves that measure the remaining supply of oil, but this quantity plus a much less well-defined sum that incorporates reserves believed with high probability to exist but not yet exploited. It could, of course, be the case that this total quantity has been constant so that the increase in proven reserves has not really been indicative of an improving supply position. But even accepting this more pessimistic interpretation, there is no clear reason why 1970 should be regarded as marking a change in the supply situation.

This lack of any obvious alteration in the economic circumstances affecting the market at the turn of the decade forces us to conclude that the changes must have been in expectations, in the way people perceived economic realities rather than in those realities themselves. There are a number of factors that could have contributed to such changes. One is the different position of the United States in the world oil market. During a relatively short period starting in about 1970, the USA moved from a position of substantial self-sufficiency in oil supplies to one of substantial dependence on imports. Two consequences followed from this—an increasing recognition of their bargaining power on the part of the oil-producing countries of the Middle East and South America, and a general realization that the exhaustion of resource stocks, a possibility which had been in principle recognized but had been consigned to 'the long run', could in fact become a tangible reality. Another factor contributing to these changes in attitudes was the intellectual resurgence of neo-Malthusian analyses of the world's prospects. In spite of their well-documented shortcomings, studies such as Forrester's *World Dynamics* and Meadows' *The Limits of Growth* undoubtedly had a substantial impact on the public's assessment of the likelihood and importance of resource shortages. Both of these studies argued that continuing economic growth and population growth would in the foreseeable future result in substantial shortages of important raw materials, shortages which would be sufficient to prevent further growth and possibly even lead to economic collapse. Not surprisingly, these apocalyptic findings were given considerable publicity. This once again had the effect of making oil suppliers more aware of the strength, and oil users of the weakness, of their respective positions, and also emphasized that 'the long run' in which stocks might be depleted stretched into, but possibly not much beyond, the foreseeable future. A further contributory factor may be found in the changing financial position of some of the major oil-producing countries. There is evidence that in the 1960s, a number of Middle

Eastern countries were engaged in development programmes that had high immediate foreign exchange requirements, and because of this were placing considerable pressure on oil companies to produce more royalty payments for them. Clearly the most sensible way for the companies to meet this demand in a situation where, as was certainly the case in the 1960s, the price of oil exceeded the marginal production costs and revenue payments, was for them to increase production. The alternative would have been to pay higher royalties per barrel. In this fashion, the foreign exchange needs of the develop-ing countries contributed to the downward pressure on oil prices in the 1960s. By the early 1970s the position was rather different. Although some oil-producing countries were still short of foreign exchange—Nigeria, for example—many of the major producing countries in the Middle East were by then satiated with foreign currencies, particularly dollars. Foreign currency reserves were more than adequate to meet their development needs and, with highly unsettled world currency markets, a substantial devaluation of the dollar and rapid inflation in most industrial countries, their marginal valuation of extra foreign currency holdings was clearly very low. At least one Middle Eastern Foreign Minister was heard to declare that oil in the ground was far safer than money in a bank. Because of these circumstances, some producing countries in the early 1970s were exerting pressure to reduce the production of oil from their fields. The Libyan government, for example, ordered substantial reductions in the production rates of all oil companies in Libya in 1970 and in 1971 Kuwait followed suit. Pressure to reduce output, or at least its rate of growth, would obviously help an upward trend in prices.

On this interpretation of events, it seems that the change in market behaviour in the early 1970s followed, as asserted earlier, not from any fundamental economic changes but from changes in people's interpretation of the economic circumstances, and in particular from changes in their interpretation of the long-run balance between supply and demand in the oil market. From a situation of complacency in the 1960s, traders swung sharply to one of considerable concern in the early 1970s, prompted by the changing American fuel balance and the extensive and rather alarmist public discussion of energy supplies. When referring earlier to the way in which traders' price expectations are formed, we mentioned two important factors—the trend of past prices, which might *ceterus paribus* be expected to continue, and an index of the balance

between the remaining stock of the resource and future demand for
it. One could interpret the data discussed above by saying that up
to 1970, the first of these factors was operative. Prices in real terms
had been falling and sellers, whose bargaining power at that stage
was not thought to be very strong, operated on the assumption that
they would continue to fall. This clearly gave them an incentive to
increase, rather than reduce, their sales, which contributed to
further falls in prices and to the 'glut' of the 1960s. This trend was
reinforced by a strong desire for foreign exchange on the part of
many producing countries. This mode of market behaviour only
began to change when traders came to place increasing emphasis on
the long-run balance of supply and demand, and during the early
1970s this factor began to dominate the formation of price expectations and hence the behaviour of prices. It was, of course, reinforced
by the extrapolative mechanism: once prices seemed set on a rising
trend, this provided sellers with an incentive to hold stocks off the
market in order to realize higher future prices, and this of course
contributed to the shortages and upward pressures. Confirmation of
the importance of the incentive to hold stocks off the market is
provided by the fact that in the early 1970s oil-producing countries
were, for the first time on record, attempting to cut back the rate of
production, explicitly in order to conserve their stocks but no doubt
also to benefit from, and reinforce, the rising price trend. This whole
movement was given additional impetus by several other exogenous
factors—for instance, by random interruptions to supplies in 1971-73
due to the destruction of pipelines by terrorists, by an upsurge in
economic activity in the major industrial countries in 1972-73
which led to big increases in demand and finally, by increases in
world interest rates in the periods 1969-70 and 1972-73. As we have
seen earlier, in a dynamic market equilibrium there should be a
relationship between the rate of capital gain on resources and the
rate of return available elsewhere. Hence, increases in interest rates
should be associated with accelerations in resource price movements.

It certainly seems to be the case that price movements in the oil
market are compatible with the type of disequilibrium price adjustment model suggested earlier. The factors recognized as important
there have been operative, and indeed the market has displayed
some of the instability that the earlier discussion of disequilibrium
in Chapter 8 suggested might be possible. Of course, to explain the
behaviour of the oil market fully, it has been necessary to introduce
factors such as the American energy balance or public concern

about energy supplies, which are exogenous to the models formulated earlier.

3. Uninsurable Risks

In addition to being unable to sell oil forward, traders in the oil market are on the whole unable to insure against some of the most important risks that they face, and we now turn to an examination of this aspect of the problem. One form of risk is of course the risk that future prices will be different from those that were expected. This is an inevitable concomitant of the inability to trade forward and in some measure its consequences have already been discussed. It is apt to produce a reliance on extrapolative forecasting, and a potential for instability. The reliance on extrapolative forecasting will mean that existing trends tend to be reinforced. The effect that an inability to insure against mis-estimating future prices will have on this picture depends, of course, on the attitudes of traders towards risk. If sellers are risk-averse, then it will introduce a systematic bias towards selling now rather than storing. In a period such as the 1960s, when prices are on a downward trend, this will reinforce the trend. On the other hand, in a period when other factors are making prices rise, this risk aversion will tend to moderate the increase and reduce the extent to which traders are prepared to hold stocks off the market in order to gamble on a price increase. The oil market does, of course, present risks other than those that are inevitably associated with price uncertainty. In particular, it is rich in political risks. As the bargaining position of producing countries has become stronger and their economic independence has increased, they have asked for more favourable royalty terms. There is a clearly visible upward trend in the royalty terms they have managed to negotiate, and companies operating oil concessions must be aware of the possibility that this will continue. Obviously, this provides an encouragement to increase the depletion rate. Oil now is worth more in net revenue terms than oil in the future, and this is equivalent to an increase in the discount rate applied to future earnings.

Over and above the risk that higher royalties will be demanded, there is in many cases a non-negligible risk that concessions will be ended earlier than agreed, or that operations will be expropriated. It can be shown that the effect of such terminal date uncertainty is to increase the rate of depletion by profit-maximizing firms. According to this argument, the fact that oil companies face an undoubted risk of expropriation in some countries will increase the rate at which they deplete oil fields in those countries. Although a plausible argument, this is in fact a difficult one to substantiate. The risk of expropriation is often difficult to gauge *ex ante*, and data on the rates at which individual fields are depleted are often hard to find. However, there is very interesting evidence to show that the rate of depletion of oil concessions in Libya was increased sharply at a time at which President Gaddafi was making increasingly militant and threatening statements about foreign concerns operating in Libya. This seems a clear example of depletion rates rising as the risk rises. However, one should not jump too quickly to a conclusion of cause and effect, as other factors might have contributed to the change in depletion rates—for example, the proximity of Libyan oil to the rapidly growing Western European market, particularly at a time when the Suez Canal was closed. It may be worth noting that there is a possible feed-back effect here; and increase in the rate at which a concession is depleted because of a perceived political risk may well displease the host government, particularly if this had indeed planned to take control of the oil itself or if prices are rising so that storage seems a sensible policy, and this displeasure may in turn increase the chances of expropriation.

4. The Price of Oil

An empirical issue of some substance, to which we might reasonably address the theory developed in earlier chapters, is contained in the question: 'is the price of oil (US \$12.5 per bl in late 1978) too high?' That this question is not purely academic, in the pejorative sense of that word, is made clear by the repeated insistence of US government economic officials and of financial journalists in many countries that the price is too high. For example, on 5 November 1974, US Treasury Secretary William Simon commented that 'We are convinced, however, that no truly satisfactory solution to the present international energy problems can be achieved as long as petroleum prices remain at their present high level. In saying this, we are not simply voicing the age-old preference of consumers for low prices. We recognize that the natural inclination is for sellers to want high prices. Our studies have convinced us, however, that lower oil prices are in the long-run best interests of both producer and consumer nations.' These remarks were followed on 19 November by a reference to '. . . the costs imposed on the world

economy by exorbitant oil prices . . .' and by the statement that
'I can think of no single change that would more improve the outlook
for the world economy than a substantial decrease in the price of
oil'. Such statements naturally invite a definition of what exactly is
meant by 'too high'—an invitation rarely accepted. A reasonable
interpretation would surely be that the price of oil is too high if it
exceeds the price that would rule in a competitive spot market, if
there were no important divergences between private and social
costs associated with oil use and extraction, and there was accurate
information generally available about future supplies and demands.

Having defined a benchmark price to be used as a norm in
determining whether the market price is too high or too low, it
would seem natural to proceed by working out what numerically
this benchmark price is, and then comparing it with the present one.
Though we shall in due course consider an attempt to do this, we
shall initially proceed more obliquely and enquire into the reasoning
that might lead people to suppose, as many of them clearly do,
that $12 US per barrel exceeds the competitive price. It seems that
there are two major items of evidence that could be regarded as
supporting this point of view. One is that the present price is much
higher than that which used to prevail, and the other is the fact
that the present price exceeds marginal extraction costs (roughly
US$0.30 per bl) by an enormous margin. But it is clear that this
evidence is nothing like sufficient to prove the point at issue. Thus
the fact that the present price exceeds the earlier price by a large
margin, although there has been no commensurate change in the
long-run balance of supply and demand, proves only that at least
one of these two prices must have been 'wrong'. Further analysis
would be needed to decide whether this is the earlier or the later
one—or indeed, whether both are 'wrong', possibly in opposite
directions. Obviously, the findings of the previous section on the
movement of oil prices from the early 1950s to the early 1970s
would be very important in that further analysis. And the rather
surprising protracted and substantial fall in the price of oil during
a period of rapidly growing demand would provide a limited basis
for arguing that prices in the 1960s and early 1970s were too low,
thus countering the argument that because the 1974–75 prices are
historically high, it follows that they are too high. Another interesting and suggestive item of information is the following: if the real
price of oil had risen by about 10% per annum from 1950 on, then
by 1974 it would have been nearly US$10 per bl. And 10% per

annum is perhaps not too far from the real rate of return that could have been obtained on industrial investment over the period so that, if the prices of the early 1950s were competitive prices and the market had subsequently been in dynamic equilibrium, then one would have expected 1974 prices not too dissimilar from those actually ruling. According to our earlier analysis, the net marginal product of oil would have risen at about 10% per annum. As extraction costs have risen very little over the period—certainly no more than 10¢ per barrel in real terms—this means that the marginal product and hence price should also have risen at about 10% per annum. But, of course, there is really no more reason for taking the prices of the early 1950s as correct and a benchmark than there is for letting those of the late 1960s play this role. Hence, there is no alternative to returning an open verdict on attempts to decide whether the present price is too high or too low by reference to past prices—but one can undoubtedly return a verdict of 'not proven' on statements to the effect that the present oil price must be too high because it is so much higher than past prices.

In view of this, we should perhaps turn to the other item of evidence mentioned earlier—the substantial divergence between market price and marginal extraction costs—and see what conclusions, if any, can be drawn from this. We have already discussed, in Chapter 6 section 4, the relationship that would exist between the price and the extraction cost of a resource in a competitive market, and it was shown there that price would in general exceed extraction costs—the only exceptions being resources whose total supply exceeds the maximum amount that could profitably be used in all future periods. Only in this case would unit resource concessions become free goods so that their price—the net marginal product or the difference between the market price of the resource and its marginal extraction cost—would become zero. It follows that a market oil price in excess of extraction costs can only be accepted as evidence that the price of oil is too high if it is argued that unit oil concessions have no value, either private or social. Few people, one suspects, would be willing to argue this case though we should note in passing that much of the social value that oil concessions do currently have stems from balance of payments constraints and related institutional factors, and not from resource shortages *per se*. And it should also be noted that, although the price of oil under competitive conditions undoubtedly should exceed its marginal extraction cost, nothing in the foregoing discussion indicates the margin by which it should do so. Calculation of this margin would require a great deal of information about future supplies and demands, and about the effect of technological changes on the productivity of oil. This was made clear in Chapter 6.

5. Simulation Studies

In Chapter 11 we reported on a simulation study aimed both at explaining the oil price rise of 1973 and predicting the future price of oil. The analysis was based on the monopoly of OPEC. In an earlier work Nordhaus (1973) attempted to estimate the competitive price of oil on the basis of a simpler model. Recall the analysis in Chapter 6 section 4(ii), and in particular equation 6.23:

$$q(t) = p_0 \exp(rt) + b$$

where $q(t)$ is the competitive price of oil at date t, b and r are respectively the constant extraction cost and the discount rate, and p_0, a constant of integration, represents the initial royalty which grows at rate r. p_0 is determined by the terminal conditions that the price path has to satisfy, which in this case are that the initial stock should be exhausted at a date and price at which a backstop technology can take over.

Using available data to estimate extraction costs and terminal conditions, Nordhaus concluded that for a discount rate of 10%, the competitive price of oil in the early 1970s should have been $1.50–$2.00 per bl; at lower discount rates it was naturally higher.

A later study is that of Pindyck (1976), mentioned in the notes of Chapter 11. The model was in many ways similar to that of Nordhaus; from a theoretical point of view the main difference was in the specification of extraction costs. Pindyck's model contained variable average extraction costs given by

$$b_t = M/S_t$$

where S_t is the stock of the resource remaining at time t. The movement of extraction costs thus depends on the rate of resource depletion and becomes endogenous. This tends to raise the marginal social cost of extraction, and hence the competitive price, as discussed in Chapter 6. The point is that the marginal cost now includes both the direct resource cost of extraction b_t and also a term to reflect the impact of a decrease in the remaining stock on future costs.

In spite of the difference in cost specification, Pindyck's results for the 10% discount rate case are very similar to Nordhaus's: these and the results for a 5% discount rate are given in Table 15.1.

The implication of these studies is clearly that unless one regards a discount rate of significantly less than 5% as appropriate, the present prices *are* well above competitive levels. However, even competitive prices could be much above past prices, and indeed much above present extraction costs. This confirms the point

Table 15.1. Competitive price of oil

	$r=5\%$	$r=10\%$
1975	4·62	1·55
1977	4·85	1·71
1977	5·09	1·88
1978	5·35	2·06
1979	5·62	2·27
1980	5·90	2·50
1985	7·53	4·02
1990	9·60	6·47
1995	12·26	10·43
2000	15·65	16·79
2005	19·97	27·05
2010	25·48	

Note: All prices in 1975 US $.

already made on theoretical grounds—reference to past prices and extraction costs establishes nothing.

6. Conclusions on Oil

Although we have emphasized the difficulty in proving conclusively that the price of oil is too high, in the sense of exceeding the competitive price associated with an efficient allocation, we would of course not wish to deny that the increase in late 1973 and early 1974 has imposed severe strains on the world economy; but this is just as adequately explained by the previous price being too low, as it is by the 1974–75 price being too high. And it is perhaps even better explained by saying that the 1973–74 price change was *too rapid*— a statement which is logically quite separate from any statement about price levels. It was too rapid in the sense that the lags inherent in an adjustment from one set of relative prices for different energy sources to another very different set, are necessarily very substantial; the changes required for this adjustment involve alterations in the type of capital equipment used in generating electricity, heating and providing transport, and it is simply not possible to make major alterations in these areas in less than five years. Hence, from 1974 to the end of the decade, most economies will be operating with capital stocks appropriate to one set of factor prices, yet with a very different set of factor prices prevailing. Obviously if there had been more warning of the price increase, either from forward markets or from a more gradual upward trend in the price, the problems of adjustment would have been less serious. Equally, they would have been less serious if the capital equipment associated with oil use had been less specific to this source of energy, so that the lags and costs associated with adjustment were lower. The implications for policy are obvious: the world needs better information about likely future resource–price movements and, in fields where this cannot be provided, there should be more recognition of the merits of flexibility.

Another issue relevant to a conclusion on this subject, but not really touched on by our models, is whether the oil producers can raise the *real* price of oil to any level they choose. The point is of course that an increase in oil prices may lead to rises in the prices of goods made and sold by oil-using countries (i.e. to inflation), thus cancelling out some part of the intended increase in the real price. To the extent that this is true, it is a factor that should be taken into account in simulation studies such as those reported in section 6 above.

7. The Influence of Interest Rates

The discussion of this chapter has so far been limited to oil. Clearly there are good reasons for focusing on this market first: oil is a very important commodity and, of all exhaustible resources, it has one of the lowest stock-flows ratios. But the theory of the previous chapters is certainly of more general applicability, and in this section we shall illustrate this point by reference to a number of other commodities. Chapter 8 was devoted to an analysis of the way in which competitive resource markets might evolve under a variety of different assumptions about price adjustment behaviour and expectation formation. In this section we shall develop a model closely related to those, though a little more complicated, and report the results of testing it against data generated by the markets for several metals.

In this model, we shall suppose that there is a basic demand for the metal which is a function of its price and of the level of industrial output: this will be written

15.1 $$D = P^{\eta_P} Y^{\eta_Y}$$

where P stands for price, Y for industrial output, and η_P and η_Y are the elasticities of demand with respect to price and output, assumed to be constant. However, equation 15.1 is not a complete specification of demand conditions: we assume that, in addition to depending on price and output, demand depends on anticipated price movements. If users expect the future price to exceed the current price, they are encouraged to buy now and add to stocks, and similarly expectations of price falls encourage them to delay purchases and run down stocks. To be more precise, expectations of price increases lead to anticipatory buying if the proportional increase in prices is expected to exceed the return available on other assets that might be held instead of stocks. This introduces an opportunity cost element into the process of deciding whether to alter current demand to anticipate price movements: if the price is expected to rise by 5%, and 5% is also the opportunity cost of funds to be invested in stockbuilding, it will be a matter of indifference to the trader whether or not he anticipates the price rise by purchasing now for future use. If, however, the opportunity cost remains at 5%, whereas the expected price increase exceeds this, then stockbuilding becomes a good investment relative to other uses of funds and present demand for the resource is scaled up above that predicted by 15.1. And, of course, when the expected price increase falls below the return available elsewhere, the reverse happens.

In order to allow for these effects, we modify 15.1 to:

15.1' $$D = P^{\eta_P} Y^{\eta_Y} \left[\frac{\tilde{P}/P}{\tilde{O}/O} \right]^{a_1}$$

where $\tilde{P}$ is the expected future price of the resource, O is the price of some other asset, $\tilde{O}$ its expected future price, and $a_1 \geqq 0$ is a constant. The expression within the square brackets is thus equal to unity if the expected return to holding the commodity equals the return expected elsewhere: if the former exceeds the latter, it exceeds unity, and vice versa. And provided that $a_1 > 0$, this means that demand is scaled up or down in a way that depends on expected rates of return in commodity and other asset markets. The sensitivity of current demand to these expectations depends on the value of a_1, which is of course something we would like to measure empirically.

In order to complete the model, it is still necessary to specify several other components—a supply equation, and equations describing how the expectations $\tilde{P}$ and $\tilde{O}$ are formed. The supply function is very simple. Supply is just a function of price, though to allow for lags in the response of supply to price changes supply is a function of a weighted average of past prices, rather than of current prices only. We thus write:

$$S = S(\bar{P})$$

where $\bar{P}$ is a weighted average of past prices. The equality of supply and demand then implies that

15.2 $$S(\bar{P}) = P^{\eta_P} Y^{\eta_Y} \left[\frac{\tilde{P}/P}{\tilde{O}/O} \right]^{a_1}$$

Note that it would be reasonable to suppose suppliers to engage in speculation on future price movements, so that the supply function might also contain a term in the ratio of expected returns, raised perhaps to the power b. But it is clear from 15.2 that a_1 and b could not be identified separately, but that only their difference $(a_1 - b)$ could be identified. We can henceforth regard a_1 as this net exponent.

Taking logarithms of both sides of 15.2 and differentiating with respect to time,

15.3 $$\frac{\dot{S}}{S} = a_1 \left(\frac{\dot{\tilde{P}}}{\tilde{P}} - \frac{\dot{\tilde{O}}}{\tilde{O}} \right) \quad a_1 \left(\frac{\dot{P}}{P} - \frac{\dot{O}}{O} \right) + \eta_P \frac{\dot{P}}{P} + \eta_Y \frac{\dot{Y}}{Y}.$$

For simplicity of notation, set $\dot{P}/P = r_c$ (the return to the commodity), $\dot{O}/O = r$ (the return on other assets), $\dot{\tilde{P}}/\tilde{P} = \tilde{r}_c$, $\dot{\tilde{O}}/\tilde{O} = \tilde{r}$, and $\dot{Y}/Y = g$, the growth rate.

It is assumed that $\tilde{r}_c$ and r are exponentially weighted averages of past values of r_c and $\tilde{r}$ respectively, so that

15.4 $$\tilde{r}_c(t) = a_2 \int_{-\infty}^{t} r_c(\tau) \exp\{-a_2(t - \tau)\} \, d\tau$$

and

15.5
$$\tilde{r}(t) = a_3 \int_{-\infty}^{t} r(\tau) \exp\{-a_3(t-\tau)\}\, \mathrm{d}\tau.$$

It can be shown that these expressions imply that $\tilde{r}_c$ and $\tilde{r}$ satisfy the differential equations:

$$\dot{\tilde{r}}_c = a_2(r_c - \tilde{r}_c)$$
$$\dot{\tilde{r}} = a_3(r - \tilde{r})$$

which mean that r_c and r are formed by a process of adaptive expectations—expectations are always revised in such a way as to narrow the gap between actual and expected values of the variable, so that $\tilde{r}_c$ is raised if $r_c > \tilde{r}_c$, and vice versa. This is a very natural way to form and revise expectations, and one which has survived fairly extensive use in empirical analysis.

The weighting which determines $\bar{P}$ as a function of past values of P is more complex, and is given by the equation

15.6
$$\bar{P}(T) = \int_{0}^{T} l(1 + 9lt - \frac{9}{2} l^2 t^2)\exp(-rlt)P(t)\, \mathrm{d}t.$$

It can be shown that the weights in this expression, instead of declining exponentially into the past as in 15.4 and 15.5, rise to a peak in the recent past, and then tail off exponentially. This weighting scheme has been chosen because delays in the production of resources are often such that current supply is influenced more strongly by past than by current prices. The precise lag with which the peak weighting occurs under this system depends on the parameter l in 15.6 and in empirical studies this is usually one of the items to be estimated. Now that $\bar{P}$ is defined, it only remains to define $S(\bar{P})$: this is assumed to take the form

15.7
$$S(\bar{P}) = P^{a_4}, \qquad a_4 > 0,$$

commendably largely for its simplicity.

Substituting 15.4–15.7 into 15.3 produces, after a little manipulation

15.8
$$\ddot{r}_c(a_1 + a_4 - \eta_P) + \dot{r}_c(a_1 a_3 + a_2 a_4 + a_3 a_4 - \eta_P a_2 - \eta_P a_3)$$
$$+ r_c(a_2 a_3 a_4 - \eta_P a_2 a_3) = a_1 \ddot{r} + a_1 a_2 \dot{r} + \ddot{g}\eta_Y + \dot{g}(a_2 + a_3)\eta_Y$$
$$+ g a_2 a_3 \eta_Y$$

which is a second-order differential equation relating the rate of change of a commodity price (r_c) to the rate of return on other assets (r) and to the rate of growth of output (g). In order to test this, it was reformulated as a difference equation: the appropriate reformulation is

15.9
$$r_c(t) = A_1 r_c(t-1) + A_2 r_c(t-2) + A_3 r(t) + A_4 r(t-1)$$
$$+ A_5 r(t-2) + A_6 g(t) + A_7 g(t-1) + A_8 g(t-2)$$

where (t) denotes the value of a variable this period, $(t-1)$, a value last period, etc., and

$$A_1 = 2 - a_3 - \frac{a_2 a_4}{a_1 + a_4 - \eta_P} + \frac{\eta_P a_2}{a_1 + a_4 - \eta_P} - \frac{a_2 a_3 a_4}{2(a_1 + a_4 - \eta_P)}$$
$$+ \frac{\eta_P a_2 a_3}{2(a_1 + a_4 - \eta_P)}$$

$$A_2 = -1 + a_3 + \frac{a_2 a_4}{a_1 + a_4 - \eta_P} - \frac{\eta_P a_2}{a_1 + a_4 - \eta_P} - \frac{a_2 a_3 a_4}{a_1 + a_4 - \eta_P}$$
$$+ \frac{\eta_P a_2 a_3}{a_1 a_4 - \eta_P}$$

$$A_3 = \frac{a_1}{a_1 + a_4 - \eta_P}$$

$$A_4 = \frac{a_1 a_2 - 2a_1}{a_1 + a_4 - \eta_P}$$

$$A_5 = \frac{a_1 - a_1 a_2}{a_1 + a_4 - \eta_P}$$

$$A_5 = \frac{\eta_Y}{a_1 + a_4 - \eta_P}$$

$$A_7 = -\frac{2\eta_Y}{a_1 + a_4 - \eta_P} + \frac{\eta_Y a_2}{a_1 + a_4 - \eta_P} + \frac{\eta_Y a_3}{a_1 + a_4 - \eta_P}$$
$$+ \frac{1}{2} \frac{\eta_Y a_2 a_3}{a_1 + a_4 - \eta_P}$$

$$A_8 = \frac{\eta_Y}{a_1+a_4-\eta_P} - \frac{a_2\eta_Y}{a_1+a_4-\eta_P} - \frac{a_3\eta_Y}{a_1+a_4-\eta_P}$$

$$+ \frac{1}{2}\frac{a_2a_3\eta_Y}{a_1+a_4-\eta_P}$$

The estimation of the coefficients A_1 to A_8 in 15.9, and of the parameters η_Y, η_P and a_1 to a_4, poses severe econometric problems, which are discussed in detail in Heal and Barrow (1979). For present purposes it is sufficient to note that 15.9 and similar equations, based on slightly different assumptions about the lags involved in the response of supply to price and in the formation of expectations, give quite good explanations of observed price movements for some resources (lead, zinc and tin in particular), and those that of the parameters η_P, η_Y and a_1 to a_4 that can be estimated from the data generally have values that accord with reasonable prior expectations. For example, when 15.9 was tested against monthly data from three-month forward transactions in zinc on the London Metal Exchange over the period December 1965 to December 1976, the values of the coefficients were:

$A_1 = 0.768*$ $\quad A_2 = 0.0007$ $\quad A_3 = 0.540*$ $\quad A_4 = -0.680*$
$A_5 = 0.147$ $\quad A_6 = -0.131$ $\quad A_7 = 0.153$ $\quad A_8 = -0.071.$

Those marked by asterisks were significantly different from zero. In this estimation, r, the return on the other asset, was taken to be the return to 91-day Treasury bills, and g was taken to be the rate of growth of an index of industrial production for all OECD countries. All variables were expressed in real terms. It is clear, then, that the basic hypothesis being tested has reasonable explanatory power, and that there are significant relationships between the return to holding a commodity and that on other capital assets. But in fact it is interesting to note that the empirical work just quoted suggests that this relationship is rather different from that which theory would predict in a set of efficient intertemporal markets.

This point is best seen by noting that the three interest rate coefficients in equation 15.9 sum to zero—i.e.

$$A_3 + A_4 + A_5 = 0.$$

Clearly the numerical estimates reported above confirm that the estimated coefficients do indeed satisfy this restriction—and, as reported in detail elsewhere, this confirmation is strikingly repeated in studies of other markets. Now, an equation with this adding-up property can be written:

$$r_c(t) = b_1 r(t) + b_2 r(t-1) - (b_1 + b_2) r(t-2)$$

or

$$r_c(t) = b_1 \{ r(t) - r(t-1) \} + (b_1 + b_2) \{ r(t-1) - r(t-2) \}$$

or

$$r_c(t) = b_1 \Delta r(t) + b_2 \Delta r(t-1)$$

where $\Delta r(t) = r(t) - r(t-1)$, etc. The rate of change of the resource price is therefore seen to depend not on the level but on the rate of change of the interest rate—a subtle but important difference from the relationship that would characterize an efficient allocation. As the model analysed above predicts this outcome, it should be possible to use it to provide an explanation of the phenomenon: to derive this, it is necessary to consider the full relationship between r_c and r:

$$r_c(t) = A_1 r_c(t-1) + A_2 r_c(t-2) + A_3 r(t) + A_4 r(t-1) + A_5 r(t-2).$$

Collecting terms, this can be rewritten as

$$\begin{aligned} B_1 r_c(t) + B_2 \Delta r_c(t) + B_3 \Delta r_c(t-1) &= b_1 \Delta r(t) + b_2 \Delta r(t-1) \\ &\quad + A_6 g(t) + A_7 g(t-1) + A_8 g(t) \end{aligned}$$

15.10

where b_1 and b_2 are as before, and

$$B_1 = 1 - A_1 - A_2, \qquad B_2 = A_1 + A_2, \qquad B_3 = A_2.$$

The relationship between r_c and r in this equation is asymmetric, in that one has on the left hand side both the current value of r_c and its current and lagged rates of change: r, however, appears *only* in rate of change form. This reflects an asymmetry to be found in equation 15.8, where $\ddot{r}_c$, $\dot{r}_c$ and r_c all appear on the left, while only $\ddot{r}$ and $\dot{r}$—the rates of change but not the level—appear on the right. In fact the basic asymmetry can be traced back further, to the demand function 15.1. Here demand is shown as depending on both the level of the resource price (via P^{η_P}) and on its rate of change (via $\tilde{P}/P$), while it depends only on the rate of change of the price of the other asset. It is easy to confirm that if one were to set $\eta_P = 0$ and $a_4 = 0$, establishing a symmetric treatment of the two prices in the demand and supply functions, then $A_1 + A_2 = 1$ and $B_1 = 0$, so that in 15.9 both r_c and r appear only as current and lagged differences. An alternative condition that would yield symmetric treatment is that $a_2=0$ or $a_3=0$—that is, that in one of the two markets concerned, traders should have static expectations about rates of return. This would also imply that $A_1+A_2=1$. But it is easy to confirm from the empirical estimates that $A_1+A_2\neq1$, so that it is neither the case that $\eta_P=a_4=0$, nor that $a_2=0$ or $a_3=0$, and the asymmetry postulated by the model seems justified.

Of course, the causes of this asymmetry give us some indication of the reasons why the present model behaves rather differently from the efficient, competitive model. Let us consider carefully the two possible sources of this discrepancy, which are (i) the asymmetric treatment of the two prices in the demand and supply equations, and (ii) the processes by which expectations are formed.

What, in economic terms, is the justification for the differences in the treatments of the two prices and thus of r_c and r? The point is that the model reflects two types of demand for the resource—speculative demand depending on price changes, and a user demand depending on the demand for final products and the prices of substitutes. This latter is naturally a function of the price level—hence the inclusion of this term in the demand function—whereas the speculative demand is a function of resource price movements relative to movements elsewhere. This is clearly as it should be, and cannot of itself be the source of the discrepancy between the present model and an efficient outcome. For in a competitive market the price would, under suitable and familiar assumptions, rise at the rate of return elsewhere, leaving resource owners completely indifferent about the date at which they supply their resource. The time-pattern of use would then be determined by users (i.e. by derived demand), who would equate the marginal productivity of the resource to its price at each date.

It thus seems completely natural that both the level and the rate of change of price should enter into the demand function for the resource, so we must seek the source of the discrepancy under discussion in the facts that $a_2\neq0$ and $a_3\neq0$. (Heal and Barrow (1979) present direct evidence that these are coefficients non-zero.) Consider for a moment the implications of $a_2=a_3=0$. These are that $\dot{\tilde{r}}_c=\dot{\tilde{r}}=0$, so that $\tilde{r}_c$ and r are constant. The return on the other asset is expected to be constant, as is the return on the resource. The resource price is thus expected to grow exponentially over time at a constant rate. Hence if $a_2=a_3=0$, expectations may be compatible with efficient functioning of the market, in that efficiency requires that if r is constant then the resource price rises at rate r, and when $a_2 = a_3 = 0$, traders may expect such a situation. We emphasize that one can say only that they may expect such a situation; they are not precluded from doing so, though whether or not they actually do so depends on initial conditions, which are historically given and exogenous to the model. We are, of course, already familiar, from the theory of Chapters 6 and 8, with situations where the efficiency of the system depends on initial conditions.

The general, albeit tentative, conclusion from this empirical work seems to be that there is a relationship between the movements of resource prices and the returns to other assets, and indeed this relationship is quite strong, though it is not of the form that would be generated by efficient markets. The principal cause of this difference would seem to be the manner in which expectations are formed.

There is one simple but important point that ought to be made about the interpretation of the results just discussed. This is that the metal prices used in the studies were all prices of refined metals. However, the decision on whether or not to deplete is a decision about unextracted and unrefined ones, not about refined metals, and is therefore influenced by the rate of change of the ore price and not the rate of change of the metal price. But as the demand for ore is a derived demand, derived from the demand for the metal, these two are clearly connected. We can see this connection by calculating an imputed or implicit price for the ore: this will obviously be the price of the refined product, P_R, minus the marginal costs of extraction and refining:

15.11 $$P_0 = P_R - C(Q)$$

where P_0 is of course the imputed price of ore, and $C(Q)$ is the unit cost of extraction and refining, which may depend on Q, the amount processed. Note that $C(Q)$ will of course depend on the quality of the ore, being lower for higher grade ores. There will therefore be an imputed price P_0 for each grade of ore.

From 15.1 it follows that the imputed rate of return to a particular grade of ore is

15.12 $$\frac{\dot{P}_0}{P_0} = \frac{\dot{P}_R}{P_R - C} - \frac{C'\dot{Q}}{P_R - C}.$$

In the case when $C(Q)$ is independent of Q—i.e. unit costs are independent of the level of production—this simplifies considerably to

15.13
$$\frac{\dot{P}_0}{P_0} = \frac{\dot{P}_R}{P_R} \quad \frac{1}{(1 - C/P_R)}.$$

The term $1/(1 - C/P_R)$ is unity when $C=0$, and tends to infinity as C tends to P_R, it is therefore small for high-grade ores where cost is small relative to refined price, but very large for low-grade ore for which the reverse is true. It thus emerges that when costs are constant, the imputed return to the ore is equal to the return to the refined product multiplied by a number which might by analogy with financial terminology be called a gearing factor, which rises as the quality of the ore falls. One can see from this that low-grade ores are more risky than high-grade ores, in that equal variations in the return to the refined product induce much larger fluctuations in the return to the former than in the return to the latter.

The case of non-constant unit costs is a little more complex: the second term in 15.12 is no longer zero, but can be rewritten as

$$\frac{\dot{Q}}{Q} \frac{C'Q}{(P_R - C)}$$

and on the assumption of a linear marginal cost schedule with a zero intercept, this reduces to

$$\frac{\dot{Q}}{Q} \frac{C/P_R}{(1 - C/P_R)}$$

and the whole expression in 15.12 is then

$$\frac{\dot{P}_0}{P_0} = \left(\frac{\dot{P}_R}{P_R} - \frac{\dot{Q}}{Q} \frac{C}{P_R}\right) \frac{1}{(1 - C/P_R)}$$

so that the return imputed to the ore depends not only on the return on the refined product and the gearing factor, but also on the rate of growth of production. Obviously, if this is zero and output is held constant, we are back once again to the relatively simple expression in 15.13.

It should be clear from this that the relationship between $\dot{P}_0/P_0$ and r will not, particularly over relatively short periods, be qualitatively different from that between $\dot{P}_R/P_R$ and r. It is thus reasonable to suppose that relationships such as those found between r_c and r also hold for $\dot{P}_0/P_0$ and r.

8. The Work of Barnett and Morse

In addition to the relatively recent studies already mentioned, there is a pioneering study by Barnett and Morse (1963); no survey of empirical work could be complete without reference to this. They compiled and analysed data on the prices and costs of a number of resources produced in the United States over the period 1870–1957. The salient features of their data are:

(1) that for almost all extractive products, the average cost of extraction, in constant prices, fell over this period;

(2) that for almost all extractive products, price fell slightly relative to an index of output prices during the period studied. The data supporting this second conclusion are reproduced in Diagram 15.5.

Barnett and Morse use this data to test the hypothesis that resources were becoming increasingly scarce in the United States during this period: and they concluded that as neither prices nor costs rose, this could not have been the case—the assumption here being that increasing scarcity would manifest itself in cost or price increases. In fact, it is not at all clear that this is the only interpretation, or indeed, the most persuasive interpretation, that can be drawn from this data. To see this, we consider it in the context of the models analysed earlier. The fact that average extraction costs declined over the period suggests that the most appropriate model will be one with extraction costs independent of the level of cumulative extraction, but perhaps declining at an exogenously given rate because of technical progress in the extractive industries. In such a case, the difference between price and marginal extraction costs would grow at the interest rate in a competitive situation. Letting $p(t)$ be the competitive price at t, $M(t)$ the marginal extraction cost at t, and r the interest rate, this implies that

$$\frac{\dot{q}(t) - \dot{M}(t)}{q(t) - M(t)} = r$$

or

$$q(t) = M(t) + \{q(0) - M(0)\} \exp(rt)$$

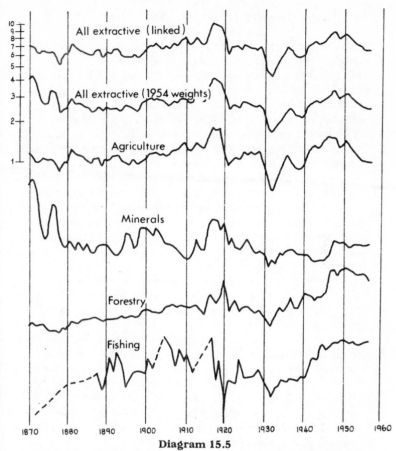

Diagram 15.5

Note: Solid lines connect points in annual series, dashed lines connect points
over a year apart. (From Barnett and Morse, p. 210.)

where $q(0)$ depends on the size of the initial stock of the resource.
A change in the perceived resource stock at some date after the
initial one would lead to a change in this constant and hence to a
discrete jump in price, downwards in the case of unanticipated
discoveries of new stocks. For the moment we take it that known
resource availabilities are constant, and consider the movement of
prices in this situation. If extraction costs decline over time at a
rate α to a constant M

15.14 $\dot{q}(t) = M(0) \exp(-\alpha t) + \{q(0) - M(0)\} \exp(rt) + M,$

so that the price path may show an initial period of decline, but in the long run will rise approximately exponentially.

Now we have a theory and some data: what conclusions can be drawn? Barnett and Morse chose to phrase their conclusions in terms of 'increasing scarcity' of resources. It is not clear that this is a felicitous choice of terminology, as in some absolute sense exhaustible resources are by definition scarce. But this is essentially a terminological point, and it is certainly open to anyone to propose as a measure of scarcity the marginal or average extraction cost. If we accept the latter as a measure of scarcity, then the Barnett–Morse data make the conclusion of decreasing scarcity unavoidable. But it is not really clear that this definition of scarcity—and the question to which it naturally leads—is the most penetrating and helpful approach to the issue. In many ways it seems more natural to take as a benchmark the rate of depletion that would be attained in competitive markets, and then enquire whether depletion thus far has exceeded or fallen short of this rate. In the former event, there would seem to be grounds for worrying about excessive scarcity. Of course, a sufficient condition for depletion to date to exceed the competitive depletion level is that prices to date should have fallen below their competitive levels; in approaching this matter it is thus natural to proceed by comparing the actual and competitive price paths. Unfortunately there is no simple (or even complex) way of computing the competitive path for the whole period 1870–1957. However, it does seem reasonable to claim that it would have taken exceedingly high and sustained rates of cost-reducing technical progress in extractive industries to generate a competitive price path that was declining over so long a period— especially in view of the undoubted incidence of diminishing returns in several sectors of the extractive industry. We can therefore suggest rather tentatively that, while the actual prices of extractive products fell over the period studied, competitive equilibrium prices would have shown a rising trend for at least the later part of this period. Now of course this observation on its own is not sufficient to establish that there is any part of the period during which the competitive path lay above the actual, as Diagram 15.6 demonstrates. To establish convincingly what one is tempted to infer from this observation—namely that for at least part of the period resources were under-priced and over-consumed—requires considerably more research. But the inference is nevertheless tempting, because for a period as long as that studied the positive exponential term in 15.14 seems bound to dominate. Thus setting $r=0.10$ at $t=87$, $\exp(rt)$ exceeds 1500 and is growing rapidly, whereas for $t=87$ the first term will be approximately constant at zero. One would thus expect that the price would be high by historical standards, and rising rapidly. Such an inference is obviously contrary in spirit to the rather comforting conclusions that Barnett and Morse drew from their own study.

The above arguments are all based on the premise that at the beginning of the period under discussion the total available resource

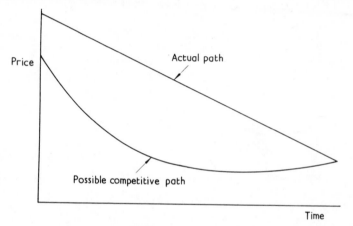

Diagram 15.6

stock was known with certainty. Such a premise is evidently unreasonable, as over the interval studied there have been large increases in the known reserves of most resources, with the great majority of these increases being unanticipated. A simple and appealing intuitive argument might suggest this as the source of the disparity between the theoretical model just constructed, and Barnett and Morse's results. For it may seem plausible that an increase in the stock of a resource will result in a period of falling resource price. In fact, of course, the analysis in Chapter 6 tells us that this will not be the case. Ignoring extraction costs for the moment, we know that if additional reserves are discovered in the future, and if these discoveries are fully anticipated, there will be a discontinuous drop in the price of the resource at the dates of discovery, provided these discoveries are separated by sufficiently large intervals of time.[1] But during intervals separating these discoveries the spot price of the resource will rise at the rate of interest. But the situation we wish now to envisage is one where the discoveries are not anticipated with certainty. By assumption both the magnitude and the timing of new discoveries are uncertain. This being the case earlier reserves will not have been entirely depleted at the dates of new discoveries. Therefore, those who hold earlier reserves at these random discovery dates will experience capital losses on their holdings.[2] It follows that even if resource owners are

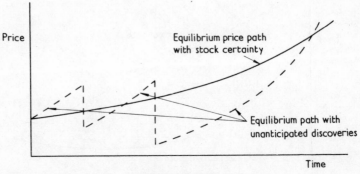

Diagram 15.7

risk-neutral the resource price must, between discovery dates, rise at a rate exceeding the (sure) rate of interest so that the *expected* rate of return to holding stocks does not fall short of the sure rate of interest.[3] We then arrive at the conclusion that random discoveries of new deposits lead to discontinuous drops in price (at the dates of discovery) and to price paths which rise at rates exceeding the sure rate of interest in the intervals between discoveries. Diagram 15.7

[1] We proved this formally in Chapter 6 section 4 for the case where the discovery is of a backstop technology. The reader can confirm that the argument holds even if the discovery is of an additional reserve, and indeed if there is a sequence of anticipated discoveries.

[2] As the discussion in Chapter 6 section 4 made clear, this will not happen if the discoveries are fully anticipated. Either there will not be a fall in price (if the intervals between discoveries are short) or, if there is, past reserves will have been entirely depleted at the discovery dates.

[3] This is proved formally in Dasgupta and Stiglitz (1976).

illustrates this along a sample path. The effect of a rapid set of unanticipated discoveries of additional reserves is thus more complex than a simple fall in the price trend. It increases the upward trend in the price, but the price drops with each new discovery.

Because of the complexity of this effect, it is difficult without further detailed quantitative study to know how far it should be allowed to qualify the earlier very tentative inference that resource price paths have been below their competitive levels. Indeed, the answer would almost certainly vary from case to case, because additions to known reserves have varied greatly from mineral to mineral.

9. Conclusions

The object of this chapter has not really been to establish conclusions—at least, not conclusions about its apparent subject matter: actual depletion rates and market biases. Just as the *a priori* analyses indicate that markets may over- or under-conserve, depending on circumstances, so the various empirical studies cited seem capable of conflicting, or ambiguous, interpretations. However, given the paucity of empirical work in this field, such a situation is to be expected. The real purpose of the chapter has been to indicate that working within the theoretical framework established earlier does give valuable insights into empirical phenomena, and does enable one to pose questions about the desirability of current resource-depletion rates in a manner which is intellectually rigorous and yet still in principle capable of empirical resolution. This is, we feel the reader will agree, no mean achievement.

Notes to Chapter 15

A standard source of data on the world oil market is Adelman (1972), and a good reference on legislation affecting petroleum extraction in the United States, especially as it affects common property resource problems, is MacDonald (1971). The empirical analysis of oil prices presented in section 3 is similar to that developed by Heal (1975a): the same volume contains useful surveys of empirical matters in the energy field by Robinson (1975) and Surrey and Page (1975).

Nordhaus's analysis is presented with an interesting discussion, in Nordhaus (1973); Kay and Mirrlees (1975) have an argument which is related to Nordhaus's about the time-path of the relationship between price and extraction cost.

The results presented in summary and non-technical form in section 8 are presented in detail in Heal and Barrow (1979); although the hypothesis of a relationship between changes in resource prices and interest rates is an obvious one to test, there seems to be little other work directed at this issue. Probably most closely related is the analysis of Barnett and Morse (1973), which is discussed in section 9. As indicated there, they are not explicitly concerned with evaluating the efficiency of markets, but do produce interesting data on the long-run behaviour of prices and costs. Most of their data is drawn from a very valuable compendium by Potter and Christy (1962); a more recent analysis of this material can be found in Smith (1974).

CHAPTER 16

CONCLUSIONS

Introduction

One of the most striking aspects of the problems analysed in the foregoing chapters is the intellectual breadth and depth of the issues involved, and this makes conclusions particularly difficult to draw. One is perhaps more conscious of unsolved problems than of clear-cut conclusions, and indeed one function of this chapter must be to emphasize the substantial deficiencies that still exist in our under-standing. But before doing so let us take stock of some of our major conclusions.

Besides providing a guide for future strategies, this can also give valuable reassurance that problems, which seem impossibly difficult at first sight, may eventually be viewed from an angle which makes their basic structure clear and tractable. Our conclusions in this chapter are offered in this spirit of providing guidance and re-assurance rather than attempting to provide categorical and simple answers to the questions we have studied.

Among the problems that have been our concern, at last two can be stated very simply: under what conditions will a market system allocate exhaustible resources in such a manner that the marginal social value of a resource is equal in all uses and constant over time, so that the benefits accruing from its use are maximized? And how should a government construct plans or conduct project evaluation exercises to achieve the same ends?

1. The Behaviour of Markets

At a formal level, an answer to the first of these questions is easily given, in the form of the sufficient conditions mentioned in Chapters 2 and 4 supplemented by the additional conditions intro-duced in connection with uncertainty in Chapter 14. Taken together, these are as follows:

(1) That there should be perfect competition, no externalities, and no non-convexities in either production possibility sets or preferences;

(2) that at the initial date there should exist a complete set of forward contingent commodity markets, on which it is possible to buy or sell goods for delivery in any future time-period and state of the world;

(3) that the only budget constraint faced by transactors should be one requiring that the present value of net revenues be non-negative.

These conditions are unusually restrictive, and are clearly not in general satisfied. We have focused attention on two particular types of violation of this ideal—the non-existence of a complete set of markets and the non-competitive nature of markets.

Externalities arise when property rights in a resource are not readily defined; in consequence, they may play an important role in determining the depletion rates of both exhaustible and renewable resources. The phenomenon is exemplified by 'slant drilling' and the 'rule of capture' in the oil industry, and also by various informational externalities associated with the process of bidding for resource concessions. With renewable resources, the role of externalities is more dramatic and underlies the continuing international disputes over the law of the sea as it affects fishing and mineral exploitation rights in the open seas. Behaviour that was conditioned by, and in turn gave rise to, the existence of significant externalities, may also have been instrumental in leading to the erosion of once valuable grazing lands and the extinction of some animal species. It is clear, then, that externalities are an important problem. Fortunately the problem is one that economists understand fairly well, and in Chapters 3 and 5 we analysed a variety of legislative devices that might be used to overcome the allocative ill-effects of externalities. The possibilities mentioned were the introduction of markets in the external effects, the use of legislation to enforce private property rights on a previously common-property resource, or the control of individual agents by taxation or regulation. There are, of course, situations where none of these approaches will work, but nevertheless they constitute a range of options which will probably prove useful in all but the most complex cases.

The problems associated with the non-existence of a suitable set of forward markets may well be more important and less tractable than those arising from externalities. The simpler of the analytical problems to which this gives rise is the inability of traders to insure against significant future risks. As we have seen in Chapters 13 and 14, the impact of this on resource allocation will, not surprisingly, depend on attitudes towards risk; with risk-aversion, presumably the common case, there is a presumption that it will lead to 'excessively rapid' depletion. Besides leading to uninsurability, the non-existence of markets means that traders have no systematic way of obtaining information on future prices or, equivalently, on future supplies and demands. A consequence of this, which has been noted and exploited by some of our more entrepreneurial professional colleagues, is the existence of a substantial demand for what purport to be accurate forecasts. A more serious consequence is that traders' expectations about the future play a crucial role in determining the allocation of resources. As we saw in Chapter 8 many outcomes are then possible, and few of them are efficient. The empirical analysis of Chapter 15 seemed, albeit tentatively, to confirm one's a priori suspicion that the time-paths generated by resource markets may bear little relationship to efficient paths.

Obviously, it is not easy to give appropriate policy responses to the problems just summarized, simply because they are so basic to the operation of the system. Policy measures which provided better information about the future would obviously be appropriate, as they would both reduce the volatility and increase the accuracy of expectations, and also reduce the risks that traders perceive. At a rather mundane level, better information about the future could be made available by encouraging the development of better forecasting techniques and by widespread dissemination of forecasts. It should not be overlooked that government policy is an important determinant of future economic conditions, so that a reduction in governmental secrecy about future intentions may be a necessary precondition for better forecasting. A slightly more substantial point is that it may be easier to provide better information about the future if the future is made more predictable. This suggests that governmental commitments to the maintenance of economic stability could yield benefits in terms of more efficient intertemporal resource allocation. This line of analysis might seem to be linked with recent discussions of the possibility of stabilizing the behaviour of commodity markets. The Lomé Convention signed in January 1975 between the European Economic Community and a number of associated developing countries contained provisions for the stabilization of the export earnings of commodity-producing countries, and similar schemes have been discussed by the Commonwealth Prime Ministers' Conference, by the US Government and by the International Monetary Fund. In fact these schemes aim to compensate for fluctuations in the export earnings of commodity-producing countries by providing transfer payments or liberal credit facilities when prices are low, rather than by stabilizing prices. They are therefore aimed at reducing the macro-economic uncertainty facing the exporting countries rather than at reducing the price uncertainty facing traders, and so are not directly relevant to the issues we have been discussing, except in so far as they may contribute to overall economic stability.

Although none of the schemes under development involves price stabilization, there have been proposals which would involve price stabilization, and indeed this is the approach adopted on many domestic agricultural markets. Could such an approach prove valuable on international resource markets? The problem seems to be that stabilization can only reduce the uncertainty associated with the operation of a market if those who run the stabilization scheme have better information than traders about future market conditions. This is unlikely to be the case. Indeed one can argue that it should not be the case, as it is implicit in our earlier arguments that the best information should be made available to all. If stabilizers are no better informed than traders, all that they can hope to do is to change the form of the uncertainty; they may transform price uncertainty into uncertainty about the amounts to be sold at relatively constant prices, or into uncertainty about the size of stabilization agency stockpiles and losses. This type of transformation may be beneficial; for example, there may be distributional gains from transferring risks from traders to those who finance a stabilization agency, though with metals and energy sources this seems unlikely. There might in addition be resource-allocation gains if the transfer of risks from traders to a stabilization agency leads to their being spread more widely, or to their being borne by those who are risk-neutral. In either case, the risks will have less impact on individual, and therefore on market, behaviour.

2. Planning

Perhaps not surprisingly, the problems of constructing plans or conducting project evaluation exercises in such a way as to ensure welfare-maximizing use of exhaustible resources are not significantly easier than those of designing policies to ensure the same outcome from markets. Fundamental to both sets of problems are the existence of substantial uncertainty about relevant future parameters and the need to take a very long-term view. In the absence of uncertainty or, more interestingly, in the presence of certain types of uncertainty which are equivalent to terminal date uncertainty, it is possible to produce a relatively simple characterization of the optimal depletion policy for a closed economy. The optimal rate of resource-depletion depends on parameters such as the discount rate, the elasticity of marginal felicity, the elasticity of substitution between resources and produced inputs, and the marginal productivity of produced inputs at very low levels of resource use. It is intuitively plausible that these parameters should enter in the way that they do, and the simple formulae that result enable us to produce very rough estimates of appropriate depletion rates for closed economies or for the world as a whole. Obviously, these estimates can be no better than extremely rough because of the dearth of firm statistical estimates of the technological parameters concerned, and because of the inevitable subjective nature of any choices of parameters relating to the objective function.

3. Research and Development

There are a number of important problems in the field of resource depletion that we have merely glanced at in the preceding pages. We shall mention one of the most important and difficult ones here— the allocation of resources to research and development (R and D) aimed at loosening the resource constraints currently operative. As a general rule, technical progress on its own is hard to model. The problems of modelling the effects of R and D are therefore particularly acute: it is necessary both to describe the occurrence of technological change and to specify the relationship between the allocation of effort to R and D and the resulting effect on changes in technology. Almost certainly, an important aspect of this relationship is that it contains a significant random element in that it is impossible to predict in advance the results of a particular research programme. In view of these complexities it is fortunate that a number of important points can be made without any explicit modelling of the R and D–technological change link. These are all statements about the extent to which one could rely on market forces to produce an optimal allocation of resources to R and D.

In Chapter 14 we noted a number of reasons why a market system cannot be expected to produce, an optimal allocation of resources to R and D, and that these are all related to the types of market imperfection that have been exemplified often in the preceding pages. It is therefore an unavoidable conclusion that there will in general be a strong case for government support for activities designed to promote a technological advance, and this is indeed the typical situation even in the most market-orientated economies. Obviously, the fact of such substantial involvement raises a new set of issues, concerning the nature of the policy that a government should pursue in this field. Can one make any progress in defining an optimal policy towards R and D? This is a major question which is still substantially unanswered, but there have been a small number of rather tentative attempts to derive conclusions. We shall end this section by discussing briefly such an attempt of our own.[1]

It seems appropriate to consider R and D as a form of investment; it is an investment with a particularly uncertain return designed to alter future production possibilities. With this point in mind, we can consider a simple model of a system similar to those used for studying optimal depletion policies in Chapter 10. The technology is initially such that a resource and capital goods are used to produce output, which may be either consumed or reinvested or used in R and D. There is only a finite amount of the resource, but there is the possibility that at some random future date a substitute for the resource may be discovered. The parameters of the probability distribution describing the possible occurrence of this substitute are not fixed, but can be altered by R and D. There are thus two forms of investment that are alternatives to current consumption: conventional investment in capital equipment, and investment in altering the chances of a major technological advance which will effectively abolish the resource constraint.

Within the context of such a model, one can analyse the factors that influence the optimal allocation of current output to R and D. Two types of parameter seem to have a bearing on this in the long run: parameters relating to the structure of the preferences embodied in the objective function, and parameters describing the way in which the probability of technological change responds to the accumulation of knowledge as a result of research. Obviously, this latter class of parameters is extraordinarily difficult to specify *a priori*, and there seems to be no empirical data on which to base guesses.[2] We shall therefore concentrate on the former. The two relevant items here are the felicity discount rate and the elasticity of marginal felicity. The felicity discount rate in particular seems to play a very important role in the long-run behaviour of an optimal R and D policy. This is perhaps something not generally

---

[1] See Dasgupta, Heal and Majumdar (1977).
[2] But see Koopmans *et al.* (1978).

recognized in the literature on R and D, though it should not be of great surprise. R and D is, as we have said, a form of investment with an uncertain and possibly long-delayed payoff, and it is natural that the desirable allocation of resources to such an activity will be sensitive to the discount rate. It is also relatively easy to see why the elasticity of marginal felicity is important. The opportunity cost of research is current consumption forgone, and the benefit is extra consumption in the future. The higher is the absolute value of the elasticity of marginal felicity and thus the more sharply curved is the felicity function, the greater are the costs of forgoing consumption and the less the benefits (see Chapter 10).

Before concluding our discussion of R and D, it is worth observing that model-building in this area presents some peculiarly difficult problems, problems which the foregoing discussion has firmly eschewed. The point is that many of the most important products of research activities have been concepts and techniques that were completely unknown only a quarter of a century prior to their discovery. Examples are the invention of antibiotics or transistors. Of course, much of the output of R and D is more predictable and consists of predictable developments and refinements of existing technologies. This is the type of activity modelled in the analysis outlined in the earlier part of this section. The development of fusion reactors provides an interesting illustration of these points. The principles of the technology are known and understood, but there is considerable doubt about the date by which, and the costs at which, it might be implemented. These uncertainties can easily be represented analytically, and indeed are so represented in the work we referred to. However, modelling the allocation of resources to the discovery of ideas and techniques that we cannot even conceptualize at present, and of whose potential existence we are completely unaware, is altogether a different matter. Indeed, philosophers of science writing in the Popperian school have placed considerable emphasis on the impossibility, in principle, of predicting future developments in the state of knowledge. They argue that to predict such developments one must describe them, and one can only describe a state of knowledge if one possesses that knowledge already. Thus, according to this viewpoint, one cannot even aspire to the construction of models of the rational allocation of resources to fundamental research, but only to development; fundamental research must remain a speculation governed by the 'animal spirits' of the Keynesians.

Just as an awful warning of the solecisms that even the most distinguished authorities can commit in this field, we conclude with a quotation from the September 1876 *Scientific American*. 'A recent lecture was given by Professor Carey Foster, F.R.S., at South Kensington on "Electricity as a Mode of Power". Dr. Siemens, F.R.S., took the chair. Professor Foster first showed with a number of experiments that by very simple arrangements light bodies can be moved by electricity . . . Although we cannot say what remains to be invented, we can say that, so far as is presently known, there seems no reason to believe that electricity will be used as a practical mode of power. There is always power lost by the inverse current. Work of some kind must be done to produce electricity, and this can more economically be done by employing that power directly.'

4. Are There Exhaustible Resources?

Intellectual and political fashions are very fickle. In the early 1970s there was widespread agreement that the exhaustibility of a number of significant resources was a fact of great importance. Five years later, the pendulum is perhaps swinging back again. One now hears much more emphasis placed on the availability of substitutes, both natural and synthetic, for resources that are in relatively short supply, and on the existence of very extensive low-grade resource deposits. Does this then mean that exhaustibility is no longer seen to be an important characteristic of resources? The answer to this must be negative, for two reasons.

One is that, even if there are synthetic substitutes or low-grade deposits, the prime high-grade deposits of a resource will still in due course be depleted, and we must worry about the rate and timing of this depletion and of the transition to the alternative source. This is the type of issue discussed in Chapter 6, where we considered the sequential depletion of a number of ore deposits of different costs, and also the transition to a backstop technology. A related issue arose in Chapter 11, when we considered the influence of imperfect market structures on the date at which a backstop would be introduced. We have seen that in properly functioning markets, all of these transitions would be made smoothly and would be accurately anticipated by market participants. There is, however, little doubt that market failures, leading to incorrect or inadequate anticipation of these transitions or to price jumps rather than to smooth price movements during the transitions, could in practice cause major economic dislocations. This was the type of effect we were referring to in Chapter 15, when we argued that the most striking feature of the oil price movements in 1973 was that they were too sudden.

The second reason for being concerned with exhaustibility, even though substitutes may be available, is that there is little definite information in this area. Statements about the availability of synthetic substitutes often contain at least an element of techno-logical speculation, and those about the existence of low-grade ores usually contain assumptions that not all geologists would find acceptable. This is very clear in the field of energy resources. There are many technologies which might in some measure act as sub-stitutes for exhaustible resources—solar power, wave power, etc.—but there is so much doubt about estimates of their costs and performances that there would clearly be some element of risk in relying on these. In general, we encounter situations where there is certainly a possibility of substitutes for exhaustible resources, but where this possibility is sufficiently ill-defined that no single estimate of the cost, quantity or date of availability can be accepted. In such situations, it would clearly be foolhardy to rely on any par-ticular estimates for the substitute. The only sensible approach is to recognize that at present the characteristics of the alternative must be viewed as random, and as described by a distribution which may well assign positive probability to its non-availability. Such a recognition forces us once again to deal with the consequences of exhaustibility, though admittedly as one of several possibilities rather than as a datum.

5. Final Remarks

Obviously, a principal aim in writing a book on the economics of exhaustible resources must be to define the economic problems relating to the use of such resources, to analyse the manner in which economic systems are likely to use such resources, and to attempt to set up ideal standards of resource-use by comparison with which actual outcomes may be judged and on which policies may be based. These are the standard stages in an economic analysis of any problem. In writing the present book, we have also had a subsidiary objective: that of demonstrating that many of the important problems in this area do have a substantial economic dimension and that the existing corpus of economic theory is capable of posing interesting questions in this field in a tractable way. We have felt a need to make explicit reference to this point because one of the most conspicuous characteristics of some of the more widely publicized studies of the impact of resource depletion has been their lack of any economic framework or analysis—though to be sure this is not the only fault that the critics have found with them. In so far as this omission stemmed from a judgement by their authors that economic analysis had little to contribute to the problems they were studying, we hope that we have shown it to be based on a false premise. But it is also possible that the omission stemmed from a feeling that, although economists might have much to say, they had few simple and clearcut answers to give. Obviously, we would not dissent from such a judgement. Indeed we would rather like to emphasize it. The world in all of its empirical and institutional glory is a remarkably complex place, and a willingness to recognize this to the extent of eschewing simple and striking statements for less glamorous but more complex conclusions must be regarded as a sign of intellectual maturity. No doubt the attractions of being a prophet, be it of economic doom or of economic redemption, are very great; but the social value of prophecy, as opposed to careful and dispassionate analysis of the logic and facts of a problem, has never been notable. So we hope that our analysis of the logic and facts of resource depletion will lead to a fuller awareness of the complexities of the situation and a more critical reception of some of the rather naive analyses often advanced.

Notes on Chapter 16

As the first three sections of this chapter are referring back to earlier sections of the book, little amplification is needed. There are relatively few references that we can give on R and D. Arrow (1962), Nelson (1962) and Dasgupta and Stiglitz (1978) discuss in some detail the inadequacy of a market system as a way of supporting R and D, and the earlier part of our analysis leans heavily on their writings. The model of optimal R and D referred to is that discussed in Dasgupta et al. (1977) Kamien and Schwartz (1978) and Davison (1978). Of the various non-economic analyses of problems relating to resource depletion, the most widely known are undoubtedly Forrester (1971) and Meadows (1972). An equally interesting though less widely known volume is Daly (1973). A detailed critique of the work of Forrester and Meadows is given in Cole (1973) and a briefer appraisal from an economic viewpoint is given by Nordhaus (1973).

BIBLIOGRAPHY

Adelman, M. A. (1972) *The World Petroleum Market*, Johns Hopkins Press, Baltimore and London.

Allingham, M. (1975) 'Towards an Ability Tax', *Journal of Public Economics*, **4**, 361–376.

Anderson, K. P. (1972) 'Optimum Growth when the stock of the Resource is Finite and Depletable', *Journal of Economic Theory*.

Arrow, K. J. (1953) 'Le role des valeurs boursieres pour la repartition la meilleure des risques', *Econometrie*, Centre National de la Recherche Scientifique, Paris, Vol. XI, 41–48.

Arrow, K. J. (1959) 'Towards a Theory of Price Adjustment' in M. Abramovitz (ed.), *The Allocation of Economic Resources*, Stanford University Press.

Arrow, K. J. (1962) 'The Economic Implications of Learning-By-Doing', *Review of Economic Studies*, Vol. XXIX, 155–73.

Arrow, K. J. (1964) 'The Role of Securities in the Optimal Allocation of Risk Bearing', *Review of Economic Studies*, XXXI (2), 91–96.

Arrow, K. J. (1965) *Aspects of the Theory of Risk-Bearing*, Yrjo Jahnssonin Saatio, Helsinki.

Arrow, K. J. (1967) 'Application of Control Theory to Economic Growth', Technical Report No. 2; Institute for Mathematical Studies in Social Sciences; Stanford University.

Arrow, K. J. (1969) 'The organisation of Economic Activity: Issues Pertinent to the Choice of Market versus Non-Market Allocation' in *The Analysis and Evaluation of Public Expenditure: The PPB System*, 44–64. Joint Economic Committee of the Congress of the United States, Washington DC.

Arrow, K. J. (1971) *Essays in the Theory of Risk-Bearing*. North Holland (Amsterdam).

Arrow, K. J. (1971a) 'Economic Welfare and the Allocation of Resources to Invention'. Originally published in National Bureau of Economic Research, *The Rate and Direction of Inventive Activity: Economic and Social Factors*, Princeton University Press 1962; Reprinted as chapter 6 of Arrow (1970).

Arrow, K. J. (1971b) 'Political and Economic Estimation of Social Effects of Externalities' in *Frontier of Quantitative Economics*, M. Intriligator (ed.). North Holland Publishing Co., Amsterdam, 3–24.

Arrow, K. J. (1973a) 'Rawls' Principle of just Saving', *Swedish Journal of Economics*.

Arrow, K. J. (1973b) 'Some Ordinalist Utilitarian Notes on Rawls's Principle of Justice' (mimeo). Harvard University.

Arrow, K. J. (1974). 'General Economic Equilibrium: Purpose, Analytic Techniques, Collective Choice', Nobel Lecture, *American Economic Review*, **3**, 253–272.

Arrow, K. J. (1975) 'Vertical Integration and Communication', *Bell Journal of Economics*, Spring, Vol. 6, No. 1, 173–183.

Arrow, K. J., Chenery, H. B., Minhas, B. S. and Solow, R. M. (1961) 'Capital-Labour Substitution and Economic Efficiency', *Review of Economic and Statistics*, **43**, 225–250.

Arrow, K. J. and Debreu, G. (1954) 'Existence of Equilibrium for a Competitive Economy', *Econometrica*, **22**, 265–90.

Arrow, K. J. and Fisher, A. C. (1974) 'Preservation, Uncertainty and Irreversibility', *Quarterly Journal of Economics*, **87**, 312–319.

Arrow, K. J. and Hahn, F. H. (1971) *General Competitive Analysis*, Holden Day (San Francisco). Also North Holland (Amsterdam), 1978.

Arrow, K. J. and Kurz, M. (1970) *Public Investment, the Rate of Return and Optimal Fiscal Policy*, Johns Hopkins Press; Baltimore.

Arrow, K. J. and Lind R. (1970) 'Uncertainty and the Evaluation of Public Investment Decisions', *American Economic Review*, **60**, 364–378.

Arrow, K. J. and Nerlove M. (1958) 'A Note on Expectations and Stability', *Econometrica*, Volume 26.

d'Aspremont, Cl., and Gevers, L. (1977) 'Equity and the Informational Basis of Collective Choice', *Review of Economic Studies*, XLIV, 199–210.

Atkinson, A. B. (1970) 'On the Measurement of Inequality', *Journal of Economic Theory*, **2**, 244–263.

Atkinson, A. B. (1973) 'Maxi-min and Optimal Income Taxation' (mimeo). University of Essex.

Atkinson, A. B. and Stiglitz, J. E. (1976) 'The Design of Tax Structure: Direct vs. Indirect Taxation', IMSSS Technical Report No. 199, Stanford University.

Aumann, R. (1967) 'A Survey of Cooperative Games without Side Payments' in M. Shubik (ed.), *Essays in Mathematical Economics in Honour of Oskar Morgenstern*, Princeton University Press (New Jersey).

Barnett, H. J. and Morse, C. (1963) *Scarcity and Growth: The Economics of Natural Resource Activity*, Johns Hopkins Press, Baltimore.

Baumol, W. J. and Oates, W. (1975) *The Theory of Environmental Policy: Externalities, Public Outlays and the Quality of Life*, Prentice Hall (New Jersey).

Becker, G. (1964) *Human Capital*, Michigan University Press.

Beckerman, W. (1972) 'Economists, Scientists and Environmental Catastrophe', *Oxford Economic Papers*.

Bergstrom, T. C. (1975) 'How to Discard "Free-Disposability"—At No Cost', *Journal of Mathematical Economics*, **2**, 131–134.

Berry, R., Heal, G. and Salamon, P. (1978) 'On a Relation between Economic and Thermodynamic Optima', mimeo. University of Chicago.

Bevan (1974) 'Savings, Inheritance and Economic Growth in the Presence of Earnings Inequality', mimeo (Oxford).

Bewley, T. (1972) 'Existence of Equilibria in Economies with Infinitely Many Commodities', *Journal of Economic Theory*, **4**, 514–540.

Bliss, C. J. (1975) *Capital Theory and the Distribution of Income*. North Holland (Amsterdam).

Boiteux, M. (1956) 'Sur la Gestion des Monopoles Publics astreint a l'Equilibre Budgetaire', *Econometrica*, **24**, 22–40.

Brannen, G. (ed.) (1975) *Studies in Energy Tax Policy*, Ballinger.

Brown, G. (1974) 'An Optimal Programme for Managing Common Property Resources With Congestion Externalities', *Journal of Political Economy*, Vol. 82, No. 1, 163–173.

Buchanan, J. M. and Karfoglis, M. Z. (1963) 'A Note on Public Goods Supply', *American Economic Review*, **53**, 403–414.

Burmeister, E. and Turnovsky, S. J. (1976) 'The Specification of Adaptive Expectations in Continuous Time Dynamic Economic Models', *Econometrica*, **44**.

Cairncross, F. (1973) 'Booby Price', *The Guardian*, December 14.

Cass, D. (1965) 'Optimum Growth in an Aggregative Model of Capital Acumulation', *Review of Economic Studies*, **32**.

Cass, D. (1972) 'On Capital Overaccumulation in the Aggregative, Neoclassical Model of Economic Growth: A complete Characterisation', *Journal of Economic Theory*, 4, No. 3, pp. 200–223.

Cass, D. and Shell, K. (1975) 'The Structure and Stability of Competitive Dynamical Systems', IMSSS Technical Report No. 160, Stanford University.

Cass, D. and Yaari, M. (1966) 'A Re-examination of the Pure Consumption Loans Model', *Journal of Political Economy*, 74, 353–367.

Cass, D. and Yaari, M. (1967) 'Individual Saving, Aggregate Capital Accumulation and Efficient Growth', in Essays on the Theory of Optimal Economic Growth (ed.) K. Shell, MIT Press, Cambridge, Mass.

Chakravarty, S. (1962) 'Optimal Savings with Finite Planning Horizon', *International Economic Review*, 3, 338–355.

Chakravarty, S. (1969) *Capital and Development Planning*, MIT Press, Cambridge, Mass.

Chambers, T. D. (1957) 'The Vale of Trent 1670–1800: A study of Economic Change', *The Economic History Review*. Supplement III. Cambridge University Press.

Chipman, J. S. (1965) 'The Nature and Meaning of Equilibrium in Economic Theory', in *Price Theory*, H. Townsend (ed.), Penguin Books, London, 1971.

Christy, Jr. F. T. and Potter, N. (1962) *Trends in Natural Resource Commodities*, Johns Hopkins Press, Baltimore.

Cohen, J. and Weitzman M. (1975) 'A Marxian View of Enclosures', *Journal of Development Economics*.

Cole, R. S. D. et al. (1973) *Thinking About the Future: A Critique of the Limits to Growth*, Chatto and Windus, for Sussex University Press.

Coase, R. H. (1960) 'The Problem of Social Cost', *Journal of Law and Economics*, 3, 1–44.

Crabbe, P. J. and Spry, I. M. (1978) 'Lewis Cecil Gray: Pioneer of the Economics of Exhaustible Resource' (mimeo), Department of Economics, University of Laval.

Cremer, J. and Weitzman, M. (1976) 'O.P.E.C. and the Monopoly Price of World Oil', *European Economic Review*, 8, 155–164.

Crutchfield, J. A. and Zellner, A. (1962) 'Economic Aspects of the Pacific Halibut Fishing', *Fishing Industrial Research*, U.S. Department of the Interior, Washington, DC.

Dales, J. H. (1968) *Pollution, Property and Prices*, University of Toronto Press.

Daly, H. E. (1973) *Toward a Steady-State Economy*, W. H. Freeman (San Francisco).

Das Gupta, A. K. (1977) 'The Problem of an International Economic Order', Second G. L. Mehta Memorial Lecture, Madras, India.

Dasgupta, P. (1969) 'On the Concept of Optimum Population', *Review of Economic Studies*, XXXVI (3), No. 107, pp. 295–318.

Dasgupta, P. (1974) 'On Optimum Population Size', in *Economic Theory and Planning*, A. Mitra (ed.). Oxford University Press (Calcutta).

Dasgupta, P. (1974a), 'Some Recent Theoretical Explorations in the Economics of Exhaustible Resources', in H. Gottinger (ed.), *Systems Approaches and Environmental Problems*,Vandenhoeek and Ruprecht(Gottingen),pp.193-214.

Dasgupta, P. (1974b) 'On Some Problems Arising from Professor Rawls' Conception of Distributive Justice', *Theory and Decision*, **4**, 325-344.

Dasgupta, P. (1974c) 'Some Alternative Criteria for Justice between Generations', *Journal of Public Economics*, **3**, 405-424.

Dasgupta, P. (1977a) 'Resource Depletion, Research and Development, and the Social Rate of Discount', in R. Lind (ed.), *Energy Planning and the Social Rate of Discount*, Johns Hopkins Press for Resources for the Future (forthcoming).

Dasgupta, P. (1977b) 'The Economics of Common Property Resources: A Dynamic Formulation of the Fisheries Problem', in M. Dempster (ed.), *Animal Economics*, Academic Press (forthcoming).

Dasgupta, P., Eastwood, P. K. and Heal, G. M. (1978) 'Resource Management in a Trading Economy', *Quarterly Journal of Economics*.

Dasgupta, P., Gilbert, R. and Stiglitz, J. E. (1977) 'Invention, Innovation and Market Structure: The Case of Natural Resources' (mimeo), London School of Economics.

Dasgupta, P. and Heal, M. G. (1974) 'The Optimal Depletion of Exhaustible Resources', *Review of Economic Studies*, Symposium.

Dasgupta, P., Heal, G. M. and Majumdar, M. K. (1976) 'Resource Depletion and Research and Development' in Intriligator M.D. (ed.), *Frontiers of Quantitative Economics*, Vol. IIIB, North Holland Publishing Co (Amsterdam).

Dasgupta, P., Marglin, S. A. and Sen, A. K. (1972) *Guidelines for Project Evaluation*, United Nations (New York).

Dasgupta, P. and Maskin, E. (1977) 'The Existence of Economics Equilibria: Continuity and Mixed Strategies', IMSSS Technical Report 56, Stanford University.

Dasgupta, P. and Maskin, E. (1978) 'A Note on Imperfect Information and Optimal Pollution Control', *Review of Economic Studies* (forthcoming).

Dasgupta, P. and Stiglitz, J. E. (1971) 'Differential Taxation, Public Goods and Economic Efficiency', *Review of Economic Studies*, XXXVIII, pp. 151-174.

Dasgupta, P. and Stiglitz, J. E. (1976) 'Uncertainty and Resource Extraction Under Alternative Institutional Arrangements'. IMSSS Technical Report 1979, Stanford University.

Dasgupta, P. and Stiglitz, J. E. (1977a) 'Tariffs vs. Quotas as Revenue Raising Devices under Uncertainty', *American Economic Review*, **67**, 975-981.

Dasgupta, P. and Stiglitz, J. E. (1977b) 'Market Structure and Research and Development', Invited paper presented at the World Congress of the International Economic Association on *Economic Growth and Resources*, Tokyo (Mimeo), London School of Economics.

Dasgupta, P. and Stiglitz, J. E. (1978a) 'Market Structure and Resource Depletion: A Contribution to the Theory of Intertemporal Monopolistic Competition', *Journal of Economic Theory* (forthcoming).

Dasgupta, P. and Stiglitz, J. E. (1978b) 'Resource Depletion under Technological Uncertainty', *Econometrica* (forthcoming).

Dasgupta, P. and Stiglitz, J. E. (1978c) 'Market Structure and the Nature of Innovative Activity', *Economic Journal* (forthcoming).

Dasgupta, P. and Stiglitz, J. E. (1978d), 'Uncertainty, Market Structure and the Speed of R & D, *Bell Journal of Economics* (forthcoming).

Davidson, R. (1978) 'Optimal Depletion of an Exhaustible Resource with Research and Development Towards an Alternative Technology', *Review of Economic Studies*, XLV (2), No. 140, pp. 355–468.

Debreu, G. (1952) 'A Social Equilibrium Existence Theorem', *Proceedings of the National Academy of Sciences of the U.S.A.*, **38**, 886–893.

Debreu, G. (1954) 'Representation of a Preference Ordering by a Numerical Function', in *Decision Processes*, R. M. Thrall, C. H. Coombs, R. L. Davies (eds.), New York, Wiley, pp. 159–165.

Debreu, G. (1959) *The Theory of Value: An Axiomatic Analysis of Economic Equilibrium*, Cowles Foundation Monograph 17, Wiley (New York).

Debreu, G. and Scarf, H. E. (1963) 'A Limit Theorem on the Core of an Economy', *International Economic Review*, **4**, 235–246.

Diamond, P. A. (1965) 'The Evaluation of Infinite Utility Streams', *Econometrica*, **33**, 170–177.

Diamond, P. A. (1965a) 'National Debt in a Neoclassical Model', *American Economic Review*, **55**, 1126–1150.

Diamond, P. A. and Mirrlees, J. A. (1971) 'Optimal Taxation and Public Production', *American Economic Review*, LXI (3), pp. 261–278.

Diamond, P. A. and Mirrlees, J. A. (1973) 'Aggregate Production with Consumption Externalities', *Quarterly Journal of Economics*, Vol. LXXXVII, pp. 1–24.

Dixit, A. (1968) 'Optimum Development in the Labour—Surplus Economy', *Review of Economic Studies*, **35**, 23–34.

Dixit, A. (1976) *The Theory of Equilibrium Growth*, Oxford University Press.

Farrell, M. J. (1959), 'The New Theories of the Consumption Function', *Economic Journal*, **69**, 678–696.

Finley, M. I. (1973) *The Ancient Economy*, University Hall Press (Berkeley, L. A.).

Fisher, A. C. and Krutilla, J. V. (1975) *The Economics of Natural Resource Environments*, Resource for the Future, Johns Hopkins University Press.

Fisher, A. C. and Peterson F. A. (1976) 'Natural Resources and the Environment in Economics', *Journal of Economic Literature*, Vol. 14.

Foley, D. (1970) 'Lindahl's Solution and the Core of an Economy with Public Good', *Econometrica*, **38**, No. 1, pp. 66–72.

Forrester, J. W. (1971) *World Dynamics*, Wright Allen Press.

Foss, P. O. (1960) *Politics and Grass: The Administration of Grazing on the Public Domain*, University of Washington Press (Seattle).

Gaffney, M. (1967) *Extractive Resources and Taxation* (ed.), University of Wisconsin Press.

Gale, D. (1967) 'Optimal Development in a Multi-Sector Economy', *Review of Economic Studies*, **34**, 1–18.

Garg, P. C. (1974) *Optimal Economic Growth with Exhaustible Resources*, Ph.D. Thesis, Stanford University.

Gaskins, D. (1971) 'Dynamic Limit Pricing: Optimal Pricing under Threat of Entry', *Journal of Economic Theory*, **3**, 306–322.

Gilbert, R. J. (1976) 'Optimal Depletion of an Uncertain Stock', IMSSS Technical Report No. 207, Stanford University.

Gilbert, R. J. (1976a) 'Search Strategies for Non-renewable Resource Deposits', IMSSS Technical Report No. 196, Stanford University.

Gilbert, R. J. (1978) 'Dominant Firm Pricing in a Market for an Exhaustible Resource', *Bell Journal of Economics* (Autumn).

Gordon, H. Scott (1954) 'Economic Theory of Common Property Resources', *Journal of Political Economy*.

Gorman, W. M. (1957) 'Convex Indifference Curves and Diminishing Marginal Utility', *Journal of Political Economy*, 55.

Gorman, W. M. (1968) 'The Structure of Utility Functions', *Review of Economic Studies*, 45, 367–390.

Gray, L. C. (1914) 'Rent Under the Assumption of Exhaustibility', *Quarterly Journal of Economics*, 28, 466–489.

Grayson, C. (1960) *Decision under Uncertainty: Drilling Decisions by Oil and Gas Operators*, Harvard University.

Green, J. (1973) 'Information, Efficiency and Equilibrium'. Discussion Paper No. 284, Harvard Institute of Economic Research.

Green, J. (1976) 'A Third Type of Information Externality' (mimeo), Harvard University.

Green, J. and Laffont, J.-J. (1977) 'A Characterisation of Satisfactory Mechanisms for the Revelation of Preferences for Public Goods', *Econometrica*, 45, 427–438.

Griliches, Z. (1957) 'Hybrid Corn: An Exploration in the Economics of Technological Change', *Econometrica*, 25, 501–522.

Grossman, S. J. (1976) 'A Characterization of the Optimality of Equilibrium in Incomplete Markets', IMSSS Technical Report No. 209, Stanford University.

Grossman, S. J. (1978) 'The Existence of Future Markets, Noisy Rational Expectation and Informational Externalities', *Review of Economic Studies*, 44, 431–450.

Grossman, S. J. and Stiglitz, J. E. (1976) 'Information and Competitive Price Systems', *American Economic Review*, 66, 246–253.

Groves, T. and Ledyard, J. (1977) 'Optimal Allocation of Public Goods: A Solution to the "Free-Rider" Problem', *Econometrica*, 45, 783–810.

Guesnerie, R. and Jaffray, J.-Y. (1974) 'Optimality and Equilibrium of Plans, Prices and Price Expectations', in H. J. Dreze (ed.), *Allocation Under Uncertainty: Equilibrium and Optimality*, Macmillan, London.

Guesnerie, R. and de Montbrial, T. (1974) 'Allocation under Uncertainty: A Survey', in J. H. Dreze (ed.), *Allocation under Uncertainty: Equilibrium and Optimality*, Macmillan, London.

Guha, A. (1974) 'A Critique of the Overtaking Criterion', in *Economic Theory and Planning: Essays in Honour of A. K. Das Gupta*, (ed.) Ashok Mitra, O.U.P., Delhi.

Hahn, F. H. (1966) 'Equilibrium Dynamics with Heterogeneous Capital Goods, *Quarterly Journal of Economics*, 88, 65–94.

Hahn, F. H. (1968) 'On Warranted Growth Paths', *Review of Economic Studies*, 35, 175–184.

Hahn, F. H. (1970) 'Some Adjustment Problems', *Econometrica*, 38, 1–17.

Hahn, F. H. (1971) 'Equilibrium with Transactions Costs', *Econometrica*, 39, 3, 417–440.

Hahn, F. H. (1973a) 'On the Notion of Equilibrium', Inaugural Lecture, Cambridge University Press.

Hahn, F. H. (1973b) 'On Transactions Costs, Inessential Sequence Economies and Money', *Review of Economic Studies*, XL (4), No. 124, 449–462.

Hahn, F. H. and Mathews, R. C. O. (1964) 'The Theory of Economic Growth: A Survey', *Economic Journal*, **74**, 779–902.

Hammond, P. J. (1976) 'Changing Tastes and Coherent Dynamic Choice', *Review of Economic Studies*, Vol. XLIII (1), No. 133, pp. 159–174.

Hammond, P. J. (1976a) 'Equity, Arrow's Conditions and Rawls's Difference, Principle', *Econometrica*, **44**, 793–804.

Hardin, G. (1968) 'The Tragedy of the Common', *Science*, **162**, 1243–1248.

Hardy, G. H., Littlewood, J. and Polya, G. (1943) *Inequalities*, Cambridge University Press.

Harrod, R. F. (1948) *Towards a Dynamic Economy*, Macmillan (London).

Harsanyi, J. (1955) 'Cardinal Welfare, Individualistic Ethics, and Inter-personal Comparison of Welfare', *Journal of Political Economy*, **63**, 309–321.

Harsanyi, J. (1976) 'Rule Utilitarianism and Decision Theory', Center for Research in Management Science working Paper CP-384, University of California, Berkeley.

Hart, O. D. (1975) 'On the Optimality of Equilibrium When Markets Are Incomplete', *Journal of Economic Theory*, Vol. II, No. 3, pp. 418–443

Hart, O. D. and Kuhn, H. (1975) 'A Proof of the Existence of Equilibrium. without the Free-Disposal Assumption', *Journal of Mathematical Economics*, **2**, 335–344.

Heal, G. M. (1973) *The Theory of Economic Planning*, North Holland (Amsterdam).

Heal, G. M. (1975a) 'Economic Aspects of Natural Resource Depletion', in D. W. Pearce and J. Rose (eds.), *The Economics of Depletion*, Macmillan, London.

Heal, G. M. (1975b) 'The Influence of Interest Rates on Resource Prices', Cowles Foundation Discussion Paper No. 407, Yale University, (October).

Heal, G. M. (1976) 'The Relationship Between Price and Extraction Cost for a Resource with a Backstop Technology', *Bell Journal of Economics*, Vol. I, No. 2, pp. 317–378.

Heal, G. M. (1978) 'Uncertainty and the Optimal Supply Policy for an Exhaustible Resource', in R. Pindyck (ed.), *Advances in the Economics of Energy and Resources*, Vol. 2, J.A.I. Press.

Heal, G. M. and Barrow, M. M. (1979) 'The Influence of Interest Rates on Metal Price Movements', *Review of Economic Studies* (forthcoming).

Heal, G. M. and Ryder, H. E. Jr. (1973) 'Optimal Growth with Intertemporally Dependent Preferences', Review of Economic Studies, **40**, 1–32.

Heller, W. P. and Starrett, D. H. (1978) 'The Nature of Externalities', in *Theory and Measurement of Economic Externalities* (ed.), Academic Press, New York.

Henry, Cl. (1974) 'Investment Decisions Under Uncertainty: The Irreversibility Effect', *American Economic Review*, LXIV, M., pp. 1006–1012.

Henry, Cl. (1974) 'Option Values in the Economics of Irreplaceable Assets', *Review of Economic Studies*, Symposium, pp. 89–104.

Herfindahl, O. C. (1967) 'Depletion and Economic Theory', in M. Gaffney (ed.).

Herfindahl, O and Kneese, A. (1974) *Economic Theory of Natural Resources*, Charles E. Merrill Books Inc. (Columbus, Ohio).

Hicks, J. R. (1939) *Value and Capital*, Oxford University Press.

Hicks, J. R. (1935) *Theory of Wages*, Macmillan (London).

Hildenbrand, W. and Kirman, A. (1976) *Introduction to Equilibrium Analysis*, North Holland (Amsterdam).

Hirsch, M. W. and Smale S. (1974) *Differential Equations, Dynamical Systems and Linear Algebra'*, Academic Press, New York.

Hirschleifer, J. (1965) 'Investment Decision under Uncertainty: Choice Theoretic Approaches', *Quarterly Journal of Economics*, **79**, 509–536.

Hirschleifer, J. (1970) 'The Private and Social Value of Information and the Reward of Inventive Activity', *American Economic Review*, **61**, 571–574.

Hoel, M. (1978) 'Resource Extraction, Substitute Production, and Monopoly', *Journal of Economic Theory*, Vol. 19, No. 1, pp. 28–37.

Hotelling, H. (1931) 'The Economics of Exhaustible Resources', *Journal of Political Economy*, **39**, 137–175.

Hubert, M. K. (1969) 'Energy Resources', in *Resources and Man*, by the Committee on Resources and Man of the National Academy of Sciences—National Research Council. W. H. Freeman (San Francisco).

Hudson, E. A. and Jorgenson D. W. (1974) 'U.S. Energy Policy and Economic Growth, 1975–2000', *Bell Journal of Economics and Management Science*, Vol. 5, No. 2 (Autumn).

Hurewicz, W. (1958) *Lectures on Ordinary Differential Equations*, M.I.T. Press (Massachusetts).

Hynilicza, E. and Pindyck, R. S. (1976) 'Pricing Policies for a Two-Part Exhaustible Resource Cartel: the Case of O.P.E.C.,' *European Economic Review*, **8**, 139–154.

Idyll, C. P. (1973) 'Anchovy Crisis', *Scientific American* (June).

Ingham, A. and Simmons, P. (1975) 'Natural Resources and Growing Population', *Review of Economic Studies*, pp. 191–206.

Intriligator, M. D. (1971) *Mathematical Optimization and Economic Theory*, Prentice Hall (New Jersey).

Kaldor, N. (1957) 'A Model of Economic Growth', *Economic Journal*, Vol. LXVIII, 591–624.

Kaldor, N. and Mirrlees, J. A. (1962) 'A New Model of Economic Growth', *Review of Economic Studies*, XXIX, pp. 174–192.

Kamien, M. and Schwartz, N. (1978) 'Optimal Exhaustible Resource Depletion and Endogenous Technical Change', *Review of Economic Studies*, Vol. XLV (1), No. 139, 179–196.

Kay, J. and Mirrlees, J. A. (1975) 'The Desirability of Natural Resource Depletion', in D. W. Pearce and J. Rose (eds.), *The Economics of Natural Resource Depletion*, Macmillan, London.

Kemp, M. C. (1976) 'How to Eat a Cake of Unknown Size', in M. C. Kemp, *Three Topics in the Theory of International Trade*, North Holland (Amsterdam).

Kerridge, E. (1968) *The Agricultural Revolution*, Augustus M. Kelly (New York).

Khalatbari, F. (1976) 'Exhaustible Resources, Planning and Uncertainty, Ph.D. Thesis, London School of Economics.

Khalatbari, F. (1977) 'Market Imperfections and Optimal Rate of Depletion of an Exhaustible Resource', *Economica*, **44**, 409–414.

Koopmans, T. C. (1957) 'The Price System and the Allocation of Resources', in *Three Essays on the State of Economic Science*, McGraw-Hill (New York).

Koopmans, T. C. (1960) 'Stationary Ordinal Utility and Impatience', *Econometrica*, **28**, 287–309.

Koopmans, T. C. (1965) 'On the Concept of Optimal Economic Growth', in *Pontifica Academia Scientiarum Seripta Varia*, Vol. 28.

Koopmans, T. C. (1972) 'Representation of Preference Orderings with Independent Components of Consumption', Chapter 3 of *Decision and Organization, a volume in honour of Jacob Marschak*, ed. C. B. McGuire and R. Radner, North Holland (Amsterdam).

Koopmans, T. C. (1972a) 'Representation of Preference Orderings Over Time', Chapter 4 of *Decision and Organization, a volume in honour of Jacob Marschak*, ed. C. B. McGuire and R. Radner, North Holland (Amsterdam),

Koopmans, T. C. (1974a) 'Proof for a Case where Discounting Advances the Doomsday', *Review of Economic Studies*, Symposium, pp. 117–120.

Koopmans, T. C. (1974b) 'Some Observations on "Optimal" Economic Growth and Exhaustible Resources', in Bos, Linemann and de Wolff (ed.), *Economic Structure and Development*, North Holland.

Koopmans, T. C. (1977) 'Concepts of Optimality and their Uses', *American Economic Review*, Vol. 67, No. 3, 261–274.

Koopmans, T. C., Diamond, P. A. and Williamson, R. (1964) 'Stationary Utility and Time Perspective', *Econometrica*, **32**, 82–100.

Kurz, M. (1974) 'Equilibrium in a Finite Sequence of Markets with Transaction Costs', *Econometrica*, Vol. 42, No. 1, 1–20.

Kurz, M. and Starrett, D. (1970) 'On the Efficiency of Competitive Programmes in an Infinite Horizon Model', *Review of Economic Studies*, Vol. XXXVII (4), No. 112, 571–584.

Kwerel, E. (1977) 'To Tell the Truth: Imperfect Information and Optimal Pollution Control,' *Review of Economic Studies*, XLIV (3), pp. 595–601.

Lane, J. (1977) *On Optimum Population Paths*, Springer-Verlag (Berlin).

Legator, M. S. (1972) 'The Genetic Effects of Environmental Contaminants', in *Population and Pollution*, Proceedings of the 5th Annual Symposium of the Royal Society, ed. R. R. Cox and J. Peel, Academic Press (London).

Lipsey, R. and Lancaster, K. (1956) 'The General Theory of Second Best', *Review of Economic Studies*, **24**, 11–32.

Lipson, E. (1949) *Economic History of England*, A. and C. Black (London).

Little, I. M. D. and Mirrlees, J. A. (1969) *Manual of Industrial Project Analysis for Developing Countries*, Vol. II, OECD (Paris).

Little, I. M. D. and Mirrlees, J. A. (1974) *Project Appraisal and Planning for Developing Countries*, Basic Books, New York.

Lind, R. (ed.) (1980) *Energy Planning and the Social Rate of Discount*, Johns Hopkins University Press for *Resources for the Future*.

Lotka, A. J. (1956) *Elements of Mathematical Biology*, Dover Publications, New York.

Loury, G. C. (1976) 'The Optimal Exploitation of an Unknown Reserve', Discussion Paper, Economics Department, Northwestern University.

Lucas, R. E. (1972) 'Expectations and the Neutrality of Money', *Journal of Economic Theory*, 4, 103–124.

Lucas, R. E. and Prescott, E. C. (1974) 'Equilibrium Search and Unemployment', *Journal of Economic Theory*, **17**, 188–209.

Luce, R. D. and Raiffa, H. (1957) *Games and Decisions*, John Wiley and Sons Inc. (New York).

Maddox, J. (1971) *The Doomsday Syndrome*, Macmillan, London.

Majumdar, M. (1974) 'Efficient Programs in Infinite Dimensional Spaces: A Complete Characterization', *Journal of Economic Theory*, Vol. 7, No. 4, pp. 355–369.

Maler, K.G. (1974) *Environmental Economics*, Johns Hopkins Press (Baltimore).

Malinvaud, E. (1953) 'Capital Accumulation and Efficient Allocation of Resources', *Econometrica*, **21**, 233–268.

Malinvaud, E. (1972) *Lectures in Microeconomic Theory*, North Holland (Amsterdam).

Manne, A. S. (1974) 'Waiting for the Breeder', *Review of Economic Studies*, Symposium, pp. 47–66.

Mansfield, E. (1961) 'Technical Change and the Rate of Imitation', *Econometrica*, pp. 741–766.

Marglin, S. A. (1963) 'The Social Rate of Discount and the Optimal Rate of Investment', *Quarterly Journal of Economics*, **77**, 95–111.

Marglin, S. A. (1967) 'The Rate of Interest and the Value of Capital with Unlimited Supply of Labour', in K. Shell (ed.) (1967).

Marglin, S. A. (1976) *Value and Prices in the Labour Surplus Economy*, Oxford University Press.

Marschak, J. and Radner, R. (1972) *Economic Theory of Teams*, Cowles Foundation Monograph 22, Yale University Press, New Haven.

Marschak, T. and Selten, R. (1974) *General Equilibrium with Price-Making Firms*, Springer-Verlag (Berlin).

Marx, K. (1961) *Capital*, Vol. I, Foreign Languages Publishing House (Moscow).

Maskin, E. (1977) 'Nash Equilibrium and Welfare Optimality' (mimeo), Cambridge.

Maskin, E. (1978) 'A Theorem on Utilitarianism', *Review of Economic Studies*, **45**, 93–96.

May, K. O. (1952) 'A Set of Independent, Necessary, and Sufficient Conditions for Simple Majority Decisions', *Econometrica*, **20**, 680–684.

McDonald, S. L. (1971) *Petroleum Conservation in the United States: An Economic Analysis*, Johns Hopkins Press (Baltimore and London).

McFadden, D. (1975) 'On the Existence of Optimal Development Programmes', in J. A. Mirrlees and N. Stern (eds.), *Models of Economic Growth*, Macmillan, London.

McFadden, D., Majumdar, M. K. and Mitra, T. (1974) 'On Efficiency and Pareto Optimality of Competitive Programs in Closed Multisector Models', Discussion Paper No. 85, Department of Economics, Cornell University.

McGuire, C. B. (1972) 'Comparison of Information Structures', in C. B. McGuire and R. Radner (eds.) (1972).

McGuire, C. B. and Radner, R. (1972) *Decision and Organisation*, A Volume in Honour of Jacob Marschak. North Holland (Amsterdam).

McVay, Scott (1966) 'The Last of the Great Whales', *Scientific American*, (August).

Meade, J. E. (1952) 'External Economies and Diseconomies in a Competitive Situation', *Economic Journal*, LXII, pp. 54–67.

Meade, J. E. (1955) *Trade and Welfare*, Oxford University Press.

Meade, J. E. (1964) *Equity, Efficiency and the Ownership of the Property*, Allen and Unwin (London).

Meade, J. E. (1966) 'Life-Cycle Savings, Inheritance and Economic Growth', *Review of Economic Studies*, Vol. 33.

Meade, J. E. (1969) *The Growing Economy*, Allen and Unwin.

Meade, J. E. (1971) *The Controlled Economy*, Allen and Unwin.

Meade, J. E. (1973) *The Theory of Economic Externalities*, International Economic Series, 2, Insitut Universitaire de Hautes Etudes Internationales, Geneva.

Meadows, D. H. , et al. (1972) *The Limits to Growth*, Universe Books, New York and Earth Island Press, London.

Milliman, J. W. (1956) 'Commodities and Price System and Use of Water Supplies, *Southern Economic Journal*, XXII, pp. 426–437.

Milnor, J. (1954) 'Games Against Nature', in *Decision Processes* (ed.) R. M. Thrall, C. H. Coombs and R. L. Davis. John Wiley and Sons (New York).

Mirrlees, J. A. (1967) 'Optimum Growth When the Technology is Changing', *Review of Economic Studies*, January, Vol. 34, pp. 95–124.

Mirrlees, J. A. (1971) 'An Exploration in the Theory of Optimum Income Taxation', *Review of Economic Studies*, **38**, 176–208.

Mirrlees, J. A. (1974) 'Optimum Accumulation under Uncertainty: The Case of Stationary Returns to Investment', in *Allocation Under Uncertainty: Equilibrium and Optimality* (ed.) by J. H. Dreze, Macmillan, London.

Mirrlees, J. A. (1975) 'Indeterminate Growth Theory', mimeo. Nuffield College, Oxford.

Mirrlees, J. A. and Stern, N. H. (1972) 'Fairly Good Plans', *Journal of Economic Theory*, 4.

Mitra, T. (1978) 'Efficient Growth with Exhaustible Resources in a Neoclassical Model', *Journal of Economic Theory*, Vol. 17, No. 1, pp. 114–129.

Musgrave, R.A. (1959) *The Theory of Public Finance*, McGraw Hill (New York).

Nash, J. Jr. (1950) 'Equilibrium Points in N—Person Games', *Proceedings of the National Academy of Sciences*, U.S.A., **36**, 48–49.

Nelson, R. R. (1952) 'The Simple Economics of Basic Scientific Research', *Journal of Political Economy*, pp. 297–306.

Newbery, D. M. G. (1976) 'A Paradox in Tax Theory', Discussion Paper, Cambridge University, Department of Economics.

Nordhaus, W. D. (1973) 'The Allocation of Energy Resources', Brookings Papers on Economic Activity, 3.

Nordhaus, W. D. (1973) 'World Dynamics: Measurement without Data', *Economic Journal*, **83**, 1156–1183.

Nordhaus, W. D. and Tobin, J. (1972) 'Is Economic Growth Obsolete?' in *Economic Growth*, 5th Anniversary Colloquium, V, National Bureau of Economic Research, New York.

Page, W. and Surrey, A. L. J. (1975) 'Some Issues in the Current Debate about Energy and Natural Resources', in D. W. Pearce and J. Rose (eds.), The *Economics of Natural Resource Depletion*, Macmillan, London.

Pasinetti, L. L. (1962) 'The Rate of Profit and Income Distribution in Relation to the Rate of Economic Growth', *Review of Economic Studies*, XXIX, 267–279.

Pattanaik, P. K. (1968) 'Risk Impersonality and the Social Welfare Function', *Journal of Political Economy*, 76.

Peleg, B. and Yaari, M. (1970) 'Efficiency Prices in Infinite Dimensional Spaces', *Journal of Economic Theory*, pp. 41–85.

Phelps, E. S. (1961) 'The Golden Rule of Accumulation: A Fable for Growthmen', *American Economic Review*.

Phelps, E. S. (1965) 'Second Essay on the Golden Rule of Accumulation', *American Economic Review*, **55**, 783–814.

Phelps, E. S. (1966) *Golden Rules of Economic Growth: Studies in Efficient and Optimal Investment*, Norton (New York).

Phelps, E. S. and Pollak, R. (1968) 'Second-Best National Savings and Game Equilibrium Growth', *Review of Economic Studies*, **35**, 185–200.

Pigou, A. C. (1932) *The Economics of Welfare*, Macmillan & Co.(London), 4th ed.

Pindyck, R. S. (1976) 'Cartel Pricing and the Structure of the World Bauxite Market', M.I.T. Energy Laboratory Working Paper No. 77-005 WP.

Pindyck, R. S. (1976a) 'Gains to Producers from the Cartelisation of Exhaustible Resources', M.I.T. Energy Laboratory Working Paper No. 76-102 WP.

Pitchford, J. D. (1974) *Population in Economic Growth*, North Holland, Amsterdam.

Popper, K. (1958) *The Poverty of Historicism*, Routledge and Kegan Paul (London).

Pratt, J. W. (1964) 'Risk Aversion in the Small and Large', *Econometrica*, **32**, 122–136.

Pratt, J., Raiffa, H. and Schlaifer, R. (1964) 'The Foundations of Decision under Uncertainty: An Elementary Exposition', *Journal of the American Statistical Association*, Vol. 59.

Radner, R. (1967) 'Efficiency Prices for Infinite Dimension Production Programmes', *Review of Economic Studies*, Vo.l XXXIV (1), No. 97, pp. 51–66.

Radner, R. (1968) 'Competitive Equilibrium Under Uncertainty', *Econometrica*, **36**, 31–58.

Radner, R. (1970) 'New Ideas in Pure Theory: Problems in the Theory of Markets Under Uncertainty', *American Economic Review*, **60**, 454–460.

Radner, R. (1972) 'Existence and Equilibrium of Plans, Prices and Price Expectations in a Sequence of Markets', *Econometrica*, Vol. 140, No. 2, pp. 289–304.

Radner, R. (1972a). 'Normative Theory of Individual Decision: An Introduction', in C. B. McGuire and R. Radner (ed.) (1972).

Radner, R. (1974) 'Market Equilibrium under Uncertainty: Concepts and Problems', in M. Intriligator and D. Kendrick (ed.), *Frontiers of Quantitative Economics*, II, North Holland (Amsterdam).

Radner, R. (1976) 'Rational Expectations Equilibrium with Price Information', mimeo. Department of Economics, Berkeley.

Radner, R. and Stiglitz, J. E. (1975) 'Fundamental Nonconcavities in the Value of Information' (mimeo), Stanford University.

Ramsey, F. (1928) 'A Mathematical Theory of Saving', *Economic Journal*, **38**, 543–559.

Randers, J. and Meadows, D. (1973) 'Carrying Capacity of our Global Environment: A Look at the Ethical Alternatives', in H. Daly (ed.) (1973)

Rawls, J. (1972) *A Theory of Justice*, Clarendon Press (Oxford).

Roberts, J. and Spence, A. M. (1974) 'Effluent Charges and Licenses under Uncertainty', IMSSS Technical Report No. 146, Stanford University.

Rothschild, M. and Stiglitz, J. E. (1970) 'Increasing Risk I: A Definition', *Journal of Economic Theory*, **2**, 225–243.

Rothschild, M. and Stiglitz, J. E. (1976) 'Equilibrium in Competitive Insurance Markets: The Economics of Markets with Incomplete Information', *Quarterly Journal of Economics*.

Salant, S. (1976) 'Exhaustible Resources and Industrial Structure: A Nash-Cournot Approach to the World Oil Market', *Journal of Political Economy*, Vol. 84, No. 5, pp. 1079–1093.

Samuelson, P. A. (1948) *The Foundations of Economic Analysis*, Harvard University Press (Cambridge, Mass.).

Samuelson, P. A. (1954) 'The Pure Theory of Public Expenditure', *Review of Economics and Statistics*, **36**, 387–389.

Samuelson, P. A. (1958) 'An Exact Consumption Loan Model of Interest with or without the Social Contrivance of Money', *Journal of Political Economy*.

Samuelson, P. A. (1961) 'The Evaluation of "Social Income": Capital Formation and Wealth', in Lutz and Hayne (ed.), *The Theory of Capital*, Macmillan (London).

Samuelson, P. A. (1967) 'Indeterminacy of Development in a Heterogenous-Capital Model with Constant Savings Propensity', in K. Shell (ed.), *Essays on the Theory of Optimal Economic Growth*, M.I.T. Press, Cambridge, Mass.

Samuelson, P. A. (1970) 'The Fundamental Approximation Theorem of Portfolio Analysis in Terms of Means, Variances and Higher Moments', *Review of Economic Studies*, XXXVII (4), pp. 537–42.

Samuelson, P. A. (1971) 'Turnpike Theorem Even Though Tastes are Intertemporally Dependent', *Western Economic Journal*, 9, 21–25.

Schaffer, W. H. J. and Sonnenschein, H. (1975) 'Equilibrium in Abstract Economies Without Ordered Preferences', *Journal of Mathematical Economics*, 2, 345–348.

Scitovsky, T. (1954) 'Two Concepts of External Economies', *Journal of Political Economy*, LXII, pp. 143–151.

Scott Gordon, H. (1954) 'The Economic Theory of a Common Property Income', *Journal of Political Economy*, LXII, pp. 124–142.

Sen, A. K. (1960) 'On Optimizing the Rate of Savings', *Economic Journal*, 71.

Sen, A. K. (1967) 'Isolation, Assurance and the Social Rate of Discount', *Quarterly Journal of Economics*, 81.

Sen, A. K. (1970) *Collective Choice and Social Welfare*, Holden Day, San Francisco.

Sen, A. K. (1973) *On Economic Inequality*, Clarendon Press (Oxford).

Sen, A. K. (1974) 'Choice, Ordering and Morality', in S. Korner (ed.), *Practical Reason*, Blackwell (Oxford).

Sen, A. K. (1977) 'Social Choice Theory: A Re-Examination', *Econometrica*, 45, 53–90.

Sen, A. K. (1977a) 'On Weights and Measures: Informational Constraints in Social Welfare Analysis', *Econometrica*, 45, No. 7, pp. 1539–1572.

Shapley, D. (1972) 'Icelandic Fishing: Science in the Great Cod Fish War', *Science* (December).

Shell, K. (ed.) (1967) *Essays on the Theory of Optimal Economic Growth*, M.I.T. Press, Cambridge, Mass.

Shell, K., Sidrauski, M. and Stiglitz, J. E. (1969) 'Capital Gains: Income and Saving', *Review of Economic Studies*, 36, 15–26.

Shell, K. and Stiglitz, J. E. (1967) 'The Allocation of Investment in a Dynamic Economy', *Quarterly Journal of Economics*, 81, 592–609.

Sidgwick, H. (1890) *The Methods of Ethics*, Macmillan, London.

Smith, V. K. (1974) 'Re-Examination of the Trends in the Prices of Natural Resource Commodities, 1870–1972', Working Paper No. 44, Economic Growth Institute, State University of New York, Binghampton, New York.

Smith, V. L. (1975) 'The Primitive Hunter Culture, Pleistocene Extinction and the Rise of Agriculture', *Journal of Political Economy*, 83, 727–755.

Solow, R. M. (1957) 'Technical Change and the Aggregate Production Function', *Review of Economics and Statistics*, 39, 312–370. Reprinted in A. K. Sen: Growth Economies, Penguin Economics Reading 1970.

Solow, R. M. (1963) *Capital Theory and the Rate of Return*, North Holland Publishing Co., Amsterdam.

Solow, R. M. (1970) *Growth Theory: An Exposition*, Clarendon Press, Oxford.

Solow, R. M. (1974a) 'The Economics of Resources or the Resources of Economics', *American Economic Review*, Papers and Proceedings, Richard T. Ely Lecture.

Solow, R. M. (1974b) 'Intergenerational Equity and Exhaustible Resources', *Review of Economic Studies Symposium*.

Solow, R. M. and Wan, F. Y. (1977) 'Extraction Costs in the Theory of Exhaustible Resources', *Bell Journal of Economics*, Autumn, Vol. 7, No. 2, pp. 359–370.

Spence, A. M. (1974) *Market Signalling: Informational Transfer in Hiring and Related Screening Processes*, Harvard University Press, Cambridge, Mass.

Spence, A. M. (1975) 'Blue Whales and Applied Control Theory', in *System Approaches and Environmental Problems*, H. W. Gottinger (ed.), Vandenhoeck and Ruprecht (Gottingen).

Spence, A. M. (1977) 'Entry, Investment and Oligopolistic Pricing', *Bell Journal of Economics*, 534–594 (Autumn).

Spence, A. M. and Starrett, D. A. (1975) 'Most Rapid Approach Paths in Accumulation Problems', *International Economic Review*, 16, No. 2, 388–403.

Starr, R. M. (1973) 'Optimal Production and Allocation Under Uncertainty', *Quarterly Journal of Economics*, 82, 81–95.

Starrett, D. A. (1970) 'The Efficiency of Competitive Programmes', *Econometrica*, 38, No. 5, pp. 704–711.

Starrett, D. (1972) 'Fundamental Non-Convexities in the Theory of Externalities', *Journal of Economic Theory*.

Starrett, D. A. (1974) 'On the Nature of Externalities', Technical Report No. 129, Institute for Mathematical Studies in Social Sciences, Stanford University.

Starrett, D. A. (1973) 'Inefficiency and the Demand for "Money" in a Sequence Economy', *Review of Economic Studies*, XL (4), No. 124, pp. 437–448.

Starrett, D. and Zeckhauser, R. (1971) 'Treating External Diseconomics— Markets or Taxes?', Harvard University (mimeo).

Stern, N. (1976) 'On the Specification of Models of Optimum Income Taxation', *Journal of Public Economics*.

Stiglitz, J. E. (1974) 'Tax Policy and the Oil Industry' (mimeo), Yale University.

Stiglitz, J. E. (1974a) 'Growth with Exhaustible Natural Resources: The Competitive Economy', *Review of Economic Studies*, Symposium, 123–138.

Stiglitz, J. E. (1974b) 'Growth with Exhaustible Resources: Efficient and Optimal Growth Paths', *Review of Economic Studies*, Symposium, 139–152.

Stiglitz, J. E. (1976) 'Monopoly and the Rate of Extraction of Exhaustible Resources', *American Economic Review*, Vol. 66, No. 4, pp. 655–661.

Sweeney, J. L. (1977) 'Economics of Depletable Resources: Market Forces and Intertemporal Bias', *Review of Economic Studies*, 44, 125–142.

Uzawa, H. (1966) 'An Optimum Fiscal Policy in an Aggregative Model of Economic Growth', in I. Adelman and E. Thorbecke (eds.), *The Theory and Design of Economic Development*, Johns Hopkins University Press (Baltimore).

Vickrey, W. (1967) 'Economic Criteria for Optimum Rate of Depletion', in M. Gaffney (ed.), 1967.

Von Neumann, John and Morgenstern, Oskar (1944) *Theory of Games and Economic Behaviour*, Princeton University Press.

Von Weizsacker, C. C. (1965) 'Existence of Optimal Programs of Accumulation for an Infinite Time Horizon', *Review of Economic Studies*, 32.

Wan, H. Jr. (1970) 'Optimal Savings Programs Under Intertemporally Dependent Preferences', *International Economic Review*, 11, 521–457.

Wan, H. Y. Jr. (1971) *Economic Growth*, Harcourt, Brace, Jovanovich, Inc. (New York).

Weinstein, M. C. and Zeckhauser, R. J. (1974) 'Use Patterns for Depletable and Recyclable Resources', *Review of Economic Studies*, Symposium, 67–88.

Weitzman, M. (1974) 'Prices vs. Quantities', *Review of Economic Studies*, XLI (4), pp. 477–491.

Weitzman, M. (1976) 'Welfare Significance of National Product in a Dynamic Economy', *Quarterly Journal of Economics*, 90, 156–162.

Weitzman, M. (1978) 'Optimal Rewards for Economic Regulation', *American Economic Review*, 68, 683–691.

Wilson, R. (1975) 'Informational Economies of Scale', *Bell Journal of Economics*, 6, 184–195.

Wilson, R. (1977) 'Risk Measurement of Public Projects', IMSSS Technical Report No. 240, Stanford University, forthcoming in R. Lind (ed.) (1980).

Wilson, R. (1977a) 'A Binding Model of Perfect Competition', *Review of Economic Studies*, 44, 511–518.

Yaari, M. (1964) 'On the Consumer's Lifetime Allocation Process', *International Economic Review*, 5.

Yaari, M. (1965) 'Uncertain Lifetime, Life Insurance, and the Theory of Consumer', *Review of Economic Studies*, 32, 137–158.

Yaari, M. (1976) 'Endogenous Changes in Tastes: A Philosophical Discussion', Research Memorandum No. 23, Center for Research in Mathematical Economics and Game Theory, Hebrew University, Jerusalem.

Yaari, M. (1977) 'Consistent Utilization of an Exhaustible Resource—or— How to Eat an Appetite-Arousing Cake', Research Memorandum No. 26, Center for Research in Mathematical Economics and Game Theory, Hebrew University, Jerusalem.

INDEX

ADELMAN: 439-40, 444, 469n.
Allingham: 263n.
American Petroleum Institute: 388n.
Arbitrage equation: 105-7, 131-2, 155-8, 162, 168, 217, 241, 369-70.
Arrow: 1, 13n, 26n, 30n, 31n, 37-8, 47, 93n, 109n, 199n, 220n, 224n, 247n, 263n, 270n, 275n, 284n, 288n, 310n, 320n, 321n, 378n, 379n, 382n, 385n, 389n, 409n, 411n, 416n, 418n, 425n, 427n, 437n.
Arrow-Debreu theory of contingent markets: 411ff.
Atkinson: 300n, 362n.
Aumann: 15n, 38.

BACKSTOP technology: 175-7, 179-81, 184ff, 191, 340, 343, 350, 468n.
Barnett and Morse: 464ff, 470n.
Barrow: 459, 462, 469n.
Baumol: 93n.
Bauxite: 344n.
Becker: 256n.
Beckerman: 426n.
Bergstrom: 28n, 92n.
Berndt: 353n.
Berry: 208n.
Bevan: 357n.
Bewley: 155n, 241n.
Bliss: 102n, 103n, 192n, 215n.
Blocking: 13-17, 20, 32, 38.
Blue whales: 133, 144-7.
Boiteux: 362n.
Brannon: 375n.
Brown: 115n, 134n, 152n.
Buchanan: 92, 93n.
Budget constraints: 26-27, 29,-30, 41, 46, 101, 110, 472.
Burmeister: 194n, 242n, 254n.

CAIRNCROSS: 352n.
Cartel: 185, 215, 336, 340ff, 352ff.
Cass: 215n, 219n, 254n, 257n, 261n.
Catching up: 266ff.
Chakravarty: 261n, 309n, 320n.
Chenery: 199n.
Christy, Jr.: 93n, 152n, 470n.

Club of Rome: 2.
Coalition: 13-17, 20, 32, 38, 58-9.
Cobb-Douglas: see Production function, Cobb-Douglas.
Cohen: 78n, 94n.
Cole: 197n, 198n, 480n.
Common property resources (static, dynamic): 21, 55ff, 73-8, 93-4, 120-1, 126, 142-4, 151, 372-5.
Competitive equilibrium: 21ff, 29ff, 42, 44-7, 50-1, 53-4, 92, 101, 109, 155, 255.
Competitive fringe: 340ff, 352ff.
Conally 'Hot Oil' Act: 75.
Concave functions: 27, 40, 54, 95ff, 139, 184, 265-7, 280, 283, 287ff, 293ff, 324, 380-1, 421.
quasi-concave functions: 27, 36, 414-5.
Contingent commodity: 379ff, 411ff, 433ff.
Convex set: 23.
Core: 15, 21, 58.
Cremer: 351n, 352n, 356n.
Crutchfield: 118n.

DALES: 77n, 93n.
Daly: 312n, 480n.
Dasgupta: 180n, 181n, 187n, 192n, 225n, 238n, 247n, 253, 254n, 263n, 270n, 274n, 284n, 29n3, 295n, 296n, 298n, 301n, 302n, 310n, 319n, 320n, 321n, 342n, 358n, 362n, 396n, 404n, 409n, 418n, 419n, 420n, 438n, 468n, 476n, 480n.
Das Gupta: 358n.
d'Aspremont: 275n.
Debreu: 1, 13n, 30n, 35n, 37-8, 389n, 425n, 437n.
Depletion allowance: 368-71.
Diamond: 92n, 275n, 276n, 277n, 281n, 362n.
Discounting: 297ff, 303ff, 313.
Discount factor: 103.
Distribution, intergenerational: 255ff*
Dixit: 102n, 321n.
Dobell: 194n.
Duopoly: 337-9.